PROTEST!

Published in the United States and Canada by
Princeton University Press
41 William Street
Princeton, New Jersey 08540
press.princeton.edu

This book was designed and produced by
White Lion Publishing,
an imprint of the Quarto Group.
The Old Brewery
6 Blundell Street
London N7 9BH

Cover illustrations: (front) Josse Pickard; and (back) from top left: *Libertad Para Angela Davi*s,
Félix Beltrán (Library of Congress); *Votes for Women*, Hilda M. Dallas; *Je Suis Charlie*, Joachim
Roncin; *I Am Trayvon Martin*, Jesus Barraza, Mazatl and Melanie Cervantes (justseeds.org);
The Indivisible Unity of the Republic: Liberty, Equality, Fraternity or Death (Pictorial Press Ltd/
Alamy Stock Photo); *The Mothers of the Plaza de Mayo*, Daniel Garcia (Daniel Garcia/AFP/
Getty Images); *Calavera of a Society Belle*, José Guadalupe Posada; *Information Libre*,
Atelier Populaire (API/Gamma-Rapho via Getty Images); *feminist symbol badge*
(Contraband Collection/Alamy Stock Photo)

Every effort has been made to trace the copyright holders of material quoted in this book.
If application is made in writing to the publisher, any omissions will be included in future editions.

This book has been composed in Plantin and Dala Prisma
Printed in Singapore

978-0-691-19833-0

10 9 8 7 6 5 4 3 2 1

LIZ McQUISTON

PROTEST!

A History of Social and Political Protest Graphics

Princeton University Press
Princeton and Oxford

Contents

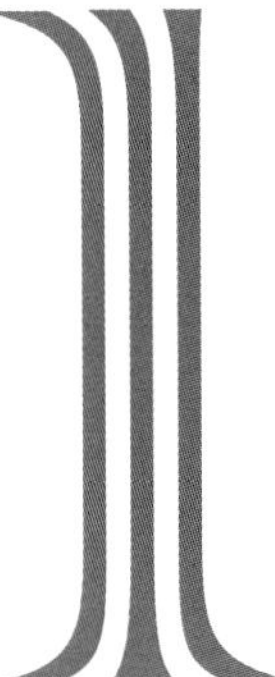

Early Developments: The Reformation and Social Comment (1500–1900)   8

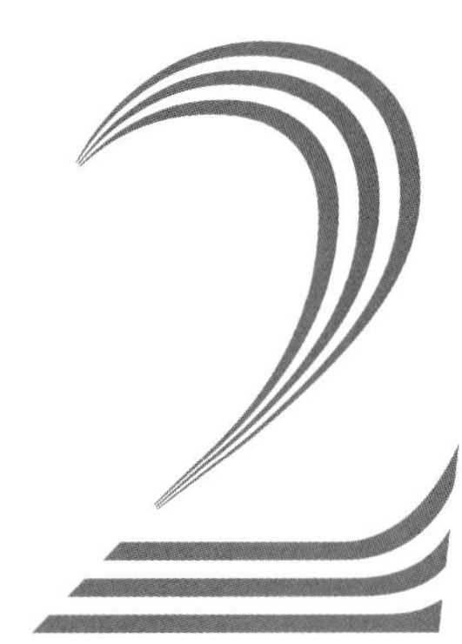

Constructing a New Society (1900–1930)   34

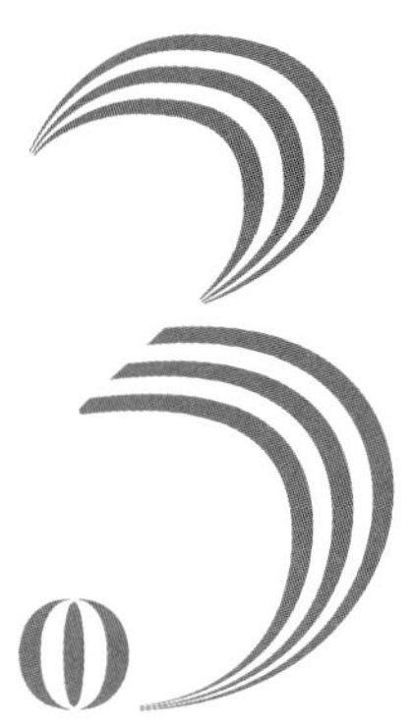

Fascism, The Cold War and The Bomb (1930–1960)   62

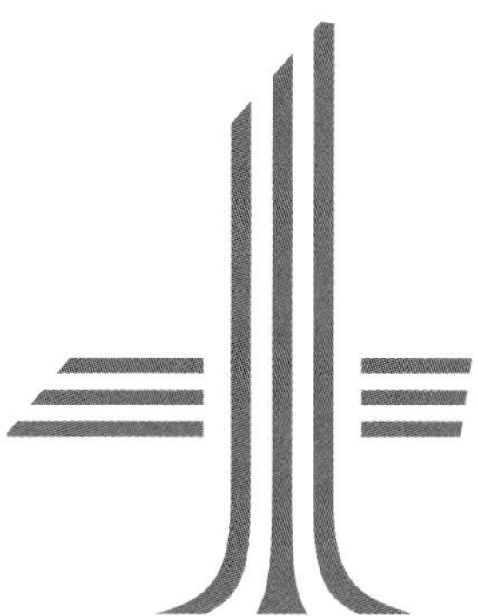

Redirection and Change (1960–1980) 86

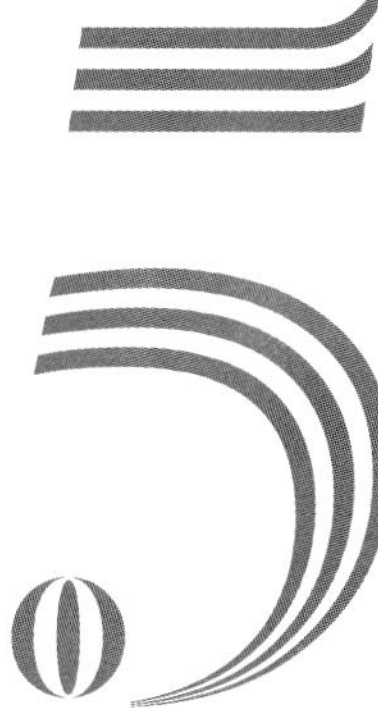

The AIDS Crisis and Other Global Tensions (1980–2000) 130

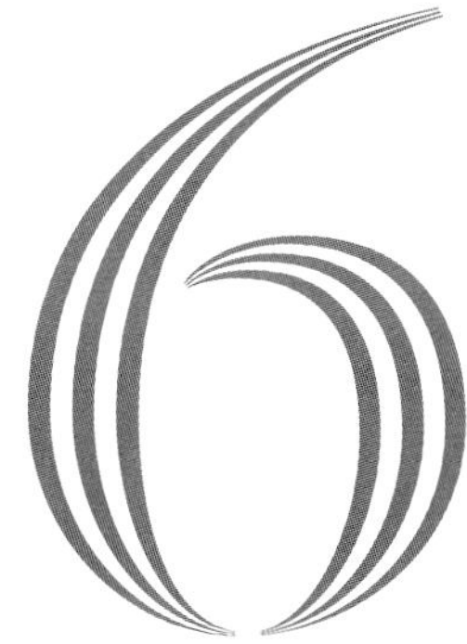

Revolutions and the Demand for Rights (2000–Present) 200

Introduction

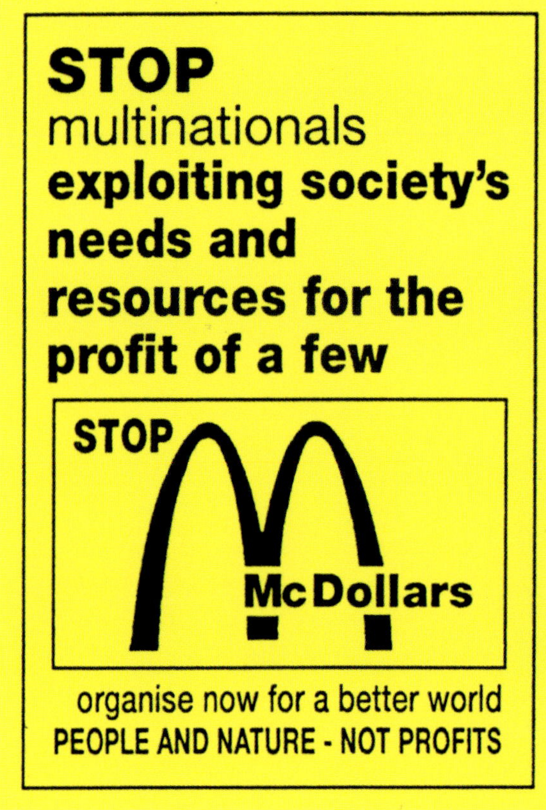

Sticker from the McLibel Support Campaign 2000

Social discontent and political protest have been expressed visually as well as verbally throughout the ages. Graffiti scribbles on a wall, pictures scattered in the street during marches, posters spread through the environment: all have played their part. For such agitational images represent a power struggle; a rebellion against an established order and a call to arms, or a passionate cry of concern for a cause. They signify, in short, an attempt to bring about change, whether driven by the cry of an individual or the heat of the crowd. It is the emotion, aggression or immediacy of this imagery that constitutes a visual power that links into the passions of the viewer.

This book's history of protest graphics can therefore be joyful as well as brutal. It is largely driven by events, both local and international, but also owes a debt to changes in technology. Consequently it begins in the 16th century with the Reformation (as by that time images could be produced in multiples). It then travels through the decades and centuries, protesting against the miseries of war, satirising the foibles of royalty, politicians, religions and society in general, calling for an end to racial discrimination and apartheid, demanding freedom from tyranny and dictatorships around the world, struggling for LGBTQ+ rights, and finally attending to current 21st-century concerns and Trumpisms.

The content encompasses an astounding breadth of emotion – from hilarious satire to utter horror. It highlights the timeless iconography of protest graphics, such as raised fists, skulls (and skeletons), mushroom clouds and missiles, and revels in the variety of its modus operandi: from posters and postcards to giant inflatables. But over and above all, this book pays tribute to the liberating concept of hard-won 'freedom of speech' throughout history, and which still has agency in current times. The power struggles of the past, and their visual communication, have meaning for us now. Such resonances occur, again and again, throughout this entire collection.

When viewing this book, don't just observe the past. Feel the present.

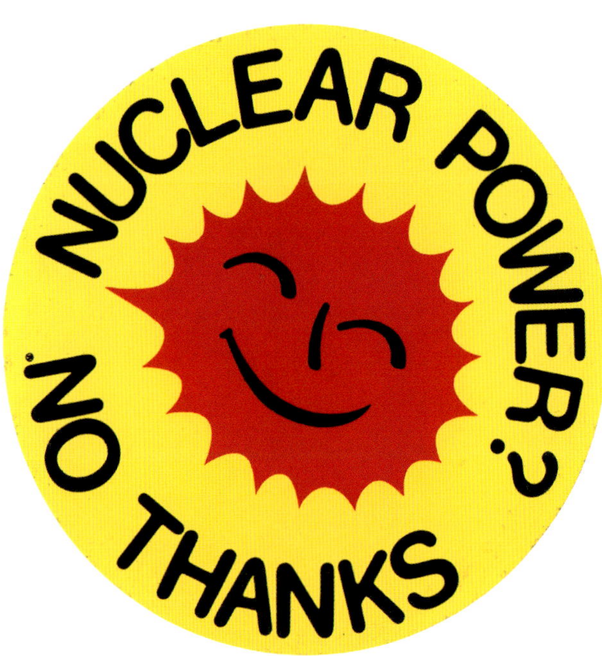

Anti-Nuclear Power sticker 1980
Logo by Anne Lind and Søren Lisberg

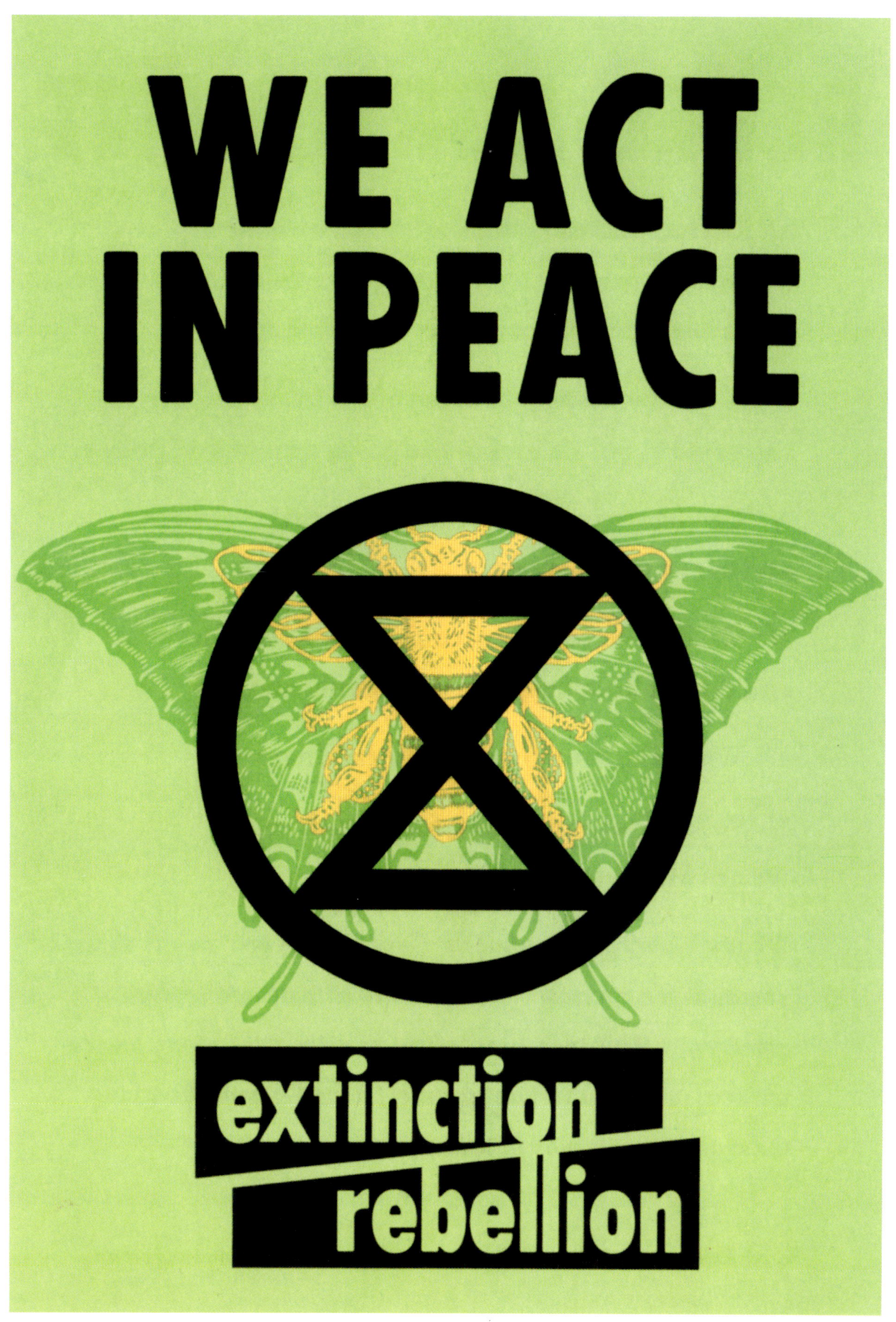

Flyer demanding government action on climate change 2019
Extinction Rebellion protest movement

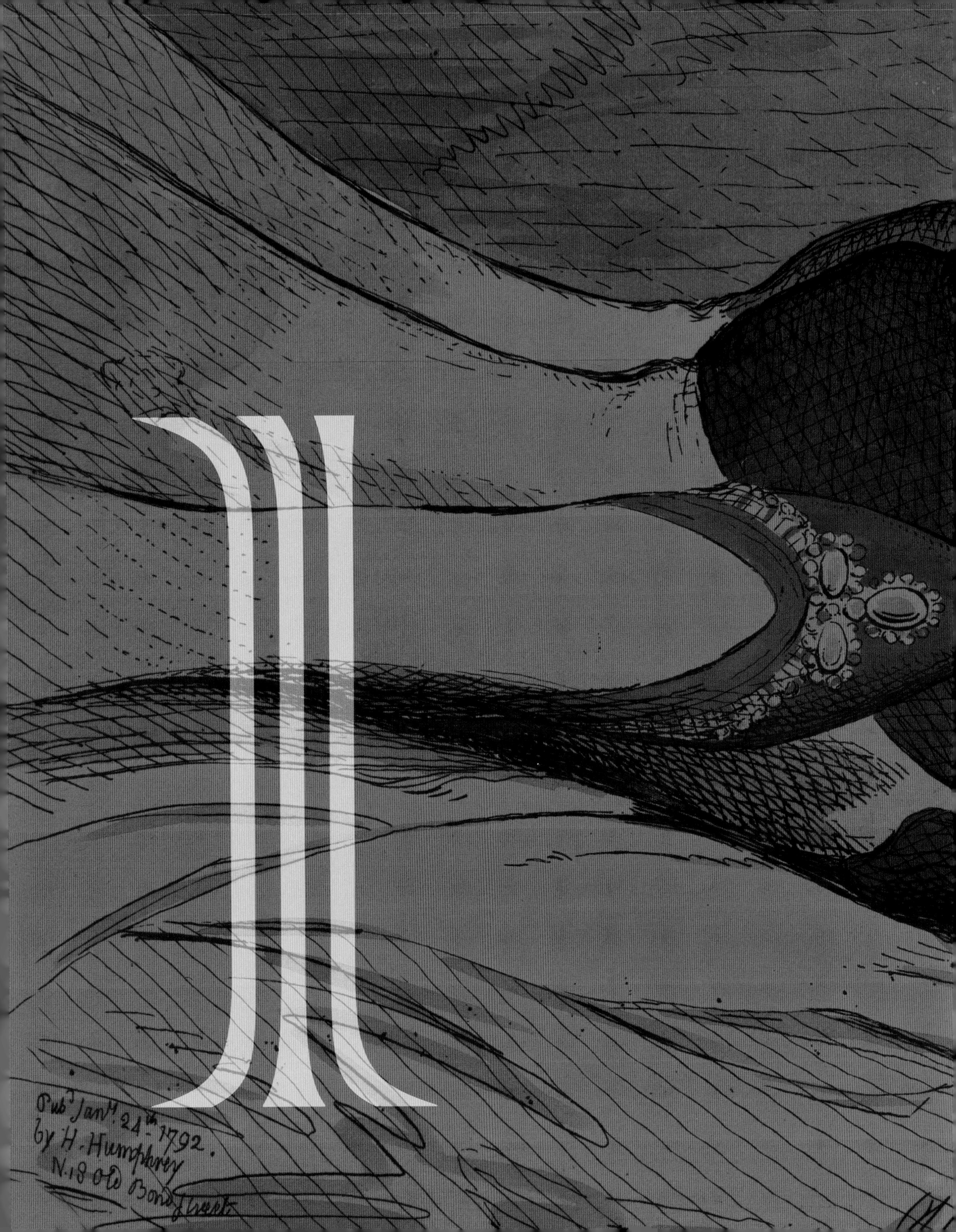
Pubd Jany 24th 1792.
by H. Humphrey
N.18 Old Bond Street

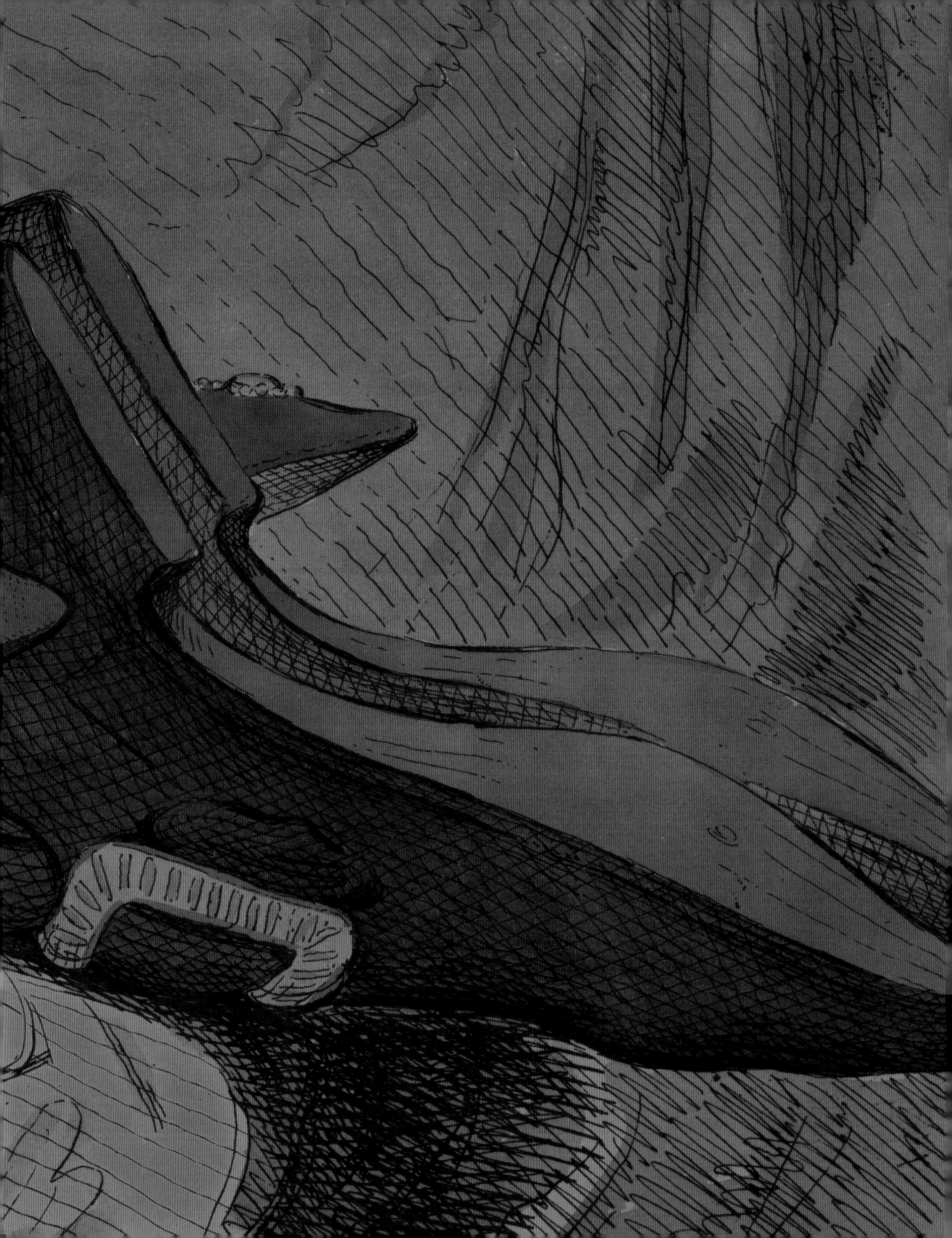

1500–1900

Early Developments: The Reformation and Social Comment

If searching for early examples of visual defiance against authority, it is tempting to use the beginning of the 20th century as a starting point. After all, that century defines an era, more or less, of living memory (ours or our relatives), and the centuries before that seem too vast and too distant. The vastness is true: disputes and protests and their visual expression, stretch far back in time, and are of such quantity as to offer a whole study in itself. But the *distance*, conceptually speaking, is false. Even a superficial glance at those earlier centuries is startling, for many of the issues at the centre of the protests, as well as the way that artists communicated them, are surprisingly similar to those of the present.

This chapter therefore deals with the vastness of the pre-1900s by presenting particular *highlights* of graphic work, and their creators, over those earlier centuries. The Protestant Reformation provides a good starting point. The advent of the 'political print', as a tool of protest, relied heavily on the multiplication of an image as a means of spreading its anger. Both paper and print had become available to the West in the 1400s. By the early 1500s, printing allowed an image to be multiplied, important in spreading ideas to the illiterate masses. It was possible to show anger towards life's injustices or those in power, by producing crude or awful depictions of key people or actions, then reproducing them in multiples and distributing them by means of strolling printsellers. Thus such messages were carried mainly through pictures (as few could actually read).[1]

The first great movement of resistance was aimed at the power of the Catholic Church and the authority of its Pope. It came in the form of Martin Luther's Reformation, ignited in 1517 by his posting of his *Ninety-Five Theological Theses* on the door of the church in Wittenberg. Illustrations became one of the Reformation's most productive forces of propaganda and communication. Many of the German artists at that time were against Rome, particularly those close to Luther such as his friend Lucas Cranach the Elder, as well as Mathias Grünewald, Albrecht Dürer and others. The artwork, artistically, tended to be extremely aggressive and crude. Messages tended to be simple, direct and devoid of broader arguments or ethical discussion. Unlike books, which were largely appreciated by a small, intellectual set of the population, prints were for the masses – and often oppositional, showing anger, demanding justice or applying cruel humour to the controllers above them.[2]

'The Miseries and Misfortunes of War' (1632–33), by Jacques Callot (1593–1635), is often experienced through the display of only one of its most distressing images, entitled 'The Hanging Tree'. It is in fact a morality tale, told in a sequence of 18 small etchings, each measuring roughly 8.1 cm high by 18.6 cm wide (3.5 × 7.5 in). It is considered to be one of the first attempts to show how the horrors of war impact on the very fabric of society, particularly the common people. But it is also a tale about the notion of 'going to war': what happens to those who are recruited, transformed by the insanity of battle, and then run berserk, killing and maiming innocents and committing atrocities. The recruits then suffer gruesome punishment by

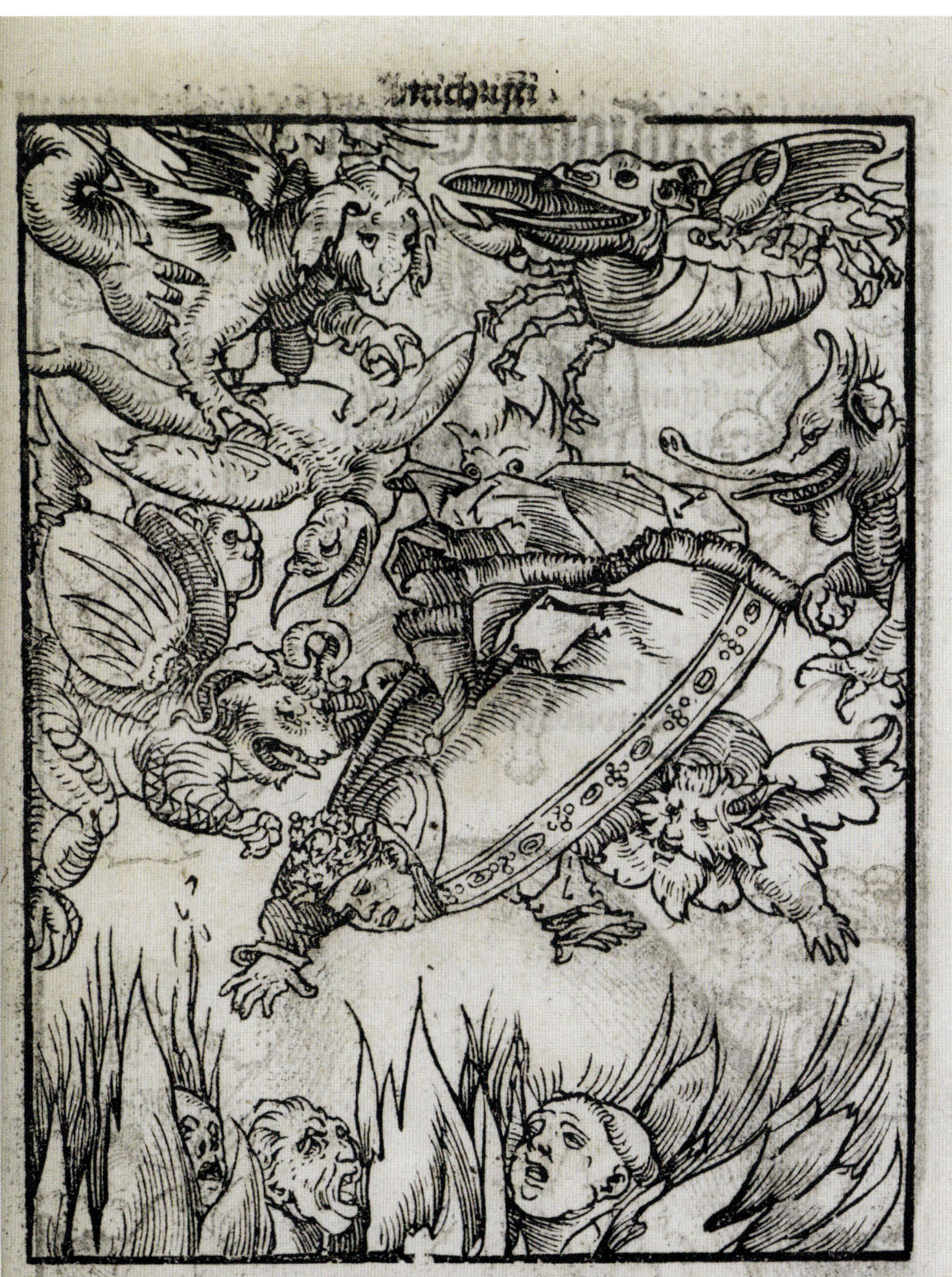

Es ist ergriffen die Bestia vñ mit yr d falsch prophet der durch
sie zeychen than hat do mit er vorfurdt hat/ die ßo ßeynt zeychē
von yme genommen /vnd sein bildt angebet ßeynt versenckt yn
die teuffe des fewirs vnd schweffels vnd seynd getodt mit dem
schwerdt des der do reydt offim weyssen pferdt/ das auß seynē
mauel gehet. Apocal:19. Danne wirdt offenbar werden der
schalckhafftige denn wirdt der herr Jesus toeten mit dem atem
ßeyns mundts vnd wirdt yn sturtzen durch die glori ßeyner zu
kunfft. 2. ad Tessa. 2.

The Pope Descending to Hell 1521
Lucas Cranach

their commanding officers (who catch up with them), and even worse, by peasants seeking to avenge the innocents.[3]

Callot was born in the Duchy of Lorraine, apparently of noble birth. Throughout much of his life, he was known to enjoy and keep company with the poorer sectors of society as well as with the rich and powerful. The latter would have been necessary as etching was an expensive process and he would have been in need of a patron or two along the way. The French army invaded Lorraine in 1633, wreaking havoc and carnage on a grand scale, and therefore providing the backdrop against which 'The Miseries' were created, and must be read.[4]

Our modern spirit of revolution, embedded in the smallest protest or uprising, has often mythologized or claimed its historical roots in the French Revolution of 1789. The French Revolution desired and manifested earth-shattering changes. It produced the 'Declaration of the Rights of Man and the Citizen', presenting the new and crucially democratic idea that 'the state' was not the property of a king or royal dynasty, but was composed of its people, thereby giving birth to the idea of 'nationhood'. (For men only; unfortunately the revolution had no interest in giving political rights to women.) In January 1793 King Louis was guillotined, and later in the year so was his wife Marie Antoinette. Hence the revolution also produced bloodshed: harsh divisions formed between the revolutionaries (Jacobins) and the moderates (Girondins). The Jacobins seized power and the Committee of Public Safety, headed by the overly fastidious Robespierre, began exterminating the opposition. In the Reign of Terror (Sept 1793–July 1794), over ten months it is estimated around 40,000 people were guillotined throughout France, until Robespierre himself was finally guillotined, followed by a period of calm until Napoleon Bonaparte's takeover in 1799.[5]

The initial five-year period produced a genuine attempt at making radical changes to society, at many different levels. For example, in 1793 the Jacobins introduced a new calendar of ten-day weeks, and renamed the months. The revolution produced new pictorial symbols, such as the Phrygian cap of liberty (*bonnet rouge*) and tricolor cockades (in the revolutionary colours of red, white and blue), often worn together. Such symbols, when worn, identified 'patriots', or the '*sans-culottes*' (meaning literally 'without-breeches'), a term used to describe people of the street.[6]

The 18th-century British artist and engraver, William Hogarth (1697–1764), was a pioneer of social satire and criticism. His career saw the rise of political satire, although Hogarth's main interest lay in exposing social hypocrisy through narrative series, such as 'The Rake's Progress', or through contemporary London interiors or street scenes. In 1751 he produced his arguably most famous print, 'Gin Lane', an image of poverty and moral decay (but not without humour): a baby falls out of its drunken mother's arms, a dog and a beggar chew on the same bone. Funny or not, it is a call for social reform.[7]

The golden age of British satire flourished from 1780 to 1830. Artists included James Gillray, Thomas Rowlandson,

Isaac Cruikshank and his sons Robert and George, and many others. Two particularly stand out, and both were professionally trained. James Gillray elevated the practice of caricature and satire to a professional discipline. He produced brilliantly offensive 'political satire' (i.e. having a poke at politicians), introducing complex compositions full of distorted yet recognizable likenesses, and venomous attacks. Importantly, he cut free from the classic academic models of the time, preferring 'Romantic' dream imagery and weird imaginings (he apparently influenced Goya). His prints became nightmare creations; those relating to the French Revolution are bloody, dripping with sensationalism. Thomas Rowlandson's subjects, by contrast, arose from observation; he dealt with the follies of everyday behaviour. He also excelled at developing humour from the depiction of contrasts: young and old, fat and thin, the grotesque and the beautiful, and so on. It is through his watercolours and drawings that the dramas and catastrophes of contemporary life in London were revealed, presenting a true 'mirror of an age'.[8]

In December 1807, France and Britain were at war. Napoleon marched French troops into northern Spain on the false pretext of protecting his Spanish allies from the British. In spring 1808, French troops took over Madrid, and Napoleon declared his brother, Joseph, King of Spain. A guerrilla war broke out between Spanish civilians and the occupiers. The artist Francisco Goya responded to the savagery of the conflict, producing 80 etchings and aquatints over 10 years. The series was titled 'The Disasters of War' (1810–20), and divided into three groups: the war, the year of famine (1811–12) and the *caprichos enfaticos* (striking caprices) which were against the Catholic Church.[9]

Atrocities were committed on both sides. French soldiers committed rape and left naked, mutilated corpses hanging or impaled on trees to demoralise the Spanish people. The Spanish peasants were depicted fighting back and butchering the enemy with their farm tools, with anguish and insanity in their eyes. Goya's message was clear: the war turned both sides into animals or monsters. The war (and French occupation) ended in June 1813. Due to the depicted horrors and anti-establishment tone of the images, the copperplates of Goya's 'The Disasters of War' were locked away after his death in 1828, and remained unpublished for 26 years.[10]

Long after the French Revolution of 1789, when memories of Napoleon's victories were fading and the shadows of republican ideals were about to be reinstated, a new, liberal revolution took place in France. The July Revolution of 1830 brought the 'King of the French people' Louis-Philippe to power, who then proclaimed freedom of the press. Three months later Charles Philipon, who had gathered a team of brilliant artists, founded the satirical weekly *La Caricature* in 1831 and almost immediately took 'a step too far', publishing a drawing (in four stages) of the king's head metamorphosing into an over-ripe, rotting '*poire*' or pear-head. ('*Poire*' is also French slang for fool or simpleton.) Philipon was hauled into court and, story has it, avoided prison by making sketches for

the jury, demonstrating that the resemblance was true and
therefore not his fault – so he was acquitted of the charge
of defamation. He launched another (more savage) satirical
paper *Le Charivari* in 1832. Meanwhile 'Les Poires' became an
emblem of resistance against authority, and continued to have
a needling effect, appearing in Philipon's papers in as many
annoying variations as possible. When Louis-Philippe decreed
the 'image' must no longer exist, Philipon published articles
in which the pear-head image was not drawn, but was formed
out of the arrangement of the type, thereby skirting around the
decree. Not surprisingly, by September 1835 the entire French
free press was censored on political subjects.[11]

Considered by many as the father of American political
cartoons, in 1870 Thomas Nast created his famous visual
campaign against big city corruption. William Marcy Tweed
(aka 'Boss' Tweed) was a New York politician who gained power
over Tammany Hall, the Democratic Party's political machine
in New York City. He was therefore able to influence the
appointment of city officials, control the city government and
through his 'Tammany Hall Ring' of allies, access public money.
At *Harper's Weekly* magazine, political cartoonist Nast was
committed to ending Tweed's reign of corruption. Nast created
a caricature of Boss Tweed as a power-mad, over-fed thug, as
well as the frightening 'Tammany Tiger' prowling the streets of
New York City.[12]

From 1867–76 (and particularly 1870–71) Nast stalked his
prey, creating cartoons intended to undermine Tweed's power
and turn the electorate against him, as 1871 was an election
year. *The New York Times* joined the fray, with ongoing articles
mentioning rumours of corruption, and finally, documented
evidence from leaked financial records (which it ran on its front
page). Although never actually working together, both Nast and
The New York Times were instrumental in exposing the criminal
actions of Tweed and his friends, and inciting public outrage.
Tweed's fury at the pictures, and obviously their effect, resulted
in the famous quote 'Let's stop those damned pictures. I don't
care much what the papers write about me – my constituents
can't read; but damn it, they can see pictures!'[13]

He was right. In the 1871 election, the public – literate or
not – voted many Tammany candidates out of office. A large
number, including Tweed himself, ended up in prison. In
1875 Tweed escaped and headed for Spain, but was caught
and extradited back to a New York jail. A Spanish officer had
recognised him from a Nast cartoon![14]

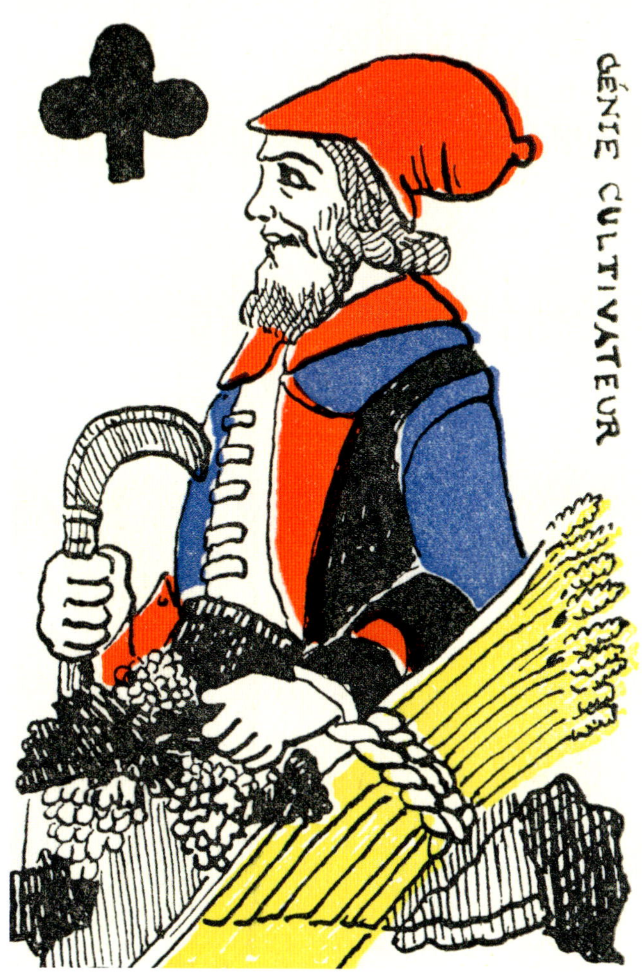

**French Revolution playing card: the 'King of Clubs'
transforms into 'genius of cultivation'** 1794
Henri Mouton

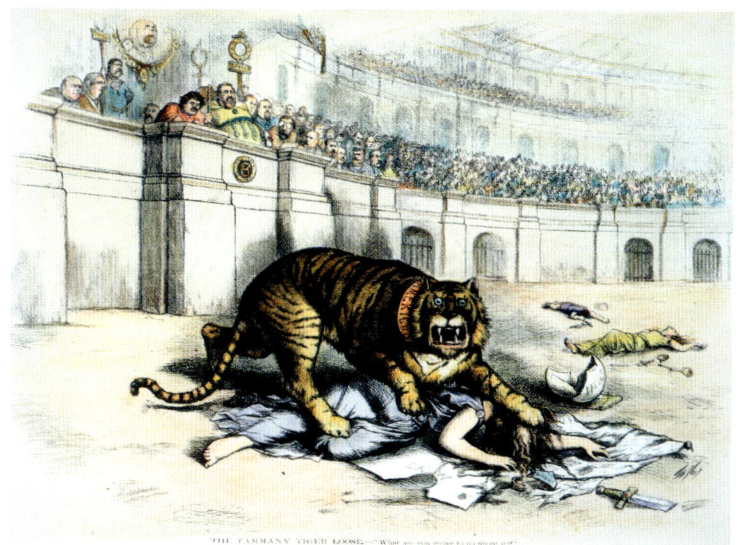

The Tammany Tiger Loose 1871
Thomas Nast

Martin Luther and the Reformation

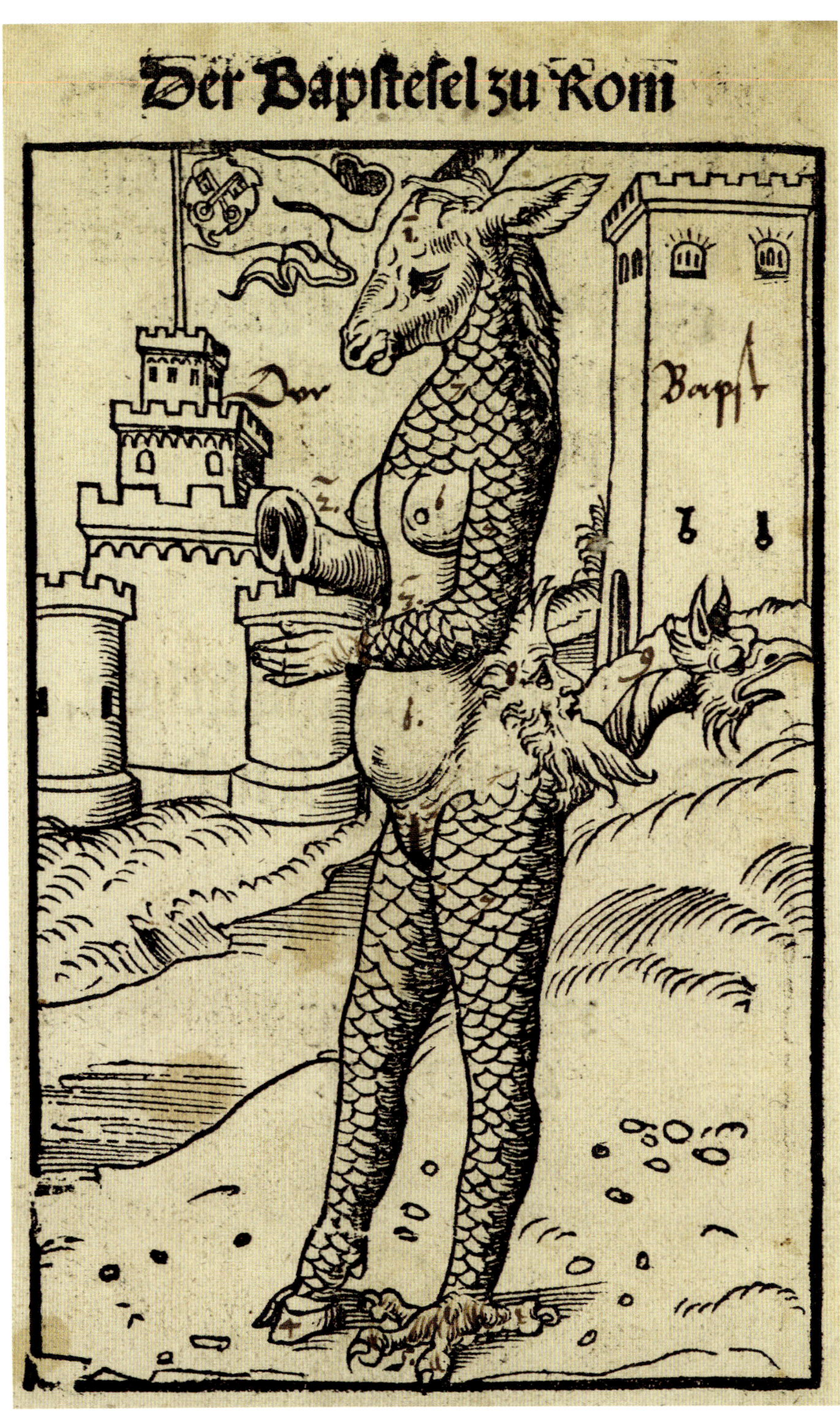

The Donkey-Pope of Rome 1523
Lucas Cranach
Woodcut

In 1517 Martin Luther posted his *Ninety-Five Theological Theses* on the door of a church in Wittenberg. This launched the Reformation, an outright act of resistance to the power and authority of the Catholic Church and its pope. Illustrations were powerful propaganda for an illiterate audience, and Luther relied on his dedicated artist friends (such as Lucas Cranach) to create such messages, often produced as prints or broadsides for the masses. 'The Donkey-Pope of Rome' is actually a re-drawn copy of an earlier engraving that recorded the alleged appearance of a monster standing on the banks of the River Tiber in Rome. It was then given new meaning and satirical purpose by Cranach. Modern interpretation therefore lies with the viewer: it is possible to ponder some complex meaning in the grotesque combination of a donkey's head, a woman's body, a dragon's tail and so on. But it is also possible (and perhaps more likely) to see it simply as coarse 16th-century mischief and a sniggering view of the 'monster' pope with a demon emerging from his arse.

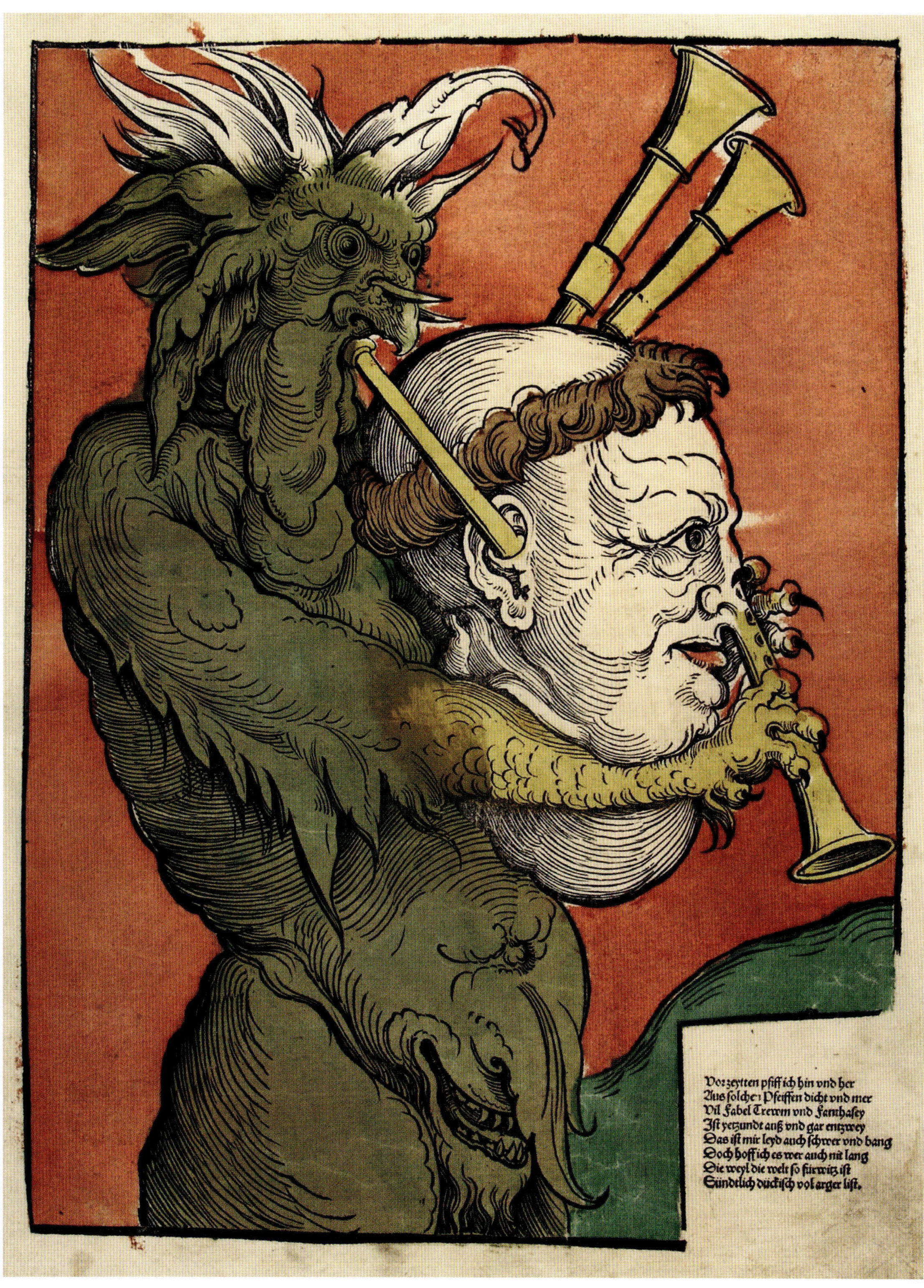

The Devil Playing the Bagpipes *c.* 1530
Erhard Schön
Woodcut

Many broadsheets such as this were produced during the Reformation by its 'reformers' in their tirade against the Catholic Church. The devil is shown here, playing the head of a monk like a bagpipe.

Such images were very popular; it was a common belief that monks were the instrument of the devil, or that the devil searched through monastic orders hoping to find a suitable monk through which to 'play his tune'. The bottom right-hand corner of such images was often left clear of detail, as a letterpress message of anti-Catholic sentiment was printed or pasted there, before posting the broadsheets around the town. It is sometimes thought that this image was produced by the Counter-reformation, and that the monk shown here is Martin Luther, but there is no evidence to prove this. However, it is not far-fetched to think that such broadsheets may have been altered for use as propaganda by both sides.

Jacques Callot: 'The Miseries of War'

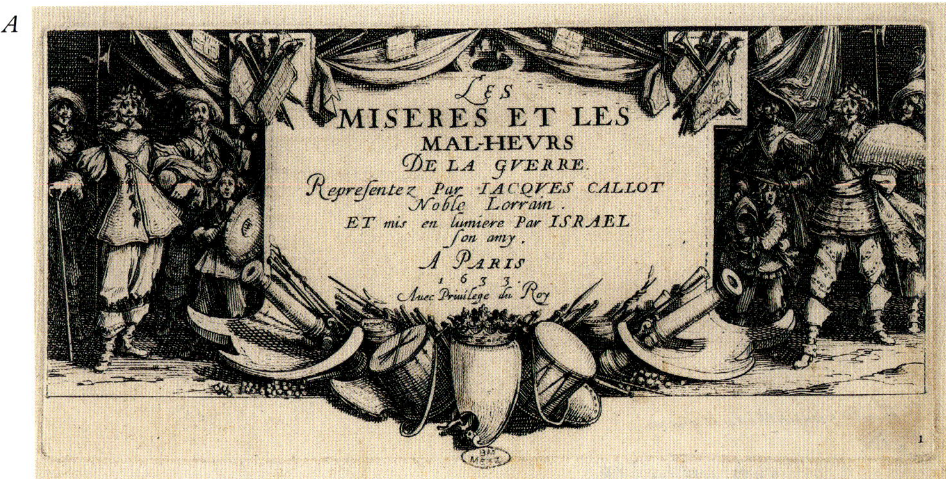

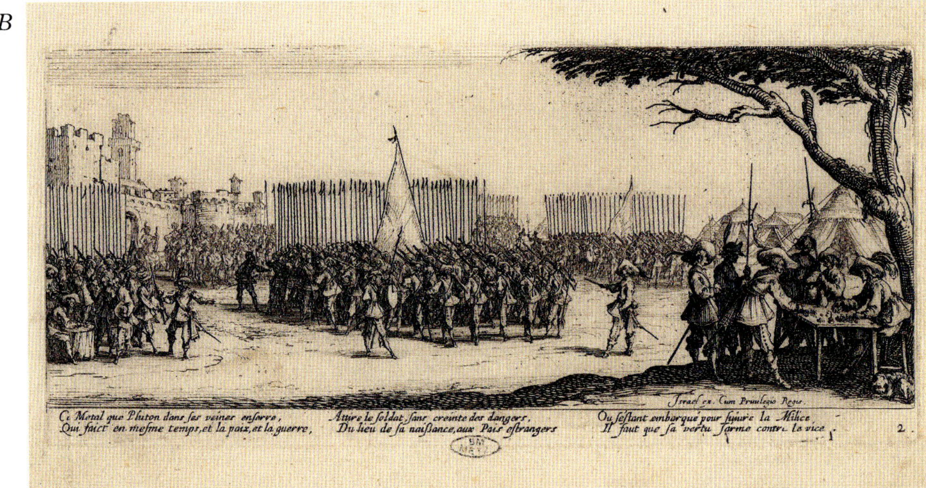

The Miseries and Misfortunes of War 1632–33
Jacques Callot
Etchings: 6 of a total of 18

Jacques Callot's 'The Miseries and Misfortunes of War' is a morality tale, told in a sequence of 18 small but highly detailed etchings, each measuring roughly 8.1 cm high x 18.6 cm wide (3.5 x 7.5 in). Produced against the backdrop of the French invasion of his home province of Lorraine, it is considered to be one of the first attempts at showing how war impacts on the very fabric of society. But it is also a tale about 'going to war': what happens to those who are recruited, transformed by the insanity of battle, then run berserk, killing and maiming innocents and committing atrocities. In the end, they suffer gruesome punishment by their commanding officers (who catch up with them), and worse by peasants avenging the innocents. Callot is an expert storyteller. Despite showing complex scenes and working at a miniaturist's scale, he avoids confusion of events and people by providing an identifier: the tiny buttons that form a line down the side of the breeches worn by the French army. Following those buttons from one etching to another allows identification of the French army as well as its punishment of its own recruits. The title page and five etchings are shown here; a link to the entire sequence can be found in the Bibliography at the end of this book.

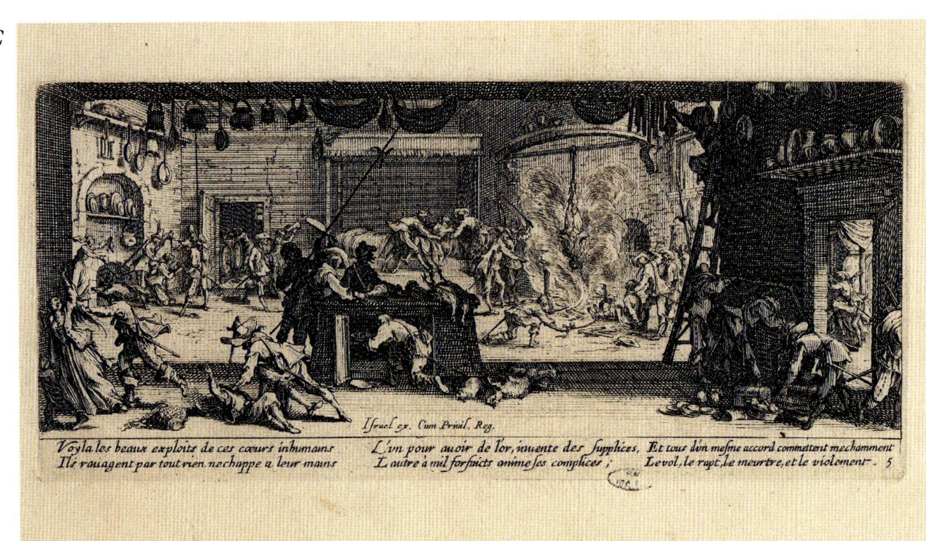

D

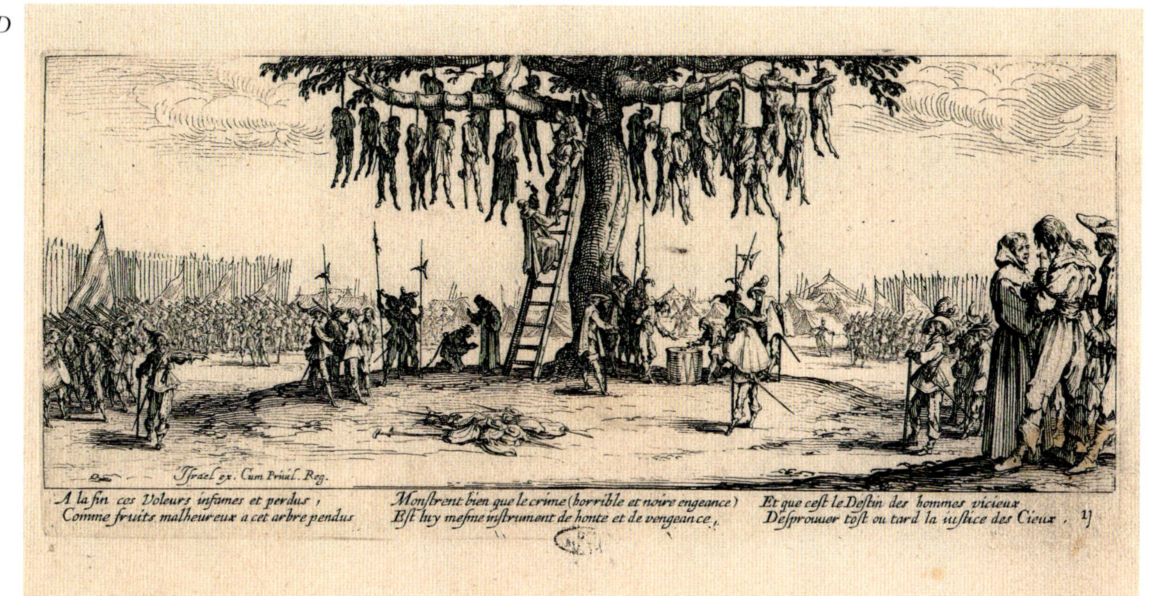

A la fin ces Voleurs infames et perdus , Monstrent bien que le crime (horrible et noire engeance) Et que c'est le Destin des hommes vicieux
Comme fruits malheureux a cet arbre pendus Est luy mesme instrument de honte et de vengeance, D'esprouuer tost ou tard la iustice des Cieux . 11

E

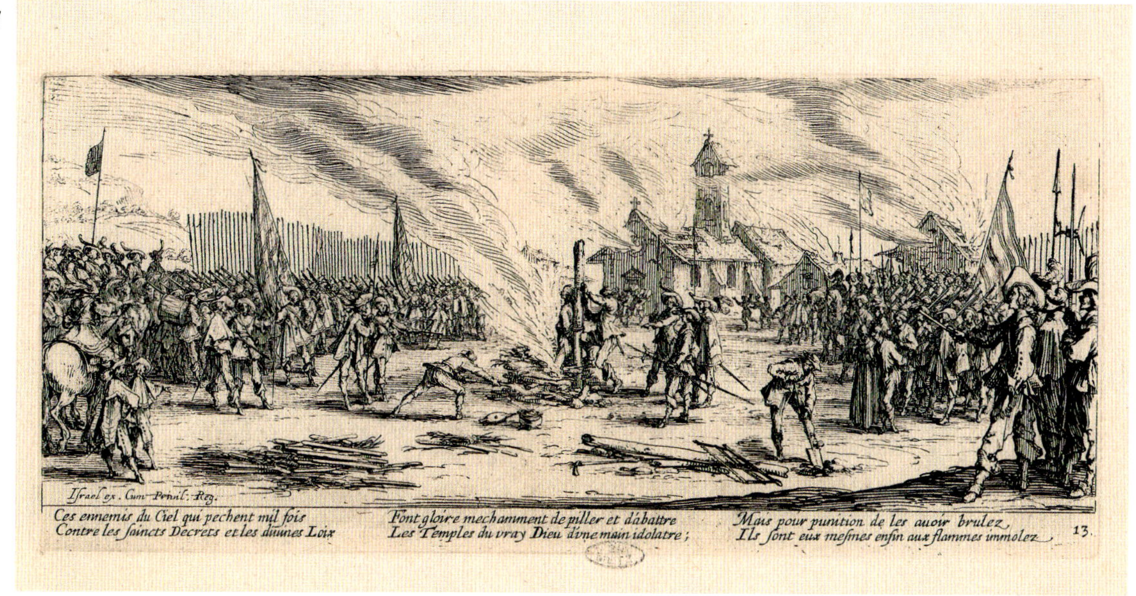

Ces ennemis du Ciel qui pechent mil fois Font gloire mechamment de piller et d'abattre Mais pour punition de les auoir brulez,
Contre les saincts Decrets et les diuines Loix Les Temples du vray Dieu d'vne main idolatre ; Ils sont eux mesmes enfin aux flammes immolez 13

F

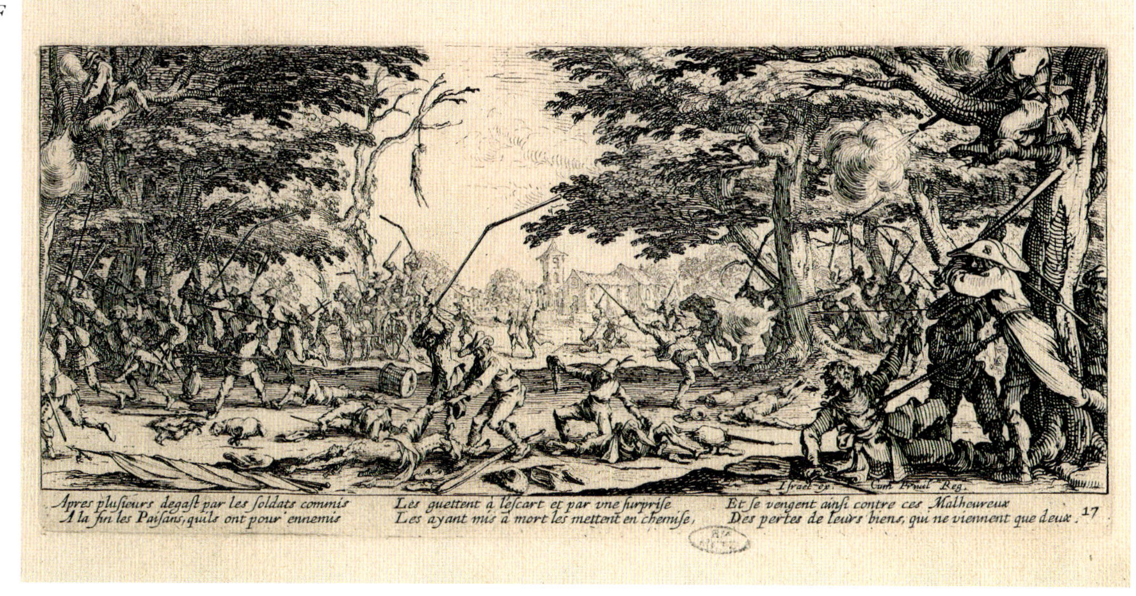

Apres plusieurs degast par les soldats commis Les guettent à l'escart et par vne surprise Et se vengent ainsi contre ces Malheureux
A la fin les Paisans, qu'ils ont pour ennemis Les ayant mis à mort les mettent en chemise Des pertes de leurs biens, qui ne viennent que d'eux . 17

The French Revolution

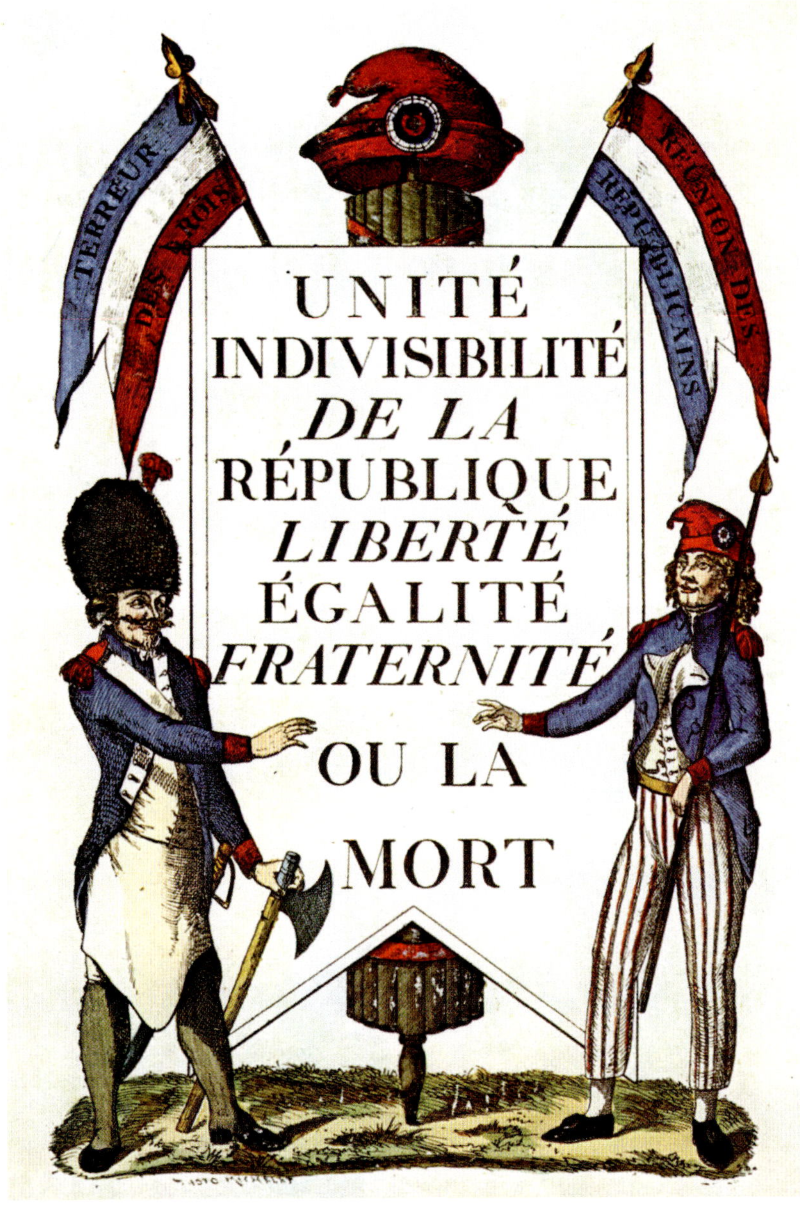

The revolution did not declare political rights for women, but that did not stop them from participating. Hence the patriot 'look' belonged to both men and women. Women rejected the extreme fashions of the time, and wore a simple skirt and apron plus a tricolor cockade. In addition, they were usually depicted carrying weapons.

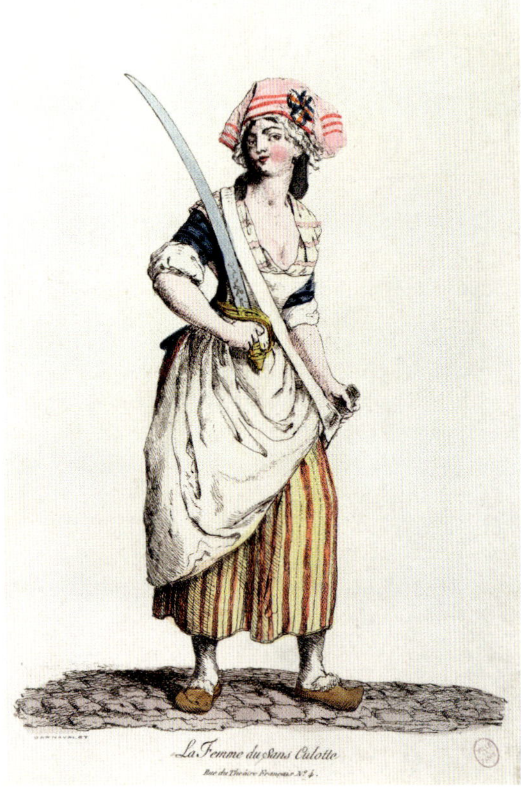

↑ **The Indivisible Unity of the Republic: Liberty, Equality, Fraternity or Death**
c. 1793
Artist unknown
Poster

The French Revolution of 1789 will forever be remembered (and admired) for its production of 'The Declaration of the Rights of Man and the Citizen', which gave birth to the idea of 'nationhood' (the 'state' was formed of its people; it was not the property of a royal dynasty). It then attempted to completely redesign society at all levels, according to its Republican vision. Fortunately these changes were pictorialized. The poster shown here carries a statement of commitment: 'The Indivisible Unity of the Republic: Liberty, Equality, Fraternity or Death'. The colours of the Republic are flying at the top, and the Phrygian cap of liberty (*bonnet rouge*) with its tricolor cockade, one of the great symbols of the revolution, towers over all. The man on the left is from the Army of the Republic (a builder or engineer), the man on the right is a patriot or *'sans-culotte'*; both are coming together in a message of shared respect. The *sans-culotte* (meaning literally 'without breeches') were people of the street. The men rejected notions of aristocratic dress with its buttoned breeches, and instead wore simple trousers with braces, a Phrygian cap and cockade, tended to carry a pike (a cheap but effective weapon, as shown here) and answered to the name of 'Citizen' rather than formal modes of address. They were people who had existed at the bottom, poorer end of society, but who knew their time had come – and were ready for revenge and a good fight.

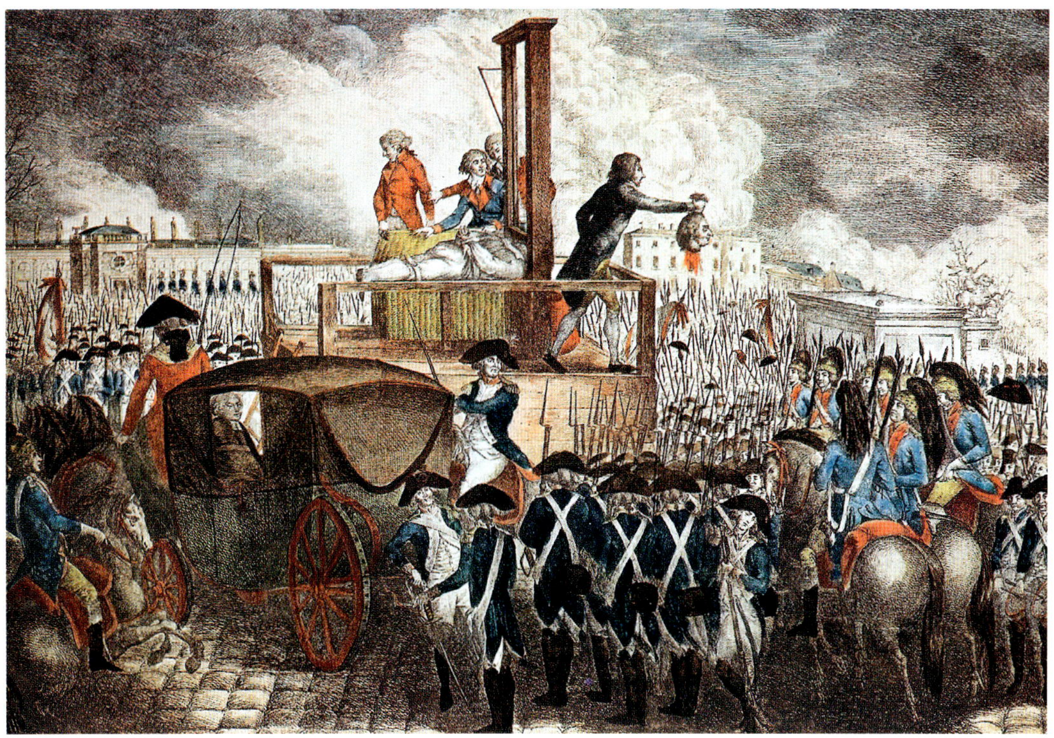

↑ **The Execution of Louis XVI** 1793
Georg Heinrich Sieveking
German copperplate engraving

Political change went hand-in-hand with social
transformation. In the autumn of 1792 France
declared itself a republic. In January 1793 King
Louis XVI was executed by guillotine, followed later
in the year by his extravagant wife, Marie Antoinette
(otherwise known as 'Madame Déficit'). The new
National Assembly, divided by two factions, shed
the weaker one and established a revolutionary
government which ruled by 'the nation's razor',
the guillotine. Mass executions took place until
1794: a period labelled the 'Reign of Terror'. Thus
the menacing image of the guillotine became the
enduring symbol of the revolution over the centuries.

→ **Vendémiaire** 1793
Illustrator unknown
Lithograph

The revolution even restructured time, or the
calendar. Year I of the French Republic was decreed
to be 1792 (not 1789). Time was decimalized: a
week was changed to 10 days. The year was split
into 12 months, but further divisions made matters
even more confusing. Months were given names
that linked to nature. 'Vendémiaire' related to the
new month of the '*vendanges*' or vine harvest; it
replaced September and marked the beginning of
the year. Irregardless of the confusion, however, it
was best to follow along; the penalty for living in
what was called the 'old style' was death.

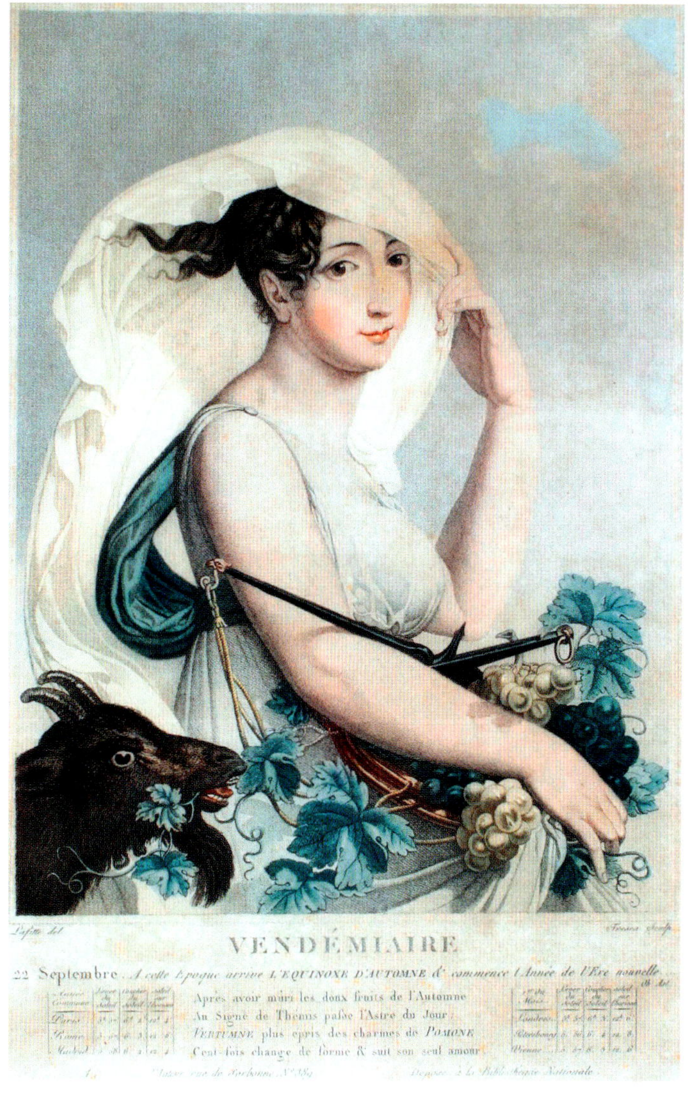

The Golden Age of British Satire

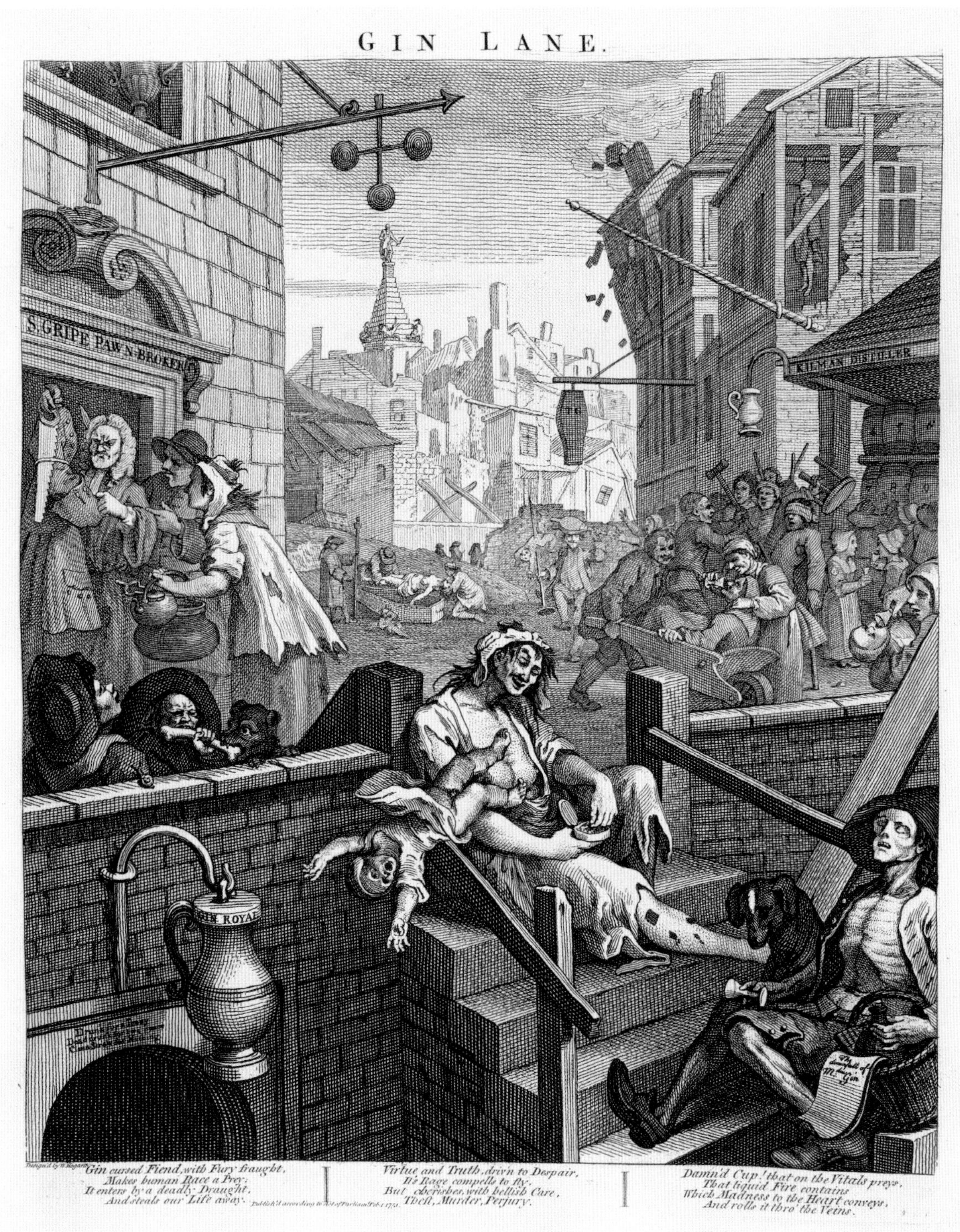

Gin Lane 1750–51
William Hogarth
Etching and engraving

The 18th century artist William Hogarth is widely acknowledged as the father of British satirical art. His main interest lay in exposing social hypocrisy through the creation of narrative series, or through contemporary London interiors or street scenes. He witnessed the rise in popularity of 'caricature' (the comic exaggeration of a person's physical features), but insisted that he drew 'characters' from observation or reportage, and considered caricature to be 'flippant'. His most famous social satire, and surely a demand for social reform, is 'Gin Lane': a tale of modern – and morbid – urban life. Its complexity would have provided much enjoyment for London's semi-literate audience.

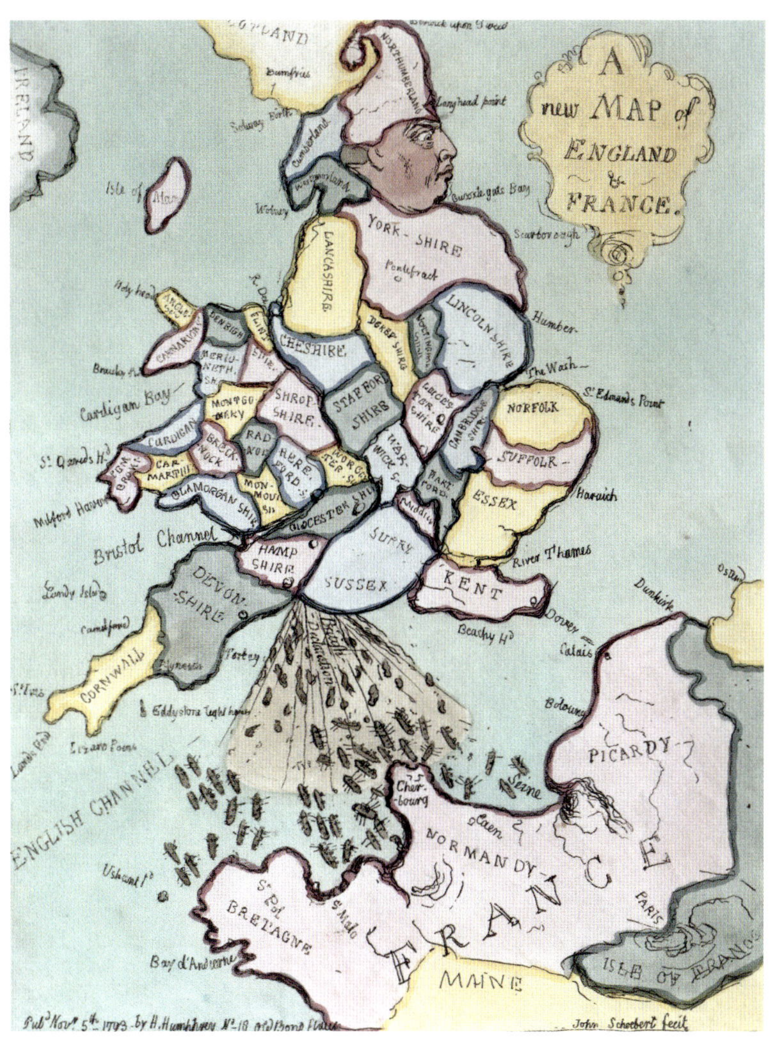

← **The French Invasion; – or – John Bull Bombarding the Bum-Boats** 1793
James Gillray
Engraving

James Gillray elevated the practice of caricature and satire to a professional discipline. His complex compositions were full of distorted (yet recognizable) likenesses, political ridicule, and venomous attacks. Gillray also fused political satire or social commentary with the bawdy, and scatological, tastes of the time. This image shows John Bull – a personification of England, with the face of King George III – heavily defecating on France and its 'bum-boats' (a sneering name for the small supply boats that accompanied large fleets) as a way of warding off the French threat of invasion.

↓ **Maniac Ravings or Little Boney in a Strong Fit** 1805
James Gillray
Hand-coloured engraving on paper

Gillray's personification of Napoleon Bonaparte as Little Boney was one of the most vicious in a stream of anti-French prints produced from 1798 onward. Boney was depicted as a ranting, raving, kicking, fretting, lunatic, evil dwarf, subjected to various indignities. It became powerful propaganda, and soon grew to be the international image or 'idea' of Napoleon. By the early 1800s, Gillray's fame was as international as Boney's.

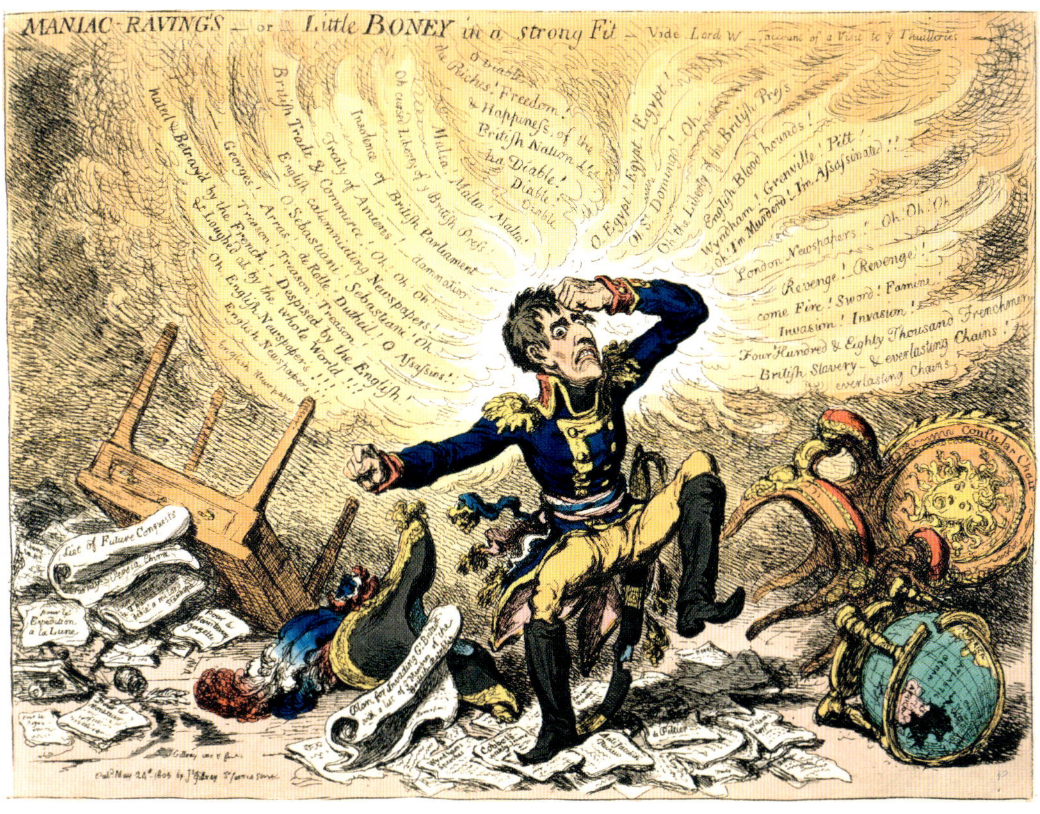

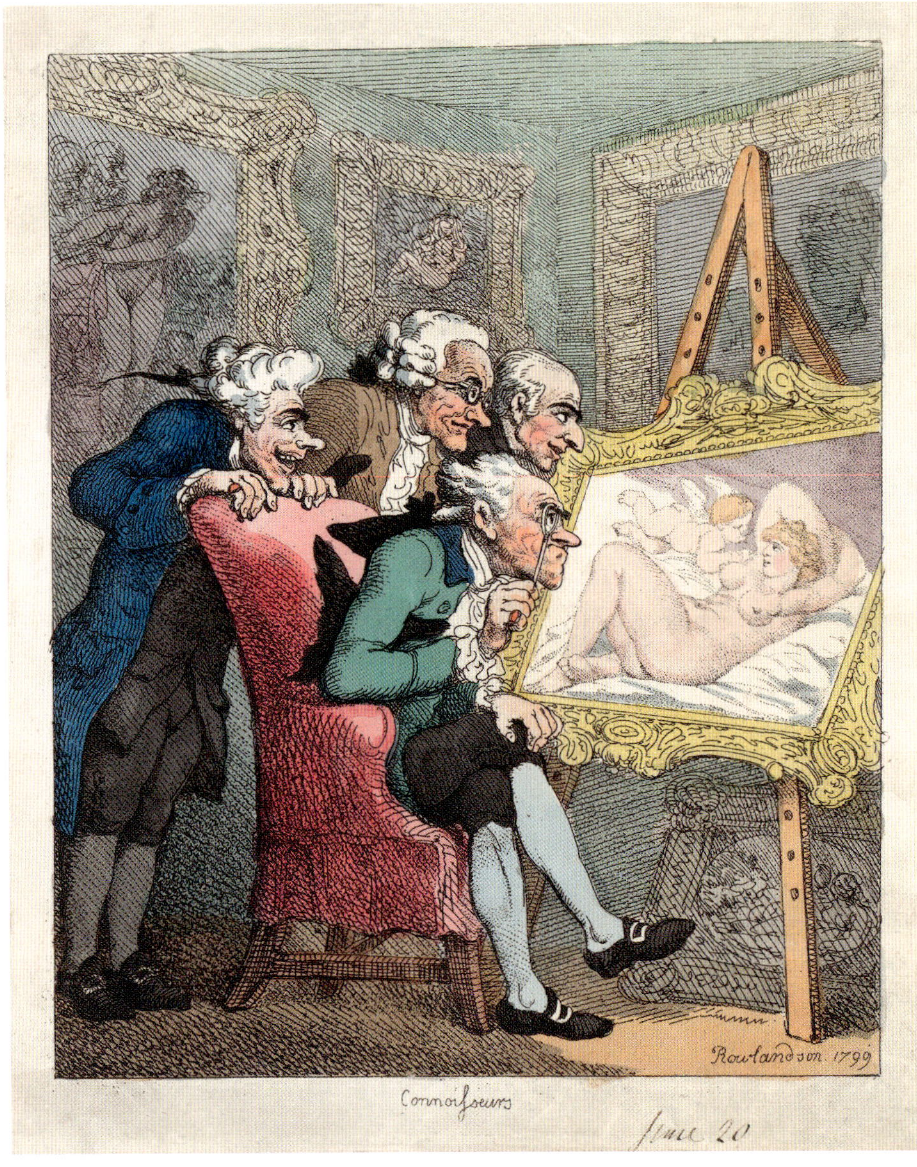

← **Connoisseurs** 1799
Thomas Rowlandson
Hand-coloured etching

Thomas Rowlandson's humour
was derived from his observations
of London life and particularly the
foolishness of human behaviour,
irrespective of age, rank or social class.
He excelled at depicting – at times
rather savagely – the silliness to be
found in contrasts: old and young, fat
and thin, and so on. A number of these
contrasts are at work in 'Connoisseurs':
the grotesque and the beautiful, the old
and young, the dark threatening colours
of the men's clothing and the pale
nudity of the woman (Venus) in the
painting. All work to produce a funny
but uncomfortable image of lecherous
desire for what cannot be had.

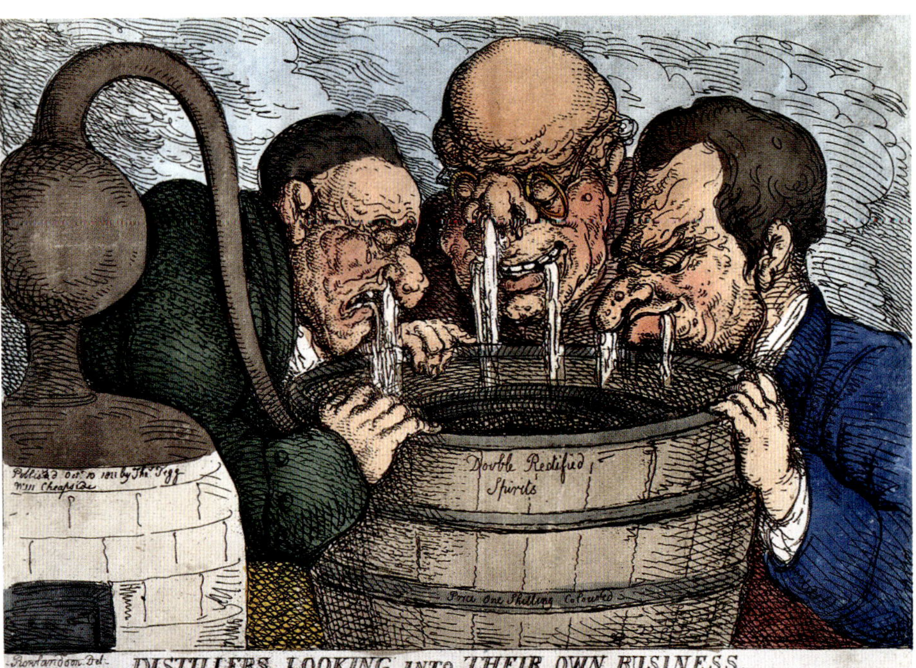

← **Distillers Looking Into
Their Own Business** 1811
Thomas Rowlandson
Etching with publisher's
watercolour on paper

At this point in time, cheap gin was
viewed as the source of, or at least
a contributor to, a variety of social
problems and was therefore heavily
regulated. As a result, it was also
produced in a variety of illegal forms
(i.e. bootleg). This image, sickening but
laughable, makes a protest by imagining
the worst that could happen.

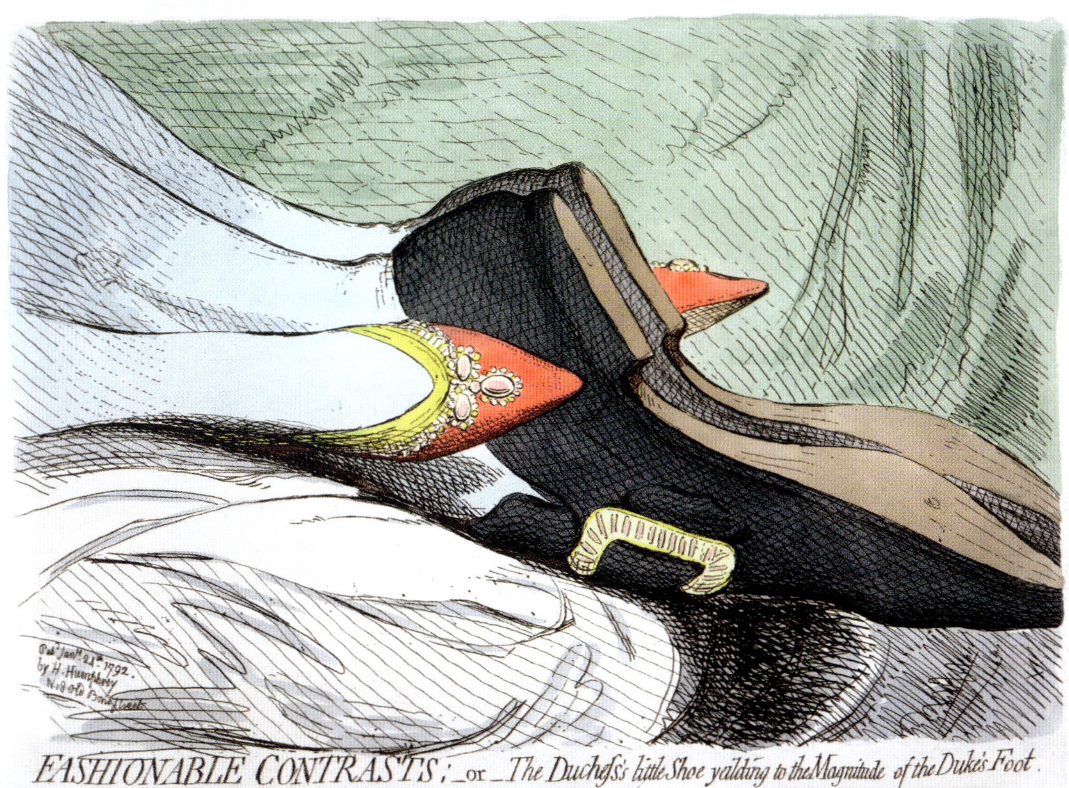

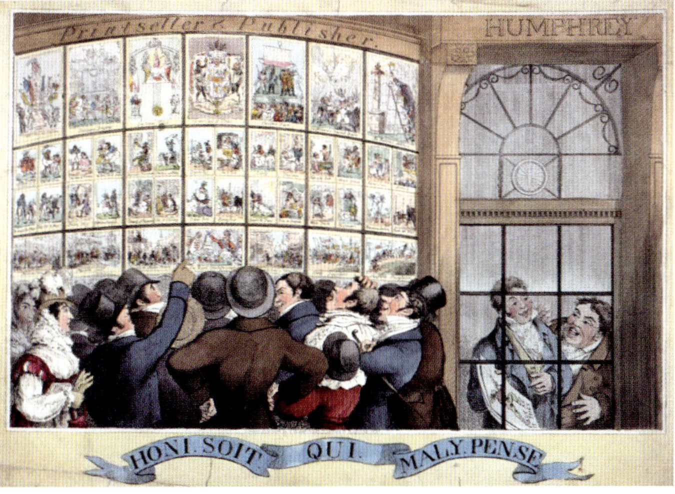

↑ **Fashionable Contrasts; – or – The Duchess's Little Shoe
Yielding to the Magnitude of the Duke's Foot** 1792
James Gillray
Engraving

In an alarmingly contemporary gesture relating to intercourse
(and a view which has appeared in advertising and poster work
up to the present day), James Gillray has a poke at aristocracy.
This satirical statement summarizes the union of the newly
married Duke and Duchess of York. The Duke – huge, self-
centred, over-indulgent and soon to be King – is more or
less burying the Duchess. It is doubtful she will survive the
experience happily.

← **Honi Soit Qui Mal Y Pense
(Shame be to him who thinks evil of it)** 1821
Theodore Lane
Etching and engraving, with publisher's watercolour on paper

By the late 1700s, satirical artists such as James Gillray and Thomas
Rowlandson had become the newsreaders, social commentators
and critics of their time. They targeted all aspects of society: the
government, military, politicians, fashionistas, as well as the poor
and homeless. They gained international renown, as their work
travelled abroad. At home, their work was revered by rich collectors
(even those who had been satirized) and displayed publicly in
the windows of print-shops, allowing broad public access to and
enjoyment of the imagery: an 18th-century version of newspaper
headlines or online news. There was an enormous demand for
satirical prints in London, causing the proliferation of print-shops
throughout the city – at least ten were located in The Strand alone.

Francisco Goya: 'The Disasters of War'

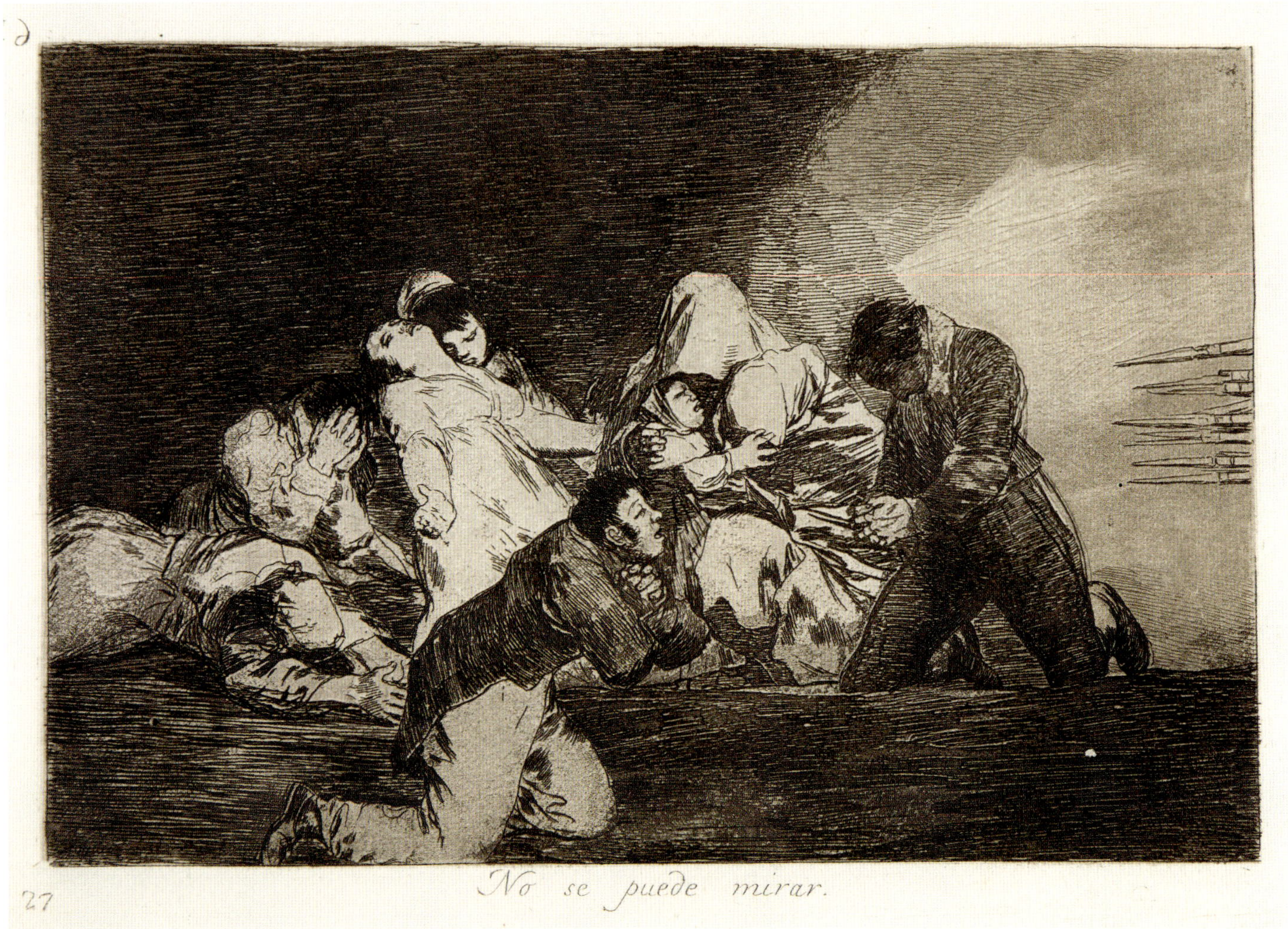

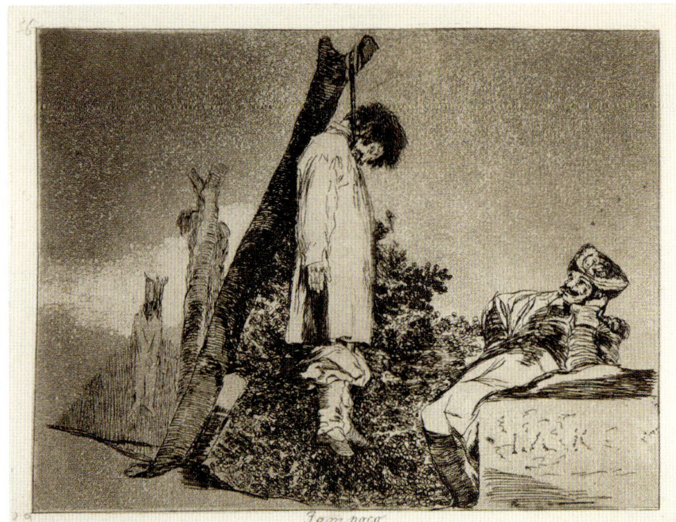

I Can't Bear to Look

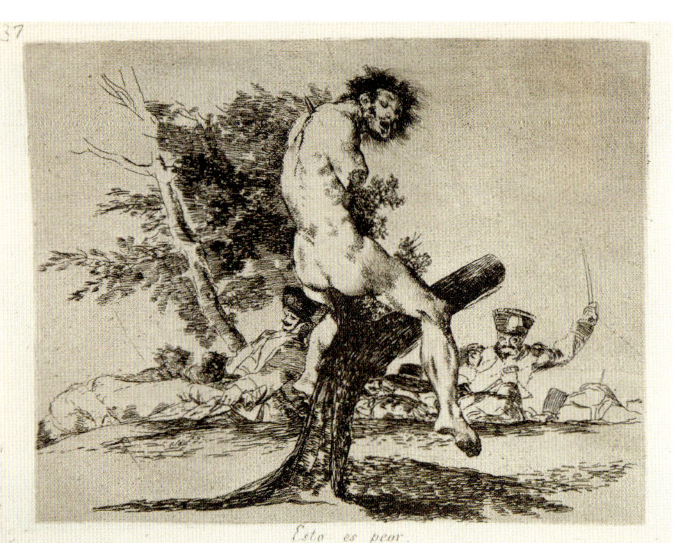

This is Worse

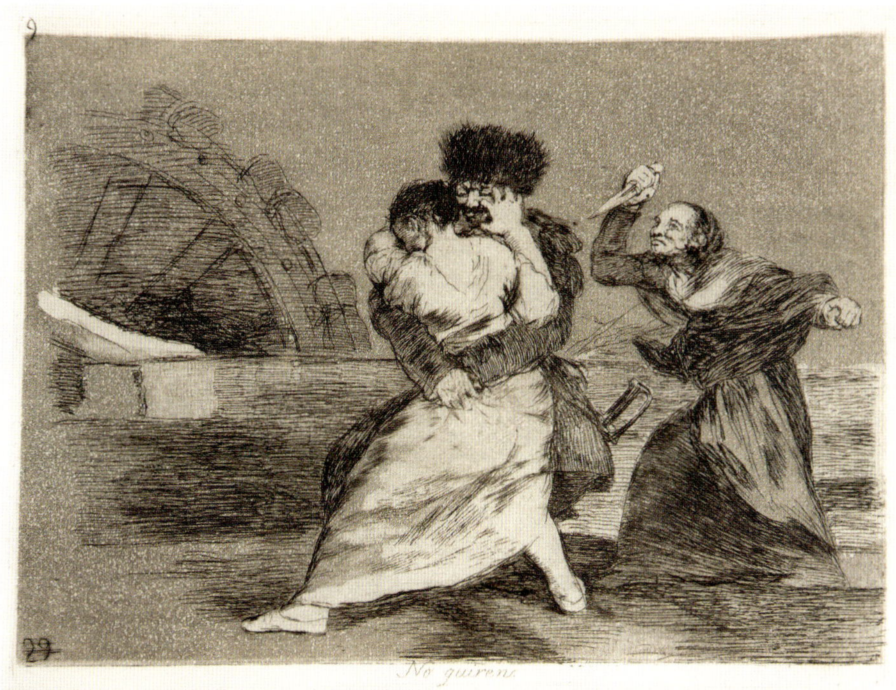

They Don't Want To

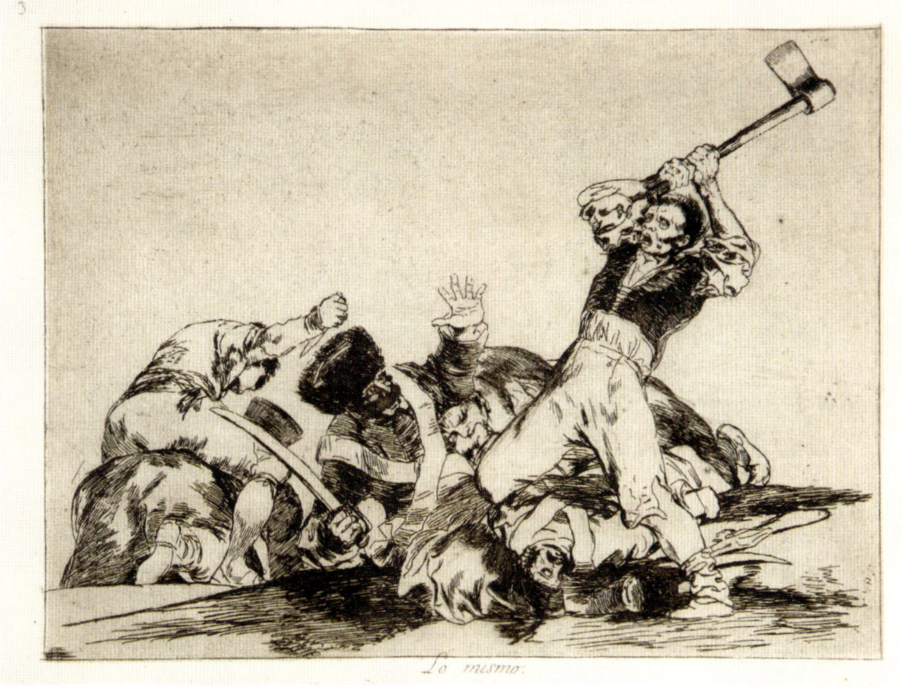

The Same

The Disasters of War 1810–20
Francisco Goya
Etchings and aquatints

Napoleon Bonaparte established himself as Emperor of France in 1804. Still looking for areas in which to expand his empire, in 1807 he marched French troops into northern Spain. In 1808 he occupied Madrid and declared his brother, Joseph, King of Spain. But Spanish civilians fought back, in a savage guerrilla war against the occupiers.

Atrocities were committed on both sides: French soldiers impaled their conquests on trees to demoralize the peasants; the peasants hacked the French to pieces with their farm tools. The guerrilla war, and the French occupation, lasted for five years, ending in 1813. Spanish artist Francisco Goya responded to the savagery, producing a series of 80 etchings over ten years (1810–20) entitled 'The Disasters of War'. Goya's blatant depictions of the carnage sent out a clear message: war turned both sides into monsters. But his prints remain some of the most chilling images of war to this day. The blatant carnage is horrific enough, but what disturbs even more is the pleasure shown in mutilating: the (French) soldier smirking and taking pleasure at viewing the figure hanging from the tree with his trousers around his knees, signifying that he has been castrated. It is little wonder that Goya's etchings were locked away after his death in 1828, and remained unpublished until 1863.

French Satire and Comic Papers

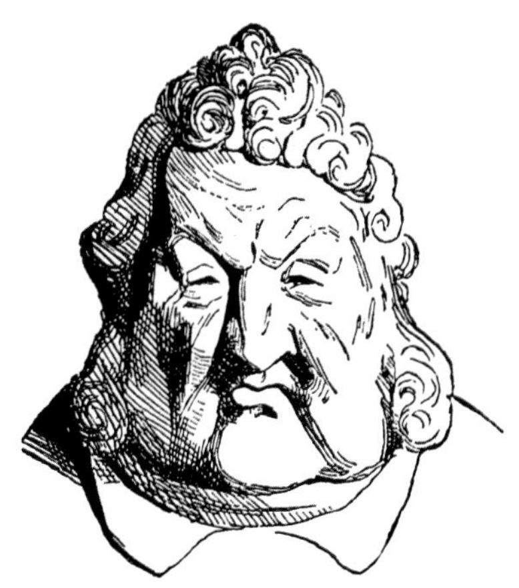
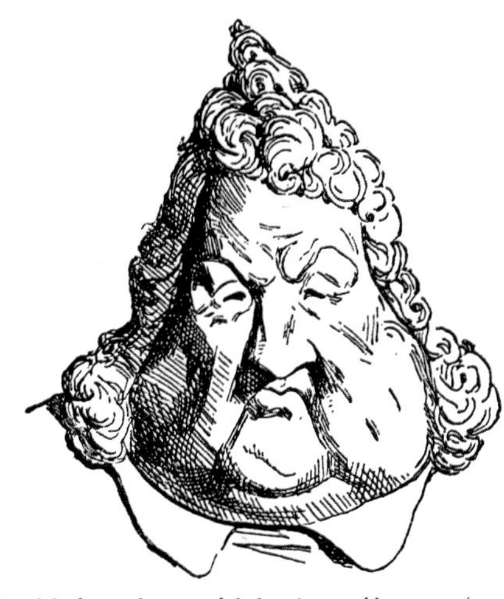
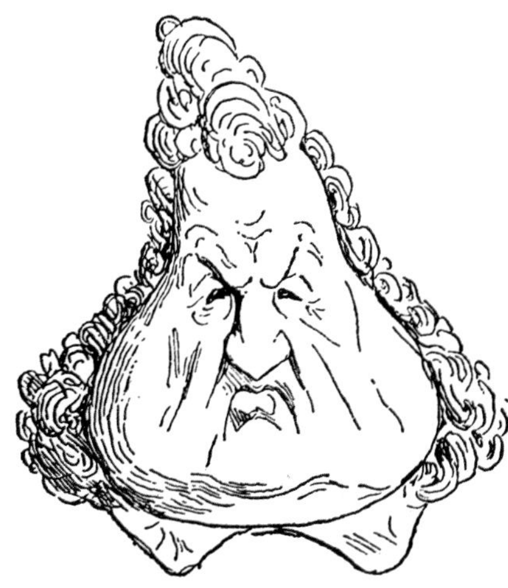
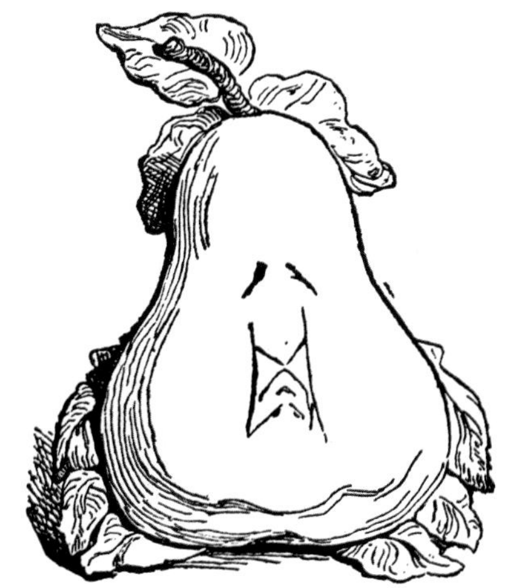

↑ *Les Poires* (The Pears) 1831
Charles Philipon
Engraving

When memories of Napoleon Bonaparte's victories were fading, the July Revolution of 1830 brought the liberal 'King of the French People', Louis-Philippe, to power, who then proclaimed freedom of the press. Soon after, Charles Philipon gathered a team of brilliant artists and founded the satirical weekly, *La Caricature* (1831). Immediately taking 'a step too far', he published a drawing of the King's head, metamorphosing in four stages to a rotting 'poire' (pear-head), also French slang for 'fool'. Philipon was hauled into court and, as legend has it, avoided prison by demonstrating the resemblance – of King to pear – to the jury, by means of sketching and (very likely) verbal panache. He was acquitted of the charge of defamation: a victory for the cause of satire that would trigger the continuation of further ridicule.

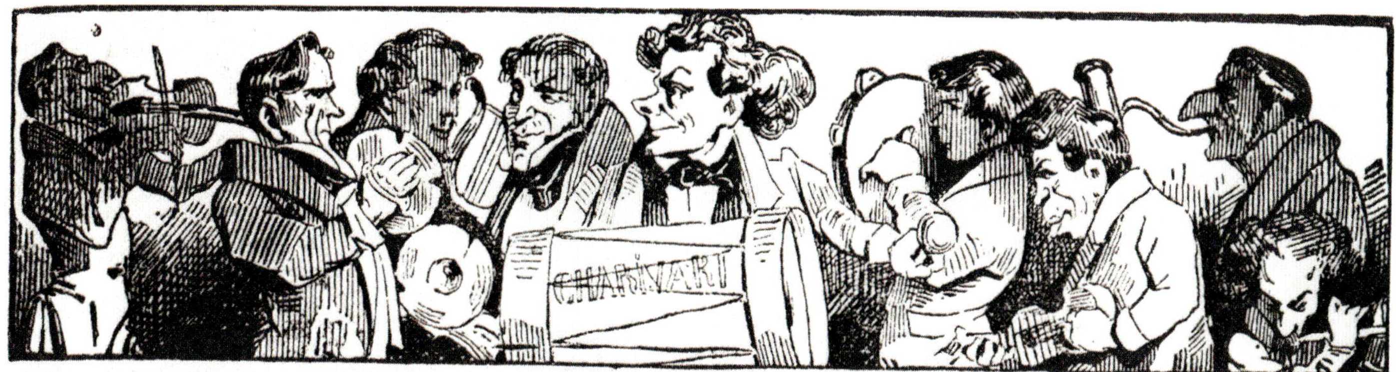

↑ Masthead for *Le Charivari* *c.*1832
Honoré Daumier
Engraving

Honoré Daumier's lively masthead for Philipon's *Le Charivari*, launched in 1832, presents portraits of a few of the artists associated with Philipon's early satirical papers. Banging a drum at the centre is Charles Philipon himself; the young Honoré Daumier is on tambourine (fourth from the right); 'Traviès' or Charles-Joseph Traviès des Villers, one of the first regular caricaturists on *Le Charivari*, is second from the right; and 'Grandville' or Jean-Ignace-Isidore Gérard Grandville, who often parodied people as animals, is far right. (In the same year as Philipon's *Les Poires* incident, young Daumier's drawing of Louis-Philippe as Gargantua sitting on a commode also appeared in *La Caricature*. He was not only arrested, but also received a short prison sentence.)

→ *Le Charivari* 1834
Charles Philipon
Front page, print

Having survived his trip to court over *Les Poires*, Philipon launched a more savage satirical paper in 1832 entitled *Le Charivari*. He also ensured that *Les Poires* became an emblem of resistance against authority, appearing in his papers in annoying variations. When Louis-Philippe banned the drawn image from sight, it appeared instead in further variations, formed out of an arrangement of type (quite a feat as they would have been hand-set in metal type), thereby skirting around the ban or decree. The needling would, once again, go too far. In September 1835, the entire French free press was censored with regard to political subjects.

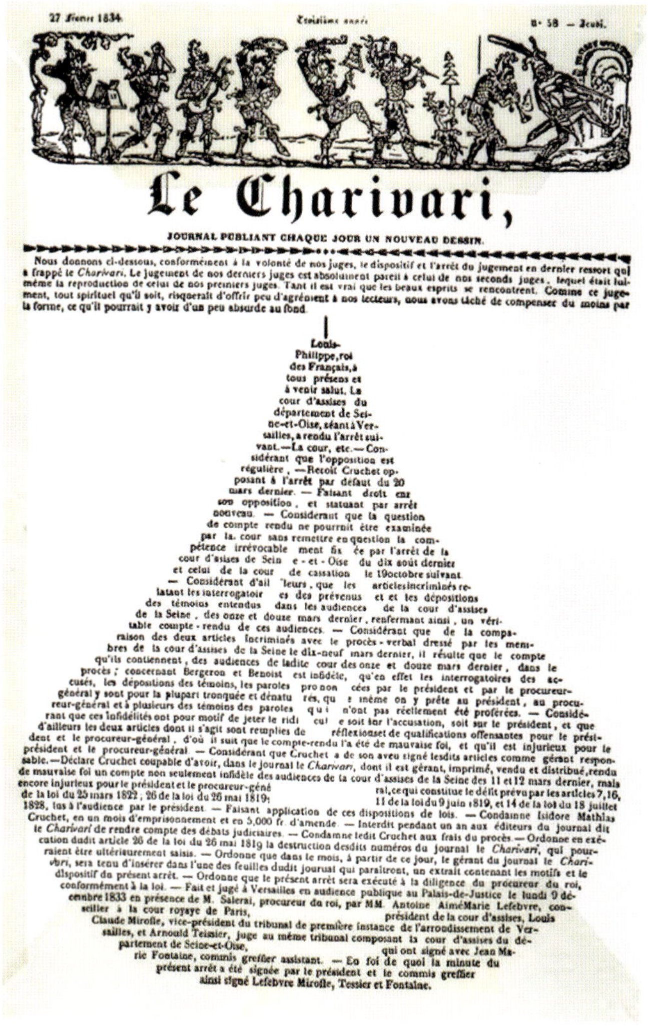

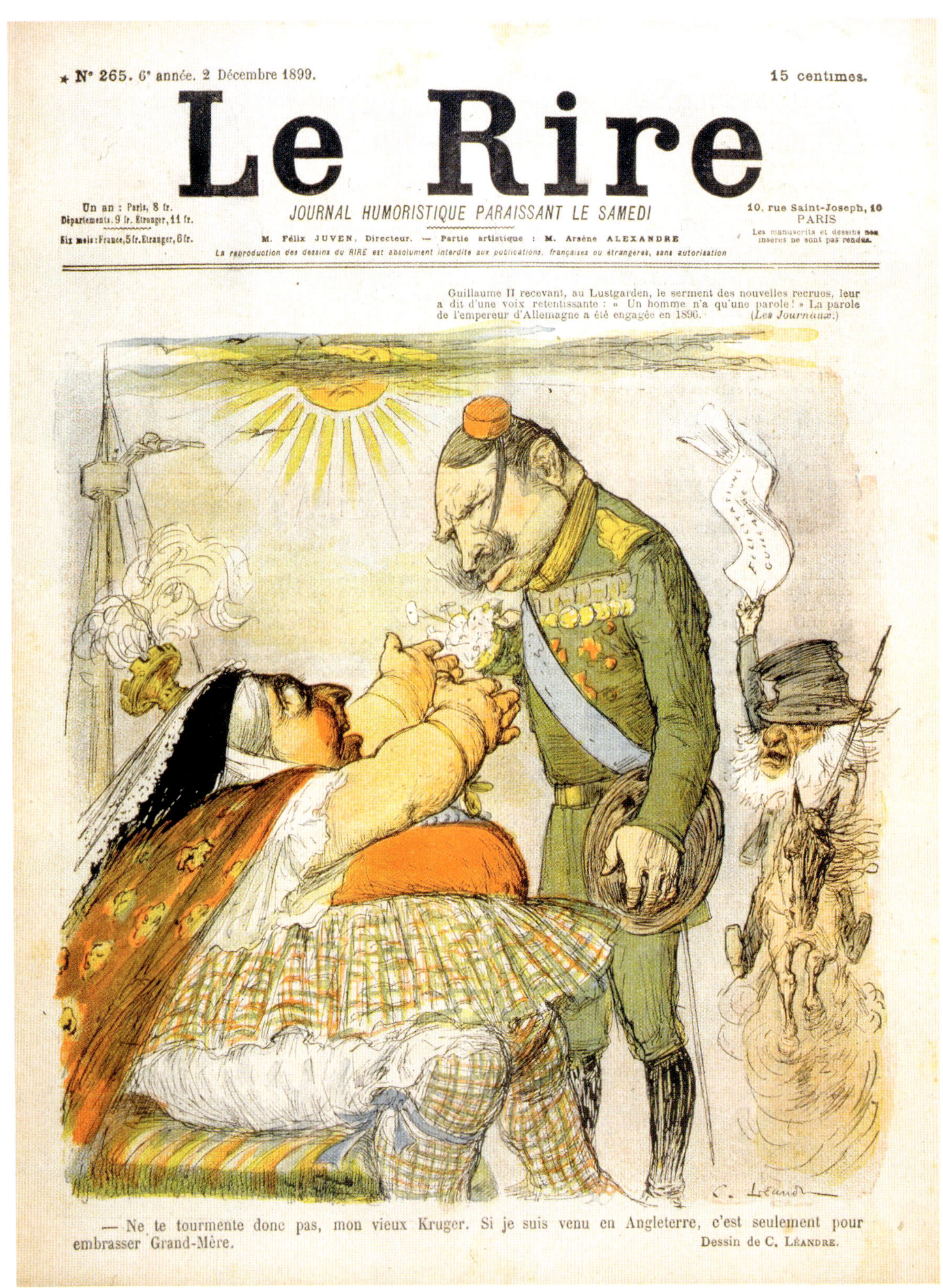

Le Rire (The Laugh),
2 December 1899
Artist: Charles Léandre
Satirical paper

Although censorship struck in 1835 with regard to political subjects, French comic papers and their caricaturists continued to thrive. Prevented from critique or ridicule of the government or those in office, they instead critiqued French (especially Parisian) society. *Le Charivari* was still in operation in 1862; other papers launched included *Le Rire* (The Laugh) in 1895 and *Le Sourire* (The Smile) in 1899. This front page of *Le Rire* shows the German monarch Kaiser Wilhelm II (standing, with a bouquet) who in 1896 had congratulated the Boer leader, Kruger, on a British defeat, but in 1899 has turned pro-British. He is passing off his shifting loyalty in the guise of familial affection for Queen Victoria (who is, in fact, his grandmother).

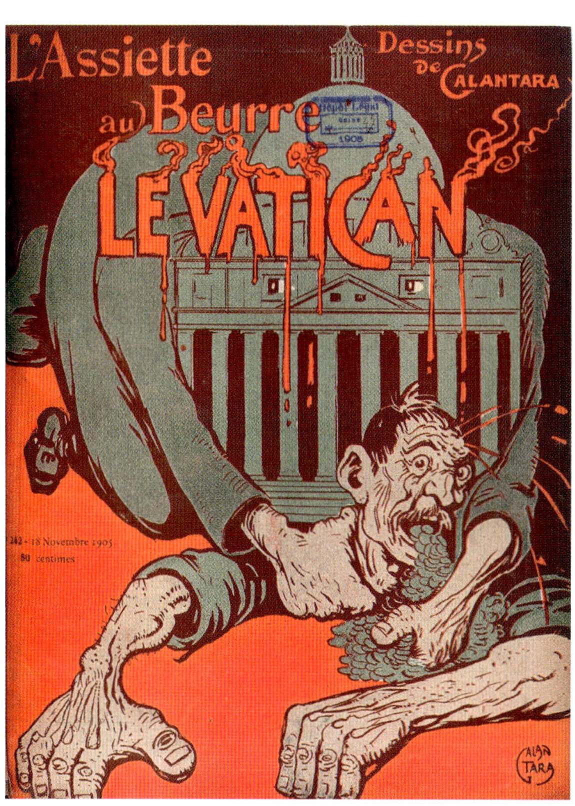

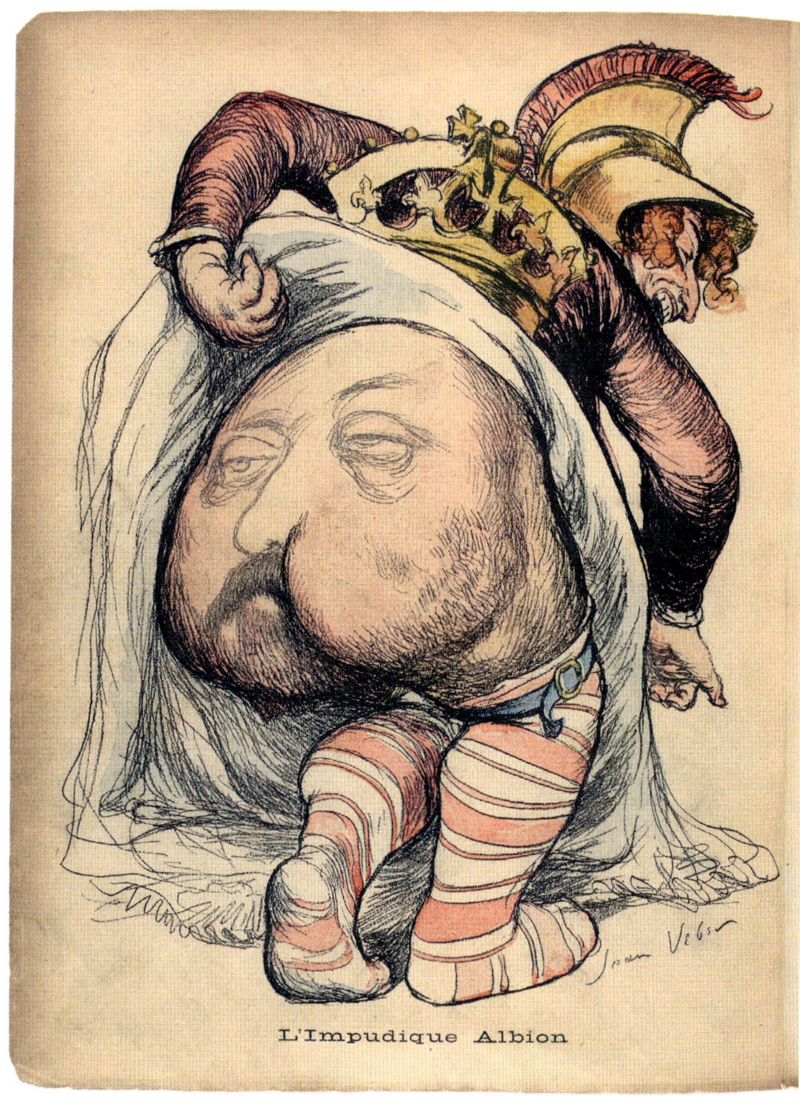

L'Assiette au Beurre (The Butter Dish),
18 November 1905
Illustration: Gabriele Galantara
Satirical paper

Samuel Schwarz founded the satirical weekly *L'Assiette au Beurre* (The Butter Dish) in 1901, appropriately named for the despised members of the governmental bureaucratic machine who connived at handing out favours to ordinary citizens for a price. (The name itself is a slur about wealth, as butter was a highly valued commodity.) The satirical paper's mission was to attack 'The Butter Dish' and the ruling classes, as well as the hierarchy and influence of the Catholic Church. It did so with energy. The socio-political content was mainly visual; text was minimal, and its issues often included current events or international personalities, Britain being a favourite target. This vicious front page illustration shows another favourite target: notice the building's shifty eyes, pig's nose and huge, gaping mouth.

L'Assiette au Beurre (The Butter Dish),
28 September 1901
Illustration: Jean Veber
Satirical paper

One of *L'Assiette au Beurre's* most famous caricatures was produced in September 1901 by Jean Veber, who became a regular contributor. Entitled 'L'Impudique Albion' (Shameless Albion, or Shameless Britain), it features a portrait of King Edward VII imprinted on the posterior of a jesting Britannia. After years of the decorum and seriousness of Queen Victoria, who died in 1901, her heir Edward VII had a reputation for being a bit of a playboy, prone to gambling and mistresses (often located in France), and so representing a very different side of British behaviour and monarchy. This French satirical tradition, particularly in its earlier, scabrous years, can be seen as having spiritual descendants in modern French satirical comics such as *Charlie Hebdo* (founded in 1969).

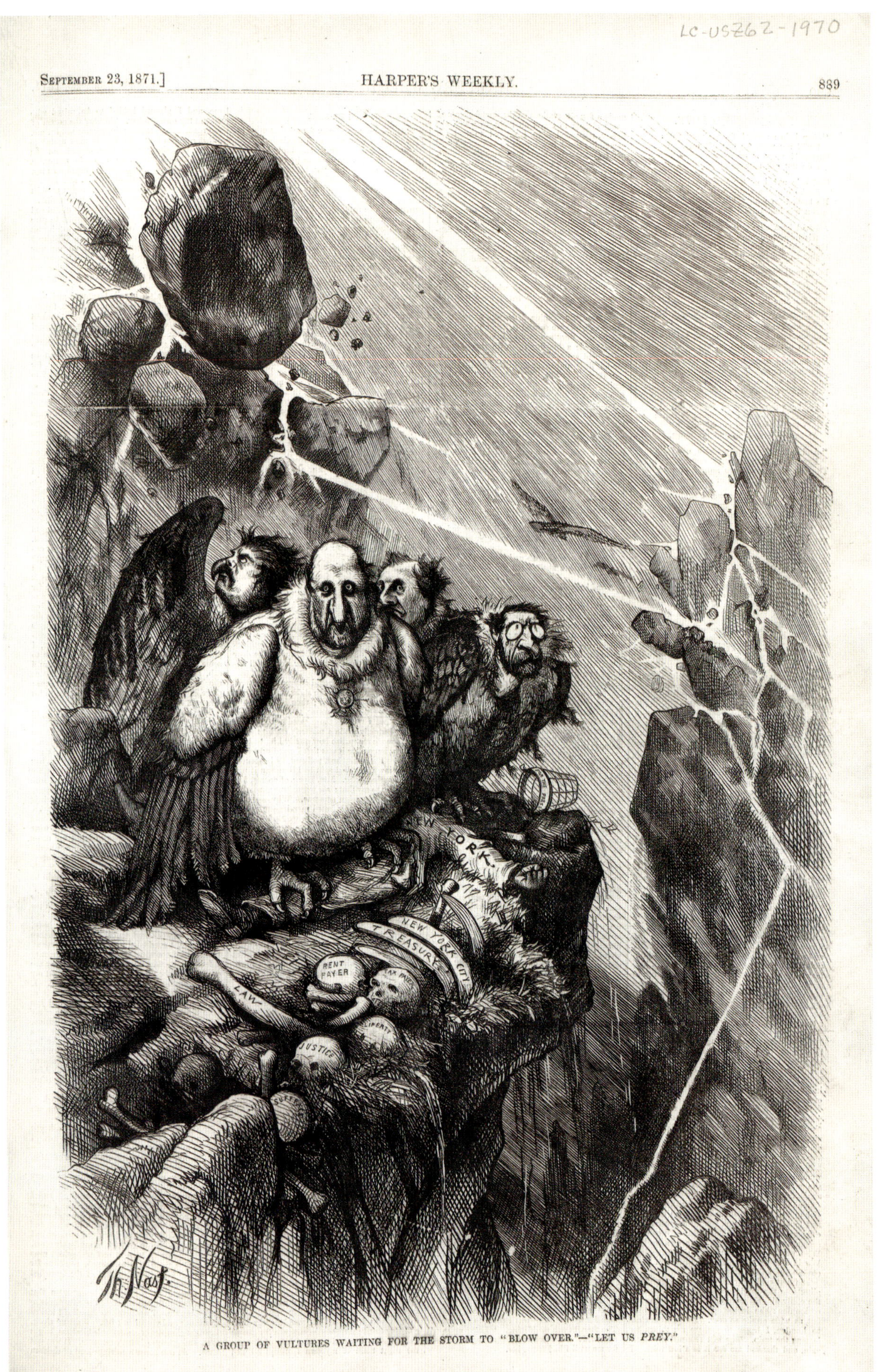

A GROUP OF VULTURES WAITING FOR THE STORM TO "BLOW OVER."—"LET US *PREY*."

Thomas Nast Targets 'Boss' Tweed

← **A Group of Vultures Waiting for the Storm to 'Blow Over' – 'Let Us Prey'** 1871
Artist: Thomas Nast
Political cartoon – *Harper's Weekly*, 23 September 1871

New York politician William Marcy Tweed (also known as 'Boss' Tweed) notoriously gained power over Tammany Hall, the Democratic Party's political machine. He was therefore able to influence the appointment of city officials, control the city government and, through his 'Tammany Ring' of allies, access public money. Thomas Nast, political cartoonist at *Harper's Weekly* magazine, committed himself to ending Tweed's reign of corruption by turning the electorate against him. Nast depicted Tweed as a power-mad, over-fed thug, and created the frightening 'Tammany Tiger' and other caricatures in a visual campaign that lasted from 1867 to 1876, particularly aiming for 1871, an election year. In the final stretch of Nast's visual campaign, *The New York Times* joined the fight with on-going articles against Tweed and, finally, ran documented evidence of corruption – from leaked financial records – on its front page. Both Nast and *The New York Times* fanned public outrage, but Nast's constant needling through his imagery had caused Tweed to break out in fury along the way, spitting out his famous quote: 'Let's stop these damned pictures. I don't care much what the papers write about me – my constituents can't read; but damn it, they can see pictures!' In the end, his much maligned constituents voted him and many Tammany candidates out of office. Many of them (including Tweed) also ended up in prison. This image shows Tweed and his cronies as vultures, waiting to ride out the storm of public disapproval. Boss Tweed is the big white vulture (wearing his trademark diamond shirt-stud). He and his friends are squatting upon the flattened figure of New York City. The scattered bones of the law, suffrage, justice and other aspects of democracy are lying at their feet.

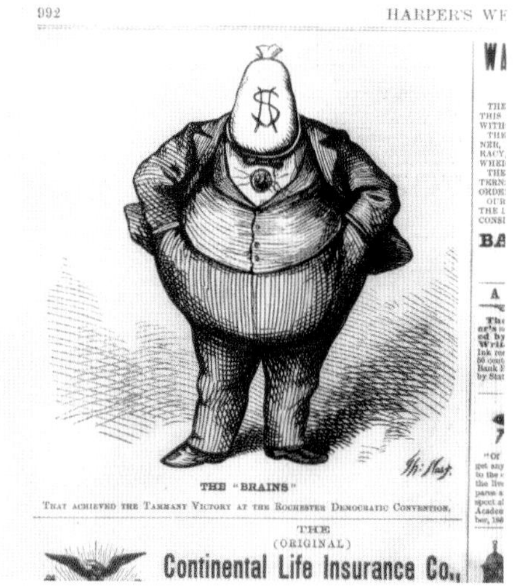

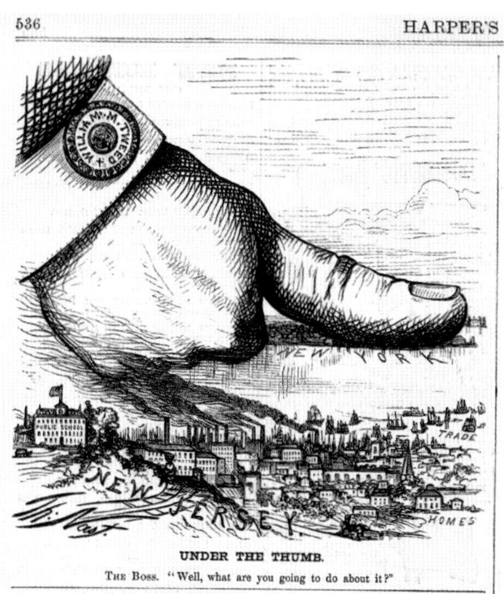

↑ **The 'Brains' That Achieved the Tammany Victory at the Rochester Democratic Convention** 1871
Artist: Thomas Nast
Political cartoon – *Harper's Weekly*,
21 October 1871

'Boss' Tweed smugly celebrates a Tammany victory at the Rochester Democratic Convention, a state nominating convention. His head is a money bag; his face a dollar sign. The inference is that Tammany won the nominations through bribes and coercion. His over-sized diamond shirt-stud shines.

↑ **Under the Thumb. The Boss. 'Well, what are you going to do about it?'** 1871
Artist: Thomas Nast
Political cartoon – *Harper's Weekly*,
10 June 1871

A cartoon showing Tweed's power over the city he has 'under his thumb', with the added taunt, 'What are you going to do about it?' Again, Tweed is sporting a huge diamond cufflink as a sign of ill-gotten wealth.

**The New Board of Education.
Sowing the Seed, with an Eye to the Harvest** 1871
Artist: Thomas Nast
Political cartoon – *Harper's Weekly*,
13 May 1871

As a reaction to one of Nast's cartoons, Tweed told his mates in the Board of Education to reject the bid Harper's Brothers had put in to publish textbooks for the New York City public schools. The Ring decided to have 'books of instruction' be prepared by its 'favourites' and printed by an association composed of members of the Ring. The threat of removal of Harper's textbooks from city schools prompted this cartoon, where Tweed seizes a book from a schoolboy; one of his friends pitches Harper's books out the window, and the other teaches the boys so-called 'truths'.

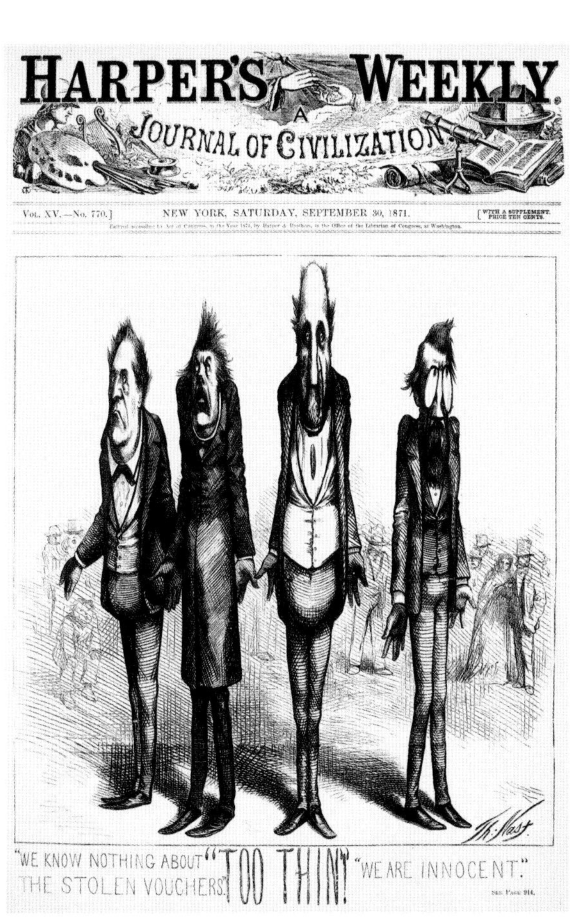

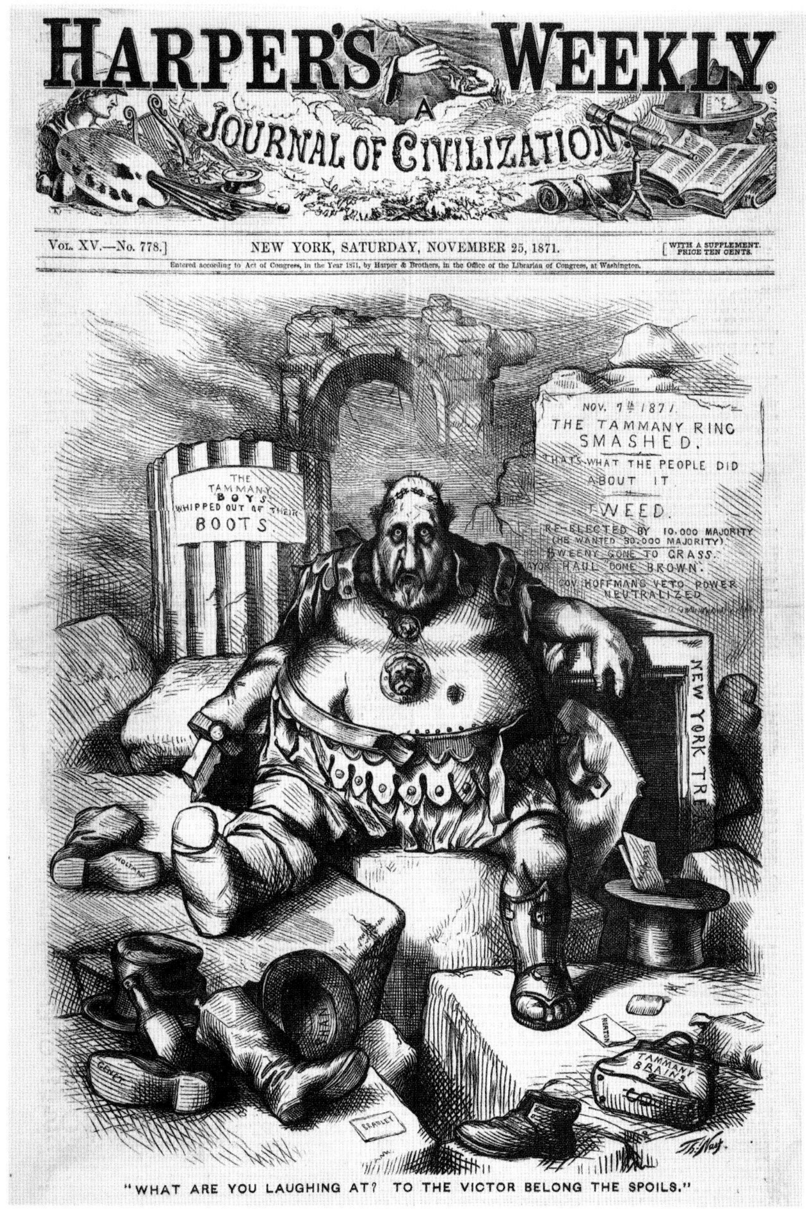

'Too Thin!' 1871
Artist: Thomas Nast
Political cartoon – *Harper's Weekly*, 30 September 1871

This cartoon refers to the suspicious theft and destruction of incriminating payment-vouchers from the offices of Boss Tweed and his Ring. The event took place soon after official requests had been made to examine city and county accounts. Boss Tweed made himself and his Ring colleagues into the victims. They received no sympathy from *The New York Times*, Nast or even City Hall officials. Instead people laughed out loud, saying the story was (in slang) 'too thin'.

'What are you Laughing at? To the Victor Belong the Spoils' 1871
Artist: Thomas Nast
Political cartoon – *Harper's Weekly*, 25 November 1871

Boss Tweed is collapsed in shock, in front of a sign (on the left) saying 'The Tammany Boys Whipped Out of Their Boots' and (on the right) 'The Tammany Ring Smashed: That's What the People Did About It', a clear riposte to the notion Tweed had the city 'under his thumb'. Tweed sits amid the rubble, dazed at Tammany's election defeat, and gazing blankly at his own questionable future. He still wears the diamond shirt-stud, but under it is a medallion of a sad-faced Tammany Tiger, looking more like a pussycat.

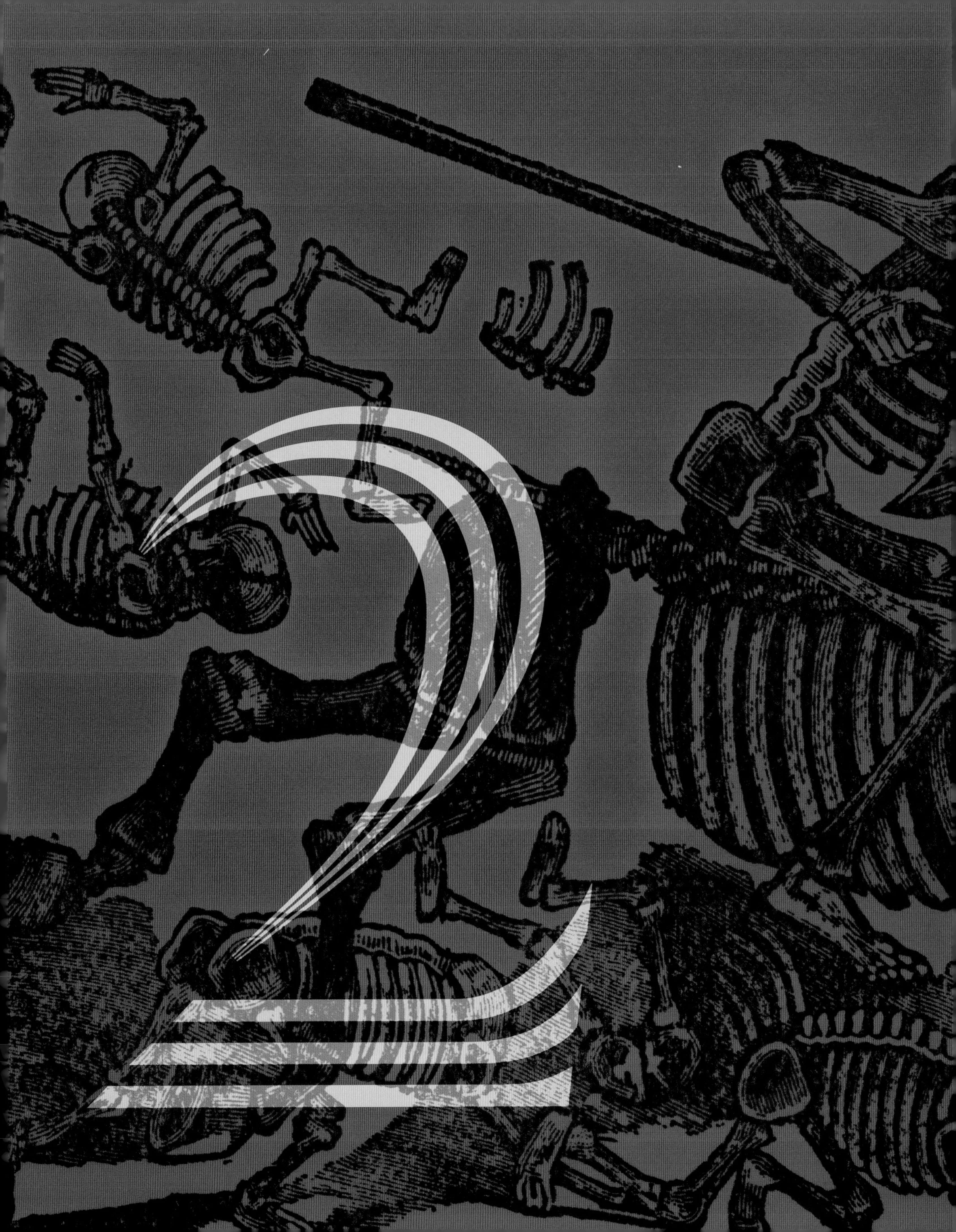

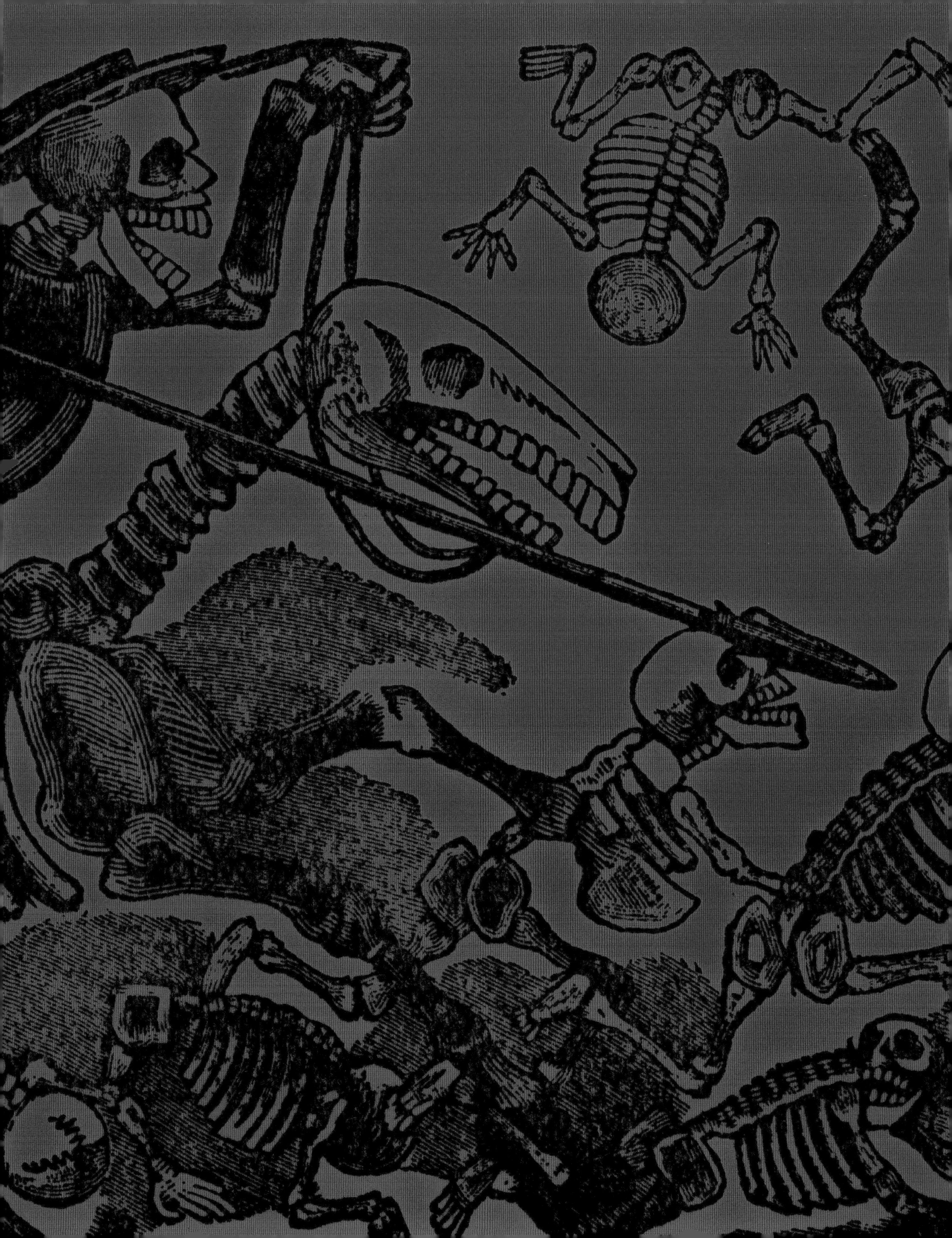

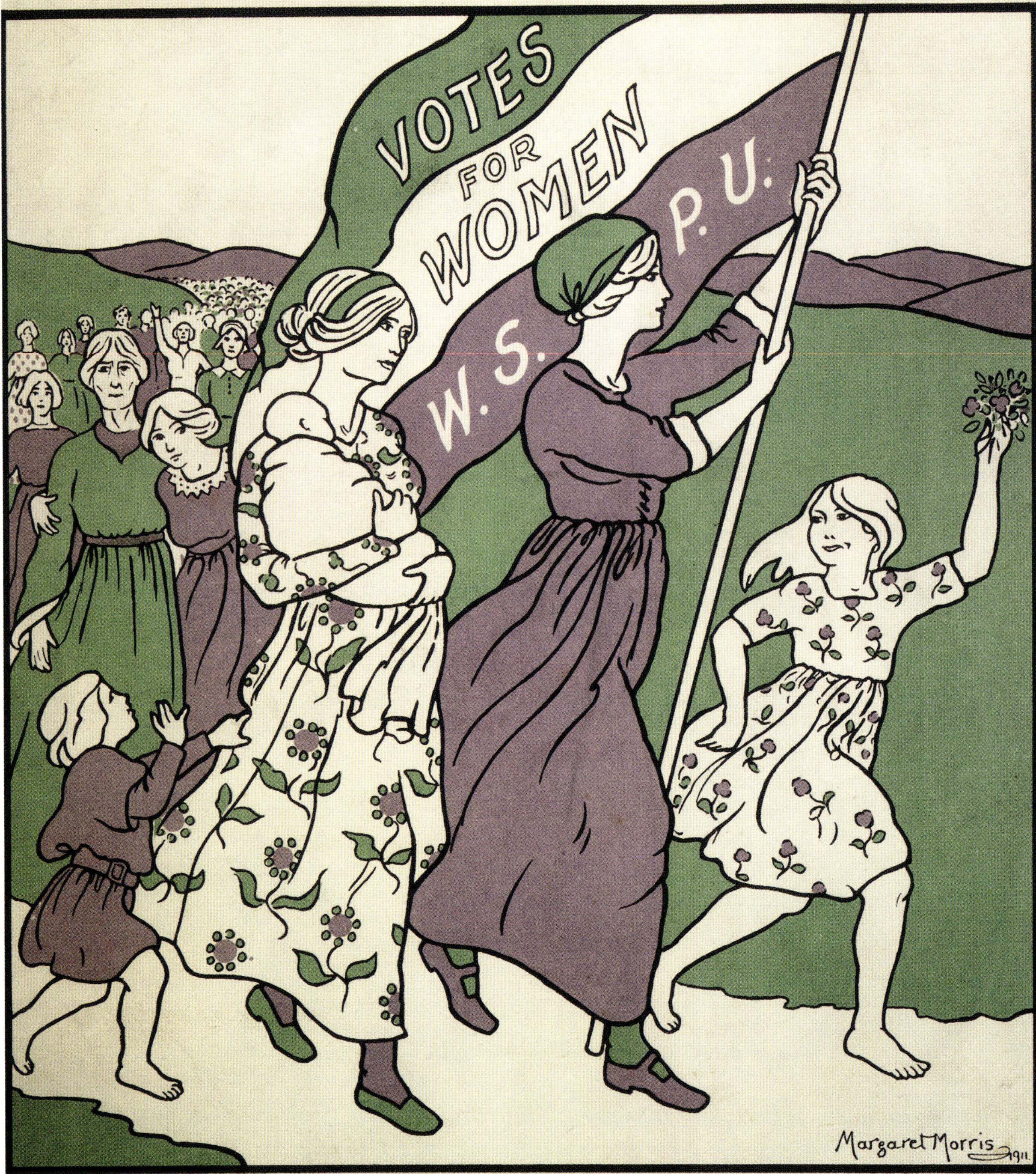

Cover of songsheet for 'The March of the Women' 1911
Drawing by Margaret Morris

1900–1930
Constructing a New Society

The beginning of the 20th century brought the promise of change. Visions of speed and industrialization, demands for social revolution, experiments with new forms of visual expression: all signalled a break with the past. And all were helped, or hindered, by a terrifying force. Within two decades, much of humanity would be plunged into the First World War (1914–18), a significant participant to the creativity unleashed during this period.

Offering a ghostly premonition of things to come in Europe, the Mexican artist and printmaker José Guadalupe Posada (1852–1913) provided an intense, satirical and at times bloody, documentary of the years leading up to the start of the Mexican Revolution in 1910. He spent much of his working life in Mexico City, and produced an incredible output of illustrations – estimated at over 15,000 – for the 'penny press', aimed at the lower, near-illiterate classes. His sensationalized depictions of news events, crimes, politics or gossip covered posters, street gazettes and broadsheets, sold at fairs and festivals. Disasters such as fires, floods and earthquakes as well as shoot-outs with the police (curiously relevant, even now) provided an exciting and at times gruesome portrayal of city life. All chronicled the interests of the common people, and especially the deep divisions between rich and poor. Posada is best known, however, for the use of macabre, humorous 'calaveras', the dancing skeletons of death (derived from ceremonies such as the Day of the Dead, 2 November, when barriers between worlds are transgressed and the living and dead coexist). Ambiguous agents of good or evil, they laugh, play, smoke cigars and

invariably convey a feeling of impending doom or death, contributing to the unsettling effect of much of his work.[1]

At the same time, a different social revolution was brewing in Britain. Emmeline Pankhurst founded the Women's Social and Political Union (WSPU) in 1903 with her daughters Christabel and Sylvia. The WSPU represented the new spirit of militancy in the British women's suffrage movement, demanding voting rights for women. Its members were dubbed 'the suffragettes' by the British press. From 1906 to 1914, the WSPU ran their campaign with military precision, underpinning all of their activities with visual propaganda and protest. Their militant activities involved public speaking, the production of their newspaper *Votes for Women* (followed much later by the more militant magazine *The Suffragette*), pestering and heckling politicians, demonstrating in front of Buckingham Palace, and many other actions, often ending in imprisonment, hunger-strikes and government retaliation by means of torture (force-feeding).[2]

Also crucial to their cause were their corporate image-building activities: the introduction of 'the colours' (purple, white and green) and the 'suffragette uniform'; the use of 'spectacle' or processions, mass demonstrations and smaller ceremonies; and the merchandising of 'the suffragette look' in fashion and style. In addition they produced a wide range of accessories, novelties (dolls, games and toys) and other goods. But despite all their efforts and sacrifices, by 1912 they were still denied the vote and so resorted to a campaign of violence in the form of window-smashing, setting fire to (unoccupied) houses and other actions. With the onset of the First World

War in 1914, they immediately stopped their campaign and
backed the war effort. Much of the WSPU's campaign was
documented graphically on postcards (extremely popular
and collectable at the time), posters and in newspapers. The
broader, international movement for women's suffrage also
yielded graphics from the USA and other countries.[3]

Across the English Channel, not far away, another revolution
was taking place that would change the visual arts forever. F.T.
Marinetti's Futurist manifesto appeared on the front page of
Le Figaro (Paris) in 1909, launching the first of a number of
intellectually-based avant-garde art movements that collectively
became known as the Modern movement, embracing writers,
artists, designers and architects on an international scale.
Futurism venerated the energy of speed and the machine, as
well as the power and violence generated by war (considered
to be the ultimate Futurist sensation). It was a movement of
ideas, writings – manifestos, poetry, texts – and methods that
were exploited by, and which energized, other existing art
movements. Futurism's dynamic artistic vision changed the use
of typography and printed formats forever, allowing the free
use of type as a pictorial/graphic element in itself rather than
as a carrier of a verbal message. Its many written or recited
manifestos made a clear rejection of the 'old social order' and
its traditions, delivered with a vehemence best described by
Marinetti's caustic remark 'Every day we must spit on the altar
of art'. This sentiment would certainly have passed on to, and
excited, Dada and other art movements.[4]

Dadaism (1916) was an outright protest against the First
World War, translating the insanity of war and bloodshed into an
absurdist rejection of everything. It was anti-war, anti-society, anti-
art, and it proceeded to turn the conventions of art, performance,
writing and typography upside down. The innovation of
photomontage was one of its most powerful tools; its shocking
treatment of typography was 'calculated chaos' on the page,
and still bears a strong influence on the teaching and practice
of graphic design today. Dada was born in the Cabaret Voltaire,
Zurich with the provocative performances (poetry readings, noise-
music, riots) of a group of young artists and writers, including
Hugo Ball and Tristan Tzara. A Berlin Dada group soon evolved,
including Hannah Höch, Raoul Hausmann and John Heartfield,
all engaged in the development and use of photomontage, often
for satirical or political purposes. There were many other Dada or
anti-art movements in New York, Paris, Hanover and other cities,
developing their own versions and methods of revolution.[5]

In the early 1920s, the art movement known as
Constructivism borrowed the geometric forms and dynamic
composition of Russian Suprematism (Kasimir Malevich's
abstract art movement of 1915) and used them to develop a new
'Constructivist vision', or model for life. The Constructivists
placed their artistic talents at the service of the 1917 Bolshevik
Revolution, envisaging a new culture for a new society. Under
the title of 'Productivism', they created a utilitarian role for
art and design in the new Soviet future, producing everyday
products across a wide range of disciplines, from graphic design
and advertising to textile design, theatre design and film.[6]

Alexander Rodchenko was an early advocate of
Constructivism, exhibited widely and was one of the most
versatile in advancing the possibilities of Productivism. He
applied a Constructivist sensibility and style to typography,
graphic composition and layout, photomontage and
photography, while working across advertising (often partnered
with his friend, the poet Vladimir Mayakovsky), illustration,
logo design, book/magazine design, and poster design for
the cinema. He even ventured into the design of a worker's
suit, the furniture and interior for a Worker's Club, and other
products such as a table lamp and teapot. Varvara Stepanova,
wife and co-worker on many projects with Rodchenko, was also
an internationally recognized artist in her own right. She was
deeply committed to Productivism, especially in the area of
clothing and textile design. She produced remarkable designs
for sports clothing and textile prints, and especially enjoyed
designing specialist clothing for surgeons, firemen and pilots.
Economy of material was always an issue, often supplemented
by the use of bright colours. She also designed both costumes
and sets for the theatre and posters, as well as being involved in
the graphic design and production of magazines and journals.[7]

El Lissitzky's pioneering Constructivist experiments in
typography and layout dealt with the visual expression of sound
and the rhythm of the spoken word, or revelled in the use of
letters as pictorial material. It was art for the machine age, and
the beginning of seeing type and pictorial material as a whole.
Lissitzky was also the great connector, visiting other avant-
garde artists in Europe, forming collaborations, lecturing on
Constructivist principles, designing several Russian exhibitions
in Germany, and bringing the new Russian art and its ideas to
the attention of the West. Sadly, this period of creativity was not
to last. Lenin, the leader of the 1917 Revolution, died in 1924;
by 1928 Stalin was leader, and in 1932 he outlawed abstract art,
introducing Socialist Realism.[8]

The First World War, having ended in 1918, had exhausted
many of the European countries involved. Post-war Germany
struggled to deal with reparation payments owed from the
war. Unemployment and inflation spiralled, followed by the
collapse of the currency in 1923. Artists drew or painted
the reality they saw around them. George Grosz depicted
bloated industrialists and their struggling workers or hungry,
unemployed victims. Käthe Kollwitz's graphic art continued
to expose the poverty and oppression of the German working
class and the wider tragedies of war. Chronicling the political
developments throughout this period was the tough, satirical
weekly *Simplicissimus*, launched in 1896 in Munich, with its
famous bulldog symbol and much of its bold cover art drawn
by co-founder Thomas Theodor Heine. For three decades
its main artists/cartoonists – Bruno Paul, Olaf Gulbransson,
Karl Arnold and others – had become well known for using a
sophisticated drawing style to make aggressive comments about
capitalism, nationalism, the ruling classes and (later) Hitler.
But not surprisingly, with the rise of the Nazi Party in the early
1930s and Hitler's installation as German Chancellor in 1933,
the satirical tabloid finally had met its match.[9]

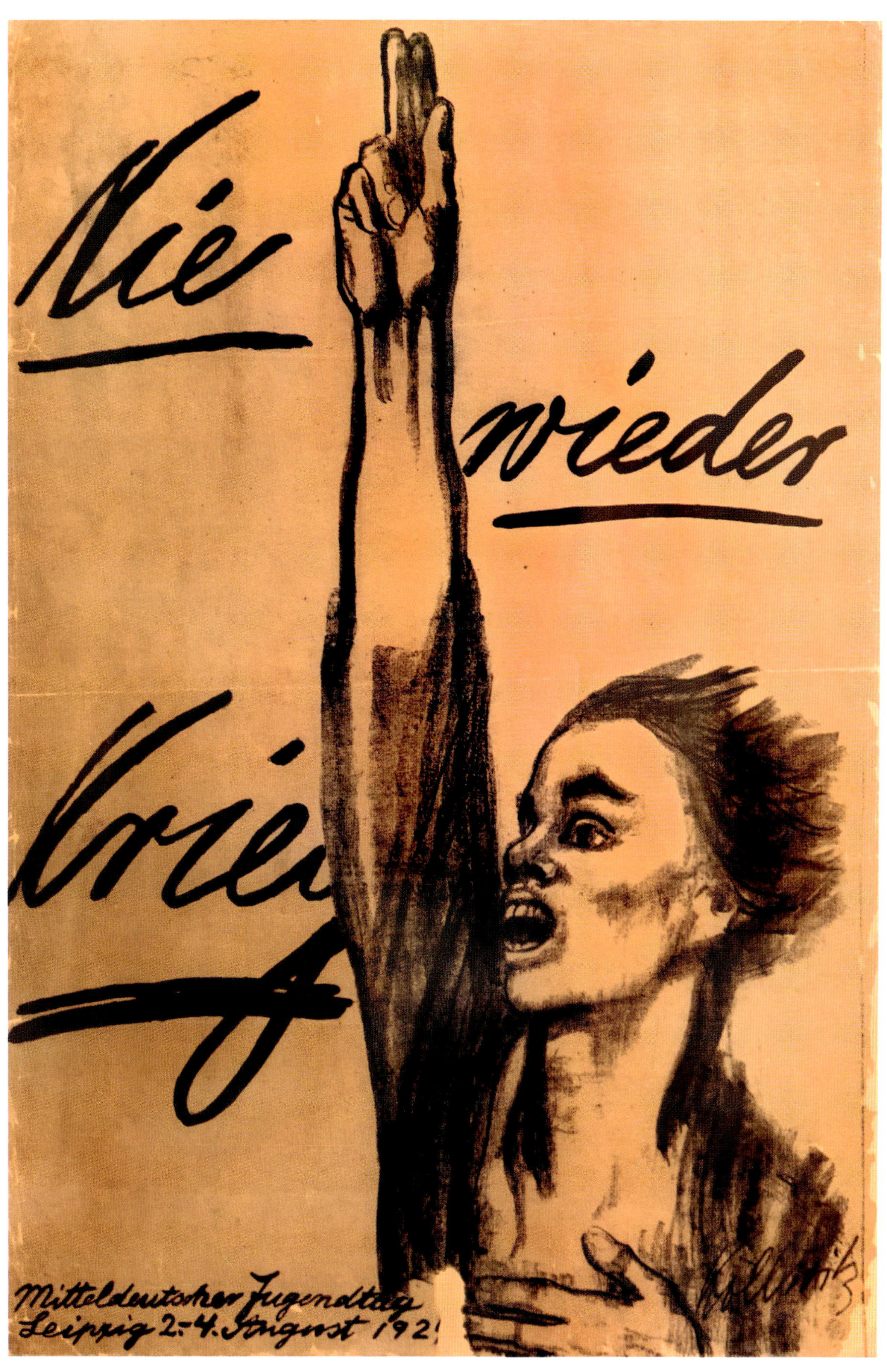

Never Again War! 1924
Käthe Kollwitz

Posada and Pre-revolutionary Mexico

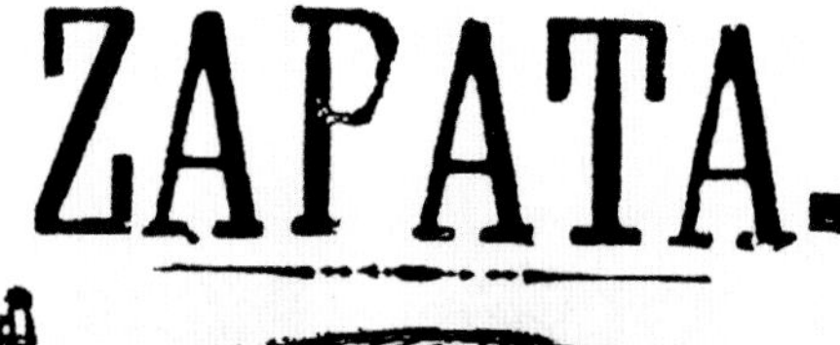

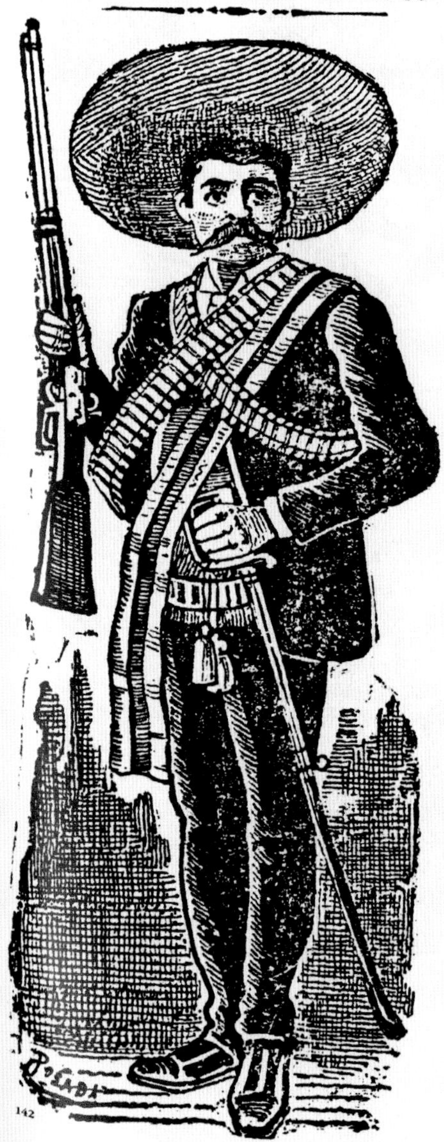

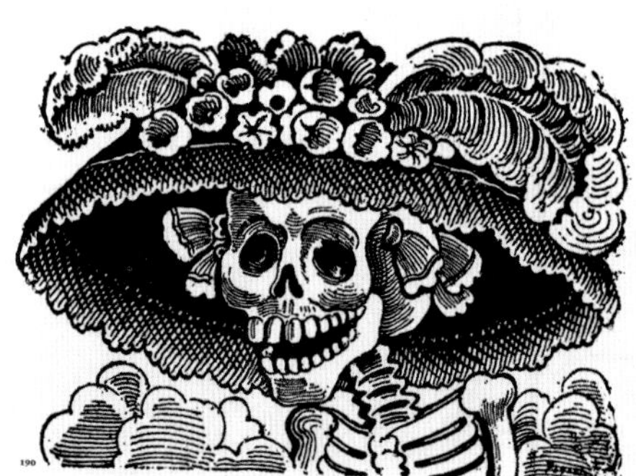

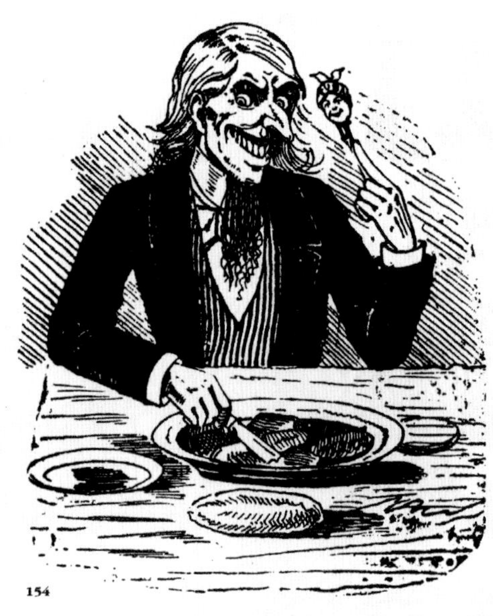

↑ **Uncle Sam Consuming Cuba** date unknown
José Guadalupe Posada
Engraving

In the Mexican War between Mexico and the USA (1846–48)
over disputed border territory, a great deal of Mexican territory
was lost to the USA. A by-product of the later Spanish-American
War (of 1898) was the Platt Amendment of 1903, giving the USA
the right to intervene in Cuba's internal affairs. It is therefore not
surprising that, by this point in time, Mexicans would see the
USA as an imperialist force that was a constant threat to Mexico
and currently devouring Cuba.

← **Emiliano Zapata** date unknown
José Guadalupe Posada
Engraving

Although at the time of this print he was probably still considered
a local bandit, at the start of the Mexican Revolution (1910)
Zapata raised an army of peasants and fought for land reform or
tierra y libertad (land and liberty). Standing up to a succession
of central governments, he took control of the southern state of
Morelos, chased out estate owners and divided their land among
the peasants. He was eventually assassinated by government forces
in 1919, but became a legendary hero, and his agrarian reform
movement is still considered relevant today.

← **Calavera of a Society Belle** date unknown
José Guadalupe Posada
Engraving

Women do not escape 'calavera' treatment, and are particularly
grotesque as skeletons when wearing fancy dress.

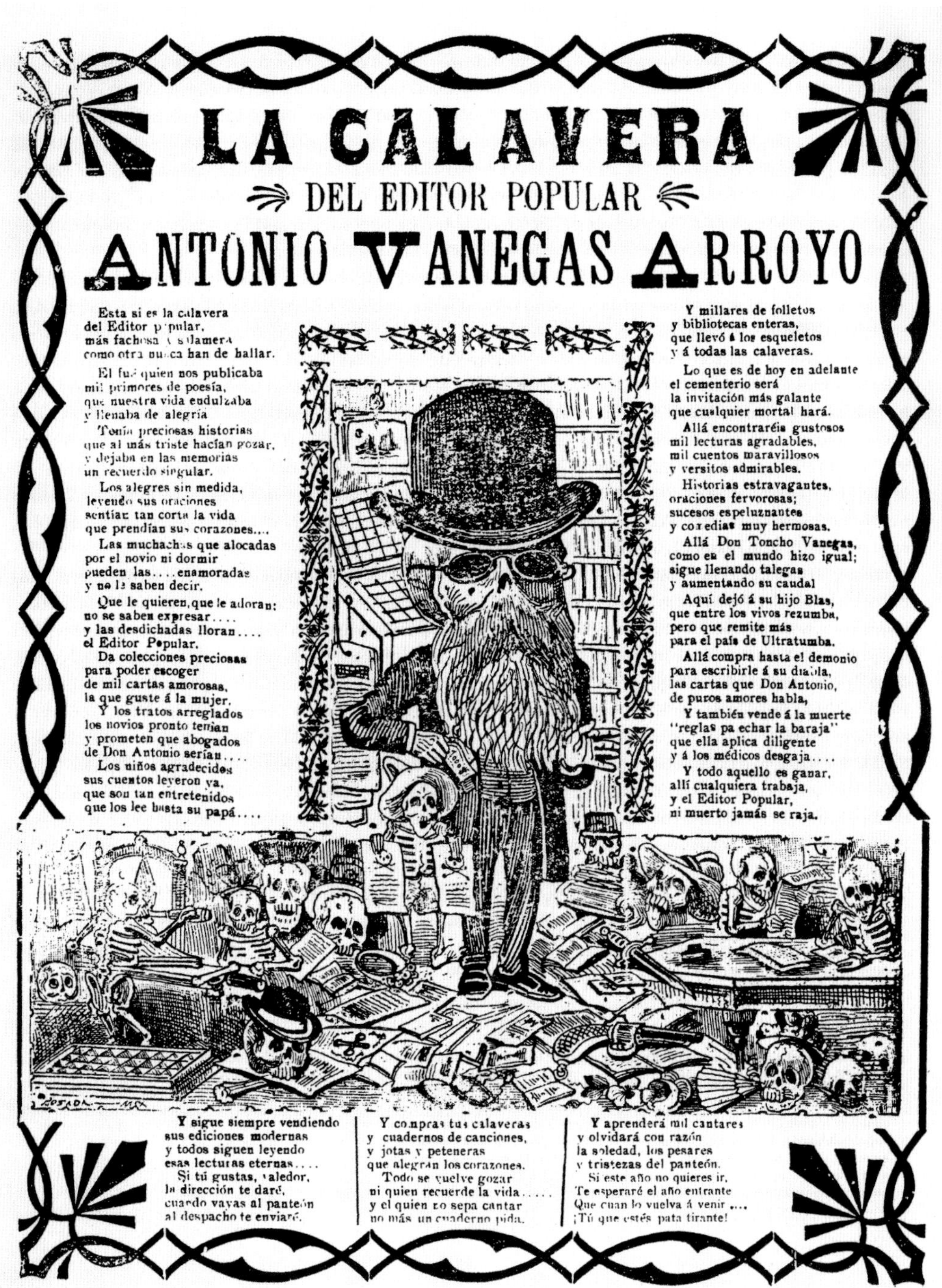

Calavera of the People's Printer Antonio Vanegas Arroyo date unknown
José Guadalupe Posada
Engraving

The Mexican printmaker José Guadalupe Posada produced his most renowned prints and illustrations for the small press owner and publisher Antonio Vanegas Arroyo in Mexico City. He began his work there in the early 1890s, producing a prolific output of illustrations depicting news, events, politics, gossip or poems for the 'penny press': cheap broadsheets aimed at the lower class, semi-literate audience and posted in the street or sold at fairs or festivals. His work chronicled the concerns of the common people, and particularly the social divisions between rich and poor. Although never an overtly 'political artist', his artistic narrative certainly included politics. His best known depictions, possibly both then and now, are his humorous 'calaveras', traditionally the macabre, grinning skeletons of death, derived from the festivities of the Mexican Day of the Dead, on 2 November, a day when the dead and the living spiritually coexist. However, the skeletons seem to overstay their welcome and appear fairly often in Posada's work, a mischievous, cigar-smoking, gambling, romantic (but scary) presence and an ominous reminder of the fragility of life. The print shown here presents a very humorous poem about the death (real or imagined) of Antonio Vanegas Arroyo. It gushes about his qualities and contributions in life throughout, while at the end joking that his pamphlets would even find readers 'in hell'.

Votes for Women: The WSPU

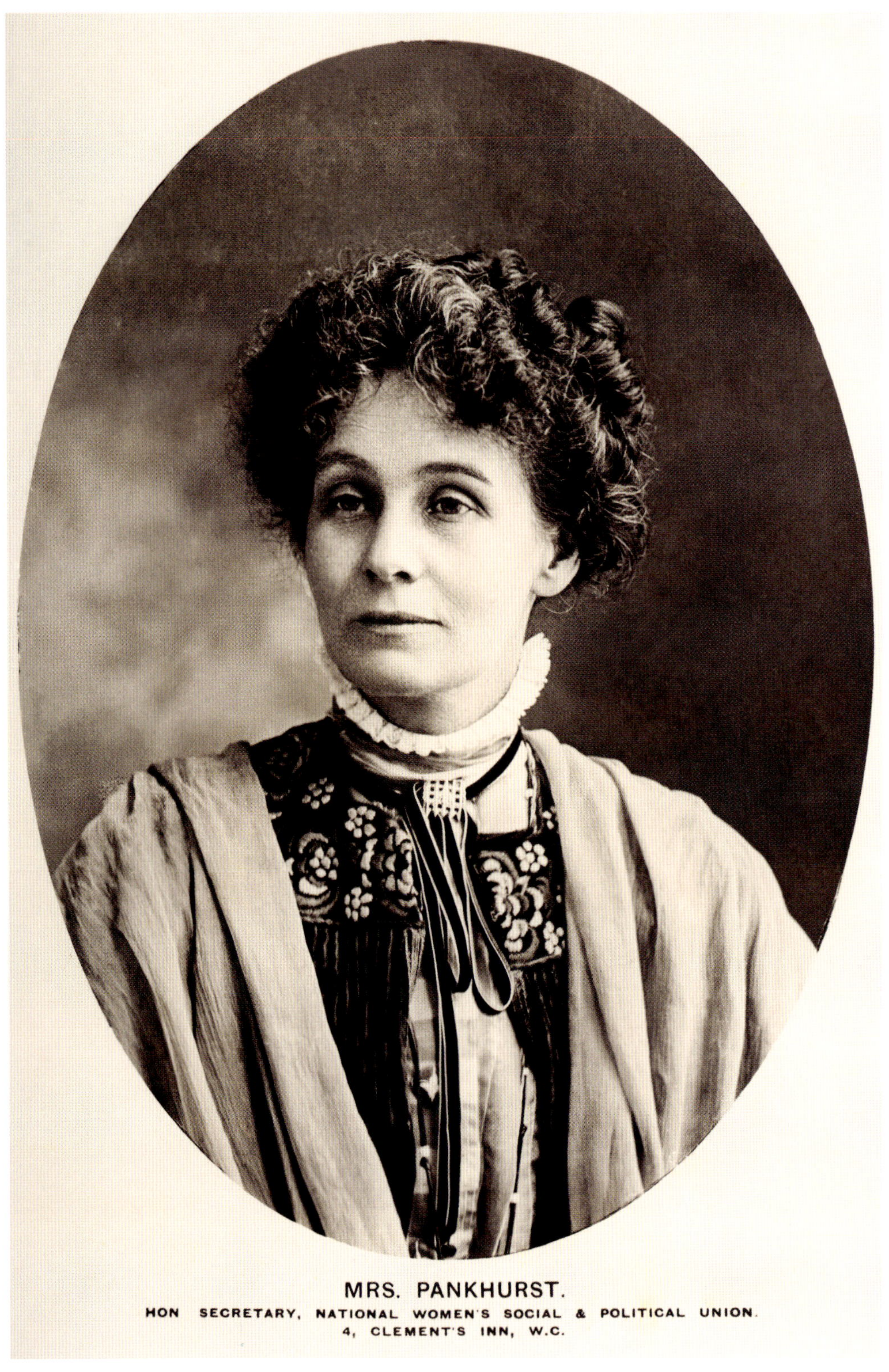

Portrait of Emmeline Pankhurst 1915
Designer unknown
Postcard

Emmeline Pankhurst, pictured in this postcard, founded the Women's Social and Political Union (WSPU) in 1903, with her two daughters, Christabel and Sylvia. Christabel would, in time, acquire a first-class law degree and was a brilliant speaker; Sylvia had studied at the Royal College of Art and was the designer-artist for the WSPU. Determined to achieve voting rights for women, the WSPU represented a new spirit of militancy, necessary as the (failed) women's suffrage campaign was already 40 years old. Also crucial to keeping the WSPU afloat were the formidable Pethick-Lawrences, Frederick and Emmeline, who were responsible for financial and propaganda initiatives. It was Emmeline Pethick-Lawrence who devised 'the colours' – a scheme of purple, white and green – and its symbolism: purple for freedom and dignity, white for purity, green for hope. Her genius was not only to apply 'the 'colours' as a uniform and corporate identity, but to also relate them to marketing and fashion as 'the suffragette look'. Due to the WSPU's civil disobedience and militant tactics, the *Daily Mail* newspaper labelled its members 'suffragettes', a slur which the WSPU adopted with pride.

→ **Votes for Women** *c.*1907
Hilda M. Dallas
Poster

This poster advertises *Votes for Women*, the official newspaper of
the WSPU from 1907 to 1912. The woman depicted is wearing
'the suffragette look'. The paper originated as a monthly but
quickly grew to weekly status. In 1912, during the last and
most violent stage of militancy, the new and more militant
newspaper *The Suffragette*, edited by Christabel Pankhurst,
became the main organ of the WSPU (although *Votes for Women*
continued to be published).

↓ **Banner** *c.*1911
Hammersmith WSPU

The WSPU made use of 'spectacle' – processions, mass
demonstrations and smaller ceremonies – as an important part
of its corporate image-building and interface with the public.
Banners became important identifiers of local groups and
associations, and carried impressive mottos such as the WSPU's
'Deeds Not Words'. This banner belongs to the Hammersmith
branch of the WSPU. It is reversible, and uses a mixture of
machine stitching, crewel stitch embroidery and appliqué. It
is fair to assume that it was handmade by WSPU members or
friends/associates.

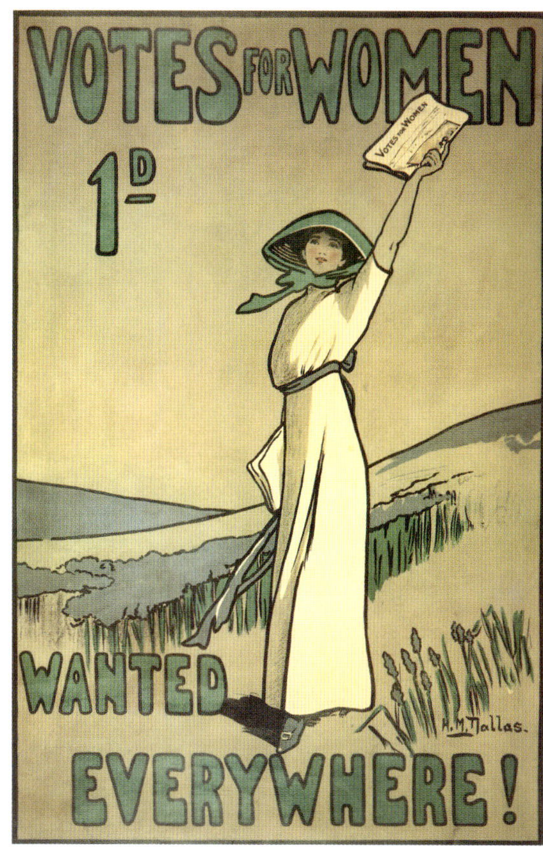

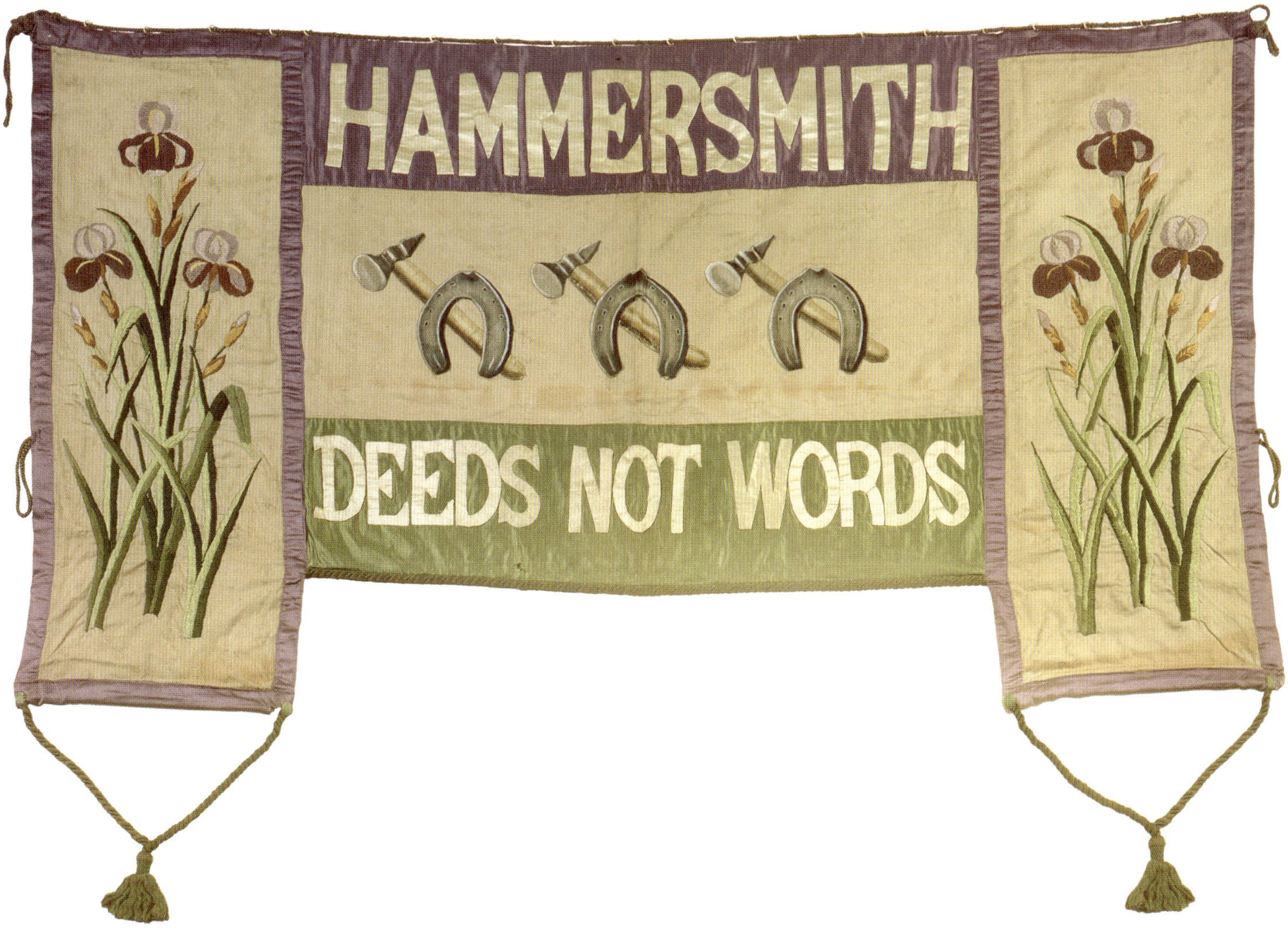

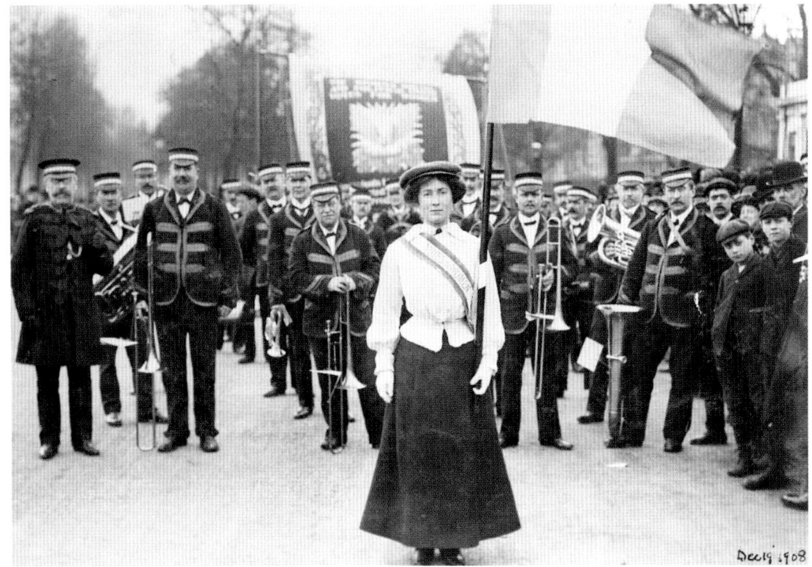

← **Daisy Dugdale, standard-bearer, and 'the uniform'** 1908
Photograph

Standard-bearer Daisy Dugdale leads a procession to welcome Mrs Pankhurst and Christabel on their release from Holloway Gaol, 19 December 1908. Daisy wears 'the uniform': a short skirt of purple or green, a white golf jersey and a simple hat of purple or green. The regalia (sash) is worn over the right shoulder, and fastened under the left arm. There was also a 'full dress uniform': a white frock with regalia and colours, usually worn only for processions. The uniform was meant to be simple and economical, so that women with very limited budgets could participate in WSPU activities and events.

↓ **The Woman's Press** 1910
Postcard

The Woman's Press was launched in 1908 at 4 Clement's Inn, London, as the WSPU's publishing imprint and distribution house for *Votes for Women* and other WSPU publications. By 1910 it had expanded into additional premises, including a shop, at 156 Charing Cross Road which acted as a focal point for its merchandising. The shop sold a wide range of novelties and products, from fashion accessories and postcard albums (collecting postcards to follow the personalities, celebrations and adventures of the movement was very popular) to packaged tea, soap and stationery, much of it sporting 'the colours'. For the period 1907–14, at least twenty-two WSPU shops were listed throughout London.

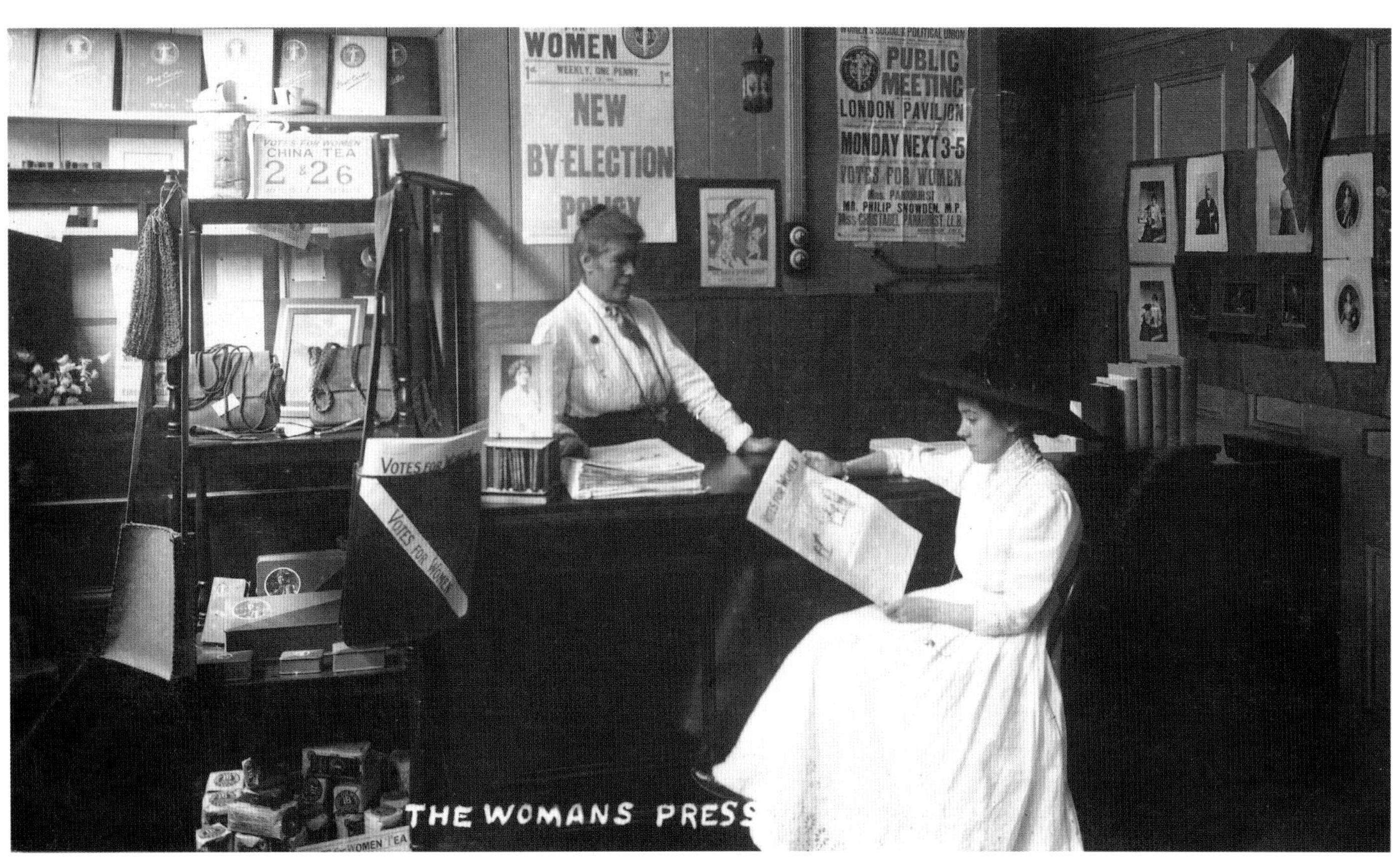

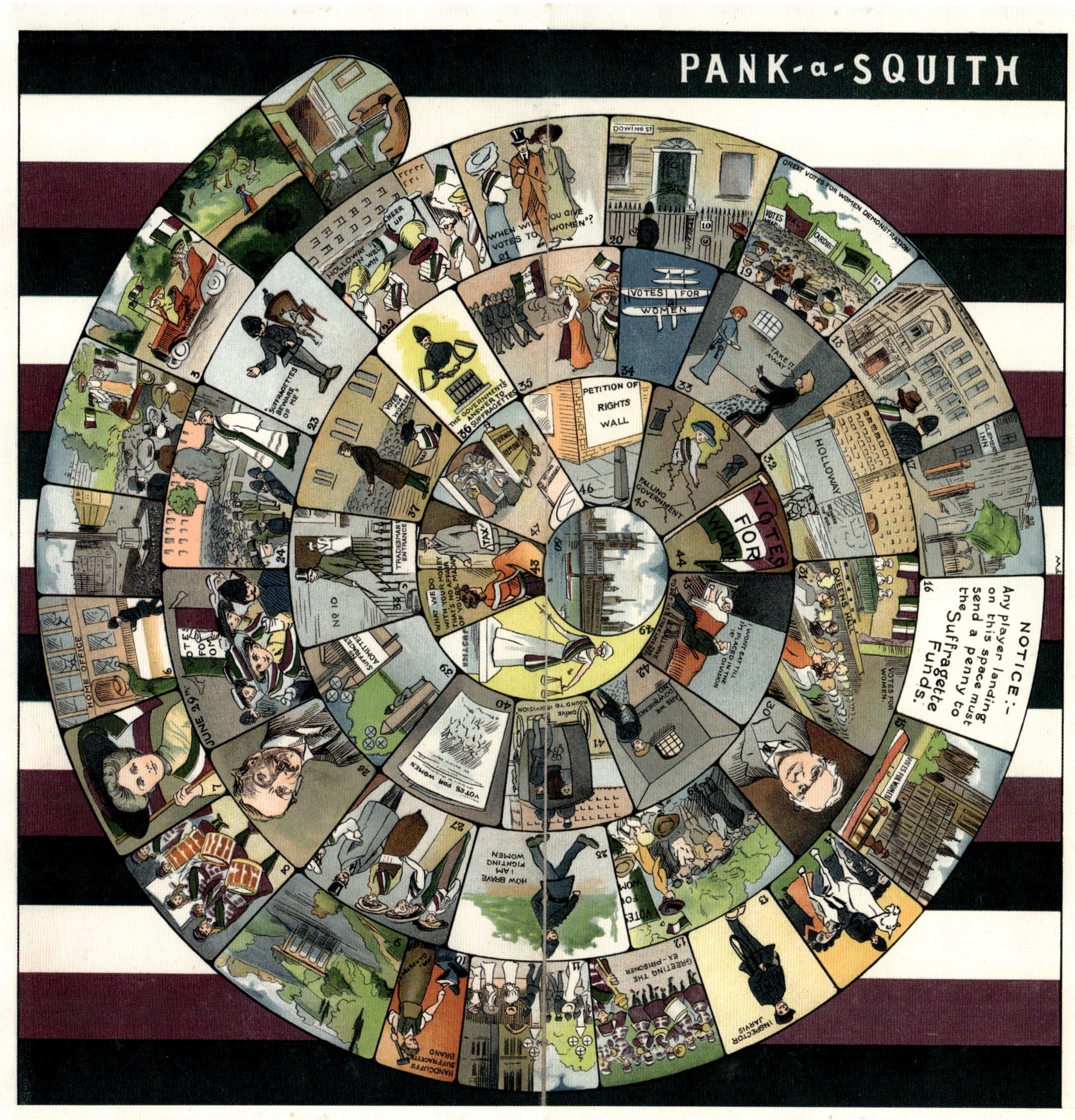

Pank-a-Squith 1908
Board game

The title of this board game can be read as 'Pankhurst vs. Asquith', for Prime Minister Henry H. Asquith was deeply opposed to women's suffrage and became one of the WSPU's main targets. Board games, card games and a range of toys were produced to help spread and support the movement. This game involved miniature metal suffragette playing pieces which, on a roll of the dice, attempted to journey from their home to the Houses of Parliament, while overcoming various difficulties. First available in 1908, from the shop of The Woman's Press, it is a good example of shrewd propaganda; it showed the suffragettes had a sense of humour and could laugh at themselves, which would have enhanced their popularity and disarmed their critics.

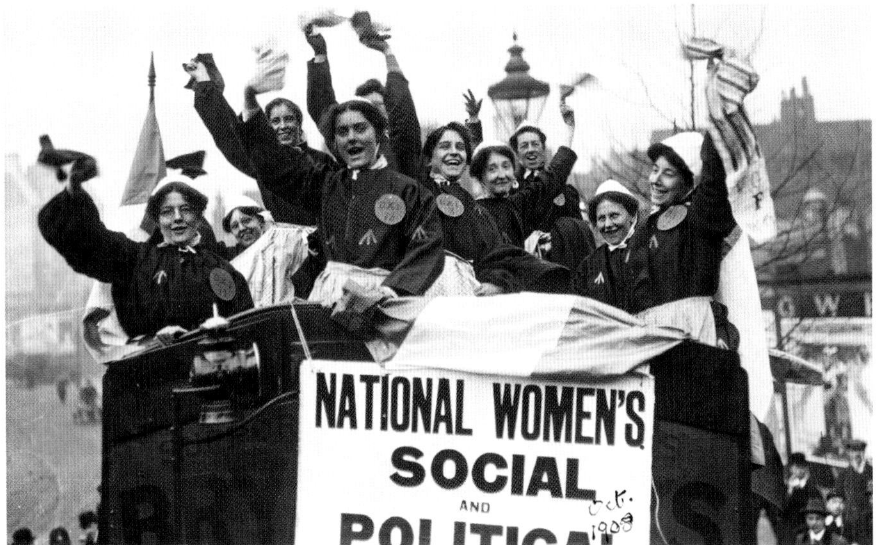

← **Suffragettes in replica prison clothing** 1908
Postcard

Suffragettes released from Holloway Prison, but dressed in replica prison clothing and badges, and riding in an open-top vehicle.

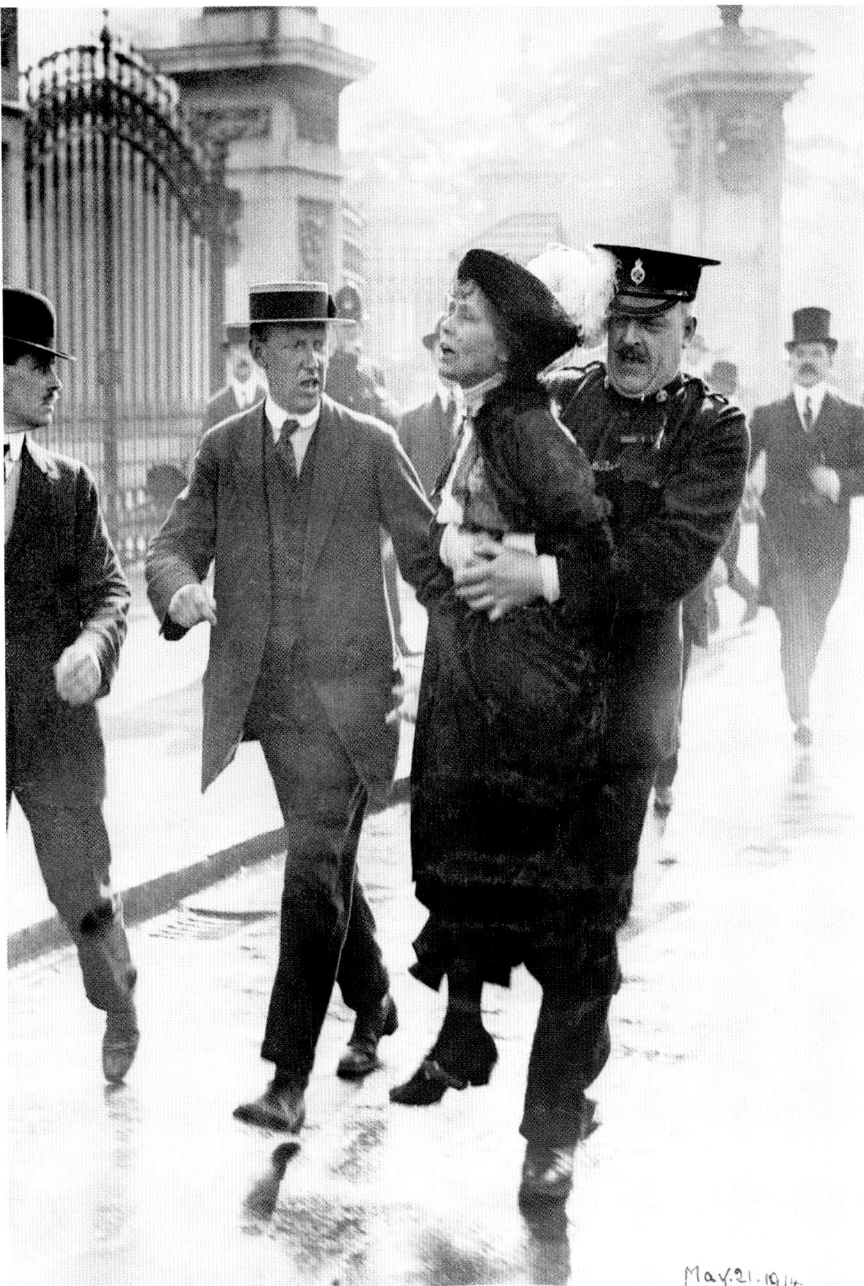

← **Emmeline Pankhurst arrested by Chief Inspector Rolfe outside Buckingham Palace** 21 May 1914
Photographer unknown
Photograph

This is one of the most commonly viewed photographs representing suffragette activities. It shows the arrest of Mrs Pankhurst (in front of Buckingham Palace) on 21 May 1914 while trying to present a petition to King George V. It was part of a volatile demonstration: 200 suffragettes attempted to break through the line of 1,500 police surrounding Buckingham Palace. Notice the formal dress and angry faces of the men surrounding the diminutive Pankhurst.

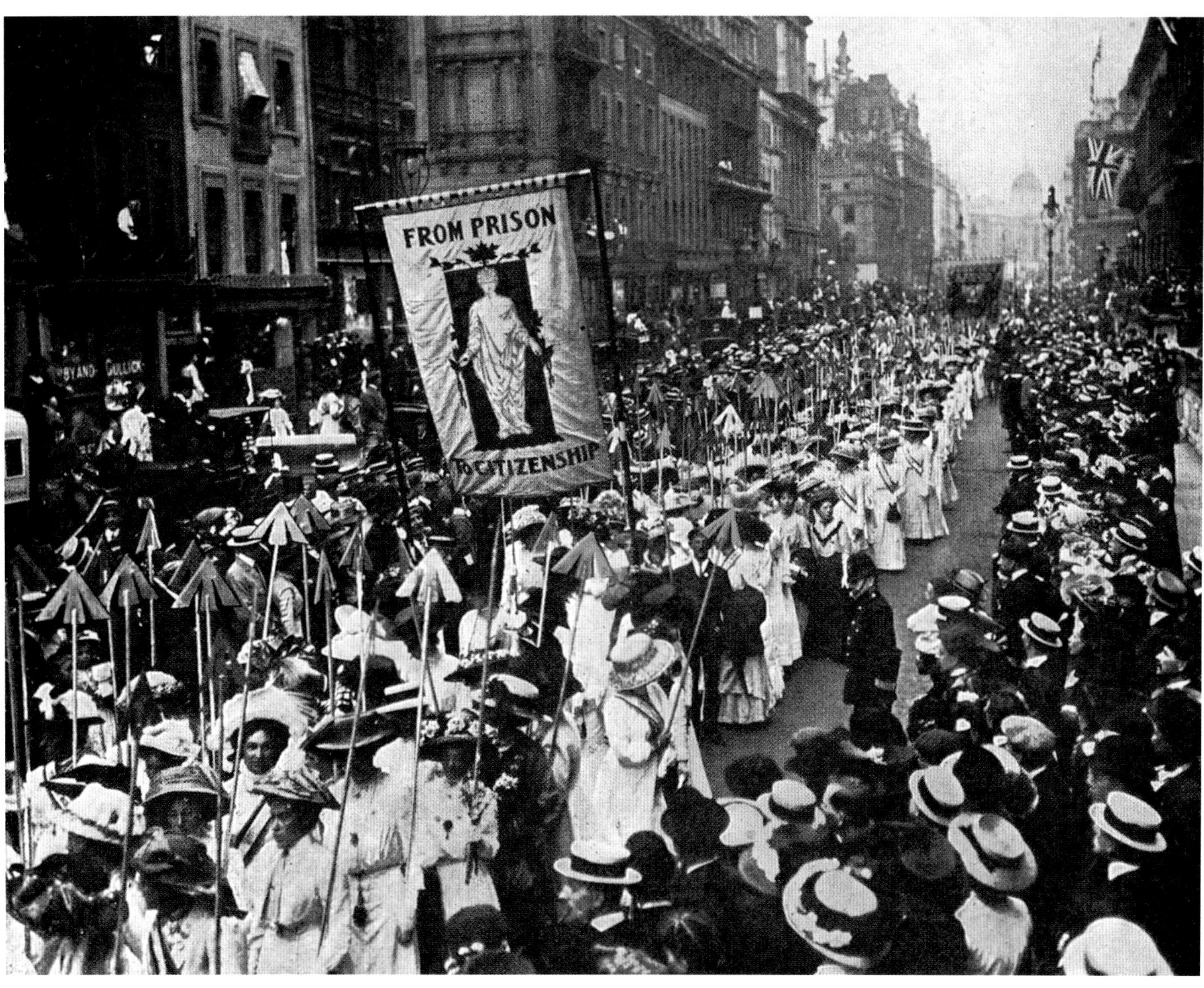

The 'From Prison to Citizenship'
Procession 1910
Photographer unknown
Photograph

Alongside their use of processions and
demonstrations for the purpose of
image-building and public interface, the
WSPU was also constantly pushing for
recognition and action in the political
sphere, through its wide range of militant
activities. This included pestering
politicians at home, canvassing against
unsympathetic government candidates at
elections, creating disturbances outside the
House of Commons, heckling politicians
(including the prime minister) at public
meetings, chaining themselves to railings,
smashing windows of government offices
and commercial properties, stone throwing
and sending deputations to the king and
prime minister. Most of these actions
ended in violence with the police, arrests
and imprisonment. When imprisoned
suffragettes went on hunger-strike, the
government retaliated with the tactic of
forcible feeding (force-feeding) as early as
1909. Again, the suffragettes fought back
by parading their martyrdom with dignity.
In processions women carried long poles
or sticks topped by broad arrows to signify
they had been imprisoned; they wore medals
of honour as a tribute to their courage; they
carried banners marked with the names
of hunger-strikers. The procession shown
here is moving through Fleet Street on 18
June 1910, in full dress uniform, with ex-
prisoners carrying broad arrows on staves.
The effect must have been stunning; 617 ex-
prisoners marched in this procession. Such
tactics sustained morale, while impressing
the public with the women's courage.

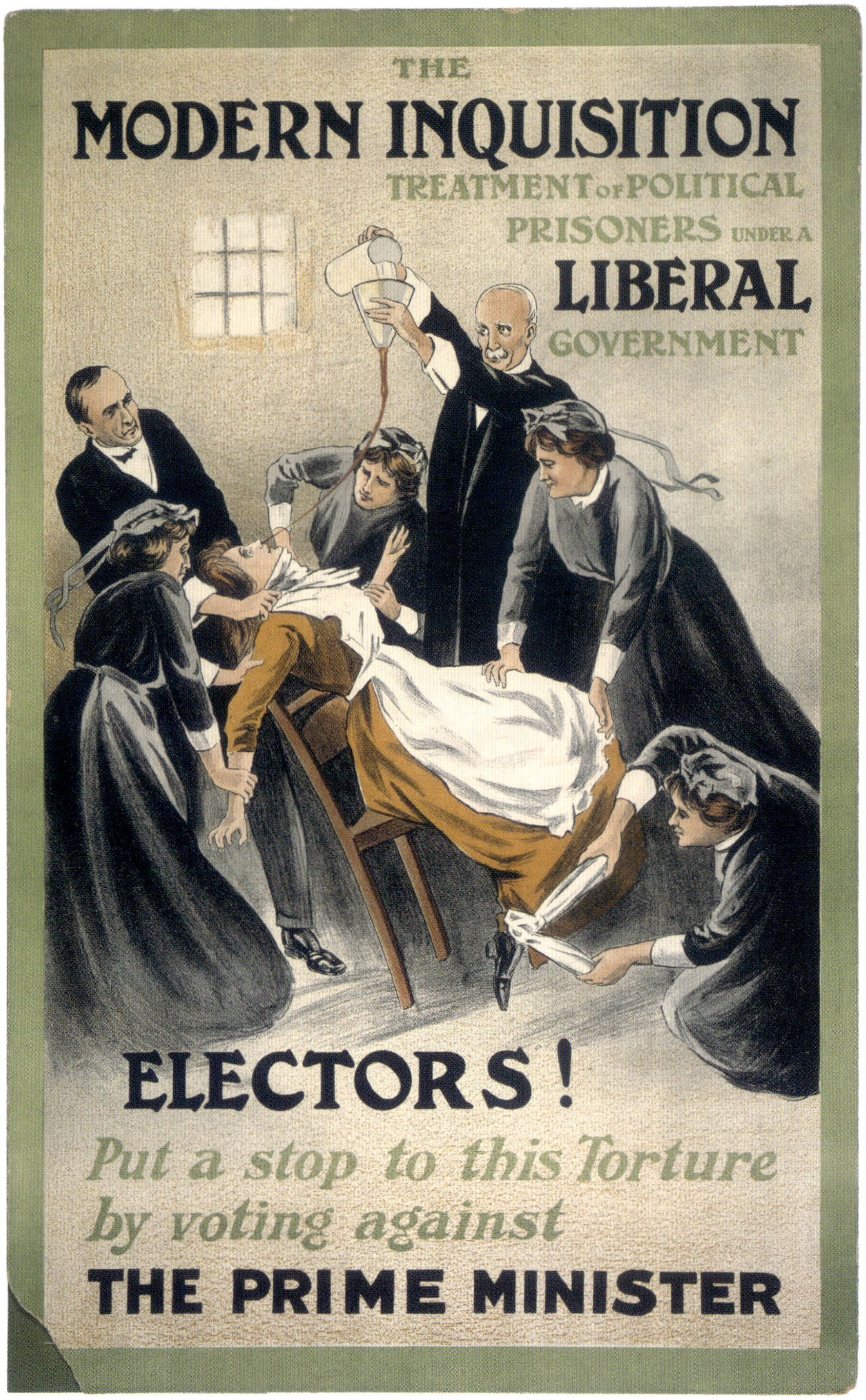

↑ **Modern Inquisition** 1910
'A. Patriot' (Alfred Pearse)
Poster

↓ **Prison badge** *c.*1909
Medal

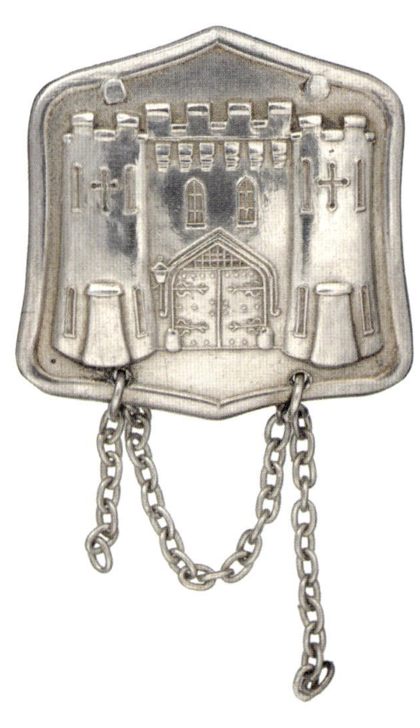

The WSPU would have awarded this badge to a suffragette who had endured a prison sentence; the woman's initials would also have been inscribed on the back, with a date.

The suffragettes' militant activities often resulted in their imprisonment, followed by hunger-striking and often accompanied by force-feeding. Introduced as early as 1909, it was regarded by militants as a form of state torture. It was, in fact, a hellish procedure. In short: women were held down, a long tube was inserted through the nose and pushed down about 20 inches, then a liquid of milk or milk and egg was poured down the other end of the tube (which had a funnel attached), causing much wretching and pain. The sacrifice was great: after repeated visits to prison, a certain amount of body-breakdown was inevitable. Consequently, the WSPU rewarded prisoners' bravery and sacrifice. Great attention was paid to ritual and ceremony. Released prisoners were met by delegations and (often) a marching band; processions and banners were used to display martyrdom; prisoners received illuminated Emancipation Certificates signed by Emmeline Pankhurst; and there were medals of honour for hunger-strikers and Holloway (prison) badges and brooches. This poster was published by the WSPU for the January 1910 general election; it represents one of the few times the WSPU depicted force-feeding. The WSPU seldom used violent imagery for fear it might brand women as victims or, even worse, allow sadistic viewers to see women 'getting what they deserve'.

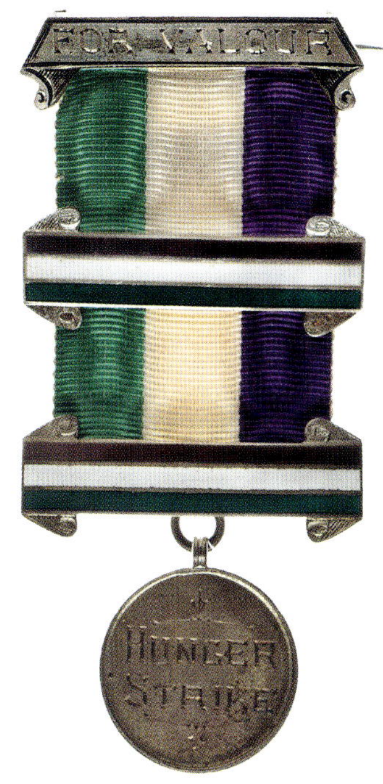

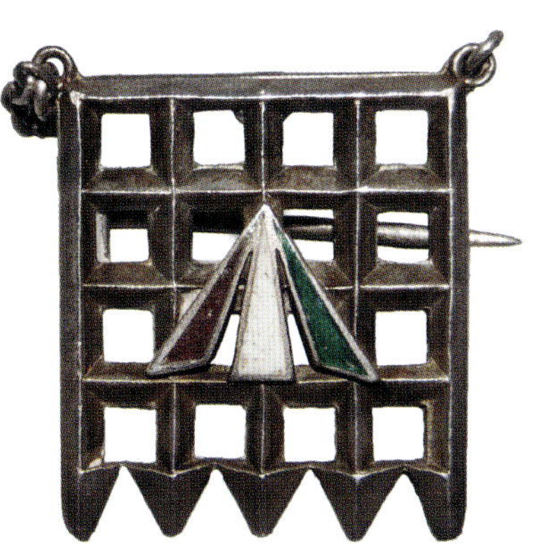

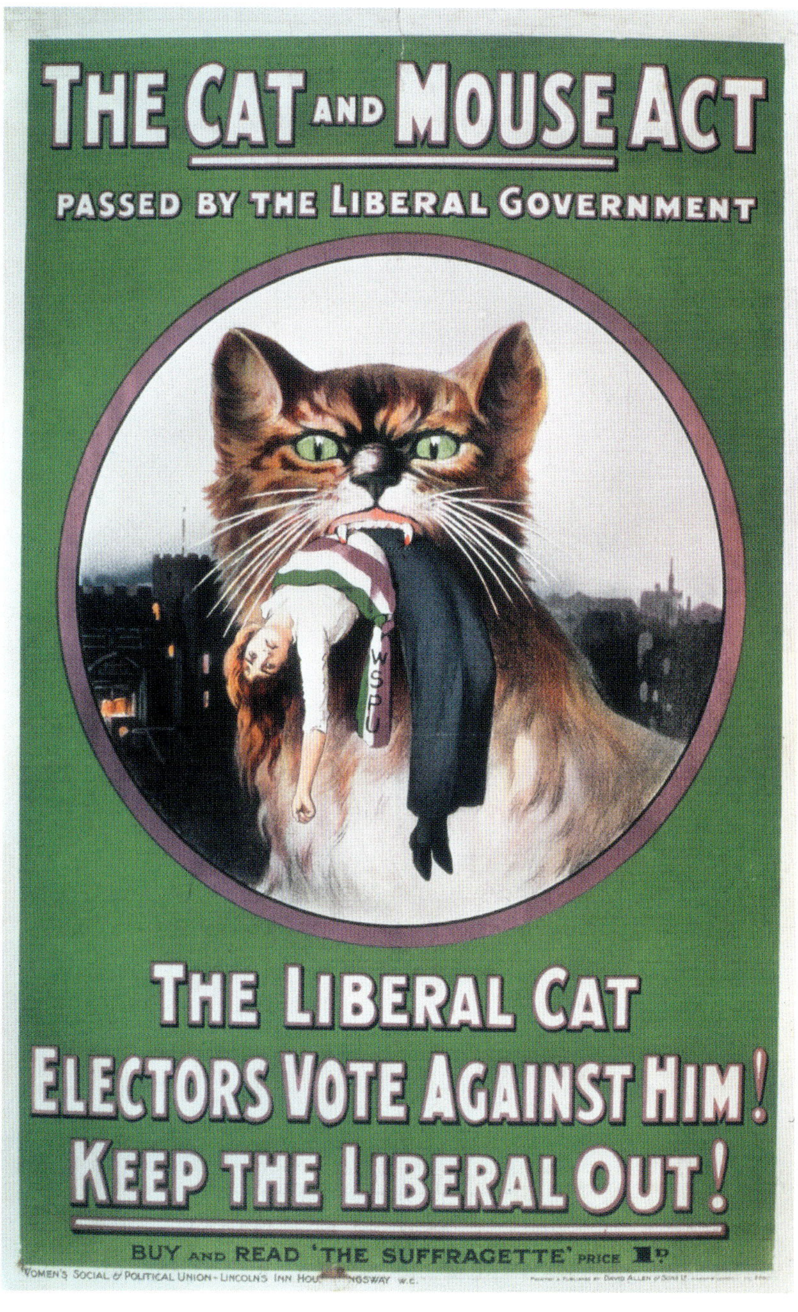

↑ **Hunger-strike medal** *c.*1909–12
Medal

This medal was awarded by the WSPU to members who endured hunger-strikes or force-feeding while imprisoned. A name and date was usually inscribed on the back, and sometimes more silver bars were added to signify force-feeding (with dates engraved on the back of the bars).

↑ **Holloway brooch** *c.*1908
Silver brooch

Designed by Sylvia Pankhurst, this silver brooch had a convict's broad arrow in purple, white and green enamel sitting on a silver portcullis (fortress or prison gate). It was awarded to suffragettes who had endured a prison sentence.

↑ **The Cat and Mouse Act** 1914
Anonymous
Poster

Published by the WSPU, this poster would have drawn attention for its use of violence. The 'Cat and Mouse Act' (as it was commonly known) was devised in 1913 and allowed the early release of prisoners suffering from ill-health due to hunger-striking or force-feeding, and then rearrested them once they were recovered in order to finish their sentence. The Act largely failed in its purpose; when released from the 'cat' (the prison authorities), the suffragette 'mice' were nursed or went into hiding, after which many of them committed even more militant acts. The typographic message is blasted out, loud and clear, in a call to arms: 'Keep the Liberal Out!'

Futurism Breaks with the Past

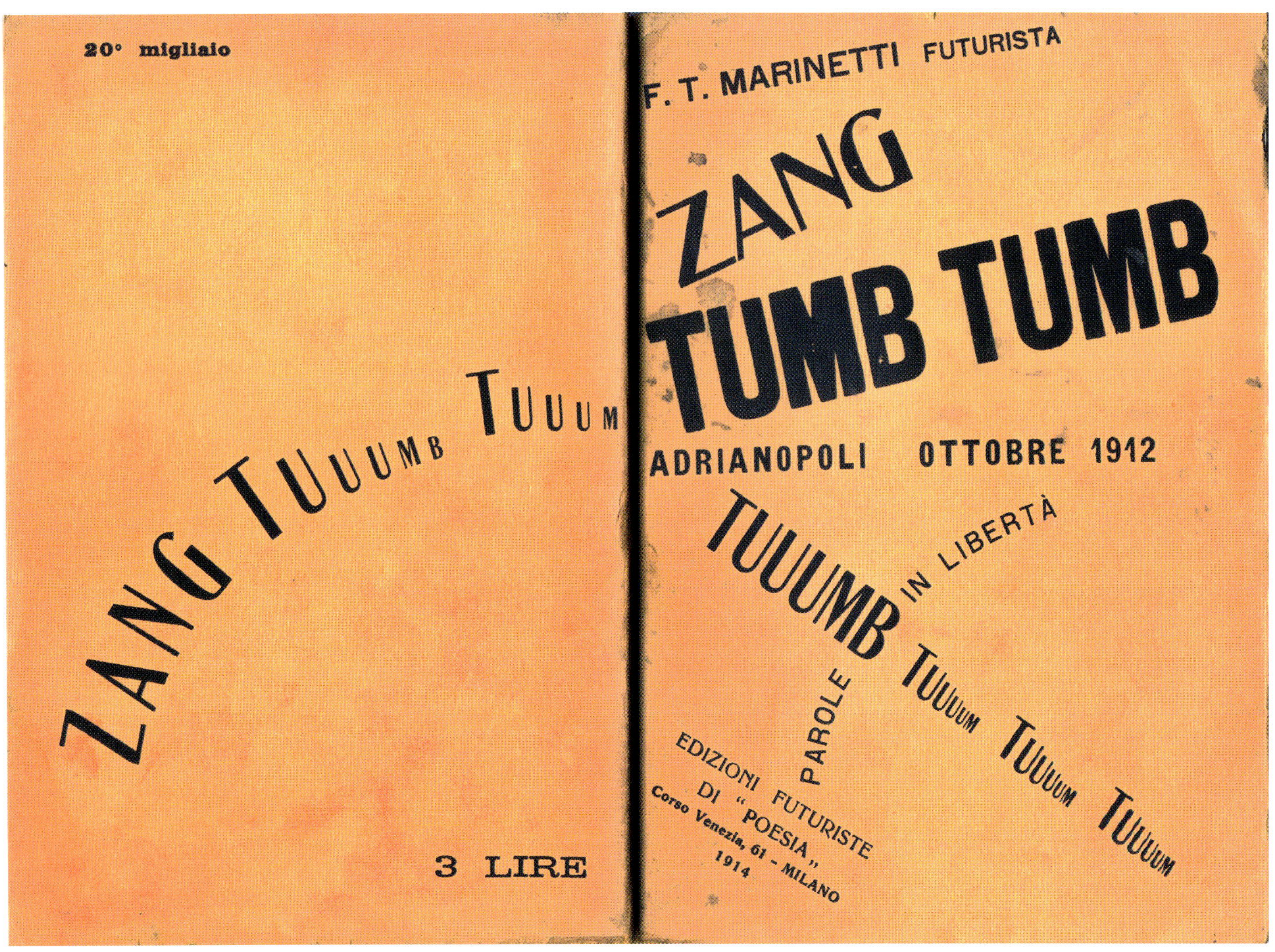

Zang Tumb Tumb 1914
Filippo Tommaso Marinetti
Book

Marinetti's 'The founding and manifesto of Futurism' appeared on the front page of *Le Figaro* (Paris) on 20 February 1909, and was immediately translated into other languages for other newspapers. It launched Futurism, a movement driven by the energy of a new century and which venerated speed, the machine, and the power and violence of war. Marinetti's following manifestos, as well as his poetry, were intended to be recited and performed with exaggerated sounds, gestures or intonation. In his poetry on the printed page, words were set free from their traditional roles of arrangement, composition and even syntax. They became '*parole in libertà*' – words in liberty, or 'free words' – and therefore able to combine to make new sounds and associations. This demanded new, revolutionary, typographic treatment, as exciting as the oral delivery. (And *Zang Tumb Tumb* was more in tune with events, as it tells the story of the Siege of Adrianople, 1912, when aerial bombing was used, possibly for the first time – and which Marinetti covered as war correspondent.) Typography therefore transformed into a new visual language: typefaces mixed with other typefaces and sizes, words changed in size and positioning, flying off the page or adopting energetic angles for dynamic effect. Words were divorced from their original function, instead appearing to merge vision and sound, appropriate for the explosions and nightmare visions that were awaiting Italy as it entered the First World War.

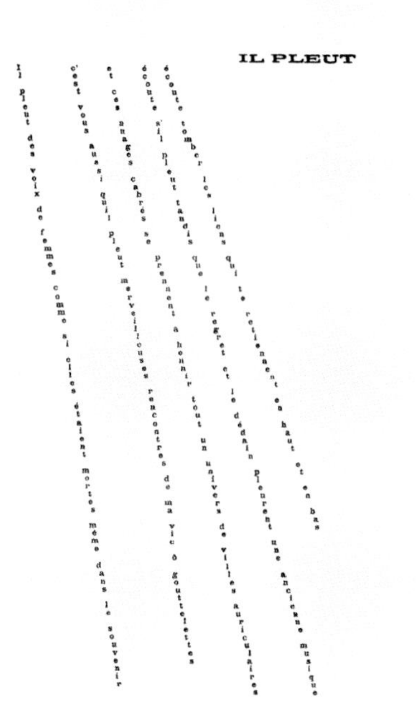

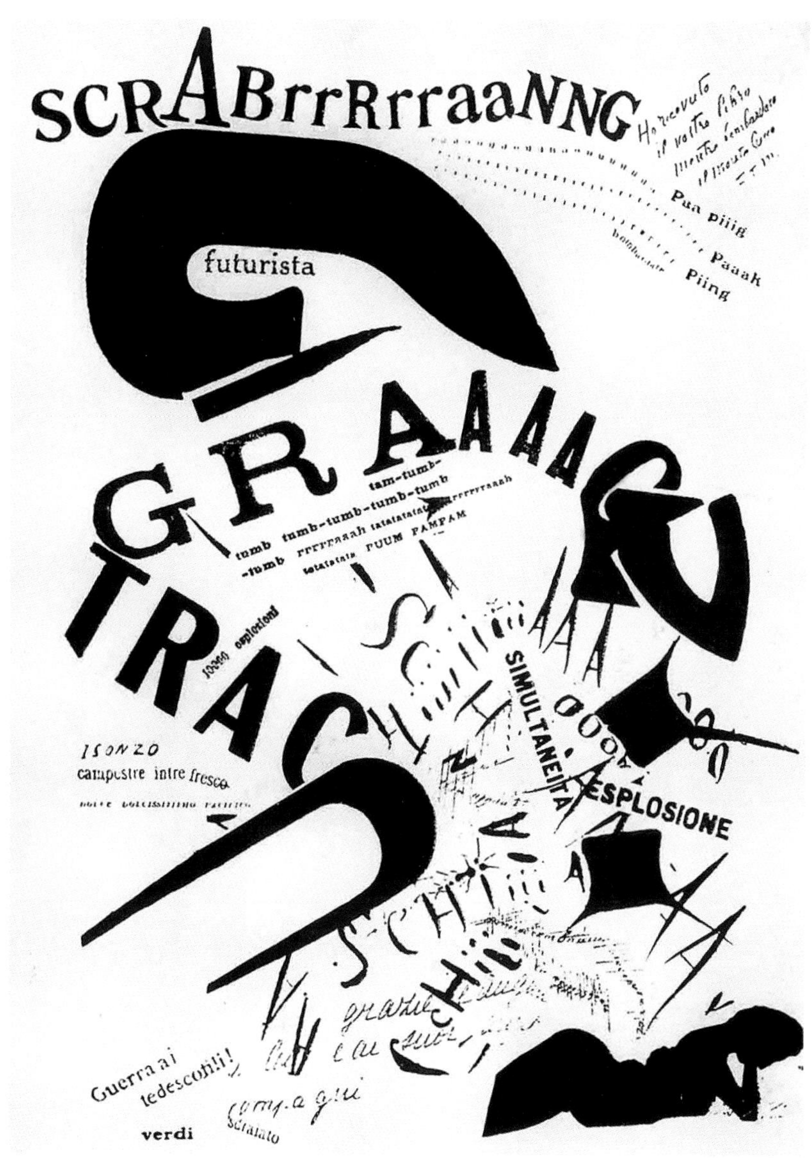

Il Pleut ('It's Raining') 1916
Guillaume Apollinaire
Calligramme for journal or magazine

Marinetti was one of a number of artists and poets intent on experimentation with language, type and sound (often derived from oral performance). Both Marinetti and French poet Guillaume Apollinaire wished to simplify language, ridding it of adjectives and other 'useless words'. Apollinaire, however, also wanted to abolish syntax, punctuation, the tenses and persons of verbs, and the structures of poetry. Literature would instead consist of free words), new words, onomatopoeic expressions and a mixture of languages.

Words in Liberty 1919
Filippo Tommaso Marinetti
One page from the book

Marinetti's later book of Futurist poetry, *Words in Liberty*, does not sustain typographic manipulation throughout the entire book, as in *Zang Tumb Tumb*. *Words in Liberty* contains both pages of typographic dynamism as well as fold-out sheets of drawings or collages. He again concerns himself with the destruction of syntax, and divorces letters from their role in written language, using them for their visual appearance and dynamic effect. The poem shown here dates from 1915, and begins: *In the evening, lying on her bed, she read again the letter from her artilleryman at the front.* The explosions and sounds of war hang above her, perhaps an expression of her imaginings.

Dadaism and its Graphics

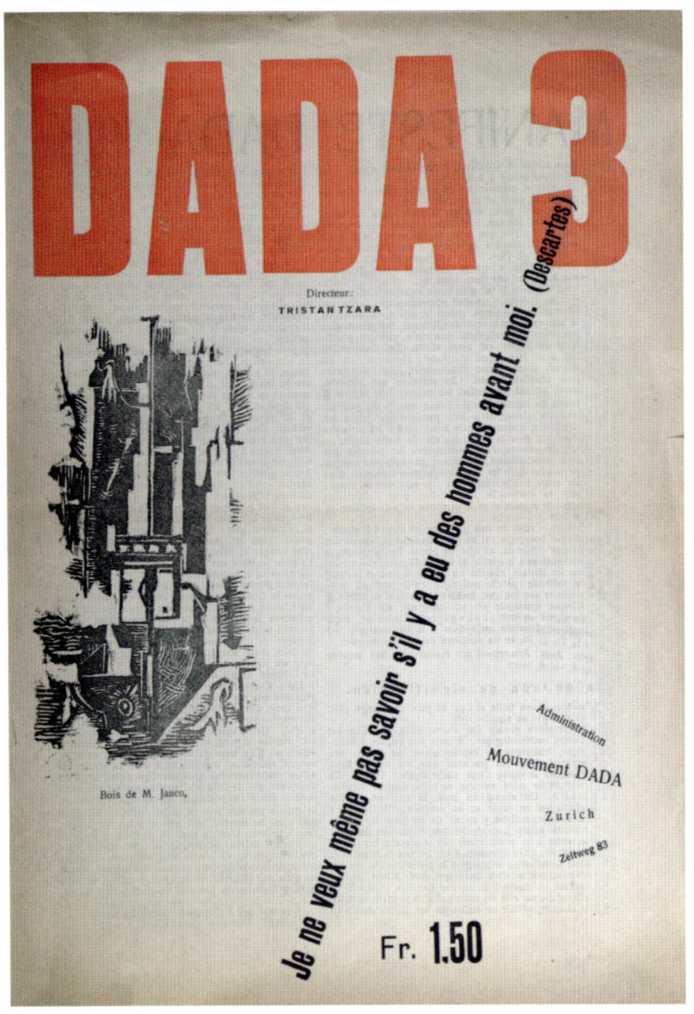

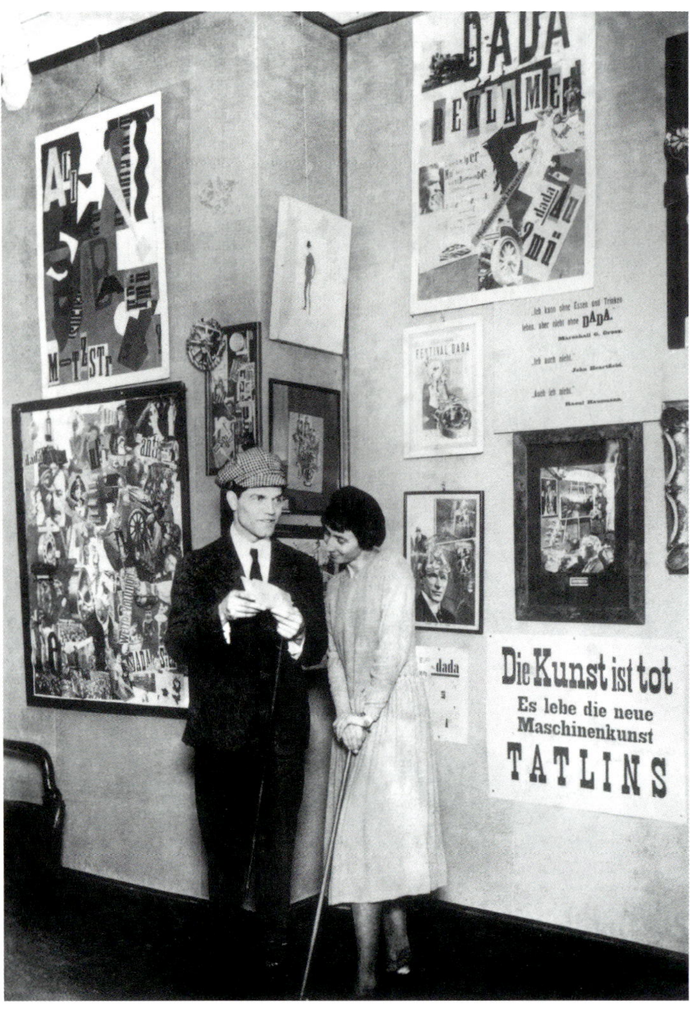

Dada 3 1918
Tristan Tzara
Journal

In 1916 Dada was born in the Cabaret Voltaire, Zurich with the provocative performances (poetry readings, manifestos, riots) of the thoughtful, restrained Hugo Ball and the fiery Tristan Tzara. Dada was an outright protest against the insanity and bloodshed of the First World War, translated into an outright rejection of everything. It was anti-war, anti-order, anti-society, anti-art and it turned the known conventions of art, performance, writing and typography upside down. Photography and particularly photomontage proved to be its most valuable weapons. Ball and Tzara were joined by other young artists and writers, and soon the spirit of Dada had networked its way to artists in Berlin and other European cities, as well as an independent anti-art movement developing in New York. Although others in the Zurich group contributed, Tristan Tzara's extraordinary energy and enthusiasm meant that he was inevitably responsible for the editing, direction, design and administration of the periodical *Dada*, shown here.

**Raoul Hausmann and Hannah Höch at the
International Dada Fair, Berlin** 1920
Photograph

Berlin was a 'hotter' place to be than Zurich (politically) and a Berlin Dada group soon evolved that included Hannah Höch, Raoul Hausmann, John Heartfield, George Grosz and others. The Berlin group's innovation of photomontage was its most powerful weapon, and suitable for tactics involving shock, protest, absurdity and violence. (The inventor of photomontage remains hotly contested, as Hannah Höch and Raoul Hausmann were experimenting with it at the same time as John Heartfield and George Grosz.) The first International Dada Fair of 1920 included work by the Berlin group. The highlight of the Fair was a stuffed dummy, dressed in a German officer's uniform with the head of a pig, which led to prosecution for defaming the German Army. Raoul Hausmann and Hannah Höch are shown here; Höch's photomontage 'Cut with the Cake-Knife' can be seen to the left of Hausmann.

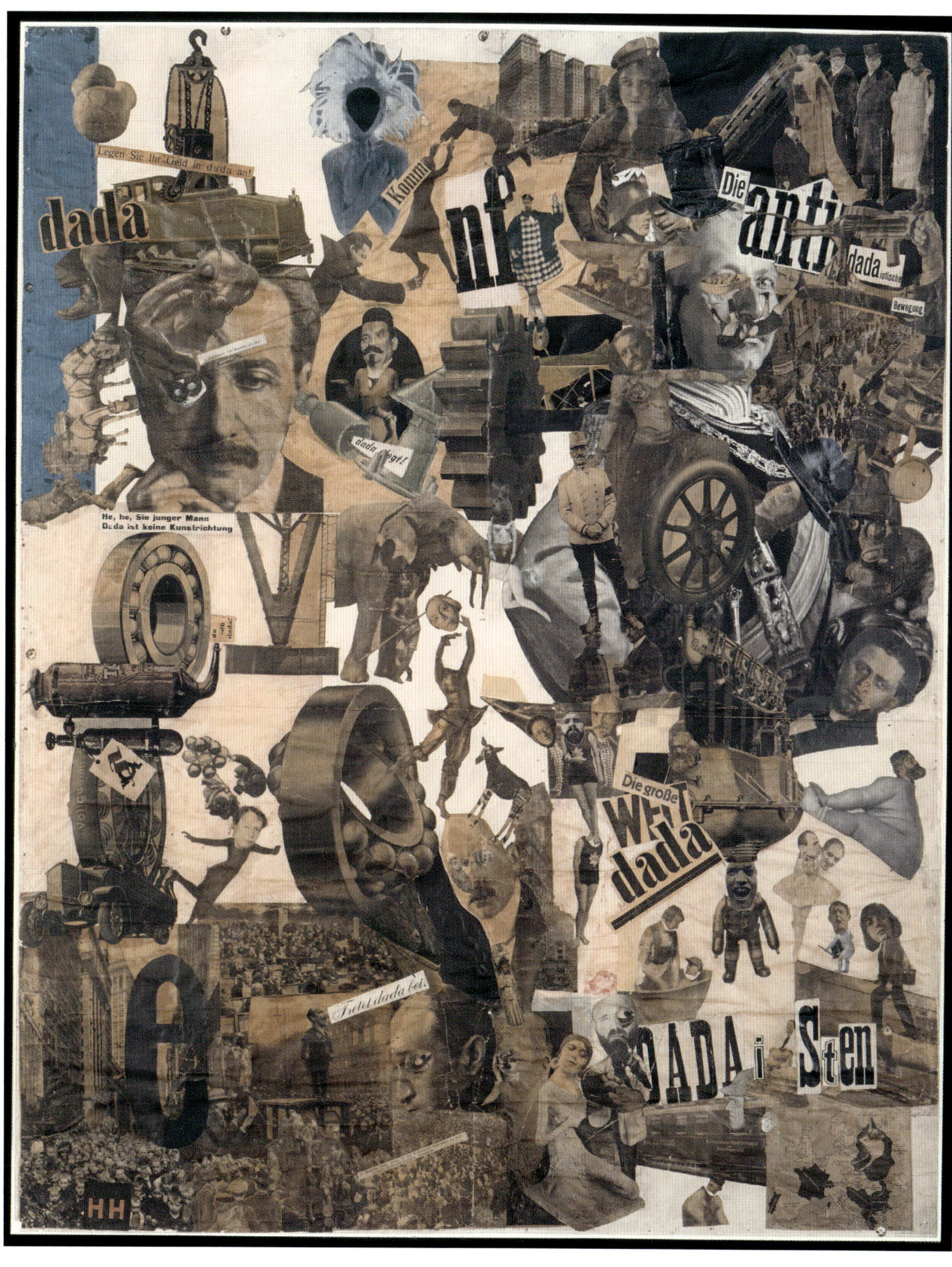

Cut with the Cake-Knife *c.*1919
Hannah Höch
Photomontage

The full-length title of this photomontage is *Cut with the Cake-Knife Dada through the last Weimar Beer Belly Cultural Epoch of Germany* (as listed in the catalogue for the First International Dada Fair, 1920). It is a large photomontage (114 × 90 cm, 45 × 35 in) and an incredible hodge-podge of carefully juxtaposed images. For Höch excels at social satire and, as with much of her work, the closer one gets, the more worrying it looks. Large bodies have small heads, men with beards have babies' bodies, and symbols of industry (cogs and wheels) seem to be mashing it all together. There is something ill-fitting and deadly about it all. Bearing in mind the year (1919), one year after the end of the First World War, when maimed and ill soldiers had returned home and inflation was climbing, it may be a suitable portrait of the Weimar Republic of 1919–33.

Photomontage and Social Critique

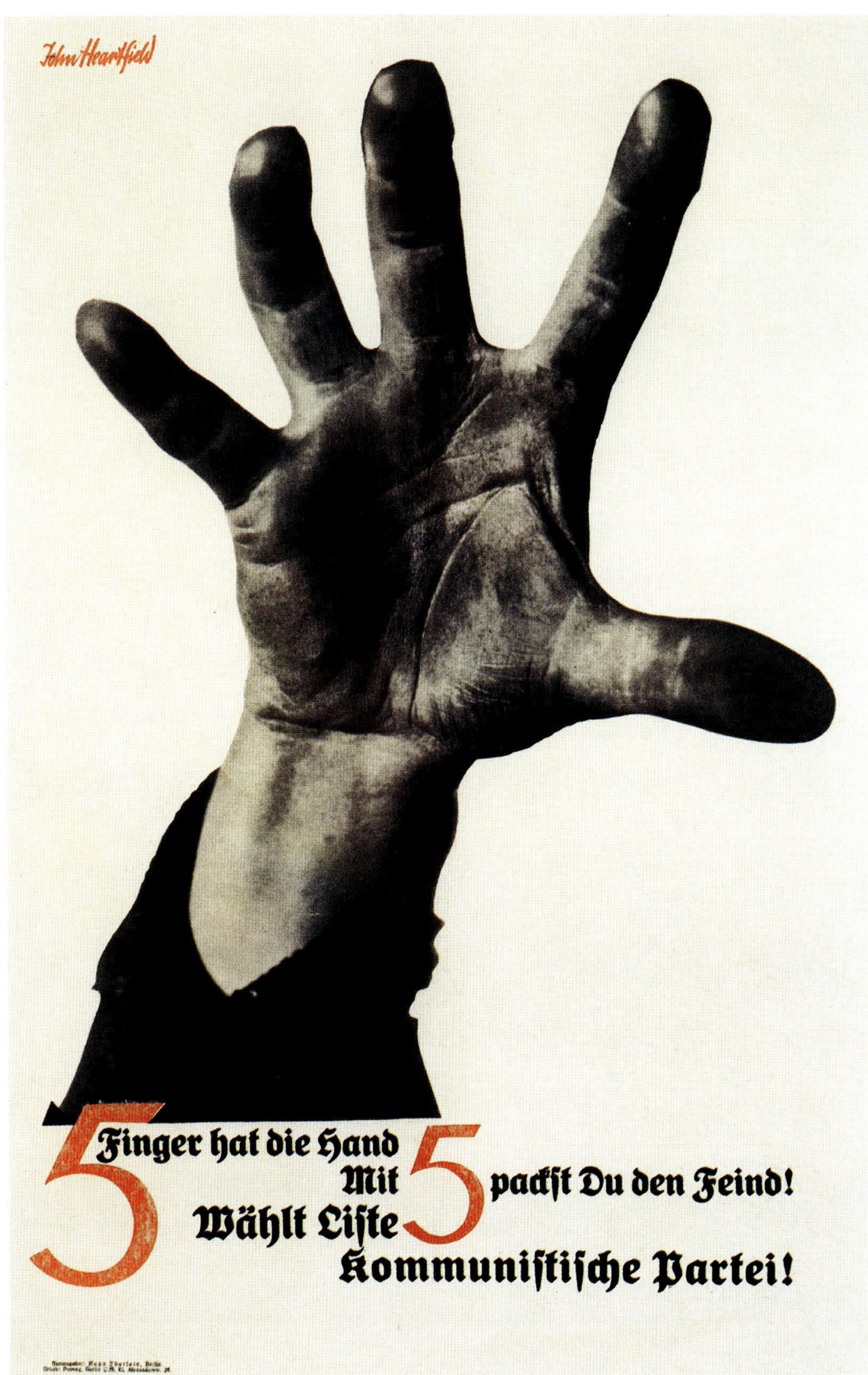

← **Fünf Finger hat die Hand (The Hand has Five Fingers)** 1928
John Heartfield
Poster

The full-length title of this photomontage poster is *The hand has five fingers. With five you seize the enemy. Vote List Five, Communist Party.* John Heartfield joined the German Communist Party, along with his brother Wieland Herzfelde and George Grosz at the end of 1918. Ten years later this poster is encouraging people to vote for the Communist Party in an upcoming election (the Communist Party is List 5 on the electoral list). As powerful as this poster is, with its hand projecting out over the typography as if to grasp the viewer, it did not achieve its goal. Within a few years, Germany began to see the rise of the Nazi Party. The poster could be seen as a desperate attempt to avoid that future.

→ **Früh um fünf Uhr (Five a.m.)** 1921
George Grosz
Cartoon

George Grosz was an outstanding satirical
cartoonist of the Weimar period, and a
close friend and working partner of John
Heartfield. The main outlet for Grosz's
books and cartoons was the publishing
house, Malik Verlag, founded by brothers
Wieland Herzfelde and John Heartfield
during the First World War. The book in
which this cartoon appeared, *Das Gesicht
der Herrschenden Klasse* (The Face of the
Ruling Class) was published by Malik Verlag
in 1921 and was one of the first examples
of a picture book designed specifically
to encourage class consciousness from a
Marxist-Leninist perspective.

→ *Deutschland, Deutschland
über Alles* 1929
John Heartfield
Book jacket

John Heartfield's attempts to produce a
new form of revolutionary graphics using
photomontage led him into designing
posters, magazines, newspapers, calendars,
pamphlets, book jackets and, as shown here,
an experimental book. In collaboration
with the writer Kurt Tucholsky, Heartfield
produced *Deutschland, Deutschland über
Alles*, a new type of satirical photo-text book
as well as the jacket for the book.

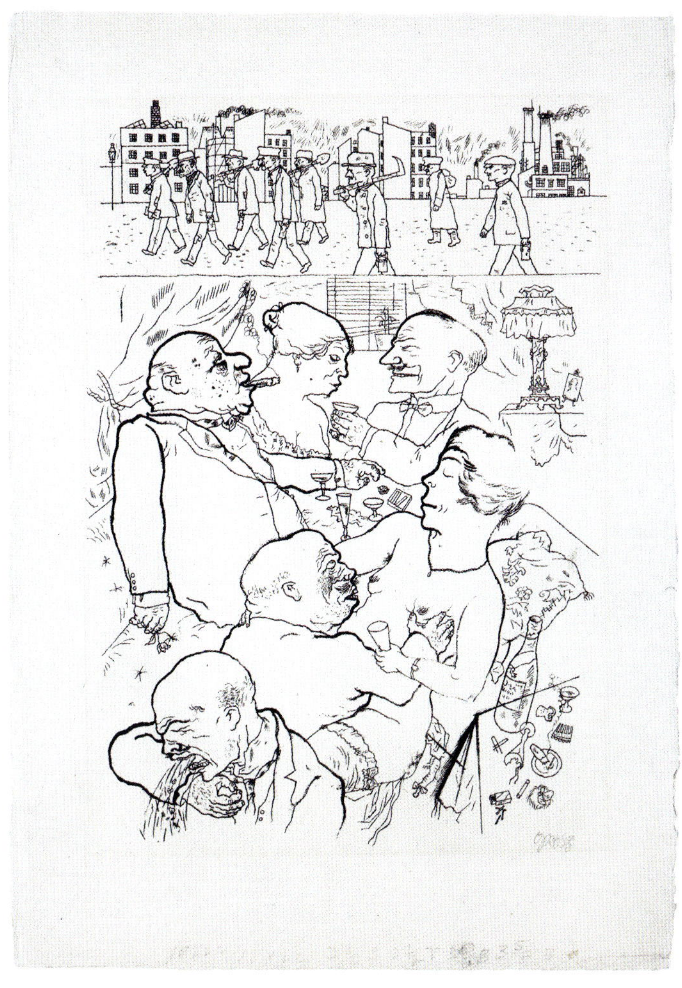

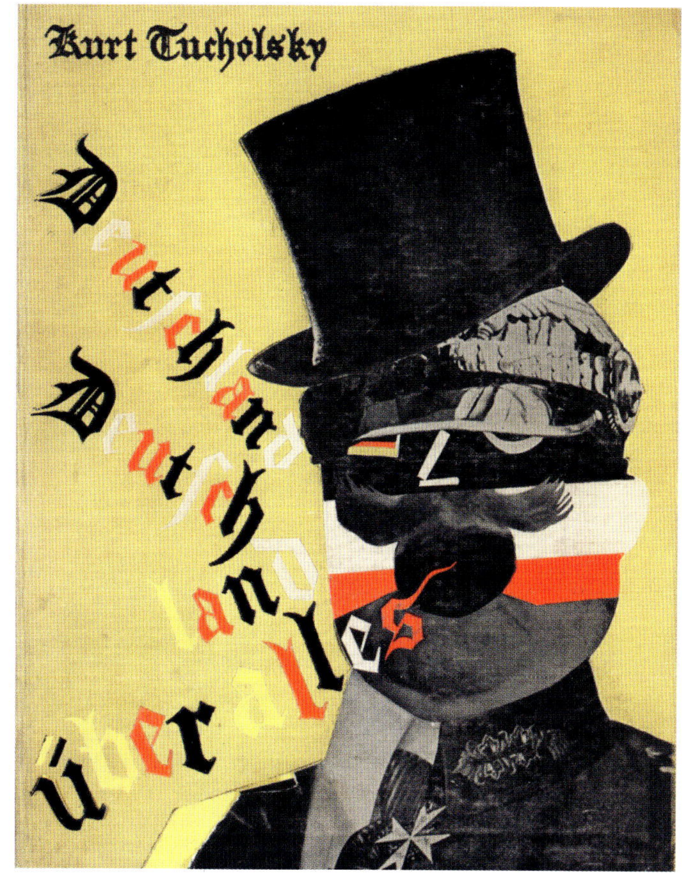

The Constructivist Style

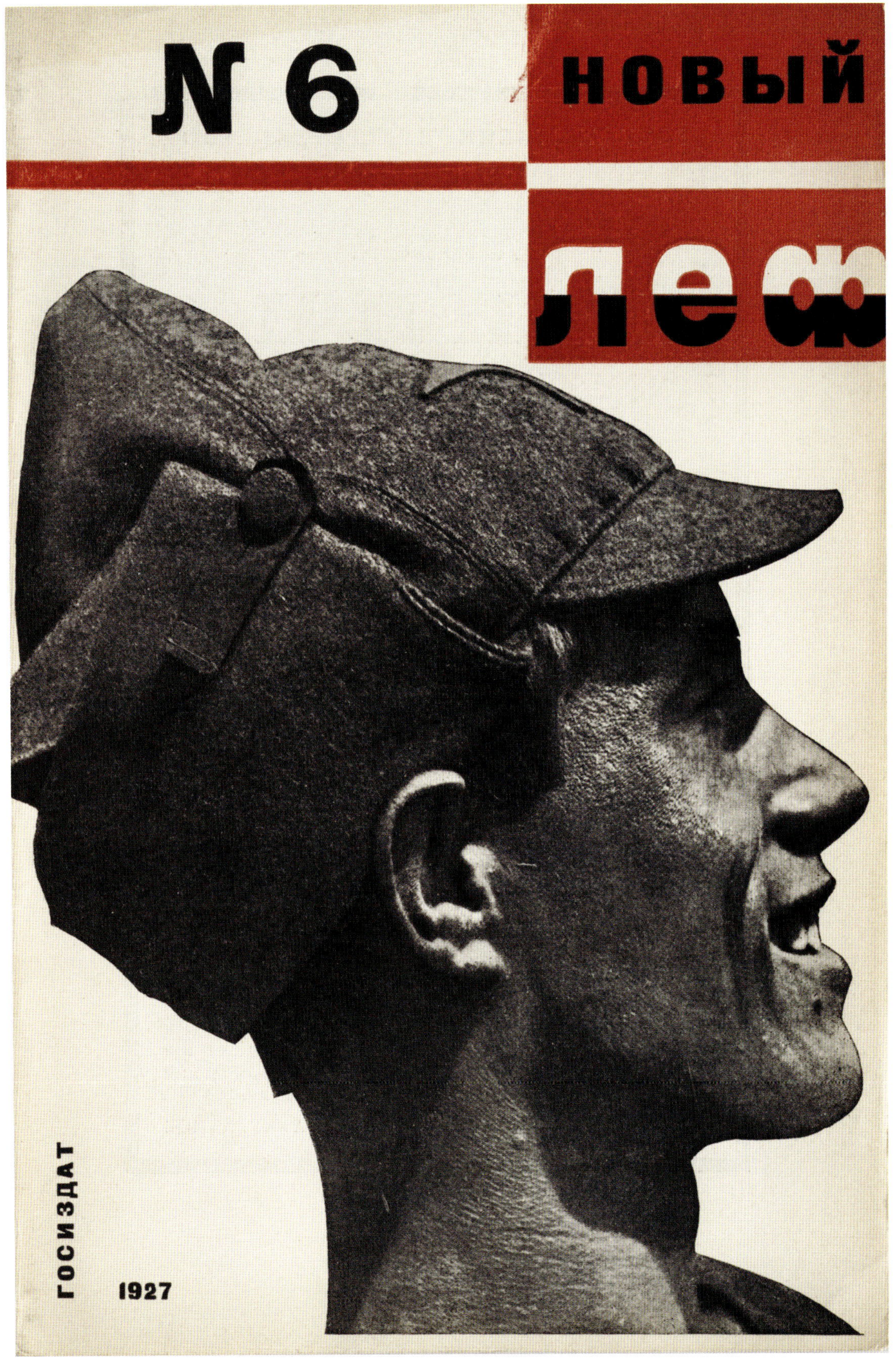

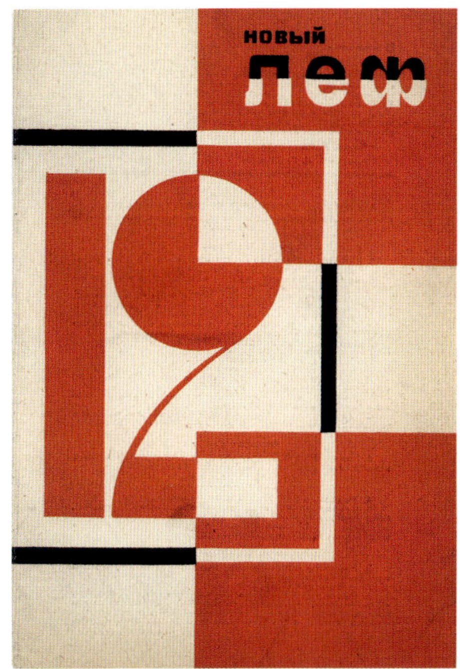

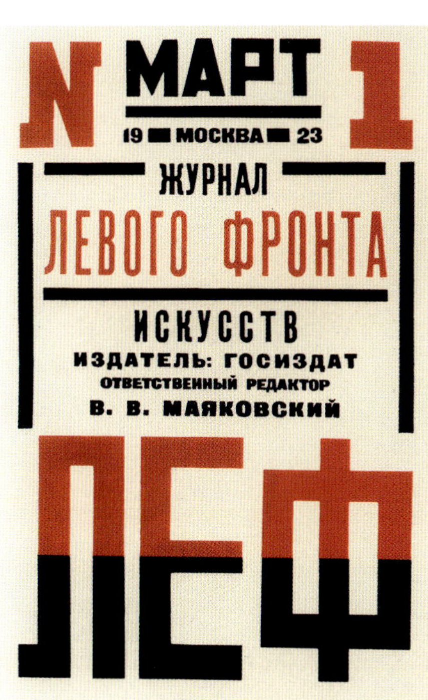

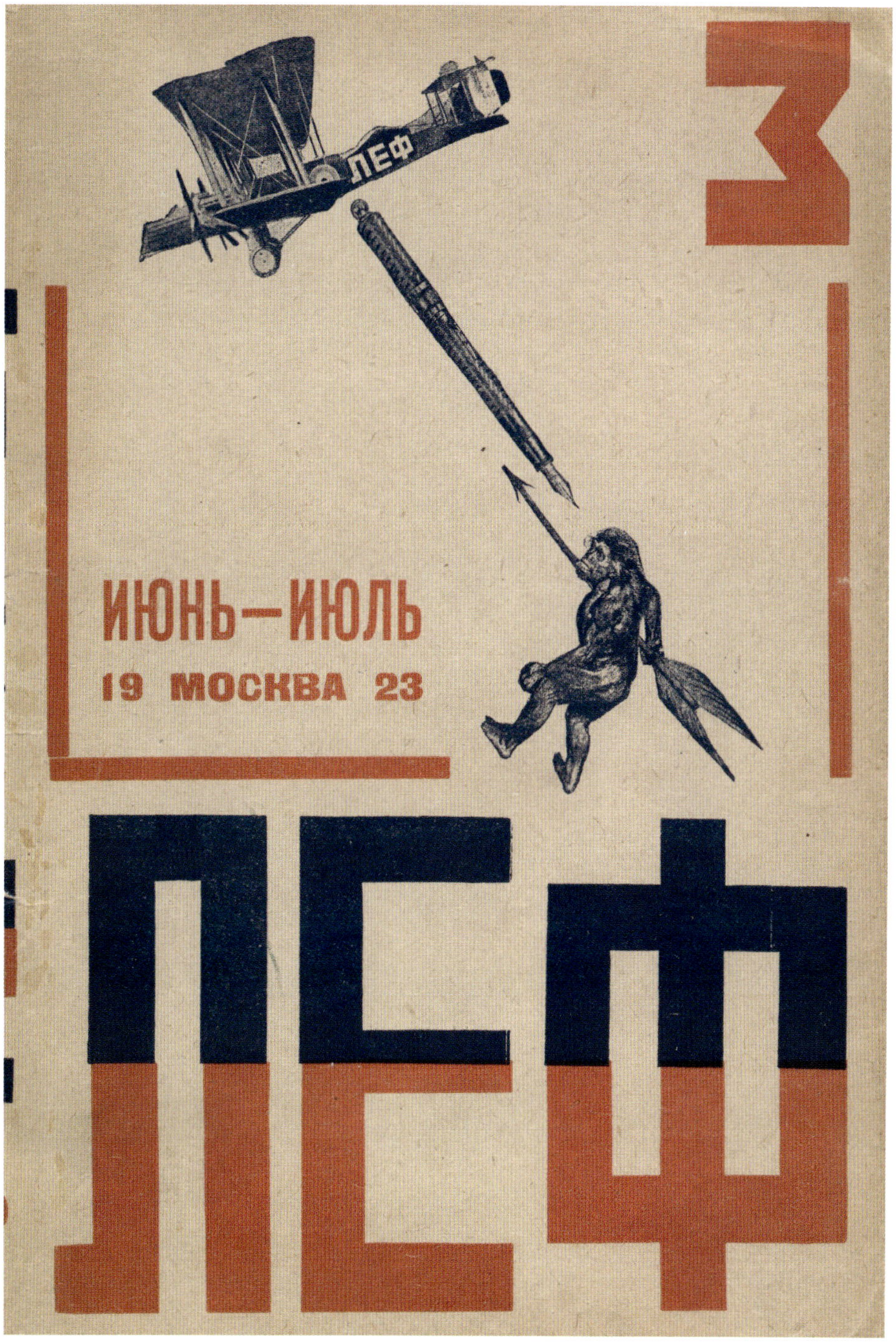

A selection of covers from
LEF and *New LEF* 1923–28
Alexander Rodchenko

The 1917 Bolshevik Revolution provided
artists with the opportunity to undertake
a central role in the building of the new
Soviet state and its culture. The artists
of Constructivism produced work that
was driven by the ideas and actions of
'construction'. They then moved towards
Productivism: designing for the functional
needs of the new society, such as workers'
clothing. They produced work across a wide
range of disciplines and, unusually for that
time period, women played a central role in
the movement. Leading practitioners were
Alexander Rodchenko and El Lissitzky
(graphic design, photography, typography)
and Varvara Stepanova (textile, theatre and
graphic design). Some of the most vibrant
examples of Constructivist graphics were
covers for *LEF*, the journal of a group of
Constructivist artists and Futurist poets
known as 'Left Front of the Arts'. It was
founded in 1923 by the revolutionary poet
Vladimir Mayakovsky (also editor-in-chief).
Alexander Rodchenko designed covers,
illustrations and layouts, and Varvara
Stepanova worked on the production. In
1925, *LEF* was terminated by the State
Publishing House following accusations
that it was incomprehensible to the masses.
It was resurrected by Mayakovsky in 1927
under the title *New LEF*, but it proved
unpopular and ceased in 1928.

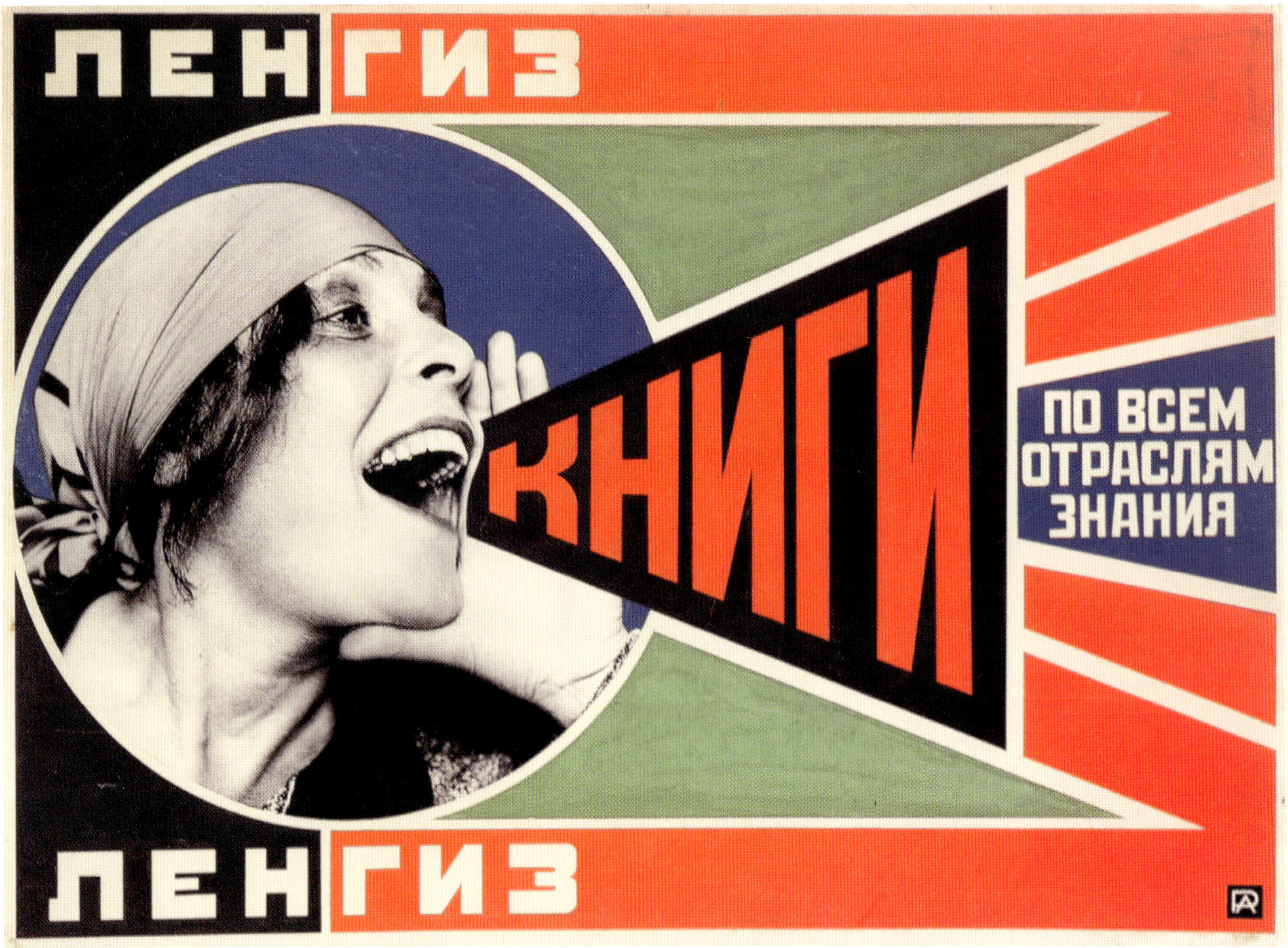

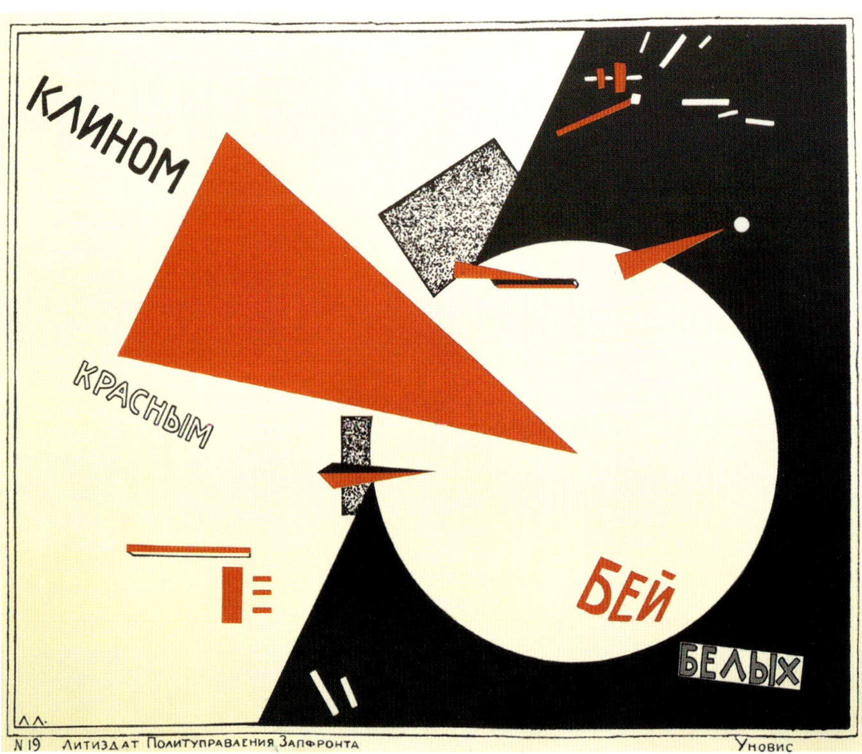

← **Beat the Whites with the Red Wedge** 1919
El Lissitzky
Poster

El Lissitzky's poster is considered to be one of graphic design's great icons of the Constructivist period. It is an abstract composition depicting the victorious Red Army (symbolized by a large red triangle) invading and crushing the White Russians (a large white circle, unable to stop the invasion of its black defences). It is now relatively easy to understand and make sense of this early, pioneering, visual interpretation of a confrontation of both people and ideas. However, its ability to communicate a political message to the semi-illiterate population, at the time it was made, could be questioned.

← 'Knigi' (Books – For Every Branch
of Knowledge) 1925
Alexander Rodchenko
Poster

Due to its bright colours and dynamic
composition, this poster remains one of
the most recognizable and best-loved
of all Constructivist posters. It was
designed by Alexander Rodchenko for
the State Publishing House Gosizdat
and made for its Leningrad branch
as part of a literacy programme,
announcing that books would be freely
available to all. (The woman shouting
is Lily Brik, actress and wife of the
critic Osip Brik: both were friends
of Rodchenko.) A large part of the
population at the time was illiterate, and
therefore simple, impactful propaganda
posters were better able to communicate
their message.

→ **Tractors** 1930
Sergei Burylin
Indienne

The young Soviet state, desperate to
promote economic reconstruction,
did not deal solely in abstract designs.
As time went on new propagandist
themes were born, shown here in a
textile design, based on representations
of industrialization and involving
subjects such as dockyards, factories,
aeroplanes and sport. The designs
appeared particularly dynamic on
lightweight cotton fabrics such
as indienne. Such 'propagandist'
fabrics (*agittekstil*) were considered
representational, both in style and as a
genre, but were still heavily influenced
by Constructivism and particularly
by the styles of Varvara Stepanova
and Liubov Popova. Despite limited
technological facilities and no more
than two or three colours, the designs
stand out for the dynamism of the
composition and the way that movement
is realized, so that tractors and other
vehicles or objects do seem to actually
travel or move across the material.

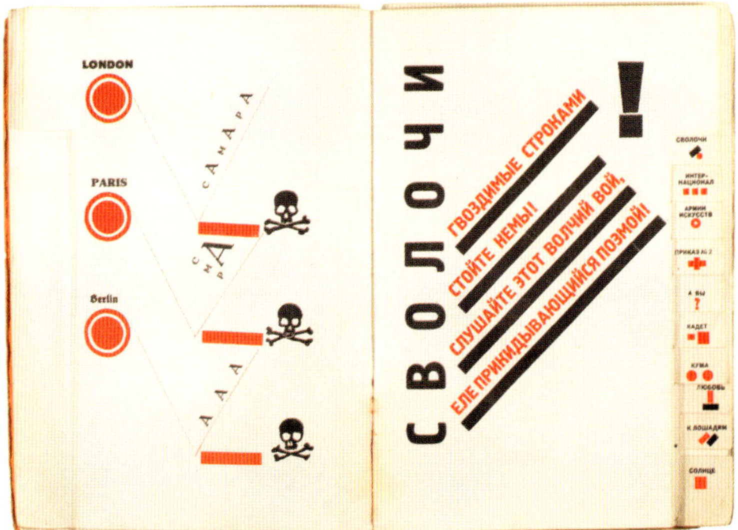

Scum

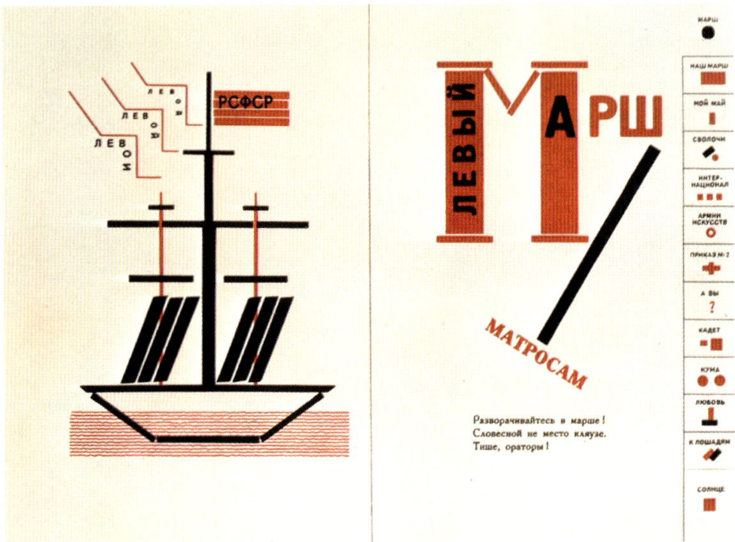

Leftward March

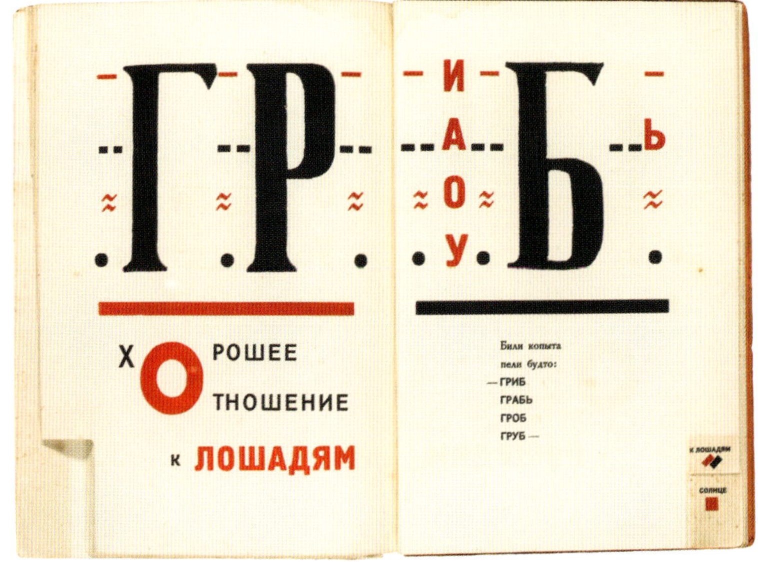

Be Kind to Horses

El Lissitzky was arguably Constructivism's
most pioneering, experimental typographer.
This book of poems, written by Vladimir
Mayakovsky, was intended to be recited
or read out loud. Lissitzky used only the
material from a compositor's type case, and
the exquisite positioning of those materials
in relation to the page (and to each other),
to create the emotion and expressiveness of
the voice or sound to be made as well as the
spoken words. A thumb index at the side
allows easy location of each poem. Three
spreads – one poem per spread – are shown
here, out of a possible dozen.

Alexander Rodchenko's poster for Dziga
Vertov's *Cine-Eye* film employs the usual
Constructivist elements of geometric
structure and bold lettering, but his
introduction of photomontage into the
poster is dramatic and meaningful. A staring
human eye represents the (all-seeing)
eye of the camera gazing at its audience;
the camera and boy's head, mirrored and
looking upward, refer to Vertov's use of
high-angle shots.

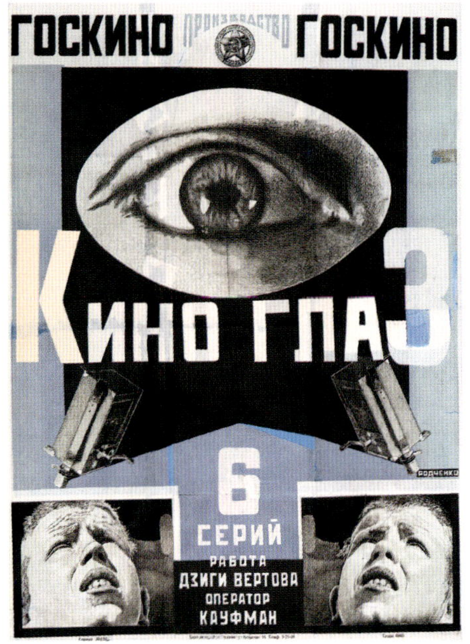

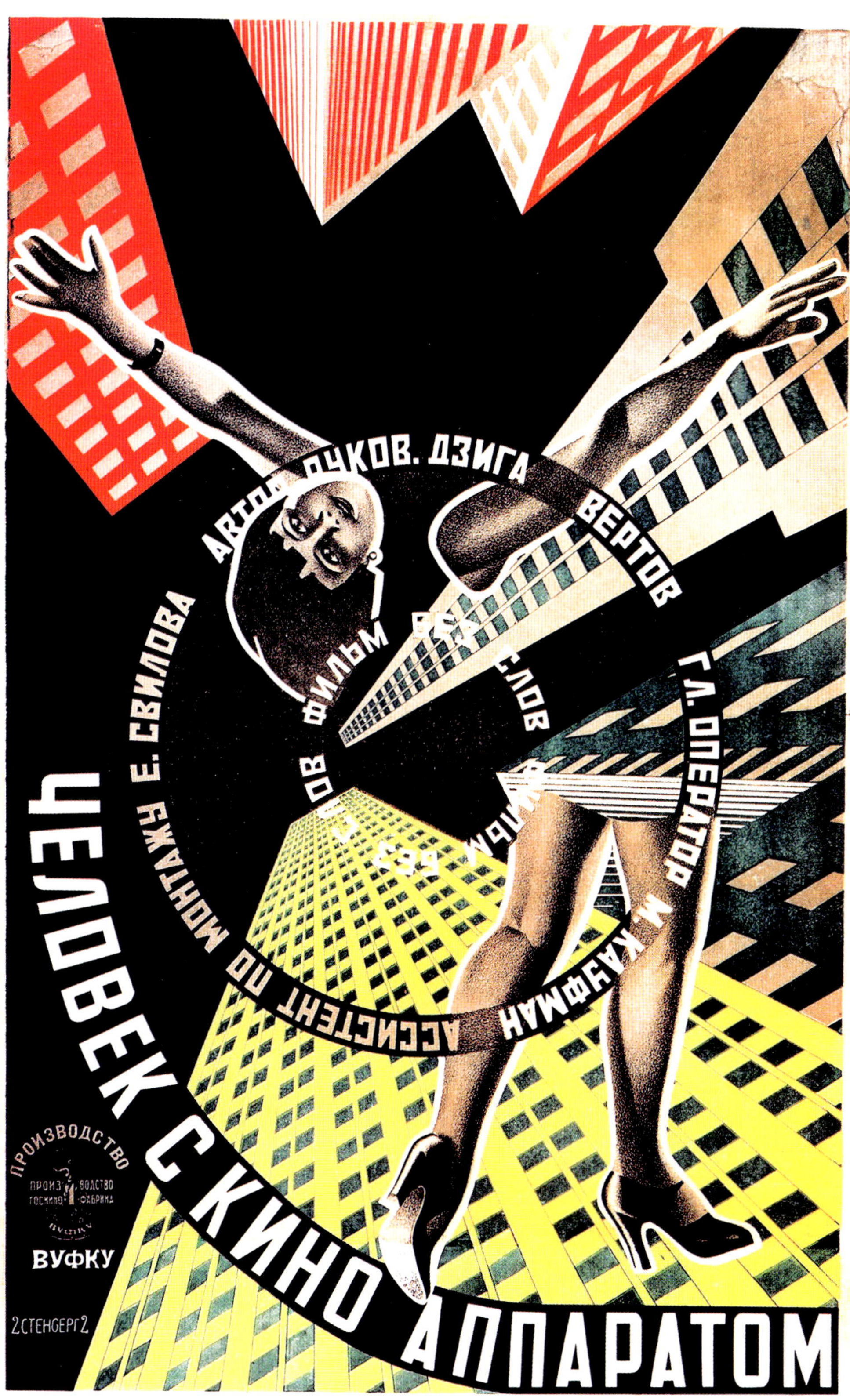

Man with a Movie Camera 1929
Georgy and Vladimir Stenberg
Film poster (lithograph)

Documentary filmmaker Dziga Vertov produced *Man with a Movie Camera* in 1929. A film without a spoken narrative, it documented the life, moods and rhythms of the city through inventive use of montage. It was fast-paced, full of experimental methods (multiple exposures, split-screen imagery, unusual camera angles), and was made to awaken Soviet citizens to their emerging new life. It is therefore suitable that this poster was created by the Stenberg brothers, Vladimir and Georgy, both Constructivist artists. Here they capture the movement and breathless quality of Vertov's film through the angled perspective of the buildings, the backward arch of the woman and the typography that seems to whirl around her.

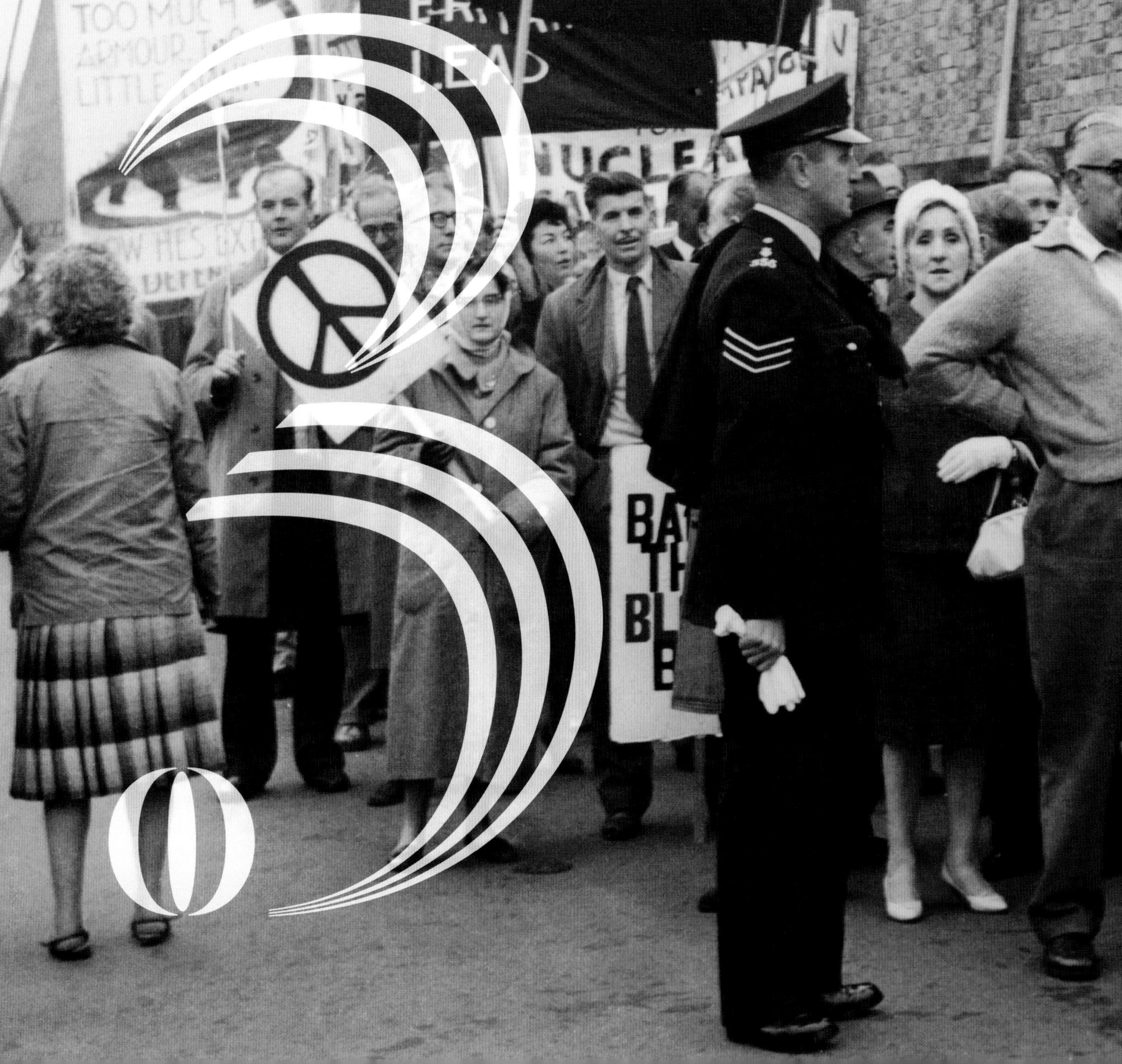

FOR
Nuclear
Disarmament
AG
H
LET H-BASES
LEAD
TOO MUCH
ARMOUR, TOO
LITTLE
BA
TH
B

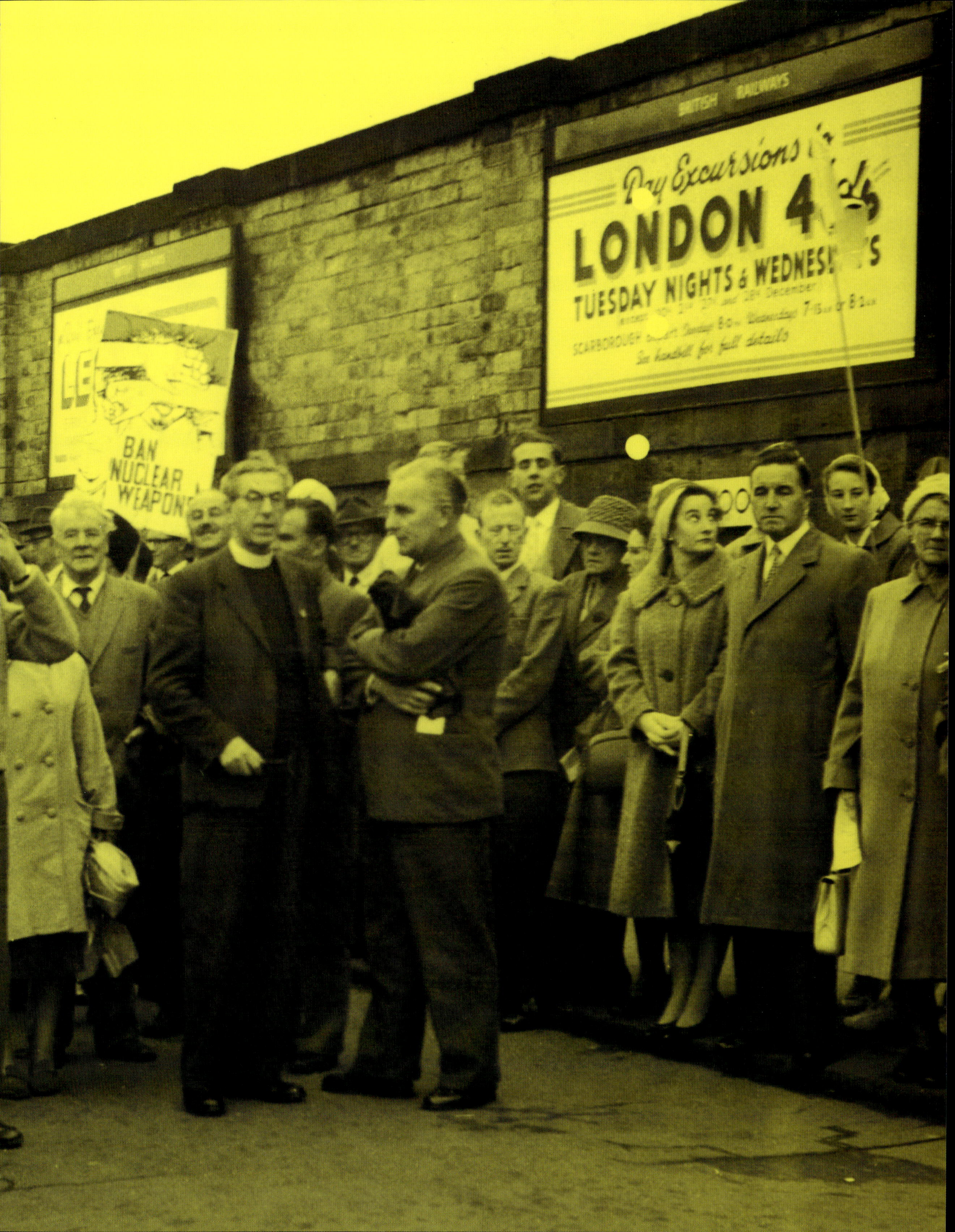
BRITISH RAILWAYS
Day Excursions
LONDON 4/-
TUESDAY NIGHTS & WEDNESDAYS
SCARBOROUGH
See handbill for full details
BAN NUCLEAR WEAPONS

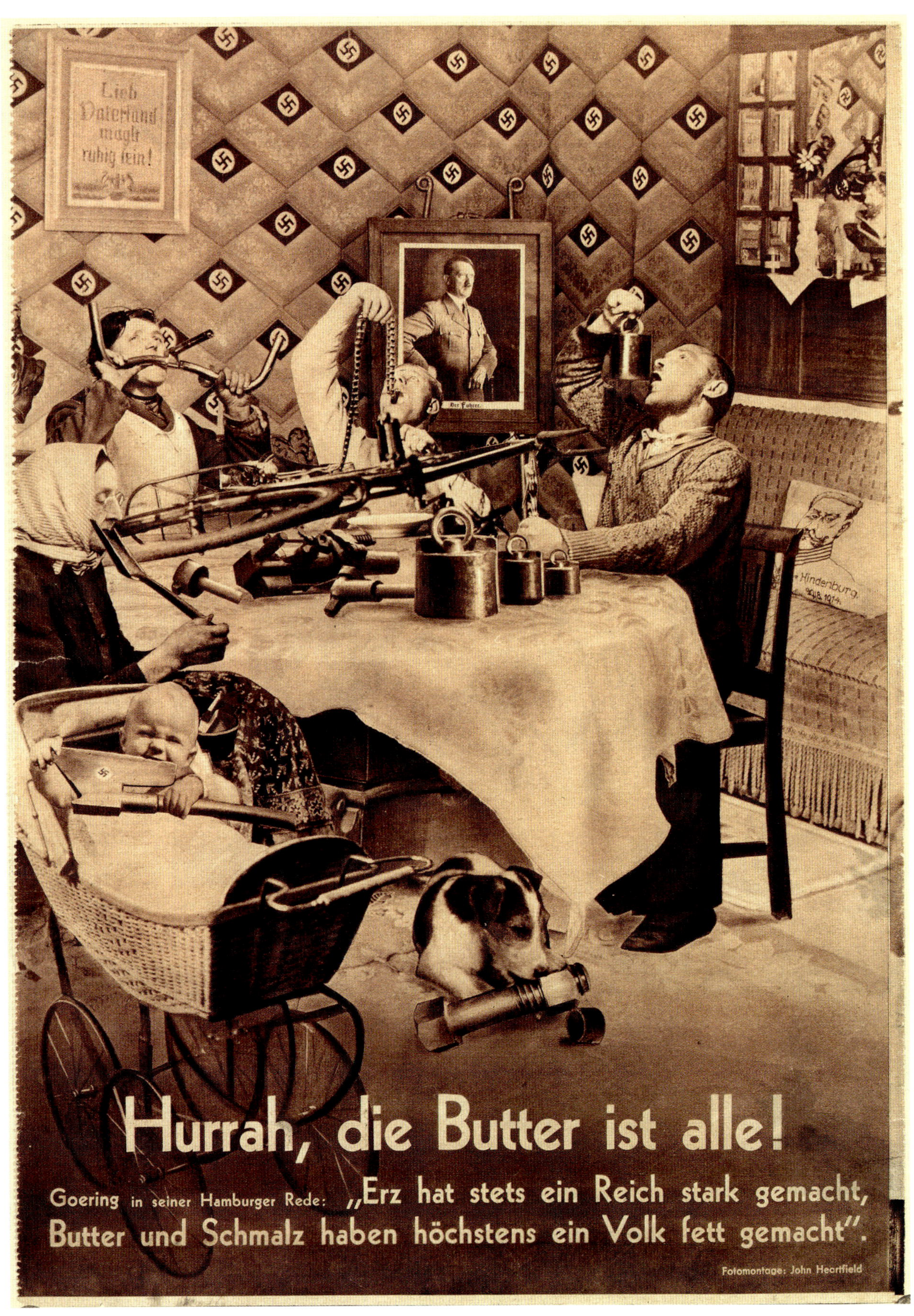

Hurrah, the Butter is All Gone! 1935
John Heartfield for *AIZ*, 19 December, 1935

1930–1960

Fascism, The Cold War and The Bomb

The end of the 1920s saw much of Europe in turmoil. Although many of the countries involved in the First World War were still attempting economic recovery throughout the decade, they were plagued by unemployment, workers' strikes (Britain's General Strike of 1926) and inflation (Germany), while the USA's economy boomed. Then, just as recovery began to be in sight for all, the US stock market crash of 1929 brought it all tumbling down, with global repercussions. This opened the door to totalitarian regimes (Fascism and Nazism) in Europe, while the USA struggled with the Great Depression. In short: the USA headed for economic collapse. Banks went bust, factories closed, unemployment skyrocketed: a million were homeless and hungry. US President Herbert Hoover could not, or would not, comprehend the tragedy, and refused to spend government money on relief programmes.[1]

In 1932 Franklin Delano Roosevelt (FDR) campaigned for the US presidency – against Hoover – and won easily. (Not surprisingly, there were campaign buttons that said 'ANYONE BUT HOOVER'.) Once in office, Roosevelt produced a series of programmes and laws under the name of the New Deal, regulating the stock market and creating work programmes or training for the unemployed. Recovery wasn't easy. By a trick of nature, from 1934–37 abnormally severe droughts and windstorms turned the Great Plains area, across seven states of the USA, into a dry desert: the Dust Bowl. But the New Deal brought hope.[2]

Throughout the 1930s, social deprivation and economic depression became the subject of the art movement known as Social Realism. Encouraged by federal arts projects under the New Deal, artists such as Ben Shahn (one of the movement's central figures and agitators) produced work that was rooted in social criticism, committing themselves to depicting the plight of the urban, or rural, poor. They drew attention to industrial workers, labour unions and labour organizing, viewed as pathways to a better future, as well as highlighting ruined land, ruined farmers and the devastation of rural communities. Such imagery produced a new expression of American identity, as well as consolidating a group of artists dedicated to social justice, while keeping an anxious (and watchful) eye on events developing in Europe.[3]

At the same time, Germany's Depression, driven by inflation and large-scale unemployment, also needed a strong leader. Adolf Hitler, leader of the (fascist) Nazi movement or National Socialist German Workers Party, was elected Chancellor of Germany in 1933 on the promise of stability and better times. But his strong nationalist movement (Nazism) had, at its centre, racism and militarism. He targeted particular groups to blame for Germany's ills – Jews, gypsies, homosexuals, the disabled – and set out to exterminate them. He built up Germany's industrial might, and by 1938 used it to invade and occupy surrounding countries including Austria, Czechoslovakia, Poland and eventually France, leading to the Second World War in Europe.[4]

In the early years of the 1930s, former Berlin Dadaist and photomontagist John Heartfield became a regular contributor of photomontages to the German magazine

Arbeiter-Illustrierte-Zeitung or *A-I-Z (Workers' Illustrated Paper)* aimed at Communists and German workers. But as time went on, he embarked on a dangerous path, producing searing and at times bloody anti-Nazi photomontages as covers or illustrations for *A-I-Z*, a number of them aiming a direct hit at Hitler or his cohorts. In 1933 both Heartfield and the magazine (now called *AIZ*) were forced to escape to Prague. There Heartfield continued to deliver his visual attack on Nazi terror. In 1938 the Nazis invaded Czechoslovakia and Heartfield made a narrow escape to London where he remained throughout the Second World War continuing his anti-Nazi activities.[5]

Not far away, Spain was fighting a civil war (1936–39) involving its beleaguered republican government pitted against the forces of the fascist rebel leader, Francisco Franco. Despite international help supplied to the republican government and its army, Franco won (aided by Hitler and Mussolini) and ruled until his death in 1975. However a product of that devastating civil war was the production of a mass of extraordinary posters, produced by or on behalf of the republican government, which drew stylistically from the Modernist advertising of the time, and are still admired, and seemingly 'modern', in the 21st century.[6]

The Second World War (1939–45) brought a spectre of weaponry that has defined global power politics to this day. In a move intended allegedly to end the war, the USA dropped an atom bomb (nuclear weapon) on the Japanese city of Hiroshima and another on Nagasaki in 1945. Within four years, another country – the USSR/Russia – had tested one. The Cold War had started, a period characterized by two superpowers (the USA and the USSR) engaged in an arms race and a space race. The testing of atom bombs by a growing number of countries wishing to be part of 'the club' continued, often taking place in the Pacific (with protests by Islanders bearing the consequences, or their sympathizers).[7]

In the early 1950s, the USA succumbed to panic about the Communist threat, fears of invasion by the Soviets (as hyped in popular culture) and an on-going craze for underground fallout shelters. Britain, however, slowly began sowing the seeds for a nuclear disarmament movement. Then on 1 March 1954 the USA set off the first hydrogen bomb (H-bomb) at Bikini Atoll in the Pacific, which had 1,300 times the power of the bomb at Hiroshima. The explosion was witnessed by the Japanese fishing boat *Daigo Fukuryu Maru* or *Lucky Dragon*. Despite being 20 miles outside of the US exclusion zone, the 23-man crew was covered with lethal fallout.[8]

In addition to the bombing of Hiroshima and Nagasaki, the *Lucky Dragon* incident added further impetus to the fast-developing Japanese peace movement. It also inspired the anti-nuclear film *Gojira* (*Godzilla*) directed by Ishiro Honda and released in 1954. Honda had visited Hiroshima after the war. Haunted by images of horror and devastation, he imbibed the film with a documentary-like directness. It opened with an incident based on that of the *Lucky Dragon*, where a fishing boat was confrontedwith a nuclear blast, which then awakened a long-dormant dinosaur-like monster. Honda made Godzilla (the monster) a representation of the destructive power of the atom bomb.[9]

With news of a hydrogen bomb, peace activists and grassroots organizations were beginning to form internationally and the 'Ban the Bomb' movement was underway. In Britain, in July 1955, world-renowned philosopher Lord Bertrand Russell drafted an appeal, co-signed by Albert Einstein, calling for scientists worldwide to work for peace. By 1957 there were hundreds of 'Ban the Bomb' groups spread across Britain, organizing meetings and marches. It became clear that they could be more effective if they banded together as a mass movement, and in January 1958 the Campaign for Nuclear Disarmament (CND) was born, with Lord Bertrand Russell as president. CND's first mass protest was a march from London to Aldermaston, the location of the government's nuclear weapons factory. Textile designer Gerald Holtom was asked to design banners and placards to be carried on the march. He also produced a logo/symbol which was adopted by CND, carried on the march and has been used by CND ever since.[10]

In 1960 Lord Russell (then in his eighties) and others split from CND to form the 'Committee of 100', favouring civil disobedience as a more urgent way of bringing attention to their cause. In their first action, in February 1961, 5,000 activists staged a sit-in outside the War Office in Whitehall, London. This was followed by other sit-ins. In September, a massive demonstration was held in Trafalgar Square in London, at which police arrested and then jailed 89-year-old Russell for a week. It made headlines around the world. But not long after, another series of events drew worldwide attention and protest, particularly among the young: the USA's intervention in the Vietnam War. Anti-war protests would overshadow many other good causes for at least a decade.[11]

The 1950s also saw a light cast on the dark practices of racial segregation in two countries. On 1 December 1955, in the USA's Deep South (Montgomery, Alabama) on her way home from work, a black woman named Rosa Parks – a 'quiet' activist since the 1940s – refused to get up from her seat on a bus and move back one row (into the black section) so that a white man could occupy her seat. In accordance with the racial segregation laws of the time, if the white section became full, the dividing line was moved back a row. But not this time. This one act of defiance set off a chain of events that ended with a Federal Court voting that segregation on buses was unconstitutional. Rosa Parks' small (but politically huge) action brought national and international attention to the USA's Civil Rights movement. Her mugshot marks the beginning of a slow transformation that would carry on for years, and still shadows the present.[12]

The 1950s brought enforced racial segregation to South Africa; it also sowed the seeds of defiance. In 1948 the National Party was voted into power, and soon introduced apartheid: a policy of white minority power over the black majority, involving an enforced system of racial segregation, economic exploitation and the denial of basic rights to blacks, as well as Indians and people of mixed race. An important tool in this system was the use of the Pass Laws, designed to control the movement of Africans, who were required to carry a Pass Book (essentially a method of tracking or restricting their movements).[13]

Africans often violated Pass Laws in order to find work, and lived under constant threat of harassment or arrest. Hatred of the Pass Laws fuelled the first Defiance Campaign (1952–54) begun by the African National Congress (ANC) Youth League, under Nelson Mandela and Oliver Tambo, and involving thousands of mass refusals to obey the new apartheid laws. Protests continued throughout the decade. Finally, on 21 March 1960, as people were burning their Pass Books in protest, police opened fire on the crowd, killing 69; it became known as the Sharpeville Massacre. The ANC called for a national 'stayaway' (stop work) in protest. The government banned the ANC and the Pan Africanist Congress (PAC). Both were forced underground, and in 1963 the ANC leader Nelson Mandela was imprisoned.[14]

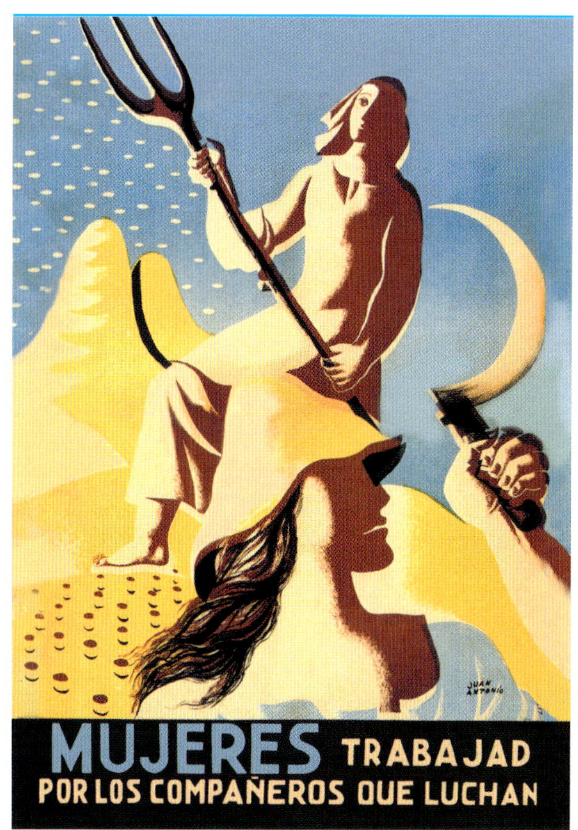

Women, Work More for the Men who Fight *c.* 1937
Juan Antonio

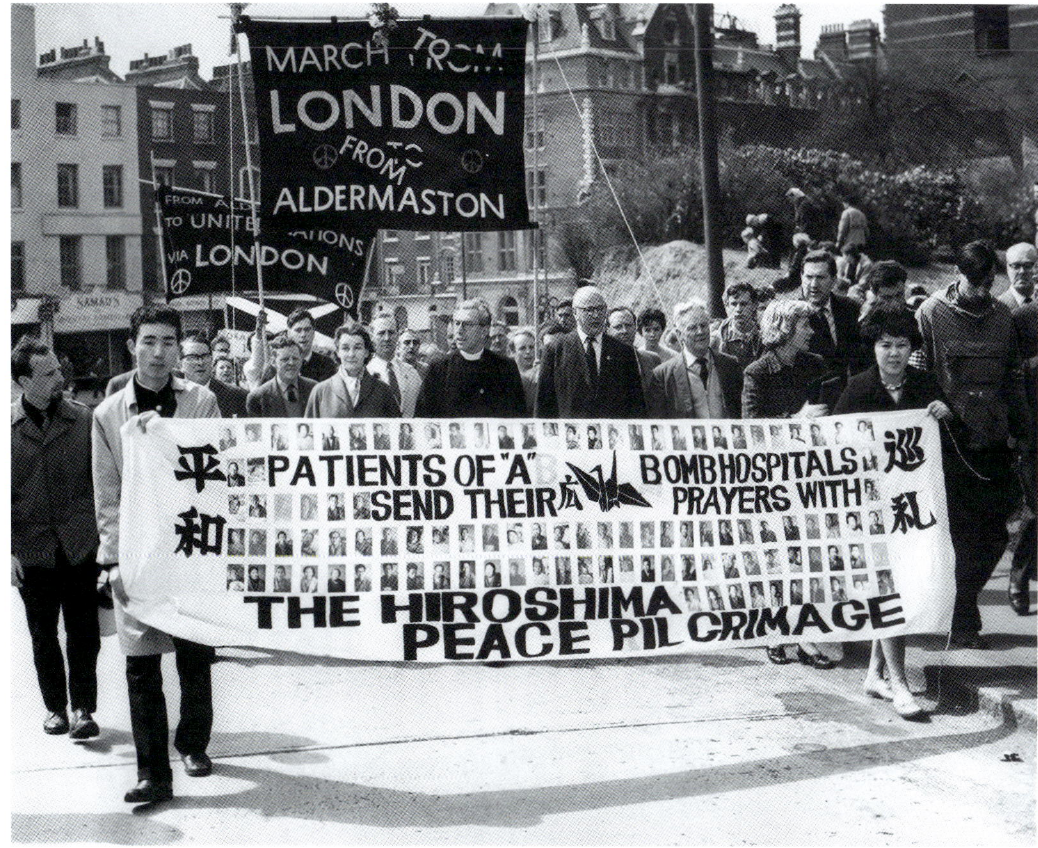

Hiroshima survivors taking part in an Aldermaston march for nuclear disarmament 1962
Photographer unknown

Ben Shahn and Social Realism

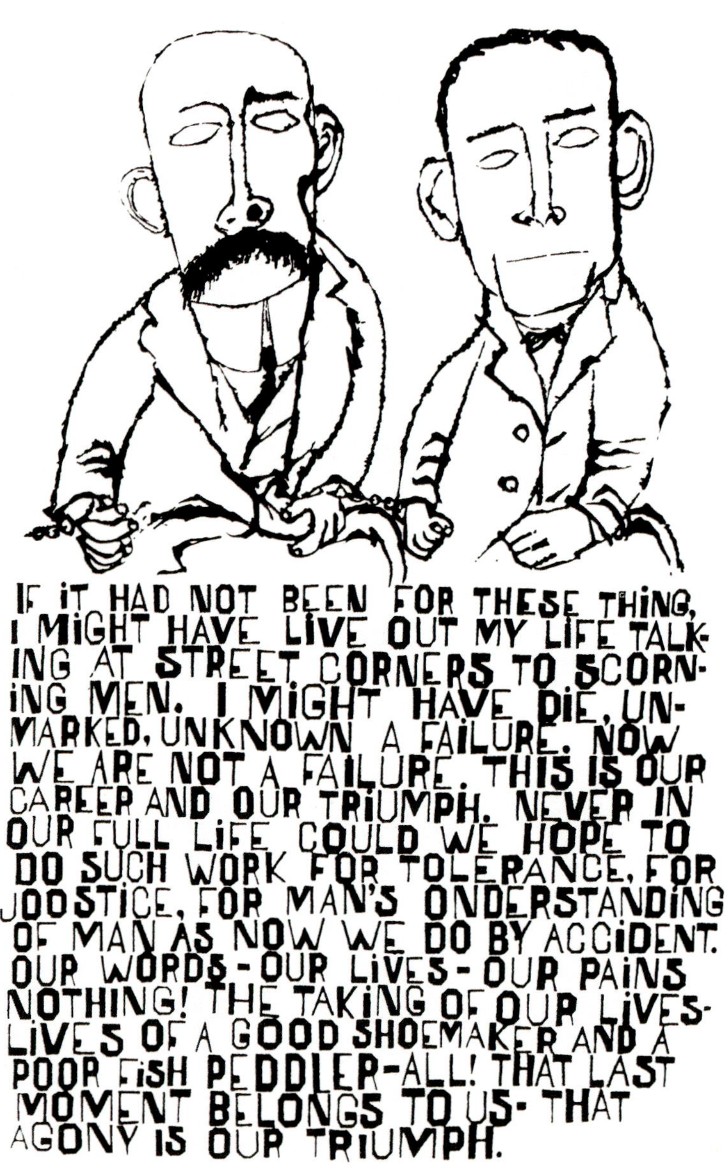

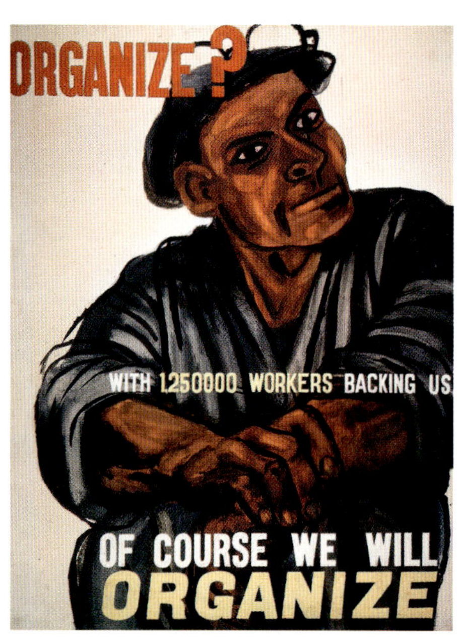

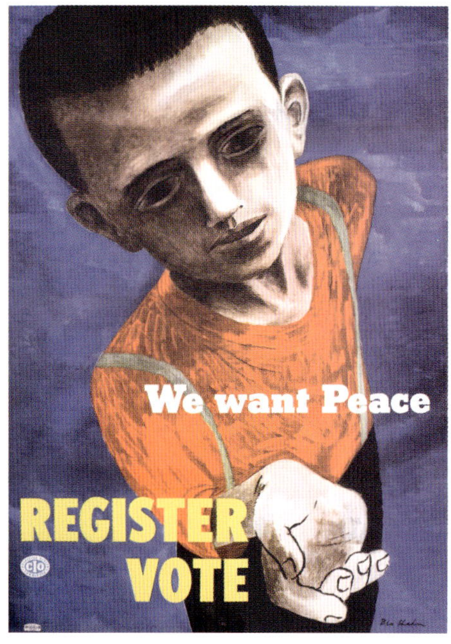

↑ **Sacco and Vanzetti** 1958
Ben Shahn
Poster, print

Throughout his life Ben Shahn used his art to expose or argue against social injustice. In the early 1930s he became known for his controversial paintings (and eventually murals) relating to the trial and subsequent execution of two Italian immigrants: Nicola Sacco, a shoemaker, and Bartolomeo Vanzetti,

a fish peddler. Arrested in 1920 in connection with the robbery and murder of two men in Braintree, Massachusetts, they were convicted the following year on largely circumstantial evidence. Despite seven appeals, in 1927 they were executed. Their conviction and execution have been argued about ever since; a more likely reason for their treatment may have been to do with the suspicion felt at that time by the authorities, and some of the public, towards Italian anarchists and immigrants

(and Sacco and Vanzetti were both). Ben Shahn maintained his fight against social injustice, as well as exercising his great love of lettering, throughout his working life. In 1958, in the twilight years of the McCarthy 'witch hunt' often aimed unjustly against 'communists' in the USA, he created this tribute to Sacco and Vanzetti by lettering a stirring quote by Vanzetti, published in the *New York World* in May 1927, immediately after their last appeal had been rejected.

Ben Shahn's concern for the common man and the hardships of workers and labourers found natural expression in the labour movement and labour organizing throughout the 1930s. As the country was trying to pull itself out of the Depression, the posters Shahn created for various trade unions were not defiant or angry; they were easy-going and positive, yet full of energy and action. Most of all, they conveyed a warm sense of hope.

Shahn joined the Political Action Committee (PAC) of the Congress of Industrial Organizations (CIO) in order to work for the 1944 re-election of President Franklin Delano Roosevelt. Once FDR was elected, Shahn became director of the CIO-PAC Graphic Arts Division. This led to the design of many posters aimed at encouraging people to exercise their democratic right to vote and see that as the road to a better future. This poster shows the emotional 'pull' of Shahn's imagery in the haunting eyes of a begging child: but a better life can be achieved through the power of the vote.

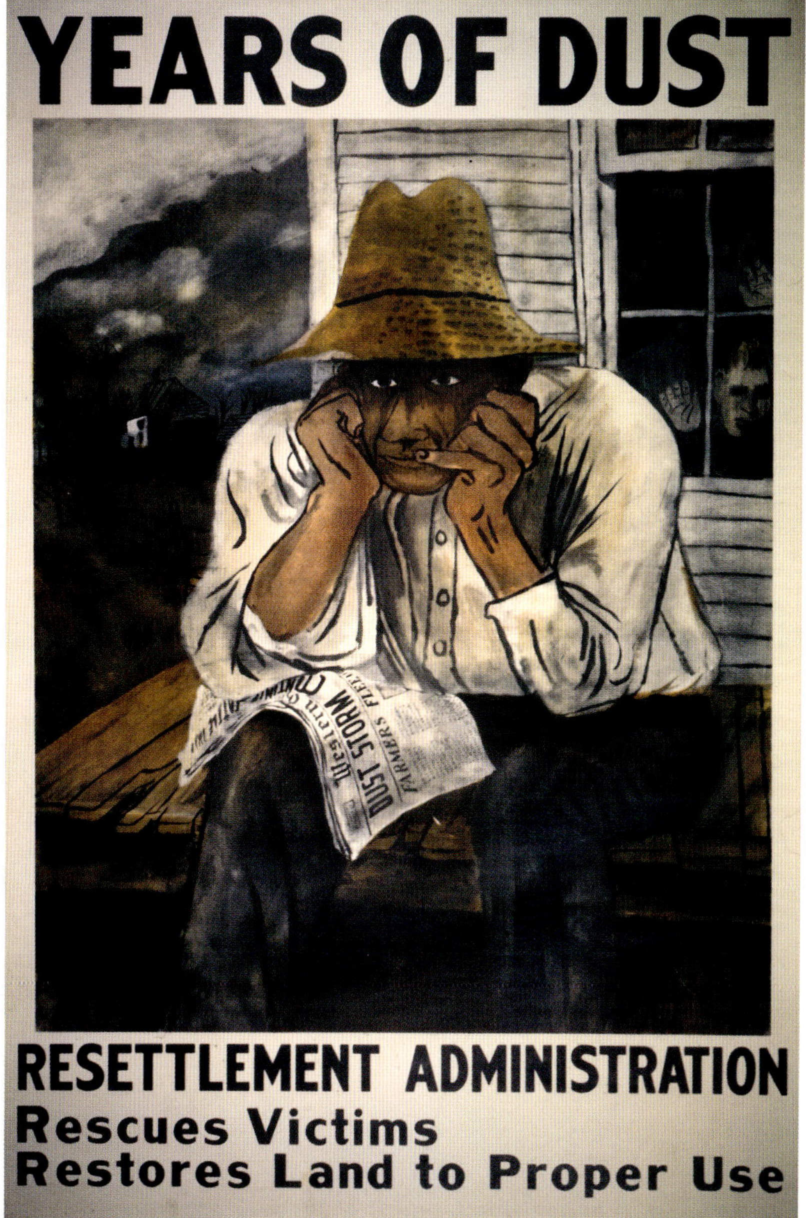

Years of Dust 1936
Ben Shahn
Poster

The US stock market crash of 1929 plunged the country into the Great Depression and economic collapse: banks went bust, factories closed, unemployment soared. In 1932 newly-elected President Franklin D. Roosevelt produced new ideas, new work programmes and new laws to help recovery, under the name of the New Deal. At the same time, from 1934 to 1937 severe droughts and windstorms turned seven states in the Great Plains area into a dry desert, referred to as the Dust Bowl. This economic depression, and the social deprivation it caused, became the subject of the art movement known as Social Realism. Aided by federal arts projects under the New Deal, artists such as Ben Shahn – one of the movement's central figures – committed themselves to social criticism and depicting the plight of the urban, or rural, poor. The poster image shown here was created by Ben Shahn for the Resettlement Administration offering resettlement for urban families, or as shown here, ruined farmers and devastated rural communities, as well as addressing problems such as soil erosion, drought, floods and financial debt.

In the Shadow of Fascism

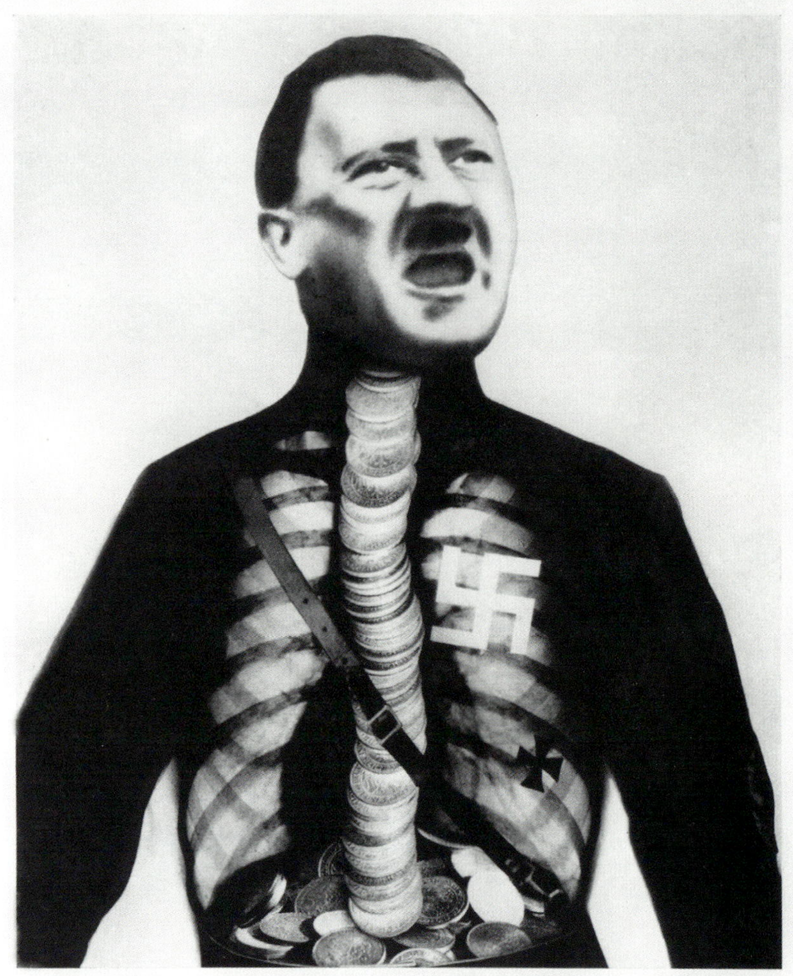

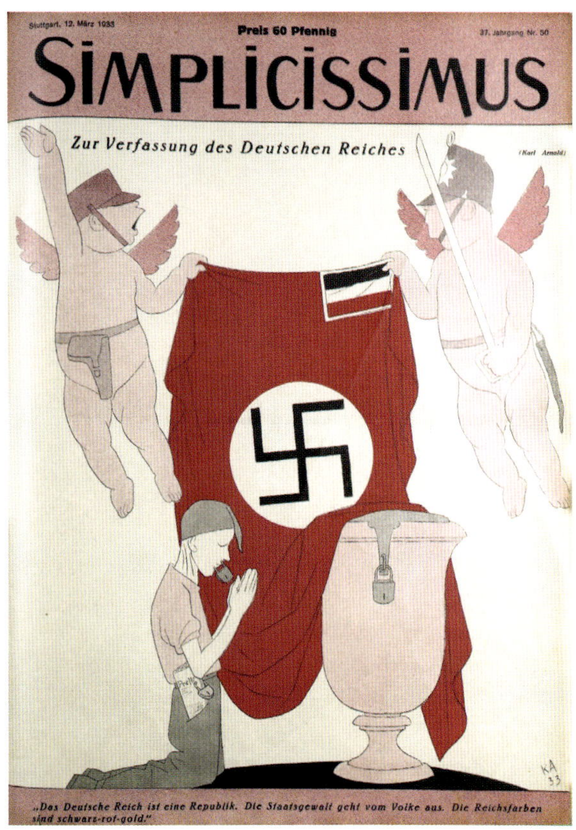

Adolf, the Superman – Swallows Gold and Spouts Junk 1932
John Heartfield
Photomontage – *AIZ*, vol XI, no.29, 1932

Former Berlin Dadaist and photomontagist John Heartfield created some of
the most vicious visual attacks on Hitler and his cohorts in existence; they were
nothing short of meticulously-constructed political weapons. They were usually
produced as covers or illustrations for the magazine *Arbeiter-Illustrierte-Zeitung*
or *A-I-Z* (Workers' Illustrated Paper), which was aimed at Communists and
German workers. (In the end, *AIZ* published over 200 of his photomontages.)
'Adolf, the superman' was a fairly early photomontage, as Hitler hadn't
been named chancellor yet. But enlarged versions were apparently pasted
up throughout Berlin, leading to fights between Communists who defended
the posters and Nazis intent on destroying them. It was one of a number of
Heartfield's photomontages implying that Hitler was backed by 'big money'
proffered by industrialists.

Simplicissimus, **March 1933** 1933
Illustration: Karl Arnold
Front page

Germany's celebrated weekly satirical tabloid,
Simplicissimus – also known as *Der Simpl* – was
bound to change when Hitler was named chancellor
of Germany on 30 January 1933. Up to that point,
Hitler had been caricatured and ridiculed by Thomas
Theodore Heine, Karl Arnold and others on the
team; now such behaviour stopped (although Arnold
continued, but with care). Not long after, co-founder
Heine was forced to flee to Norway, as he was of
Jewish heritage. Other members of the team carried
on, but *Der Simpl* didn't survive the war; it stopped
publication in 1944.

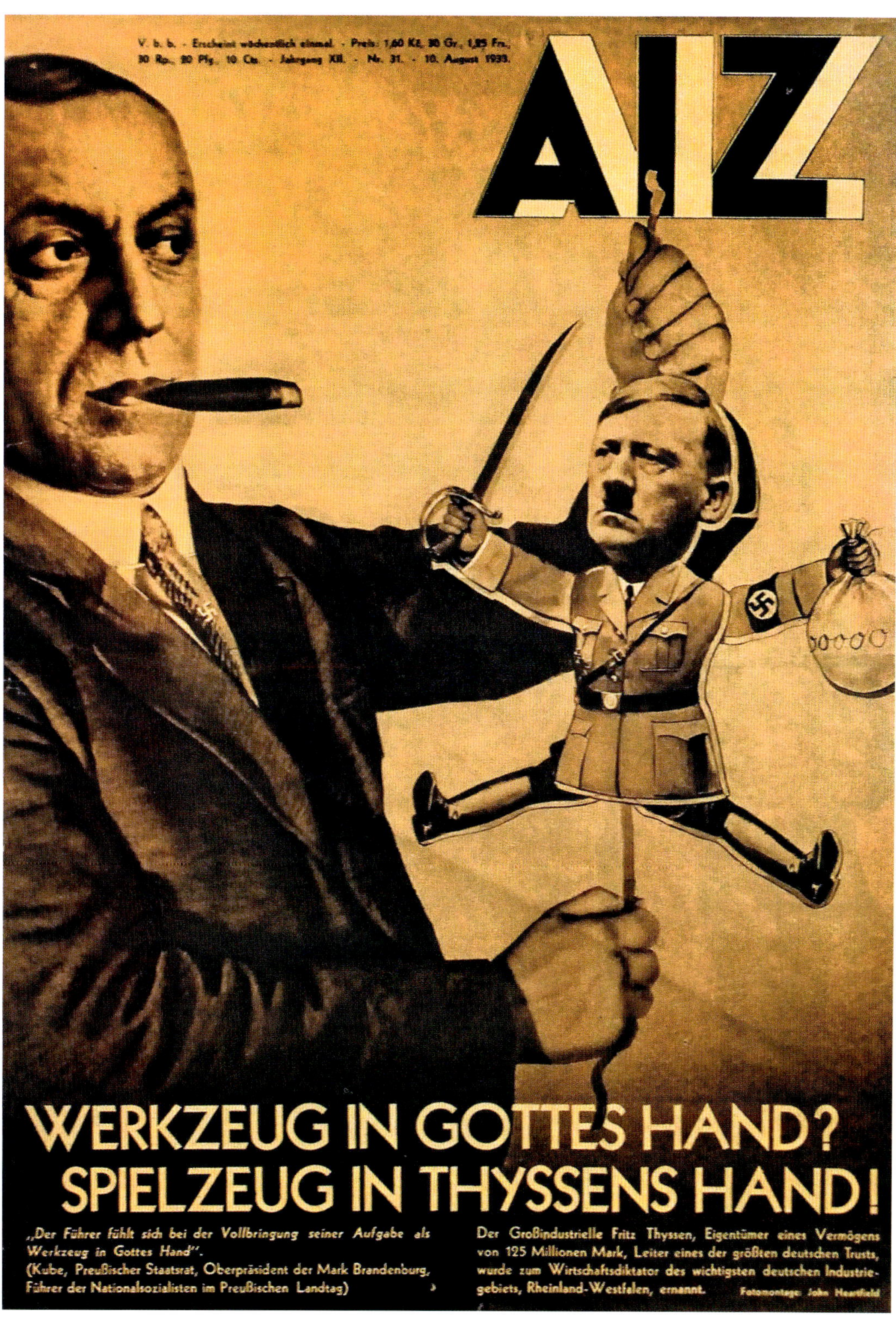

Tool in God's Hand? Toy in Thyssen's Hand! 1933
John Heartfield
Photomontage, front cover – *AIZ*, August 1933

At some point of note in 1933, Wilhelm Kube – a loyal Nazi and a committed German Christian (eventually to become a high-ranking SS officer) – referred to Hitler as a 'tool in God's hand'. Photomontagist John Heartfield then added the slur 'Toy in Thyssen's Hand!', in both text and image, on a front cover of *AIZ* magazine. The man pulling the puppet's string is industrial magnate Fritz Thyssen, a friend and financial backer of both Hitler and the Nazis from very early days. Now, in 1933, Thyssen was all-powerful: manager of one of the largest trusts in Germany and recently appointed 'economic dictator' of Rhineland-Westphalia, Germany's most important industrial region. Thus Thyssen is shown playing with his puppet ('Hampelmann') with a look of control and boredom on his face, while the toy's arms and legs click up and down with exaggerated (and ineffectual) bravado.

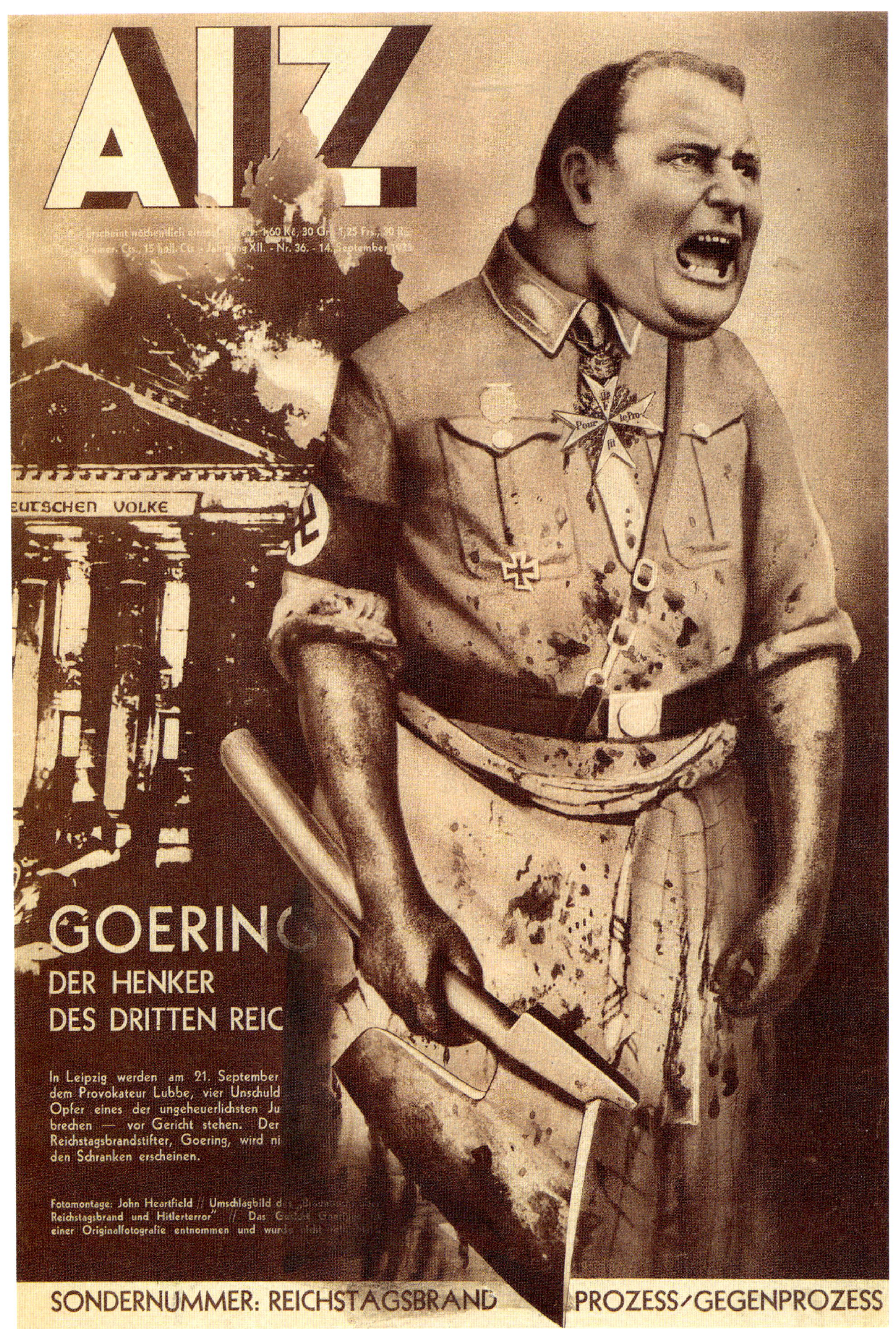
AIZ
Erscheint wöchentlich einmal. Preis: 1.60 Kč, 30 Gr., 1,25 Frs., 30 Rp.
Ermer. Cts., 15 holl. Cts. — Jahrgang XII. — Nr. 36. — 14. September 1933
DEUTSCHEN VOLKE
Pour le Pro fit
GOERING
DER HENKER
DES DRITTEN REIC
In Leipzig werden am 21. September
dem Provokateur Lubbe, vier Unschuld
Opfer eines der ungeheuerlichsten Ju
brechen — vor Gericht stehen. Der
Reichstagsbrandstifter, Goering, wird ni
den Schranken erscheinen.
Fotomontage: John Heartfield // Umschlagbild des „Braunbuches
Reichstagsbrand und Hitlerterror" // Das Gesicht Goerings
einer Originalfotografie entnommen und wurde nicht
SONDERNUMMER: REICHSTAGSBRAND   PROZESS/GEGENPROZESS

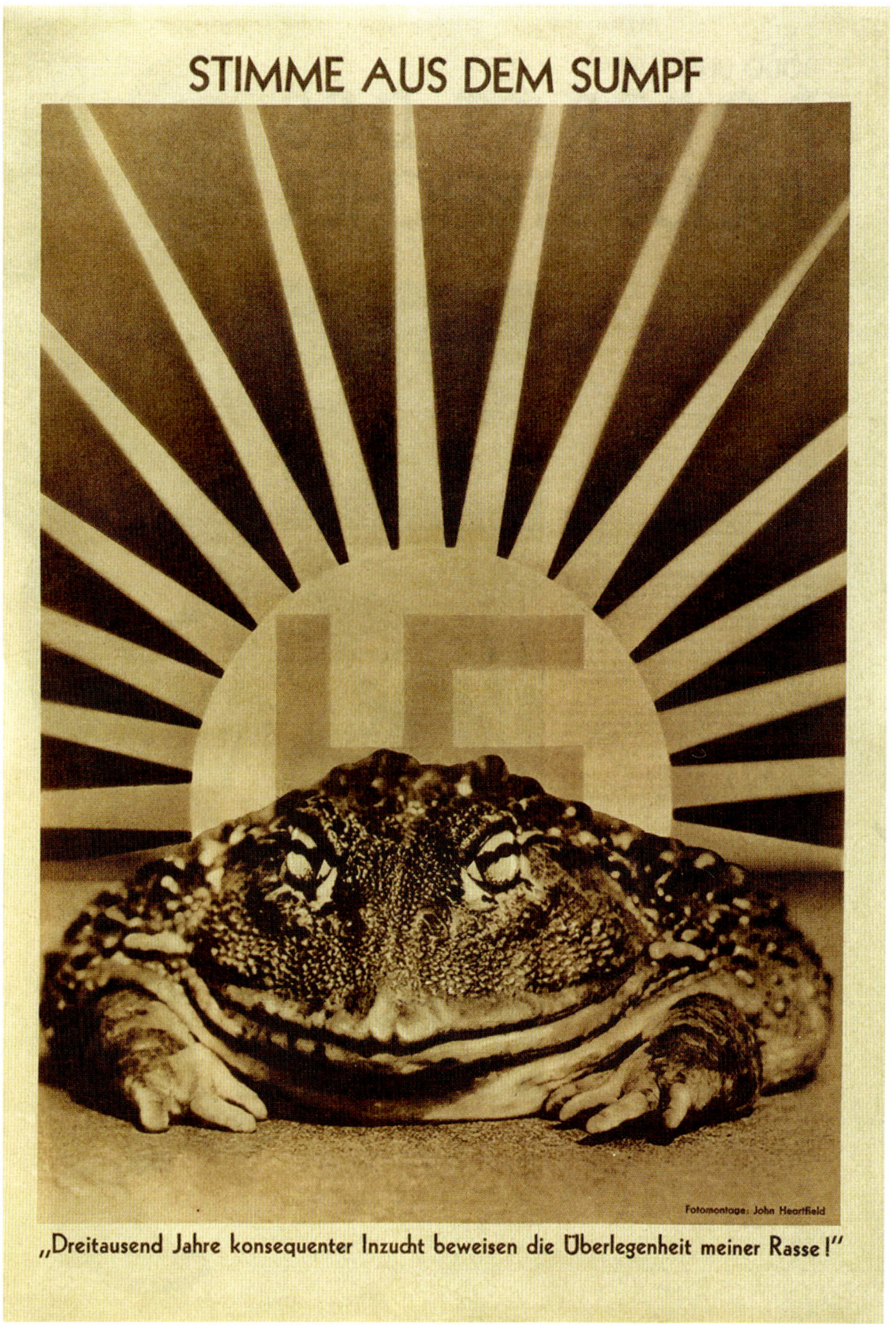

← **Goering, the Executioner of the Third Reich** 1933
John Heartfield
Photomontage, Front cover – *AIZ*,
vol XII, no.36, 1933

The Reichstag in Berlin, Germany's parliamentary building and symbol of the Weimar Republic, was set alight on 27 February 1933. It was believed to have been engineered by Goering and Goebbels as a plot to incarcerate the Communists. At any rate, the Nazis arrested mostly Communists and Socialists, citing their alleged conspiracy to overthrow the state. In the trial that followed, five Communists were accused of arson. This is one of Heartfield's most bloody photomontages, showing Goering as the executioner (or butcher) of the people. In the end, thousands of Communist Party leaders were arrested and imprisoned, and the Communist Party was outlawed.

↑ **A Voice from the Swamp** 1936
John Heartfield
Photomontage – *AIZ*, 19 March 1936

The caption to this simple but incisive photomontage states: 'Three thousand years of consistent inbreeding prove the superiority of my race!'

The Spanish Civil War

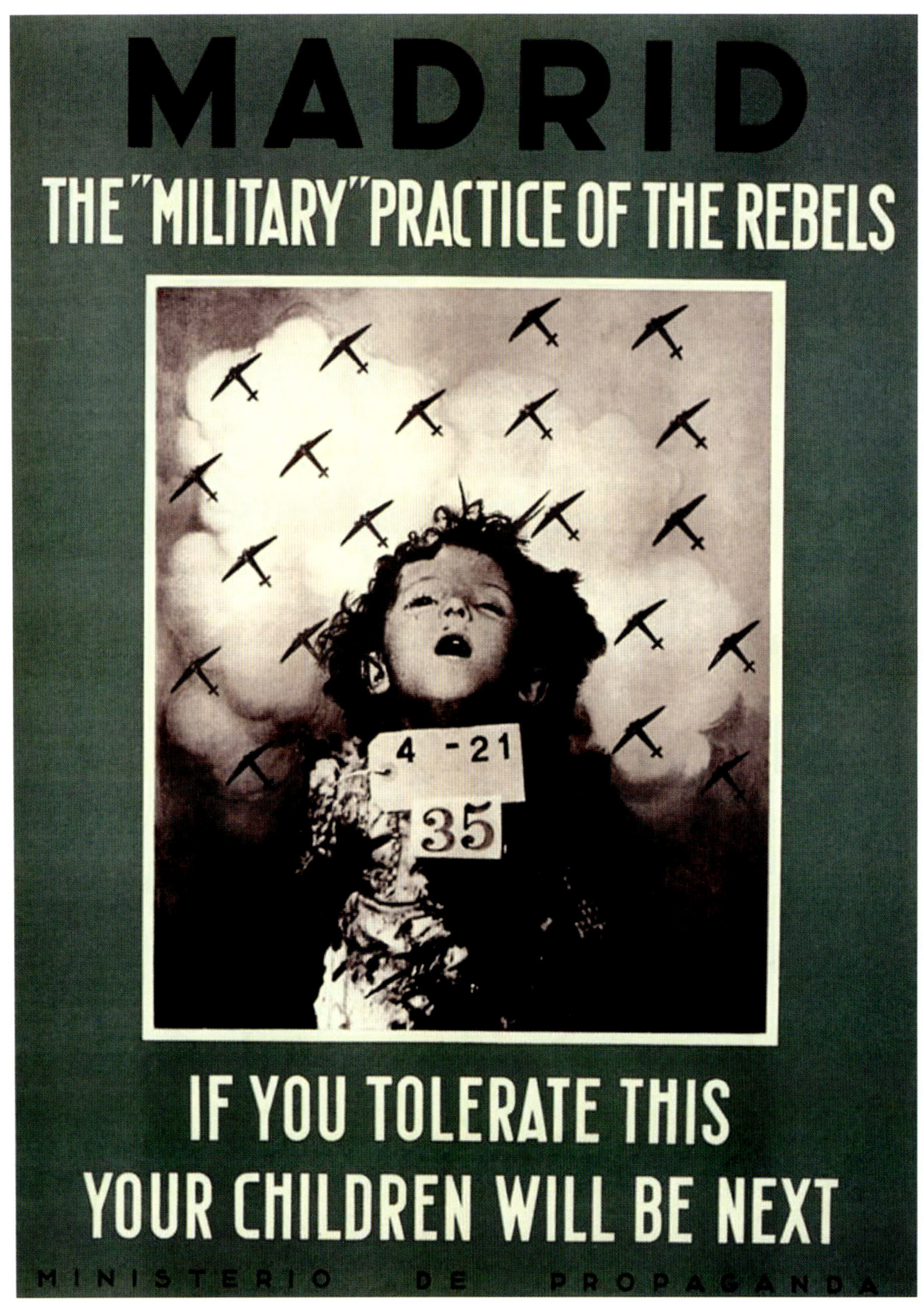

← **MADRID. 'Military' Action of the Rebels. If You Tolerate This, Your Children Will Be Next.** *c.* 1937
Artist unknown
Poster – issued by the Ministry of Propaganda (originally in English)

Not long after Hitler's rise to power in Germany, Spain found itself in the throes of a bloody, devastating civil war (1936–39). The young Spanish Republic, barely five years old, was defended by a loose combination of Communists, Socialists and other Republican factions, as well as volunteers from around the world who joined the 'International Brigades'. (Sadly, the Republicans received 'sympathy' but no substantial help from Britain, France or the USA.) The so-called 'Rebels' attacking the government were led by Francisco Franco, who received heavy backing and military help from the Italian fascists (Mussolini) and the German Nazi Party (Hitler). As the Republicans were the weaker side, they created an outpouring of posters calling for aid from other countries, targeting the enemy, supporting the morale of their people, applauding the courage of their combatants, encouraging farmwork and industry, and calling for volunteers (to fight). Artistically, the posters make extraordinary use of the visual developments of the Modern Movement, incorporating photomontage, dynamic layout and composition, symbolism and, in many cases, 'active' typography. In the end, Franco won; Spain paid a heavy price. The poster shown here was for the Republican cause, but has become a recognizable protest against any modern war. It shows a photomontage of a dead child, with a formation of aircraft flying behind her, and shames the enemy 'military' for killing children while also warning other countries 'you could be next'. It also marks the Spanish Civil War as the beginning of conflicts utilizing the power of bombing from the skies.

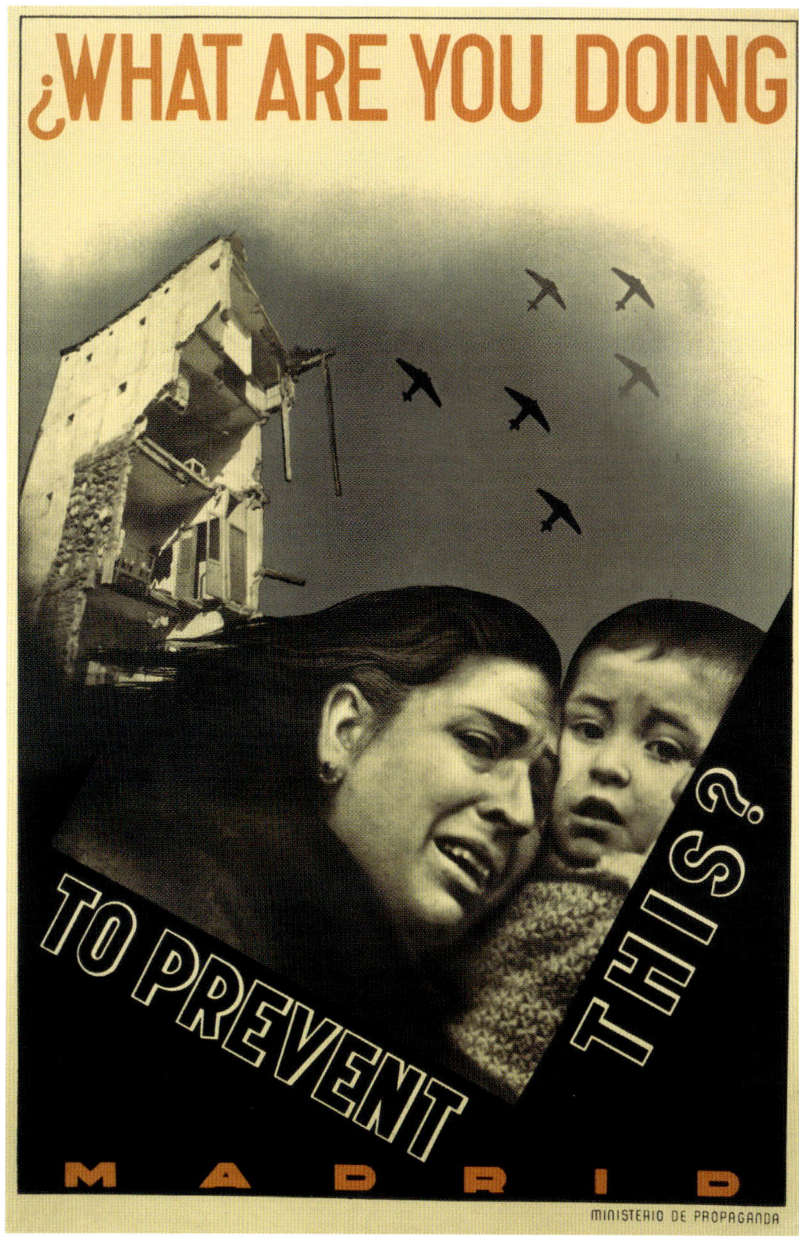

↑ **What Are You Doing to Prevent This?** *c.* 1937
Artist unknown
Poster – Issued by the Ministry of Propaganda

Photomontage is used here to make another plea for help, focusing on the aerial bombing of Madrid and particularly the targeting of women and children. Similar to the poster opposite, this poster was probably produced in different languages, including English and French, with the intention of attracting aid or funds from other countries, as well as international volunteers. However, a wide range of Republican propaganda posters were produced by myriad organizations, from trade unions and government ministries to the army and youth organizations, for internal communication and confidence-building. They united the masses, demanded commitment from all, and covered walls throughout Republican Spain. They were placed in every available space in cities, villages and along roads in farming regions, and due to swift production methods, responded rapidly to changing events.

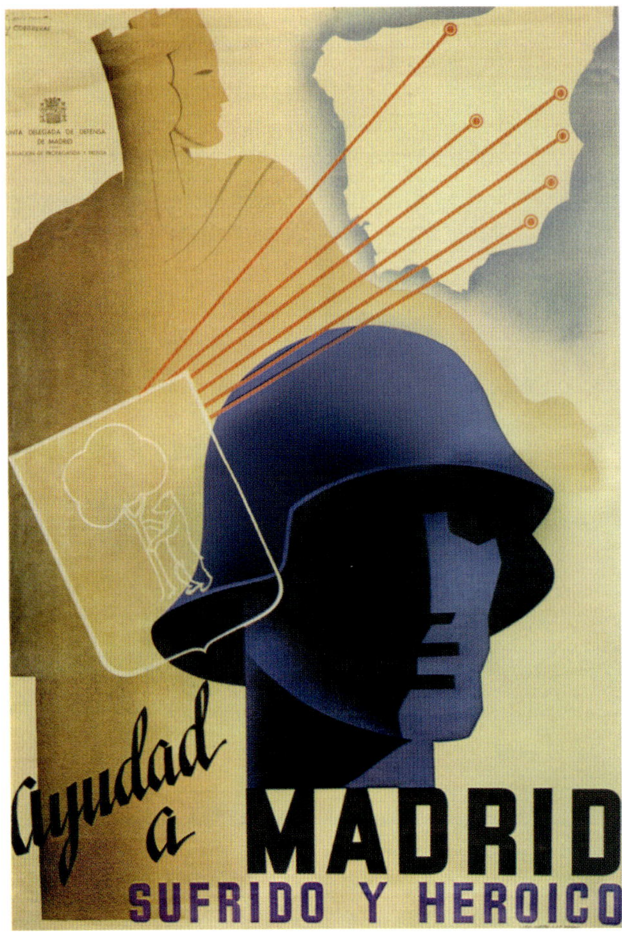

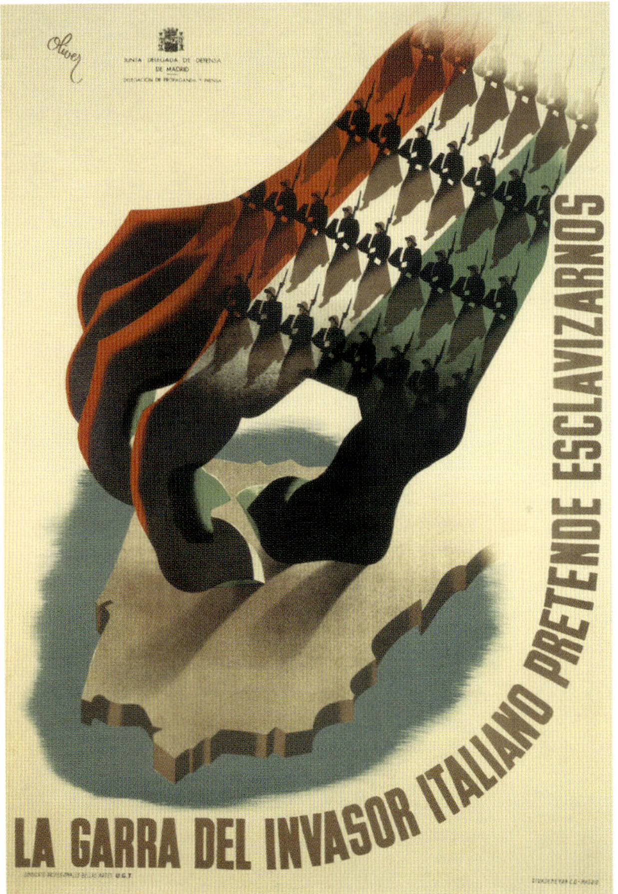

← **Help Tortured and Heroic Madrid** *c.*1937
Artists: Cabaña and Contreras
Issued by: Council for the Defense of Madrid

A number of symbols are combined here: the
head of a soldier, the revered emblem of Madrid
(the Bear and the Strawberry Tree) and, gently
but powerfully in the background, the historical
figure of Isabella I, Queen of Castile and Spain,
representing Spanish unity.

← **The Claw of the Italian Invader Grasps to
Enslave Us** *c.*1937
Artist: Oliver
Issued by: Council for the Defense of Madrid

In this poster the huge, grasping hand that threatens
to take hold of Spain, is also used to symbolize the
power of the marching Italian Army (bearing the
colours of the Italian flag – red, white and green).

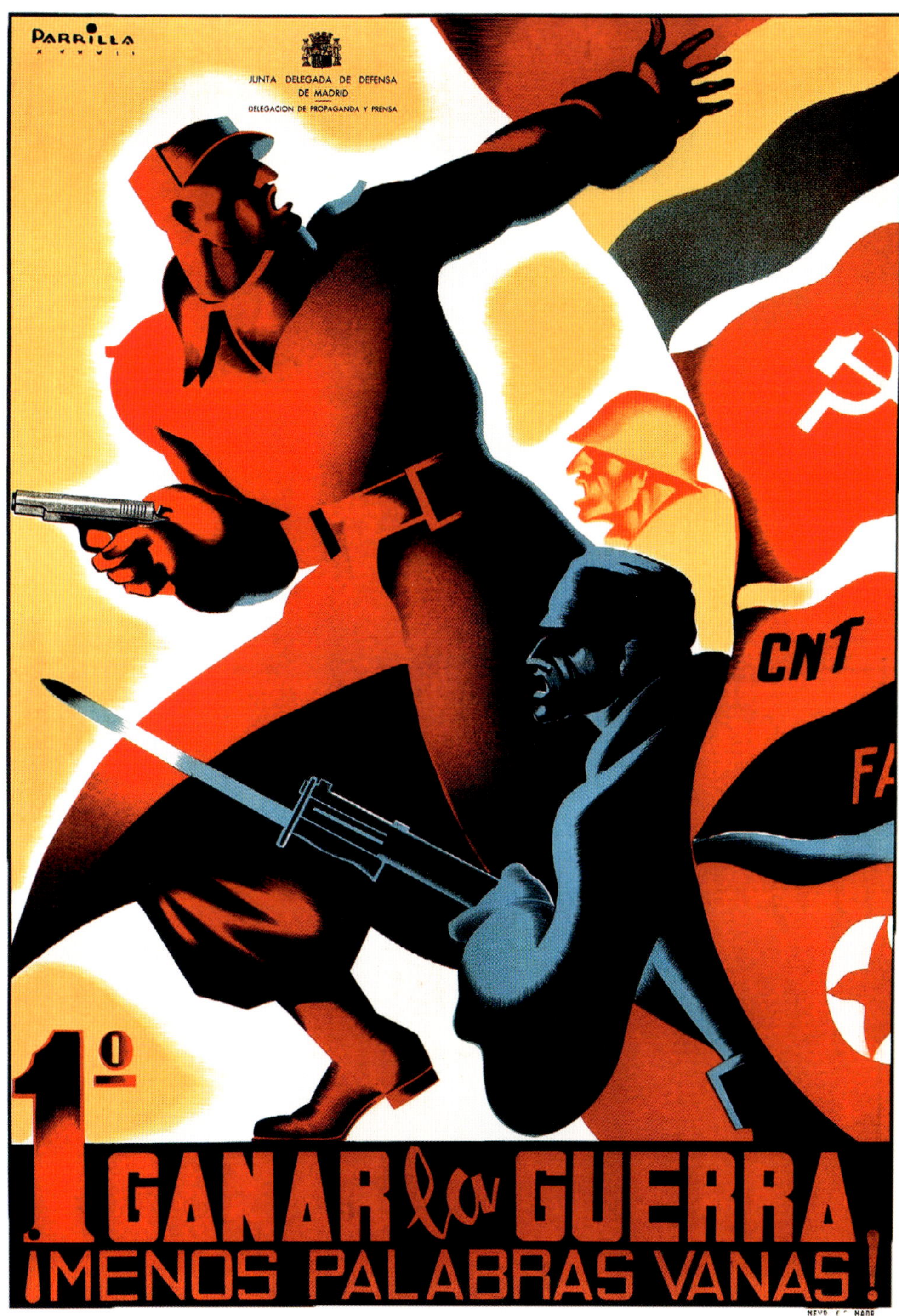

First Win the War. Fewer Idle Words! 1937
Artist: Parrilla
Issued by: Council for the Defense of Madrid

Republican Spain's fighting force depended greatly on the organization and unity of loose bands of militia and battalions as well as volunteers, both internal and international. Bringing together such disparate elements was crucial. In this dynamic poster, an officer of the Spanish Republic strikes a heroic pose, rousing his diverse co-fighters to work together and follow him into action. Floating behind them are banners belonging to different supporters: the Soviet Union (supplying aid), the CNT or Anarchist Syndicates, the FAI – another anarchist group – and others. The dynamic use of colour and composition produces a vibrant call to action. But over and above all, this is a poster proclaiming the importance of unity: it shouts 'Work together, follow me'.

'Ban the Bomb' and CND

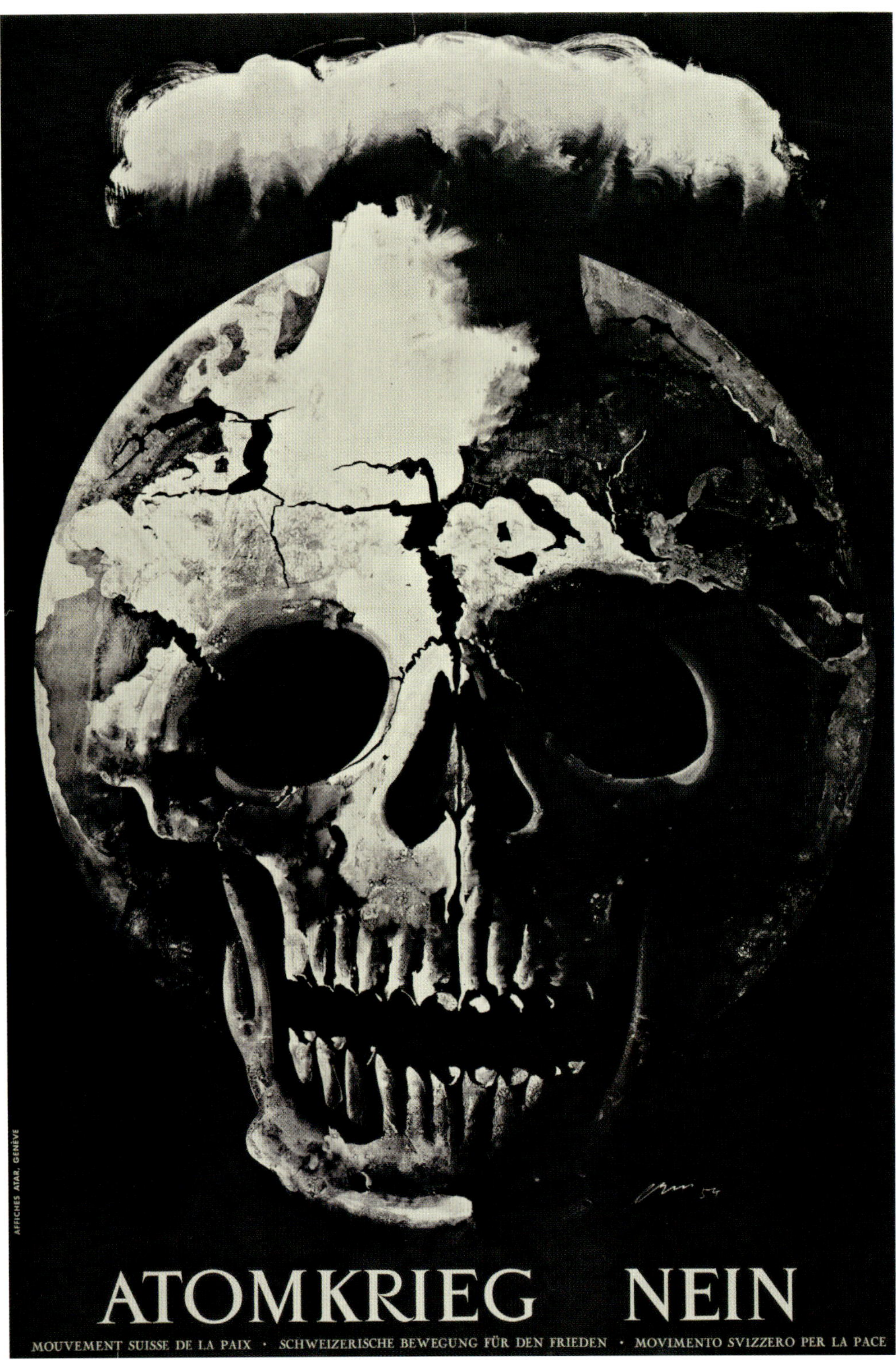

← **No Atomic War** 1954
Hans Erni
Poster

A new era of global power (and its weaponry) began when, in a move intended to end the Second World War, the USA dropped an atom bomb on the Japanese city of Hiroshima and another on Nagasaki in 1945. Within four years, the USSR/ Russia tested one, starting the Cold War between two superpowers engaged in an arms race. Slowly countries in Europe, particularly Britain, began sowing the seeds for a nuclear disarmament movement. Then on 1 March 1954 the USA tested the first hydrogen bomb (H-bomb) at Bikini Atoll in the Pacific, which had 1,300 times the power of the bomb used on Hiroshima. When news of the hydrogen bomb spread, peace activists and grassroots organizations began to form internationally. The 'Ban the Bomb' movment was underway. This poster was created by Hans Erni for the Swiss peace movement. It is one of a number of posters using the characteristic mushroom cloud or human skull (or both) to represent total annihilation and death. Both symbols would continue to be in evidence in the peace movement well into the 1980s.

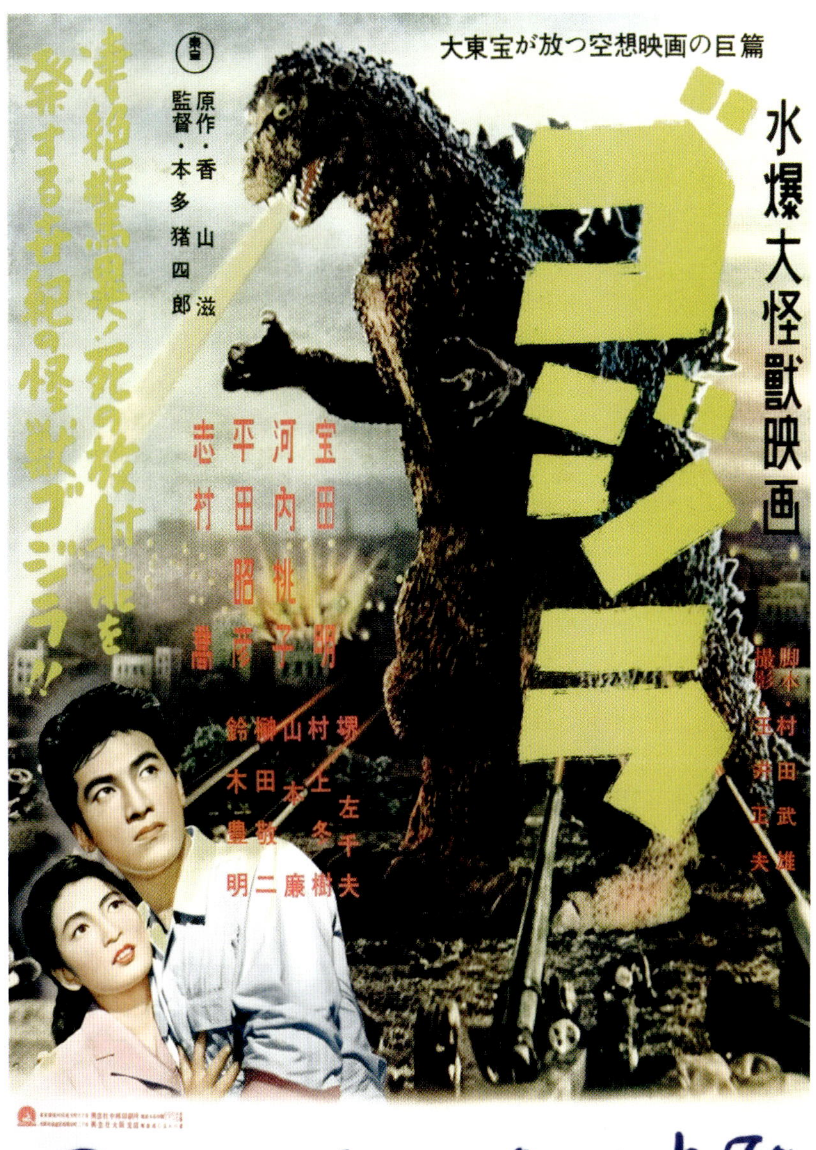
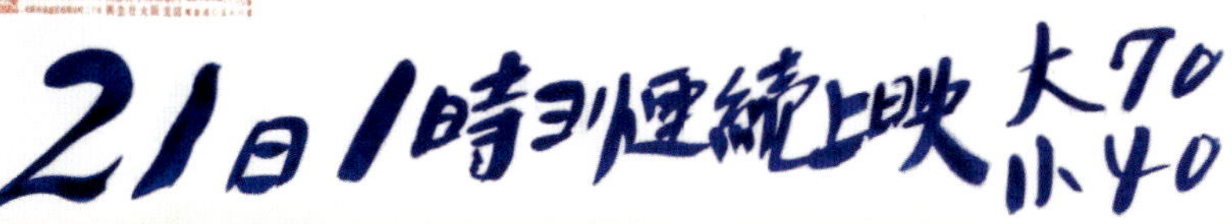
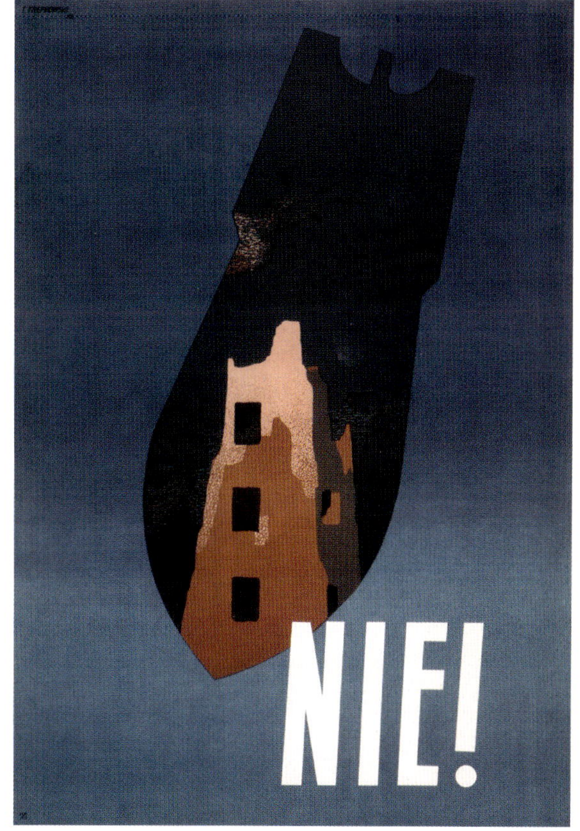

Gojira (*Godzilla*) 1954
Artist unknown
Film poster

The US testing and explosion of the first hydrogen bomb at Bikini Atoll in the Pacific in 1954 was witnessed by the Japanese fishing boat *Daigo Fukuryu Maru* or *Lucky Dragon*. Although outside of the US exclusion zone, the 23-man crew was covered with lethal fallout. All were treated for radiation burns, and at least 239 Marshall Islanders (100–300 miles from Bikini) were exposed to radiation, along with 855 other boats. The *Lucky Dragon* incident accelerated the fast-developing Japanese peace movement, and also inspired the anti-nuclear film *Gojira* (*Godzilla*) directed by Ishiro Honda. Having visited Hiroshima after the war, Honda was haunted by images of horror and devastation, and so gave *Gojira* a documentary-like directness. It opened with an incident similar to that of the *Lucky Dragon*, where a fishing boat was confronted with a nuclear blast, which then awakened a long-dormant dinosaur-like monster. Honda made Godzilla (the monster) a representation of the destructive power of the atom bomb.

NIE! (NO!) 1952
Tadeusz Trepkowski
Poster

Polish designer Tadeusz Trepkowski produced this poster at a point when two interpretations were still a part of living memory. One recalls the destruction of European cities in the Second World War. The ruins of a building are depicted within the bomb's silhouette, symbolizing the serial bombing that took place, leaving houses and buildings destroyed, cities in ruin and years of necessary reconstruction. The other interpretation is even more lethal: the recognition of one (and only one) bomb, silhouetted, fixed in blue sky. Bombs no longer need to come in groups, or in series or repetition: it only takes one for total annihilation. The isolated typographic 'NIE!' suddenly feels very urgent and powerful.

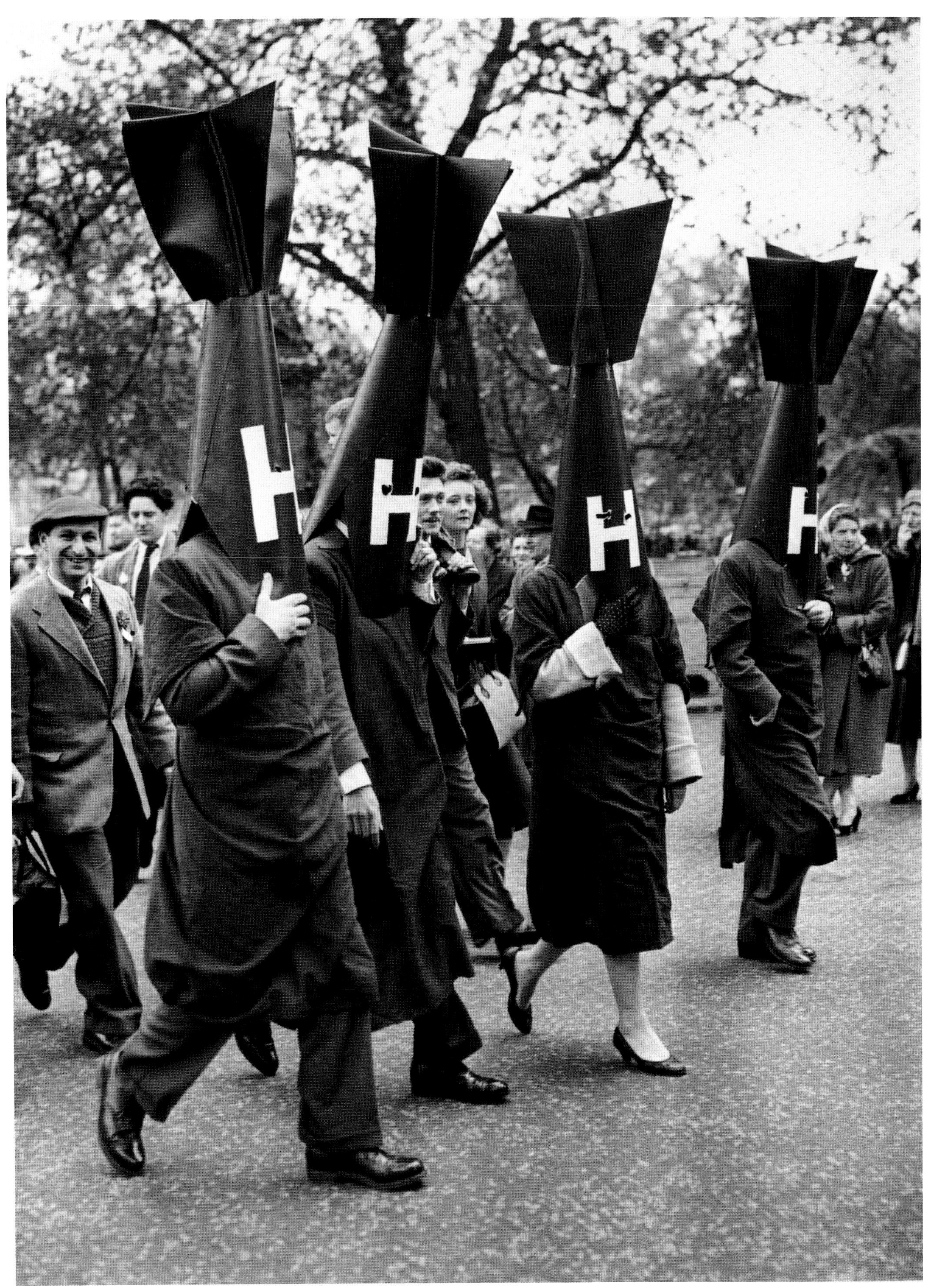

H
H
H
H

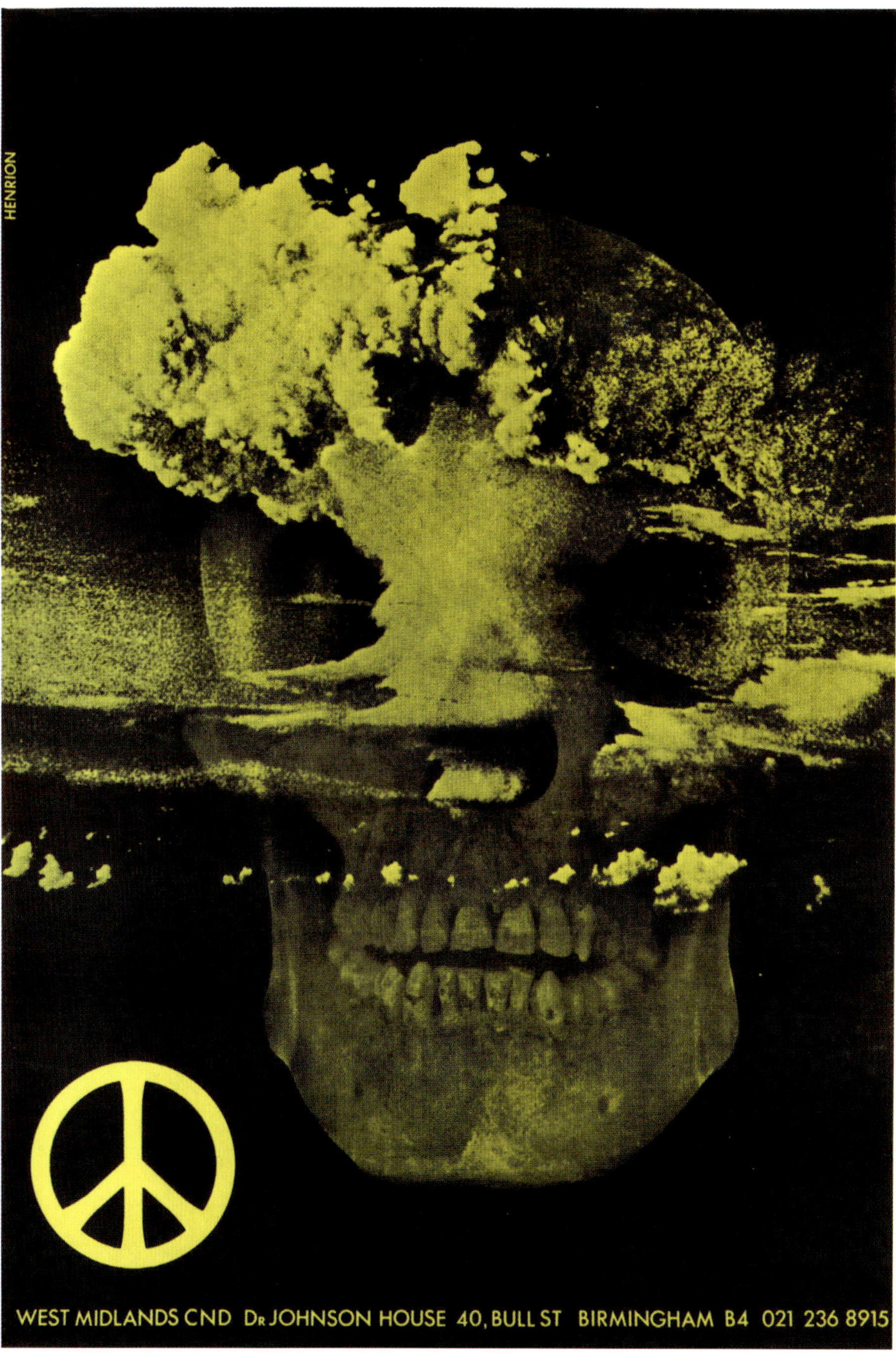

← **'Ban the Bomb' (H-bomb) demonstration in London** 1957
Photographer unknown
Photograph

With news of a far more destructive hydrogen bomb, anti-nuclear
protests increased internationally. In 1955 world-renowned
(British) philosopher Lord Bertrand Russell drafted an appeal,
co-signed by Albert Einstein, calling upon all scientists worldwide
to work for peace. By 1957 hundreds of 'Ban the Bomb' groups all
over Britain coalesced into a mass movement, and in January 1958
the Campaign for Nuclear Disarmament (CND) was born, with
Russell as president. It shifted its attention from focusing solely
on testing, to opposing the actual weapons – in other words, the
military use of nuclear energy.

↑ **Stop Nuclear Suicide** 1963
FHK Henrion
Poster

This poster by internationally-known designer FHK
Henrion was commissioned by the relatively new
Campaign for Nuclear Disarmament (founded 1958)
for placement in London Underground stations. After
a decade of Cold War hysteria, nuclear bomb testing
and mass protests by the peace movement, the Cuban
Missile Crisis followed in 1962. Henrion pulled together
two monumental images as a warning to the new
decade. The image has a respectful presence: the nuclear
blast merges with the skull. It says 'stop and think'.

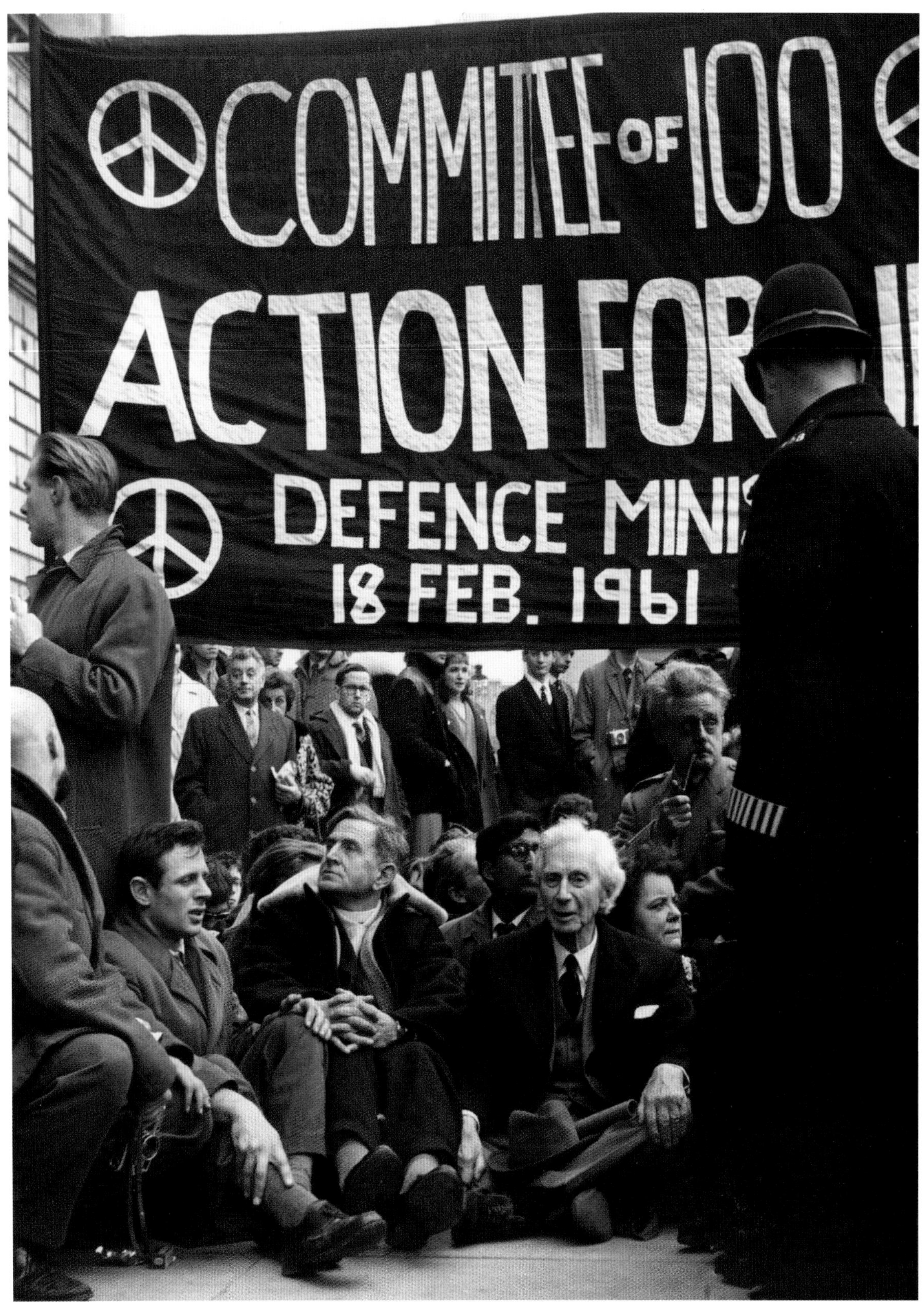

'Action for Life' Sit-in Staged in Whitehall, London, with Lord Bertrand Russell (front row; middle right) 1961
Photographer unknown
Photograph

Lord Bertrand Russell and others left CND in 1960 to form the 'Committee of 100', as they felt civil disobedience would be a more urgent way of attracting attention to their cause. This photograph captures their first action in February 1961, a 'sit-in' involving 5,000 activists outside the War Office in London. Their efforts peaked in September with a massive demonstration in Trafalgar Square, when police arrested and jailed 89-year-old Russell for a week, making headlines around the world.

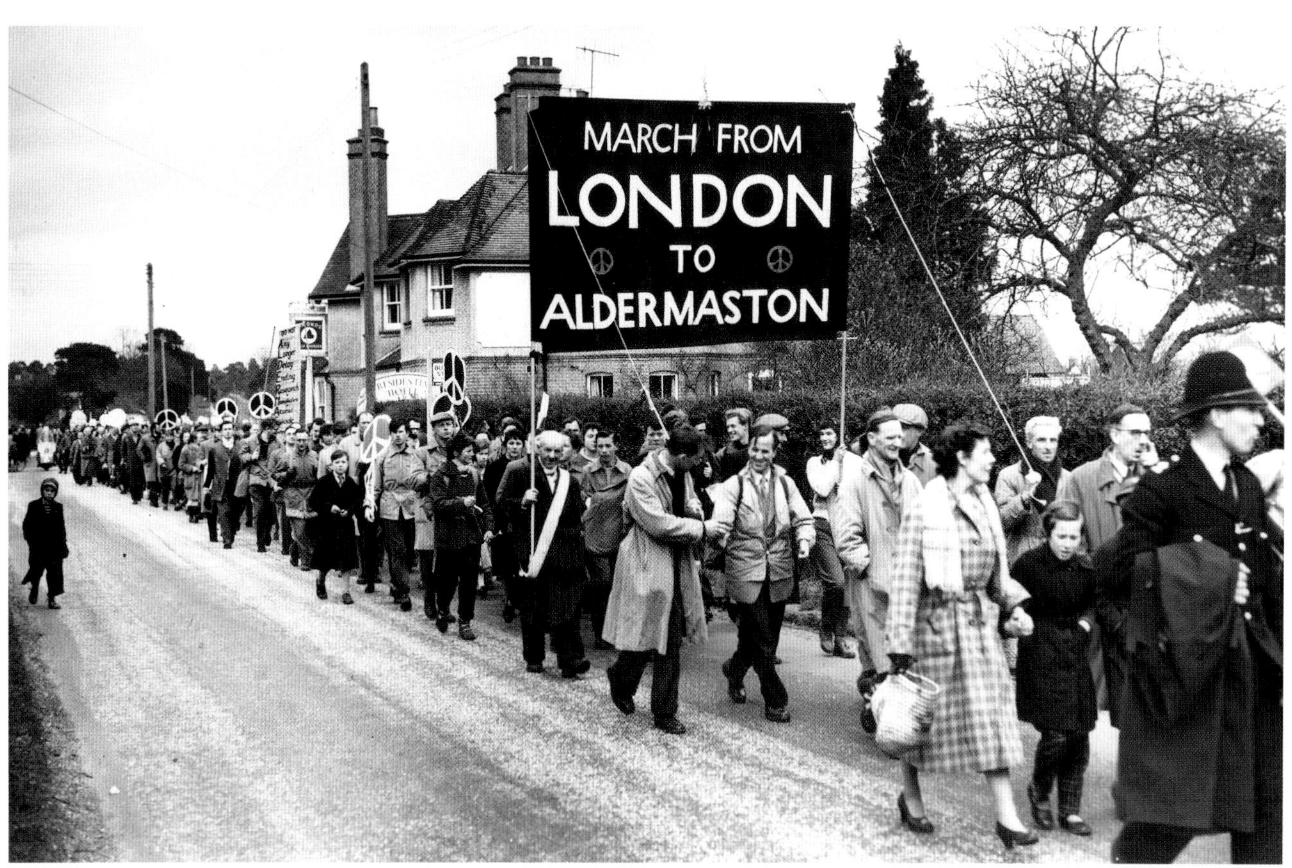

↑ **First CND March from London to Aldermaston** 1958
Photographer unknown
Photograph

This photograph shows the first CND march from London to Aldermaston, and the display of the CND symbol on the banner as well as being carried on sticks (as placards).

→ **March on London** June 1958
Photographer unknown
Photograph

A few months after the initial CND march to Aldermaston, up to 4,000 H-bomb demonstrators from throughout Britain marched to Whitehall, carrying Gerald Holtom's nuclear disarmament symbol, in order to deliver a letter to the Prime Minister calling for a ban on nuclear weapons.

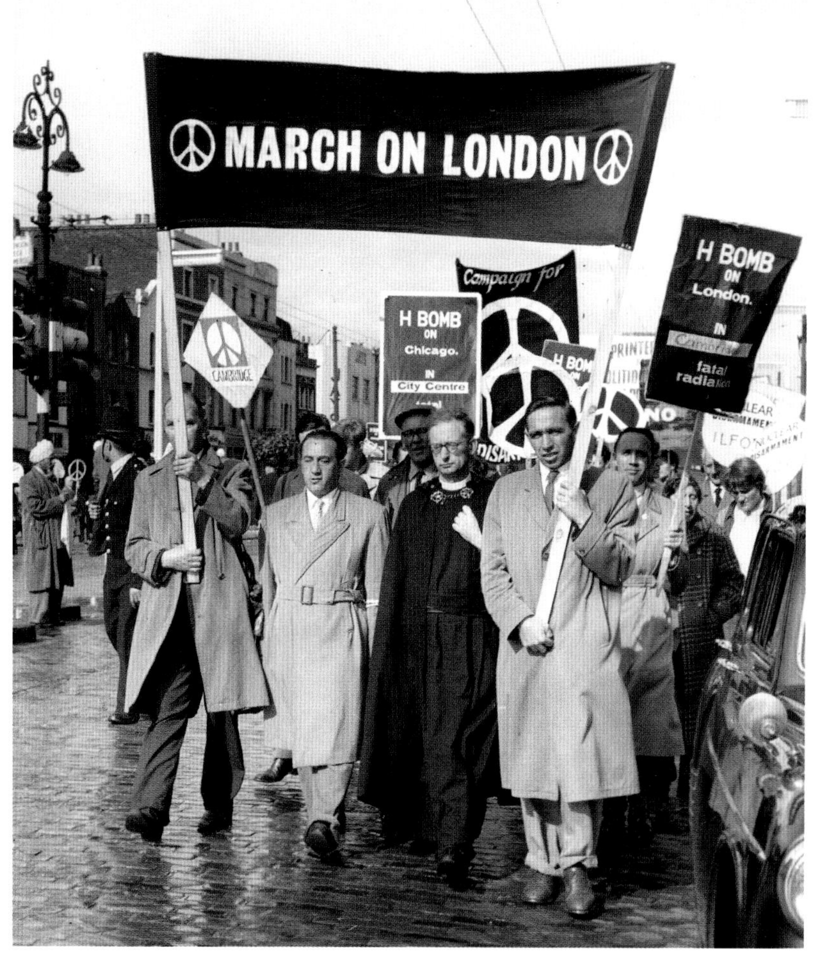

The Dawn of Defiance:
Civil Rights, Anti-Apartheid

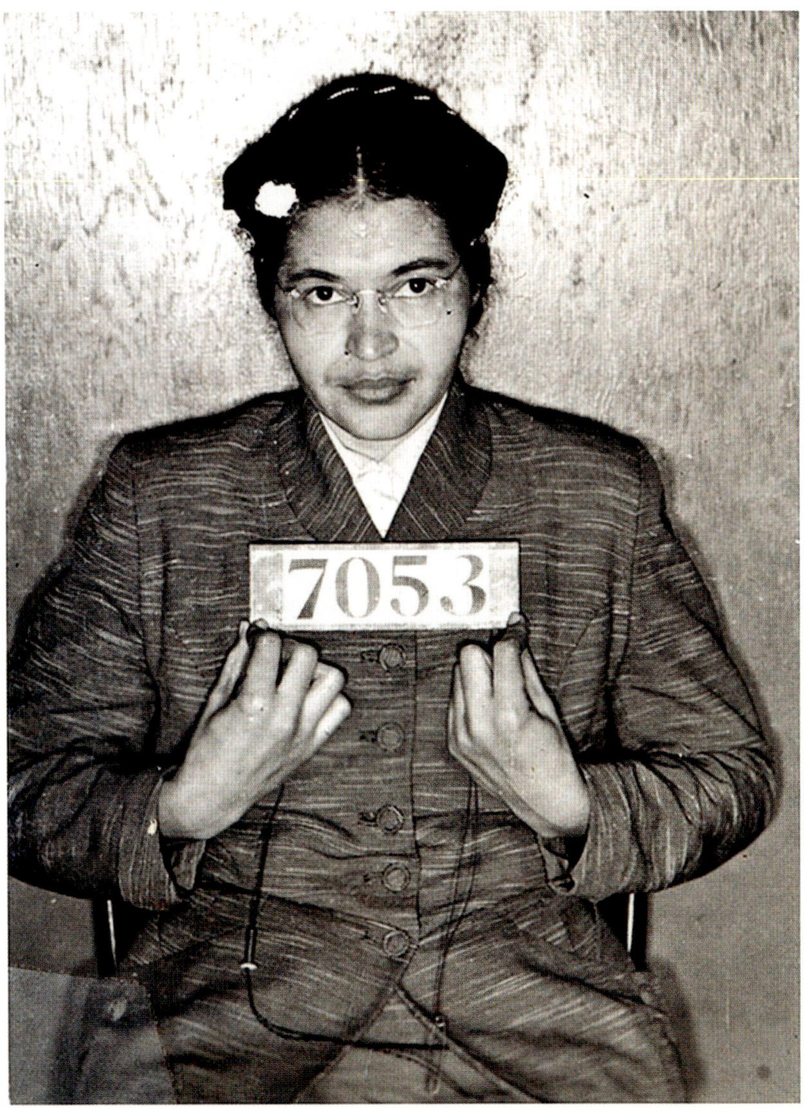

Rosa Parks' Mugshot 1955
Photographer unknown
Photograph

In Montgomery, Alabama, on 1 December 1955, a black woman named Rosa Parks, riding home from work on a segregated bus, refused to give up her seat so that a white man could occupy it. This act of defiance set off a chain of events. The white bus driver called the police, and Parks was arrested but out on bail that night. The NAACP (National Association for the Advancement of Colored People) called for a bus boycott which took place on the day of her trial. Martin Luther King got involved and extended the boycott. Churches were burned; Parks lost her job and received hate mail. The boycott continued for over a year, and finally a Federal Court voted that segregation on buses was unconstitutional. Rosa Parks' one action brought national and international attention to the Civil Rights movement. Her mugshot has come to mark the symbolic start of that movement.

→ **We the People Are Granite** *c.*1955
Artist unknown
Poster/pamphlet image reproduced in
The New Age newspaper

The 1950s also marks the beginning of mass defiance against the enforced system of apartheid in South Africa. Apartheid was, in essence, a policy of white minority power over the black majority, and included racial segregation, economic exploitation and the denial of basic rights to black people, as well as Indians and people of mixed race. An important tool of enforcement was the Pass Laws, which controlled the movements and therefore the work and lives of all Africans. Hatred of the Pass Laws fuelled the first Defiance Campaign (1952–54) begun by the African National Congress Youth League, under Nelson Mandela and Oliver Tambo, involving thousands of mass refusals to obey the new apartheid laws. Protests continued throughout the decade. This image projects the inspirational, combined strength and resistance of the people. The people are shown as huge, strong, made of granite or stone. The puny character below, wielding a straggly whip, is Hendrick Verwoerd, the architect of apartheid. The image intimates that the strength and will of the people will eventually overpower him. But it is the beginning of a long struggle, that will take at least another 30 years.

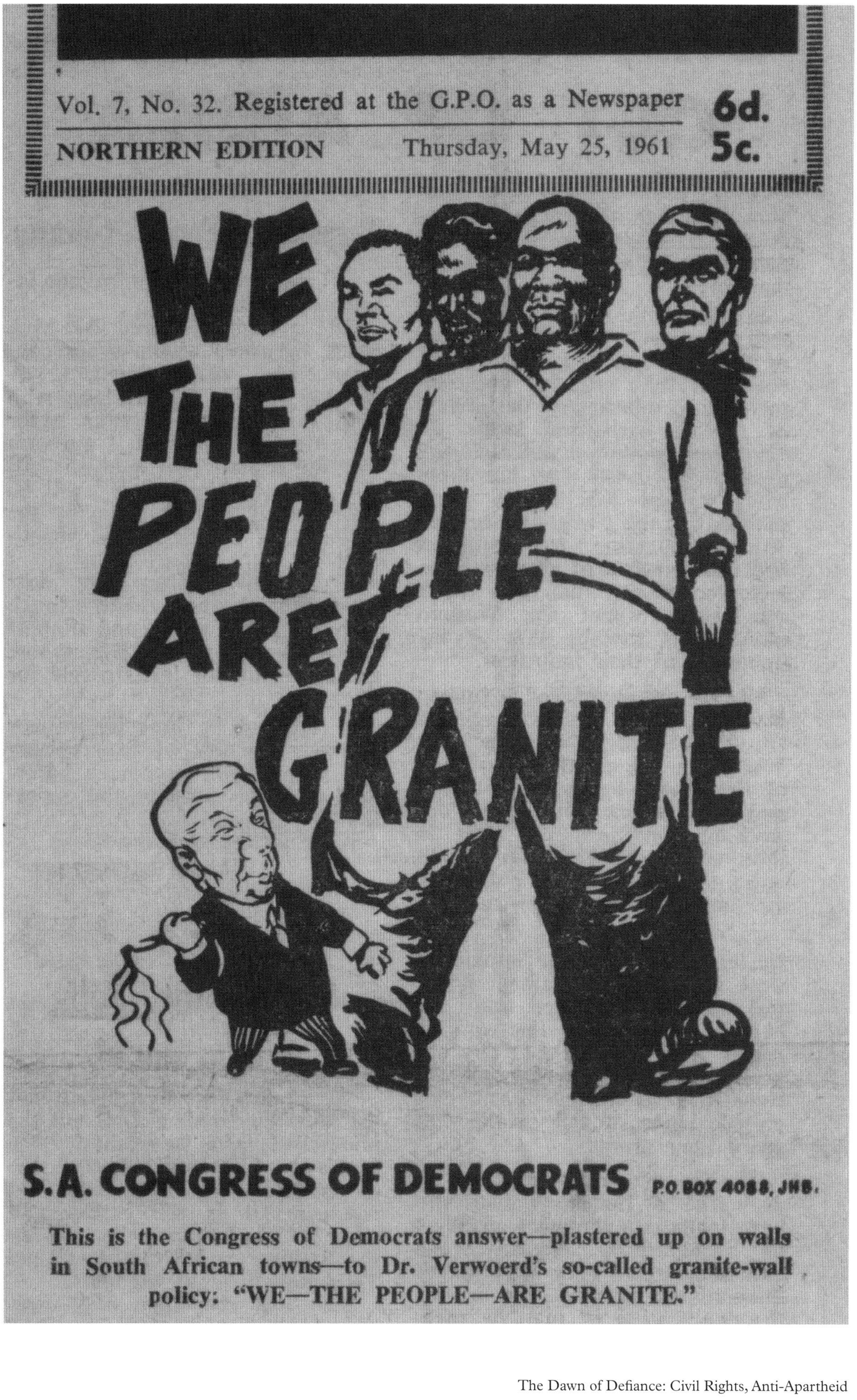

Vol. 7, No. 32. Registered at the G.P.O. as a Newspaper
6d.
5c.
NORTHERN EDITION
Thursday, May 25, 1961
WE THE PEOPLE ARE GRANITE
S.A. CONGRESS OF DEMOCRATS
P.O. BOX 4088, JHB.
This is the Congress of Democrats answer—plastered up on walls
in South African towns—to Dr. Verwoerd's so-called granite-wall
policy: "WE—THE PEOPLE—ARE GRANITE."

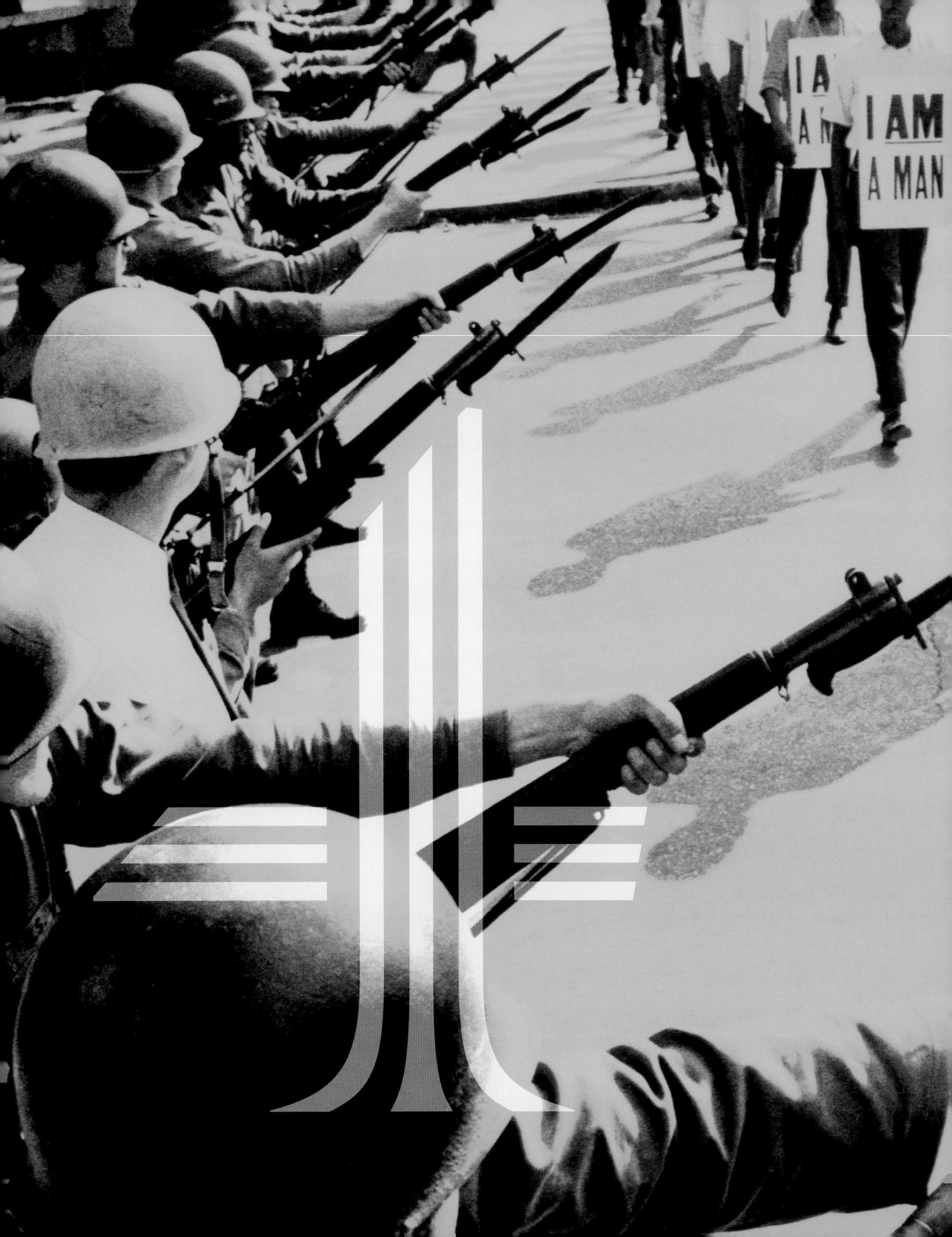
I AM
A MAN
I AM
A MAN

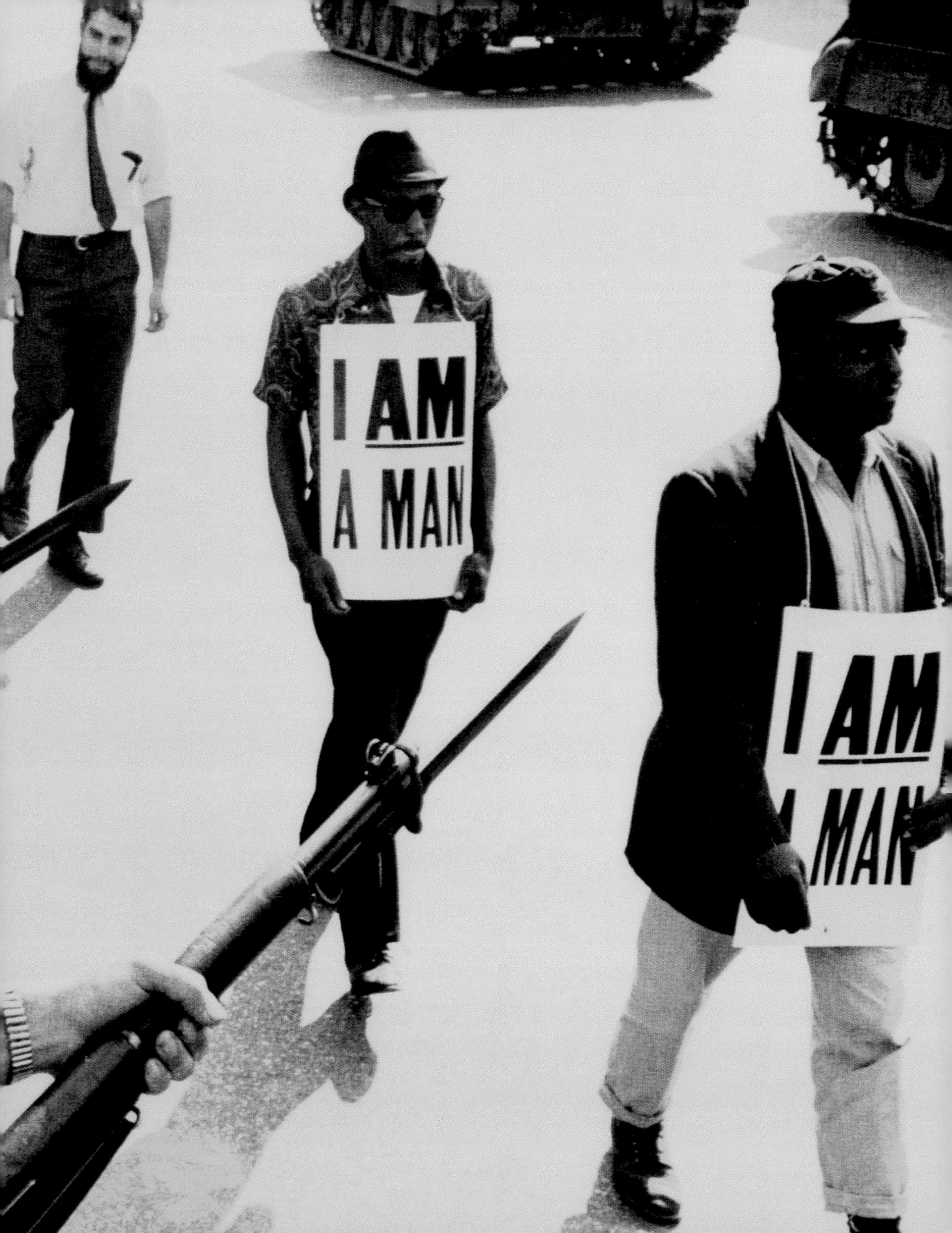
I AM
A MAN
I AM
A MAN

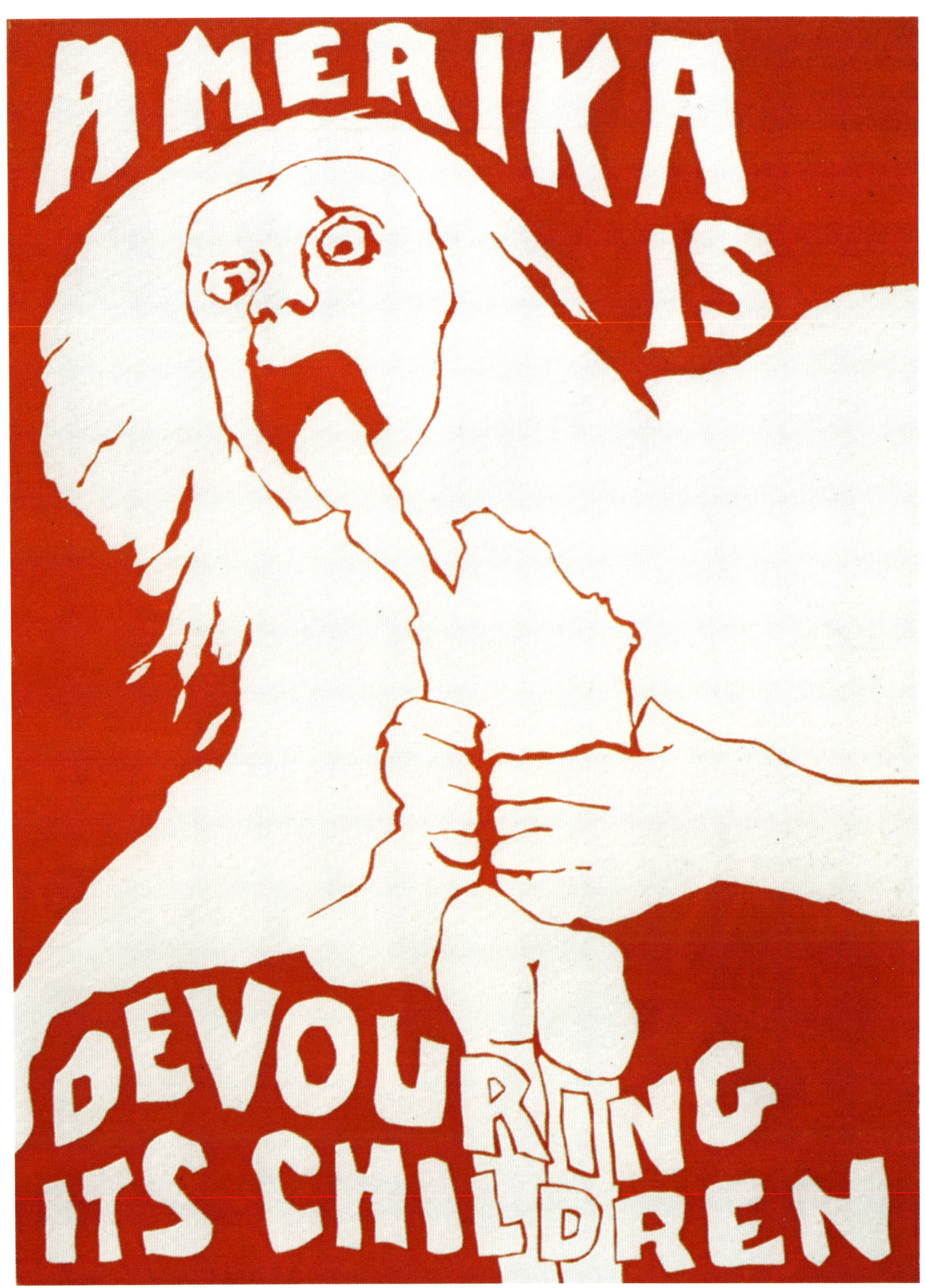

Poster against the US invasion of Cambodia 1970
Silkscreened at the University of California, Berkeley

1960–1980
Redirection and Change

Cuba's proximity to the United States has forever defined relations between the two countries. Twentieth-century Cuba longed for independence and self-sufficiency. At the same time, the USA had long-term commercial interests and land-ownership in Cuba and a tendency to intervene in Cuban internal affairs. Then in 1959, anti-imperialist Fidel Castro and his guerrilla army overthrew the existing Cuban president, Fulgencio Batista. Castro became prime minister, began social reforms, and nationalized (took over) US businesses. Matters escalated. The USA cut off diplomatic relations and imposed a trade embargo on Cuba. Castro declared Cuba a Communist state and looked to the USSR as an ally. Feeling threatened by the USA, in 1962 Castro agreed to allow the USSR to base nuclear missiles on the island. This resulted in 'the Cuban Missile Crisis': the two Cold War superpowers were headed for nuclear war, but backed away just in time. But from then on, the USA found its close island-neighbour an irritation and kept up its embargo, and Cuba viewed the USA as an imperialist threat to itself, as well as globally.[1]

Cuba celebrated its independence, and declared solidarity with other countries struggling for independence, through the publishing and distribution of large numbers of beautiful, artistic posters (as well as, at times, supplying weaponry or military support). Those posters were, and still are, models of simplicity and directness in their use of composition, colour and symbolism. They have influenced generations of artists, globally, ever since.[2]

In the USA, the mid-1960s brought revolution in many different forms. Young people rebelled against the 'Eisenhower generation' and its values. They 'dropped out', expressing themselves through new cultural codes of dress (long hair, t-shirts, jeans), as well as music, sex and drugs. San Francisco became the undeclared epicentre of hippie culture, espousing 'peace and love', but hippiedom quickly spread across the country and beyond. Popular art exploded in many exciting forms. Psychedelic posters were heavily associated with music and bands, and characterized by complex visual patterns,

bright or lurid/acidic colours and barely readable lettering, all reminiscent of a drug-induced state. The underground press (magazines or newspapers) reflected this hallucinatory art, as well as railing against 'the establishment', debating politics, reporting news or exchanging ideas.[3]

Arguably the best-loved graphics of that time were underground comics: rude, crude, over-sexed, offensive and often hilarious. Some of the best-known artists associated with underground posters, press and/or comics included Victor Moscoso, Wes Wilson, Rick Griffin and Robert Crumb. The underground press, its ideas and its art, crossed the ocean to Europe, spread by travellers or simply carried in suitcases, and soon achieved an international reach.[4]

In Britain, the early 1960s saw a new generation rebelling against the old social order with sniggering satire, giving rise to the satire boom. It started with the theatre performance of a subversive review called 'Beyond the Fringe', which mocked the government, class system, academics, politicians, royalty, religion… and Britain's loss of international status. A vital part of this scenario was the satirical magazine *Private Eye*, founded in 1961, which mocked everyone and everything. It is especially known for its notorious front-covers, and still runs to this day. Britain also produced its own underground press, publishing magazines such as *Oz*, *Ink* and *IT* (*International Times*), which reported news and protests from the USA as well as concentrating on issues closer to home.[5]

As time moved on, stronger visual signs appeared signalling protest and discontent taking place in other parts of the world: the massacre of students, demanding the release of political prisoners, on the eve of the 1968 Olympic Games in Mexico, or the death (in suspicious circumstances) of Stephen Biko, who was stirring up Black Consciousness in South Africa. Plus there were worldwide protests against the USA's involvement in the Vietnam War (1965–73). But few were as furious or passionate as those taking place within the USA itself. There were campus demonstrations, songs and performances, publications, marches and rallies, strikes, city referendums, and draft-card burnings (as troops were dragged in by conscription). A massive amount of visual protest was also produced by artists, both known and unknown: art collectives and workshops, photographers, designers, ad agencies and the ordinary person/protester in the street. Their efforts produced a US protest poster movement that has yet to be surpassed, in quality or quantity. Add to that, the large amount of work produced by protests in other countries.[6]

The volatile atmosphere also fed social tensions waiting to erupt. The US Civil Rights movement started its decade of resistance with actions that challenged segregation (such as sit-ins at whites-only lunch counters), and marches that demanded the right to vote. Martin Luther King proclaimed his stirring 'I Have a Dream' speech in a mass demonstration in Washington D.C. in 1963. Within five years he was dead: assassinated in 1968 in Memphis, Tennessee. Malcolm X, another influential voice, renounced non-violence and expressed the right of black people to define their own destiny. He also advocated armed self-defence. He was killed in 1965, and this spurred Huey P. Newton and Bobby Seale to found the Black Panther Party for Self-Defense (BPP) in 1966 on the principles of self-defence (against the police) and achieving economic justice and power for ordinary black people. They initiated over 60 community programs, including the Free Breakfast for Children Program, and grew from a group of fifty members in Oakland, California to a national organization with over 5,000 members. They also asserted a strong visual presence, through dress (black berets and leather jackets, Afro hair-style) and through their graphics, particularly their 'revolutionary posters' and newspaper, *The Black Panther*.[7]

Sexual politics was also transforming throughout this period. The Women's Liberation movement worked to change the power politics to which women were subjected. Women explored self-identity and discovered a sense of self-worth through consciousness-raising groups, protests and other activities. They achieved strength and respect by the motivation and camaraderie of an entire movement (the 'sisterhood', aided by a strong graphic symbol) which tackled issues such as regaining control of their bodies, their health and medical care; gaining equal opportunities and pay in the workplace; and combating violence against women, in all its many manifestations. Sisterhood was global, and an international network of feminist groups and presses existed all over the world, producing journals and magazines. The sisterhood was also extremely creative. Feminist writers set about examining the way women's achievements had been left out of history, and redressed the balance by producing 'herstory'. Posters, postcards and other graphics were produced by feminist collectives, presses and workshops around the world, carrying vibrant renditions of 'women's issues' or messages of solidarity.

Gay liberation was kickstarted by the Stonewall Riots of 1969, when the routine police raids enacted on a gay bar in New York City suddenly met resistance – and the gays openly fought back. The next day thousands took to the streets demanding 'Gay Power!', and riots and demonstrations continued throughout the following week. Demands for liberation by gays and lesbians brought the formation of the Gay Liberation Front (GLF) who proudly claimed the word 'Gay' for their own, organised marches, dances, consciousness-raising groups and published the newspaper *Come Out!* It soon grew a network of groups and became the main generator of the gay and lesbian political movement. In 1970 the First Gay Pride March took place in New York City, another opportunity to emphasize gay presence and demand acceptance and recognition 'in the street'.[8]

Energized by the New York scene in 1970, Britain founded its own version of the Gay Liberation Front that year. The 1967 Sexual Offences Act had recently been passed, which ceased the prosecution of men for homosexual acts. (Before that, people did not normally speak openly of their homosexuality or campaign in public.) Although the 1967 Act was not perfect, it opened new opportunities. So Britain's Gay Liberation Front started the country on a course of 'coming out' (of the closet), and gay liberation was set to change lives both publicly at work and privately. The Pride March soon followed, and is now an international showpiece of costume, colour and self-determination.[9]

The Paris Riots of May 1968 have come to represent, both artistically and politically, the revolutionary spirit of the 1960s. The mass protest was a demand for change, aimed at Charles de Gaulle's outdated government, and the strict, traditional values imposed by the education system. Unusually, students and workers joined forces in a general strike. Factories, offices and schools were occupied, and violent riots and demonstrations took place. The École des Beaux Arts went on strike, so students occupied the studios and print workshops. Under the name 'Atelier Populaire', they created an outpouring of dynamic, energized posters, produced by silkscreen, lithography or stencilling, and pasted them up in the streets all over Paris. The strike eventually came to an end, but the simplicity, directness and vitality of those posters has continued to influence students and practitioners of art and design over the years.[10]

By the mid-1970s, in the economic depression and ('no future') gloom of Britain, the revolutionary spirit of 'Punk' gave rise to self-styled creativity fuelled by subversion and the energy of the street. Young people poked fun at symbols of authority. They found creative expression in aggressive bands such as the Sex Pistols, the production of 'fanzines' (do-it-yourself small papers and magazines they could sell in the street), or the DIY assemblage of exhibitionistic fashion or 'street style'. Vivienne Westwood was one of the fashion innovators of this time, creating 'clothing as subversion'. The DIY aesthetic also impacted heavily on graphics. Jamie Reid gave Punk its graphic style and vocabulary. He worked with mixed typefaces, 'ransom' lettering, cut out or torn shapes, spontaneous layouts or screaming soapbox colours, and applied them to his posters, album sleeves and t-shirts for the Sex Pistols. Other subversive imagery could be found in more album artwork and fanzines, especially the extraordinary photomontages of the artist, Linder.[11]

A very different type of protest can be seen with the birth of the Earth Movement, also known at this time as the Ecology or Green Movement. It had its roots in the 1960s, when hippie drop-outs desired a better relationship with Mother Earth, and gathered force when the Oil Crisis of 1973 brought shortage scares to some countries. People slowly began to develop a sense of responsibility for their planet (and its limitations). The representative directory for alternative living, and self-empowerment, was *The Whole Earth Catalog* (1968–85). It expanded as time went on, with many editions and permutations, and has often been considered a forerunner of the internet. The heroes of the time were members of the environmental pressure group Greenpeace, founded in 1971, with their early attempts to 'Save the Whale'.[12]

However, one issue that drew attention and concern was the development of nuclear power as a new, reliable and supposedly safe energy source. Safety concerns were justified when in 1979, an accident occurred in one of the reactors at Three Mile Island nuclear power plant in Pennsylvania, which eroded public confidence in further developments. Another issue, often addressed by Australian poster groups, was the continued testing of nuclear bombs in the Pacific, a product of the Cold War (still taking place in the 1970s) which was considered to be affecting the environment as well as the lives of Pacific Islanders and future generations.[13]

Throughout the 1970s, news travelled of dictatorships and human rights abuses around the world. Argentina was by no means the only South American country led by a military government at this time, but it was possibly the one treated most cruelly. From 1976 until 1983, in an attempt to rid itself of any opposition, approximately 30,000 men, women and children were 'disappeared' by the military junta. Approximately 5,000 were dealt with by what was called 'destino final' (final destination). They were arrested, tortured and drugged. Unconscious, they were loaded on to military planes (known as the 'death flights'), stripped and then thrown – alive but unconscious – out of the plane and into the mouth of the Rio de la Plata, as it meets the Atlantic Ocean. Their relatives had no idea what had happened to them. On 30 April 1977, fourteen women gathered in the Plaza de Mayo in Buenos Aires, demanding information about their kidnapped children. Every Thursday they came at 3.30p.m., and their numbers grew. When police told them to move on, they walked slowly in circles around the square carrying large photographs of the disappeared, and were soon known as 'Las Madres de Plaza de Mayo' (the Mothers of the Plaza de Mayo). They became known internationally. After the military junta ended in 1983, following defeat in the Falklands War, the Mothers and (now) Grandmothers of the Plaza de Mayo continued their fight for justice and the truth. In 2018 they still maintain a presence in the Plaza de Mayo, although a small one, and the Grandmothers (Las Abuelas de Plaza de Mayo) continue their search online by means of a website (abuelas.org.ar), Facebook and Twitter. The search goes on.[14]

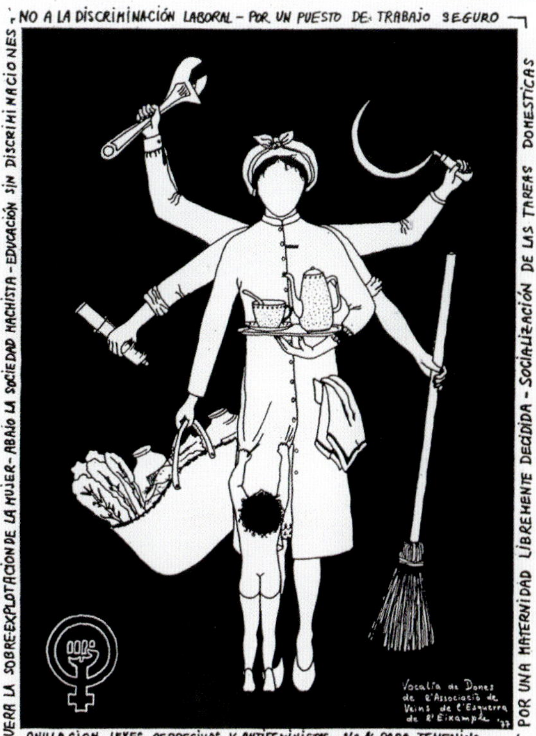

Spanish Women's Liberation Movement poster 1970s
Artist unknown

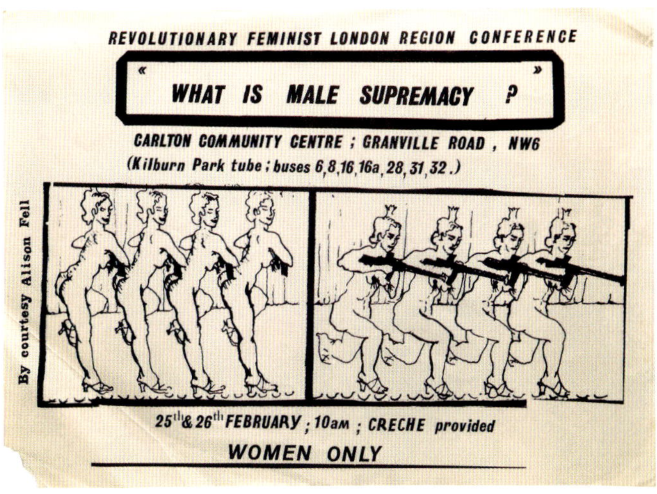

Poster announcing a Revolutionary Feminist Conference *c.* 1973
Artist: Alison Fell

Cuban Revolutionary Poster Art

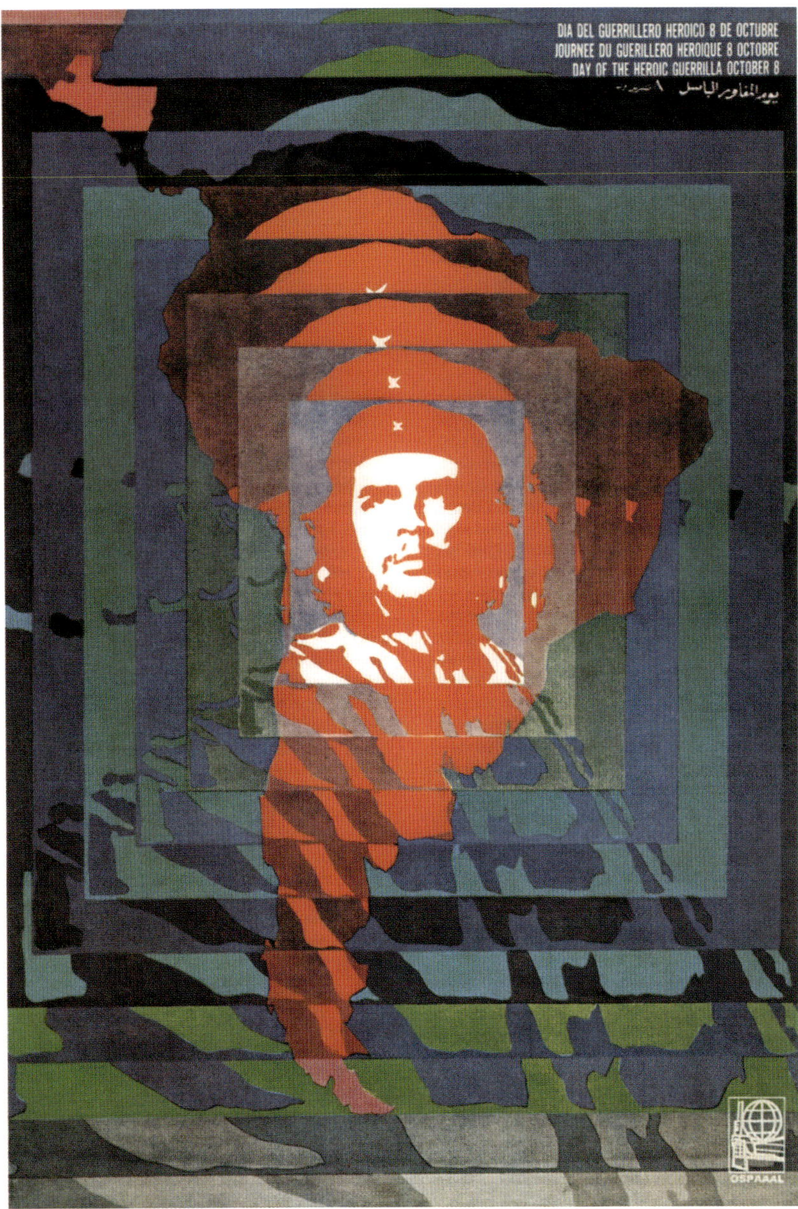

**Day of the Heroic Guerrilla
(Continental Che)** 1968
Elena Serrano
Poster (silkscreen and offset)

Cuban poster art epitomized the spirit of revolution and change in the 1960s and has influenced artists and designers ever since. Cuba had finally achieved independence in 1959 by means of the anti-imperialist Fidel Castro and his guerrilla army, including the legendary Che Guevara. Cuba's socialist leanings and rejection of US intervention and threats became embedded in the posters' role and message. The posters were (and still are) admired for their economy and boldness of style, their clarity of communication (even when employing minimal elements or shapes), their simplicity in conveying abstract ideas and their vibrant use of colour. But they also excelled in their mission: they bolstered nationalism, celebrated heroes, supported and promoted domestic campaigns (agricultural, educational and so on) and expressed solidarity with movements or countries struggling for political change or national liberation all over the world, especially those engaged in armed struggle. The artists worked both independently or as a group, and production was handled by three main agencies, of which the best known was OSPAAAL: it's distribution was massive and spanned the world, thanks to having the audacity to ignore artistic convention and fold the posters, then insert them in a magazine for mailing. The Cuban 'Day of the Heroic Guerrilla', 8 October, commemorates the life of Che Guevara (killed in Bolivia on 9 October 1967) and is one of the most celebrated of all Cuban posters. Utilizing Alberto Korda's famous photograph of Che as a revolutionary, it projects both the legendary image and the dreams of liberation, reverberating throughout Latin America and the whole world.

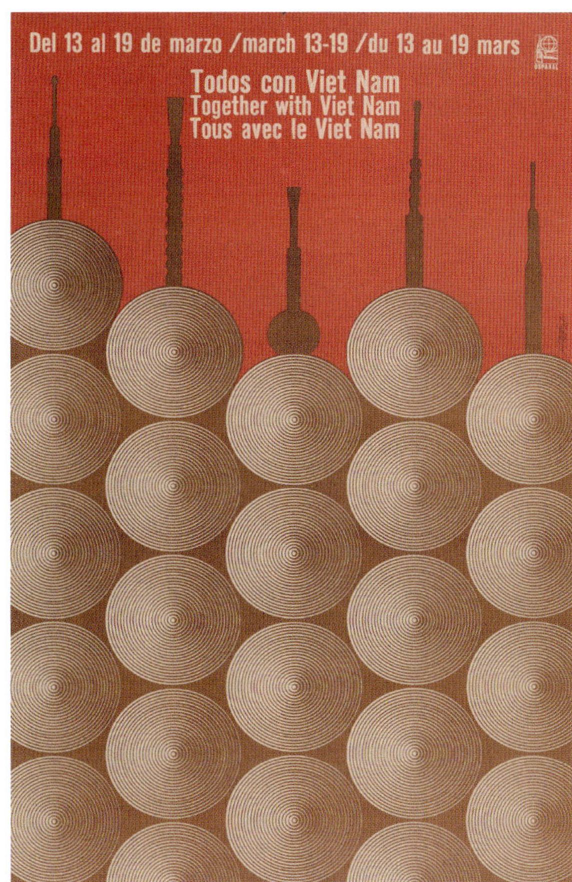

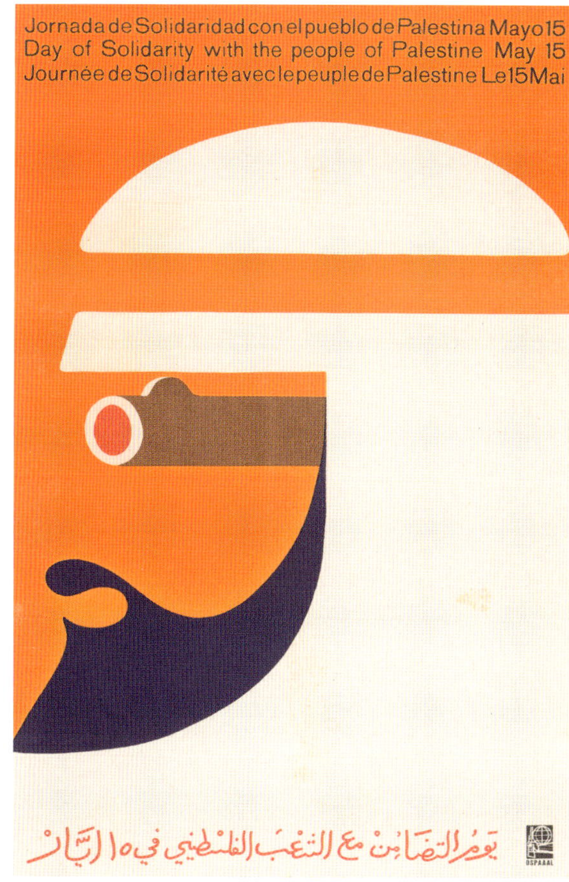

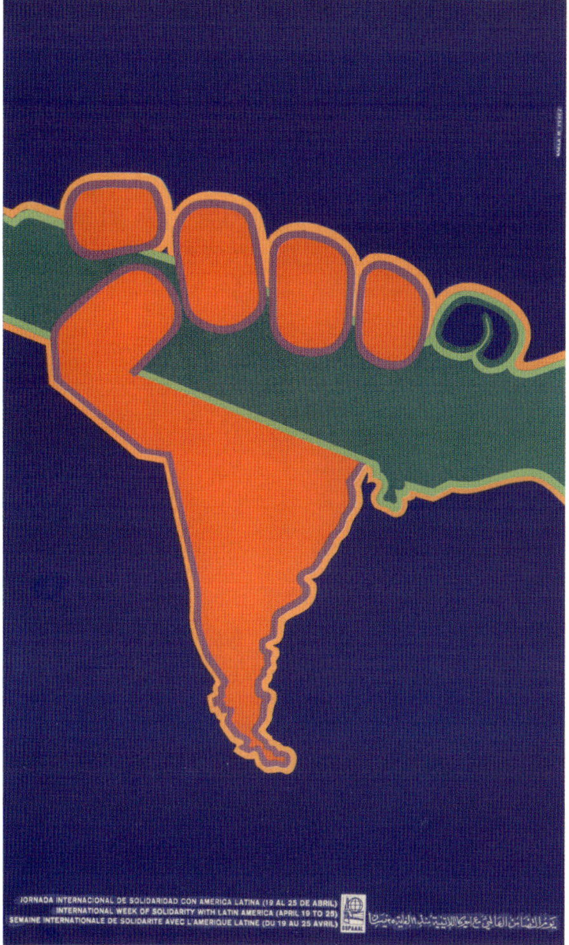

↖ **Together with Vietnam** 1971
Ernesto Padrón
Poster (offset)

This poster makes textural use of simple circular shapes which signify Vietnamese headwear, but the real achievement is the slow recognition of barely visible brown bars emerging from the red background (and the brown bars are guns). The poster depicts an aerial view of an advancing group of Vietnamese guerrilla fighters.

↑ **Day of Solidarity with the People of Palestine** 15 May 1968
Faustino Pérez
Poster (offset)

Solidarity with armed struggles often brought the inclusion of weapons in inventive ways as part of the poster's composition.

← **International Week of Solidarity with Latin America (19 to 25 April)** 1970
Asela Pérez
Poster (silkscreen)

South America grasps a gun, conveying the notion of, or desire for, liberation throughout the continent whether achieved peacefully or, more likely, through armed struggle.

Counter-Cultures

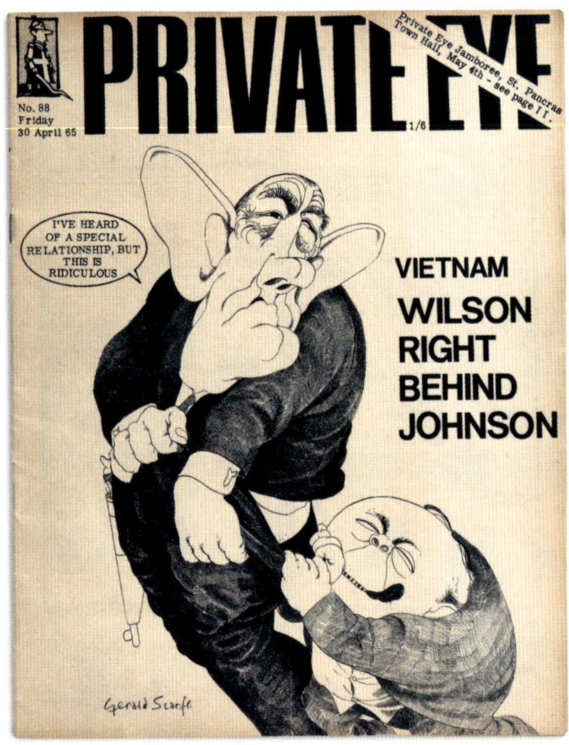

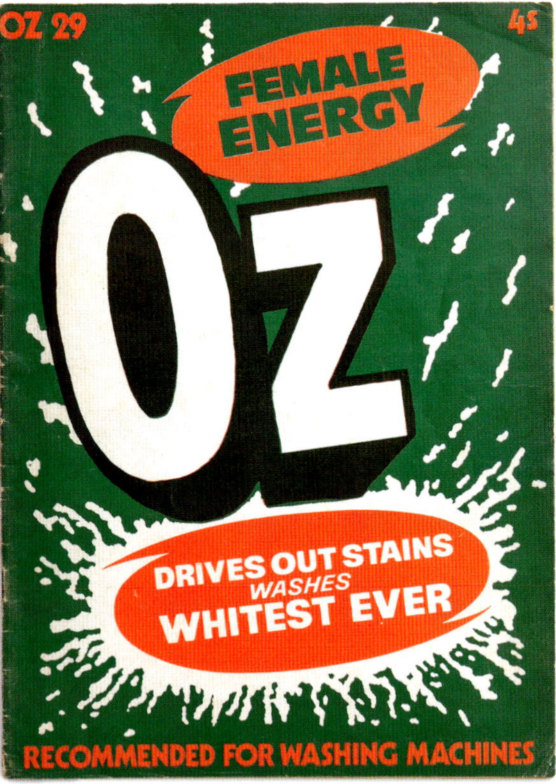

← *Private Eye*, No. 88 30 April 1965 1965
Illustration: Gerald Scarfe
Magazine

Founded in 1961 as part of the satire boom, the British satirical magazine *Private Eye* mocked everyone and everything, particularly the government, royalty and politicians (and continues to do so today). This front cover from April 1965 takes aim at current events. Labour Prime Minister Harold Wilson was newly elected on a narrow margin in October 1964. In December President Johnson pushed him to commit British forces to help the USA in the Vietnam War as part of the 'special relationship', but Wilson stalled. By April 1965, Wilson was still stalling, but trying to keep the special relationship intact (thus is depicted licking Johnson's arse). Wilson would eventually say a resounding 'No' to committing British forces on the ground in Vietnam, a decision that would have met with the approval of much of the British public.

↙ *Oz* 'Cuntpower' issue
↓ (No. 29, July 1970) 1970
Guest editor: Germaine Greer
Magazine (offset)

The British underground press was notoriously sexist, which would eventually lead to the creation of the feminist magazine *Spare Rib* in 1972. *Oz* was one of the few British underground magazines to carry news of the new women's movement, its most blatant statement being the 'Cuntpower' issue guest-edited by Germaine Greer. However, *Oz*'s ultimate aim was to shock, and some of the erotic pictures of naked women in other issues were more likely than not to get *Oz* labelled as sexist too.

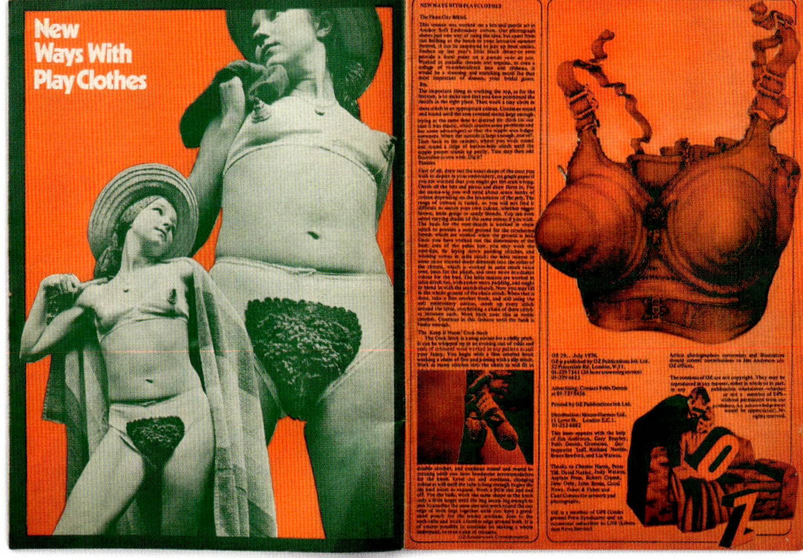

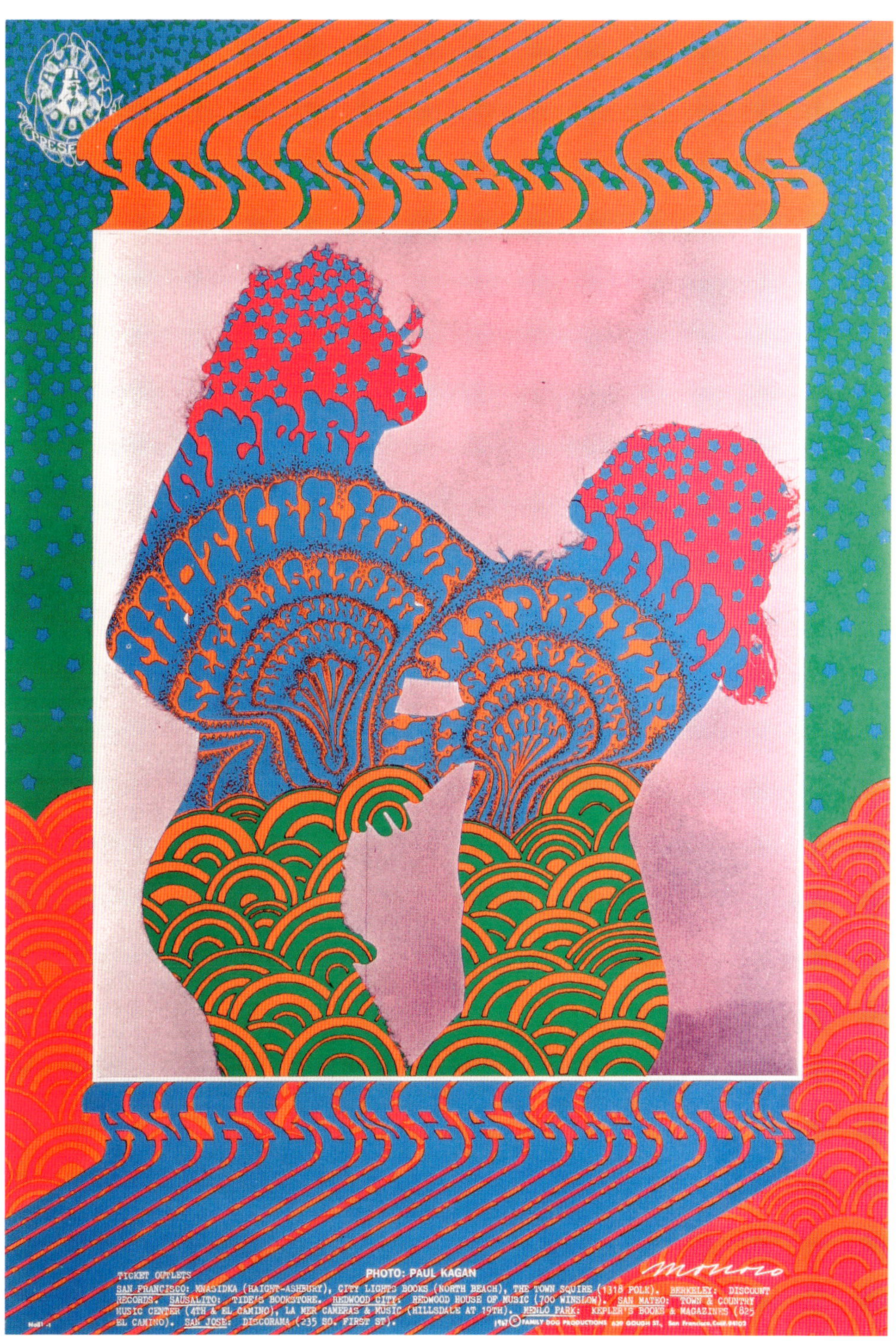

Poster for the Youngbloods folk rock band (Family Dog No. 81) 1967
Victor Moscoso
Poster

Against the backdrop of the Vietnam War and the draft (conscription), the USA experienced a massive generation-clash with regard to dress, attitudes and values: the establishment (parents) versus dropping out (young people). Hippie culture found its epicentre in San Francisco. Rock music and drug culture co-existed, and the 'underground' – radical or far-out – publishing of newspapers, magazines or comics provided news, political debate and protest, or rude, over-sexed humour and satire. Psychedelic art and posterwork belonged, to a great extent, to rock music. The hippie rock music promoters, known as 'Family Dog', had a group of artists designing their promotional material who produced some of the most iconic rock music posters in existence. Their trademark was the use of vibrant, psychedelic colours, densely detailed composition and highly decorated hand-drawn type (which was often barely readable). The best-known artists, the 'San Francisco Five' as they were called, were Rick Griffin, Alton Kelley, Victor Moscoso, Stanley Mouse and Wes Wilson, some of whom also worked on underground comics. The expression of artistic freedom, and energy of radical underground publishing, spread across the USA and on to Britain and Europe.

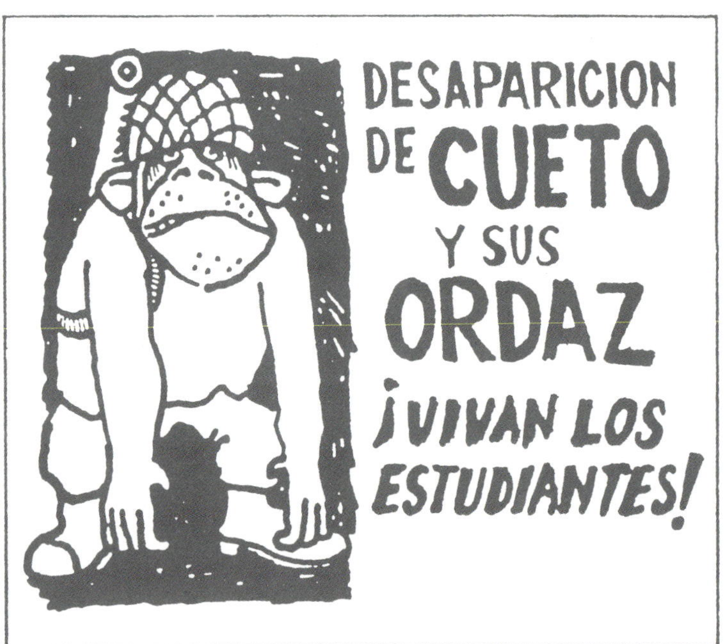

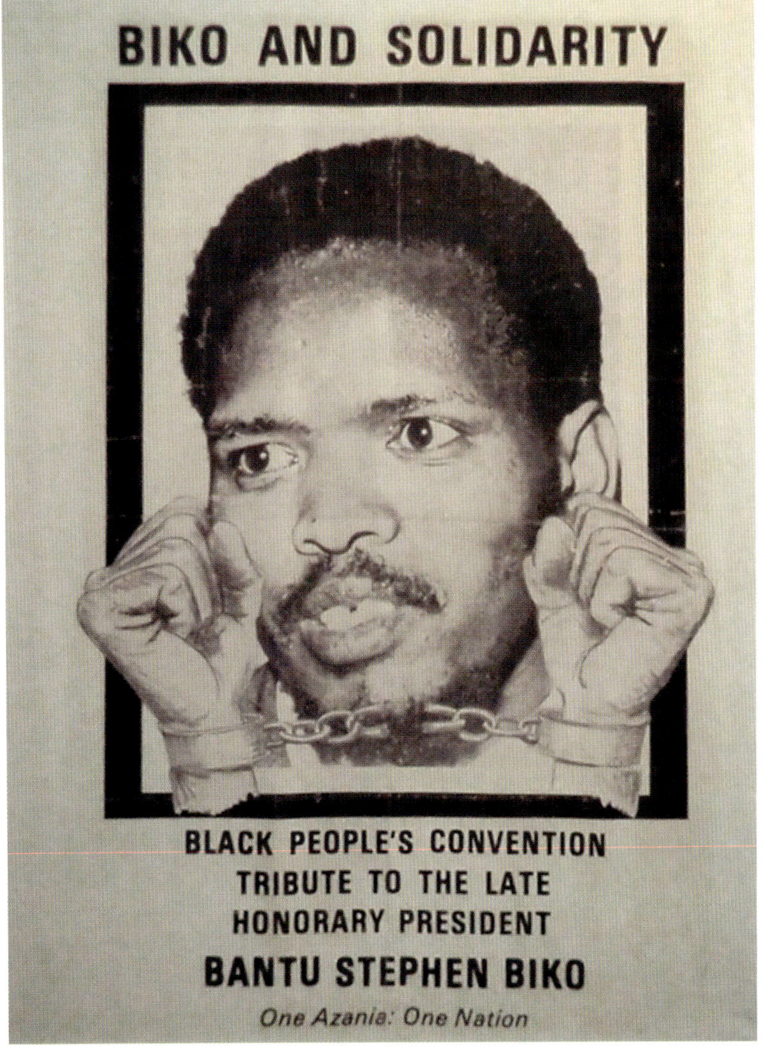

Desaparicion de Cueto y sus Ordaz 1968
Designer unknown
Sticker

On 2 October 1968, the eve of the Olympic Games in Mexico, 10,000 people crammed into the Plaza de las Tres Culturas, listening to student speakers make demands for civil liberty and the release of political prisoners. Not wanting student demonstrations to ruin the prestige of the Games, on the direct order of Díaz Ordaz, leader of the corrupt ruling party (PRI or Institutional Revolutionary Party), tanks and troops showed up and opened fire on the crowd. Sixty people were dead; hundreds were injured. The next day the president of the International Olympic Committee stated that he had been assured by the Mexican authorities that nothing would interfere with the entrance of the Olympic Flame into the stadium on 12 October. Elsewhere: a campaign immediately begins to boycott the Games, and students demonstrate in Nicaragua, Holland, Chile, Italy, France and Britain. The Mexican sticker shown here reads: 'Get rid of Cueto and his Ordaz. Long live the students!', a protest against the Mexican chief of police (Cueto) and the president (Ordaz).

Biko and Solidarity *c*.1977
Designer unknown
Poster

Steve Biko was the founder of the Black Consciousness Movement in South Africa, and was particularly inspirational to the black student community. He was only 30 when he died. His death in detention (in suspicious circumstances) sparked the beginning of a global focus on apartheid in South Africa. This poster was a tribute from the 'Black People's Convention', an organization of black consciousness groups which Biko co-founded in 1972.

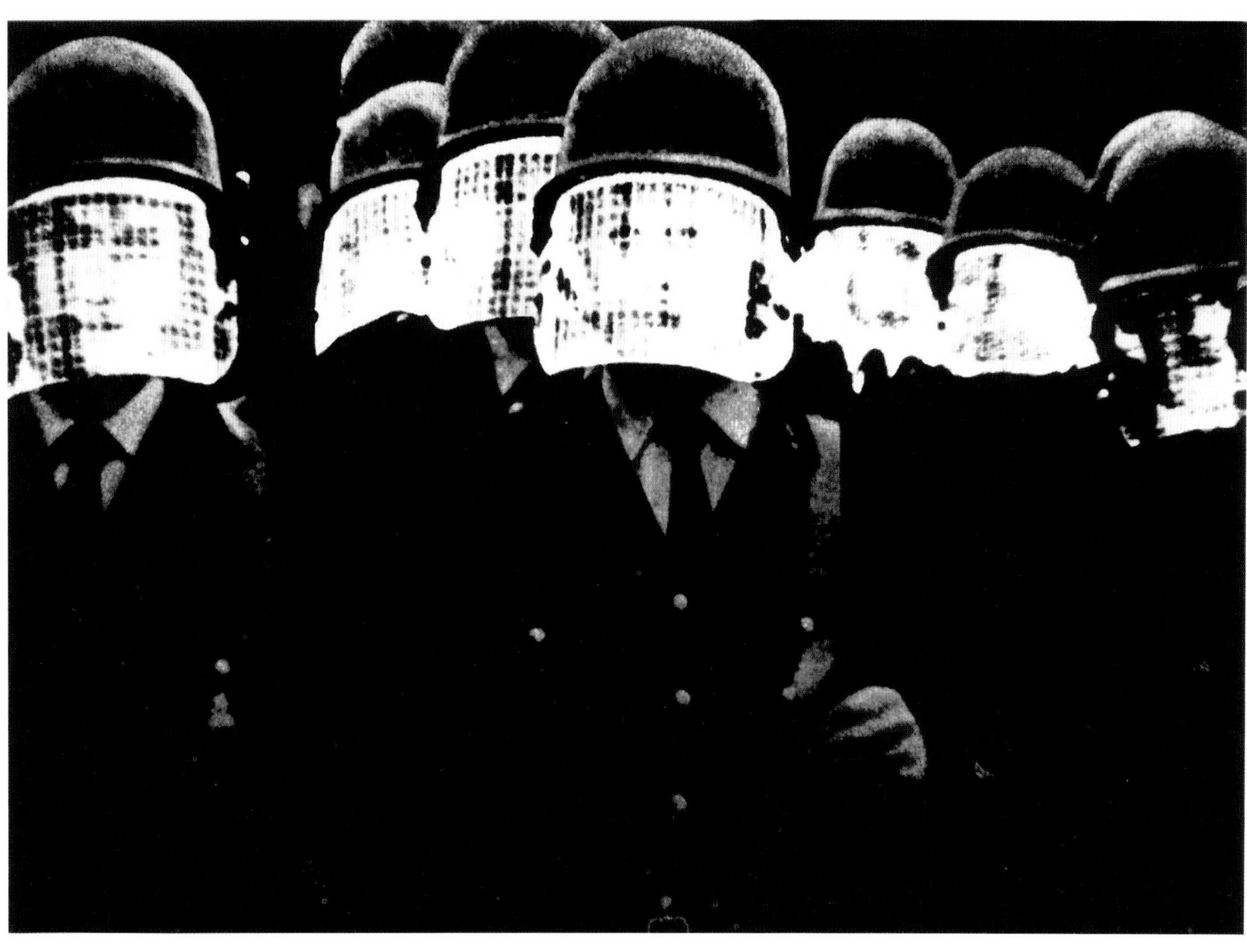

Law and Order 1970
Klaus Staeck
Postcard

Klaus Staeck is a prominent, long-standing and respected figure in the world of creative arts and art education in Germany. He is also an activist, lawyer, graphic artist and publisher of posters and postcards (in Heidelberg) since the 1960s. Most importantly, he remains one of the chief critics and satirists of German politics and society, and his posters and postcards have traditionally been met with disapproval or outright anger by politicians and other 'targets'. His critique has not been confined to Germany: Staeck's graphic statements have been particularly acidic when taking on global issues (refugees, global warming and so on) and the damage done by global corporations and brands. The postcard shown here is an early one, commenting on a society of heavy-handedness and control. Over the years, 41 attempts have been made to legally ban posters or postcards by Klaus Staeck: not one has been successful.

Protests Against the Vietnam War

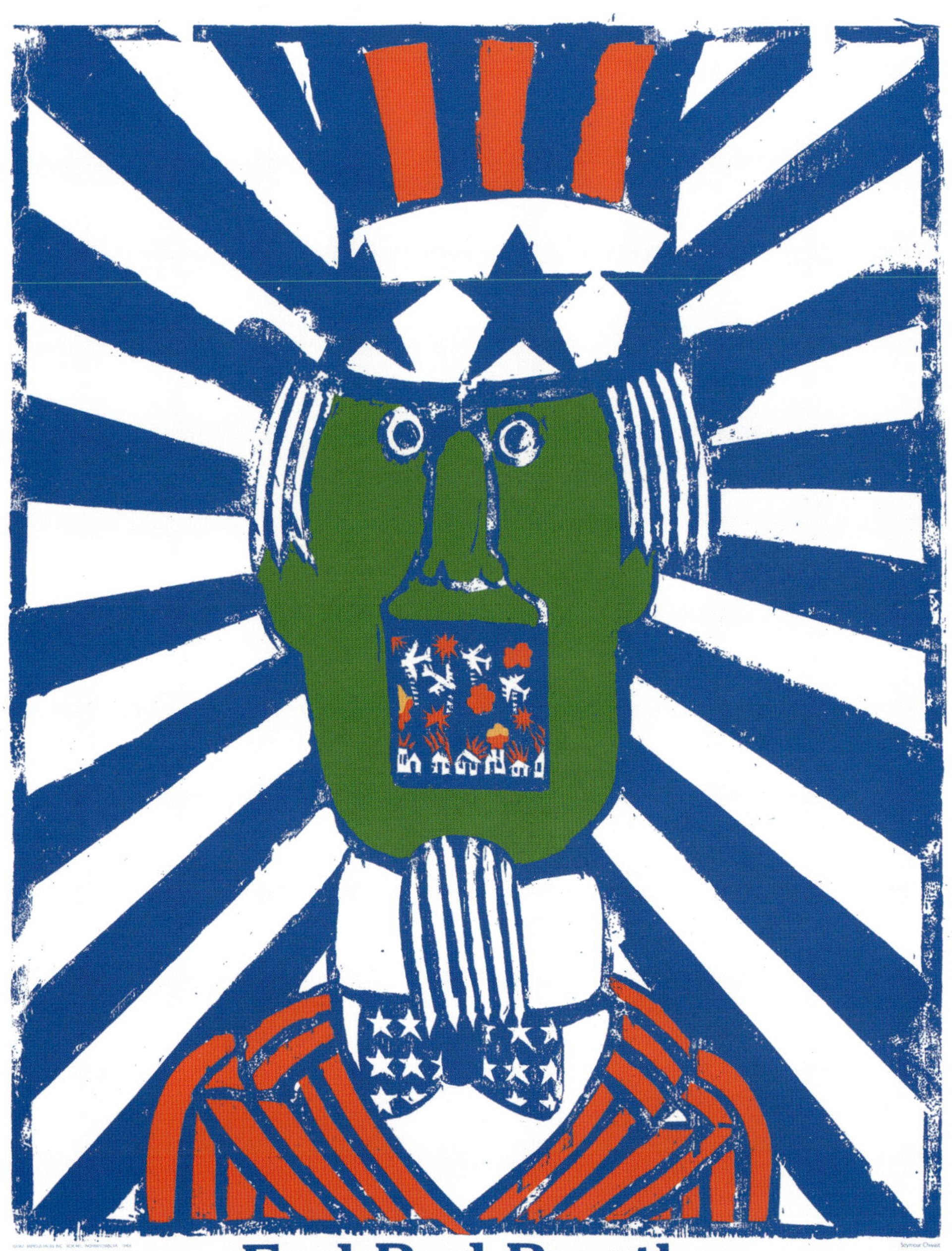

End Bad Breath 1967
Seymour Chwast
Poster

The US symbol of Uncle Sam appears in this poster as if in a toothpaste or mouthwash advertisement, and the 'bad breath' of which it speaks is the carnage being created by the USA's role in the Vietnam War (in his mouth, planes are shown bombing villages). Produced by Seymour Chwast, co-founder of the renowned Push Pin Studios in New York, the poster is highly memorable and representative of the immense outpouring of anti-war protest posters produced at that time by artists, illustrators, design studios, ad agencies, and people in the street. There was tremendous variety in approach and treatment, ranging from line sketches and cartoons to the use of news footage or photography. Emotions were wide-ranging, including humour, cynicism and anger. But all joined together in a protest which became a movement unequalled in the visual arts ever since, and became a vizualisation of the public anger that was instrumental in forcing withdrawal from Vietnam in 1973. The posters remain an important graphic reference point today.

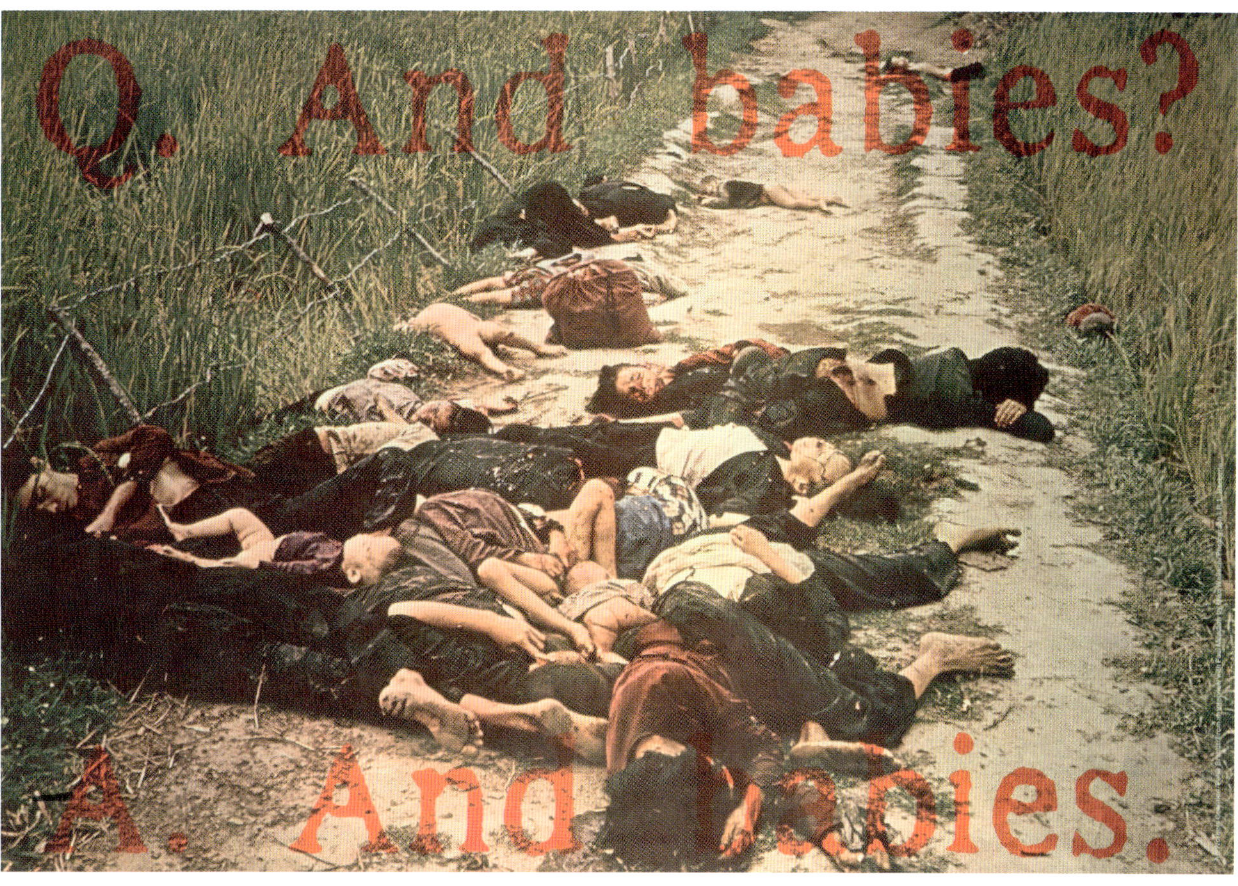

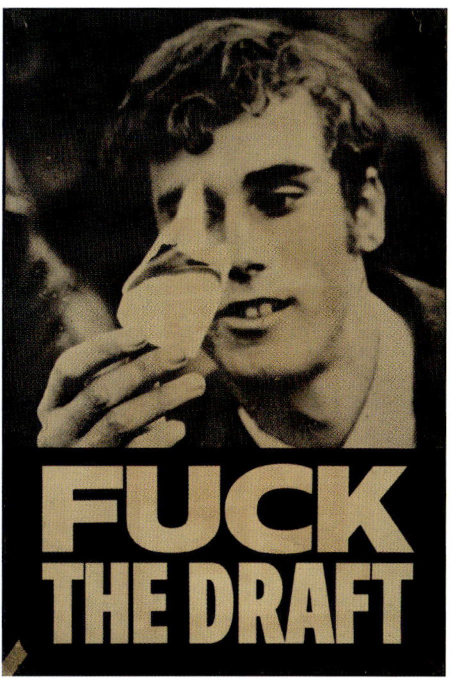

↑ **Q. And Babies? A. And Babies.** 1970
Art Workers' Coalition poster committee
(Frazer Dougherty, Jon Hendricks, Irving Petlin)
Photography: Ron L. Haeberle
Poster (offset)

This poster was produced in outrage at the disclosure in 1969 (by an ex-serviceman) of events that became known as the 'My Lai Massacre'. The massacre took place in the South Vietnamese village of My Lai on 16 March 1968, when many Vietnamese civilians were killed by US soldiers. (The number of those killed varies wildly, from 106 to 347.) The people who died were initially described by a US Army spokesman as a Vietcong unit, but the photographs provided later by the Army's own photographer proved otherwise, showing men and women, old and young. On the poster, the Art Workers' Coalition used Army combat photographer Ron L. Haeberle's photograph, which had been published in *Life* magazine. The title was a quote taken from one of the participants in the massacre who had been interviewed about the events that took place.

← **Fuck the Draft** *c.*1965
Dirty Linen Corp., New York City
Poster

Public protests within the USA against the Vietnam War took many different forms: citywide referendums, election campaigning, campus and mass demonstrations, marches, sit-ins, strikes and draft card burnings. The draft (conscription) was in operation from 1964–73; draft age was 18–25. Draft card burning started around 1965, and increased as time went on, but it was illegal and involved risking imprisonment.

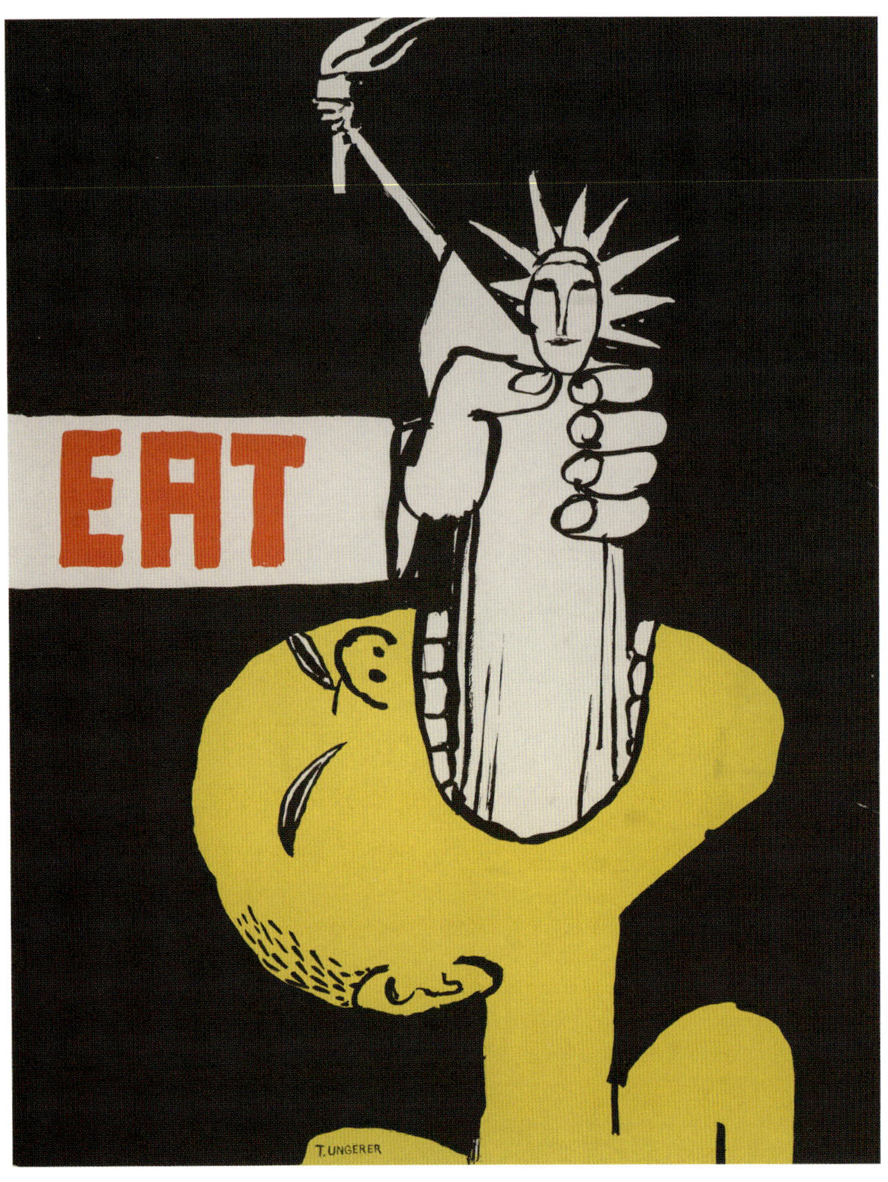

↑ **EAT** 1967
Tomi Ungerer
Poster

In protest against the Vietnam War, renowned artist and illustrator Tomi Ungerer
self-published a series of posters that take a vicious view of the intentions behind
the war. Using his bold, spontaneous, cartoon-like drawing style, he shoves
an image of the Statue of Liberty down the throat of a crudely-caricatured
southeast Asian man (intended to be Vietnamese), accompanied by the red-
lettered command 'EAT'. Hence the Vietnamese man must swallow American
values, commercialization, democratic ideals and so on, whether he likes it or
not. It is a violent image, uncomfortable in its rendering and unsettling in its
message … but powerful nevertheless in its revulsion of the USA's intentions.

↓ **Johnson, Pull Out Like Your Father
Should Have** 1967
Designer unknown
Poster

The brightly-coloured American eagle
delivers a direct, insulting message to
President Lyndon Baines Johnson in
colourful razzmatazz type: the text is a pun
on the phrase 'pull out'. The message is,
more or less: if you pulled the US out of
Vietnam, the world would be a better place
– if your parents had used restraint during
sex and you had never been born, the world
would be a better place.

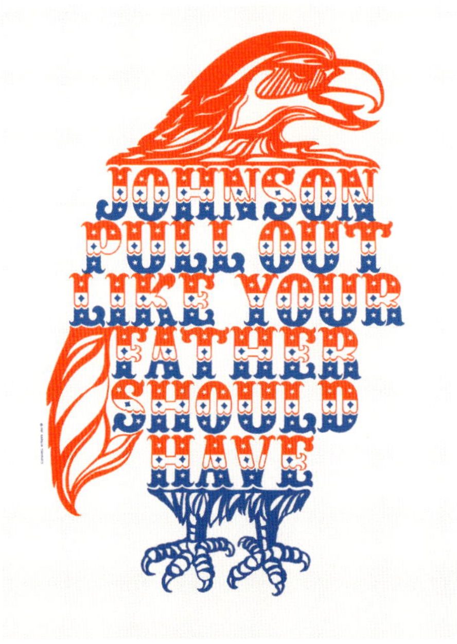

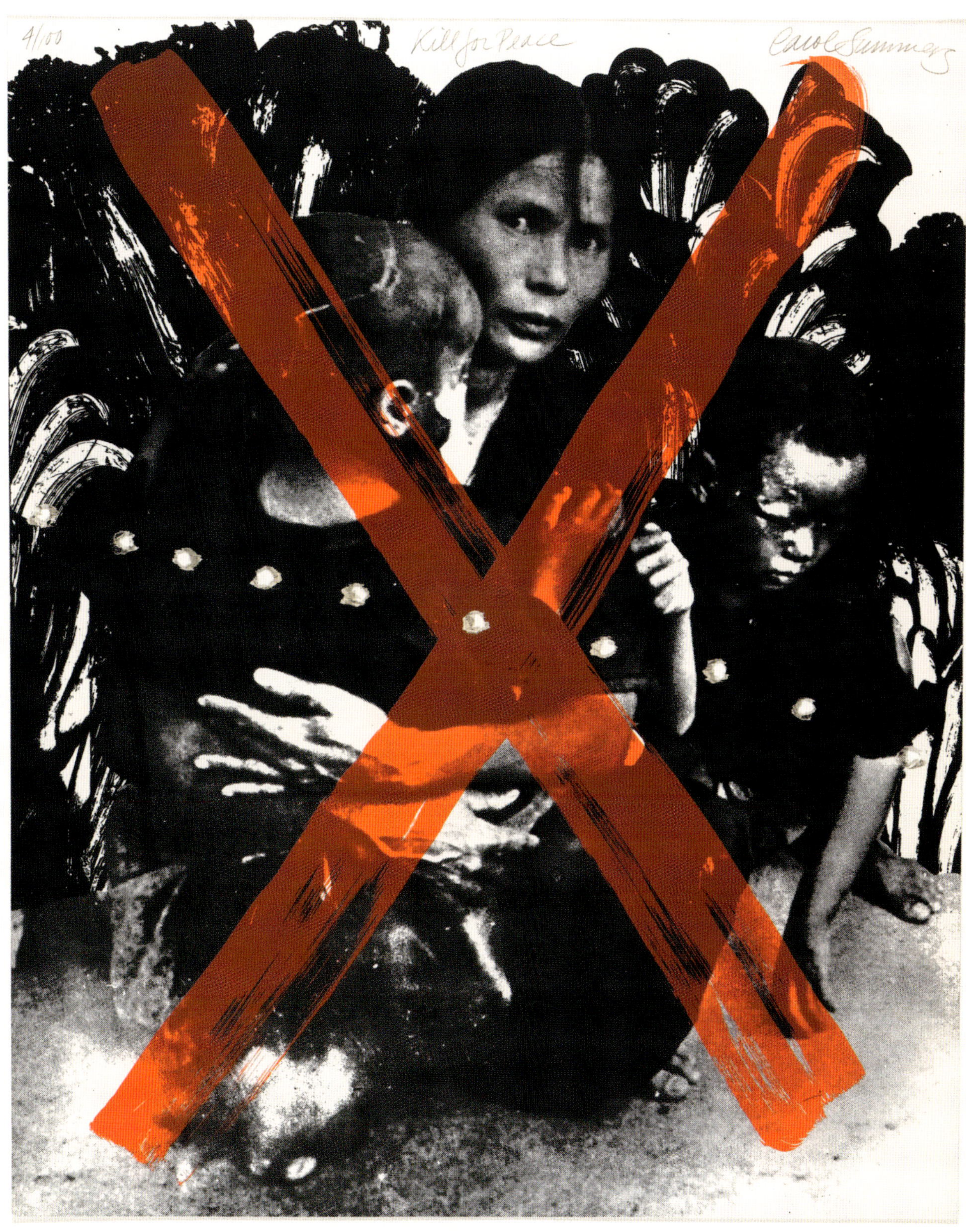

Kill for Peace 1967
Carol Summers
Poster (screenprint and photo-screenprint
on board)

Interestingly, this poster was produced
before the My Lai Massacre, although it
can't help feeling related to the incident.
The mother is huddling protectively with
her children. We don't know if she is from
North or South Vietnam, but does it matter?
Either way, she is looking directly at the
viewer with deep suspicion; and the huge
'X' which fills the image represents a brutal
action, giving the impression that she and
her children are soon to be exterminated
(if it hasn't happened already). If produced
in quantity and displayed as multiples (in
repetition), the effect would be even more
shocking.

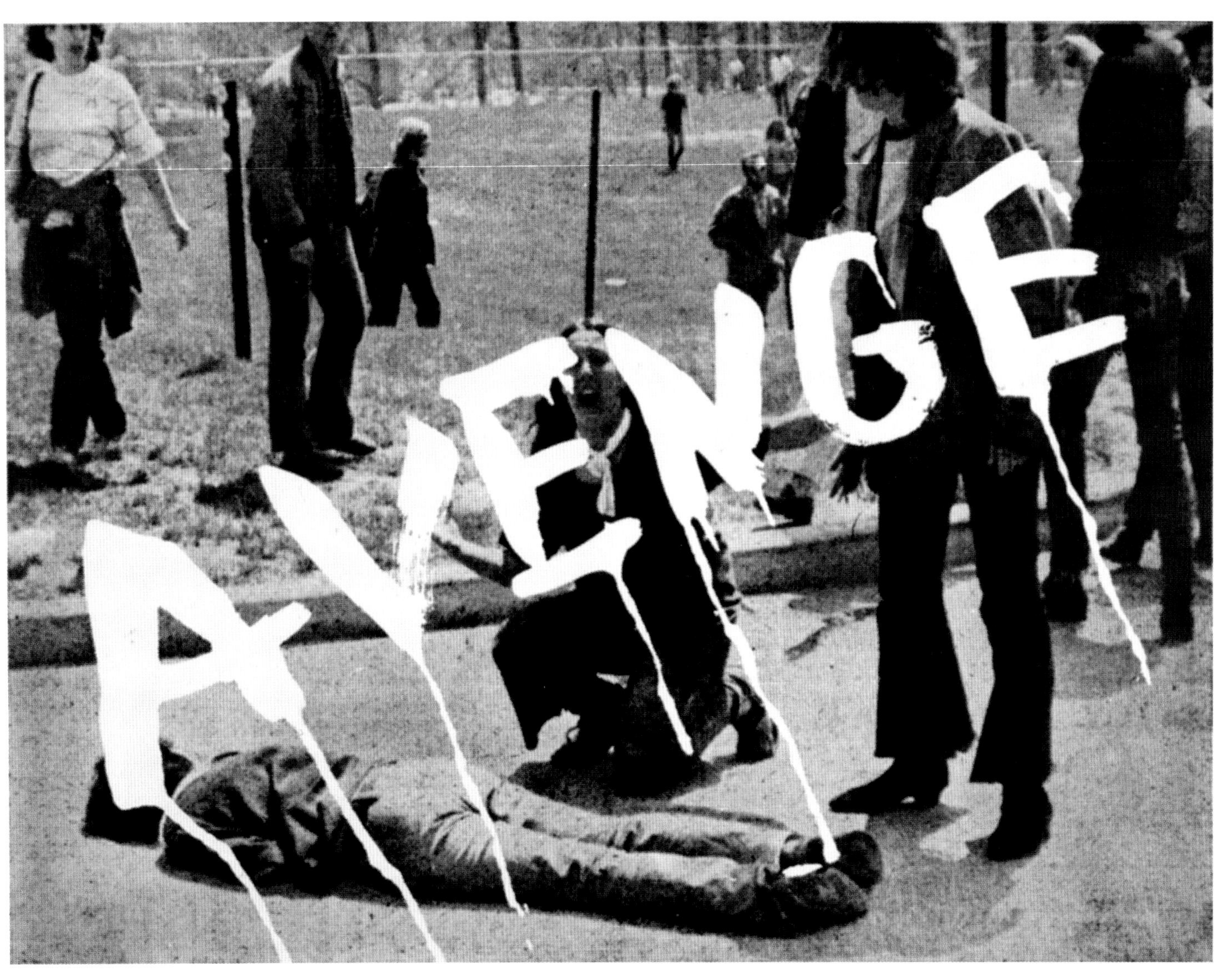

Avenge 1970
Valley Daily News (Pennsylvania) via AP
(photograph)
Poster (offset lithography)

US President Richard Nixon's announcement in 1970 of the expansion of US military operations into Cambodia added fuel to an already volatile phase of student activism. The Ohio National Guard had previously been placed on the campus of Kent State University to keep anti-war activism under control. But on 4 May a midday rally on campus turned ugly, with students shouting abuse and throwing rocks and other objects, and guardsmen firing tear-gas canisters at the crowd. When matters reached fever pitch, one group of guardsmen opened fire on the students. Four students lay dead, and nine were wounded. A student photographer snapped a few pictures of Mary Vecchio kneeling and crying out in agony over the body of her dead friend. The photographs immediately hit national newspapers and magazines, along with the label 'The Kent State Killings'. In the poster shown here, one of the photographs placed in the *Valley Daily News* has been enlarged to poster size and a message scrawled across it saying 'AVENGE'. It promises further protests and reprisals and could have been produced anywhere in the USA. The incident sparked off memorials such as rock musician Neil Young's song 'Ohio', which became an anthem in universities all over the USA due to its persistent, accusatory refrain 'Four Dead in Ohio'.

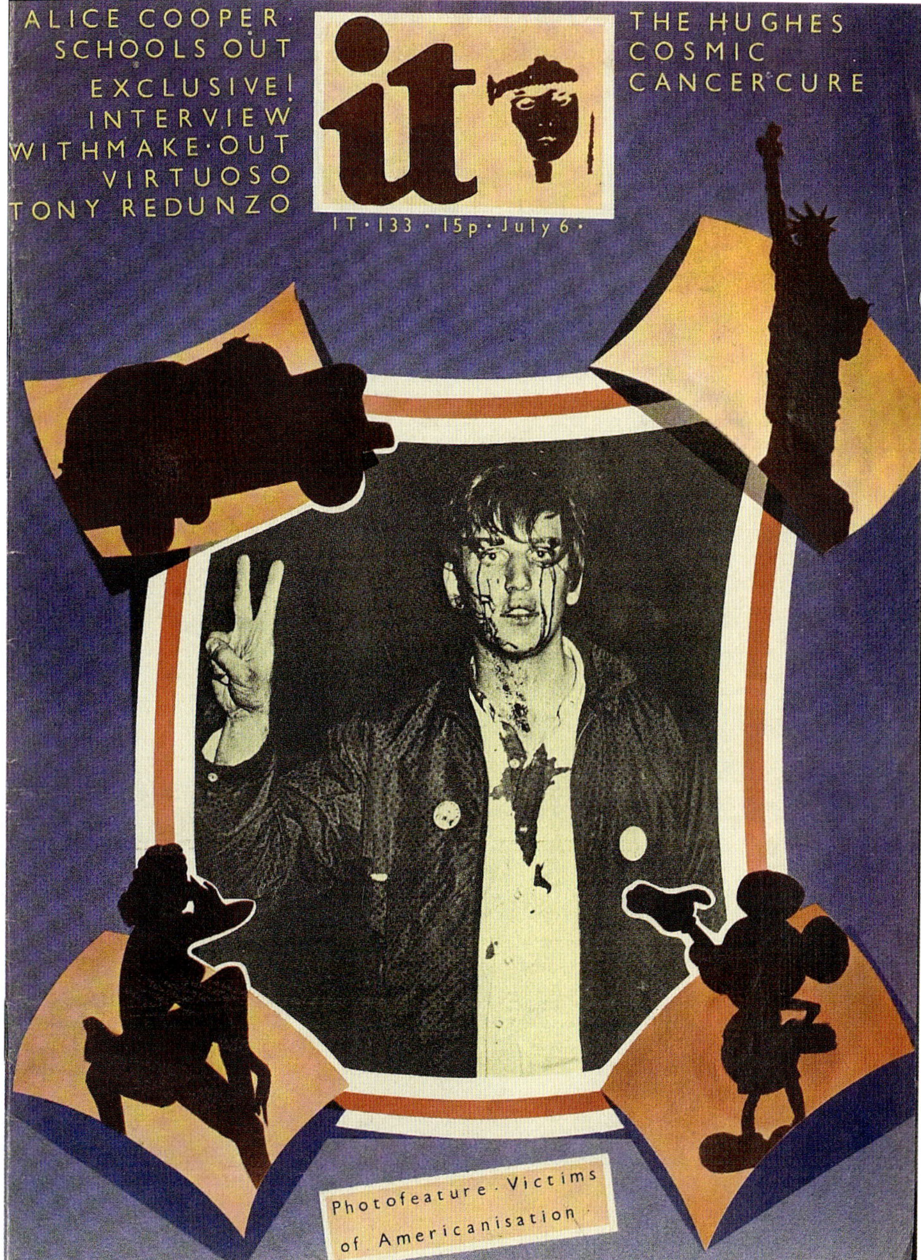

→ **Cover and inside spread,** *IT*
↓ *(International Times,* **No.** 133) *c.* 1970
Magazine (offset lithography)

Underground magazines based in
London kept a watchful eye on anti-war
protests taking place in the USA. This
cover shows a well-known photograph
of a US student demonstration at
Columbia University in 1968. Violence
and bloodshed were already common
occurrences in campus riots by
1967–68, and the term 'police brutality'
was ever-present in the reportage of the
USA's underground press.

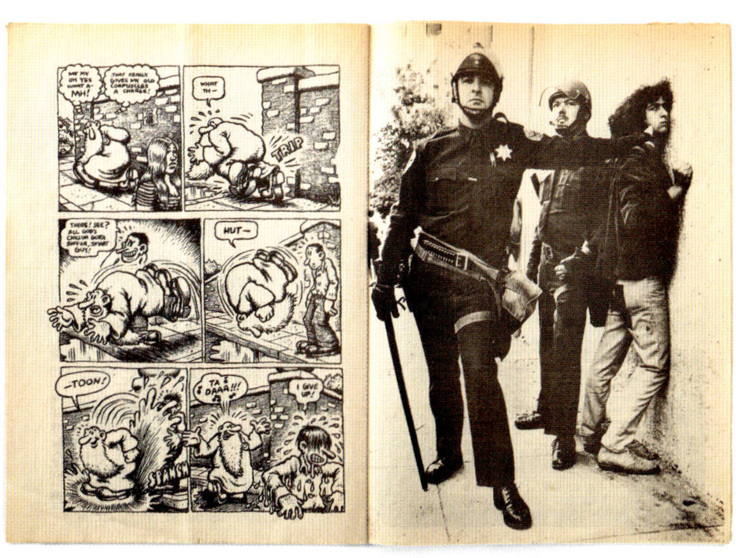

The Civil Rights Movement

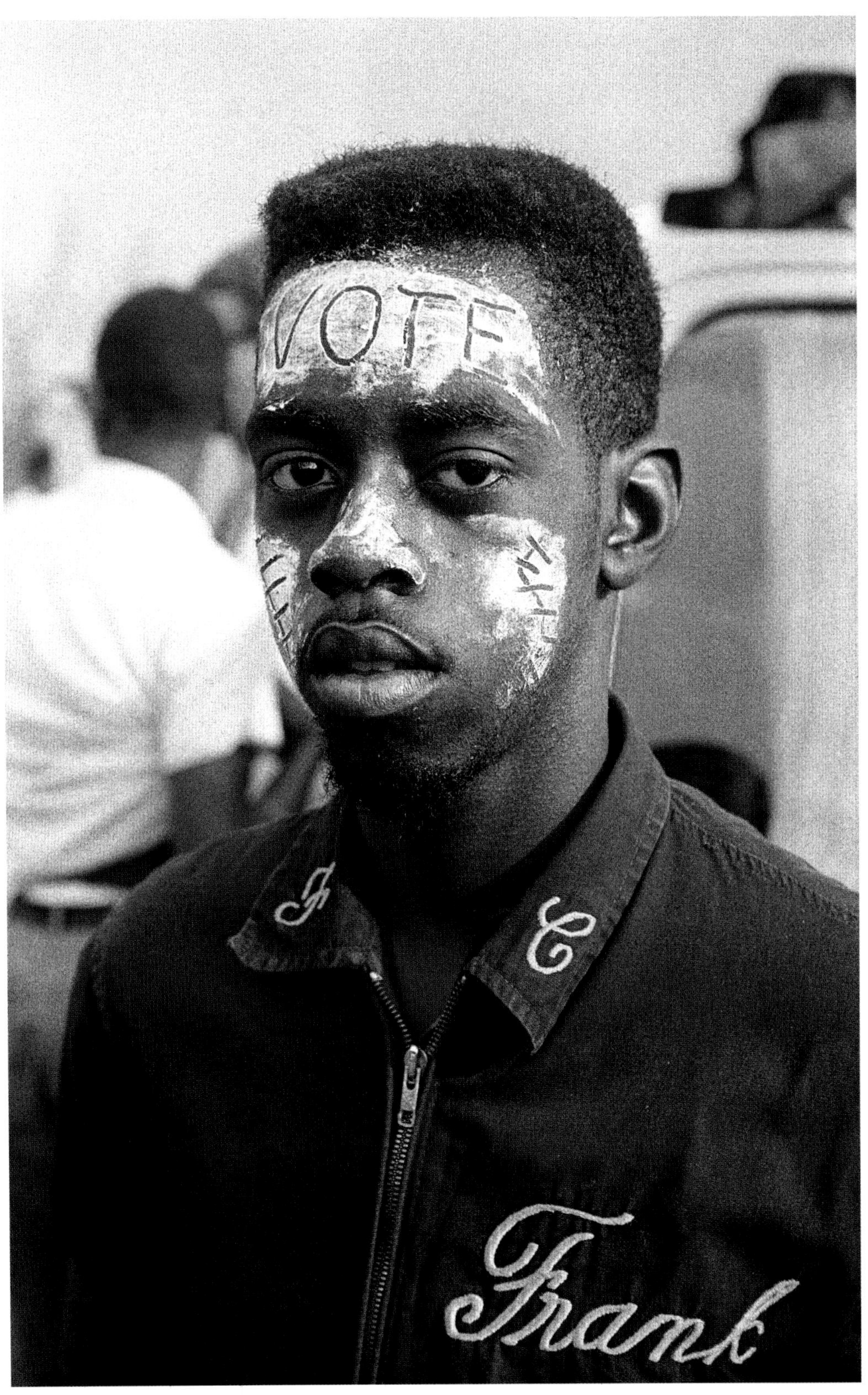

'VOTE' Marcher 1965
Photograph: Stephen F. Somerstein

Having gained a leader in the young, charismatic Martin Luther King, the 1960s saw the US Civil Rights movement embarking on a decade of demonstrations, marches, riots and assassinations, in its effort to challenge segregation and achieve equality and voting rights. In 1965 attention was focused on the pivotal events surrounding the Selma Marches and Alabama's denial of voting rights to black people. After a number of incidents of brutality inflicted on those who even tried to register to vote, mass demonstrations began and eventually Martin Luther King attended marches aiming to walk 50 miles from Selma to Montgomery, the state capital, to put forward their grievances. After two attempts to march (that were disrupted by violence and killings) the third march finally went on its way, guarded by US Army troops and National Guardsmen sent by President Lyndon Johnson. The march took five days. It started with 3,200 marchers but, with the nation watching and people joining along the way, it arrived in Montgomery with over 25,000. Five months later Johnson signed the Voting Rights Act of 1965. This photograph shows the zinc oxide that marchers put on their faces to prevent sunburn in the blistering heat, as well as the strength of conviction they carried.

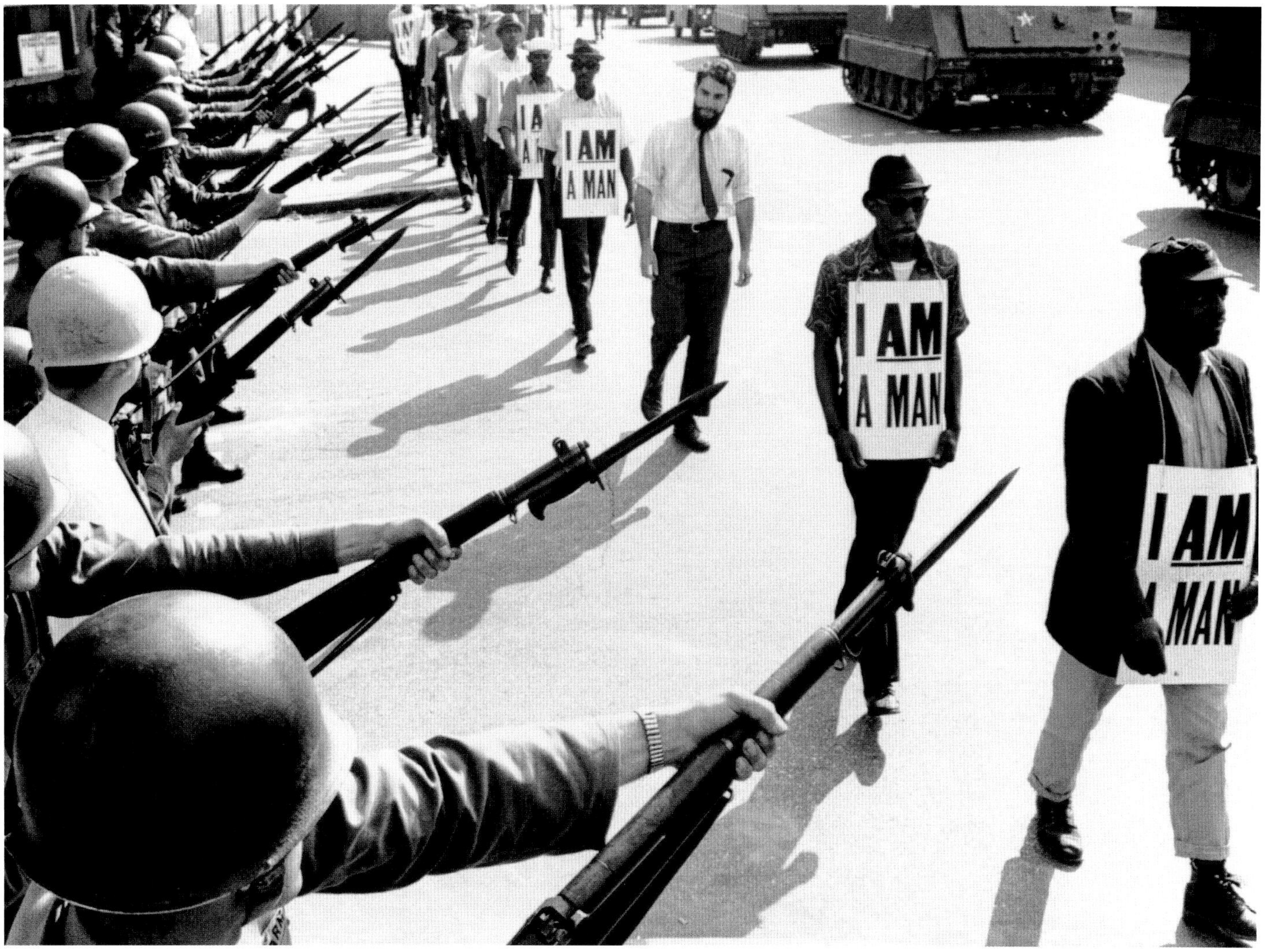

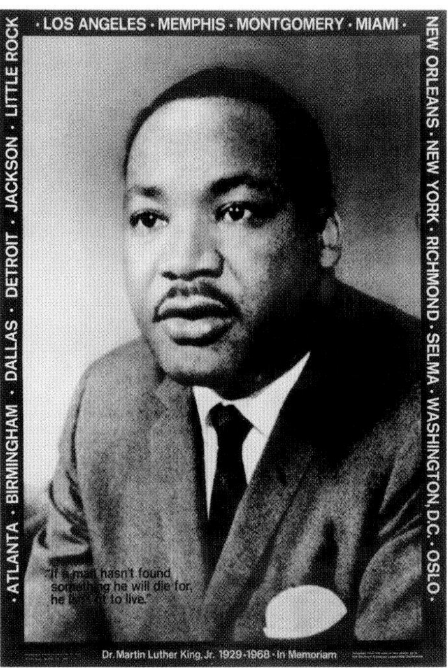

↑ **Striking Sanitation Department Workers** 1968
Photograph: Richard L. Copley

In Memphis, Tennessee (April 1968), 1,300 African American sanitation workers went on strike and marched in protest against low wages and unsafe working conditions, triggered by the deaths of two co-workers from faulty equipment. The signs/placards they carried were printed with a statement of significance that has resonated over the years: 'I <u>AM</u> a man' was a marker of identity and an assertive demand for recognition and rights.

← **Memorial Poster for Dr. Martin Luther King, Jr** 1968
Produced by the Southern Christian Leadership Conference
Poster (offset)

Martin Luther King delivered his stirring 'I Have a Dream' speech to a peaceful mass demonstration in Washington D.C. in 1963. He was assassinated five years later in Memphis, Tennessee. A well-loved and respected figure, his death was a devastating blow. But instead of weakening the movement, it made it stronger. An advocate of progress by peaceful means, King inspired strength and carried the spirit of the Civil Rights movement through its crucial early years, when it was subjected to vicious intimidation and violence. The Black Power leaders that followed would not have his patience.

Black Power and the Black Panthers

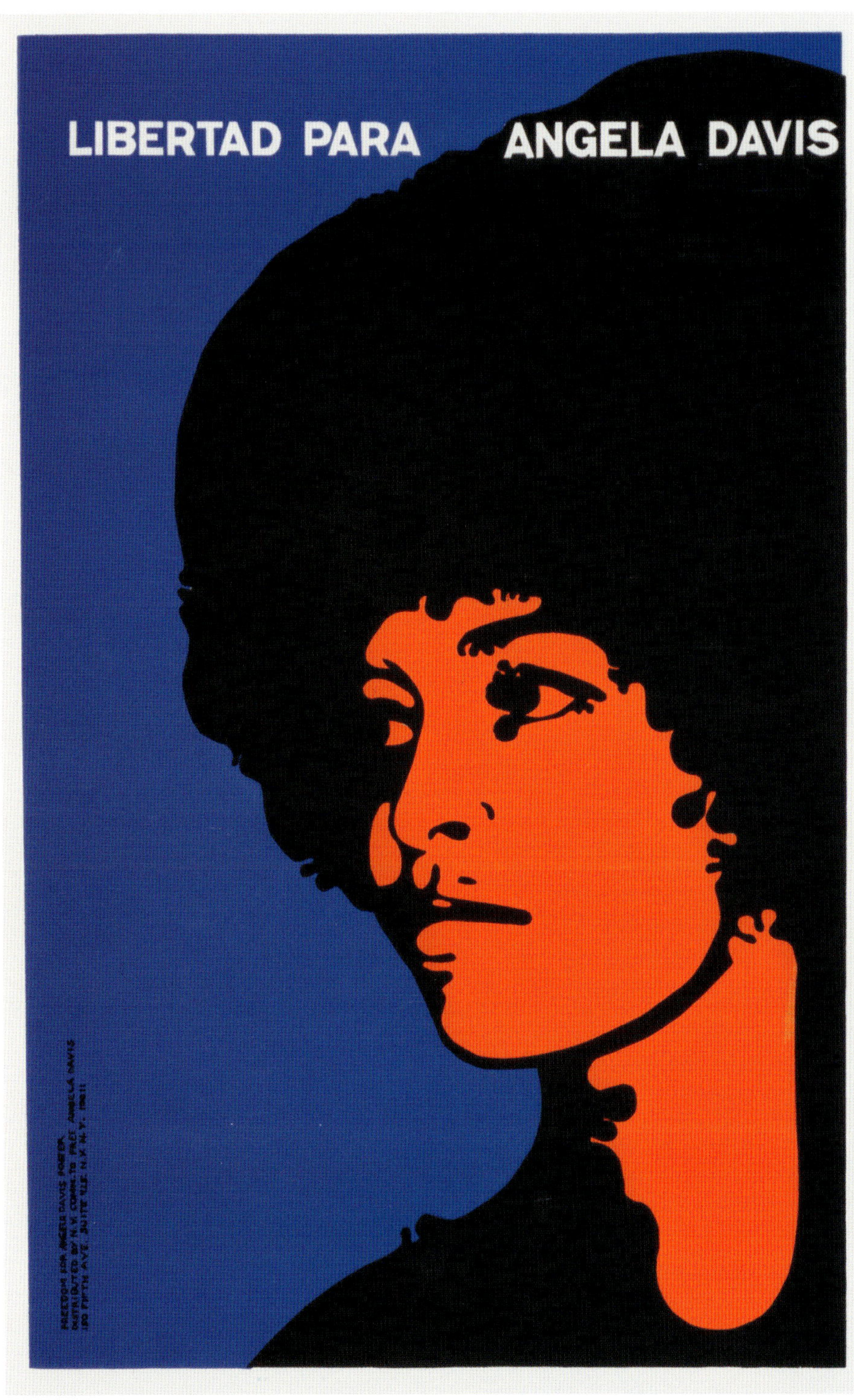

Libertad Para Angela Davis (Free Angela Davis) 1971
Félix Beltrán
Poster

In 1966 Huey P. Newton and Bobby Seale founded the Black Panther Party for Self-Defense or BPP on the principles of self-defence (against the police) and achieving economic justice and power for ordinary black people. Based in Oakland, California, they initiated over 60 community programmes, including the Free Breakfast for Children Program, and grew to become a national organization with over 5,000 members and Panther offices around the country. They also made the decision to (legally) arm themselves in defence against police harassment. The US government considered them a threat to the internal security of America, and by 1969–70 most of their leaders had been jailed and their offices attacked around the country. Political activist Angela Davis joined the Black Panthers in the late 1960s and worked to free the Soledad (Prison) Brothers held in California. In 1970 an escape attempt from Marin County's Hall of Justice left the trial judge and three other people dead. Davis was implicated as the guns used had been registered in her name. She fled and was immediately placed on the FBI's Top 10 Most Wanted Criminals list. She was captured in New York, imprisoned for 18 months (during her trial), then cleared of all charges in 1972. During this time, an international 'Free Angela Davis' movement had taken hold. This Cuban poster was produced in 1971, calling for her release from prison.

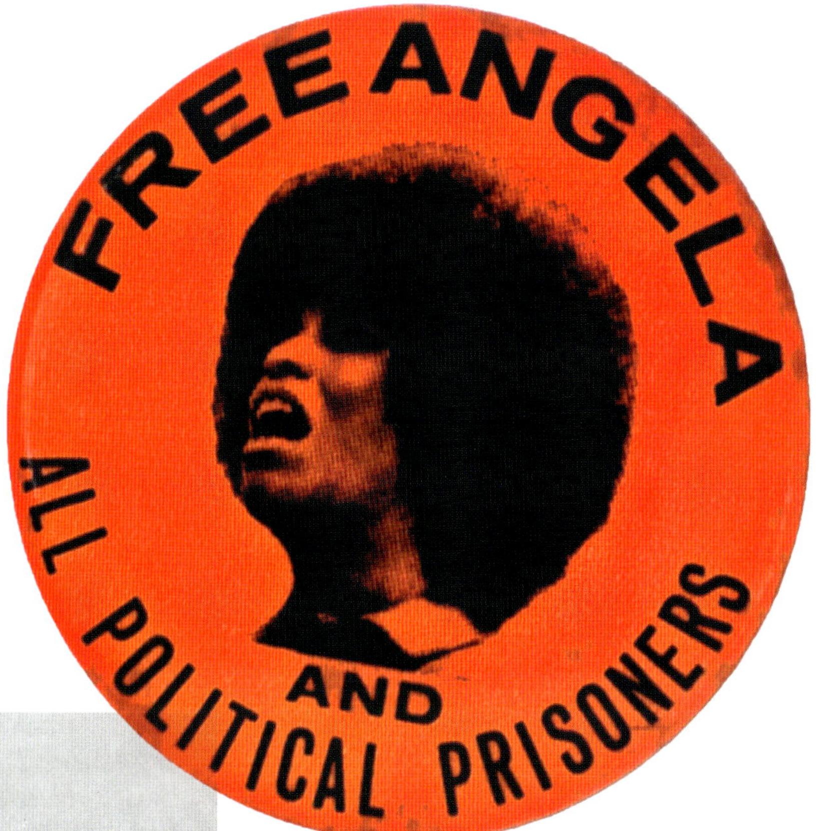

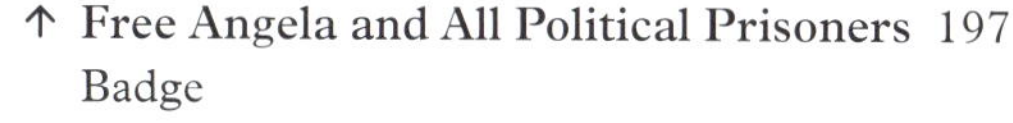

↑ **Free Angela and All Political Prisoners** 1971
Badge

In 1971, the words 'Free Angela' accompanied by the iconic Afro hairstyle could only have referred to political activist Angela Davis, imprisoned by the US government. Calls for her release, as shown on this badge, emanated from around the world.

← **Black Power salute** 1968
Photograph
Photographer unknown

A historic moment occurs during the medal awards ceremony on 16 October 1968 at the Olympic Games in Mexico. In a silent and dignified gesture, two black American winners – gold medallist Tommie Smith and bronze medallist John Carlos – raised their fists in the Black Power salute while the US national anthem was played. The next day they were expelled from the US team, and the day after that three more black American athletes resolutely mounted the rostrum and as the national anthem was played, gave the Black Power salute.

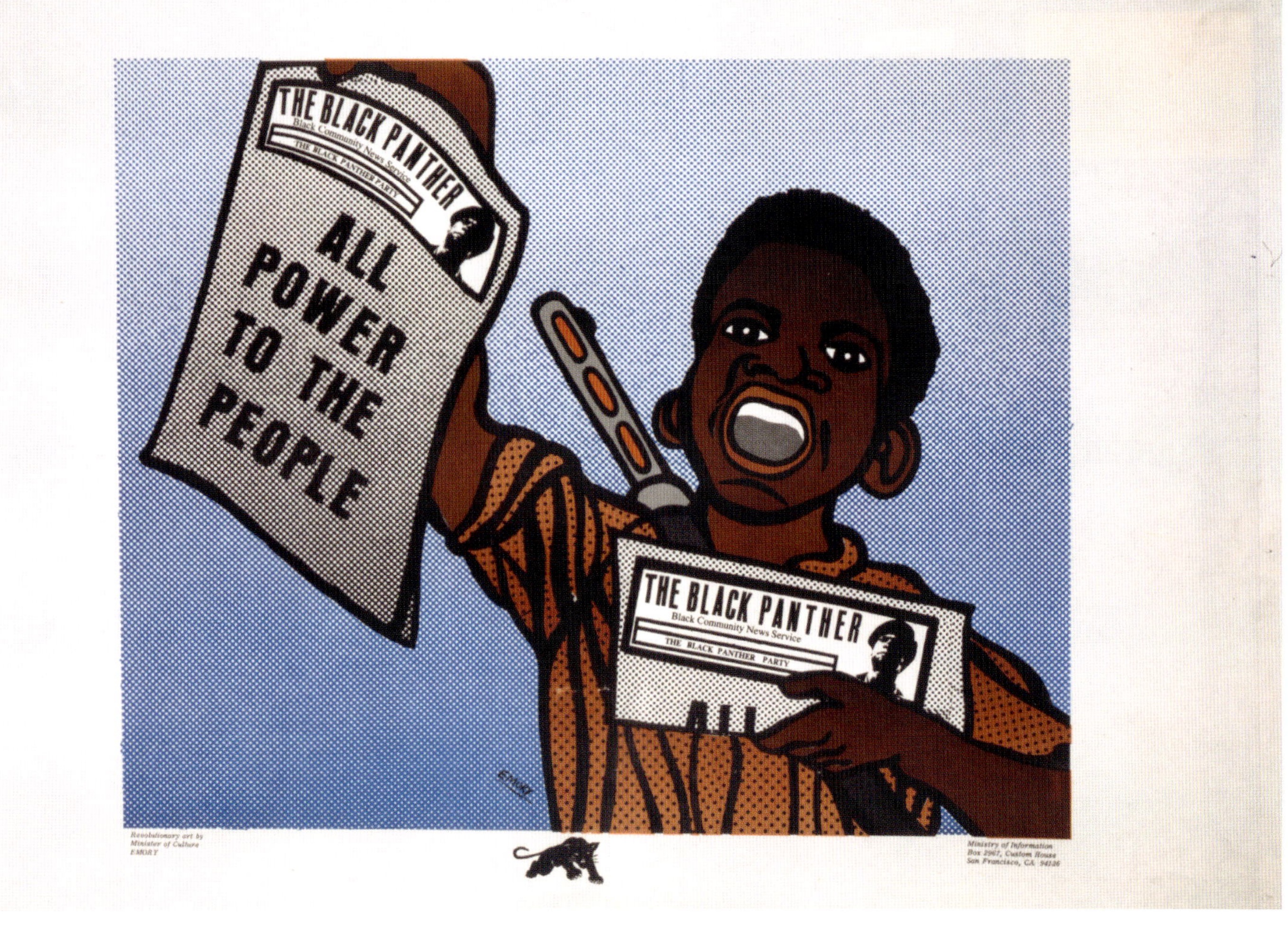

Posters for *The Black Panther* newspaper and the Black Panther Party (BPP) *c.*1967–72
Design and illustration: Emory Douglas
Two posters

Both Bobby Seale and Huey P. Newton recognized the value of a strong visual presence and were responsible for the uniform that became the hallmark of the Black Panthers: black berets, black leather jackets and black slacks. Together this combination represented unity, while the Afro-haircut represented political style. Also, in the BPP newspaper, Bobby Seale was keen to communicate to the community through strong graphics as well as text (thinking that many people wouldn't read endless columns of text). Seale created *The Black Panther: Black Community News Service*, the BPP newspaper. Eldridge Cleaver was writer and editor of the newspaper, and Emory Douglas – already a member of the Black Arts movement – became the BPP Minister of Culture, responsible for all of the graphics for the newspaper. He produced 'revolutionary posters' which could be bought, front and back covers for the newspaper (back covers were for use as posters), plus other illustrations of anger or empowerment. Douglas's distinctive illustrations became the visual voice of the BPP. The newspaper grew a circulation of more than 400,000 weekly – and expanded to 52–60 tabloid pages.

(Image A)   Promotional poster for *The Black Panther* newspaper, *c.*1967–72

(Image B)   BPP poster, The Slaughter of Black People Must Be Stopped!
By Any Means Necessary!, 1969

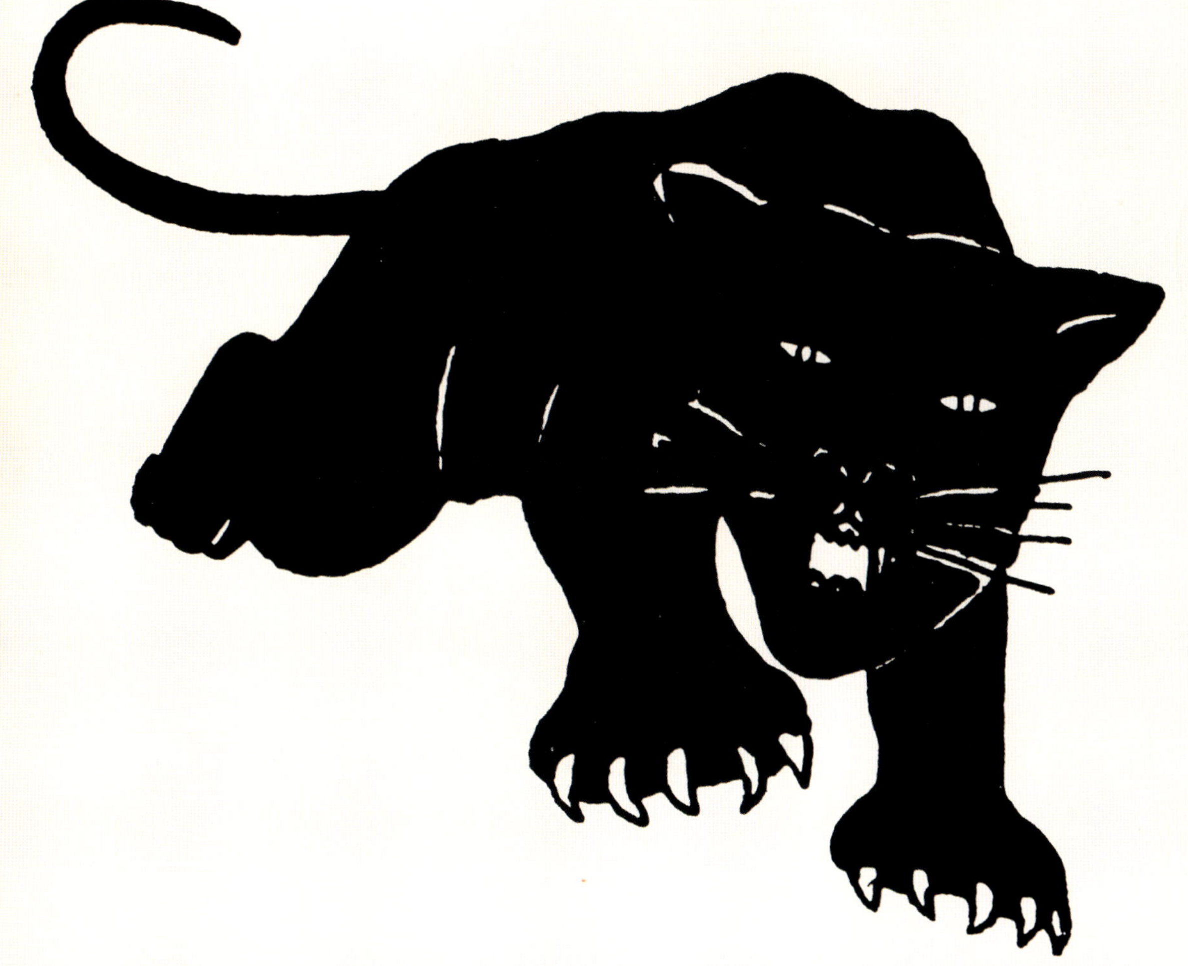

An Attack Against One
Is An Attack Against All

The Slaughter of Black
People Must Be Stopped!
By Any Means Necessary!

Distributed by The Robert Brown Elliott League, 540 McAllister Street, San Francisco, Calif.

Women's Liberation: The Second Wave

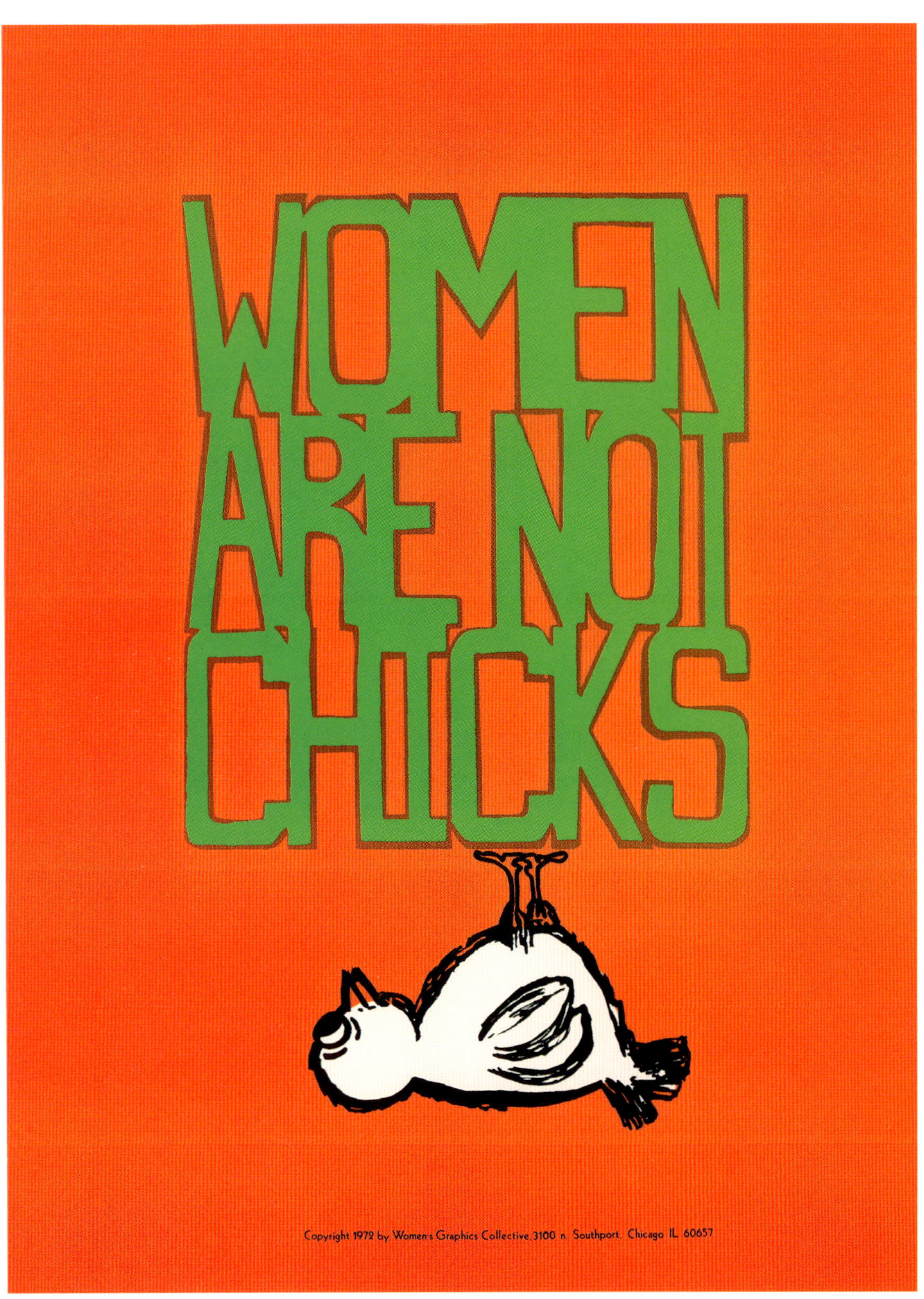

Women Are Not Chicks 1970–71
Chicago Women's Graphics Collective
Poster

Within the volatile climate of change and liberation taking place in late 1960s USA, a movement of young radicalized women organized to bring about an end to their oppression. The Women's Liberation movement called upon all women to challenge the existing politics of male/female power relations. Their machinery for bringing about direct change included consciousness-raising, networking and direct action, as well as the celebration and promotion of women's achievements. (Inspired by the 'First Wave' of early 20th century suffrage societies and militant suffragettes, they became the 'Second Wave'.) Graphic formats such as posters, postcards and magazines were important carriers of the new ideas and messages to an international audience, and became part of the search for a new visual language that expressed women's struggles and concerns. Radical poster groups often worked collectively: an important rejection of what was seen as 'male' hierarchical systems. This assertive poster by the Chicago Women's Graphics Collective (one of their earliest) immediately takes issue with the undermining character of ordinary, so-called 'innocent' labels applied to women.

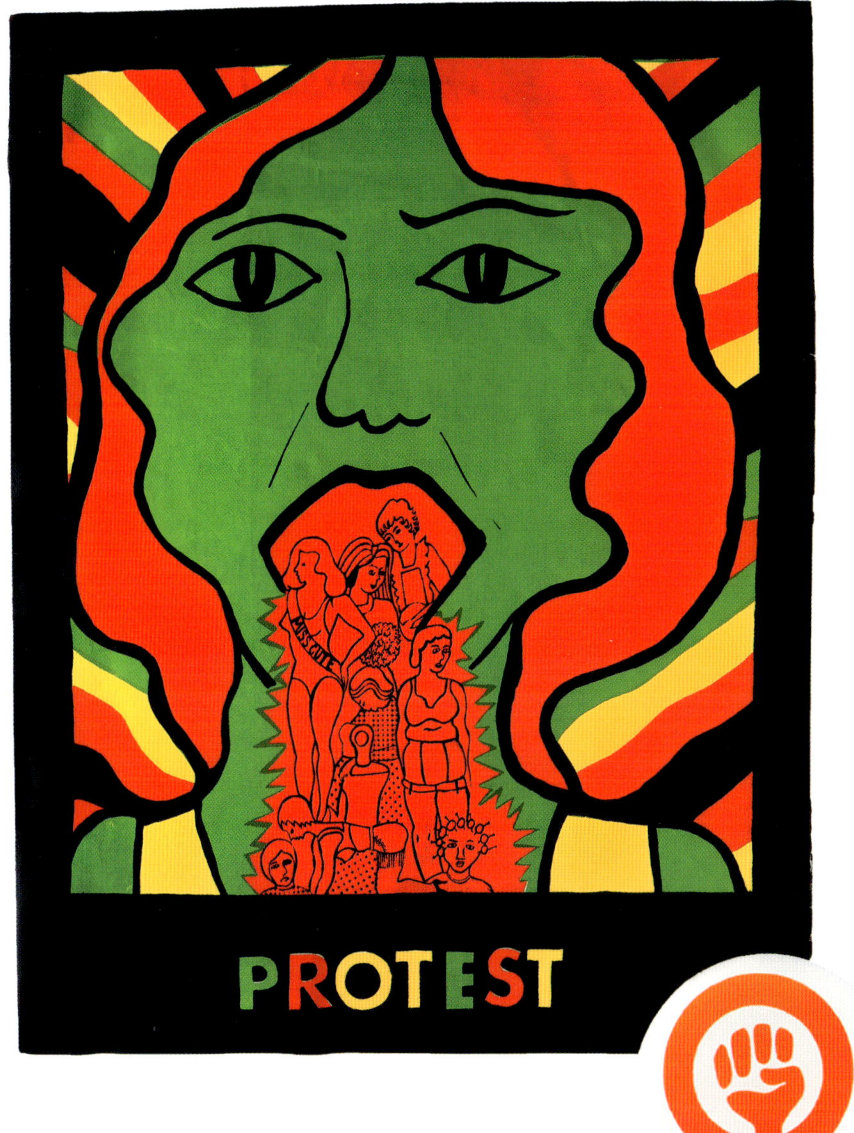
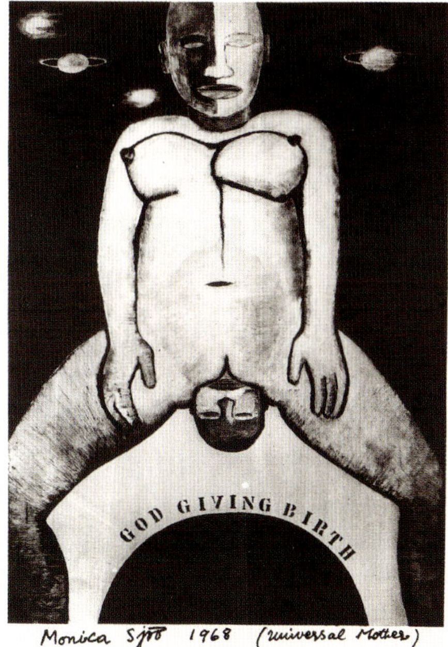

↑ **Protest** 1973
See Red Women's Workshop
Poster (silkscreen)

See Red Women's Workshop became one of Great Britain's best-known and longest-lasting women's poster collectives (*c.*1973–90). This poster rails against beauty contests and women's objectification.

↗ **Feminist Symbol with Raised Fist** 1970
Badge

The Women's Liberation movement was fortunate in having a brilliant graphic symbol – the female biological sign – as its emblem. It developed a multitude of artistic variations (such as the one shown here, with a raised fist) and its simplicity allowed it to be scribbled or drawn by anyone on anything.

God Giving Birth
(Universal Mother) 1968
Monica Sjöö
Poster reproduction of painting

Monica Sjöö's painting 'God Giving Birth', depicting the goddess as the great cosmic and creative power giving birth to all life, became an important feminist icon in Britain. Its public exhibition led to Sjöö being threatened with prosecution for 'obscenity and blasphemy'. Subsequently, in venues around Britain, it was removed by police and banned from exhibition.

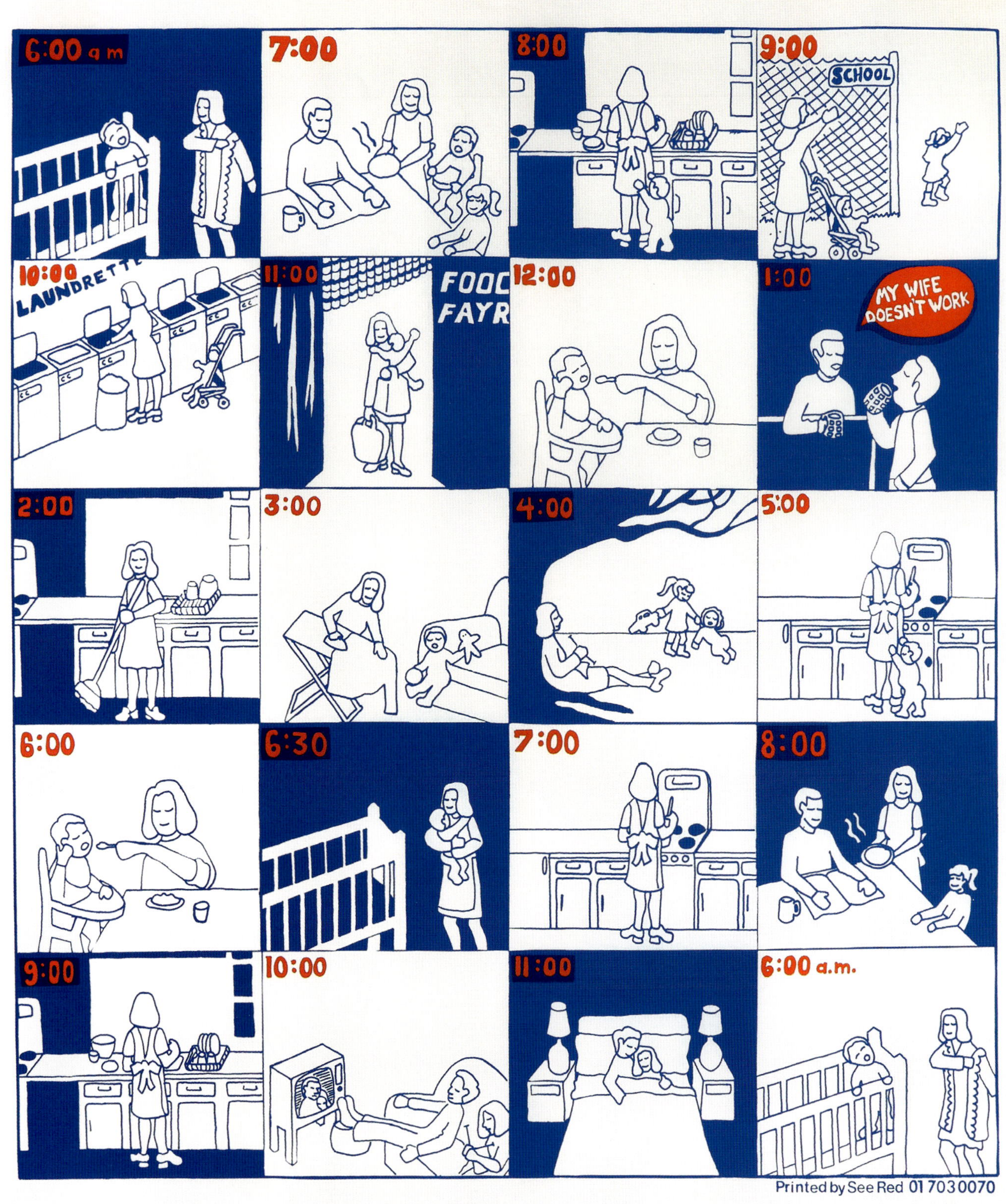

My Wife Doesn't Work 1976
See Red Women's Workshop
Poster (silkscreen)

In addition to celebrating women's lives and achievements, See Red Women's Workshop also excelled at visualising the notion that 'the personal is political', thereby attacking some of the established views and prejudices that affected women's lives. This included the 'hidden' difficulties of holding an outside job while also caring for the home, and the overriding view that men's work in the factory (or wherever) was of much greater value than women's work in the home, as shown in 'My Wife Doesn't Work'.

This powerful cartoon shows Wonder Woman brandishing her speculum and clobbering representatives of US medical professions and institutions, plus religious, legal and other advisors (all male). The use of the speculum (for self-examination of the vagina) became an important part of women's liberation consciousness-raising, and was symbolic of women's desire to take over control of their bodies and their health. This was first demonstrated in the USA in 1971, and by 1975 the Women's Health Movement had carried it to a dozen other countries.

↓ **Free Castration on Demand:**
A Woman's Right to Choose 1970s
Pen Dalton
Poster (silkscreen)

In addition to poster groups, individual poster artists such as Pen Dalton (in Britain) produced work of extraordinary energy, celebration and anger, while expressing many of the same issues and concerns.

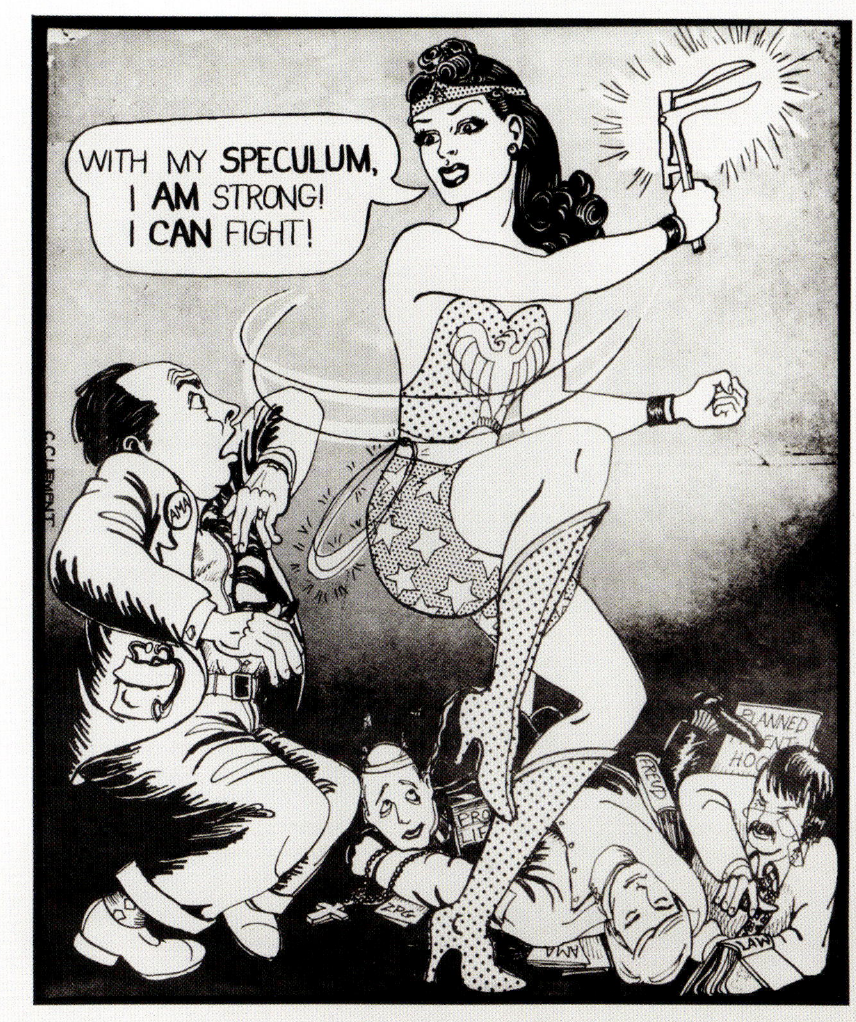

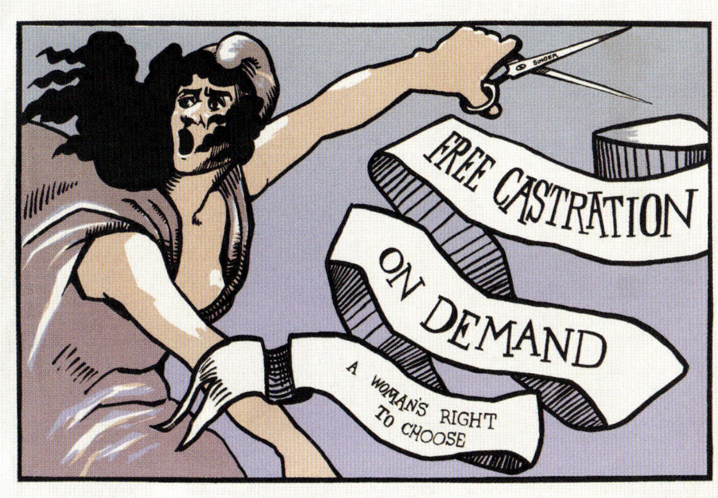

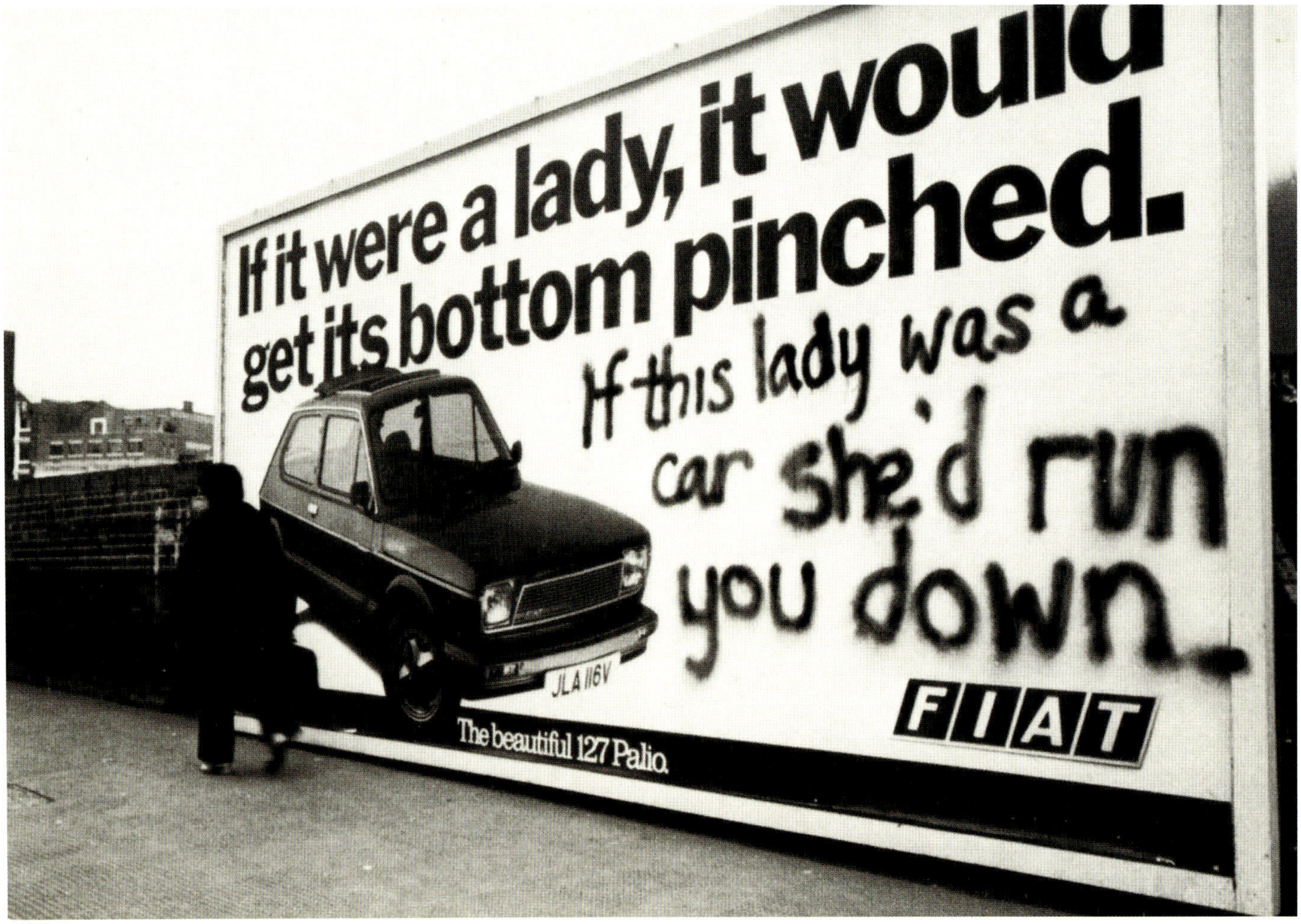

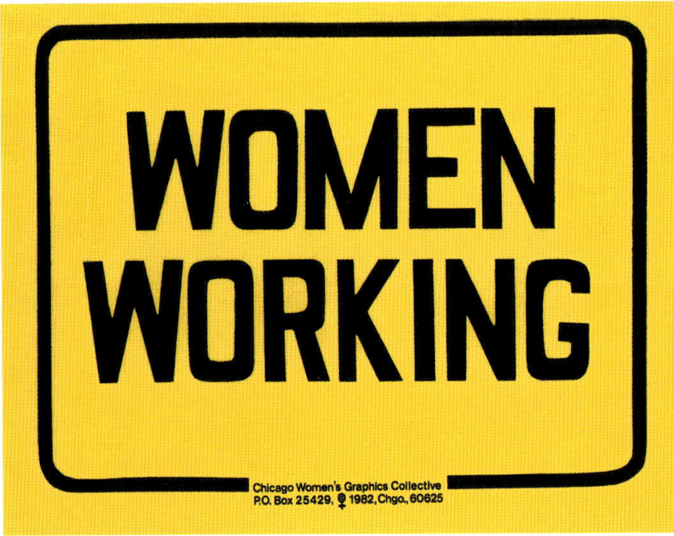

↑ **If it were a lady …** 1979
Photograph: Jill Posener
Billboard

Margaret Thatcher became prime minister of the
UK in 1979, heralding a new era of conservative
politics. Tensions soon rose between the haves
and have nots; and revolutionary movements such
as feminism and the peace movement began an
undeclared war with the government. Both groups
chose spray can graffiti as one of the ways in which
to show their anger. It was at this point that Jill
Posener began to photograph and document the
graffiti sprayed on buildings, billboards and other
parts of the city environment. She filled two books
with it: a record of social discontent, protest and,
in some cases, desperation.

↖ **Women Working** 1970s
Chicago Women's Graphics Collective
Poster

This well-loved poster is from a well-known US
poster group that proclaimed pride in women's
collaboration and achievement, while also warning
off anyone wanting to interfere.

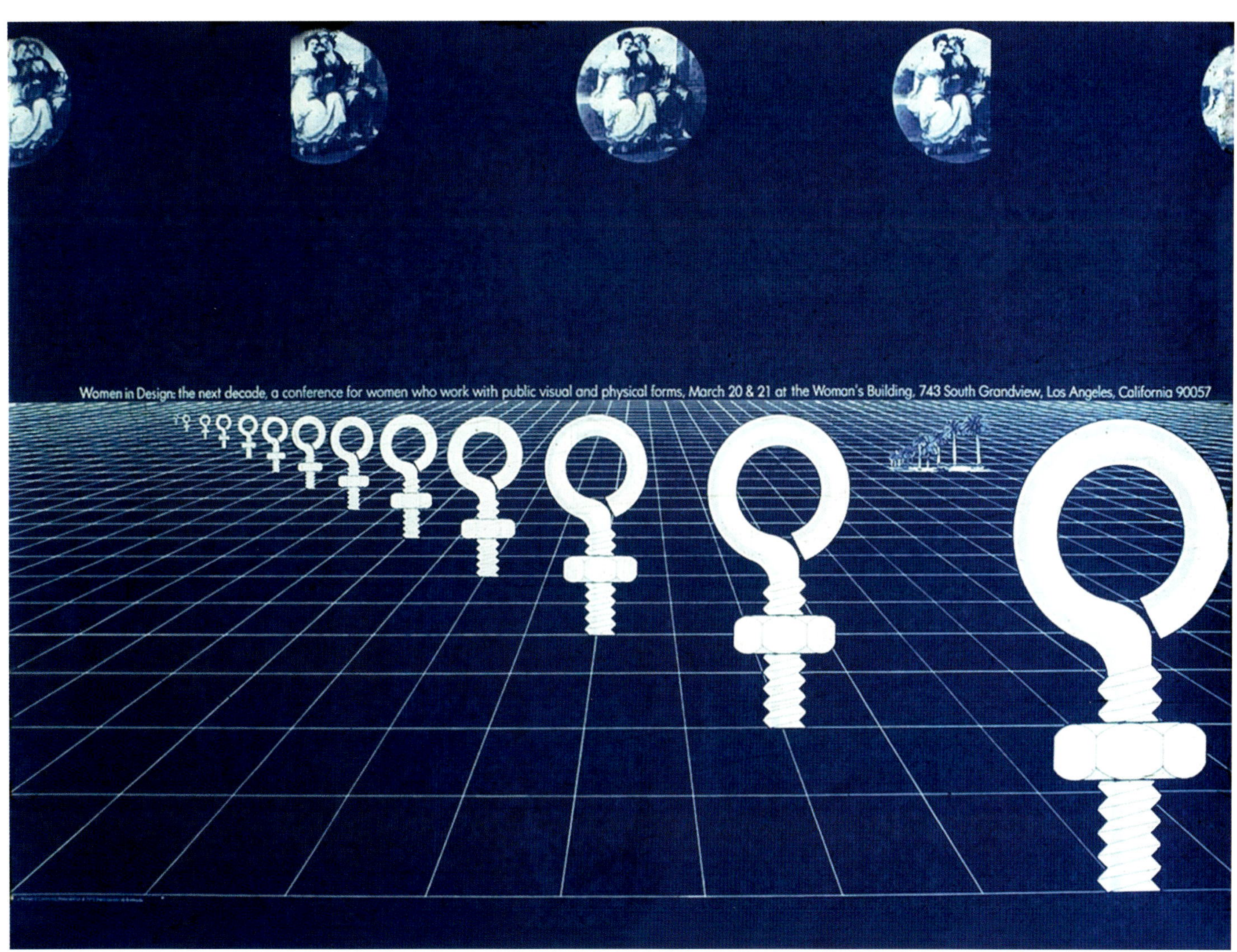

Women in Design: The Next Decade 1975
Sheila Levrant de Bretteville
Diazo poster

The first national conference on 'Women in Design: The Next Decade' was held at the Woman's Building (Grandview Street site) in Los Angeles, a public centre for women's culture founded in 1973 by Sheila Levrant de Bretteville, Judy Chicago and Arlene Raven. It offered an alternative space for feminist studies, the making and exhibiting of art and other activities, and also housed de Bretteville's Women's Graphic Center, offering teaching and print facilities to women as a way of making their own personal 'voice' or experiences visible. Sheila Levrant de Bretteville's contribution to the Women's Liberation movement, and her impact on the design world and design education in the USA, have been substantial and long-lasting.

Gay Liberation and Pride

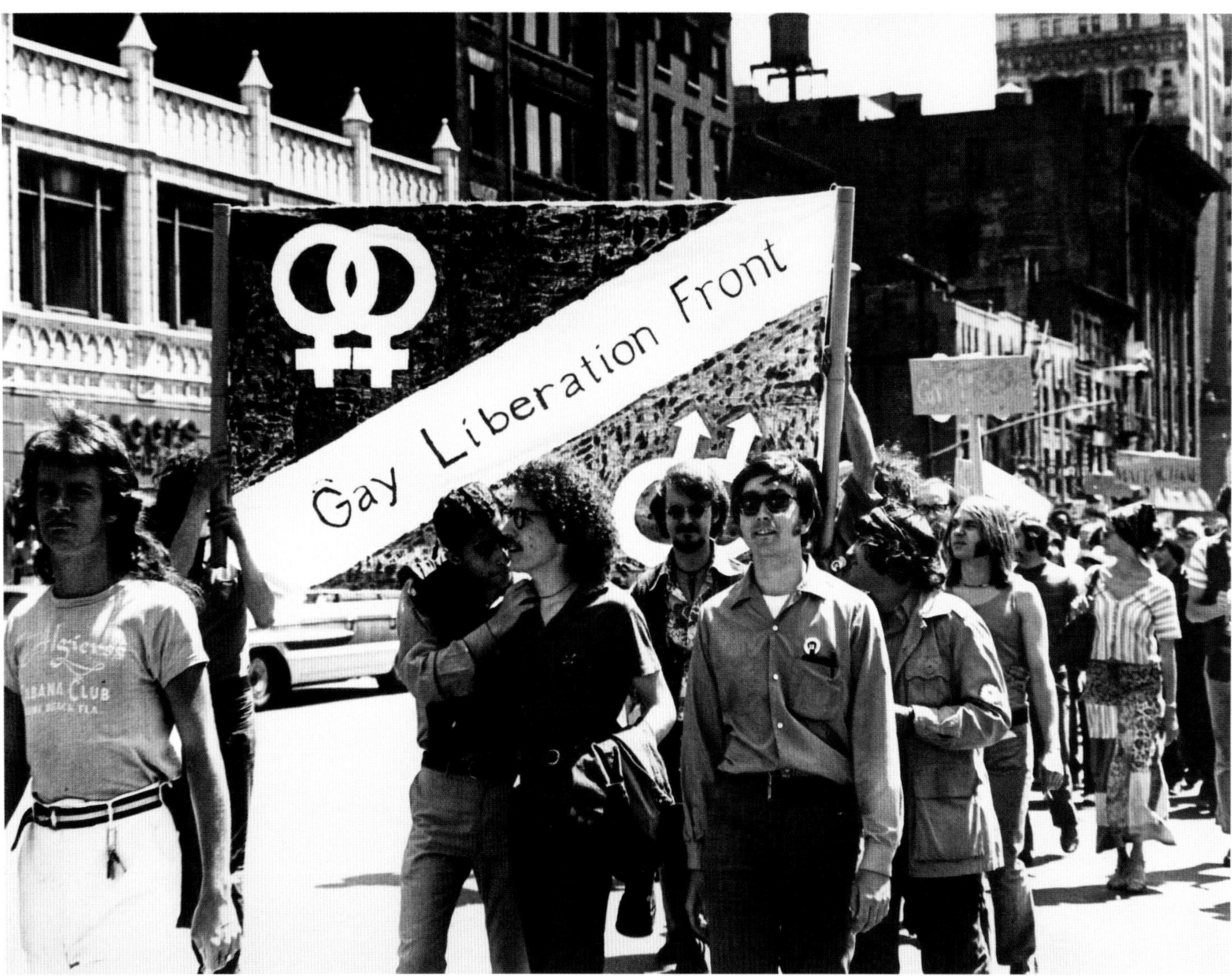

First Gay Pride March, New York 1970
Photographer unknown
Photograph

The Gay Liberation movement was born in New York City with the Stonewall Riots of 1969. The Stonewall operated as a private club and drew a devoted clientele of young gay men. It was one of the few gay clubs where patrons could dance and cross-dress. Police routinely raided the place, but it is thought the management bribed them for protection and the raids were really for show. On 24 June, another raid took place by the NYPD's First Division, rather than the local precinct, and on Friday 27 June, they returned to shut the Stonewall down (for good). But it was a day of reckoning: the clientele gathered in front of the bar. When the police van arrived to take away those arrested, the gays fought back. The riot gathered force from onlookers who turned on the bar with garbage cans and fire. The crowd dispersed the next morning, only to re-emerge the following evening as several thousand people took to the streets chanting 'Gay Power!' Riots and demonstrations continued the following week: Gay Liberation had begun. The Gay Liberation Front (GLF) soon grew a network of groups and became the main generator for the movement. One year later, on the anniversary of the riots – 27 June – the first Gay Pride March took place, as shown in this photograph: a celebration of gay presence and a demand for acceptance and recognition.

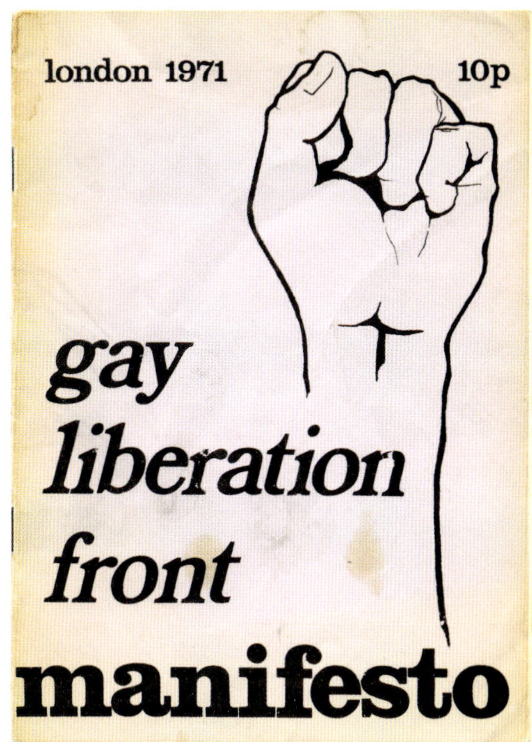

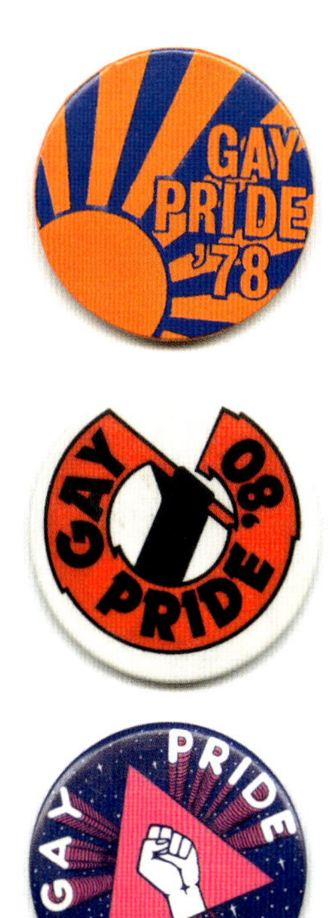

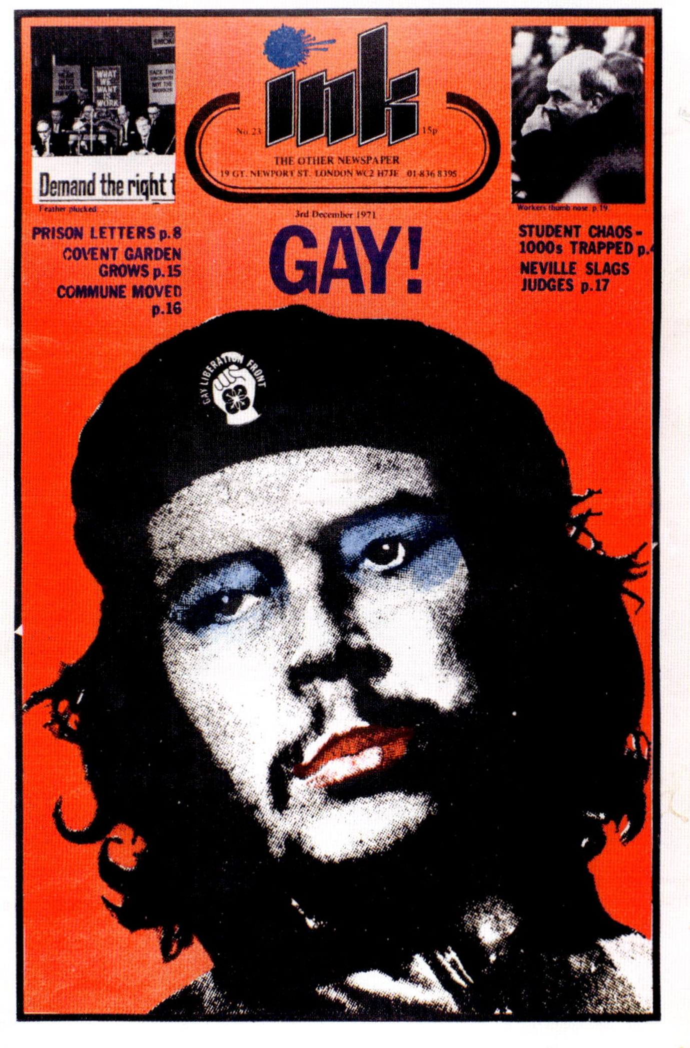

↖ **Gay Liberation Front Manifesto, London** 1971
Pamphlet

London's Gay Liberation Front, which was founded in
the London School of Economics, produced a manifesto,
published in 1971, which set out the key demands and
principles of the GLF. Although the GLF had disbanded
by the end of 1973, its manifesto (and the core principles
stated in it) would influence gay rights organisations
throughout the 1980s and 1990s.

↑ **Gay Liberation badges from Britain** 1970s–80s
Throughout the 1970s and 1980s, the Gay Liberation
movement in Britain had to continually defend
its ground and demand its rights. Therefore the
movement's most memorable images tend to be street
graphics and demo-graphics: placards, posters and
stickers as part of demonstrations or marches. Personal
identity statements, such as badges or t-shirts, also
chronicle the movement's campaigns, protests and
general concerns.

← *Ink* **underground magazine** 1971
Front cover

Ink was one of a number of underground magazines
published in Britain. The 3 December 1971 issue
is shown here, sporting a satirical 'Gay Liberation'
front cover of Che Guevara in makeup (and probably
promising to contain an article about gay issues inside).

May '68 Riots: Atelier Populaire

A

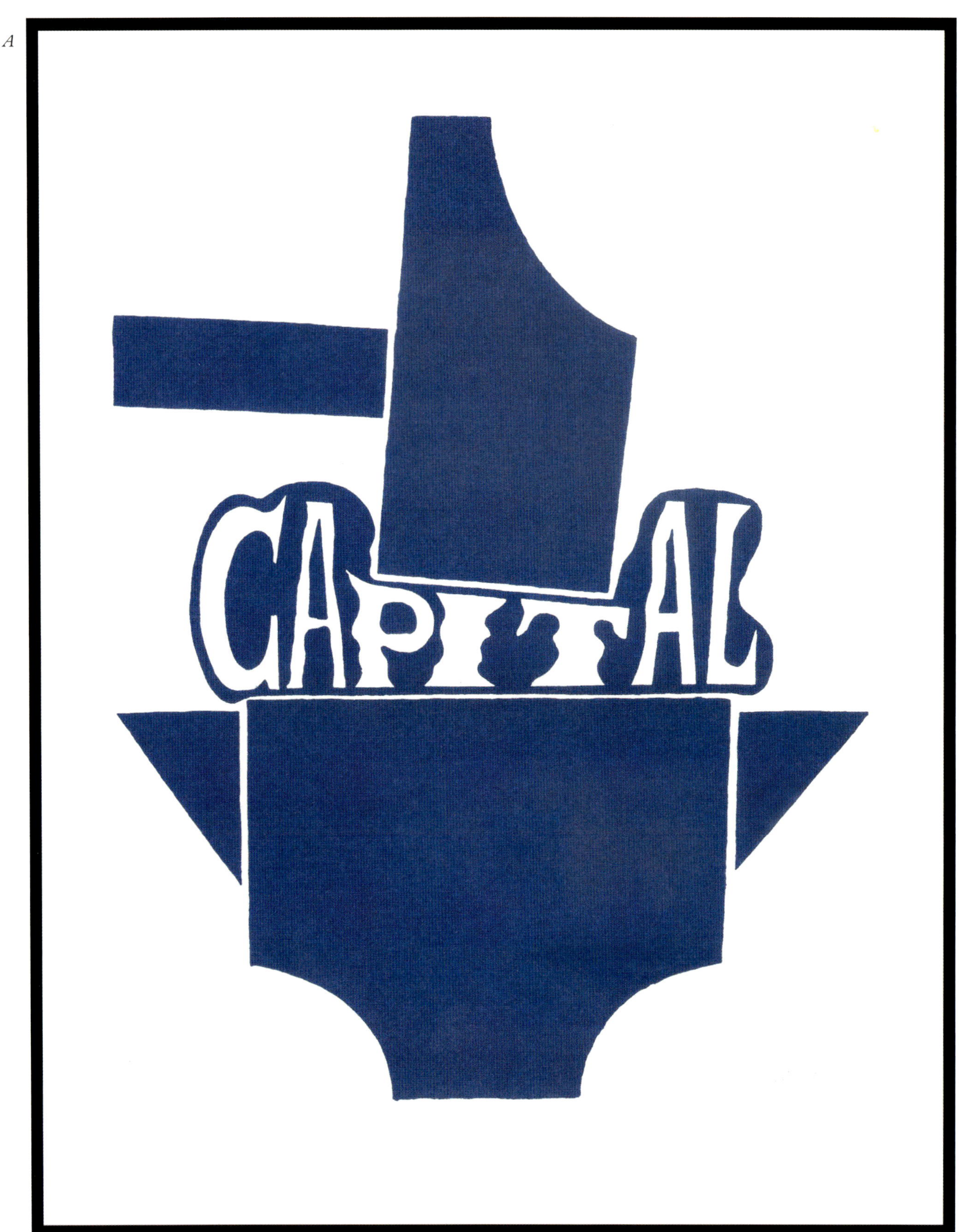

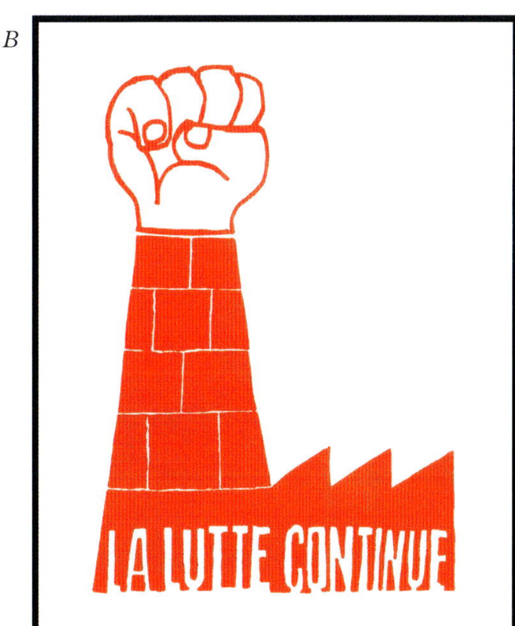

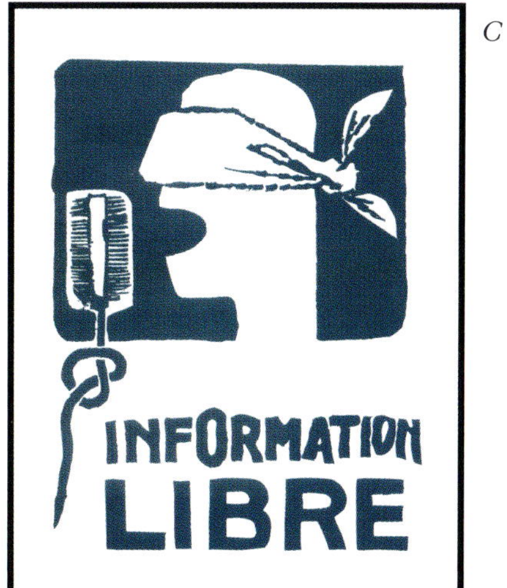

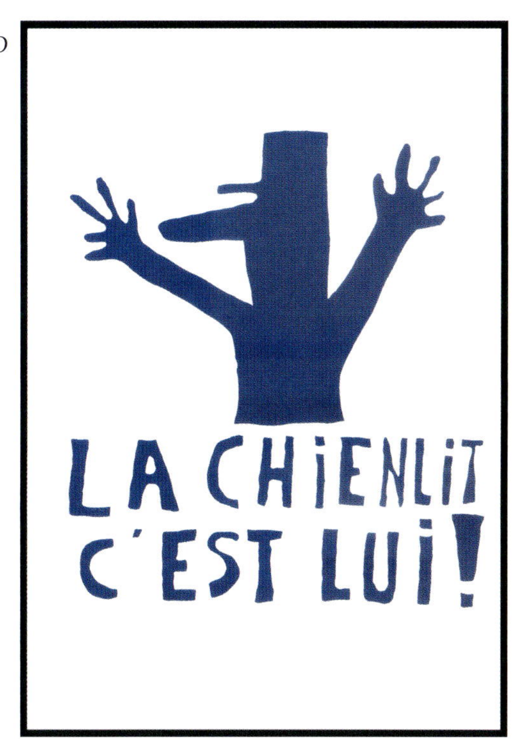

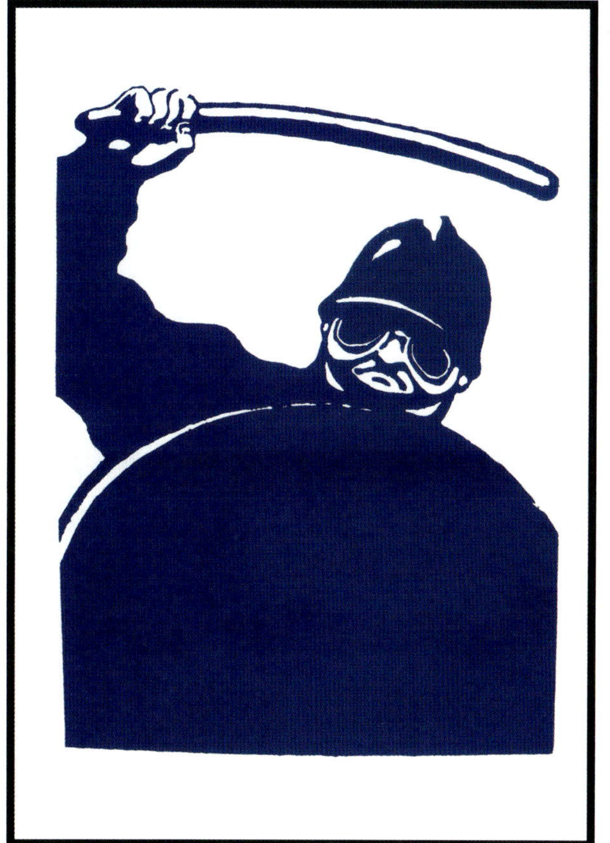

Atelier Populaire, May 1968 1968
Posters

The Paris Riots of May 1968 represented a mass protest against the rigidity of Charles de Gaulle's government and the traditional education system. Workers and students joined forces in a general strike, and factories, offices and schools were occupied. The École des Beaux Arts went on strike; its students formed the 'Atelier Populaire', producing an extraordinary number of posters which were discussed and designed collectively, produced by silkscreen (usually) and pasted up in the streets all over Paris. The drama, excitement and brutality of the events produced posters with a simplicity of shape and directness of message that has been admired ever since. Certain designs were repeated in different variations: the silhouette of De Gaulle (with a long nose), the chimney stack of a factory that becomes a raised fist, and a vicious policeman wielding a baton or club: an indicator of the riot police or CRS (Compagnies Républicaines de Sécurité), whose shield is sometimes marked with a Nazi 'SS' by the artist-protesters. The posters shown here hint at the speed, ingenuity and brilliance of it all.

Translations:
(Image A) Capital
(Image B) The struggle continues
(Image C) Free information
(Image D) He's the shitty mess! (De Gaulle)
(Image E) (From a design by Jacques Carelman)

1970s Youth Rebellion: Punk

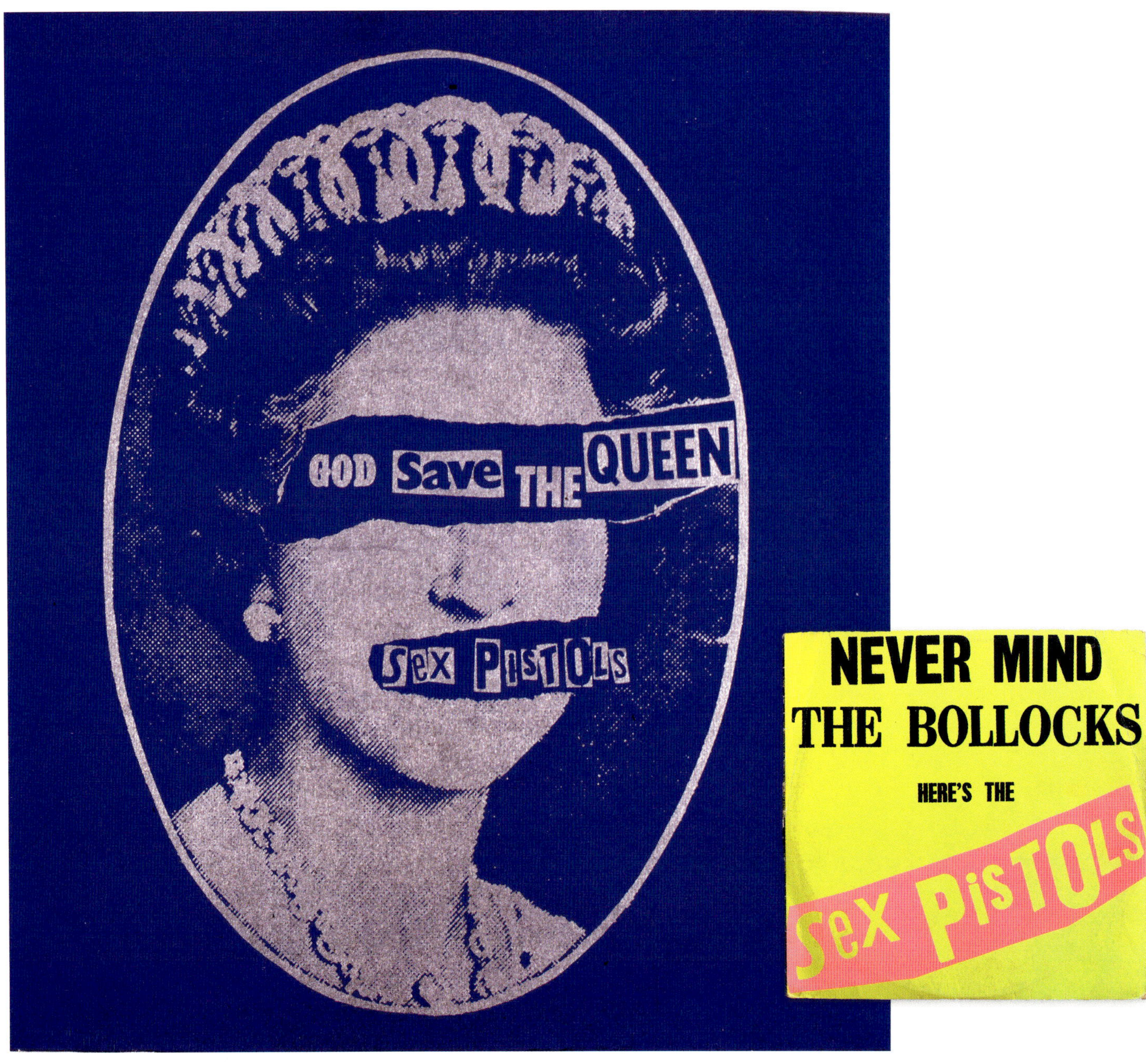

'God Save the Queen' –
The Sex Pistols 1977
Jamie Reid
Record cover (single)

In the economic depression of mid-1970s Britain, a youth revolution took hold through self-styled subversion fuelled by the energy of the street. The spirit of 'Punk' involved hating authority and the establishment, but finding excitement and creativity in the music of loud, aggressive bands such as the Sex Pistols, the enterprise of producing do-it-yourself fanzines, and the assemblage of DIY fashion or street style: the more exhibitionist and subversive, the better. Jamie Reid created a graphic language for Punk, working with mixed typefaces, collage, 'ransom' lettering, cut-out shapes or screamingly loud soapbox colours, and applied them to his promotional material for the Sex Pistols. He was therefore responsible for one of Punk's most iconic images: the poster and record cover for the Sex Pistols' single 'God Save the Queen', produced in 1977, the year of Queen Elizabeth's Silver Jubilee. It was a controversial single, with graphics to match: a well-known portrait of the Queen is more or less mutilated by placing a strip of ransom lettering across her eyes (the title of the song) and another across her mouth (saying 'Sex Pistols'). Both the song and the graphics caused outrage and offence; the spirit of Punk had achieved its mission.

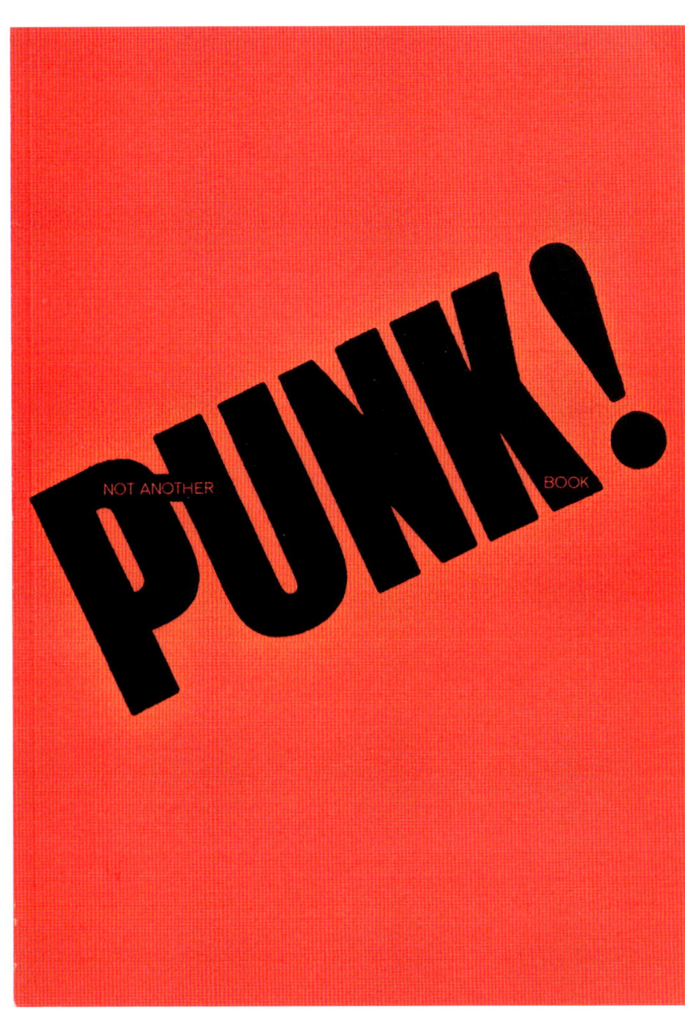

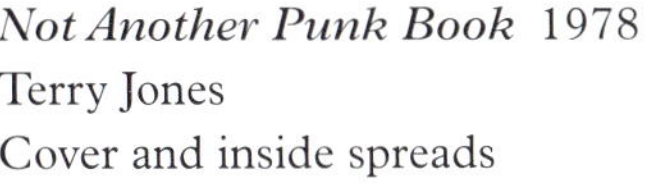

Not Another Punk Book 1978
Terry Jones
Cover and inside spreads

Terry Jones' *Not Another Punk Book* produced a
portrait of Punk's inimitable, self-styled fashion or
'street style', and the people who wore it. It includes
a young Vivienne Westwood wearing her 'Destroy'
t-shirt. Westwood's designs for Seditionaries, the
Punk clothes shop she ran with Malcolm McLaren,
created a new style direction that saw clothing as a
kind of subversion. Terry Jones lived up to notions
of Punk graphics with an anarchic sense of layout,
limited colour and a mixture of typefaces (including
the use of Dymo-tape, where lines of type are
punched into long strips of industrial tape).

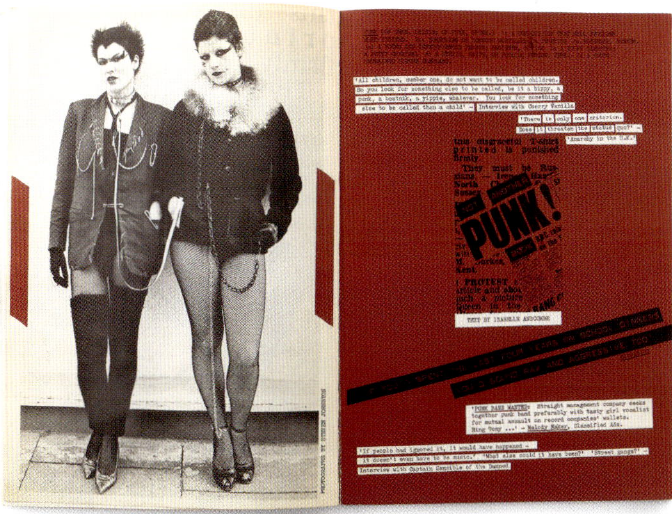

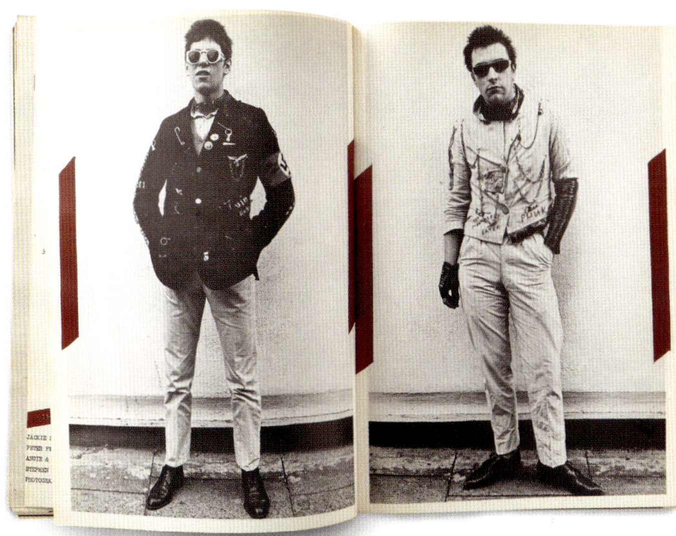

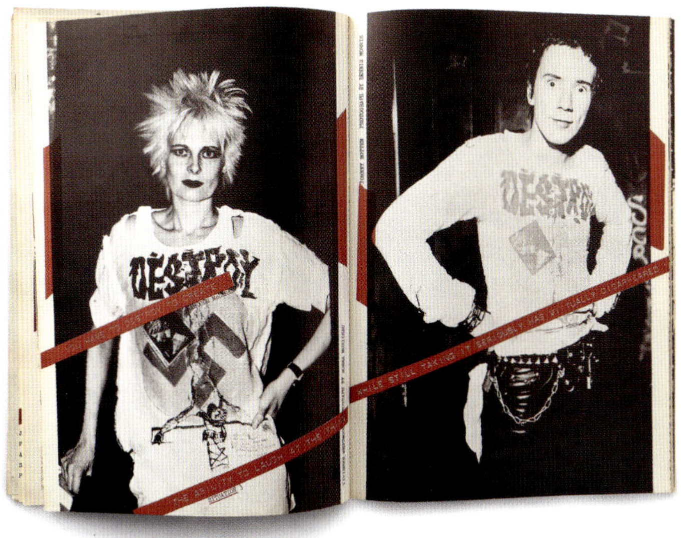

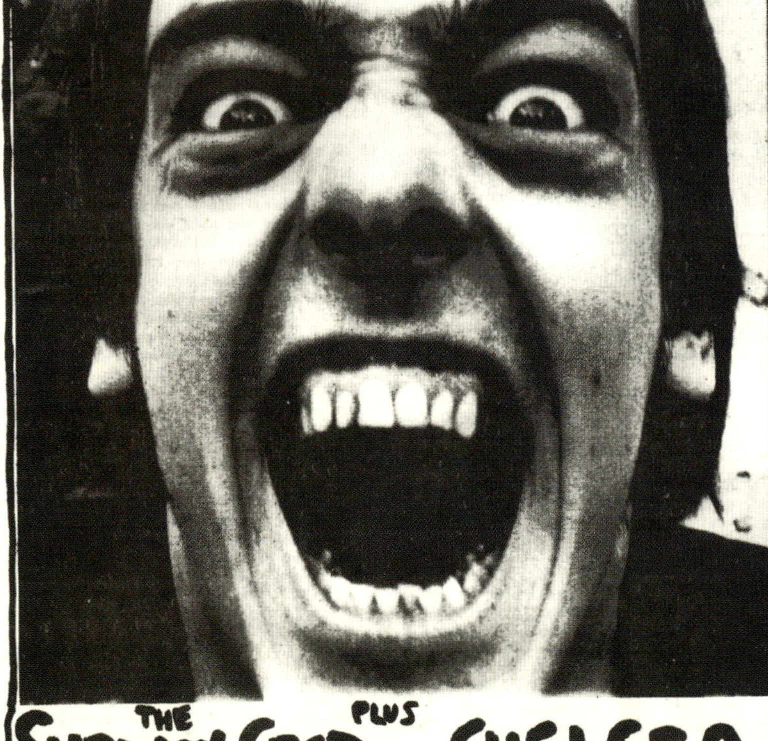

← *Sniffin' Glue*, No. 5, November 1976 1976
Mark P and others
Self-published fanzine

Punk's irreverence found a natural method of expression in cut-and-paste lettering, cheap photocopying, collage, felt-tip markers and other elements of DIY print or image-making. Self-published fanzines, or zines, were the masters of this approach, often dealing with bands, music reviews or the boredom of the everyday. (And some of their writers later transformed into journalists for national newspapers.) *Sniffin' Glue* is repeatedly voted the best of the lot, and is considered to have kickstarted Punk's zine explosion.

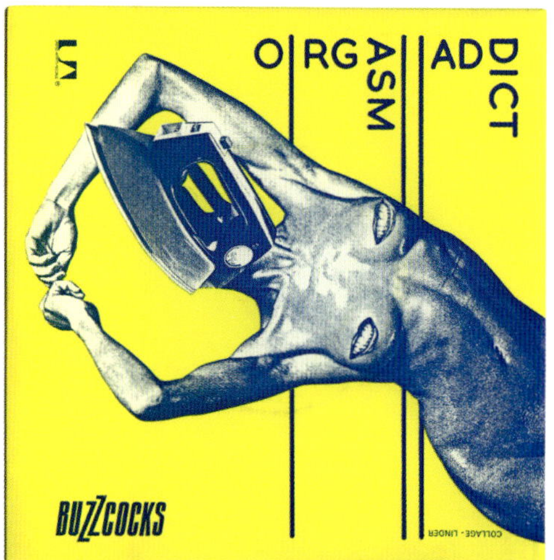

← 'Orgasm Addict' 1977
Design: Malcolm Garrett
Photomontage: Linder
Record cover (single)

This record cover for the Buzzcocks, 'Orgasm Addict' was designed by Malcolm Garrett and used an iconic Punk image by Linder.

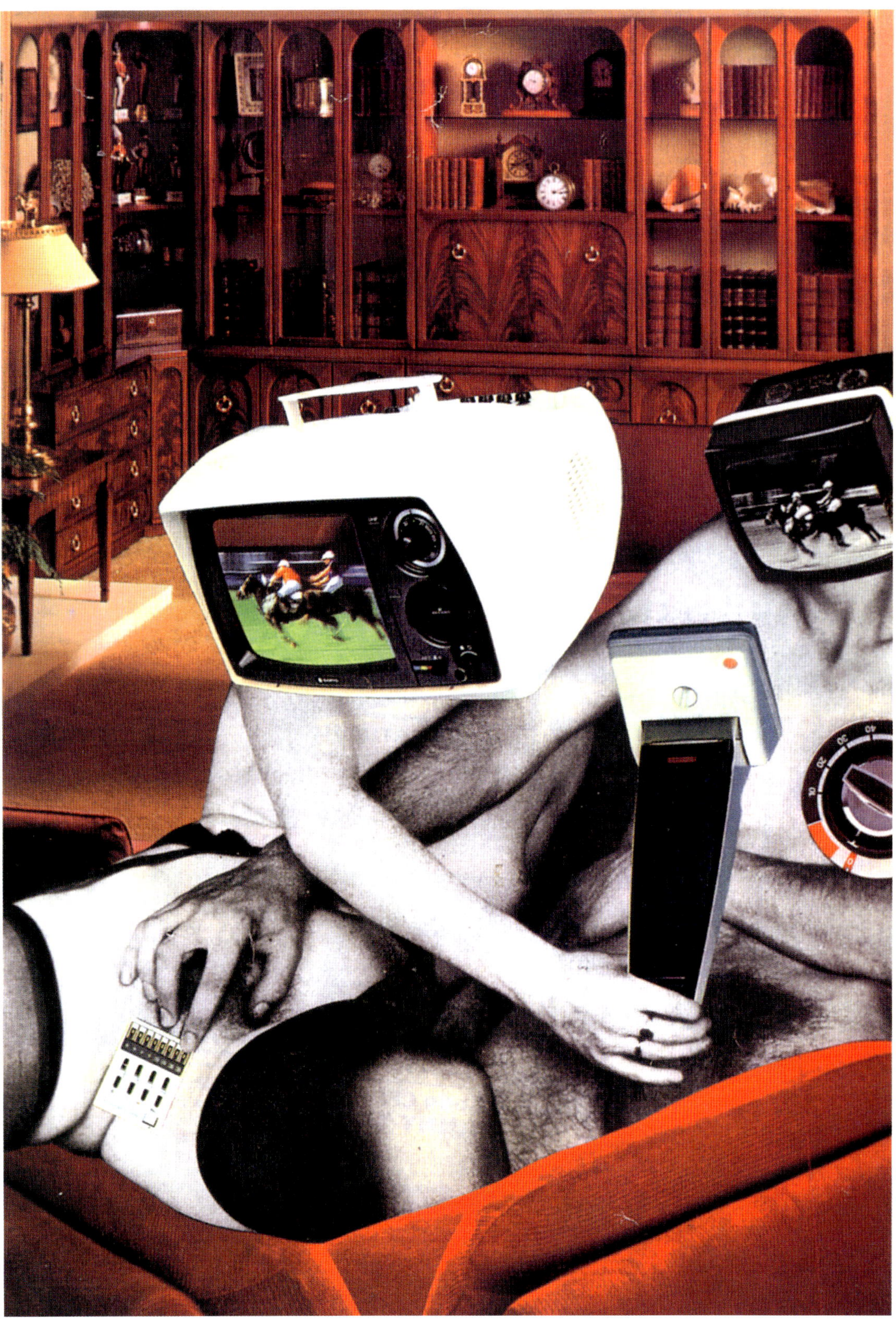

Punk photomontage *c.*1977
Linder

Punk's subversive imagery could be found in the art of music promotional material, record cover sleeves, fanzines and especially in the extraordinary photomontages of the Manchester-based artist, Linder. Often depicting the everyday (food, relationships, interiors, appliances) her graphic marriage of imagery from both men's magazines (cars, porn) and women's magazines (fashion, the home) created a disturbing world of possession and sexual demand indicative of that time period, and from which a new generation (of feminists) would plan their escape.

The Environmental Movement

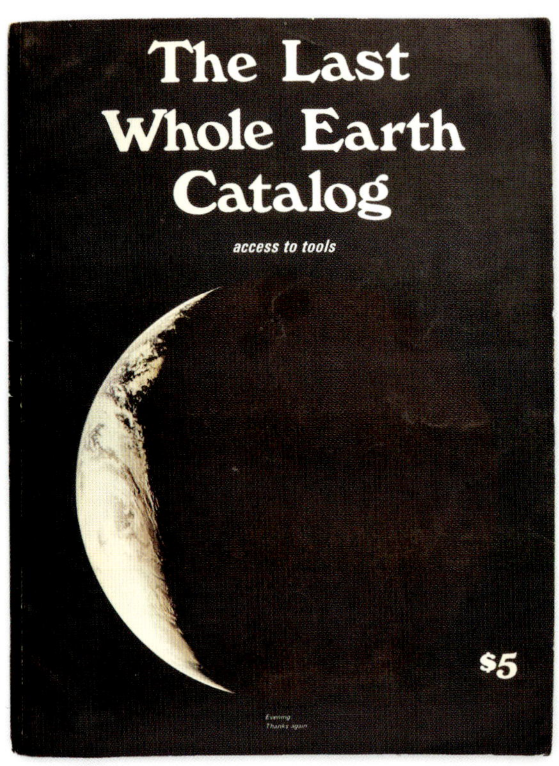

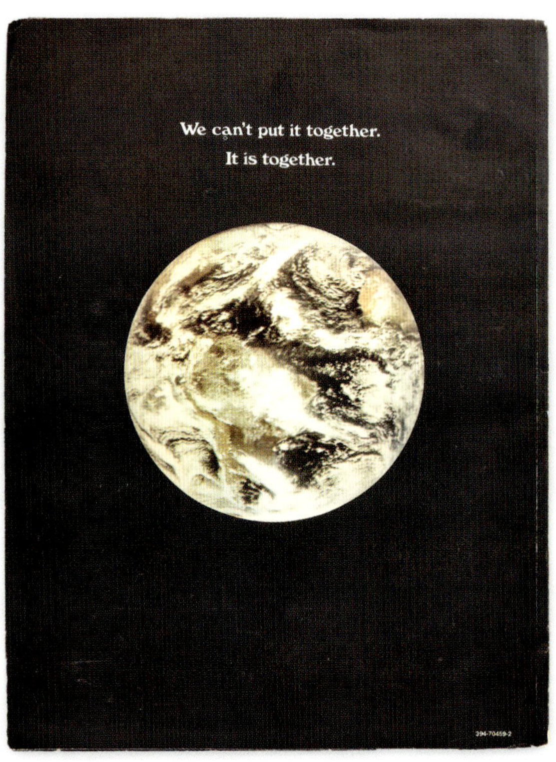

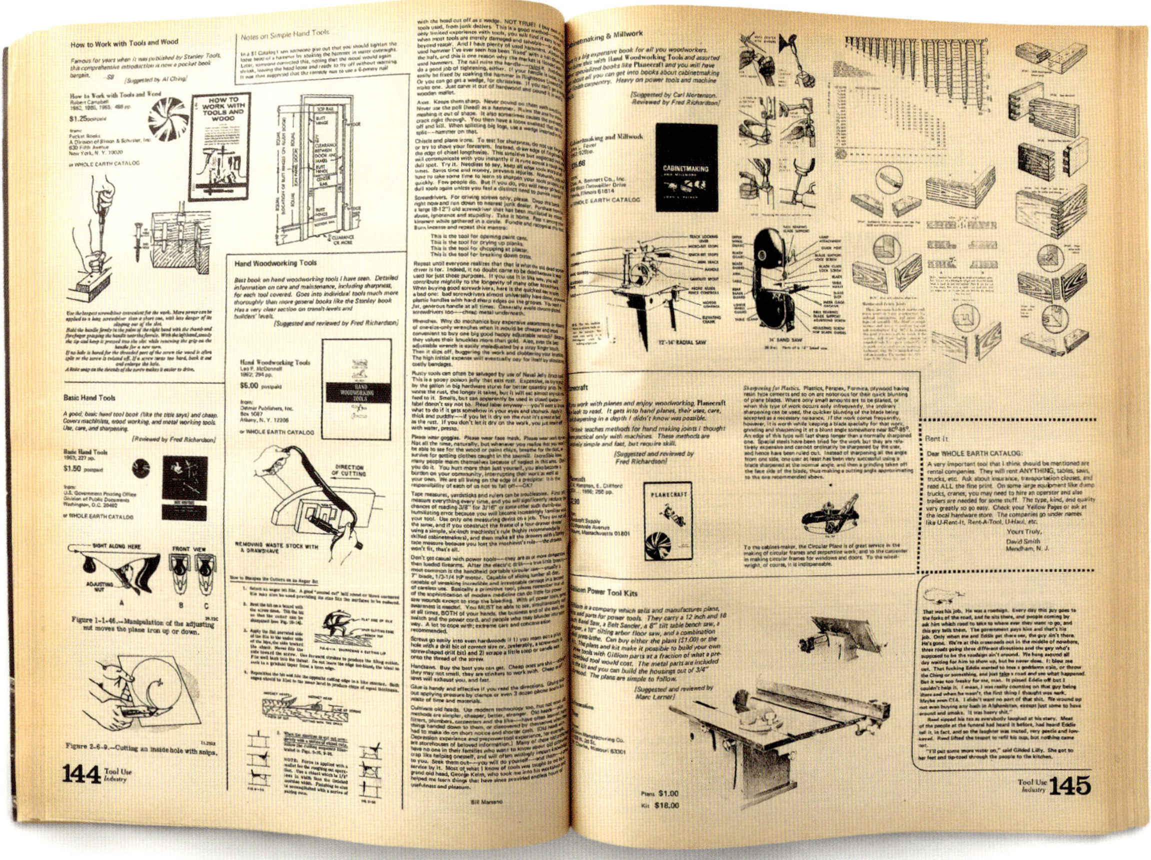

← *The Last Whole Earth Catalog:*
Access to Tools 1970
Stewart Brand
Book: front and back cover, inside spread

The Whole Earth Catalog had its roots in the visionary
thinking of 1960s US counterculture. It was a vast
compendium of 'tools' for thinking and surviving,
encouraging readers to question the power systems
and attitudes of the time, while sharing information
on the route to self-education and empowerment.
Founded, edited and designed by Stewart Brand,
entries included information about building materials,
solar energy and bee-keeping as well as yoga, self-
hypnotism and Tantra art – all accompanied by
evaluative commentary and sources. A best-seller
with many editions and permutations, the first catalog
(1968) was 64 pages and the last (1971) was over 300,
although there were further variations under the name
of 'Whole Earth' thereafter. Its main delight was, in
its later editions, its large format (about 36 x 28cm,
14 x 11in), its cluttered mass of images, headings and
fonts, and its absence of a clear pathway through the
material, which allowed the reader to make interesting
connections between different worlds of information,
leading some to see it as a forerunner of the internet.
The front and back covers bear the final lasting
statement – a photograph taken from outer space of
the 'whole earth', beautiful and fragile. Its concluding
comment: 'We can't put it together. It is together.'

→ Earth Day 1970
Robert Rauschenberg
Poster (offset lithography)

Although the seeds of environmentalism were
sown in the 1960s, the First Earth Day (USA)
was held on 22 April 1970 to focus public
attention on environmental issues and consolidate
the new, fast-growing, Earth movement. On
Robert Rauschenberg's poster for the event, the
aggressively staring bald eagle became a symbolic
guardian of the movement, emanating a sense of
responsibility and a call to action, while surrounded
by collected imagery of environmental devastation
in the background. The Earth movement, or Green
movement, would adopt more radical attitudes
and campaigns in the 1980s, but Earth Day USA
celebrations were revived in 1990 and continue
annually, a tribute to (local) community action on
environmental issues.

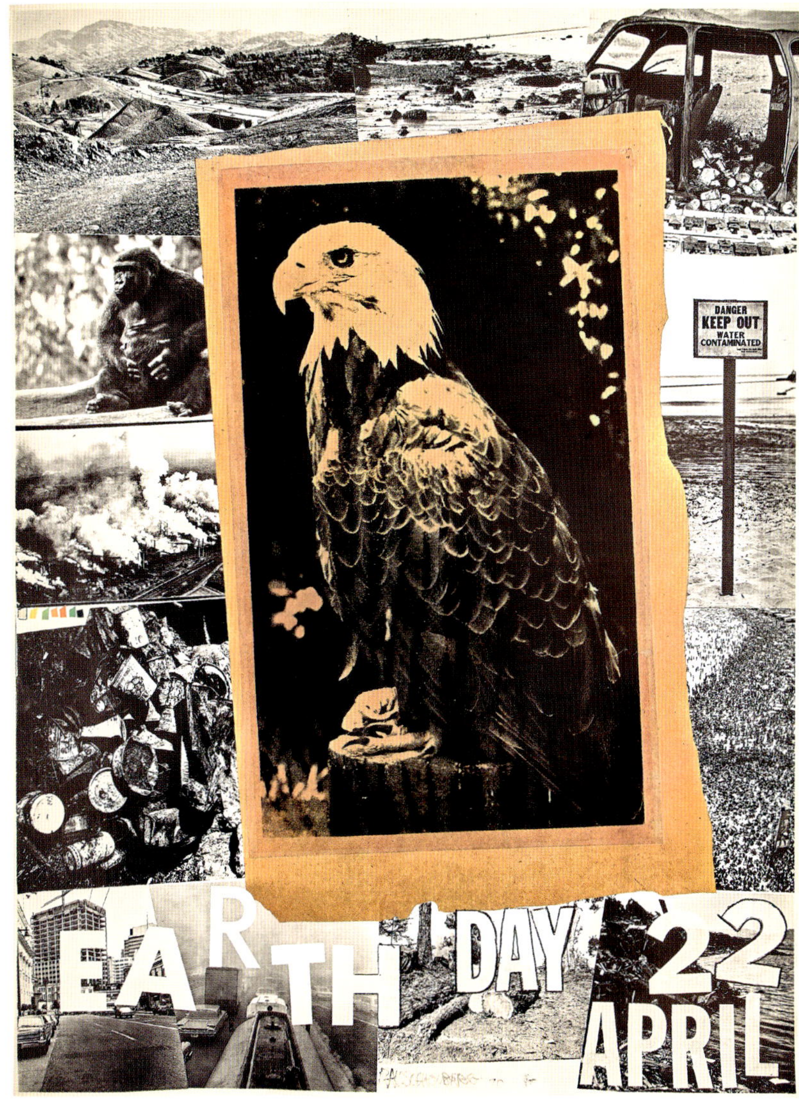

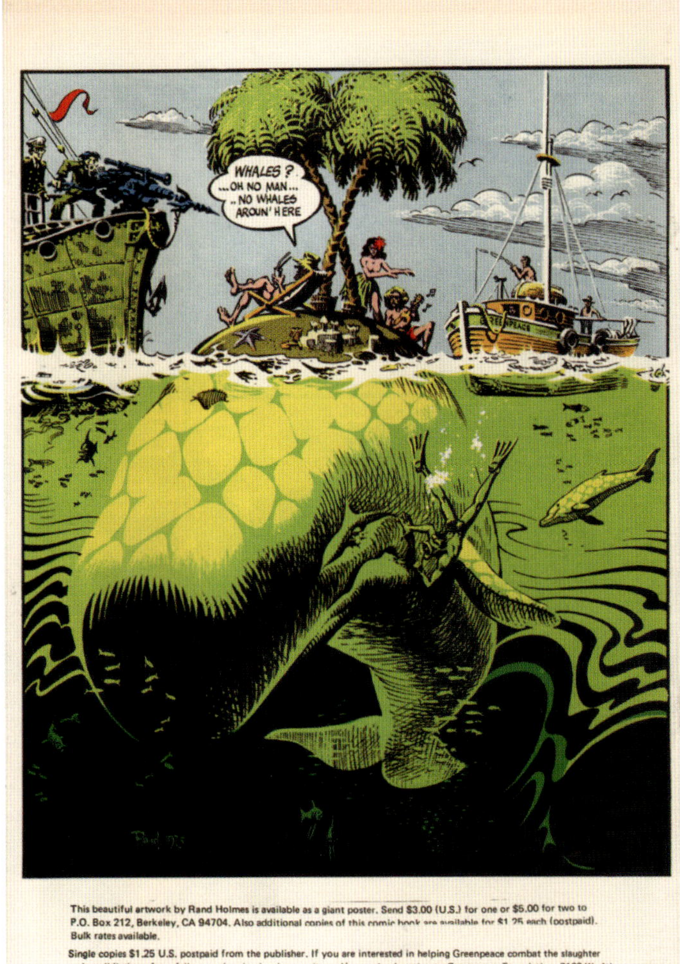

This beautiful artwork by Rand Holmes is available as a giant poster. Send $3.00 (U.S.) for one or $5.00 for two to P.O. Box 212, Berkeley, CA 94704. Also additional copies of this comic book are available for $1.25 each (postpaid). Bulk rates available.

Single copies $1.25 U.S. postpaid from the publisher. If you are interested in helping Greenpeace combat the slaughter and annihilation of our fellow earth animals, please write and/or send a donation to Greenpeace Foundation, 2108 W. 4th Ave., Vancouver, B.C. Canada V6J 1W7 or Greenpeace Foundation, Fort Mason, San Francisco, CA. 94123, USA.

↑ **Whales?** 1975
Randolph Holme
Magazine illustration (offset)

Founded in 1971, Greenpeace began its first campaign against whaling in 1975. This anti-whaling illustration is by Randolph Holme, contributor to the underground newspaper, *Georgia Straight*, which reported on early Greenpeace actions.

↗ **Critical Mass 74** 1974
Artist: Arnold Saks
Poster

Maverick US lawyer and social crusader Ralph Nader took on the automotive industry for its poor safety standards in the 1960s (and won). His consumer rights movement also investigated nuclear power.

→ **Die Grünen (The Green Party)** 1979
Poster

This was the first major poster produced by Die Grünen, the West German political party, founded and led by the dynamic Petra Kelly in 1979. It states 'We have only borrowed the earth.'

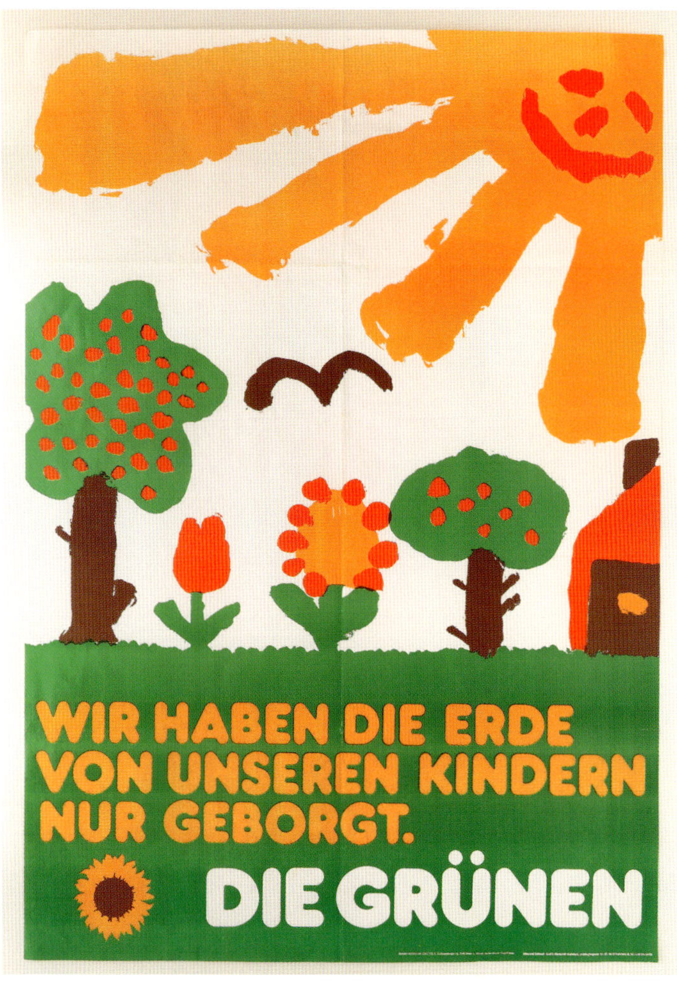

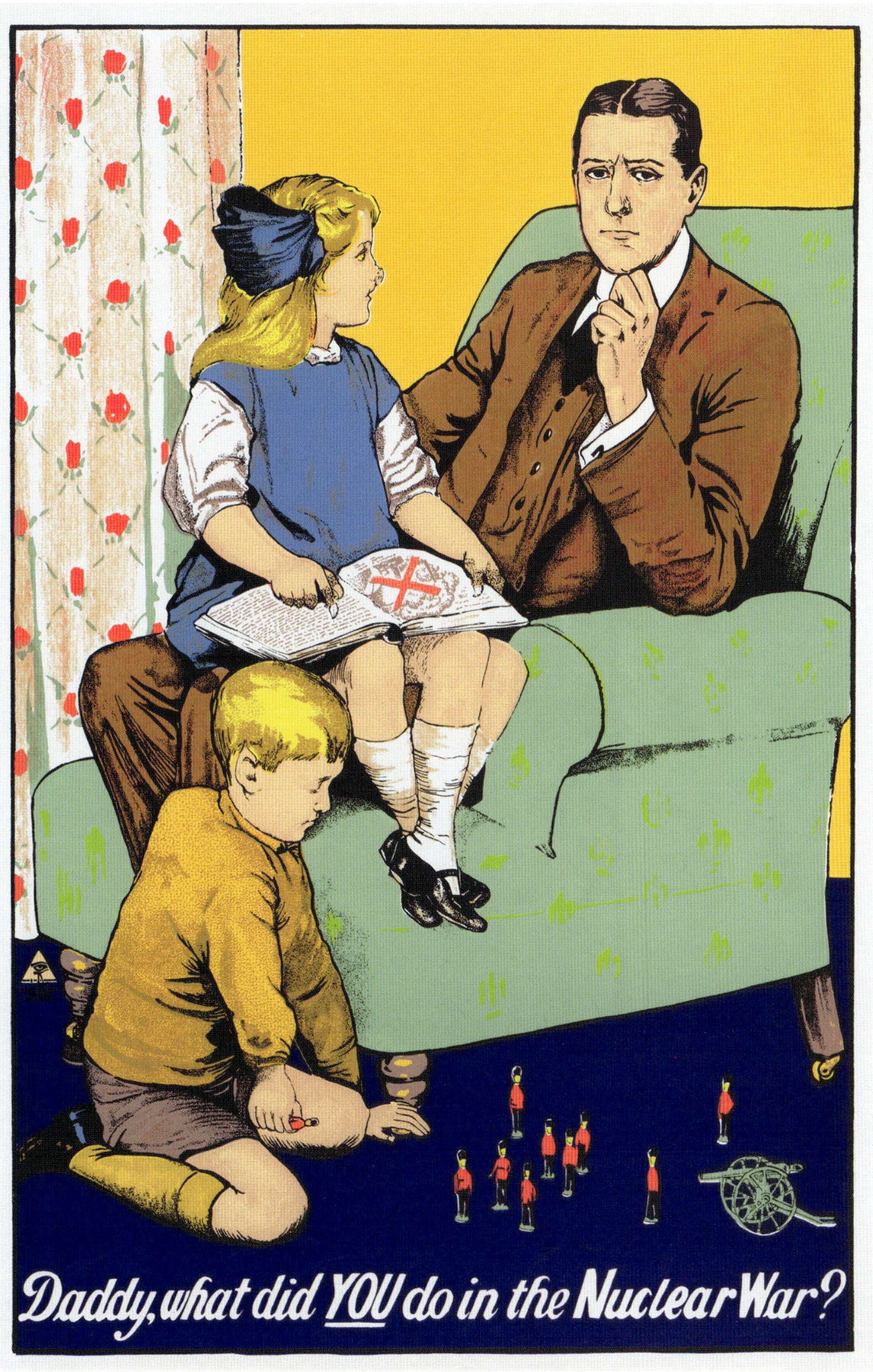

'Daddy, What Did YOU Do in the Nuclear War?' 1977
Toni Robertson and Chips Mackinolty
(Earthworks Poster Collective)
Poster

Starting in the 1960s, France tested nuclear bombs at Mururoa Atoll in the South Pacific. As testing continued in the 1970s, nuclear disarmament protests combined with human rights and environmental protests, particularly in the minds of politicized Australian poster collectives. They produced posters campaigning for a 'nuclear free Pacific' well into the 1980s, in an effort to stop such testing as well as promote awareness of its effects on the Islanders. (It wasn't stopped until 1995.) This poster is a parody of a well-known First World War recruitment poster, but its message has become distorted as an alert to other (nuclear) dangers, such as disease and generational human defects: both of the children are drawn with deformities.

International Solidarity

Las Madres de Plaza de Mayo *c.*1977
Photographer: Daniel Garcia
Photograph

In Argentina, from 1976 to 1983, up to 30,000 men, women and
children were 'disappeared' by the military junta in an attempt
to rid themselves of any opposition. (At least 5,000 of those
were subjected to the 'death flights' known as 'destino final';
they were drugged and, during the flight, thrown into the sea.)
Relatives had no idea of their whereabouts or demise, and any
enquiries went unanswered. On 30 April 1977, fourteen women
gathered in the Plaza de Mayo in Buenos Aires, demanding
information about their kidnapped children. Every Thursday
they came at 3.30p.m., and their numbers grew. When told
to move on, they walked slowly in circles around the square,
carrying large photographs of the 'disappeared', and were soon
known as 'Las Madres de Plaza de Mayo' (the Mothers of the
Plaza de Mayo). Some of the Mothers were tortured or killed,
but their numbers still grew until hundreds took part in the
protests each week, wearing white headscarves (bearing the
name of a loved one) and/or carrying large photographs of those
missing. After the military junta ended in 1983, the Mothers
and (now) Grandmothers of the Plaza de Mayo continued their
search to find out what had happened to their loved ones, or
to at least identify their remains. Although, as of 2019, a small
presence is still maintained in the Plaza de Mayo, much of their
search now takes place online by means of the Grandmothers'
website (www.abuelas.org.ar), Facebook and Twitter.

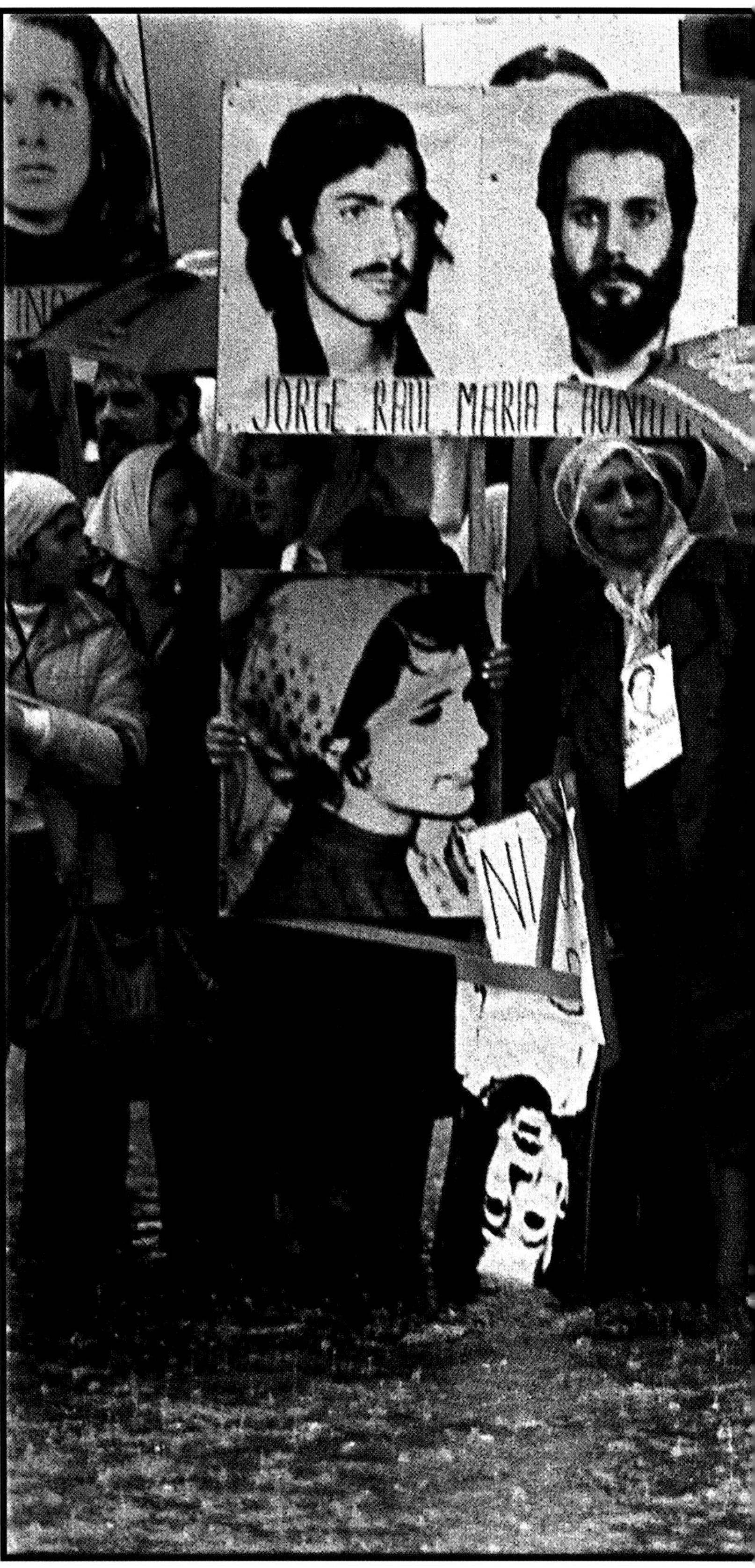

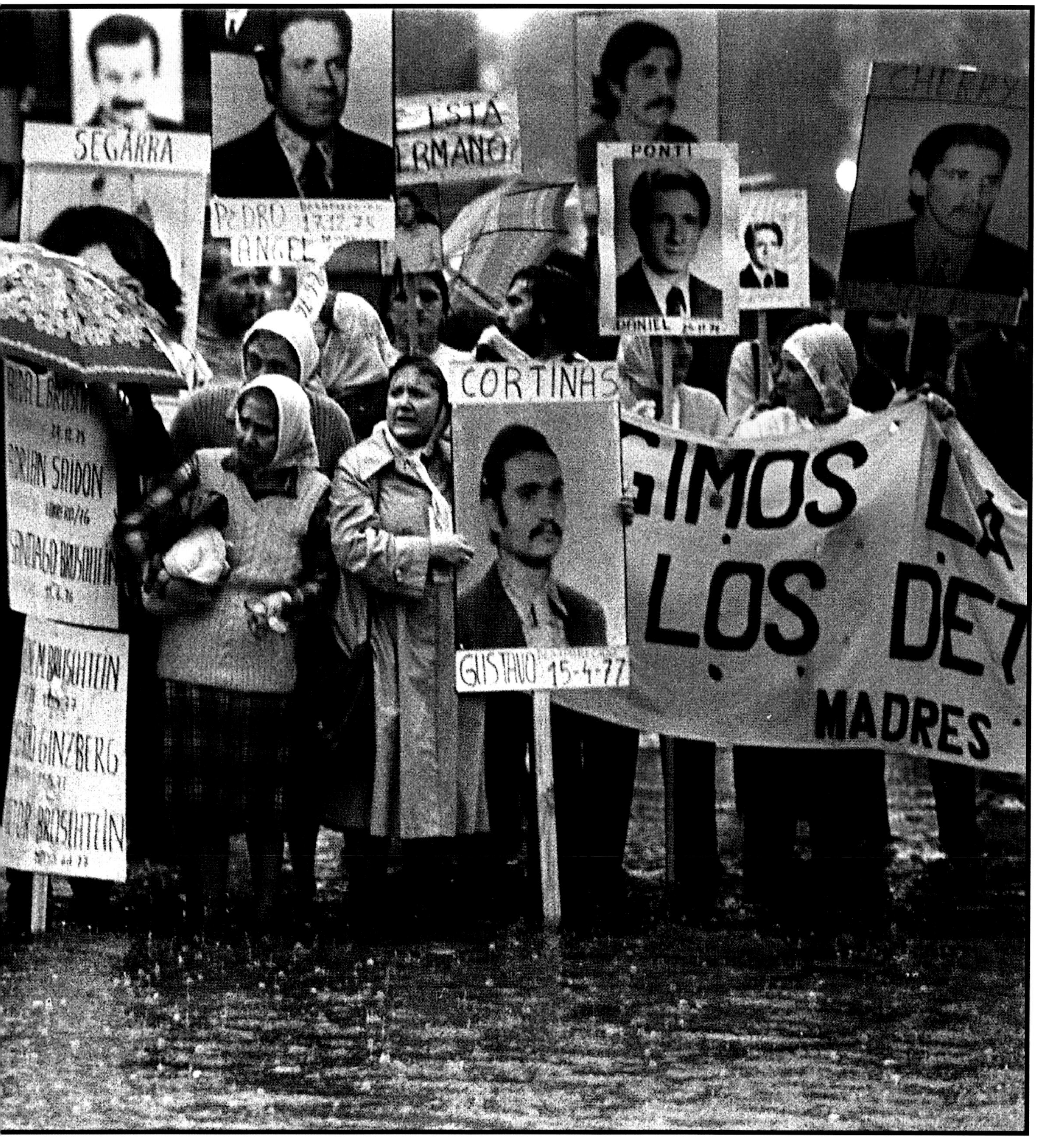

SEGARRA
PEDRO ANGEL
PONTI
DANIEL
CHERY
ESTÁ
ERMANO
CORTINAS
GUSTAVO 15-11-77
GIMOS L
LOS DE 7
MADRES

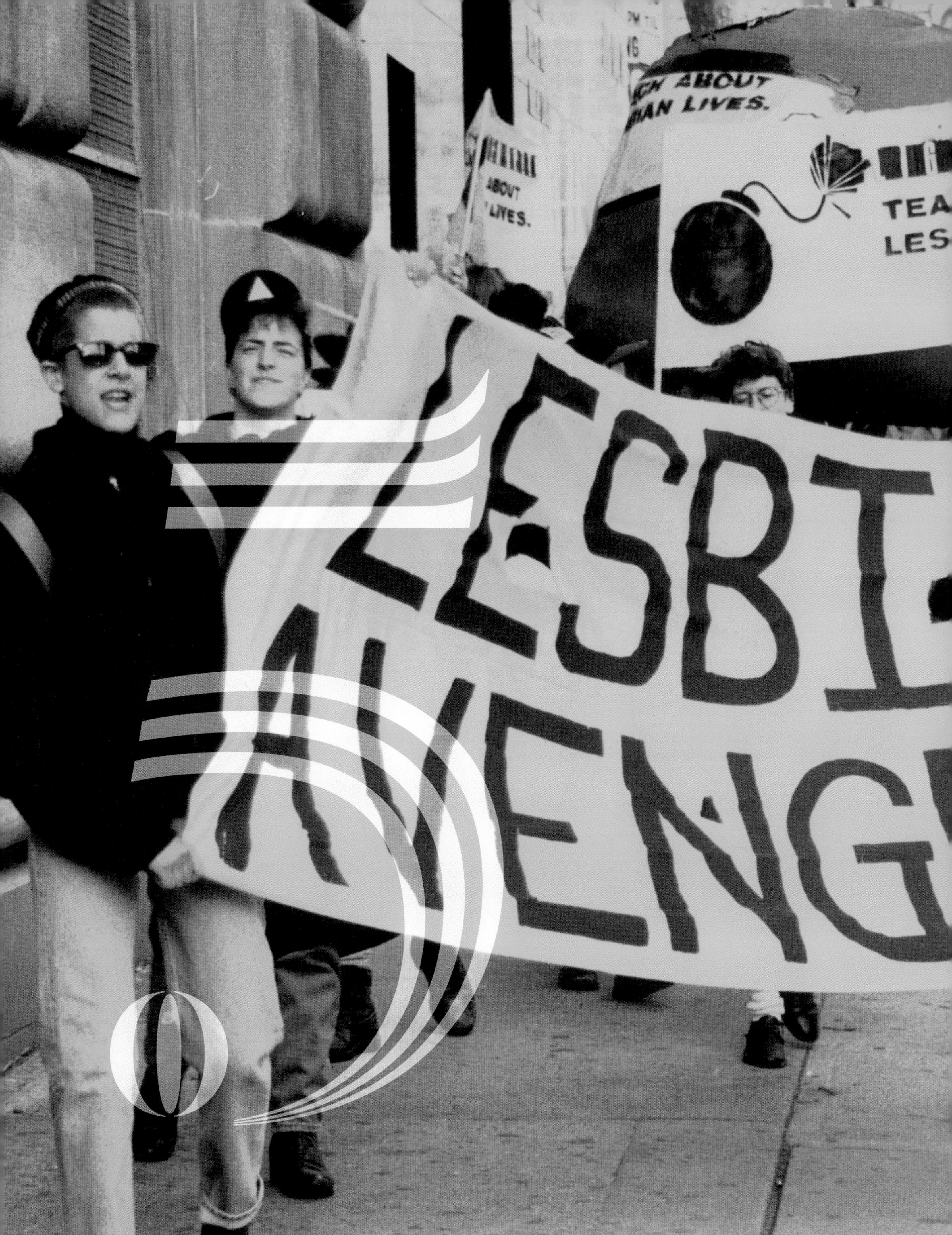

ACH ABOUT
BIAN LIVES.
ABOUT
LIVES.
TEA
LES
ESBIA
VENGE

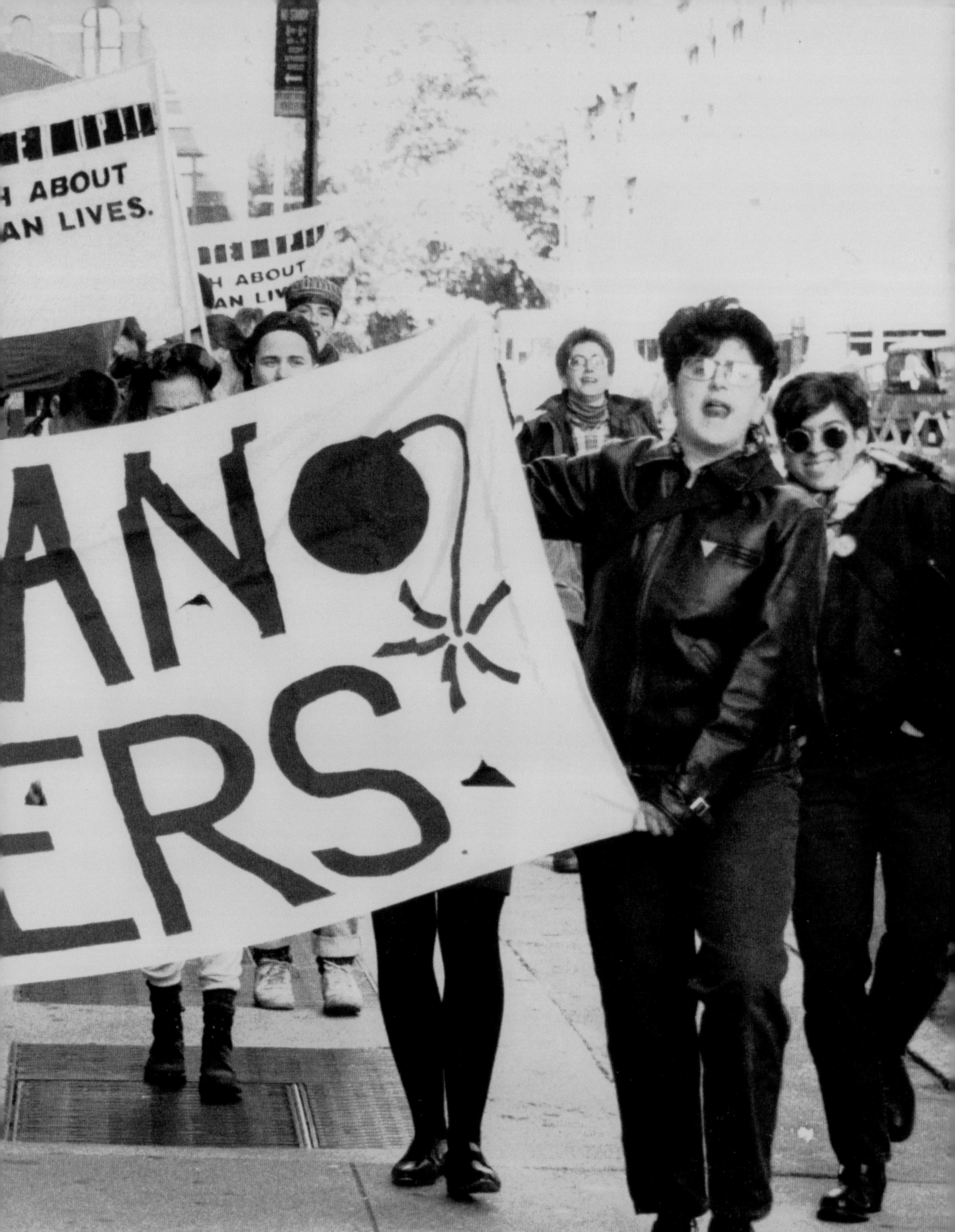

H ABOUT
AN LIVES.
H ABOUT
AN LIV
ANO
ERS

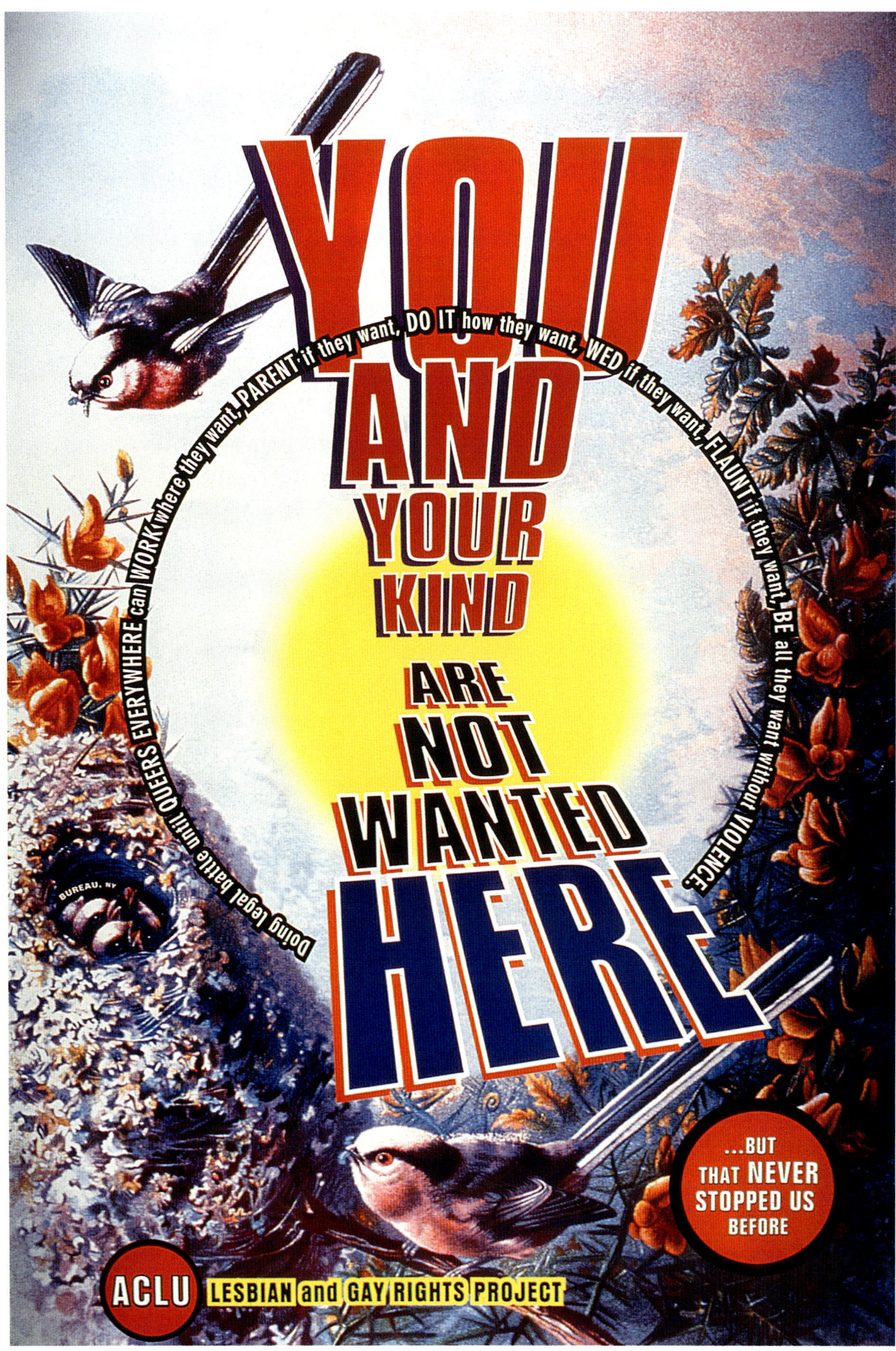

You and Your Kind Are Not Wanted Here... But that Never Stopped Us Before (ACLU Lesbian and Gay Rights Project Poster) 1994, Marlene McCarty and Donald Moffet at Bureau

1980–2000

The AIDS Crisis and Other Global Tensions

Protests staged by Britain's Campaign for Nuclear Disarmament (CND) continued throughout the 1960s, but were slowly overtaken by more violent protests against US intervention in the Vietnam War. Despite the 'special relationship', Britain refused to join the USA in active fighting in Vietnam. In the 1970s the British public increasingly felt that Britain's location between two global superpowers, locked in an arms race, made it a potential middle-stage for nuclear attack. When NATO decided to deploy US Cruise missiles in British Army bases in 1979, CND and the peace movement sprang to life with renewed energy, driven by a new, young generation of activists. Artist Peter Kennard produced extremely popular photomontages and graphics for CND and the Greater London Council, often satirizing the British government's civil defence plan and information booklet, as both were considered useless.

In 1981 a group named 'Women for Life on Earth' marched from Cardiff in Wales to the Greenham Common military base, which was due to house US Cruise missiles, and established the Women's Peace Camp at Greenham Common. The camp became known for its use of arts and crafts, including banner-making, to produce protest statements that were hung or draped on the base's perimeter fence or scattered throughout the camp. The women engaged in daring actions such as attempts to cut through, or climb over, the perimeter fence. They also received brutal treatment by the press and government of the time. Nevertheless, the camp achieved international renown, and lasted ten years, closing in 1991 when the missiles had left.[1]

Britain's satire boom of the 1960s had led the way in mocking politicians; by the 1980s (and 1990s) such public humiliation had reached new heights. Visual satire was perfected by the latex puppets of 'Spitting Image' (weekly television programme) and the political cartoons of Steve Bell and others, often aimed at Prime Ministers Margaret Thatcher or John Major. At the same time, US guerrilla artist Robbie Conal gave rough treatment to Presidents Ronald Reagan, George Bush and many others.

The 1980s was also marked by the internal struggles of particular countries, each giving rise to graphic statements that carried news of those struggles around the world, often resulting in the creation of solidarity movements. 'The Troubles' was an expression used to describe the British government's war with the Irish Republican Army or IRA, and a consequent 30-year military presence in Northern Ireland. News of the conflict, for example the hunger-strikes of republican political prisoners such as Bobby Sands, was mainly conveyed via news reports or postcards and posters from solidarity groups. But a much closer to home visualization took place in the imposing political wall murals, both loyalist and republican, created in Belfast and other locations in Northern Ireland, depicting memorials, military emblems, heroes and more. Another struggle within Britain was the Miner's Strike of 1984–85. It took place when Margaret Thatcher and her Conservative government attempted to break the power of the trade union movement, and close down 'the pits' or coal mines. At least 165,000 miners went on strike. The strike became famous for the number of riot police employed to break the picket lines, and the brutality meted out to the miners and their supporters. Such incidents were recorded through angry imagery, spread through the public by photographs, posters and postcards. The strike eventually broke and the pits closed, but the damning images remained.[2]

The Israeli-Palestinian conflict has had a long historical past; its most recent chapter started in 1948 with the creation of the state of Israel, and decades of turmoil have continued ever since. International solidarity with the Palestinian resistance was at its height during the 1980s. However, a strong peace movement was also present within Israel at that time, with Israeli organizations such as Peace Now working to bring about peaceful co-existence. Two superb designers have worked particularly hard to promote a peaceful future for both sides, while despairing at the violence occurring along the way. The prolific designer, David Tartakover, has been relentless in his calls for peace. His poster imagery has often been based in a brutal reality (using real occurrences, such as injured children). Yossi Lemel, of a more recent design generation than Tartakover, often deals in symbolic imagery, using just one or a few objects or people that have been instilled with a greater political meaning. In the difficult climate of 21st-century Israel, both designers have continued to use their art to communicate messages of humanity.[3]

A new climate of resistance (against apartheid) was also spreading across South Africa, resulting from the on-going imprisonment of ANC leader Nelson Mandela; the Soweto Uprising (June 1976) when 10–20,000 students marched peacefully and were met with gunfire; the murder of Black Consciousness leader Steve Biko in 1977; and many other tragedies. Also, due to improved global communications, the world was now watching. The growing strength of the international anti-apartheid movement produced solidarity posters, publications and events all over the world. The popular movement within South Africa peaked with the Defiance Campaign of 1989, and the apartheid system began to collapse. Nelson Mandela was released in 1990, and in 1994 he was elected president in the first democratic elections in South Africa, marking the beginning of 'the new South Africa'.[4]

The 1980s marked a move towards conservative politics, with the election of Margaret Thatcher as prime minister in 1979, and Ronald Reagan as US president in 1980, followed by George Bush in 1988. The decade therefore produced a groundswell of activism from feminists, both young and old, in what has been labelled 'Third Wave Feminism'. The art activists, 'Guerrilla Girls', founded in 1985, produced street posters (illegally posted at night) that exposed racism and sexual discrimination in the New York art world, particularly in well-known museums and galleries. The pro-life/pro-choice debate (a woman's right to choose whether she has an abortion or not) surfaced forcefully in the USA, epitomized by Barbara Kruger's outstanding poster for the Pro-Choice March on Washington in 1989. Issues such as abortion rights, violence against women, and sexism in society were all targeted by feminist activist groups such as the Women's Action Coalition, SisterSerpents, and Helaine Victoria Press (dedicated to women's history) in the USA. While in Britain publishing thrived in many forms, such as See Red Women's

Workshop (posters), The Women's Press (books) and do-it-yourself fanzines such as *Shocking Pink* and *Bad Attitude*.[5]

Despite a reported start-date of 1981, conservative governments attempted to ignore the fast-developing AIDS crisis throughout the 1980s. The US activist group known as ACT UP (AIDS Coalition to Unleash Power) was founded in 1987 to combat government inaction. Through their visual campaigns and memorable direct actions, the coalition attacked the lack of government funding for research, the drug approval process, poor access to treatment and care, and the lack of safe-sex education. Within five years they had become a large network of city chapters with an international reach. Their powerful graphic identity, a pink triangle on a stark, black background supported by the words 'Silence = Death', provided a call to action that has resonated ever since. By the early 1990s, the global spread of the disease was slowly being acknowledged. Safe-sex education was produced worldwide, often taking the form of print or poster campaigns. These showed great variety in style and approach, as well as in attitudes to the disease, according to their country of origin.[6]

Throughout the 1980s gay and lesbian communities consolidated their strength against a common enemy (AIDS); in the early 1990s new directions in activism were formed. In 1991 artist and designer Carrie Moyer and photographer Sue Schaffner teamed up to form Dyke Action Machine! (DAM!). Their work together as DAM! defined a decade of lesbian assertiveness and visibility. They critiqued prejudiced attitudes and heterosexual conceit by skillfully inserting lesbian imagery into both traditional (family) and contemporary (fashion) advertising campaigns, as well as using a film poster parody to critique lesbian representation. Most importantly, their powerful work gave lesbianism a sense of community, politics and respect.[7]

With new visibility and energy brought by AIDS activism, the initials LGB (Lesbian, Gay, Bisexual) slowly began to replace the word 'gay'. The 1990s, however, brought the desire for more exposure, more community and more radical action. The term LGBT was introduced (Lesbian, Gay, Bisexual, Transgender) and the old term 'queer' was adopted as a new umbrella term for sexual and gender minorities, but with an outspoken, in-your-face attitude and an appetite for radical activism, such as civil disobedience and direct action, as practised by the UK queer rights group Outrage! (1990–2011).

The early 1990s also saw the unravelling of the Cold War vision of the world. It began in May 1989, when a series of pro-democracy demonstrations was held by students, workers and intellectuals in Tiananmen Square in Beijing, China, generating immense global solidarity through media coverage and the art they produced, including banners and a makeshift statue of 'the Goddess of Democracy' (similar to New York's Statue of Liberty). On 4 June the world's media watched in horror as the protesters were massacred by their own army. But their spirit lived on, and is said to have ignited the following popular revolutions that travelled across Europe.[8]

The slow struggle throughout the 1980s for free elections in Poland, led by Lech Walesa, head of Poland's free trade union

Solidarity, finally achieved its goal in 1989. The Iron Curtain (staunch symbol of the Eastern bloc) collapsed and a wave of popular revolutions swept through Central and Eastern Europe, including Poland, Hungary, East Germany, Bulgaria, Czechoslovakia and Romania. An area of Europe known for its long-running poster tradition, artists produced large numbers of posters criticising the Communist Party, documenting elections or other events taking place, expressing uncertainty about the future, or showing solidarity with revolutions in other countries. Almost as if providing a grand finale, on 11 November 1989 the Berlin Wall was pulled down by the people it had divided for years.[9]

Iraq's invasion of Kuwait in August 1990 initiated the First Gulf War in January 1991, waged against Iraq by a UN-backed coalition of 36 countries led by the US military. Dubbed 'the information war', it was known for its highly censored portrayal of bloodless warfare, its gung-ho emphasis on air-strike techno-wizardry and the mythic capabilities of 'smart bombs' and precision-guided weapons. It also introduced non-messy terminology such as 'surgical strikes' and 'collateral damage'. Protest imagery of the time brought issues of oil ownership into the discussion, and a mistrust of mainstream media due to the sanitizing of information (producing a 'bloodless' war).[10]

To much of the world, the Balkan Wars presented one of the great confusions of the 1990s. A simplified explanation can be found by following the footsteps of the land-grabbing President Slobodan Miloševic of Serbia (known as Yugoslavia at that time) and his desire for constructing a Greater Serbia (as well as his talent for fanning the flames of nationalism and setting ethnic groups warring against each other). In short: he launched an offensive against Slovenia (1991), which fought him off. Then he attacked Croatia, creating a cycle of battles and purging of ethnic groups. This set off the powder keg known as Bosnia, with Bosnian Serbs, Bosnian Muslims and Catholic Croats warring against each other and exercising 'ethnic cleansing' (the purging

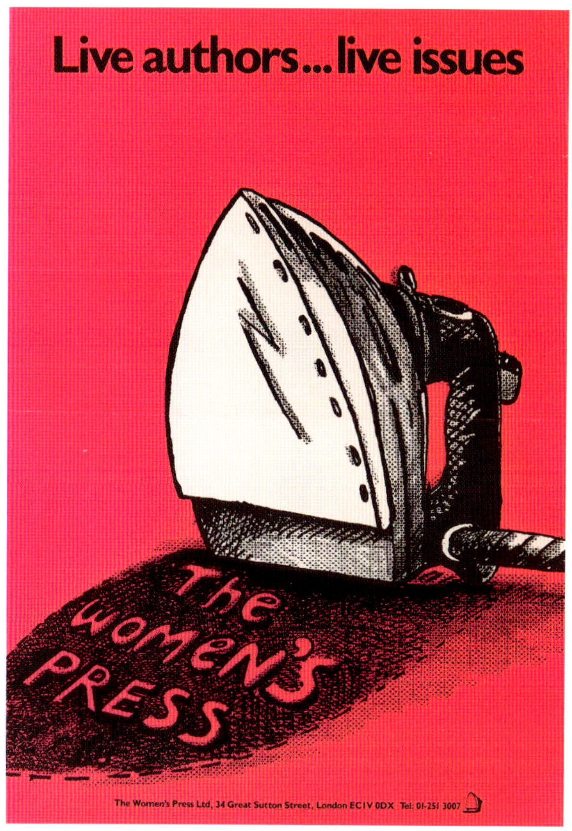

Promotional poster for The Women's Press, London 1980s
Illustration: Donna Muir,
Art Direction: Suzanne Perkins

GUERRILLA GIRLS
CONSCIENCE OF THE ART WORLD

Sticker from the US feminist art activist group
Guerrilla Girls *c.* 1990

of 'unwanted' ethnic groups from areas they wanted to control).
Also a part of this Bosnian War was the siege of Sarajevo (April
1992–Feb 1996) when Milošević's Yugoslav People's Army and
local militias blockaded, shelled and demolished the city. The
Bosnian War was brought to an end in 1995, and a shaky peace
was enforced by NATO (Sarajevo's nightmare continued into
1996). But in 1998 Milošević laid claim to Kosovo, and waged
war on the resident ethnic Albanians. Despite the confusions
and chaos, the creative communities in the countries affected
kept design studios in operation (for example, Trio in Sarajevo),
created art activism projects against violence or produced graphic
documentation of the crimes.[11]

Admirably, there was resistance to Milošević within Serbia
itself. Belgrade students and citizens demonstrated for change
between November 1996 and March 1997. They marched
through the streets, pelted the offices of the state newspaper
Politika with eggs, and other actions, but to no avail. A new spirit
of revolt appeared in 1998 in the form of the movement Otpor!
(Resistance!), founded by Belgrade University students (average
age, 20–21). It set its sights on the democratic overthrow of
Milošević in the upcoming September 2000 elections, and ran
an energetic, sophisticated campaign with brilliant graphics; by
July 2000 it claimed 40,000 members. Its symbol, a clenched fist,
appeared all over Serbia. Otpor!'s final move, the 'He's Finished!'
campaign in the run-up to the presidential elections of 24
September 2000, brought victory. Milošević didn't go easily, but
a revolt on 5 October finally ousted him, and he was on his way
to The International Court in the Hague.[12]

Throughout the 1980s solidarity campaigns existed in support
of countries in Central and South America attempting to deal
with US interference or with the machinations of military
dictators (or possibly both together). The Sandinista Revolution
in Nicaragua (1979) overthrew the corrupt Somoza dictatorship,
formed a government and set about addressing the country's
struggle for literacy, health care and land distribution. Posters
were used by the new government to address these issues and
to strengthen cultural identity. They also encouraged people to
defend themselves against the US-backed Contras aiming to
destabilize the country, and called to Central American countries
to resist American intervention (as experienced in El Salvador in
1982 and the West Indian island of Grenada in 1985). In Chile
in 1973, the democratically elected (Marxist) President Salvador
Allende was overthrown in a CIA-backed coup d'état, resulting
in the country being ruled by a military junta led by the dictator
General Augusto Pinochet. A purge of dissidents followed,
thousands were murdered or 'disappeared' and an estimated
200,000 Chileans were driven into exile. Politically-minded
poster collectives and design studios in the US, UK, Holland and
other countries continued to produce posters for international
organizations providing support and solidarity for liberation and
other struggles throughout the Americas and Africa.[13]

Leading up to the new century, an important global resistance
movement took hold incorporating anti-globalization and
environmentalism, and engaging with new developments in
digital technology. 'Anti-globalization' was, in essence, people

power vs. corporate power. It had anti-corporatism and anti-
capitalism at its core, and a deep suspicion of the power that
multinational corporations wielded over world economies
and people's lives, particularly by highly visible names such
as McDonald's and Nike. It also targeted the debt-handling
activities of Western institutions such as the International
Monetary Fund (IMF), the World Trade Organization (WTO)
and the World Bank, for stifling the progress and livelihood
of the developing world. Anti-globalisation joined forces with
environmentalism, which employed militant, uncompromising
methods of direct action, initially seen in the UK roadbuilding
protests aiming to protect trees and areas of natural beauty.[14]

Mass anti-globalization protests took place at the turn of the
century. They included J18 (18 June 1999), the International
Carnival Against Capitalism taking place in 27 countries; and the
Battle of Seattle protest in November 1999 against the IMF and
WTO, with an estimate of 50–100,000 protesters involved. There
was no turning back for graphic artists and designers wishing to
add their voices to the mix. Posters and maps were produced to
announce time and place; signs, banners and flags were carried
at protests and other events. The graphic statements (posters,
billboards, websites) aligned to anti-corporate protest – anti-
tobacco, anti-fast food, anti-advertising and so on – all turned
nasty, and the more extreme, the better. The anti-corporate
backlash included 'brand subversion', and the multinationals
controlling health, food, environment, energy and economies,
and their symbols of power (logos, symbols and mascots),
have been a target for satire and graphic opposition ever since.
Adbusters, a movement/magazine out to subvert the media and
corporates, developed a global craze for 'subvertising' (corporate
ad spoofs). Fast-food giant McDonald's found itself embroiled
in the longest running civil libel case in British history (1994–
97) against two activists: a postman and a gardener. Plus the
Marlboro Man lost his 'tough guy' image, having confessed to
another cowboy that he's got emphysema.[15]

Despite widespread support for Nelson Mandela and the anti-
apartheid movement, Britain still had problems with race at home
in the 1980s. Sparked off by issues such as the heavy targeting of
black youths by police using stop-and-search tactics, in 1981 the
anger of the black community exploded into the Brixton Riots of
south London and spread throughout the country. Against this
backdrop, new, more forceful comments emerged about life in
Black Britain from a young generation of British artists, including
Tam Joseph. The black community's mistrust of and difficult
relationship with the police would continue.

With the end of the guerrilla war for independence in 1980,
Zimbabwe (formerly Rhodesia) embarked on the building of
a new socialist state, under the elected leadership of Robert
Mugabe. By the late 1990s, and with the aid of his ruling party
Zanu-PF, Mugabe's stranglehold on power and the economy
had brought the country to near ruin. As the year 2000 elections
approached, Zimbabwean designer Chaz Maviyane-Davies
(then living in London) embarked on '30 days of graphic
activism' to encourage a vote for change, emailing daily 'Graphic
Commentaries' – including poster images, written texts, links

to websites – to individuals and civic rights groups around the world. It was a brilliantly informative solidarity project, spinning out daily events and issues, and chronicling the power abuses taking place.

When Nelson Mandela was released from prison in 1990, after 27 years of imprisonment, he began the negotiations that would lead to the dismantling of the apartheid system. The first all-race democratic elections took place in 1994, and Mandela's victory marked the beginning of the new South Africa, followed by a period of euphoria. But, of course, the shadows of apartheid (and the resentment felt by parts of the population) didn't disappear overnight. Bitterkomix was started in 1992 by Anton Kannemeyer (aka Joe Dog) and Conrad Botes while still in university, and grew with regard to the number of artists involved as well as the provocative content. It satirized (mainly) white South Africans, their fears and obsessions, and gradually cast its satirical eye on South African society as a whole. Similar to US underground comics, sex and violence were ever present, boldly (and often brashly) lifting the lid on underlying taboos and prejudices bubbling beneath the surface.[16]

Jonathan Shapiro (aka Zapiro) has been scratching beneath the surface of South Africa's psyche in a very different way. A committed anti-apartheid activist, his regular professional cartooning started around 1994. His first annual collection of cartoons produced for newspapers covered the 'Madiba years' (Nelson Mandela years, 1994–96). After that, collections of cartoons appeared annually showing Zapiro's role as expert social commentator, exposing the flaws and difficult social adjustments to be overcome in the early stages of the new South Africa, while producing hilarious depictions of the politicians involved. He also courted controversy: Jacob Zuma (president of South Africa, 2009–18) twice sued him for millions of rand on a charge of defamation of character, but then (years) later dropped the charges.[17]

Fired by the spirit of change that was circling the globe in the 1960s and 1970s, Australia saw the rise of a poster and community art tradition involving politically and socially-committed graphic arts workshops which excelled at low-cost screen printing. In the 1980s, the next generation of poster artists and printmakers (including Redback Graphix, Red Planet Workshop and others) carried on this tradition of activism, imbibed with the new graphic spirit of Punk. They placed a special focus on the oppression of the Aboriginal people, exacerbated by the 1988 Australian Bicentennial which had exposed sharp cultural divisions and produced a grassroots movement calling for historical reassessment. They also contributed heavily to the continuing campaign against nuclear testing in the Pacific, highlighting its effects on both indigenous people and their environment.[18]

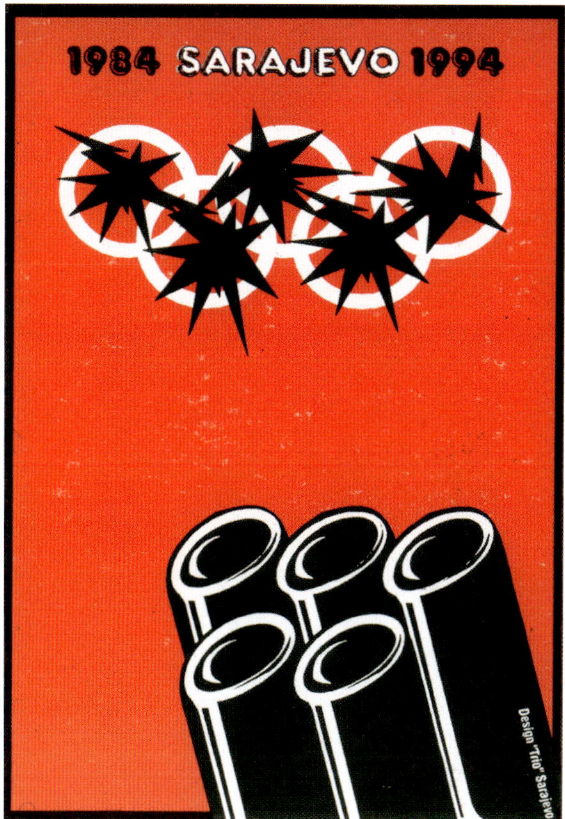

Two postcards produced during the Bosnian War 1993–94
Trio design group, based in Sarajevo

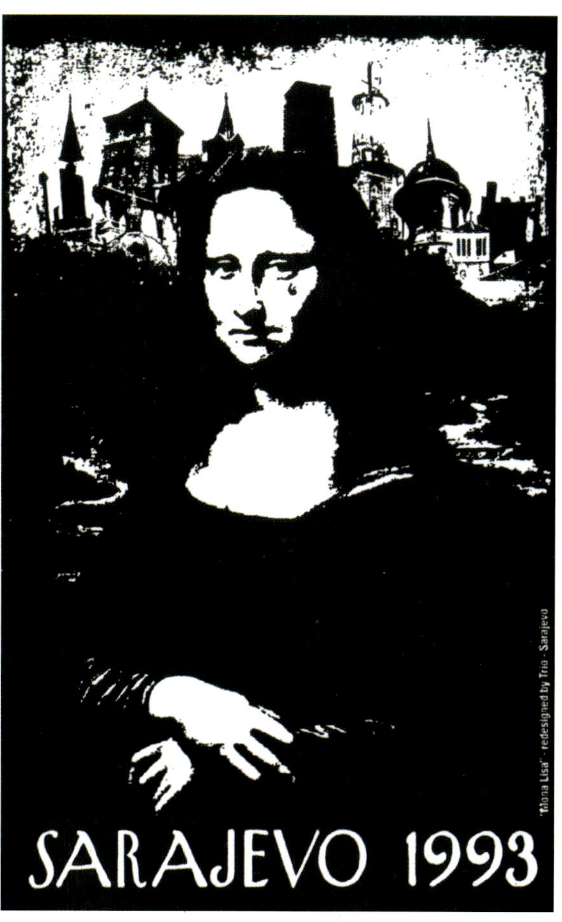

The International Peace Movement

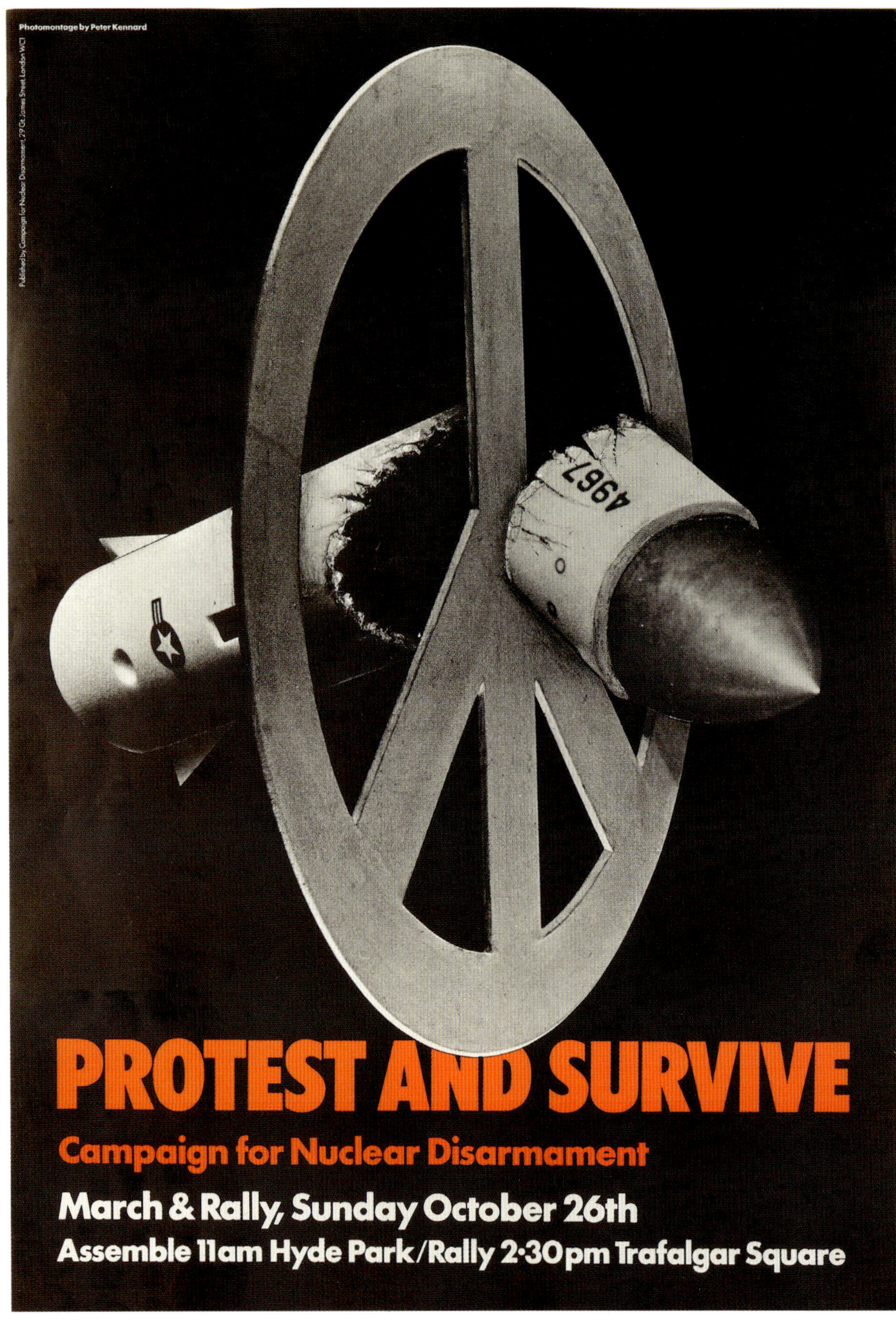

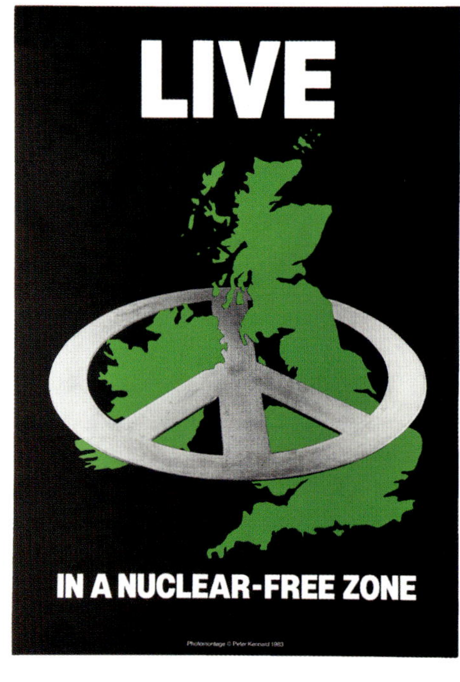

↑ **Protest and Survive** 1979
↗ **LIVE in a nuclear-free zone** *c.*1981
Peter Kennard
Poster (offset)

The mounting tension between the two global superpowers (the USA and the Soviet Union), locked in an arms race, brought back the rising spectre of nuclear war. Consequently, NATO's decision to deploy US Cruise missiles on British soil in 1979 brought the subdued Campaign for Nuclear Disarmament (CND) roaring back to life. This time it was energized by a new generation of young activists committed to applying their creative talents to work for the peace movement. Peter Kennard's photomontages for the CND and the Greater London Council led the way, and would define the new movement in Britain. The poster, on the left, aimed to revitalize CND's symbol and image for use on the first march of the revived CND; over the next five years Kennard's photomontages and other imagery provided a forceful image for the British peace movement, appearing on posters, postcards, banners and badges.

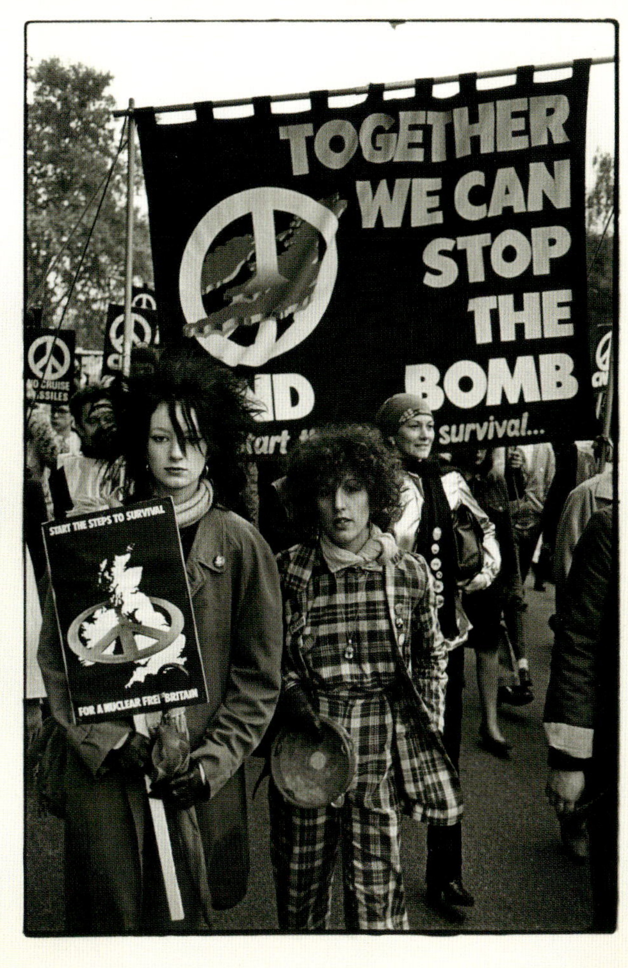

↑ **Hyde Park, October 1981** 1981
Photograph: Ed Barber
Postcard

Photographer Ed Barber documented the activities and
emotions of the British peace movement in the 1980s, including
CND marches and the Women's Peace Camp at Greenham
Common. In this photograph he captures a peace march
gathered in Hyde Park; the demonstrators are carrying posters
and banners with images by Peter Kennard. He also captures
the spirit and diversity of the moment. Some of the protesters
are dressed in the street style of Punk, while at the same time
their expression shows their clarity of purpose.

→ **'Gone with the Wind'** 1984
Bob Light and John Houston
Poster

This poster provided one of the great satirical moments of
1980s Britain. It shows US President Ronald Reagan and
British Prime Minister Margaret Thatcher in a pose intended to
mimic Rhett Butler and Scarlett O'Hara in the 1930s film *Gone
With the Wind*. It is a sarcastic statement relating to the 'special
relationship' between the USA and Great Britain, depicting
both leaders as war-mongers in cahoots as global nuclear
destruction occurs behind them.

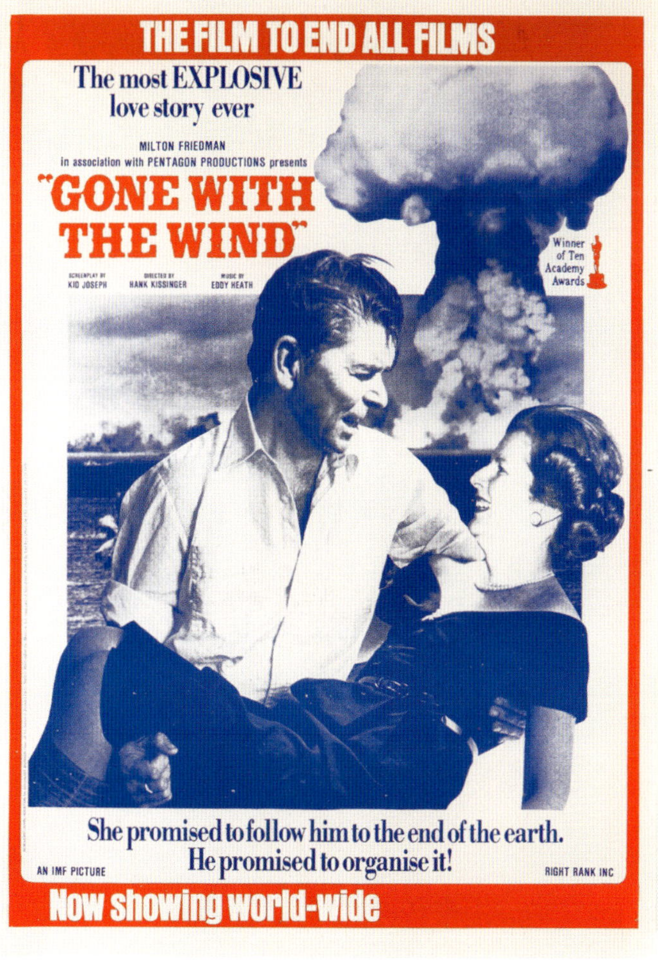

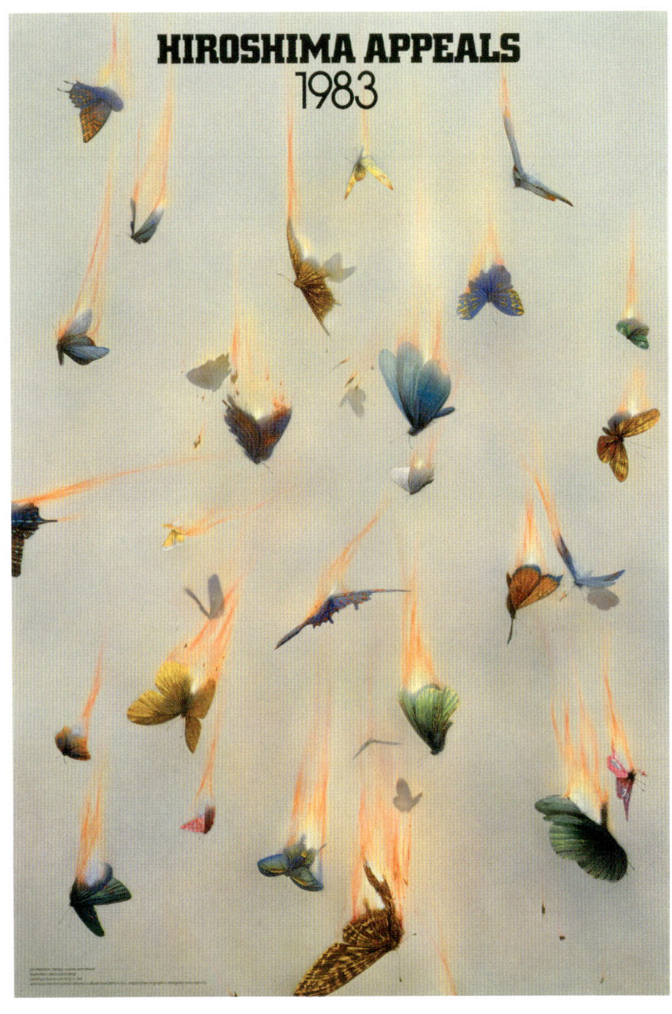

Hiroshima Appeals 1983
Yusaku Kamekura
Poster

Burning butterflies signify the horrors of the atomic blast of 6 August 1945 that incinerated the Japanese city of Hiroshima and its people. This poster launched the Hiroshima Appeals poster series. From 1983 to 1990, an annual appeal was made to the world on behalf of the people of Hiroshima to work for the cause of peace. Each year a poster was created by one of Japan's top designers to be distributed worldwide and exhibited in Hiroshima on the anniversary of the bombing. Both the poster series, and an annual peace poster exhibition, were organized by the well-known and extremely active Japan Graphic Designers Association (JAGDA).

Attention! 1981
Christer Themptander
Poster and postcard (offset)

The lunacy of the military (and other controlling figures of authority, such as banks and politicians) has always featured strongly in Themptander's work. But his photomontages remain beautifully and meticulously constructed, qualities which only seem to enhance their comedy and ongoing attempts to point out humanity's foibles.

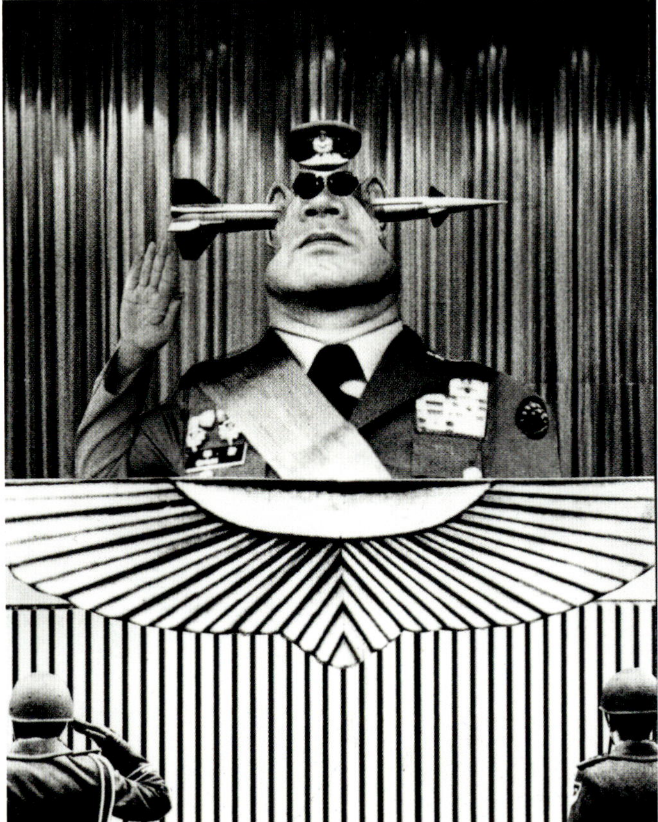

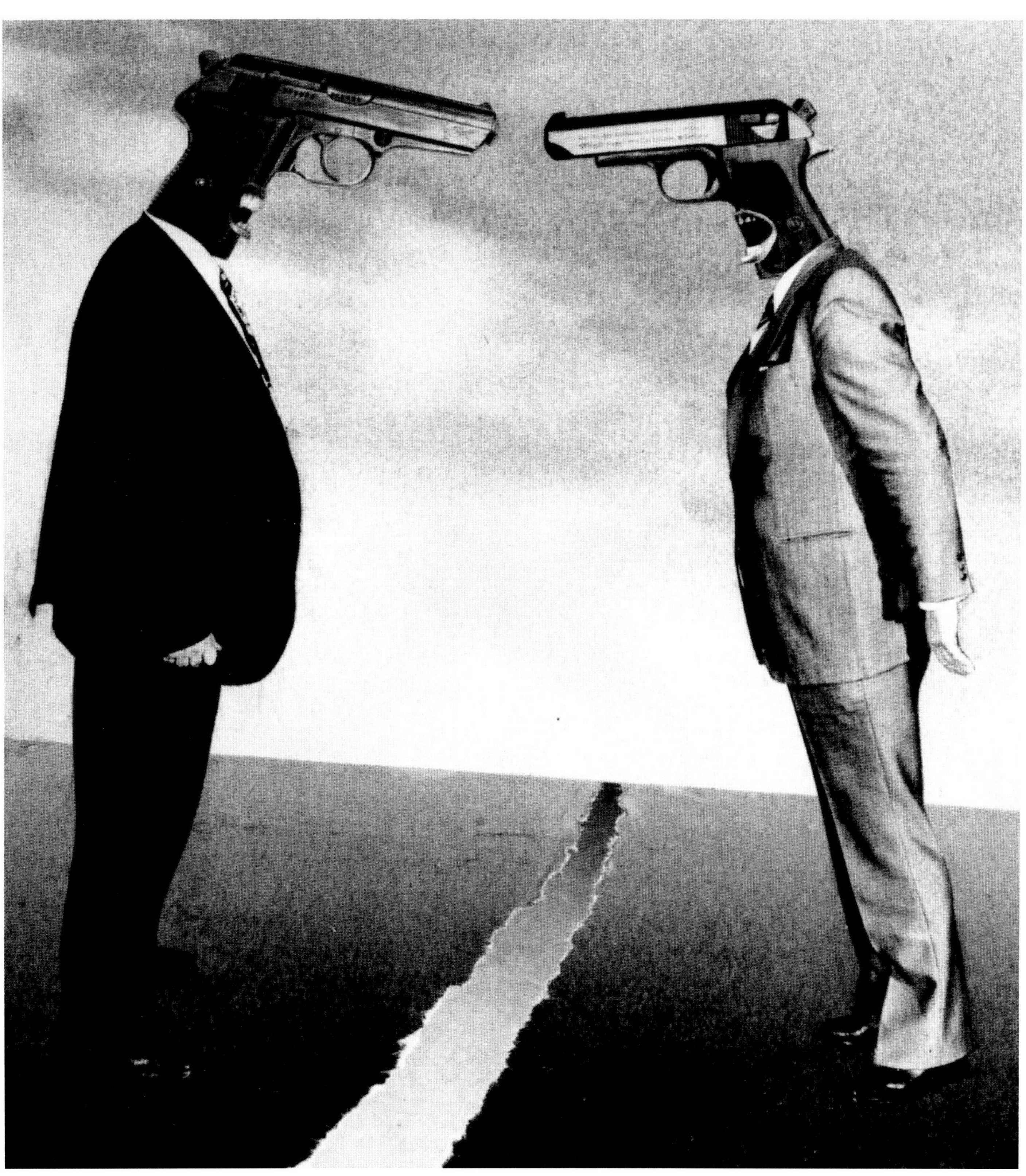

Impending Image 1984
Christer Themptander
Poster and postcard (offset)

The Swedish photomontagist Christer
Themptander has produced a large
body of anti-militarist work, executed
with razor-sharp wit and satire. His
placement of weaponry (guns, missiles
and so on) can be humorous, but also
thought provoking. One of his most
effective works is entitled 'Impending
Image'. It is a beautifully rendered image
of a frightening situation. Two men in
suits, with guns as an extension of their
heads, shout at each other. Each man
stands on one side of a dividing line,
which could be real or imagined. Although
this image was created in the 1980s, it
remains just as relevant today, and just
as disturbing.

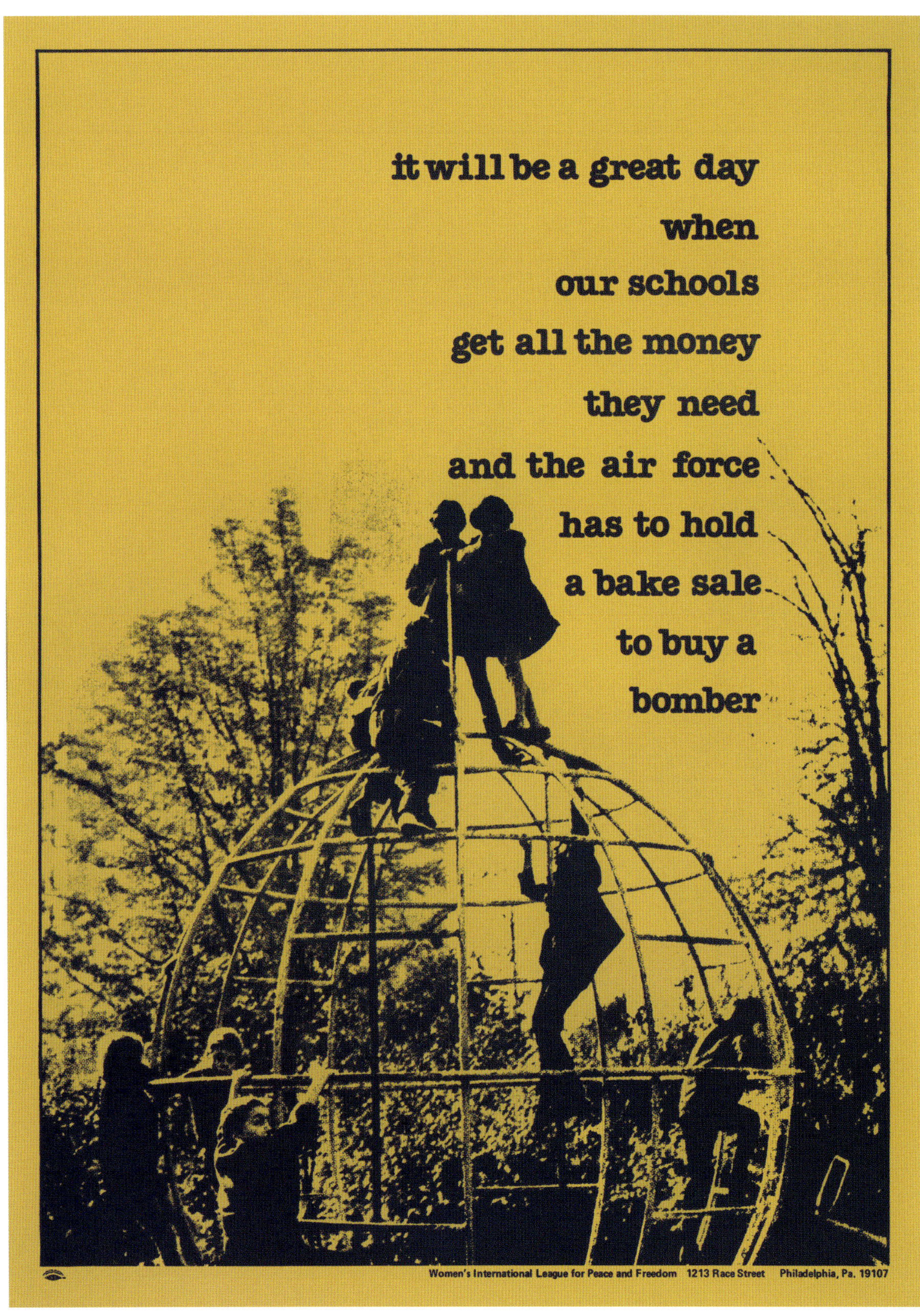

It will be a great day… 1979
Designer unknown
Poster (offset)

Ten memorable lines of text (wishful thinking that becomes a blatant protest when it finishes), and a basic black image, make for a powerful poster regardless of the size or quality of its reproduction, or the variety of stock it is printed on. It was produced by the Women's International League for Peace and Freedom (WILPF) in the USA, dedicated to working for peace by non-violent means. Founded in 1915, it is now a well-known NGO (non-governmental organization) with sections on every continent, offices in Geneva and New York and thousands of members worldwide.

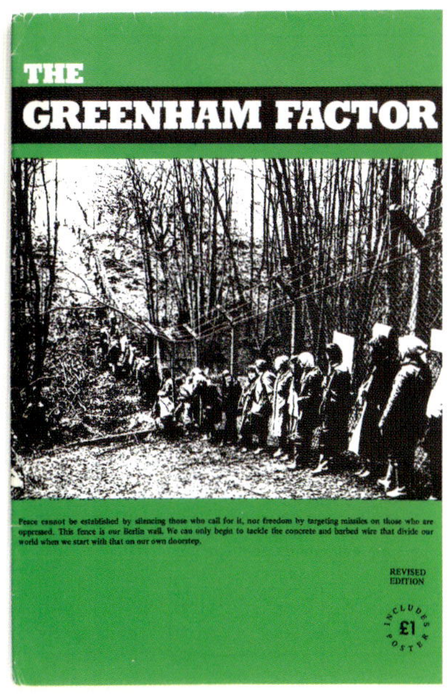
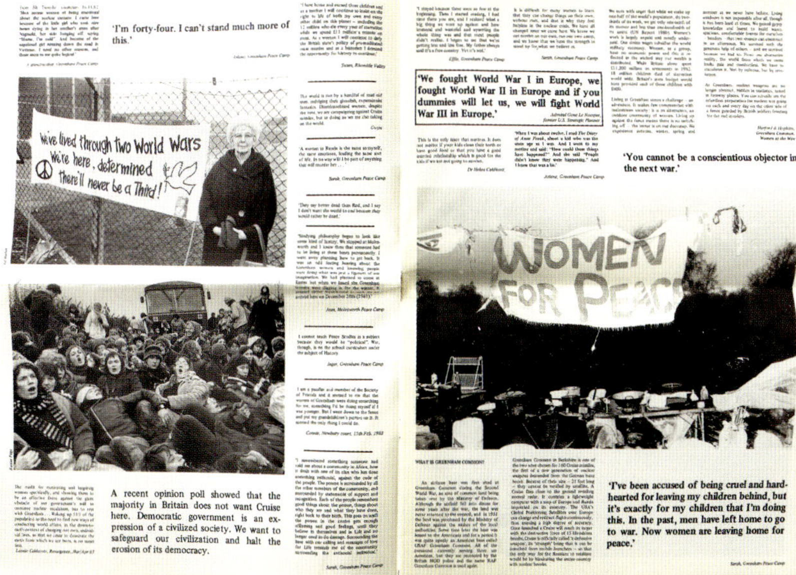

↗ **The Greenham Factor** 1983–84
↗ A4 pamphlet cover and inside spread

The Greenham Factor was a newsheet, produced to document the aspirations
and activities of those involved in the Women's Peace Camp at Greenham
Common in Britain. It was also used as a solidarity tool and to raise funds
for the camp.

→ **Banner for the Women's Peace
Camp at Greenham Common** 1983
Thalia and Jan Campbell and Jan Higgs
Photograph (also postcard)

The Women's Peace Camp at Greenham Common was established in 1981
when women (of all ages) camped outside the gates of a US military base in
Britain in an attempt to stop its receiving and housing of US Cruise missiles,
as agreed with the British government. The camp's numbers grew and shrank
periodically, but it thrived on performance and demonstrations of solidarity
and strength, and decorated the environment and perimeter fence with
drawings, paintings, banners, baby clothes and other mementos of humanity,
as well as weaving webs out of anything to hand. (Plus bannermaking
enjoyed renewed popularity.) The women performed daring actions – such as
climbing over or cutting through the perimeter fence – and held extraordinary
demonstrations, such as 'Embrace the Base' in 1982 when over 30,000 women
travelled to Greenham to link hands around the base. Plus there were injuries,
usually when women blocked entrances to the base and the police arrested
them, dragging them away. The camp became internationally renowned, as a
potent symbol of women's ability to stand up to the male military machine,
and lasted ten years, ending when the missiles left.

Dear Margaret *c.* 1983
Photographer: Brenda Prince
Postcard

A banner at the Women's Peace Camp makes a smug comment to Prime
Minister Margaret Thatcher about not buying presents (bombs) for her
'children' (her politicians). Thatcher was no friend to the women in the
Peace Camp; they stole her media headlines and interfered with her and
Ronald Reagan's shared vision of global (armed) diplomacy.

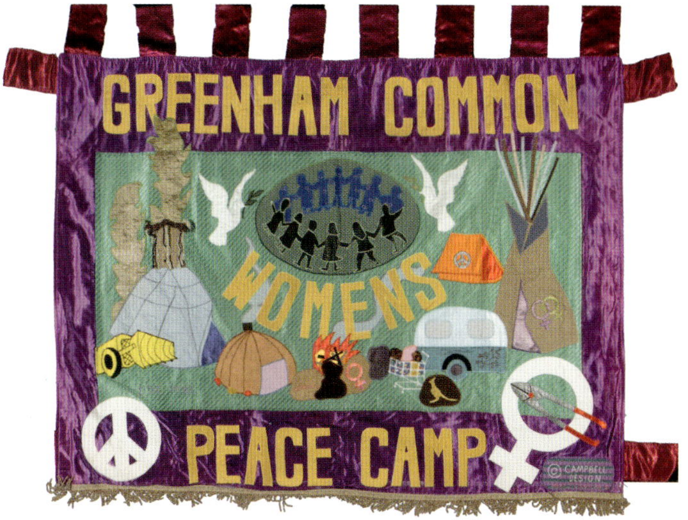

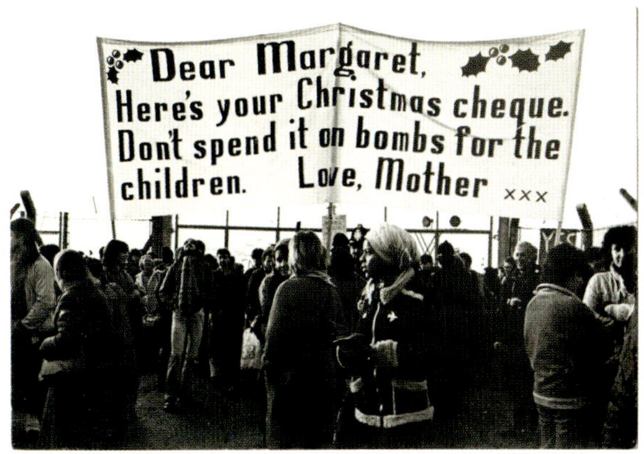

Political Satire: A Rogues' Gallery

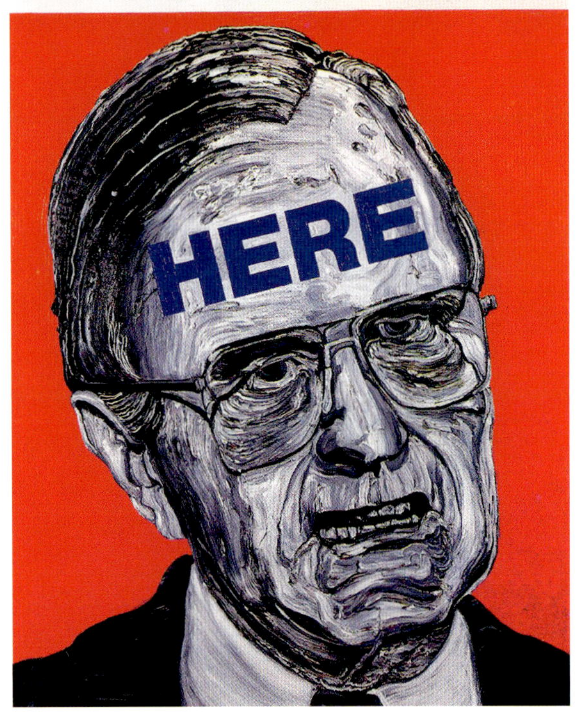

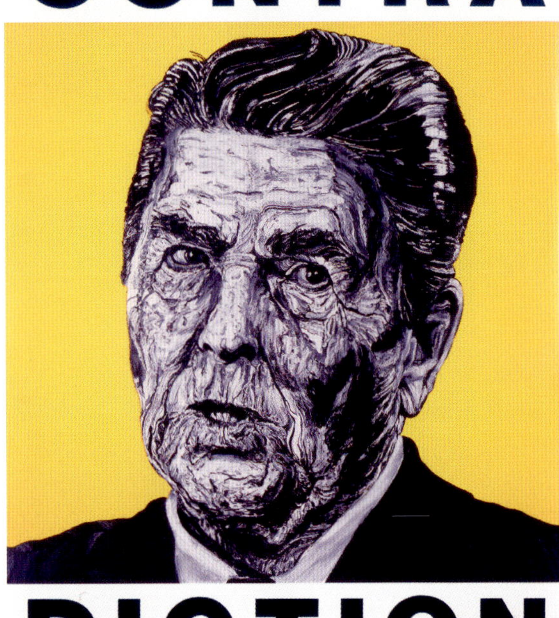

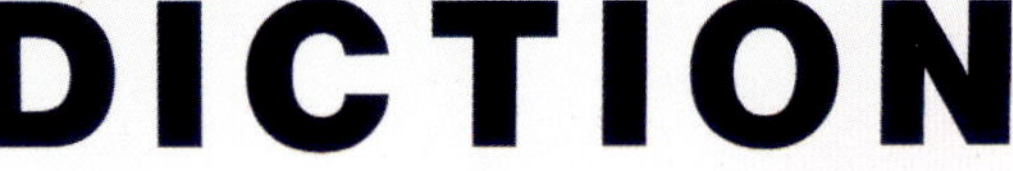

← **It Can't Happen Here** 1988
Artist of poster and original artwork: Robbie Conal
Poster

Guerrilla street artist Robbie Conal is well known for his portrait posters of 'bad guys' – including politicians and public icons – that are then wheatpasted on the streets, walls and billboards of Los Angeles (and a few other American cities). This poster shows George Bush, US president, 1989–93. Newly elected at the time this poster was made, the statement 'It Can't Happen Here' is Conal's expression of incredulity at the election of someone so boring – a 'suit' or organisation man, who had former connections with the CIA – as well as the insinuation of a certain lack of brainpower.

↙ **Contra Diction** 1987
Artist of poster and original artwork: Robbie Conal
Poster

Robbie Conal strikes again; this time the 'bad guy' is US president Ronald Reagan, targeted here for looking confused and 'failing to remember' his administration's/CIA dealings with the Contras (terrorizing Nicaragua) and their possible drug smuggling, as well as arms deals with Iran.

↓ **The Best Future for Britain** 1993
Artist: Steve Bell
Cartoon

Political cartoonist Steve Bell often drew Prime Minister John Major, Margaret Thatcher's successor, wearing his underpants over his suit in a parody of Superman. It was also meant to signify John Major's uselessness.

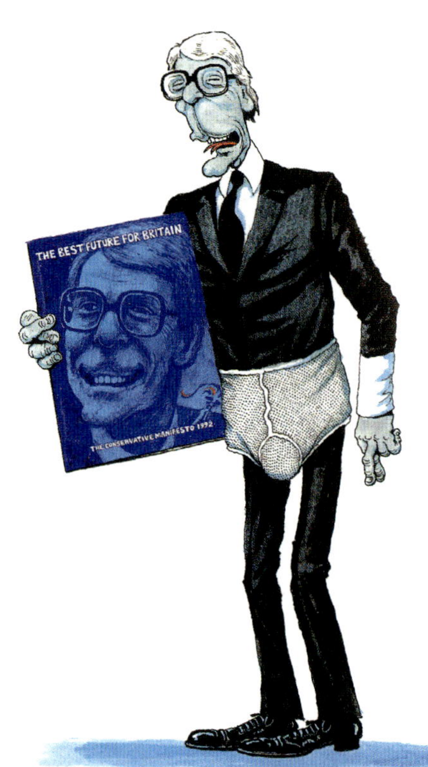

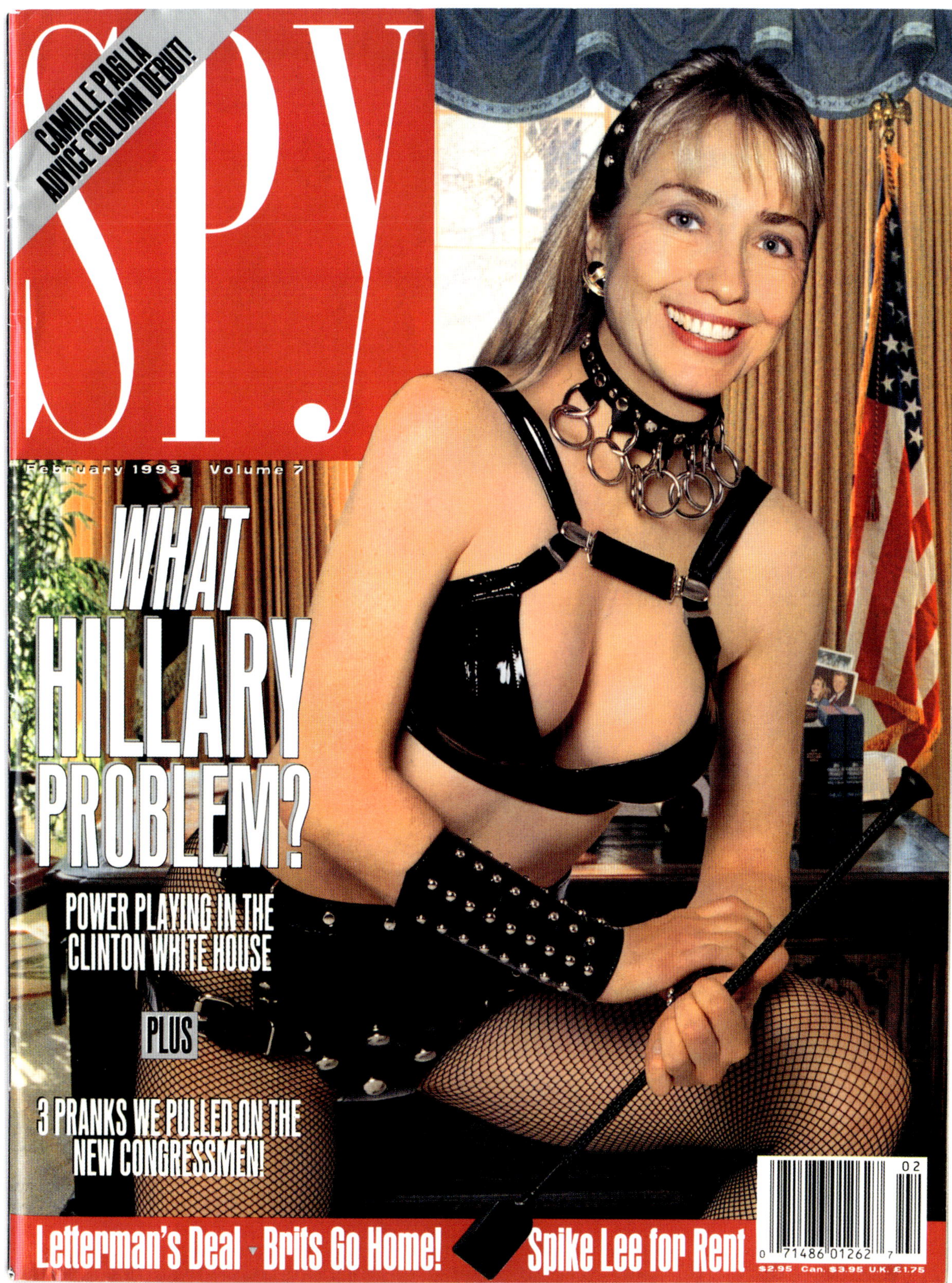

What Hillary Problem? 1993
Artist unknown
Spy magazine: front cover

Artists, cartoonists and magazines dealing in political satire were spoilt for choice in the 1980s, with conservative politicians in charge on both sides of the ocean. In the 1990s, misbehaviour ruled. Soon after Bill Clinton won the presidential election in autumn 1992, New York's satirical magazine, *Spy*, published this photomontaged cover. Hillary Clinton had just become First Lady and questions were already being raised about her influence in the White House. However, by the end of the decade it was Bill who would occupy the headlines with his affair with intern Monica Lewinsky in 1998–99 and subsequent impeachment trial.

Internal Struggles, Divided Countries

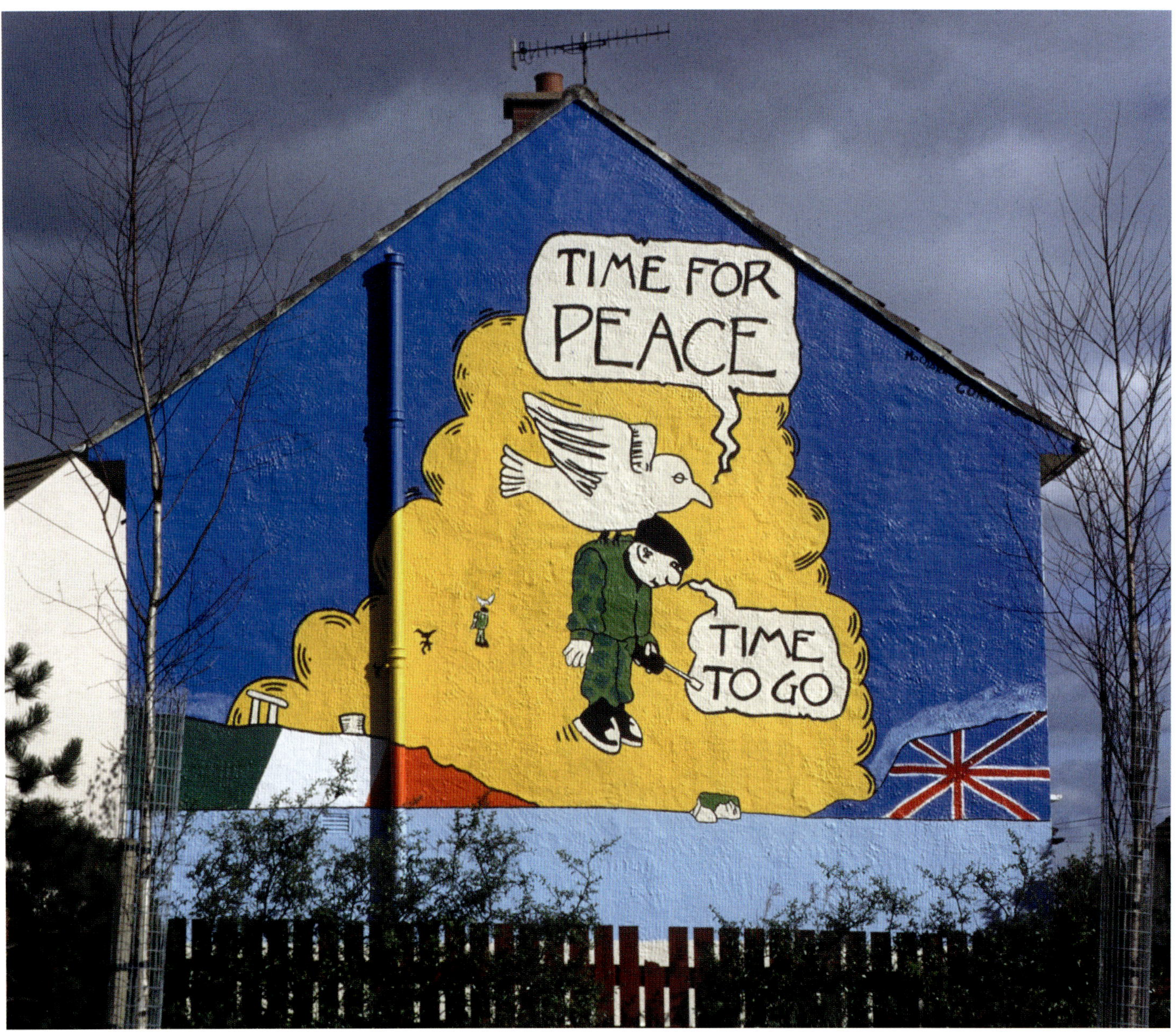

Time for Peace, Time to Go *c.*1994
Reproduction of a 'Cormac' cartoon
Political mural, Northern Ireland

The British government's war with the Irish Republican Army (IRA), otherwise known as 'the Troubles', resulted in a 30-year military presence in Northern Ireland (1968–98). Simply stated: within Northern Ireland, the largely Protestant and loyalist majority wanted to remain part of the UK; the mainly Catholic and republican minority wished to become part of the Republic of Ireland (the South). Having said that, loyalties on both sides were far more complicated, and the violence was brutal and wide-ranging, including terrorism that spread to the British mainland. News of events and protest statements developed in mainland Britain in the form of documentaries, newspapers and ephemera – badges, pamphlets and postcards – calling for a stop to the violence, protesting the use of plastic bullets by British armed forces and, as time went on, carrying the inevitable call for 'Troops Out Now'. Northern Ireland visualized its experiences, loyalties, anger and pain in the form of political wall murals, both loyalist and republican, created in Belfast and other locations, depicting memorials, military emblems, and more. By 1994, the desire for peace meant that the slogan 'Time to Go' began to appear on republican murals. The mural shown here carries a reproduction of a cartoon by 'Cormac' (Brian Moore, political cartoonist for *An Phoblact*) in which the peace dove is carrying the British soldier back home to the mainland.

↓ **Mural commemorating Bobby Sands** 1990
Artist unknown
Mural

This mural memorialises Bobby Sands, the first
prisoner to go on hunger strike in 1981 and the first
to die. It is located in Belfast and contains a quotation
from his writings. Also depicted is 'the Spirit of
Freedom', shown as a lark trapped within a ribbon
(and in other murals, trapped within barbed wire),
an image also taken from Sands' prison writings.
The logo of the republican newspaper *An Phoblacht/
Republican News* appears above him.

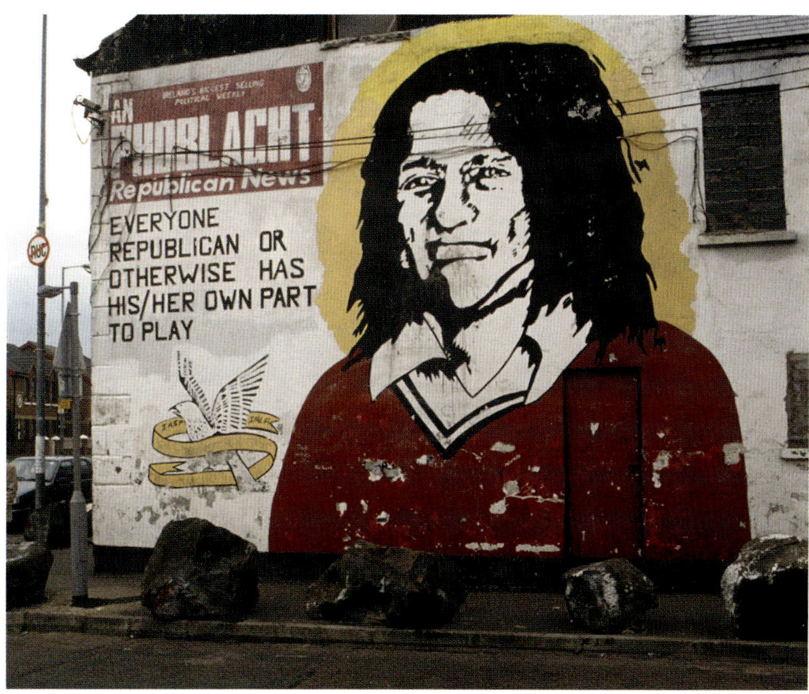

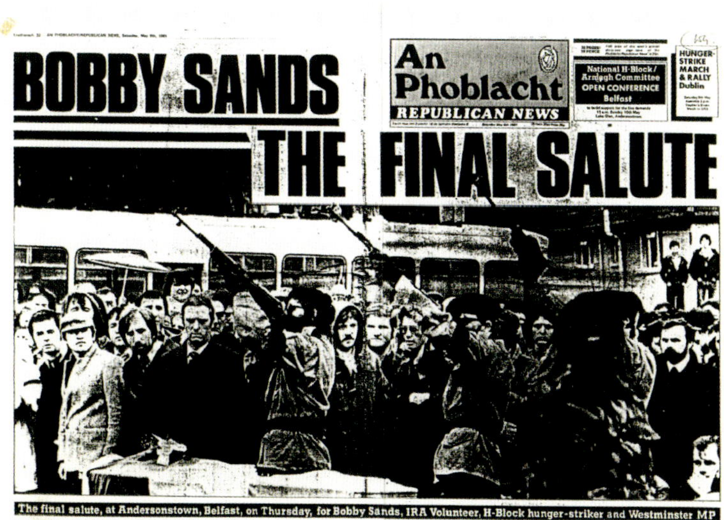

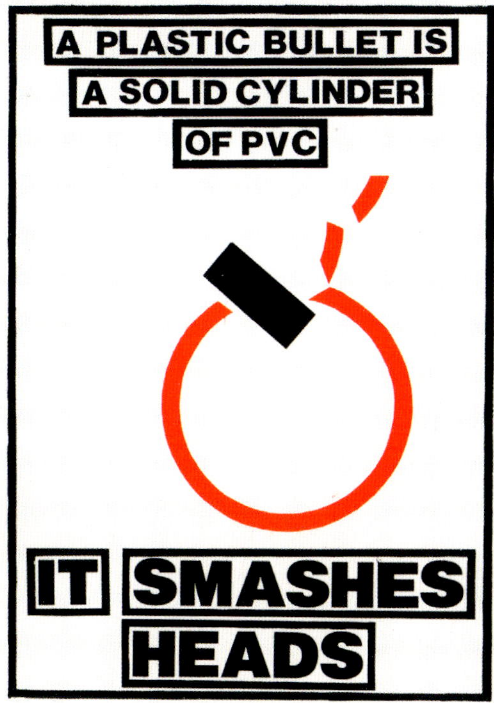

↑ **A Plastic Bullet – It Smashes Heads** early 1980s
Design: Stephen Dorley-Brown
Postcard

The Campaign Against Plastic Bullets (based in
London) produced this postcard with the aim of
banning the use of plastic (rubber) bullets by police
and armed forces in Britain and Northern Ireland.
However, the postcard had additional value in
combatting misinformation, as it was often thought
by the British mainland public that plastic bullets
weren't as bad as real bullets – but they could still
kill and maim both adults and children.

↙ **Bobby Sands: The Final Salute** 1981
Photographer unknown
Front and back pages: *An Phoblacht*

These front and back pages of *An Phoblacht*, the
republican newspaper, carried a photograph of a
memorial and final salute (by the IRA) to Bobby
Sands, who led a group of ten hunger-strikers in
Maze Prison demanding 'political prisoner status'
for republican prisoners instead of treatment as
criminals. Sands was leader of the IRA prisoners
in the Maze; during the strike he was also elected
a member of the British Parliament by a Northern
Ireland constituency. The strike began on 1 March
1981; Sands died on 5 May, 66 days after refusing
food. Nine other prisoners died before the strike
was called off on 3 October 1981. The British
government (under Margaret Thatcher) made no
concessions, 'the Troubles' worsened, and Bobby
Sands became a hero to the republican cause.

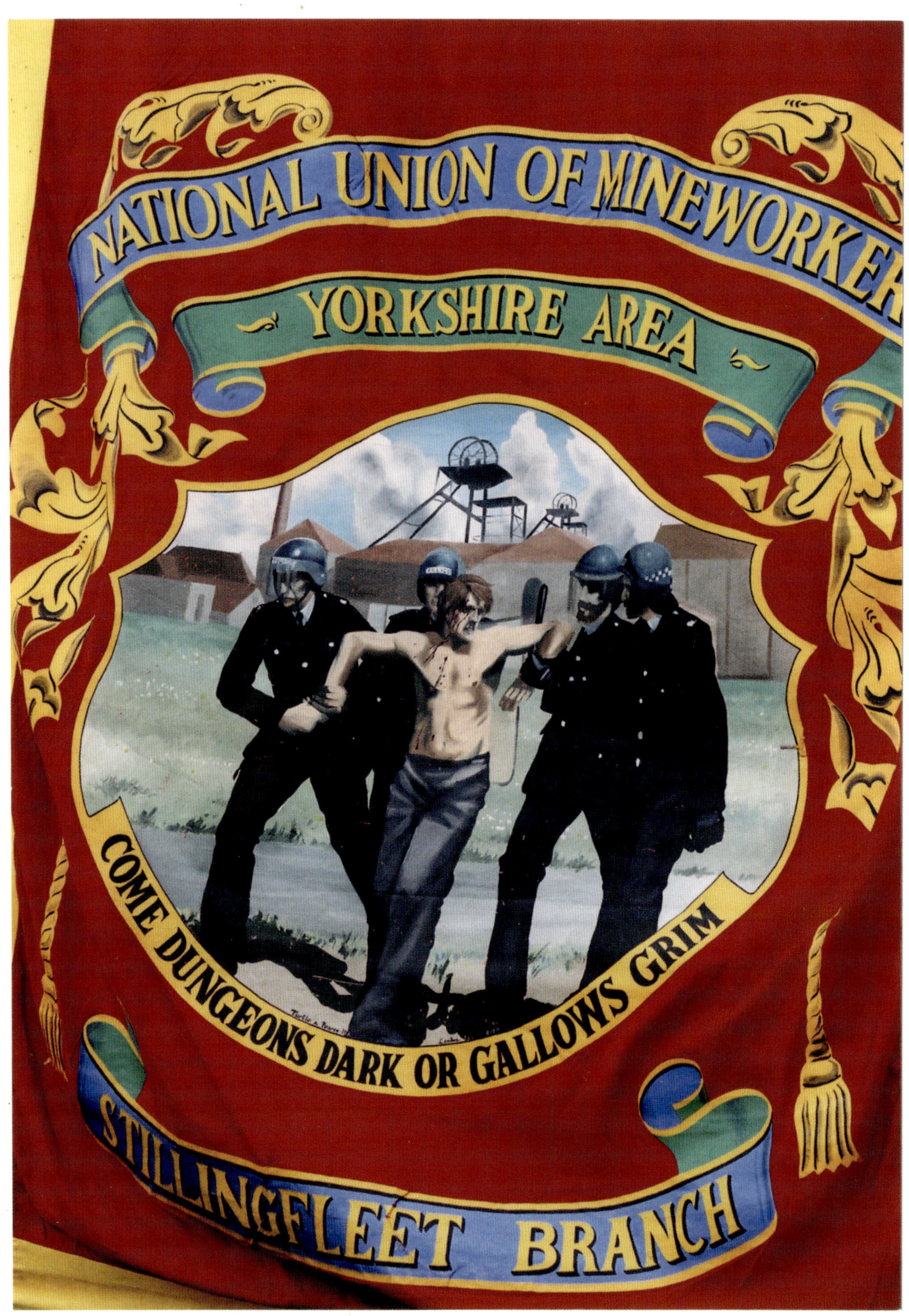

NATIONAL UNION OF MINEWORKER
YORKSHIRE AREA
COME DUNGEONS DARK OR GALLOWS GRIM
STILLINGFLEET BRANCH

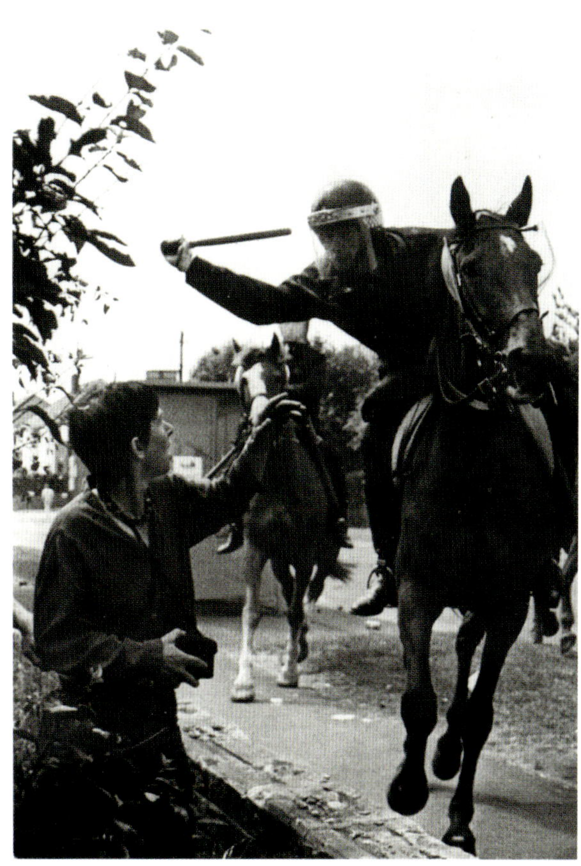

In 1984 British Prime Minister Margaret Thatcher and her Conservative government embarked on a mission to destroy the power of the trade union movement – especially the National Union of Mineworkers (NUM) – and close down the pits or coal mines. The result was the Miners' Strike of 1984–85, beginning with the closure of Cortonwood pit in South Yorkshire, the heartland of Britain, in March 1984. The miners went on strike; more strikes spread to coalfields throughout Britain due to the efforts of 'flying pickets' (strikers who moved around from one strike to another, adding strength where needed). In the end, at least 165,000 miners went out on strike. The government ordered thousands of highly trained, well-armed police to fight the strikers; the confrontations were bloody and brutal. Women activists and trade unionists delivered support (food kitchens, fund-raising and so on); the British public provided funds and heartfelt solidarity with the miners. By March 1985 it was all over; the strike was weakened. But the physical brutality remained in the public mind, as well as Margaret Thatcher's shocking reference to the miners as 'the enemy within'. Banners have traditionally acted as emblems of identity for trade unions, to be carried in marches or displayed at events. The NUM trade union banner shown here depicts one of many bloody incidents during the Miners' Strike. It was photographed at the Durham Miners' Gala, a key annual ritual where miners carried this banner (as well as other miners' banners) with members of the community, on a long march through the city of Durham, ending at Durham Cathedral where many of the banners were blessed.

↗ The Battle of Orgreave 1984
→ Photograph: John Harris
Postcard (top) and poster (bottom)

Miners from all of the striking coalfields formed a mass picket at Orgreave on 18 June 1984. 'The Battle of Orgreave' proved to be one of the most violent confrontations between miners and police. Photographs showed miners facing police baton charges, and mounted police wielding riot sticks. This photograph, taken at Orgreave, caught a member of Sheffield Women's Support Group under attack from a mounted policeman. (She was calling for an ambulance for a nearby injured miner.) It became an iconic protest image throughout the dispute and appeared on postcards, posters and in radical journals.

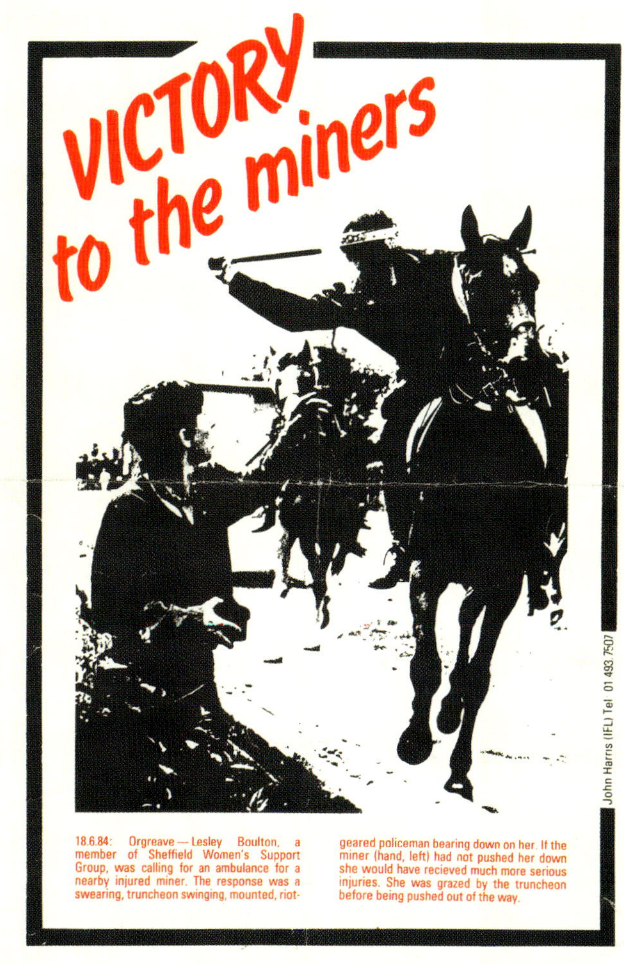

18.6.84: Orgreave — Lesley Boulton, a member of Sheffield Women's Support Group, was calling for an ambulance for a nearby injured miner. The response was a swearing, truncheon swinging, mounted, riot-geared policeman bearing down on her. If the miner (hand, left) had not pushed her down she would have recieved much more serious injuries. She was grazed by the truncheon before being pushed out of the way.

→ 'Daddy, What Are You Doing
In the Occupied Territories?' 1989
David Tartakover
Poster

David Tartakover's use of a child's drawing of a flower,
backed by the photograph of an injured child, presents
the ultimate horror: the suffering of children caught in
the conflict. This poster was published by Yesh Gvul
(There is a Limit), founded in 1982, a movement of
combat veterans who originally refused to serve in the
Lebanon War, and as time went on, also refused to serve
in the Occupied Territories. Also known as 'refuseniks',
the movement still exists today.

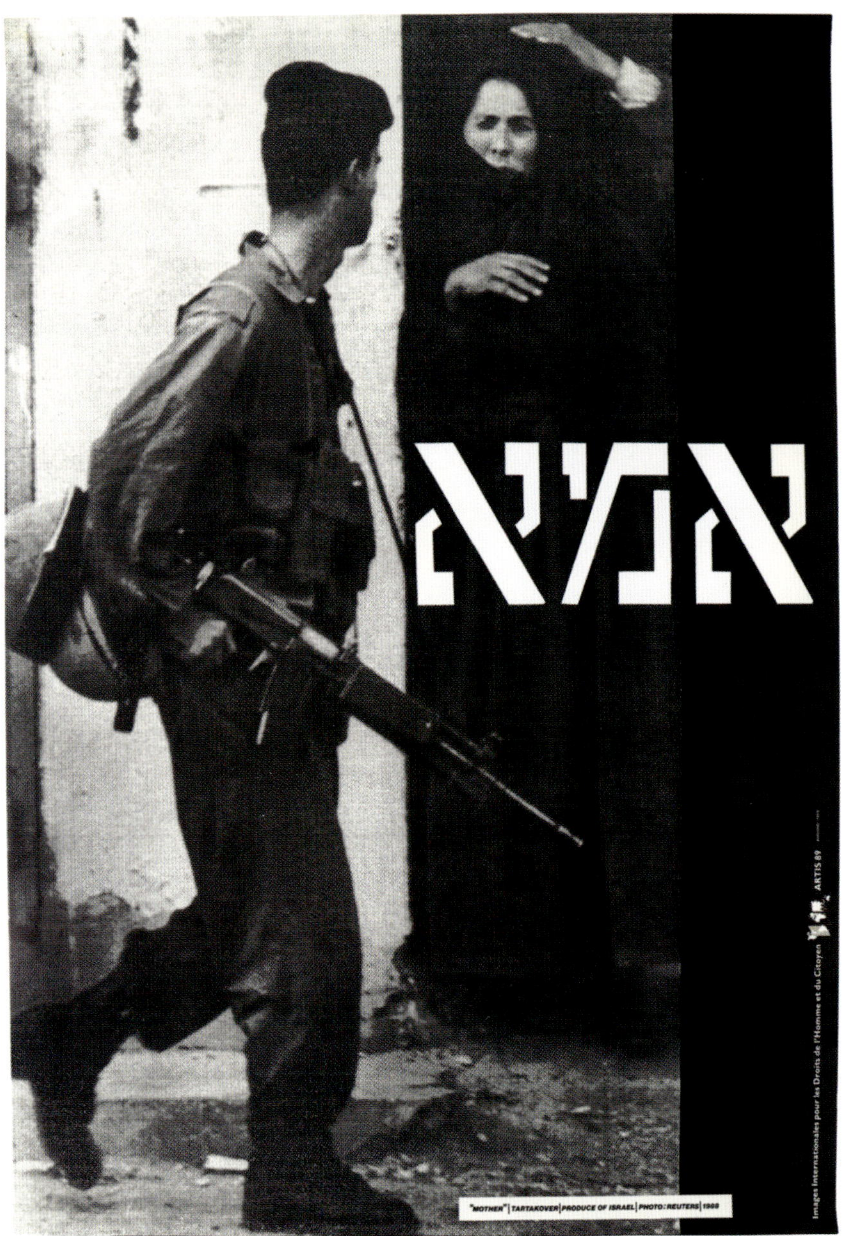

← 'Mother' 1988
David Tartakover
Poster

The most recent phase of the Israeli-Palestinian
conflict could be said to have had its roots
in the creation of the independent state of
Israel in 1948 and its consequent treatment
of the resident Palestinians ever since (as well
as their resolute retaliations). This eventually
led to the containment of Palestinians in the
'Occupied Territories' – the West Bank and
Gaza Strip – and conflict between the two
sides over at least 50 years. A strong peace
moment has been present throughout, shown
by groups such as Peace Now, Gush Shalom
(Israeli Peace Bloc), Yesh Gvul (There is
a Limit) and others, but the politics of the
situation, and lack of diplomacy, have made
real progress impossible. The prominent Israeli
designer, David Tartakover, created the 1978
logo for Peace Now and many posters along
the way, protesting the violence of the conflict
and isolating moments of truth. This 'truth' is
evident in the poster 'Mother', showing a news
photograph of an Israeli soldier passing by and
returning the gaze of a Palestinian woman. It is
a defining moment relating to mothers and sons
of both sides, and the possible pain and loss
inflicted on both.

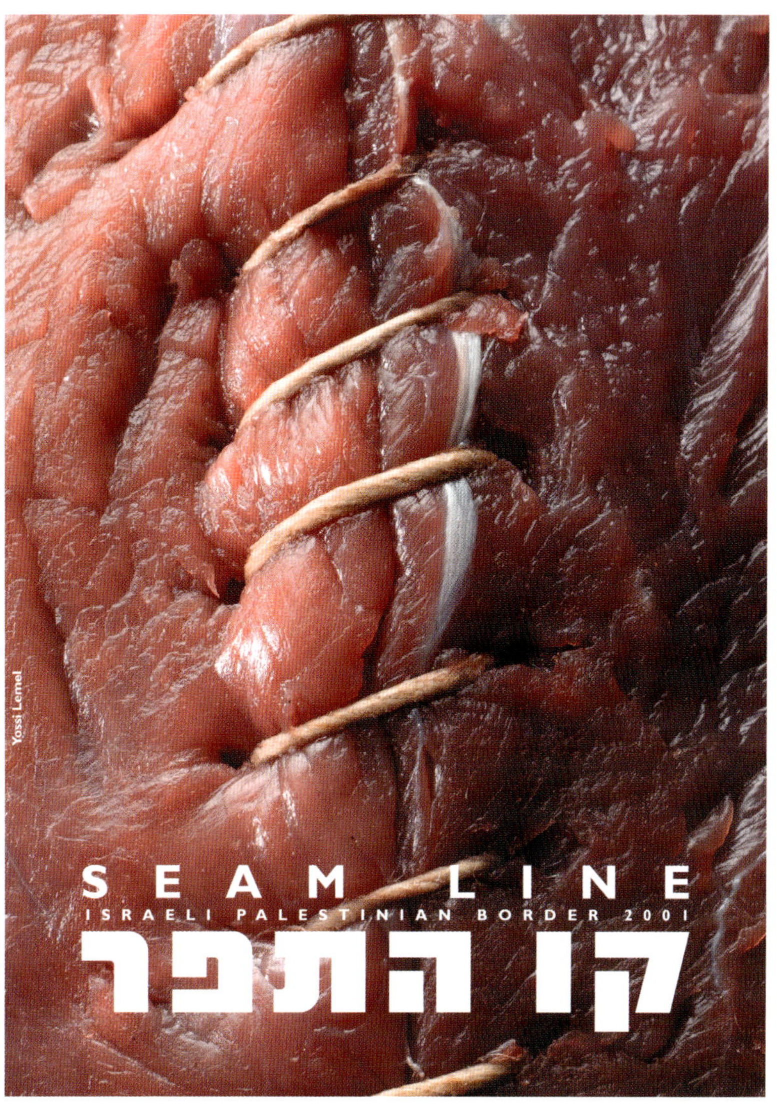

Seam Line: Israeli Palestinian Border 2001
Yossi Lemel
Poster

Yossi Lemel is also a central figure in both Israeli and international political poster design. Using distinctive, high-quality photography, his posters derive their force from the manipulation of modern signs and symbols, allowing for multiple readings. In this poster, meat becomes the bloody meat and muscle of humanity (both Israeli and Palestinian) tied together forcefully by string, rather than lying together peacefully. The punctured holes in the meat (on both sides) can be seen as the historical injuries suffered and tensions incurred over the years by the process of being forced together.

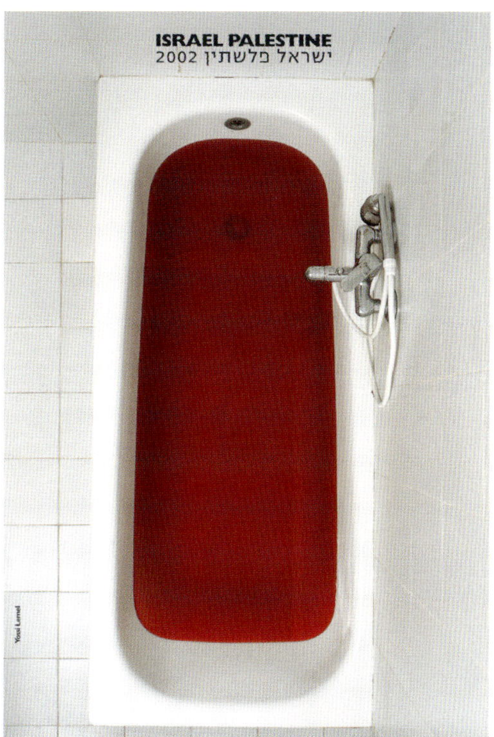

Bloodbath 2002
Yossi Lemel
Poster

Yossi Lemel pictorializes the term 'bloodbath' (meaning 'a massacre') literally, using a household bath to comment on a long period of intense violence enveloping both Israelis and Palestinians in the early 2000s. Various interpretations can be suggested here: the notion of suicide or the cutting of one's wrists as if both sides are committing suicide together; or if viewing the tub, roughly, as the shape of Israel, both sides are bleeding into Israel together. Or the bathtub can be reminiscent of a morgue, with cold, hard surroundings and dripping drains, which is where all will end up. It remains a harsh (and unfortunately timeless) statement about a country that, even now, must continue searching for a lasting peace.

The Anti-Apartheid Movement

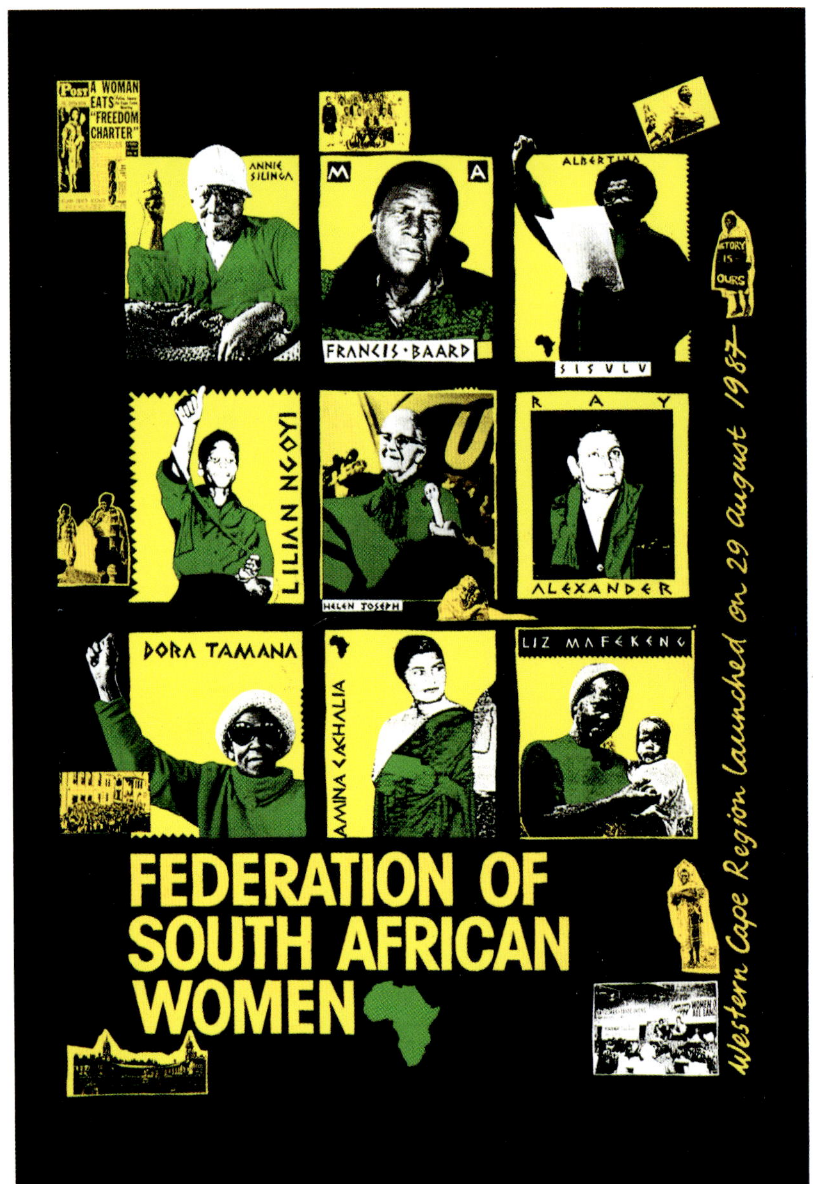

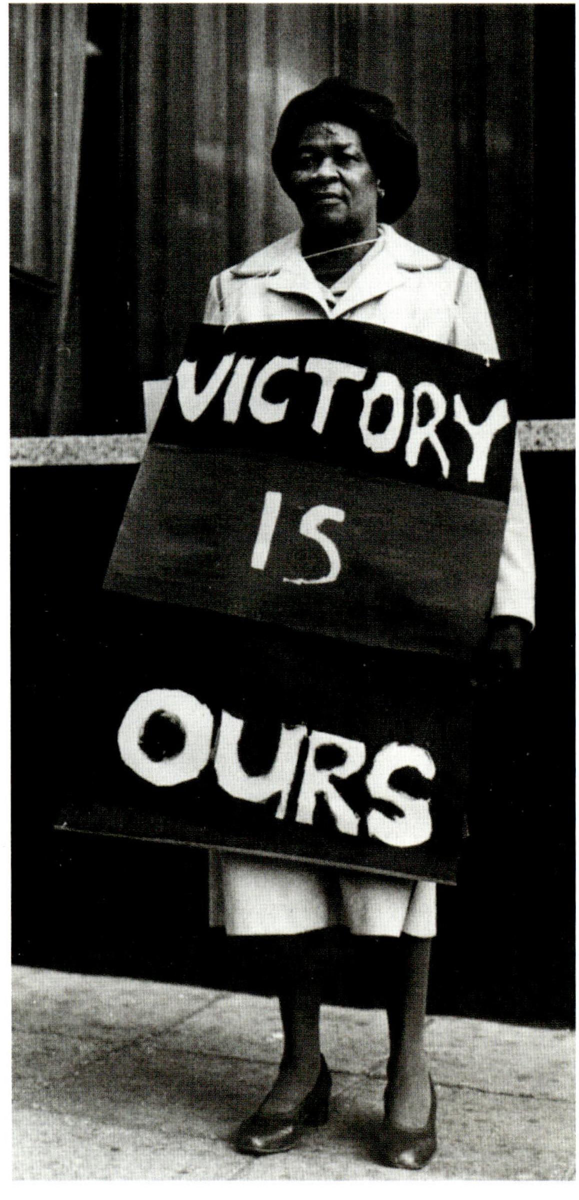

**Federation of South African Women
(Western Cape Region)** 1987
Designer unknown
Poster (offset litho)

The introduction in 1948 of apartheid (a
system of enforced racial segregation) in
South Africa was soon followed by the first
Defiance campaign in 1952: the beginning of
a struggle that would last until 1990. During
that period the black majority would endure
Pass Laws, work restrictions, punishments
and imprisonment for resistance, the murder
(or injury) of their leaders and loved ones
and countless other abuses. Throughout
those years, women always played an
important role in the struggle. Furthermore,
grassroots organizations produced posters,
particularly in the 1980s, that supported the
determination of the people. The posters
were also considered, by the state and by
the security police, to be subversive (and
therefore dangerous). The poster shown
here honours heroines of the South African
struggle, including Albertina Sisulu (above),
one of 16 United Democratic Front leaders
charged with treason in 1985.

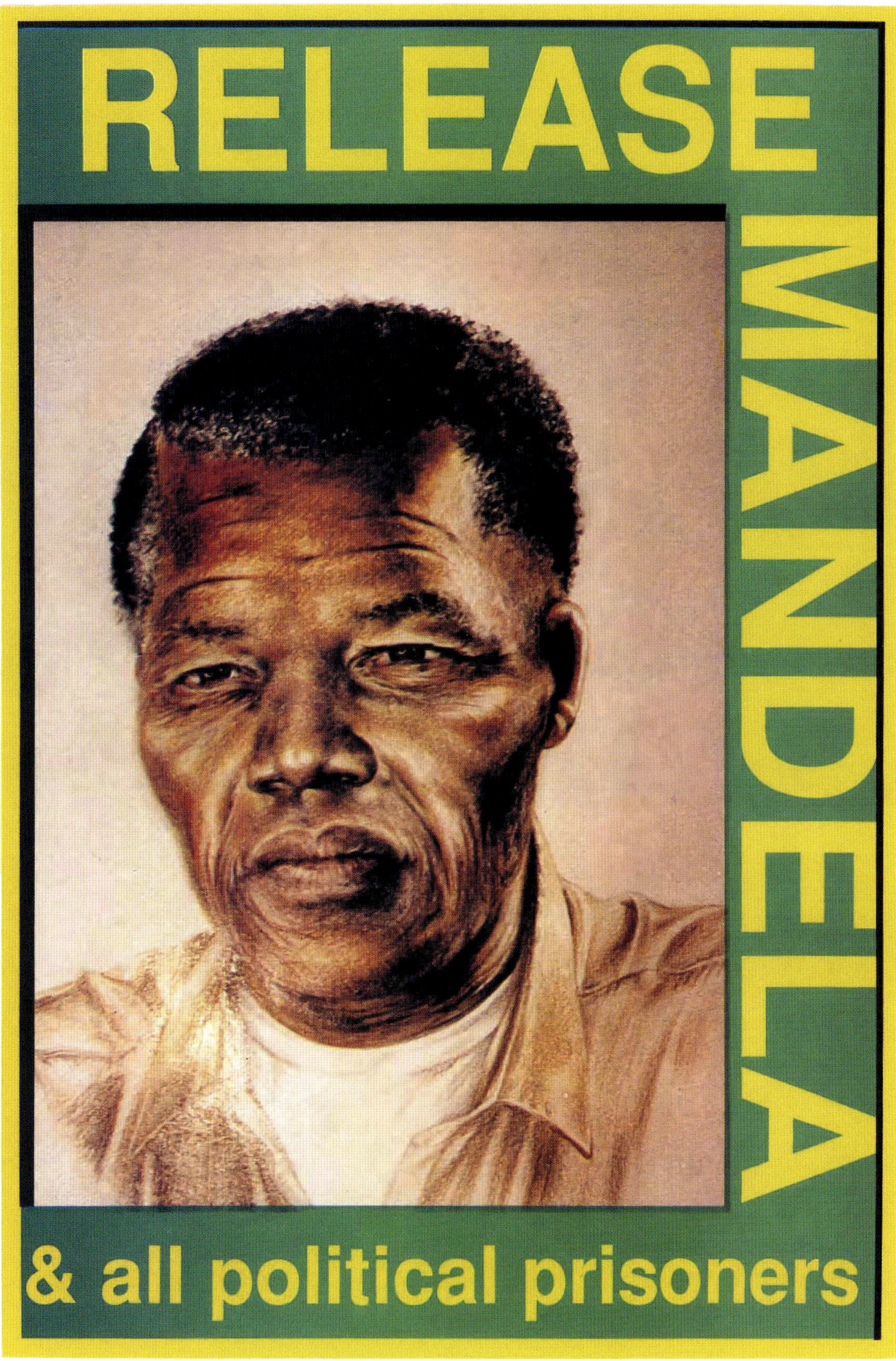

Release Mandela 1989
Designer unknown
Poster (offset litho)

This poster portrait of Nelson Mandela, made while he was still in prison, was painted from the verbal descriptions of people who had visited him. (It was illegal to publish the photograph of a prisoner.) The poster would have given strength and encouragement to many, and was produced by COSATU, the Congress of South African Trade Unions in Johannesburg.

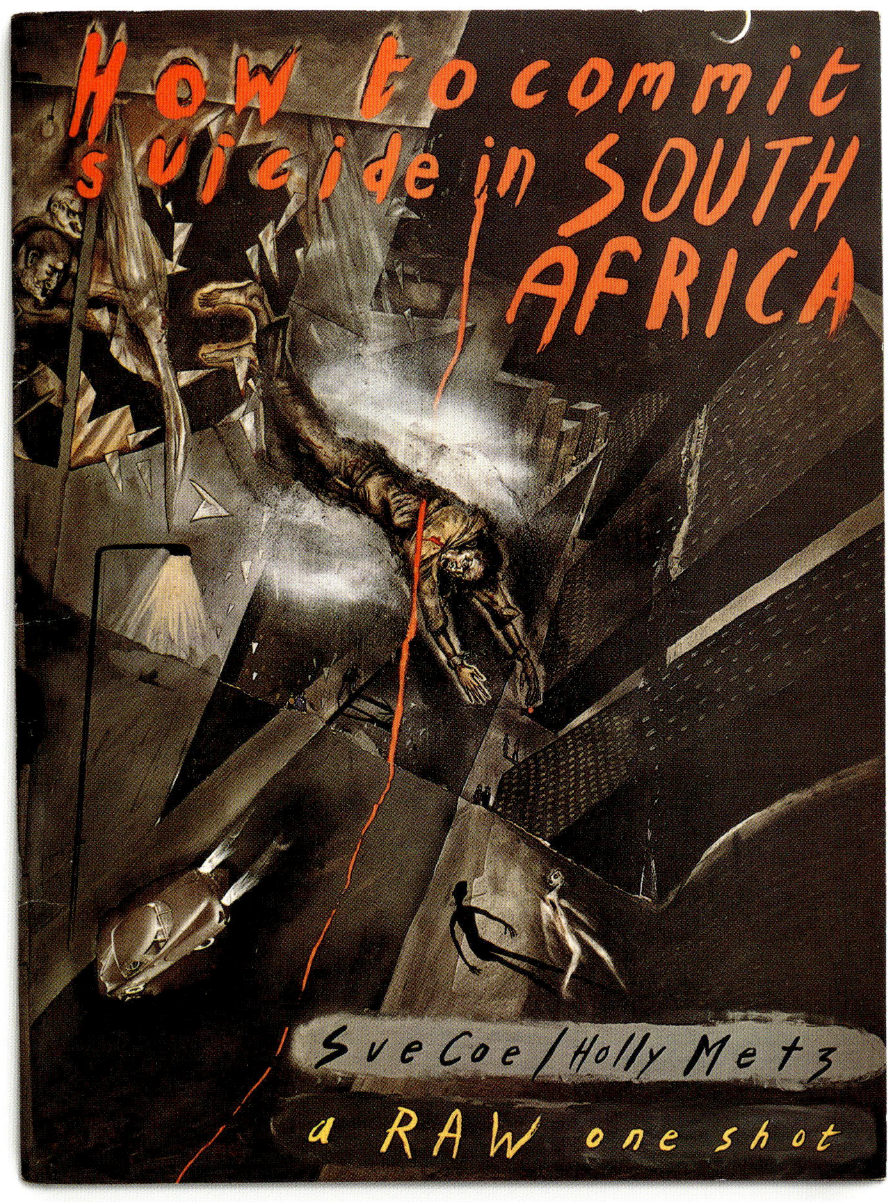

How to Commit Suicide
in South Africa 1983
Illustrations: Sue Coe
A4 booklet: cover and inside spread

Artist Sue Coe and journalist Holly Metz
created this handbook after reading about
people who died or 'committed suicide' in
detention in South Africa, including the
Black Consciousness leader Steve Biko
who died in detention in 1977. It contained
researched information concerning racism
in South Africa – historical timelines,
statistics on foreign investment and so
on – and was illustrated by Sue Coe's
dark, nightmarish imagery. It became an
important consciousness-raising document
in both Britain and the USA, and was used
as an organizing tool on US campuses when
'divestment' (the withdrawal of public funds
from companies investing in South Africa)
was being hotly debated as a potential tool
for challenging apartheid.

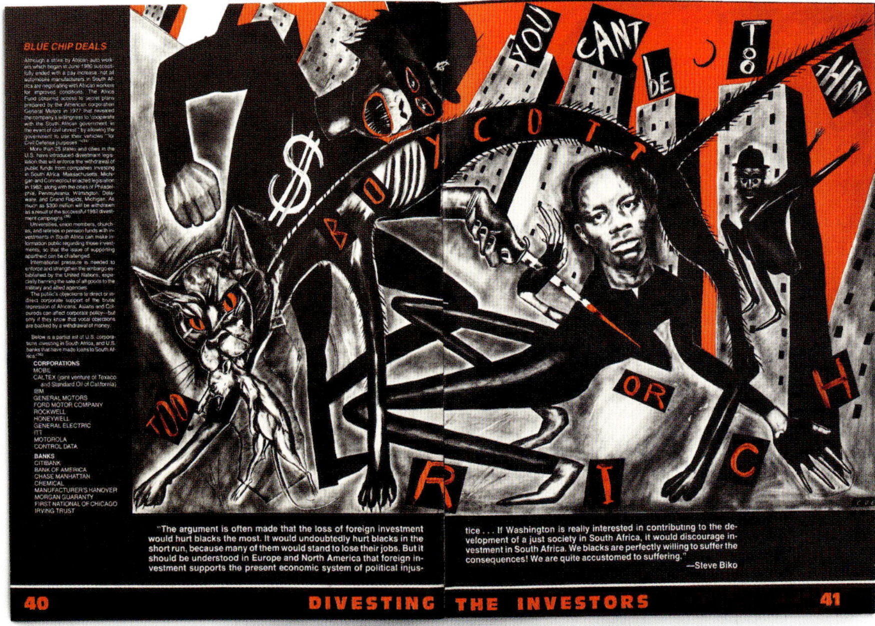

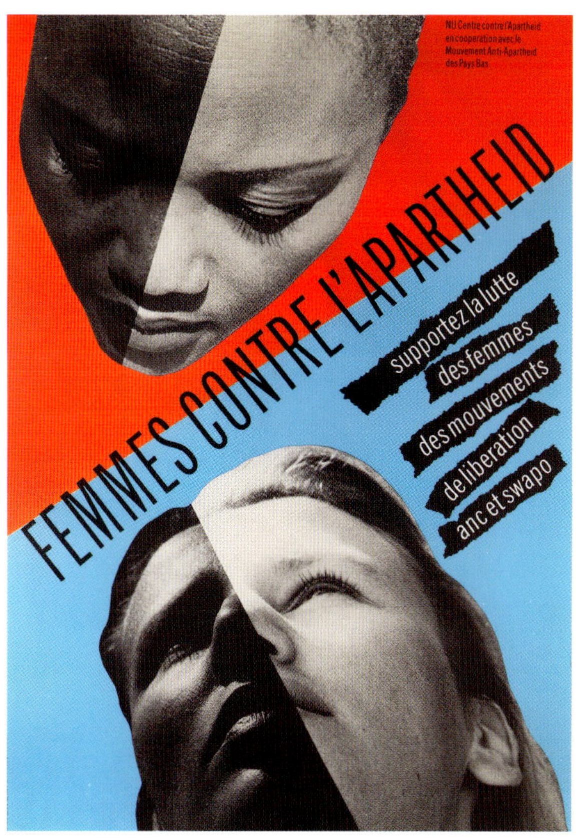

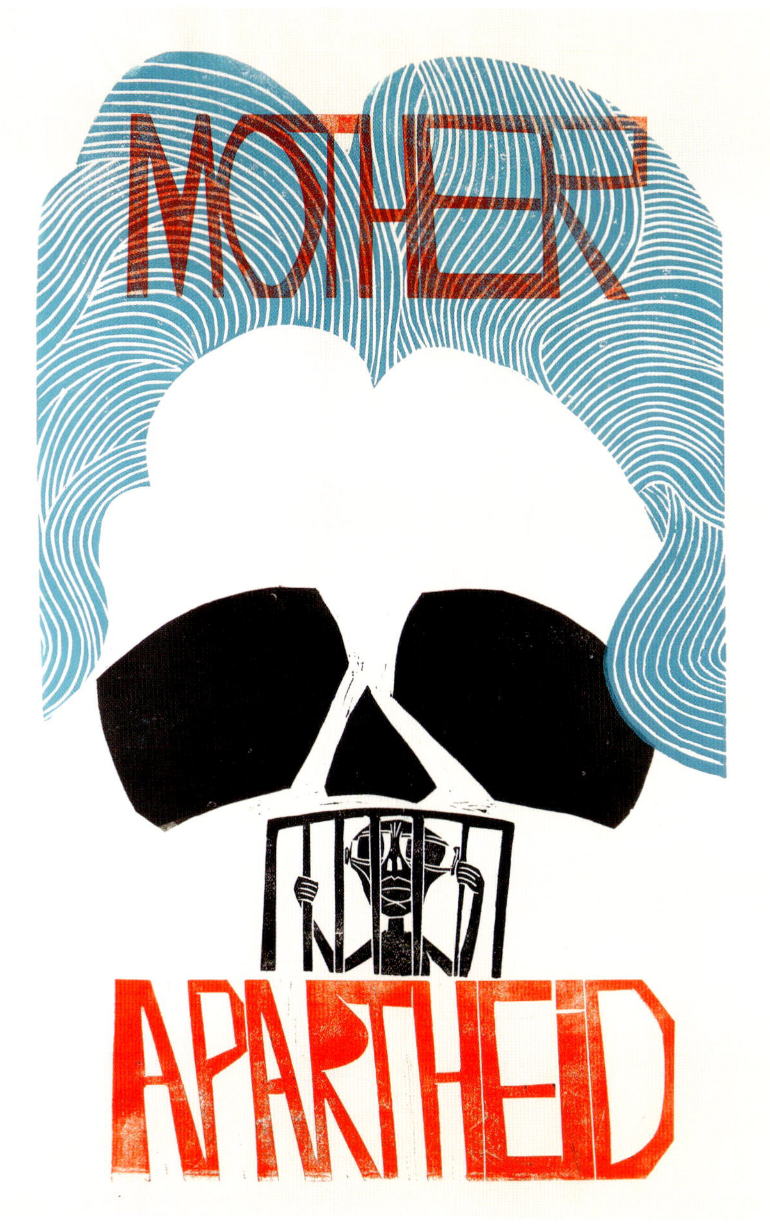

Women Against Apartheid 1984
Wild Plakken (Frank Beekers,
Lies Ros, Rob Schröder)
Poster

The full text on the poster reads: 'Women Against
Apartheid. Support the struggle of the women of
the liberation movements ANC and Swapo.' The
poster was made by Wild Plakken design group
in Amsterdam, who created many anti-apartheid
statements in photo-collage form for the energetic
AABN, the Dutch anti-apartheid movement. For
years the Dutch government subsidized the AABN,
which also received heavy support from the public
due to the past Dutch connection with South Africa.

Mother Apartheid 1987–88
Paul Peter Piech (The Taurus Press)
Poster (lino-cut)

The international anti-apartheid movement escalated in the 1960s, the
1970s and particularly the 1980s when pressure against the South African
state was at its height. In Britain, solidarity posters, postcards and badges
were highly visible. Industrial embargoes were held by trade unions,
sporting associations and the entertainment industry. Boycotts were
organized against South African goods and British companies based in
South Africa. The possibility of punitive sanctions or divestment was hotly
debated. Lastly, criticism was hurled at Prime Minister Margaret Thatcher
for her dealings with the South African government, as shown in this poster
by printmaker Paul Peter Piech, one of a number of posters he produced in
support of the anti-apartheid movement.

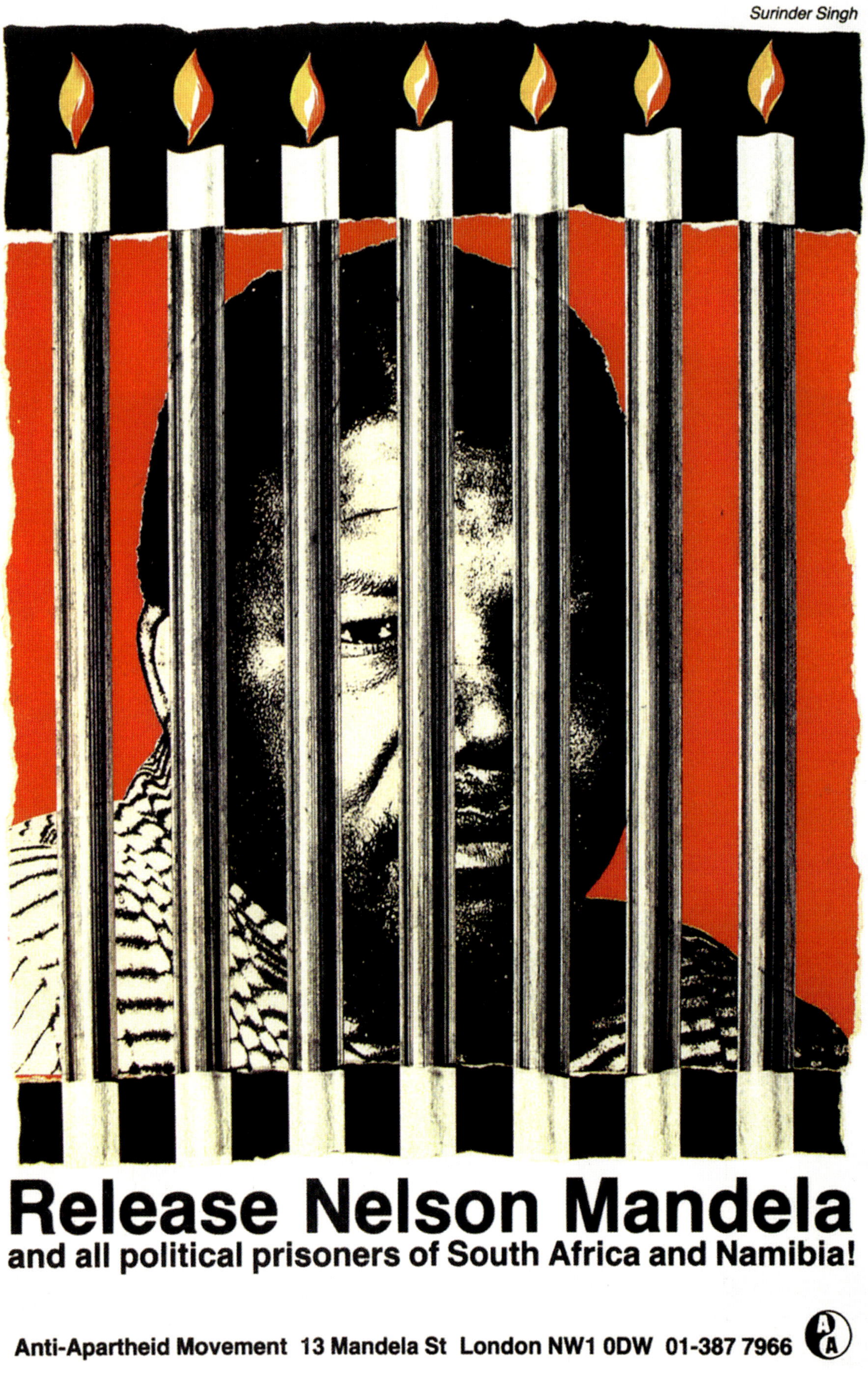

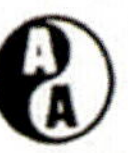

Surinder Singh
Release Nelson Mandela
and all political prisoners of South Africa and Namibia!
Anti-Apartheid Movement 13 Mandela St London NW1 0DW 01-387 7966

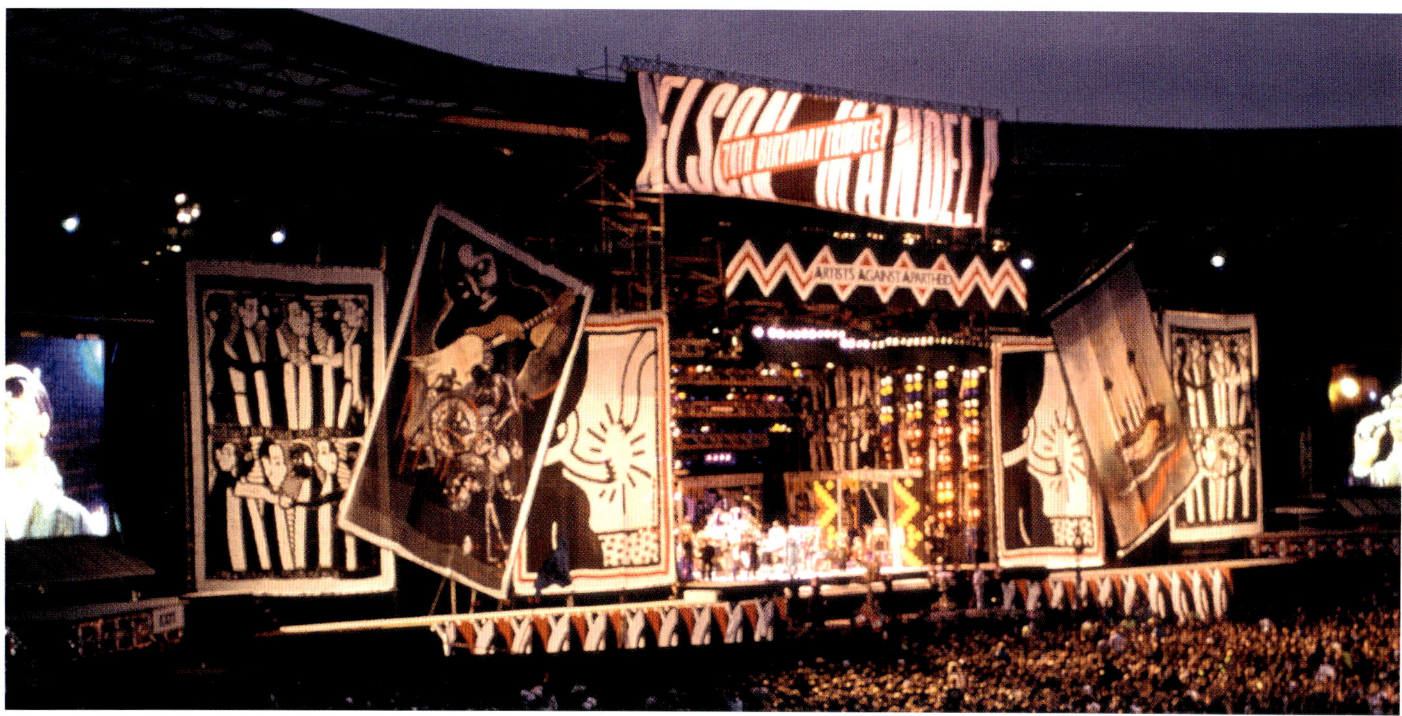

↑ **Nelson Mandela 70th Birthday
Tribute Concert, London** 1988
Photographer: John Cole
Photograph

The 70th Birthday Tribute Concert staged for the imprisoned Nelson
Mandela was held at Wembley Stadium, North London on 11 June
1988. It was organized by Artists Against Apartheid as part of the
British Anti-Apartheid Movement's 'Nelson Mandela Freedom at 70'
campaign. The concert was performed before a backdrop of work
by artists Keith Haring and Jenny Holzer (USA), John Muafangejo
(Namibia) and others. Attended by a capacity audience of 72,000,
the ten-hour concert was also watched on television by up to a billion
people in over 60 countries around the world.

← **Release Nelson Mandela** 1988
Surinder Singh
Poster (silkscreen and offset)

In 1988 the imprisoned Nelson Mandela reached the age of 70. The
British Anti-Apartheid Movement, along with other organizations and
groups, decided to stage birthday celebrations and send support and best
wishes for his release. This poster was produced by the Anti-Apartheid
Movement as part of their 'Nelson Mandela Freedom at 70' campaign.

→ **Untitled** 1988
Keith Haring
Poster

Renowned US artist Keith Haring produced images of great
directness, simplicity and impact, which not only sent a strong
message against apartheid in South Africa but also of the hope of
breaking free from other forms of oppression regardless of country.
This poster was part of the stage backdrop used in the Nelson
Mandela 70th Birthday Concert in London.

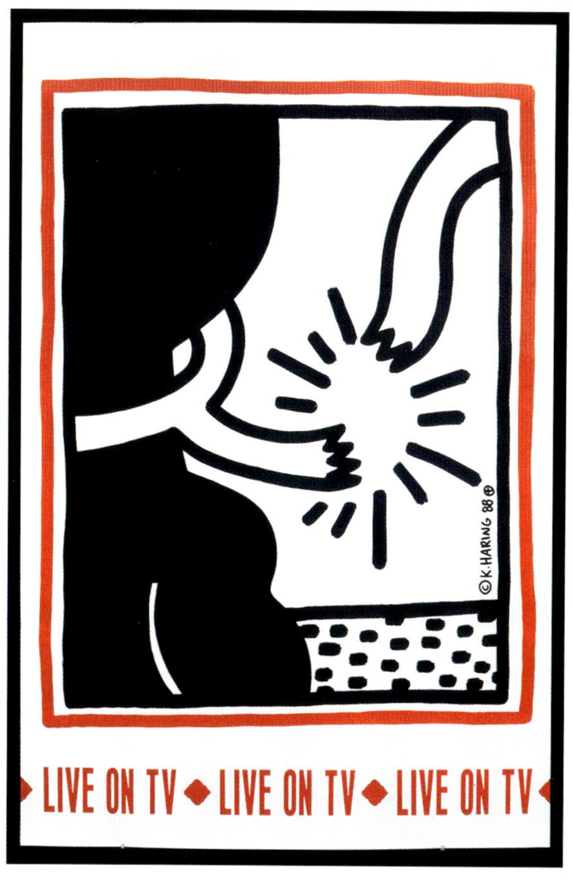

Feminism: The Third Wave

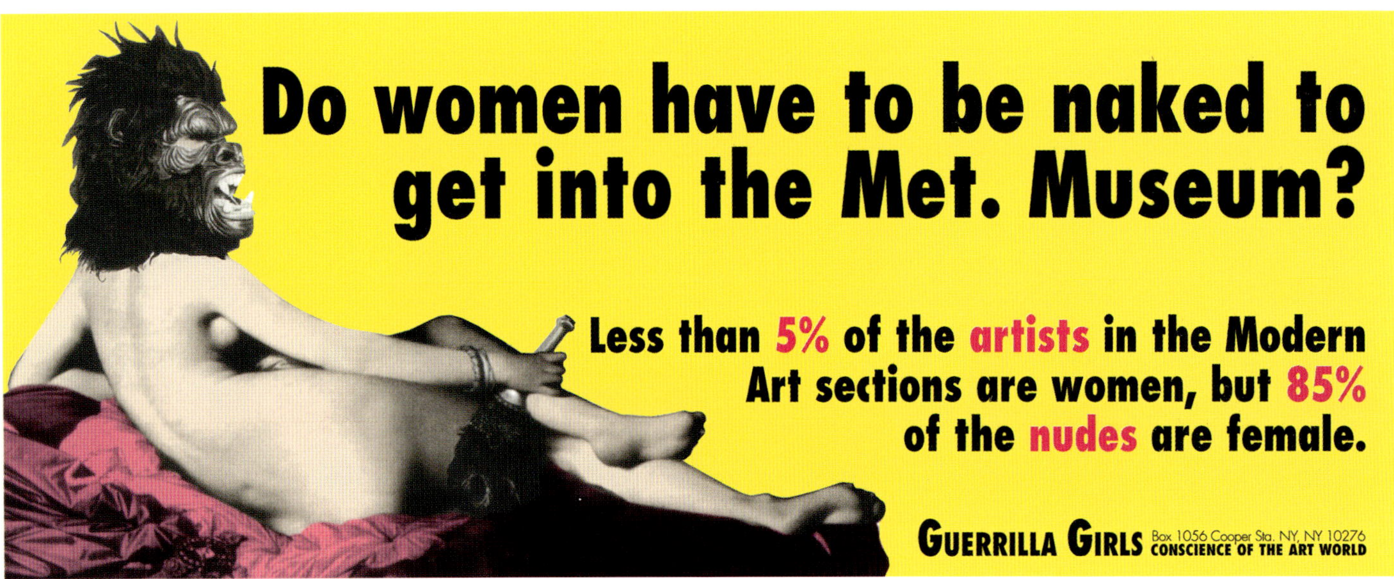

↑ **Do Women Have to be Naked …** 1989
Guerrilla Girls
Poster

The US feminist art activist group known as Guerrilla Girls began exposing sexual and racial discrimination in the New York art world in 1985. Their chosen weapons tended to be spontaneous street posters (often posted illegally at night). This particular poster, one of their most popular, was denied billboard space and so became a bus and street poster instead. Renowned for their sharp ironic humour, they have also lectured and made appearances but always dressed in gorilla masks or gorilla suits. Their anonymity is important in order to keep focus on the issues (rather than on personalities) and to avoid reprisals, for it has always been rumoured that they may be top female artists, curators or critics within the art establishment they criticize. Over the years they have produced books, travelled to other countries, and who knows if the members of the group have stayed the same. But they are still going strong, and their most recent posters and exhibitions have proved, via their statistics, that there hasn't been a great deal of improvement with regard to the status of art by women (or women of colour) in the collections of museums or the galleries of the art world.

↗ **Guerrilla Girls Street Posters** c.1990
→ Guerrilla Girls
Street posters

A few examples of the early street posters produced by the Guerrilla Girls are shown here; they would have been posted in the street at night. They attacked the New York galleries and museums by means of facts, statistics and the 'naming of names' (probably another reason that anonymity was crucial).

WHEN RACISM & SEXISM ARE NO LONGER FASHIONABLE, WHAT WILL YOUR ART COLLECTION BE WORTH?

The art market won't bestow mega-buck prices on the work of a few white males forever. For the 17.7 million you just spent on a single Jasper Johns painting, you could have bought at least one work by all of these women and artists of color.

Bernice Abbott	Elaine de Kooning	Dorothea Lange	Sarah Peale
Anni Albers	Lavinia Fontana	Marie Laurencin	Ljubova Popova
Sofonisba Anguisolla	Meta Warwick Fuller	Edmonia Lewis	Olga Rosanova
Diane Arbus	Artemisia Gentileschi	Judith Leyster	Nellie Mae Rowe
Vanessa Bell	Marguérite Gérard	Barbara Longhi	Rachel Ruysch
Isabel Bishop	Natalia Goncharova	Dora Maar	Kay Sage
Rosa Bonheur	Kate Greenaway	Lee Miller	Augusta Savage
Elizabeth Bougereau	Barbara Hepworth	Lisette Model	Vavara Stepanova
Margaret Bourke-White	Eva Hesse	Paula Modersohn-Becker	Florine Stettheimer
Romaine Brooks	Hannah Hoch	Tina Modotti	Sophie Taeuber-Arp
Julia Margaret Cameron	Anna Huntingdon	Berthe Morisot	Alma Thomas
Emily Carr	May Howard Jackson	Grandma Moses	Marietta Robusti Tintoretto
Rosalba Carriera	Frida Kahlo	Gabriele Münter	Suzanne Valadon
Mary Cassatt	Angelica Kauffmann	Alice Neel	Remedios Varo
Constance Marie Charpentier	Hilma af Klint	Louise Nevelson	Elizabeth Vigée Le Brun
Imogen Cunningham	Kathe Kollwitz	Georgia O'Keeffe	Laura Wheeling Waring
Sonia Delaunay	Lee Krasner	Meret Oppenheim	

Please send $ and comments to:
Box 1056 Cooper Sta. NY, NY 10276   GUERRILLA GIRLS CONSCIENCE OF THE ART WORLD

BUS COMPANIES ARE MORE ENLIGHTENED THAN NYC ART GALLERIES.

% of women in the following jobs*	
Bus Drivers	49.2%
Sales Persons	48
Managers	43
Mail Carriers	17.2
Artists represented by 33 major NYC art galleries	16
Truck Drivers	8.9
Welders	4.8

* Sources: U.S. Bureau of labor Statistics, Art in America Annual

Please send $ and comments to:
Box 1056 Cooper Sta. NY, NY 10276   GUERRILLA GIRLS CONSCIENCE OF THE ART WORLD

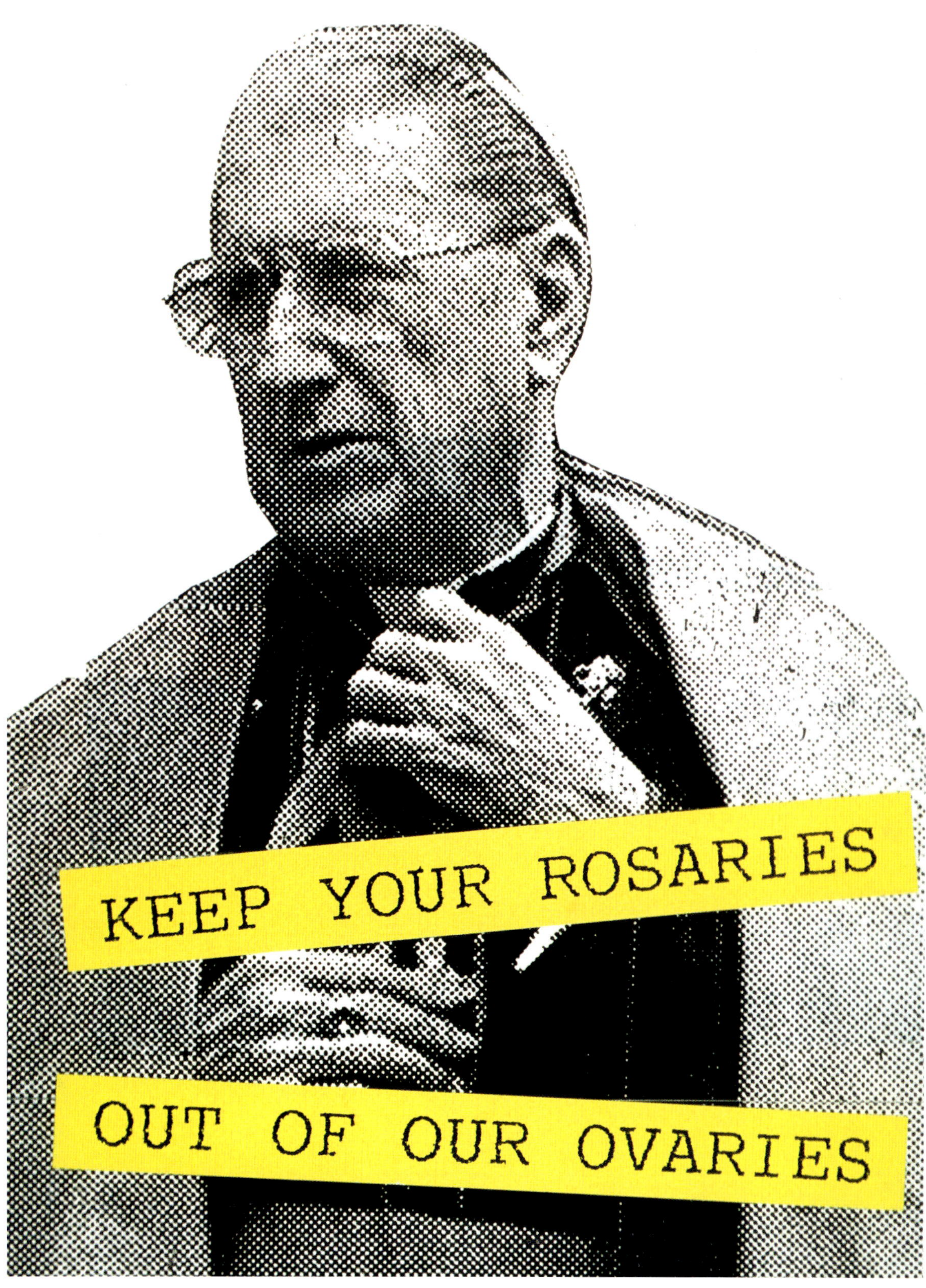

Keep Your Rosaries Out of Our Ovaries 1991–92
Marlene McCarty and Bethany Johns
Poster

The New York-based activist group, Women's Action Coalition or WAC (1992–94), committed itself to direct action on a variety of issues, particularly abortion rights and violence against women. This poster was carried outside of St Patrick's Cathedral to protest against Cardinal John O'Connor's public 'anti-choice' statements on behalf of the Catholic Church. The poster was also carried by the Women's Action Coalition at the 1992 'March for Women's Lives', a national rally for reproductive rights, and was used continuously for (pro-choice) clinic defence throughout the summer and autumn of 1992.

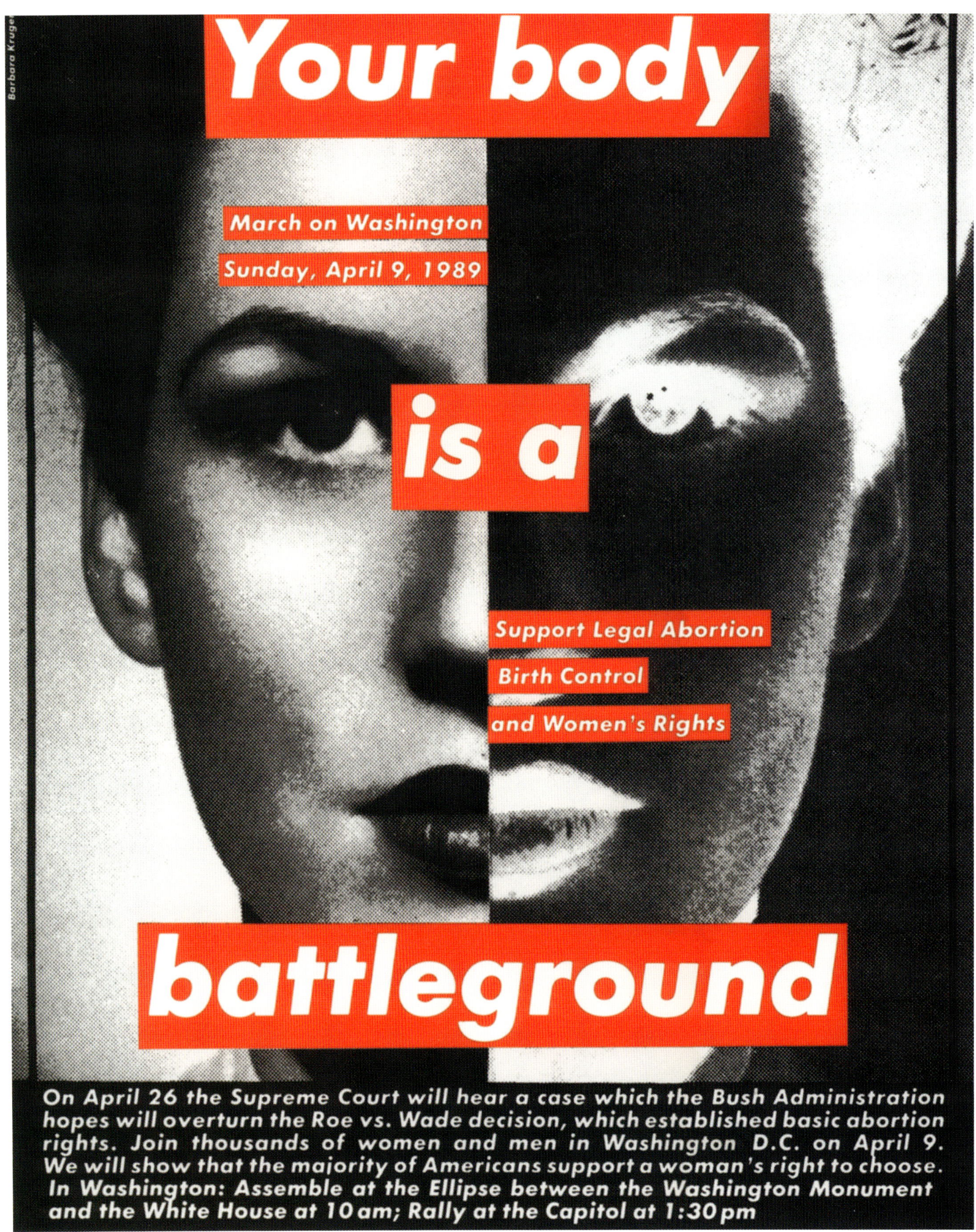

Barbara Kruger
Your body
March on Washington
Sunday, April 9, 1989
is a
Support Legal Abortion
Birth Control
and Women's Rights
battleground
On April 26 the Supreme Court will hear a case which the Bush Administration hopes will overturn the Roe vs. Wade decision, which established basic abortion rights. Join thousands of women and men in Washington D.C. on April 9. We will show that the majority of Americans support a woman's right to choose. In Washington: Assemble at the Ellipse between the Washington Monument and the White House at 10 am; Rally at the Capitol at 1:30 pm

← **Your Body is a Battleground** 1989
Barbara Kruger
Poster (offset)

After the build-up of pro-life and pro-choice forces
throughout the conservative 1980s in the USA, a
visual language of resistance emerged that would
tackle further threats to abortion rights in the
1990s. This graphic resistance was encapsulated in
Barbara Kruger's magnificent poster 'Your Body is
a Battleground', a call to arms on behalf of the 1989
march on Washington for birth control and basic
abortion rights for women. The image was also later
used to promote women's rights issues in other
countries.

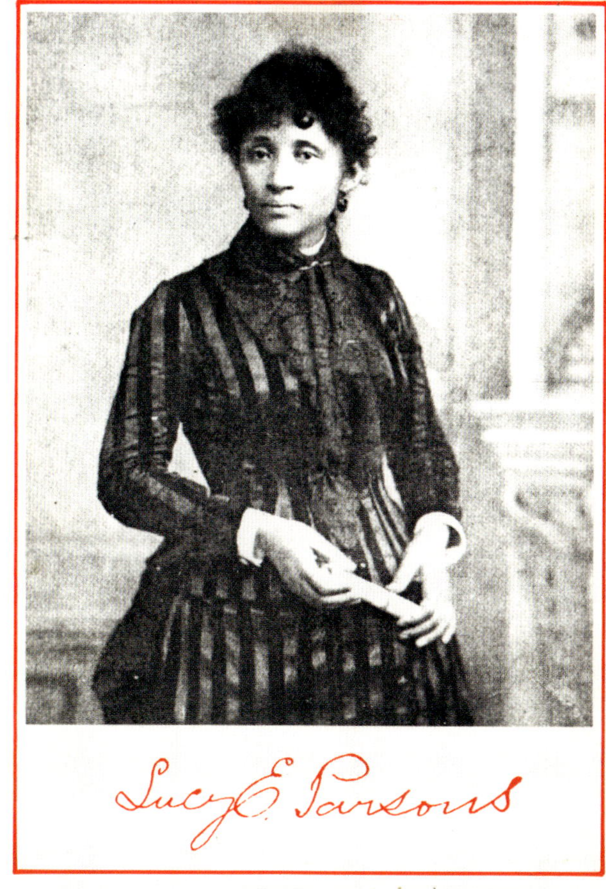

↗ **Helaine Victoria Press** 1973–90
→ Jocelyn Cohen and Nancy Poore
Postcards

Defiance towards the exclusion of women's
achievements throughout history brought about the
cultural search for 'hidden heroines', as practised by the
well-loved Helaine Victoria Press, which published mini-
histories of both ordinary and extraordinary women
within the ingenious format of the postcard (as well as
the occasional poster). Co-founded by Jocelyn Cohen
and Nancy Poore, the press researched and combined
archival photographs and potted-history captions of its
subjects into a uniquely intimate educational experience,
including both individuals and movements. Poore left in
1982, but Cohen carried on for almost a further decade
producing the distinctively designed postcards that
spanned the globe (by mail). The postcards shown here
depict Lucy E. Parsons (1852–1942), US free speech
and labour leader, and joyful ladies from the Woolworth
Workers' Sit Down Strike of 1937.

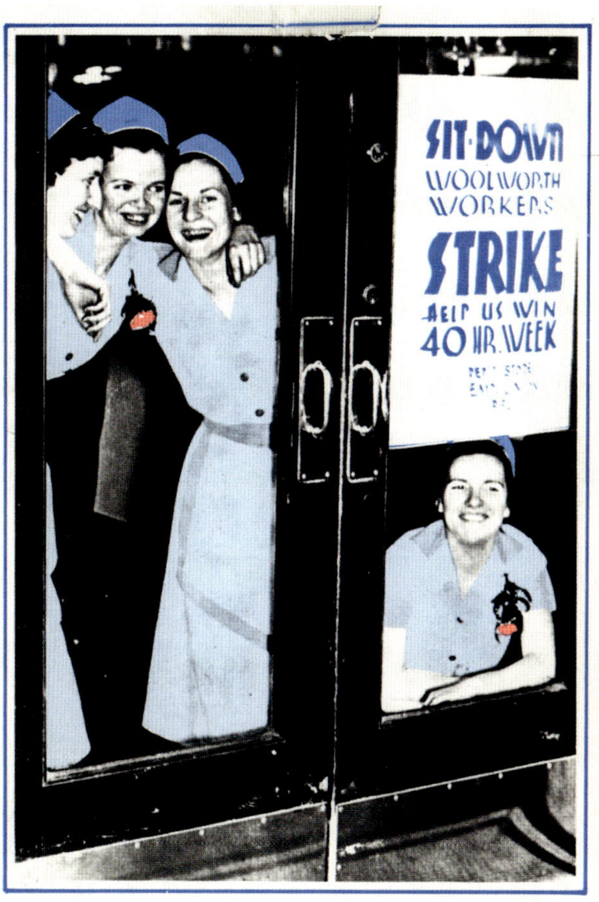

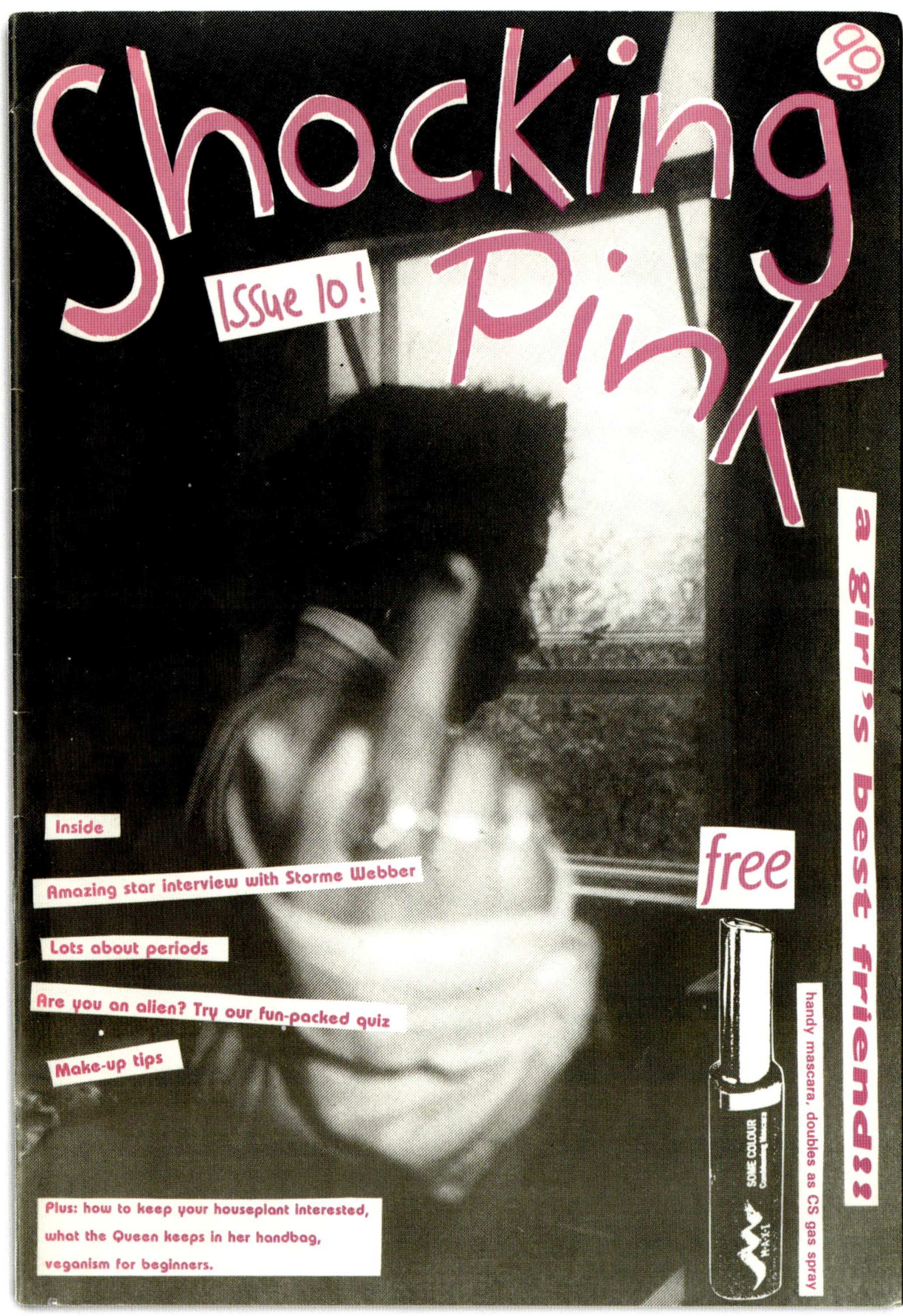

***Shocking Pink*, Issue 10** *c*.1990
Magazine/fanzine: front cover

The 1980s introduced a new generation of women with a tough, self-defined attitude and a powerful form of delivery. Both girls and women pitted themselves against the commercial media and cultural institutions that dominated and fashioned their lives. By challenging the powerlines of the media and its stereotyped roles, women found their own power: girlpower, womanpower and so on. A prime example of girlpower was the highly irreverent London-based feminist girls' magazine *Shocking Pink*. It combined Punk's fanzine tradition of do-it-yourself publishing with social critique and a feminist stance. Aimed at girls aged 10 upwards, it was produced by a collective aged 16 to 25, and was particularly keen to give space to young lesbians. They launched scathing attacks on the media and particularly on what they called the 'propaganda' of popular girls' magazines such as *Jackie*, which they accused of telling 12-year-old *Jackie* readers to 'buy more make-up' twenty-two times in each issue. Sharp-tongued and anti-authoritarian, *Shocking Pink* offered discussion and information on subjects ranging from contraception to politics.

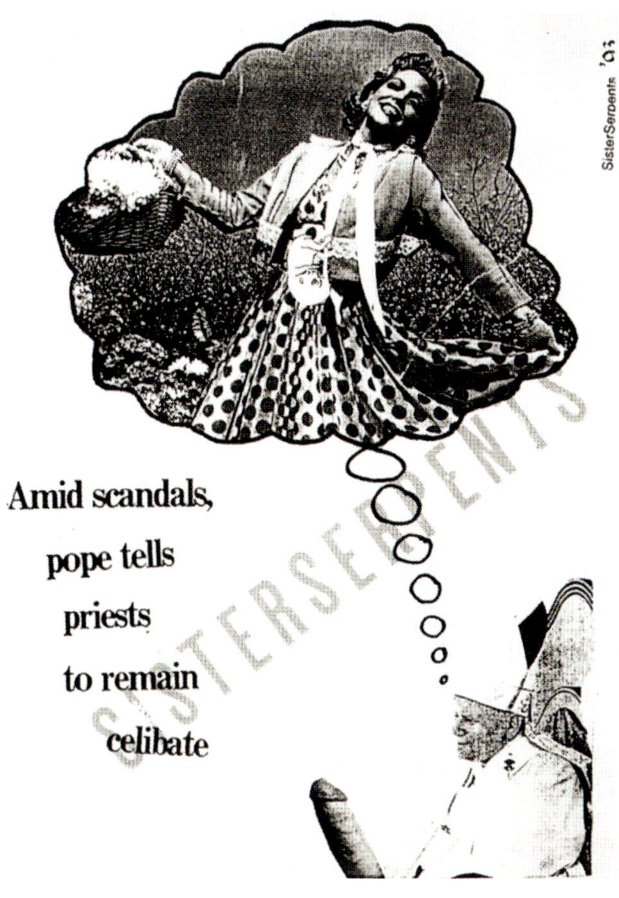

A Collection of Photo-collaged Posters by SisterSerpents 1994–95
SisterSerpents and Mary Ellen Croteau
Posters (offset and photocopy)

The Chicago-based, anonymous art activist group known as SisterSerpents (and its spokeswoman Mary Ellen Croteau) directed their venom at the many levels of sexism in society. They targeted society's varied symbols of sexism – including little boys' games, army pin-ups, and more – and their weaponry included stickers, rubber stamps, photocopies, posters and exhibitions that aimed to shock. With the battle cry 'GET ANGRY – Piss on Patriarchy', they produced some of the most provocative (and effectively uncomfortable) statements of the time. (One of them was a poster-collage of renowned cook Julia Child, holding up a kitchen knife which had a penis stuck on its point, titled 'Julia's simple method for stopping a rapist – Go for the Groin, Gals!') All created as part of a strategy they called 'idea warfare', their shocking imagery spat and railed against a system that allows the brutalization of women.

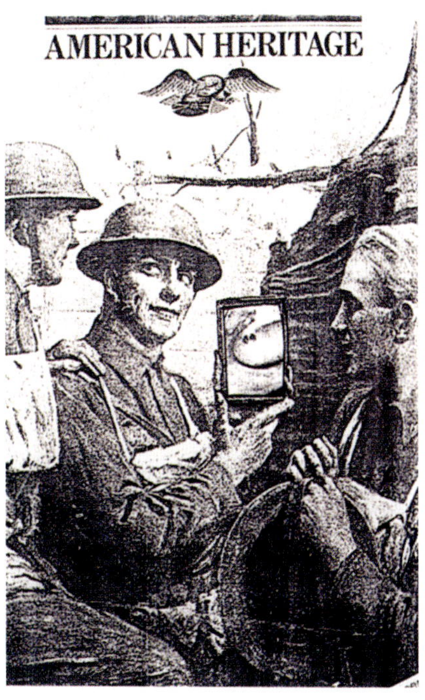

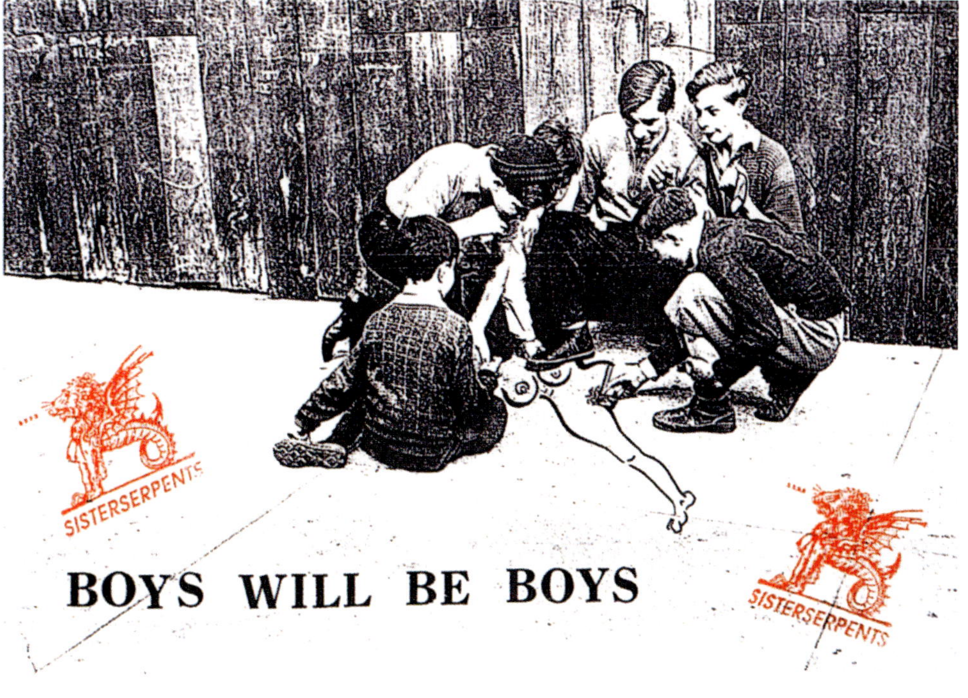

The AIDS Crisis

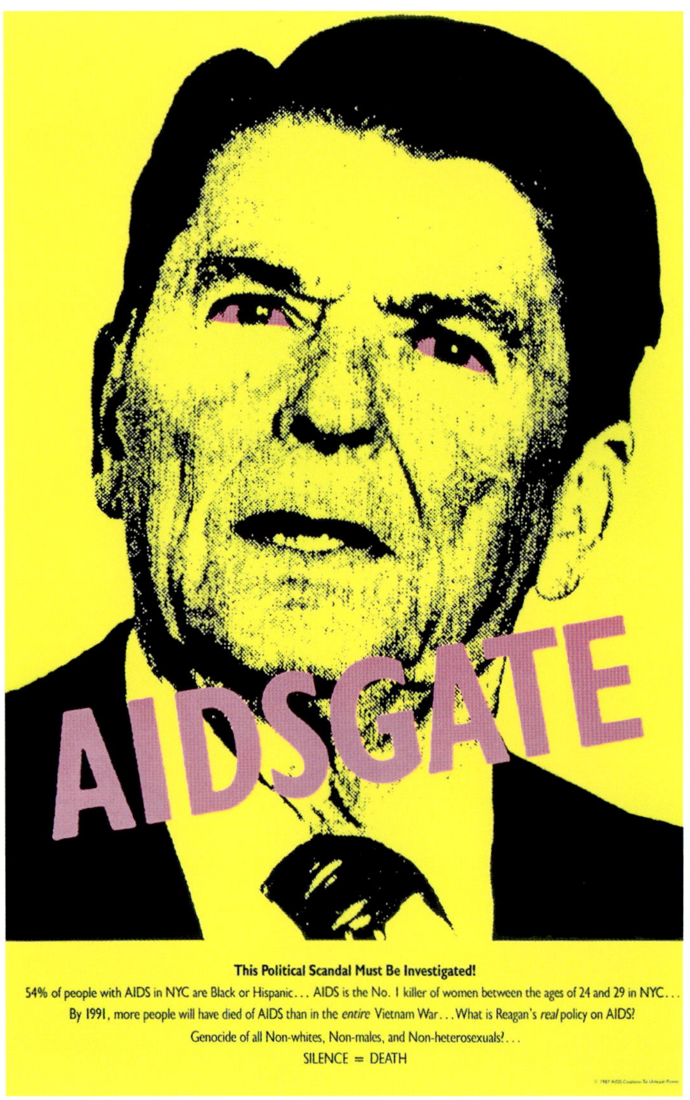

← **AIDSGATE** 1987
Silence = Death Project
Poster (offset lithography)

This poster was produced for use at the National AIDS Demonstration in front of the White House, aligned with the start of the Third International Conference on AIDS in Washington, D.C. on 1 June 1987. Both proved to be a massive gathering of AIDS activist groups aiming to protest government inaction on AIDS. When Ronald Reagan addressed the conference the night before, he made (shameful) history by saying the word 'AIDS' publicly for the first time – six years into the epidemic. By that time, ACT UP's factsheets were reporting 19,000 deaths. Thus the poster's title, AIDSGATE, refers to the scandals attributed to government inaction and Reagan's silence on the subject.

↓ **Kissing Doesn't Kill** 1989
Gran Fury art collective
Bus advertisement

Gran Fury was the art collective most heavily associated with 'exploiting the power of art to end the AIDS crisis', and produced a variety of graphics that contributed to ACT UP's distinctive style. 'Kissing Doesn't Kill' is a bus ad that ran in San Francisco and New York City, in which they made clever use of the sophisticated visual techniques of advertising.

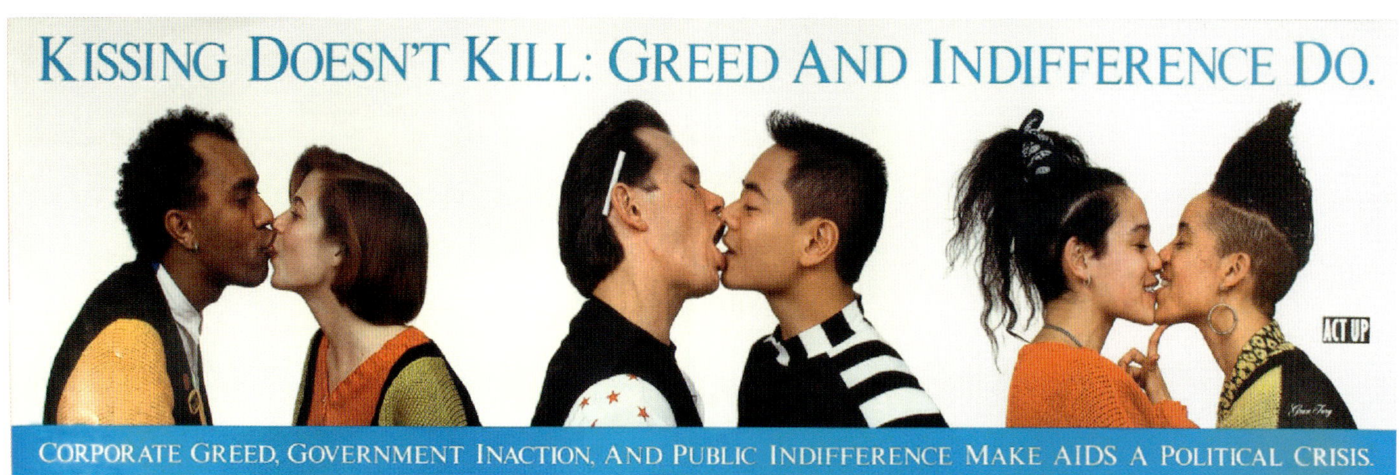

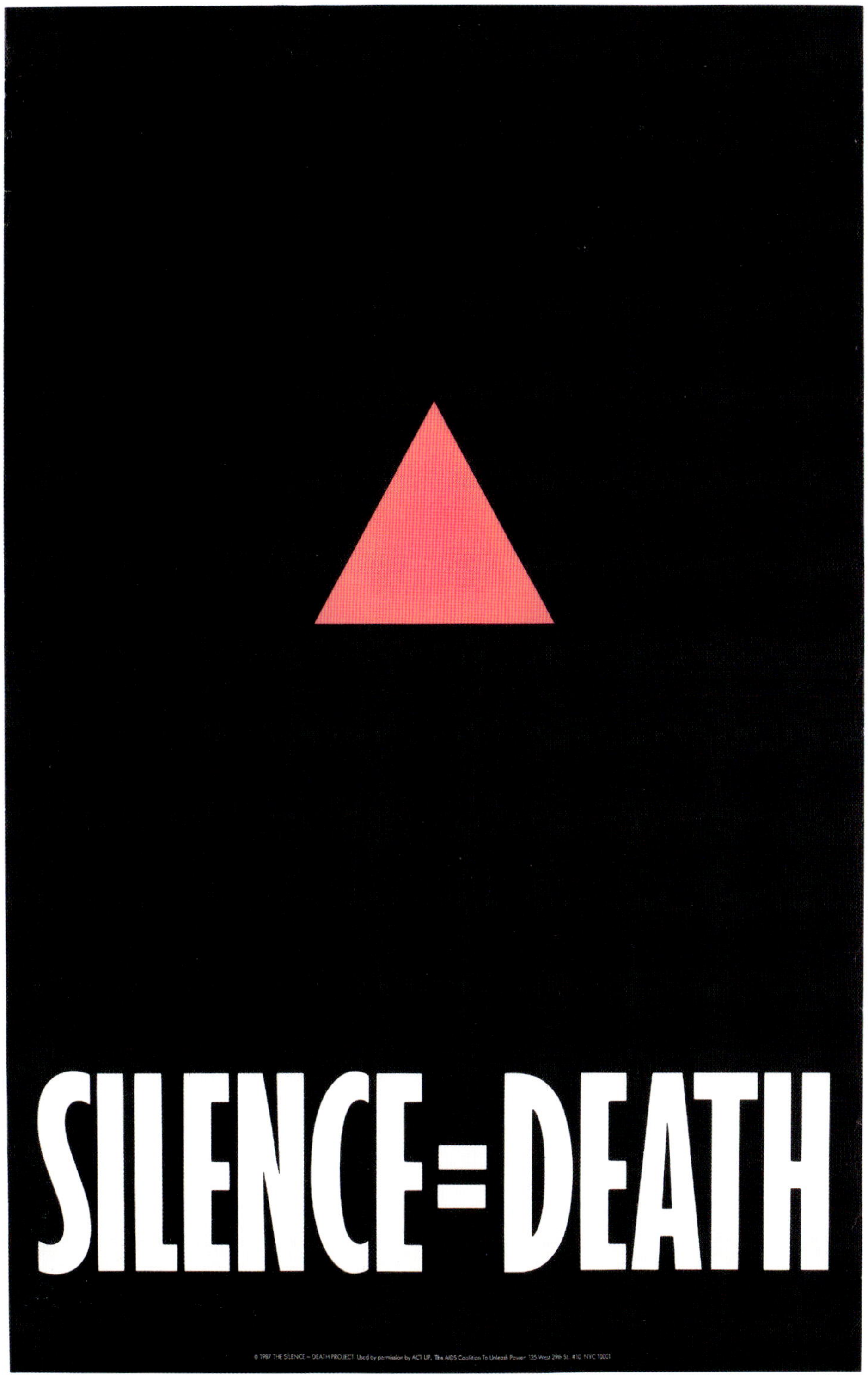

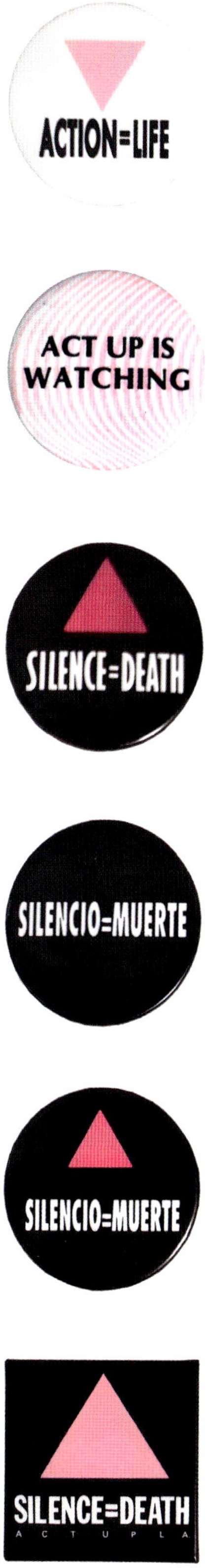

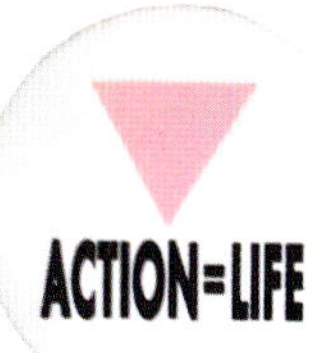

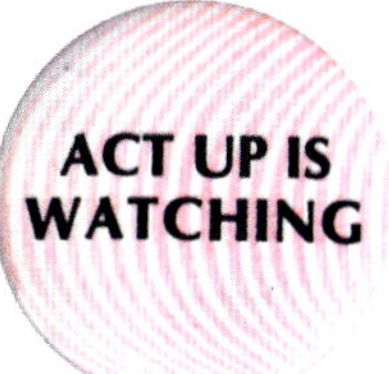

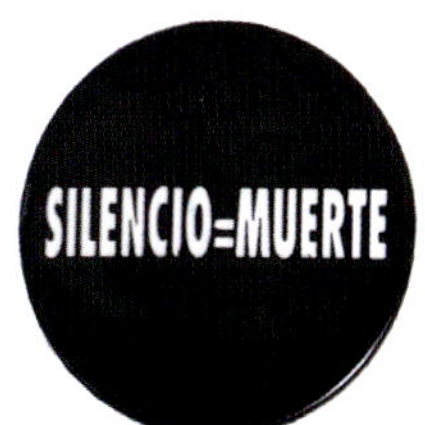

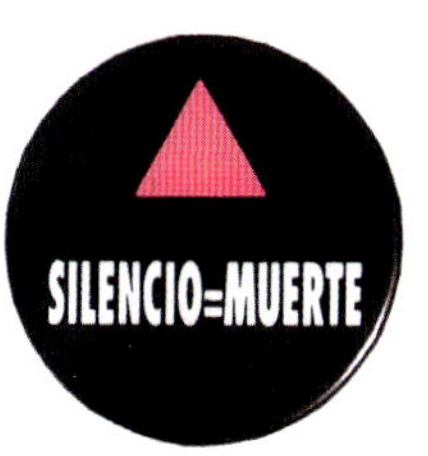

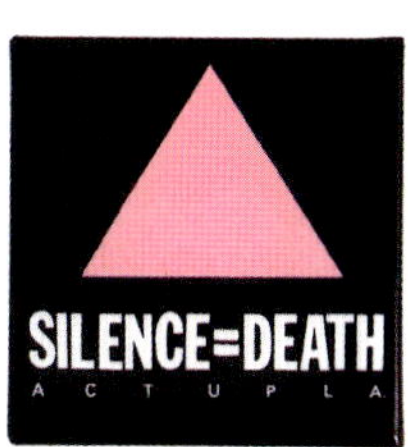

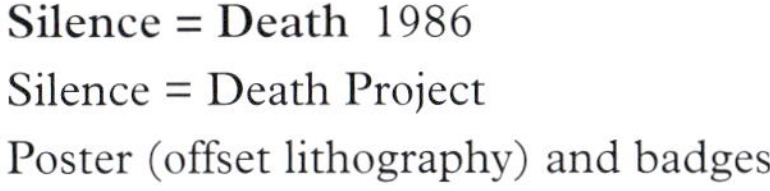

Silence = Death 1986
Silence = Death Project
Poster (offset lithography) and badges

This powerful graphic emblem was originally created by the Silence = Death Project: six gay men who produced posters of the design for display on the streets of New York City in 1986. They subsequently lent their design to ACT UP, and from thereon it became the main identifier not only for ACT UP but for AIDS activism in the United States. The use of the pink was symbolic. A pink triangle, pointing down, was the identifier worn by gay men in Nazi concentration camps in the Second World War; its inversion, pointing up, was a sign of resistance against new forces of oppression.

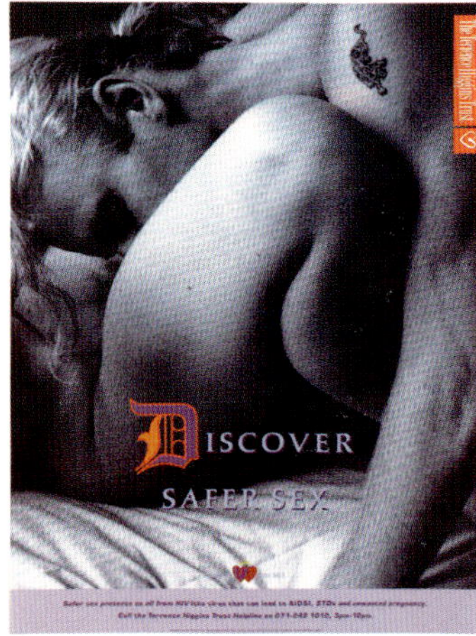

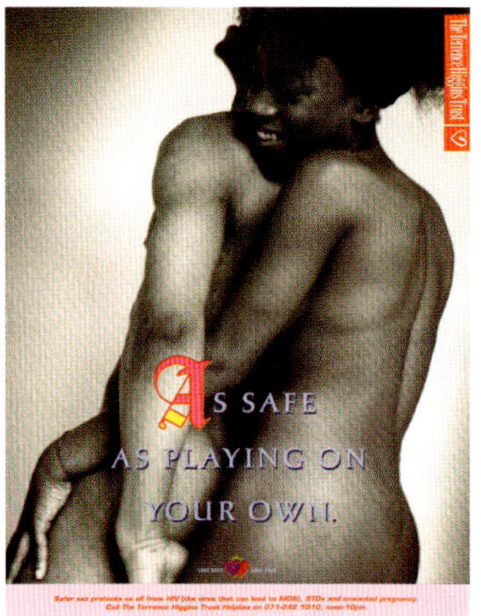

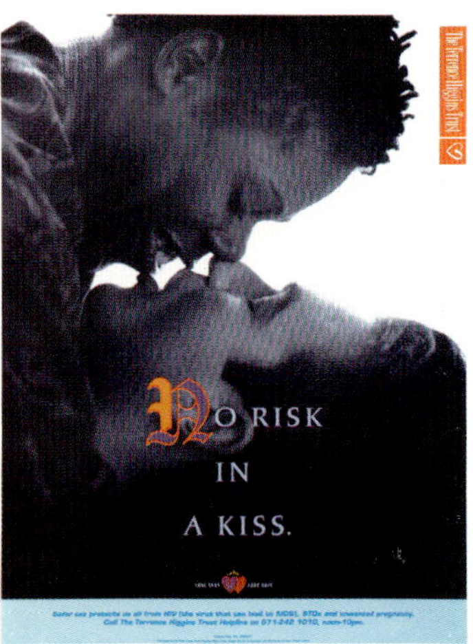

Safe-sex posters (from a series of six) for the Terrence Higgins Trust, designed by Big-Active, Britain, 1992.

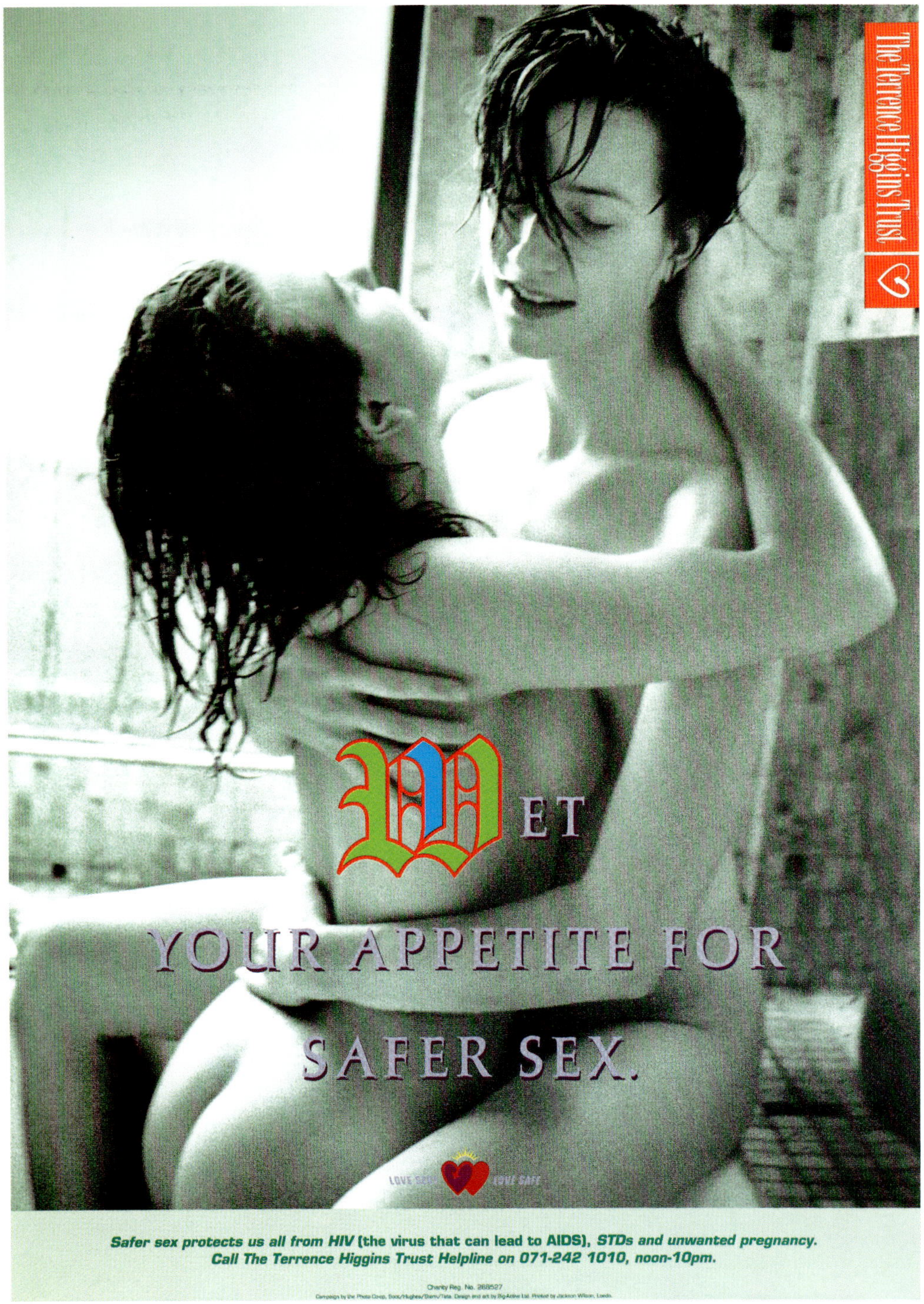

Safe-sex Education 1987–92
Artists: various
Posters (silkscreen and offset)

The fast-developing AIDS crisis was largely ignored by governments, globally, throughout the 1980s. This dreadful situation emphasizes the importance of the actions of the US activist group ACT UP (AIDS Coalition to Unleash Power) and their attacks on lack of government funding for research, treatment and care, and safe-sex education. Due to their initial efforts, by the early 1990s safe-sex poster campaigns existed internationally, and varied with regard to cultural traditions and audiences. Government campaigns normally addressed a broad general audience, and often used bland imagery, worried about offending the status quo. Campaigns produced by the community sector targeted specific audiences and tended to be much bolder in approach, as they were more directly involved with their audience. They addressed lesbians and gay men, the young, the sexually active – all those people most at risk – and rose to the challenge with imagination and energy. They realized the need to change attitudes and behaviour as well as combat misinformation and prejudice. They also had the courage to supply a sense of fun and humour, despite the dire circumstances. A selection of campaigns from community and activist organizations is shown here.

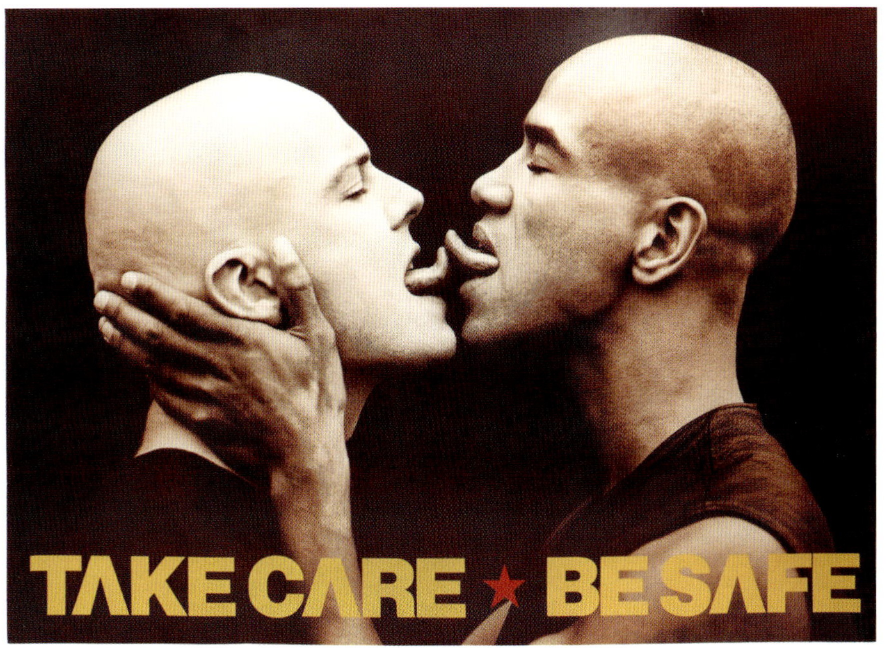

Poster from the 'Take Care, Be Safe' campaign for the Swedish Federation for Gay and Lesbian Rights (RFSL), design by Ola Johansson, photography by Robert Nettarp, Sweden, 1992.

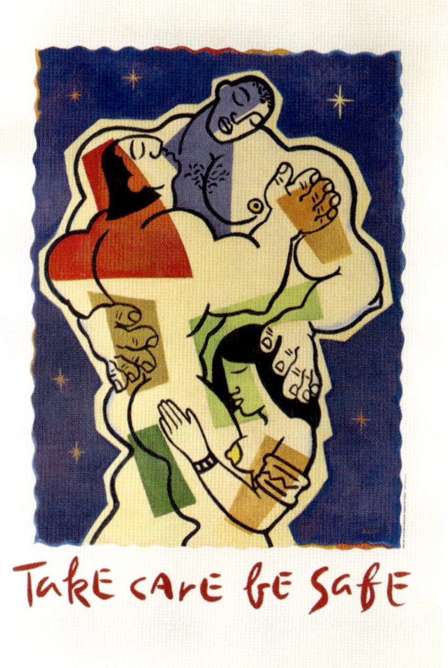

'Take Care, Be Safe', from a series of posters produced by the Swedish Federation for Gay and Lesbian Rights (RFSL) that were targeted for use in specific settings: this poster was meant for nurses' offices and surgeries in schools and similar contexts. The entire series was also used in gay bars and restaurants around the country as part of a large campaign, 1992.

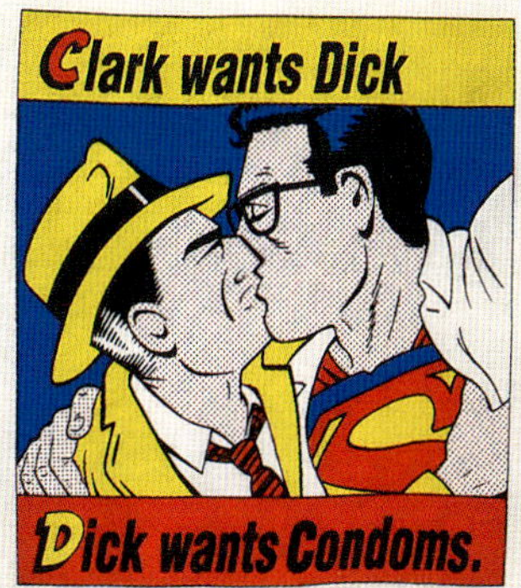

Comic book heroes: Clark Kent (alias Superman) smooches Dick Tracy, on a t-shirt produced by the Golden Gate chapter of the AIDS activist group ACT UP, USA, 1992.

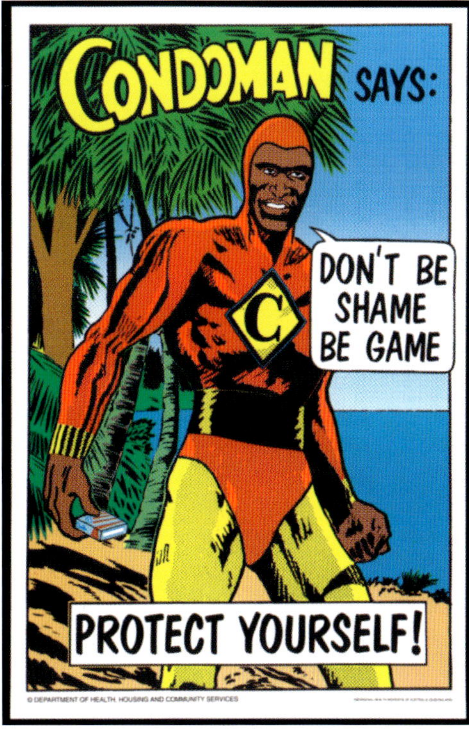

'Condoman', poster by Redback Graphix for NACAIDS, Canberra, Australia, 1987.

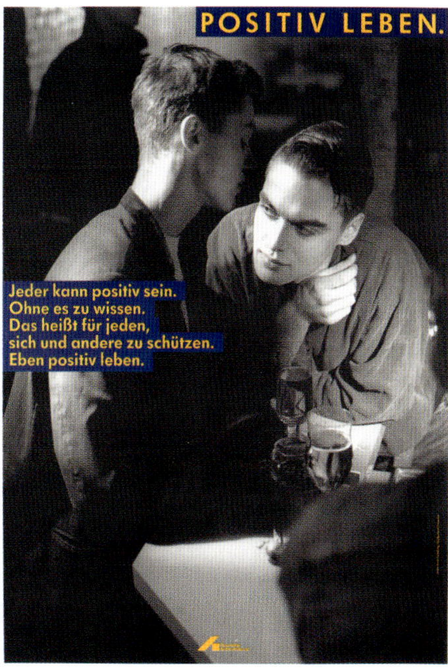

'Live Positively', supportive poster series on gay values and living by Deutsche AIDS-Hilfe; design: Detlev Pusch, photo: Jörg Reichard, Germany, 1992.

Lesbian and Gay Activism

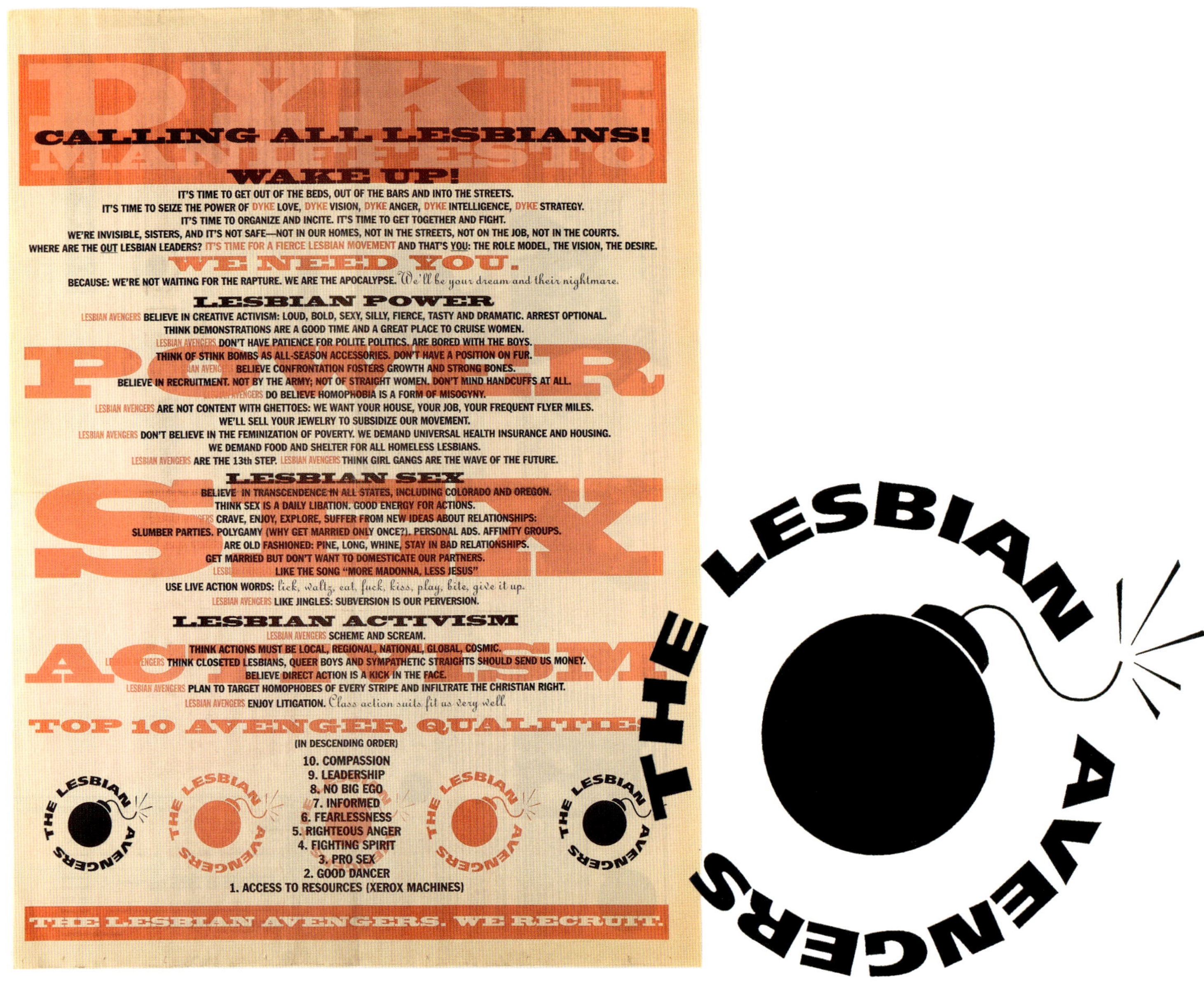

The Dyke Manifesto and Lesbian Avengers logo 1993 and 1992
Designer: Carrie Moyer
Poster (silkscreen and offset)

A new era of lesbian power and visibility surfaced in New York City in the early 1990s, with the founding of Dyke Action Machine (DAM!), the lesbian graphics project established in 1991 by painter and graphic designer Carrie Moyer and photographer Sue Schaffner, and the Lesbian Avengers, founded in 1992. The Lesbian Avengers focussed on strategies vital to lesbian visibility and survival. They became known for their direct actions: they marched with flaming torches, pestered politicians, stormed editorial offices and more. All were crucial to their mission of demanding respect for lesbians, as well as attempting to teach lesbians how to organize and think politically. Their manifesto and logo, both designed by Carrie Moyer, encapsulated their explosive energy and 'ready-to-blow-up' anger that made them a legend, and known around the world. Dyke Action Machine (DAM!) produced poster campaigns that criticized the prejudiced attitudes of mainstream advertising by inserting lesbian images into current, recognizable advertising campaigns, and then displayed the results around the city. This not only subverted the postures normally reserved for heterosexual fantasy in magazines, but also began to subvert the visual profile of society as a whole. A new view of lesbian reality was beginning to emerge. Within a couple of years they had expanded into other forums such as new technology: their website eventually became one of the most entertaining spots in cyberspace. DAM! were instrumental in creating a sense of lesbian community and pride, while at the same time placing that community loudly and soundly within society as a whole and here to stay.

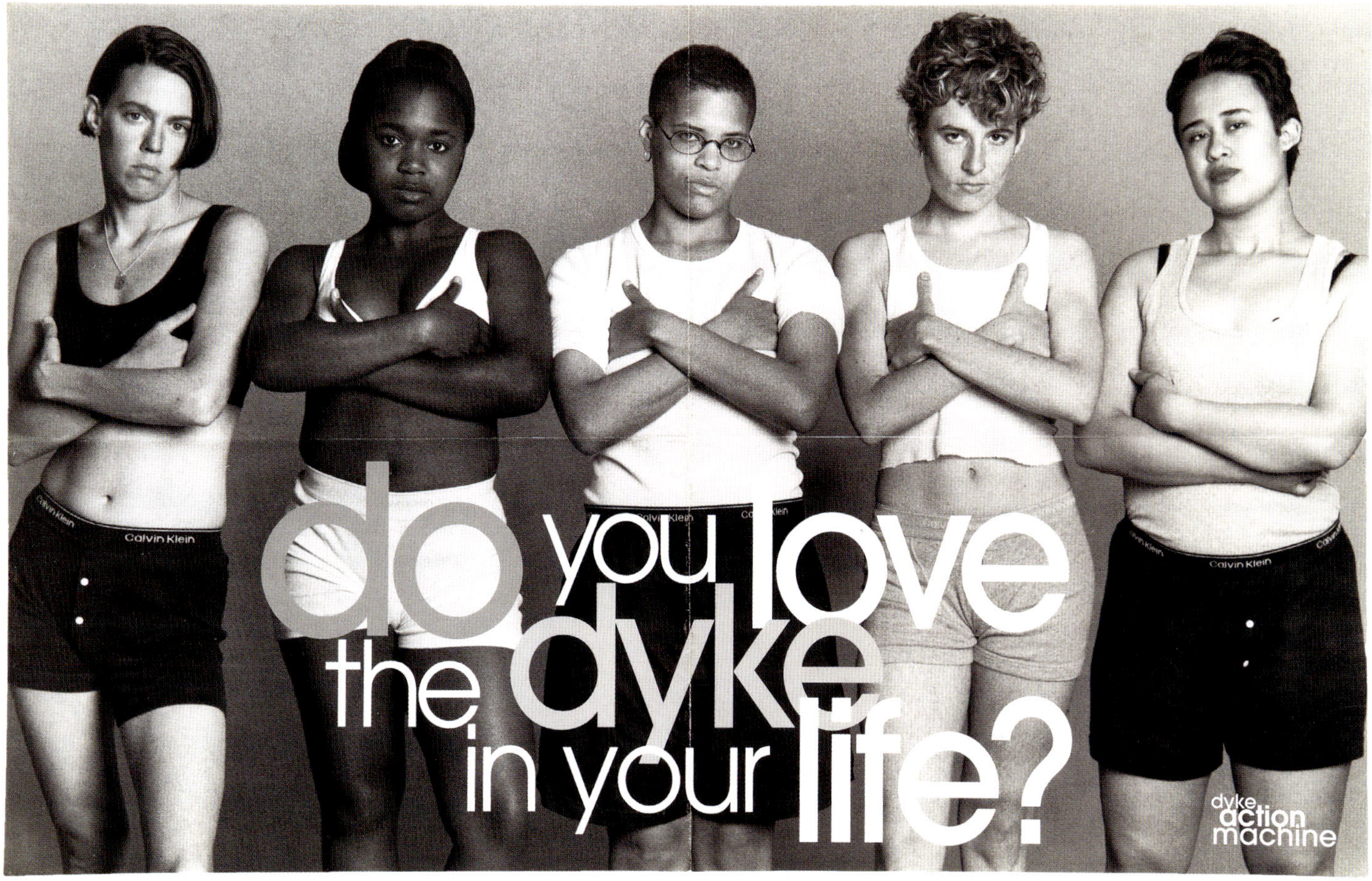

↑ **Do You Love the Dyke in Your Life?** 1993
Dyke Action Machine (DAM!):
Carrie Moyer and Sue Schaffner
Poster (offset)

This direct appropriation of a Calvin Klein campaign, by Dyke Action Machine, was one of a number of advertising parodies intended to raise lesbian visibility in the early 1990s.

→ **Straight to Hell** 1994
Dyke Action Machine (DAM!):
Carrie Moyer and Sue Schaffner
Poster (silkscreen and offset)

This poster for a fantasy film became an investigation of new approaches to lesbian representation, showing the main character's internal conflict, heavy anger and desire for 'dyke revenge', within a traditional cinema format (the action movie) as well as a political format (military propaganda).

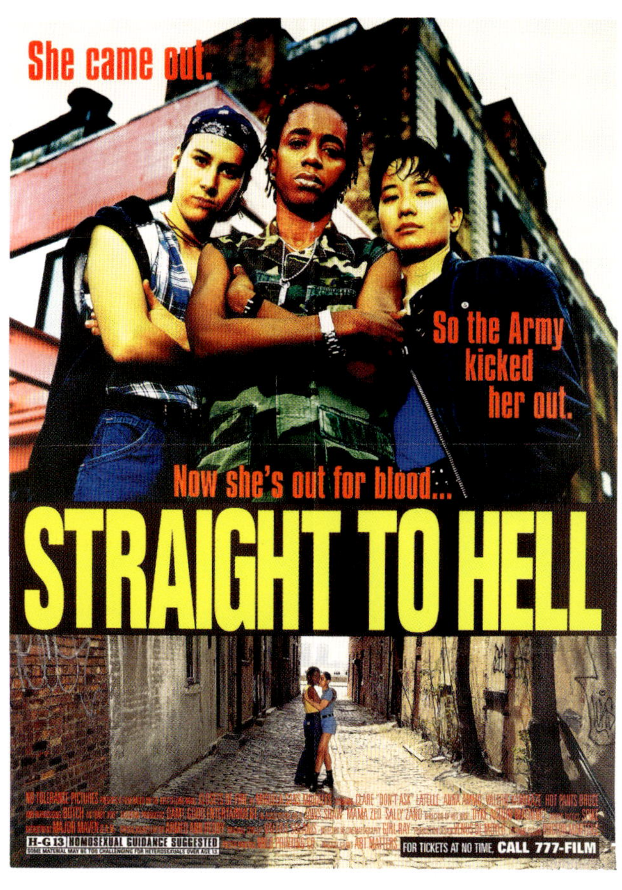

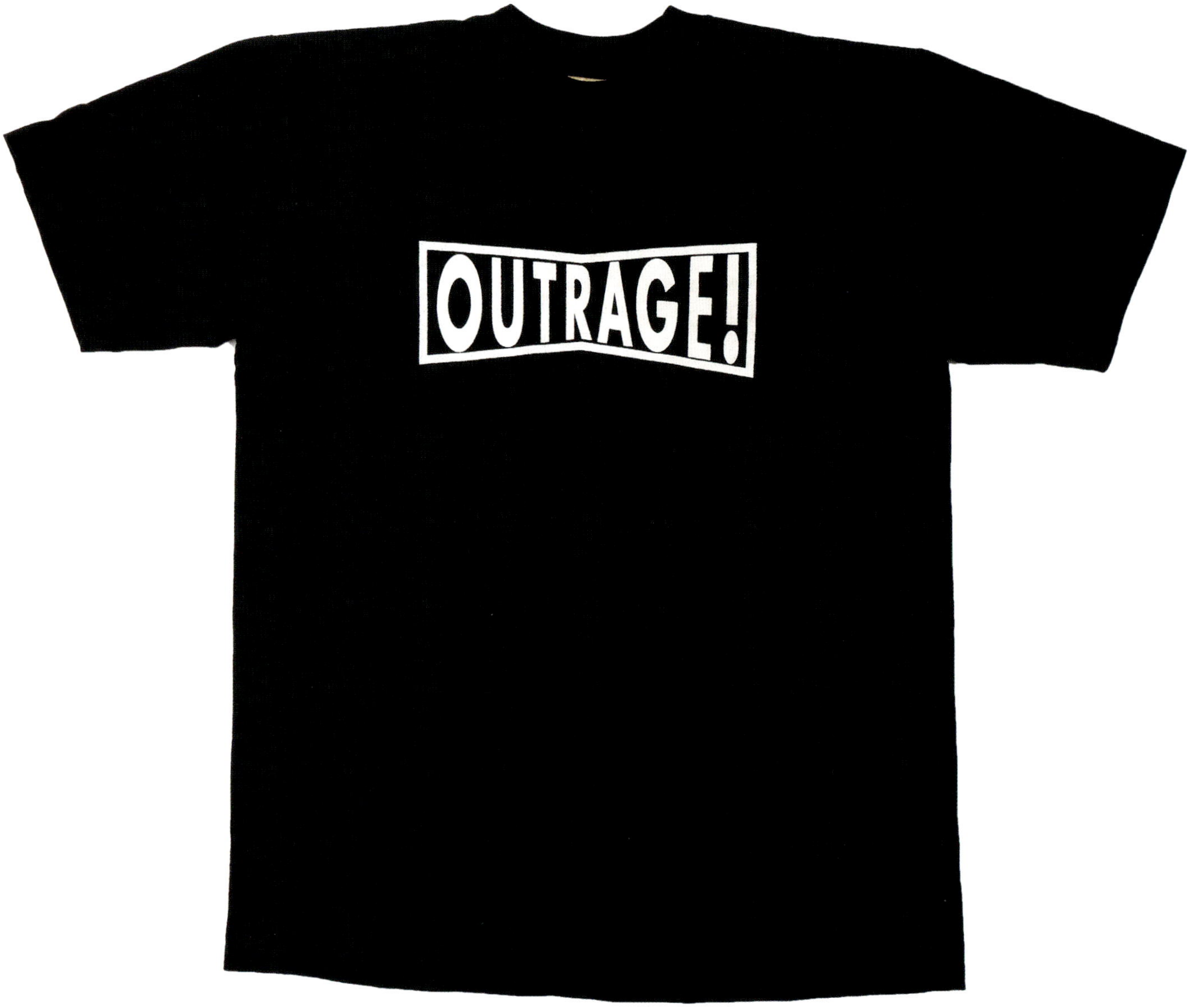

↑ **Outrage!** 1990s
Designer unknown
T-shirt

This t-shirt hails from Outrage!, the radical queer rights
direct action group, which operated from 1990 to 2011.
It used a highly irreverent style of non-violent civil
disobedience ('protest as performance') including famous
stunts such as Kiss-in, Queer Wedding, Exorcism of
Homophobia and others.

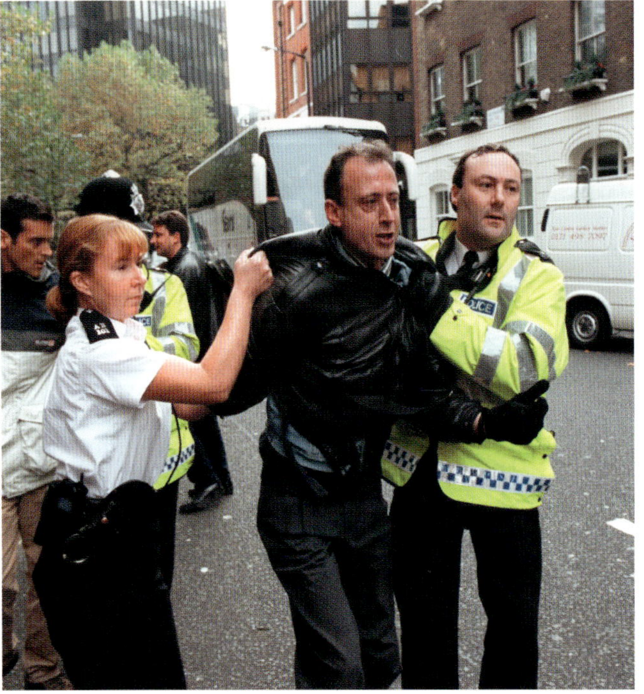

← **Citizen's Arrest of Robert Mugabe** 1999
Photographer: Neville Elder
Photograph

Peter Tatchell is a well-known British human rights
campaigner and was co-founder of the radical queer
rights group, Outrage! Tatchell and three other members
of Outrage! attempted a citizen's arrest of then-President
Robert Mugabe of Zimbabwe during his visit to London
in October 1999. The activists accused Mugabe's regime of
condoning 'murder, torture, detention without trial and the
abuse of gay human rights'.

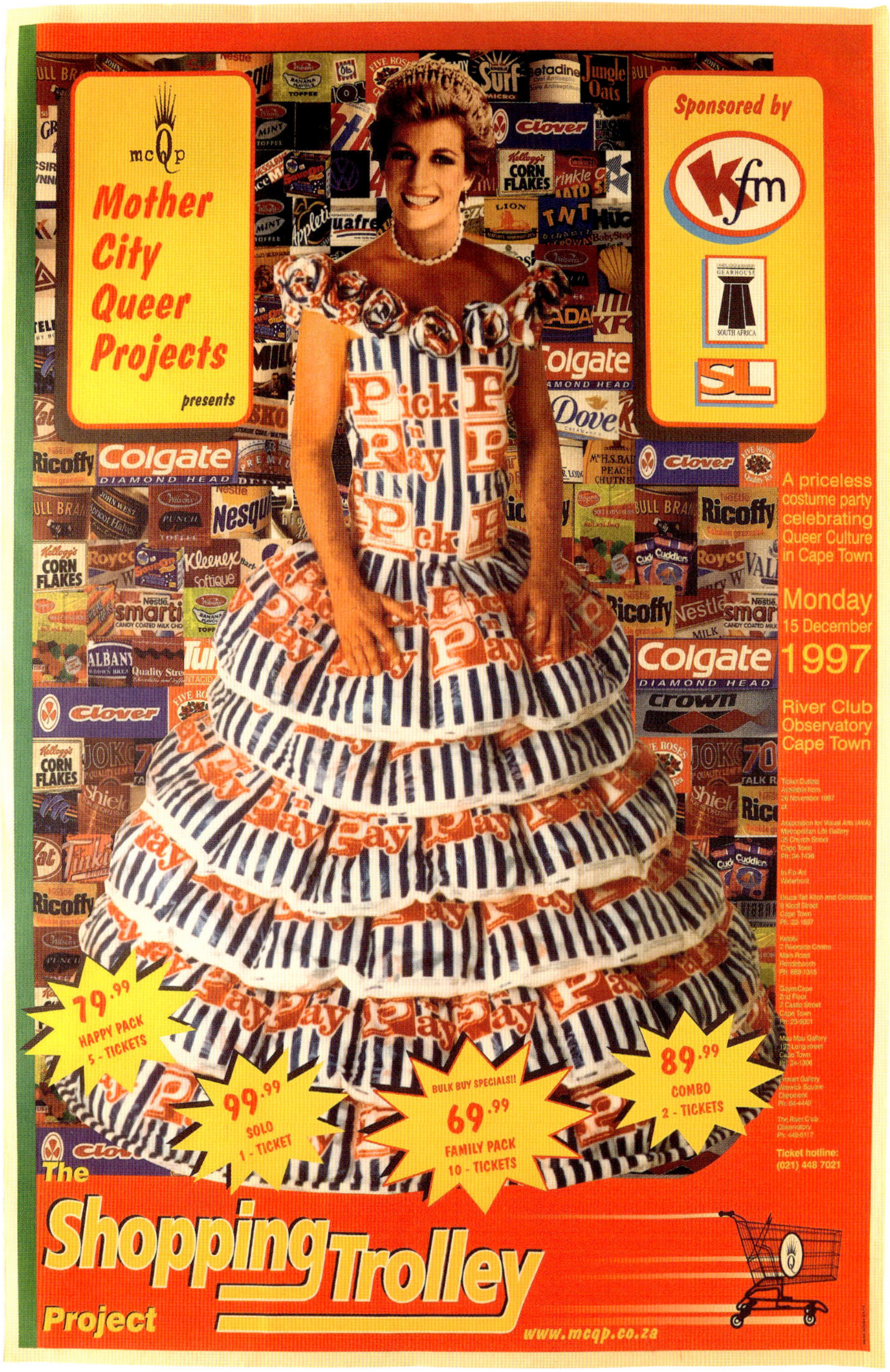

↑ **The Shopping Trolley Project** 1997
Mother City Queer Projects
Design: Manik Design South
Poster (offset)

Mother City Queer Projects (MCQP) was born when, in 1994, the newly-elected President Nelson Mandela brought a new spirit of freedom and a new constitution to South Africa, which included a 'freedom of sexual orientation' clause. MCQP devised an annual themed costume party in Cape Town as a celebration of the richness of queer culture in South Africa (the first event's theme was 'The Locker Room Project'). The costume party has grown to become an annual event on the international map of queer culture and attracts thousands of visitors. The poster shown here is from one of the earlier events – 15 December 1997 – which was dedicated to the memory of Princess Diana, a queer hero.

↓ **Happy 80th Birthday Madiba!** 1998
Mother City Queer Projects
Badge

MCQP produced this badge for Nelson Mandela's birthday, 18 July, which they celebrated every year: another hero!

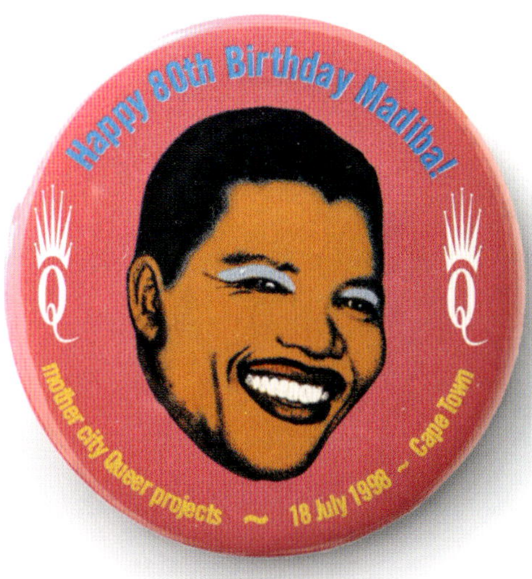

Pro-Democracy Movements

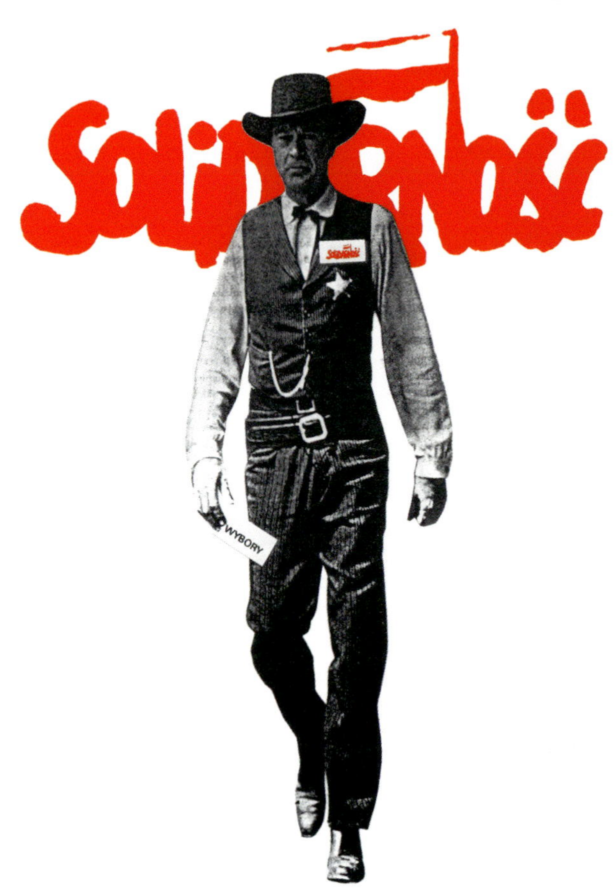

← **High Noon** 1989
Tomasz Sarnecki
Poster

The year 1989 proved to be a watershed for the pro-democracy movements in Central and Eastern Europe. A decade of struggle, starting with workers' strikes in Gdansk shipyard led by Lech Walesa, head of Solidarity (Poland's free trade union), finally achieved its goal. Free elections were about to take place on 4 June 1989. On voting night this poster was hanging on polling booths throughout Poland. Taken from the classic American western *High Noon* (1952), it shows resolute sheriff Gary Cooper striding down the street, making his way to a confrontation, holding a paper ballot instead of a gun – representing Solidarity's own resolute march to the ballot for a showdown with the Communist Party, which they won. The Communists consequently lost their grip on Europe and throughout 1989 a wave of popular revolutions swept through Poland, Hungary, East Germany, Bulgaria, Czechoslovakia and Romania. Spontaneous graphics (posters, signs, flags) played an important role, accompanying many of the demonstrations and chronicling events. Poster artists also travelled to help revolutions in other countries, offering solidarity and helping to document events taking place. It all climaxed on 11 November 1989 when the Berlin Wall, symbol of the ideological division between East and West, was breached and pulled down.

↙ **Solidarity (SOLIDARNOŚĆ)** 1980
Jerzy Janiszewski
Logo/sticker

The logo for Solidarity, Poland's independent trade union, appeared during the workers' strikes led by Lech Walesa and staged in Gdansk shipyard in 1980. It became the emblem of the national workers' movement and was soon published worldwide, hailed as the symbol for collective strength and the spirited resistance of the Polish people. It was also the first persistent symbol of the growing desire for democratic reform in Europe.

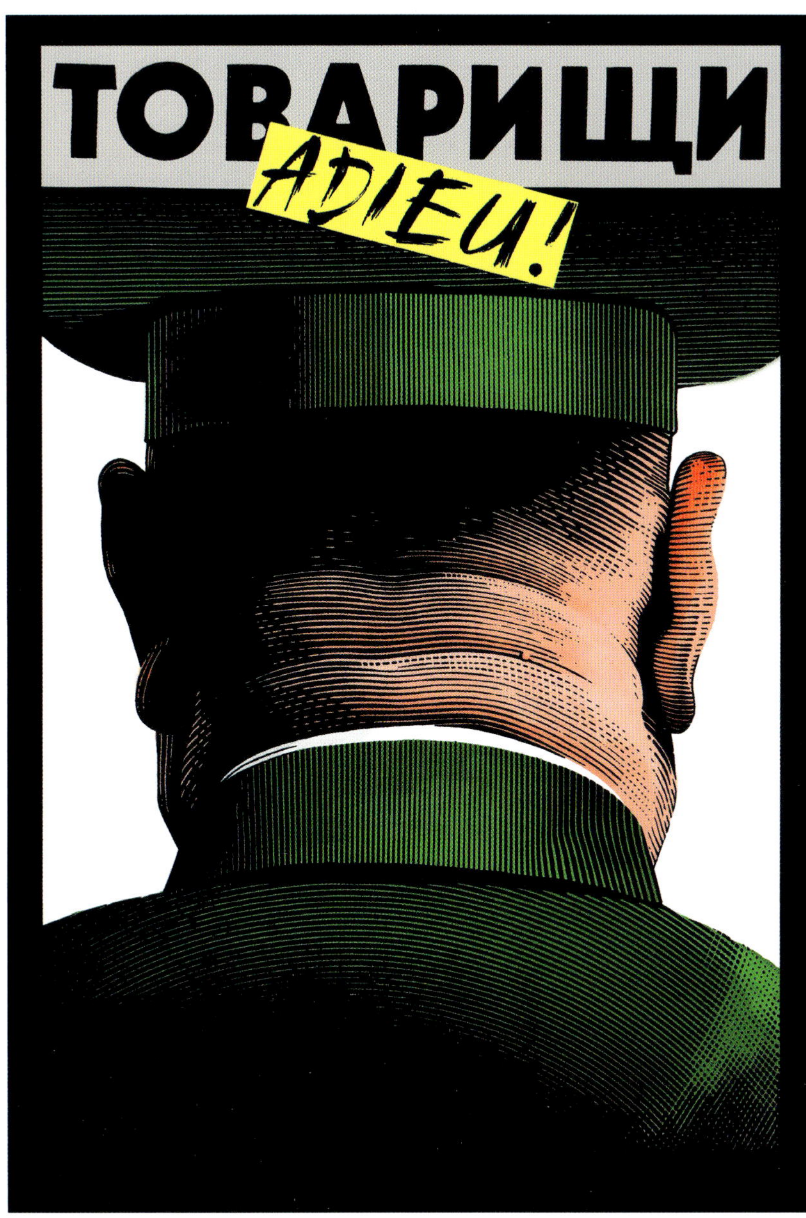

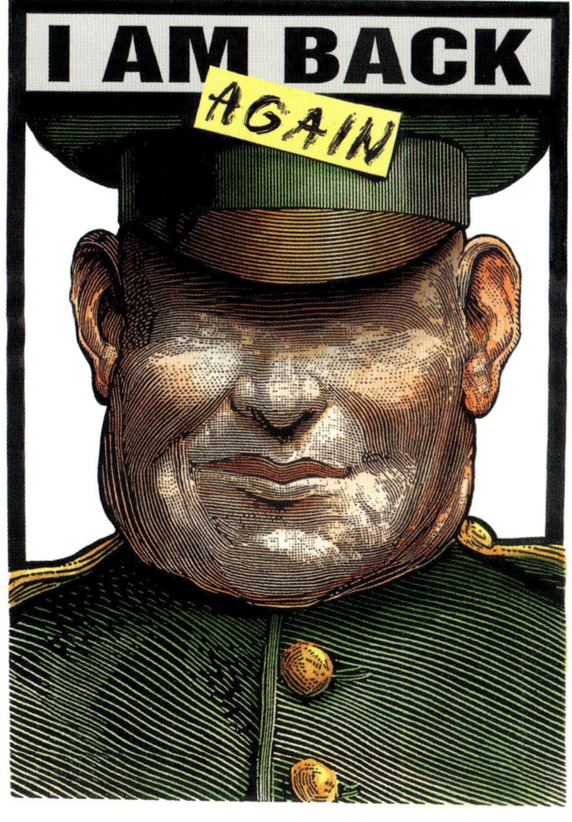

Comrades, Goodbye! 1989
I Am Back Again 1995
István Orosz
Posters

István Orosz's 'Comrades, Goodbye!' poster
reflects the happiness he felt in seeing the
withdrawal of Soviet troops from their
occupation of Hungary in 1989. Apparently,
Russian soldiers queued to buy a copy of
it when the Red Army finally left in 1991.
However, in 1995 when the Communists were
voted back into power in Hungary, Orosz
produced a less-happy sequel entitled 'I Am
Back Again'.

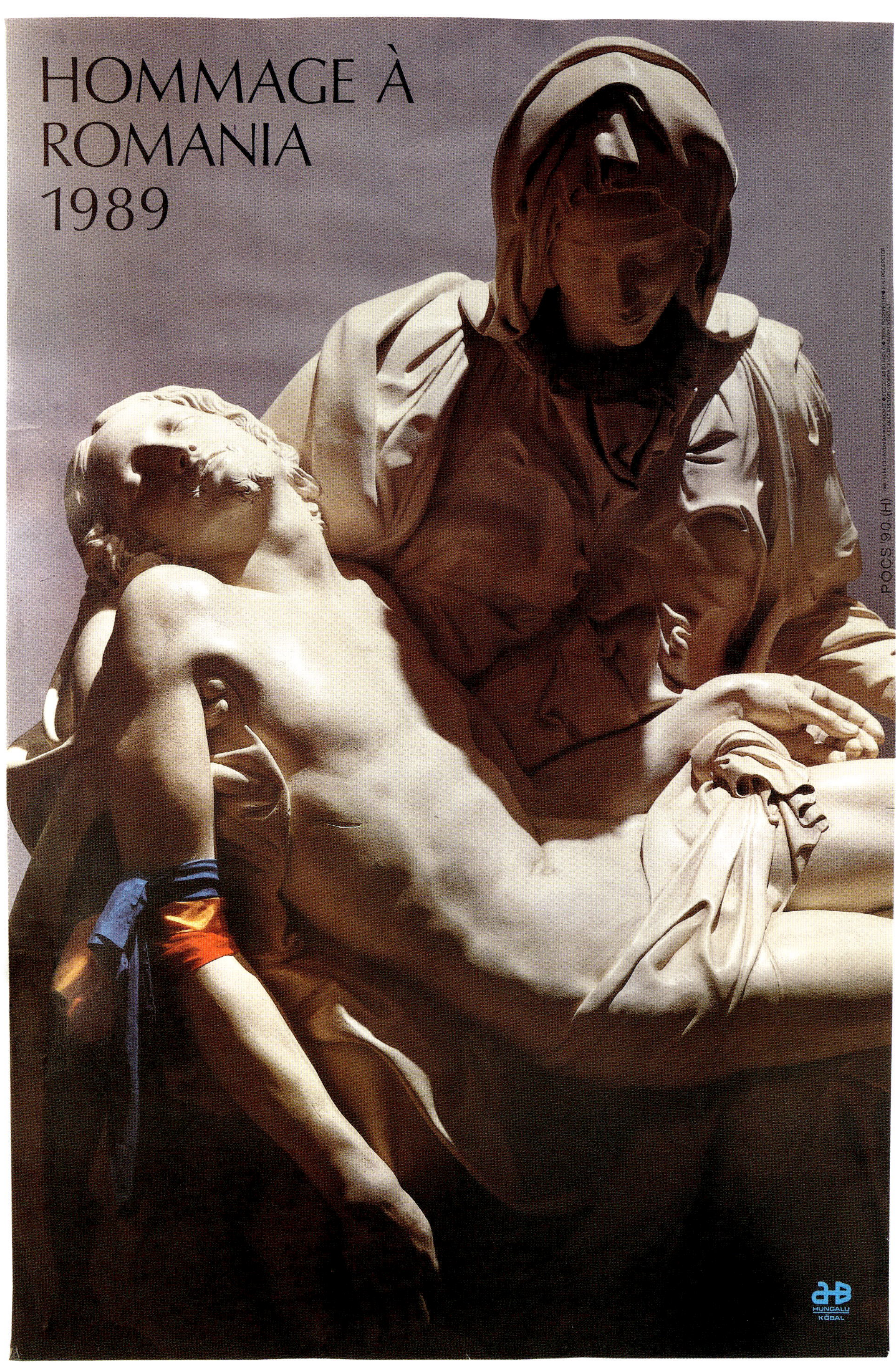

HOMMAGE À
ROMANIA
1989
PÓCS '90. (H)

← **Homage to Romania** 1989
Péter Pócs
Poster

Hungarian artist Péter Pócs created this poster
as a memorial to the victims slaughtered during
Romania's popular revolution of 1989; Romania's
colours are tied to the arm of the Christ-figure.
Romania's uprising was particularly bloody, ending
with the execution of the despot Nicolae Ceausescu
and his wife.

→ **'Students 69–89** 1989
Dusan Zdímal
Poster

A striking yet haunting image of political violence,
this poster was produced in memory of students
injured by armed police during the demonstrations
of 1968 against the Soviet invasion of Prague, as
well as students injured in the so-called 'bloodless'
Velvet Revolution of 1989. The Velvet Revolution
involved mass unrest which led to the resignation
of the Communist politburo and president, and the
foundation of a new government with writer Václav
Havel as president. Reminders of past struggles
and sacrifices were important, particularly in light
of Soviet attempts to erase, forbid discussion of or
rewrite the histories of occupied countries.

↘ **Hero City** 1990
Feliks Büttner
Poster

Applauding its role as a pain in the posterior of
what was then known as (Soviet-occupied) East
Germany, Feliks Büttner commemorates the
demonstrations of 1989 in the city of Leipzig,
which were instrumental in the downfall of the East
German state.

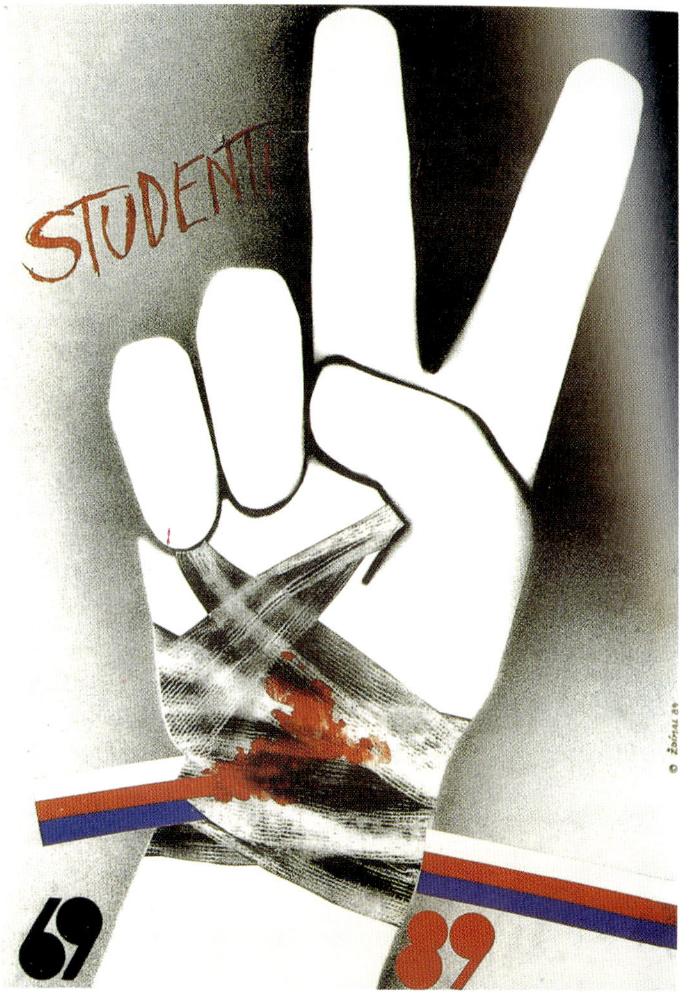

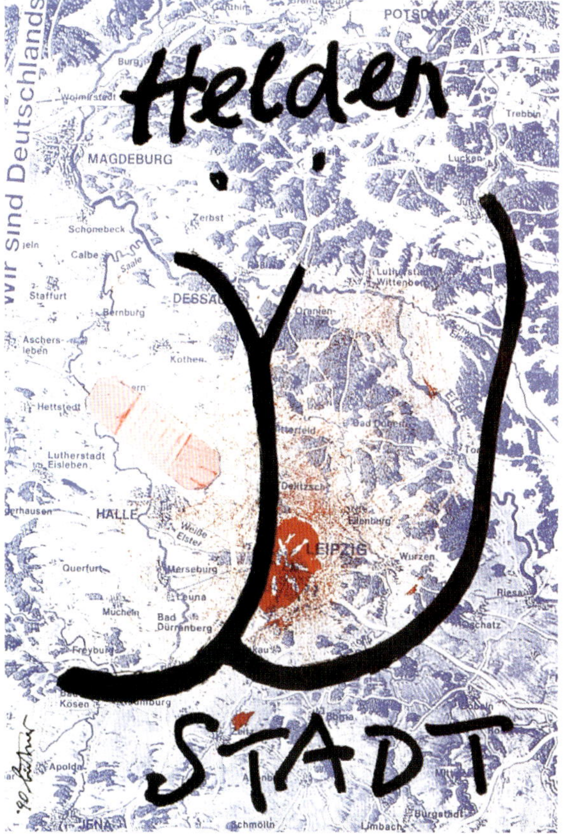

Anti-War Protests

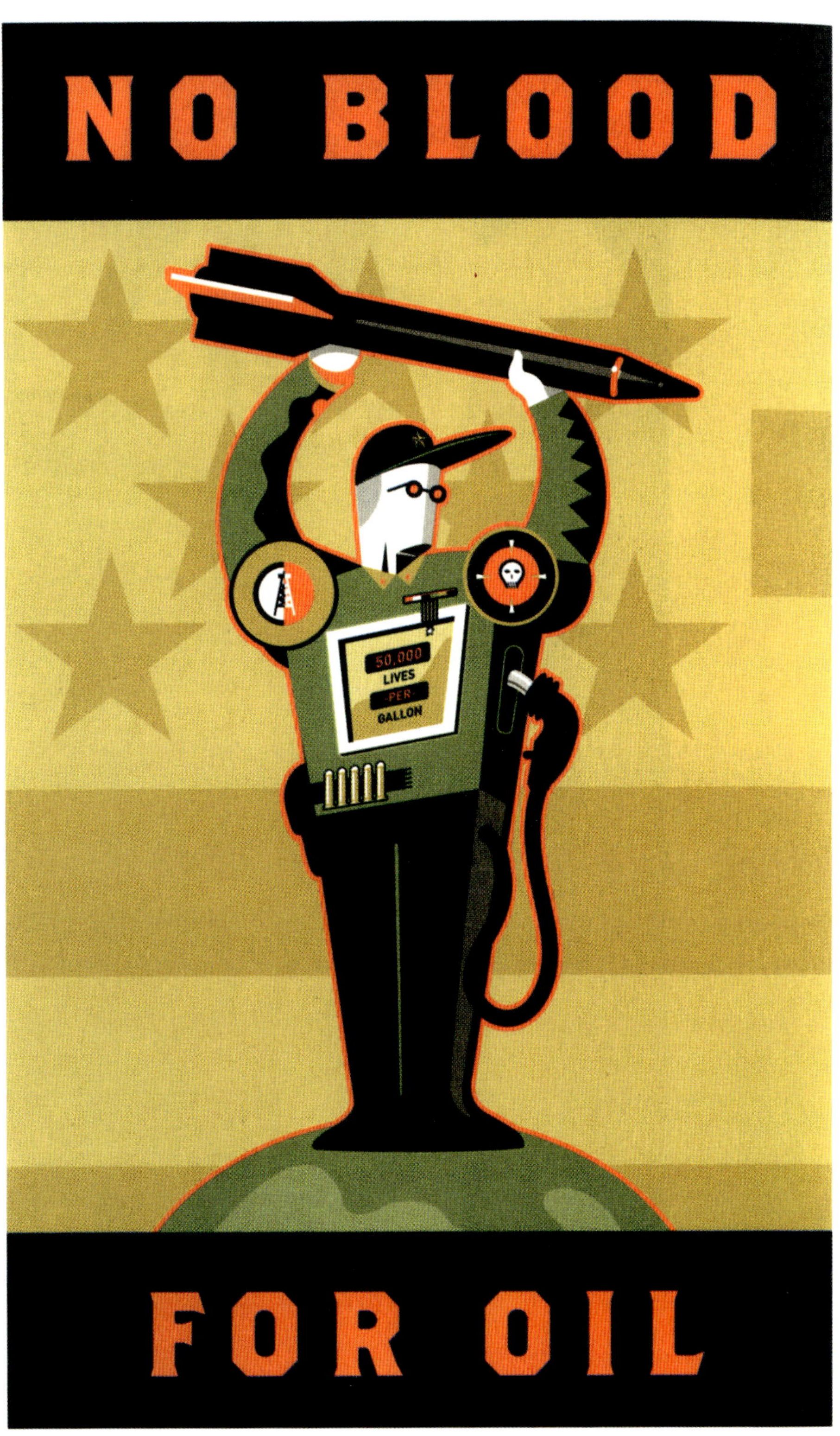

No Blood for Oil
1990 and 2003
Steven Lyons
Poster

Iraq's invasion of Kuwait in August 1990 lit the spark that started the Gulf War of January 1991. It was waged against Iraq by a UN-backed coalition of 36 countries, led by the US military with heavy support from Britain and France. It became known as 'the information war' for its censored portrayal of bloodless warfare. Mainstream media (television, newspapers, magazines) carried gloating coverage of air-strike techno-wizardry and the mythic capabilities of 'smart bombs' and precision-guided weapons, while also showing endless charts of dazzling arrays of hardware and weapons. Non-messy technological-sounding words such as 'collateral damage' and 'surgical strikes' crept into popular vocabulary. The protest imagery of the time – posters, booklets, comics – questioned the motives behind the war (suspecting the desire for possession of oil), argued the failings of the US administration, and brought blood and death back into the discussion. It also fanned a mistrust of mainstream media, and its sanitizing of information to create a bloodless war. Steven Lyons' poster addresses the issue of motives behind the war. He therefore visualized a general as a fuel pump. The poster was published in 1990 in the USA by the Emergency Campaign to Stop the War in the Middle East. It was then reprinted in 2003 to confront the second Gulf War – the Iraq War.

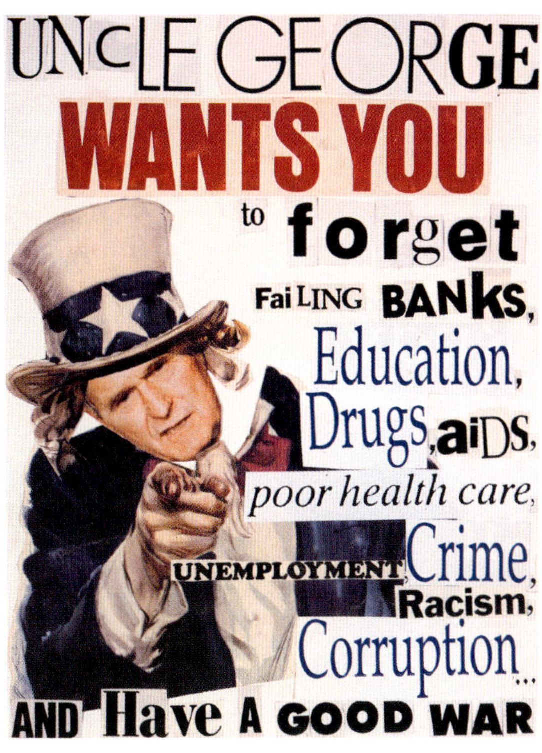

↑ Uncle George Wants You
to Have a Good War 1991
Stephen Kroninger
Poster

Although US President George Bush was
considered by some to have provided strong
leadership with regard to his handling of the
Gulf War, it was his administration's handling
of the US economy (and other ills, listed on
the poster) that was said to have denied him
a second term as President. This poster was
self-published and distributed first by the
Village Voice in Manhattan, then by *Progressive*
magazine in Madison, Wisconsin. It was also
emblazoned on t-shirts in New York City.

→ Yahoo No. 5 *c.*1991
Artist: Joe Sacco
Front cover

Comics journalist/artist Joe Sacco makes
(deadly serious) fun of General Norman
Schwartzkopf – aka 'Stormin' Norman' –
Commander-in-Chief of the coalition
forces in the Gulf. Sacco's front cover
portrait, carrying lips by Claudia Basrawi,
uses a wild, acidic yellow for the lettering
of 'How I Loved the War' as well as for the
insane eyeballs of the general.

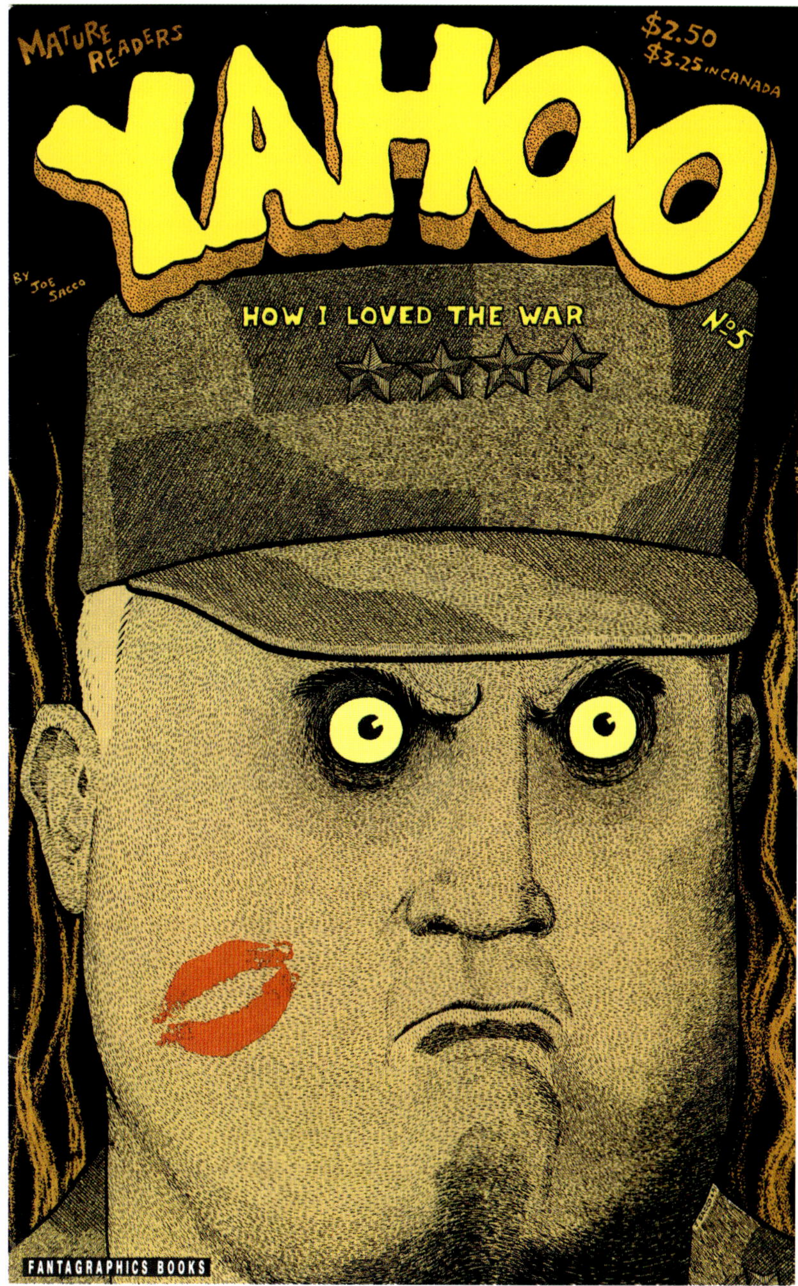

S.O.S. Croatia 1991
Ranko Novak
Poster

The Balkan Wars of the 1990s were, to a great extent, instigated by the land-grabbing activities of the Serbian leader, Slobodan Miloševic and his desire to create a 'Greater Serbia'. Miloševic and his forces attacked Slovenia, which fought them off, then wreaked havoc in Croatia, Bosnia (including the siege of Sarajevo) and Kosovo. In every case, he set ethnic groups warring against each other, inciting 'ethnic cleansing' (gaining control of an area by purging 'unwanted' ethnic groups) and bloodshed. Through the wars and sieges that took place in the 1990s, artists and creative studios kept working, producing projects protesting against the crimes being committed. Croatia suffered terrible massacres of both resident Serbs and Croats. The country also has a proud tradition of graphic design. Consequently, extraordinary posters were produced symbolizing the bloodshed taking place or documenting the devastation of Croatia's cultural heritage. This poster by Ranko Novak makes use of the pattern of the 'sahovnica', the red-and-white checked medieval shield that is Croatia's heraldic emblem.

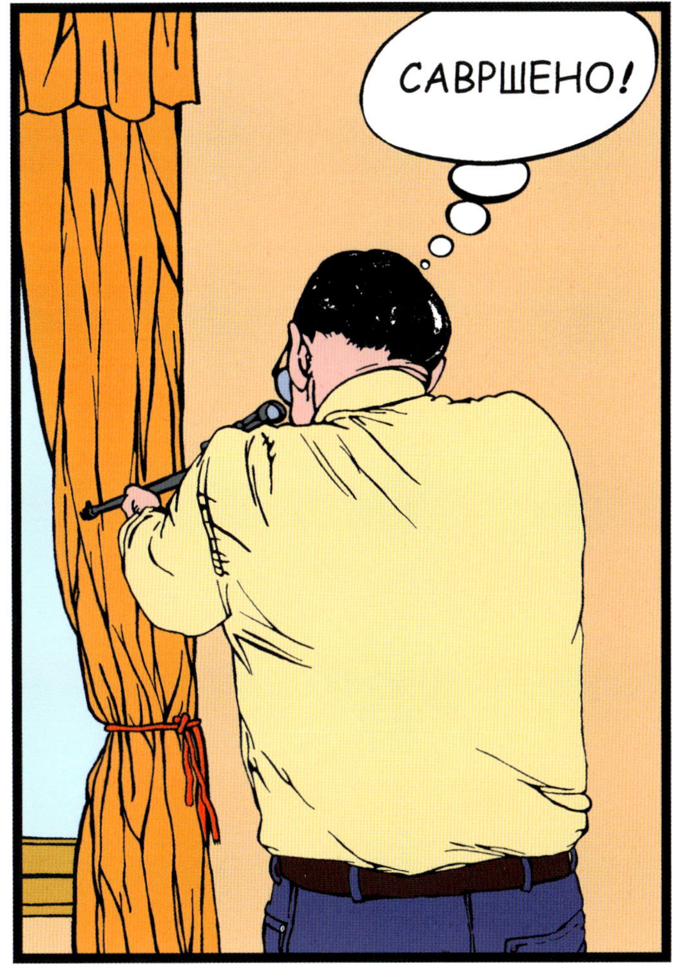

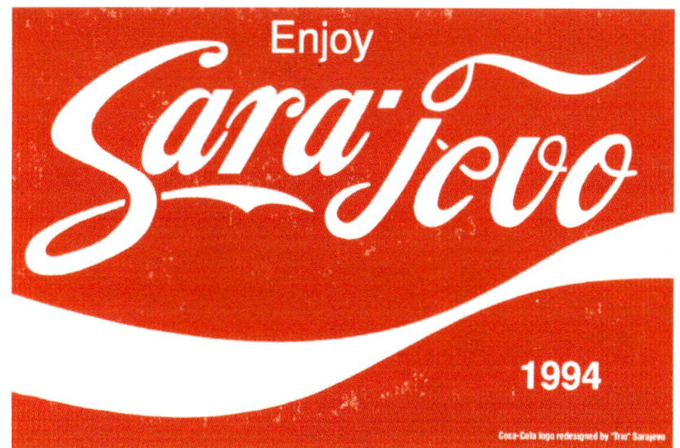

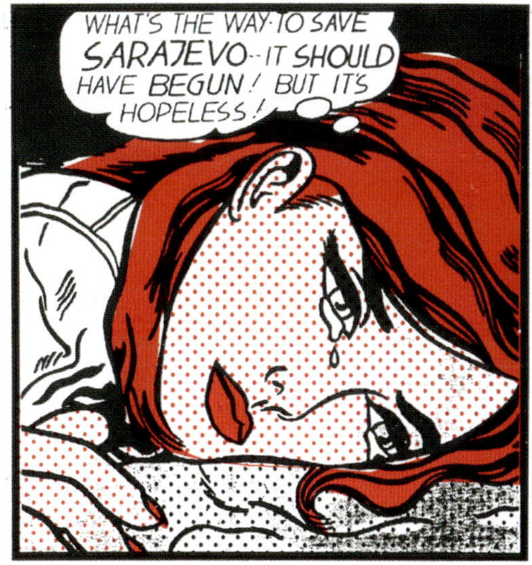

↑ **Perfect!** 1992
Asim Đelilovic
Poster

This poster is one of a series of twenty-seven, created by Đelilovic, telling
the story of the Bosnian War. (They were conceived during the war, but
not produced until after it.) The spectacled sniper taking aim symbolized
the role of Serb intellectuals in starting the Bosnian War. The poster was
also inspired by the death of Suada Dilberovic, shot on a bridge by a sniper
during a peace demonstration in 1992: the first violent death in Sarajevo.

↗ **Enjoy Sara-jevo** 1993–94
→ Trio design group
↘ Postcards

With the start of the Bosnian War, the city of Sarajevo came under siege
in April 1992. The siege lasted three and a half years, until February 1996.
Trio design group (husband and wife Bojan and Dalida Hadzihalilovic,
and others) stayed in Sarajevo and ran a commercial office throughout the
war, despite shortages of paper, ink, electricity and water. The project that
brought them international attention was a series of postcards, imbibed with
a strong sense of irony and black humour. Sarajevo's fate became a satirical
theme, expressed through reworked cultural and pop icons, such as the
Coca-Cola logo. The postcard format was chosen as the postcards could be
transported out of the city, allowing communication with the outside world,
and also because of shortages of paper and ink.

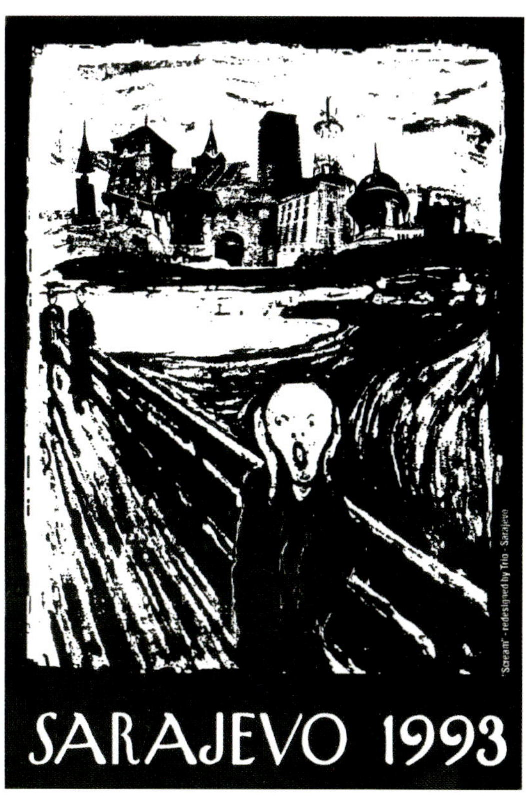

A

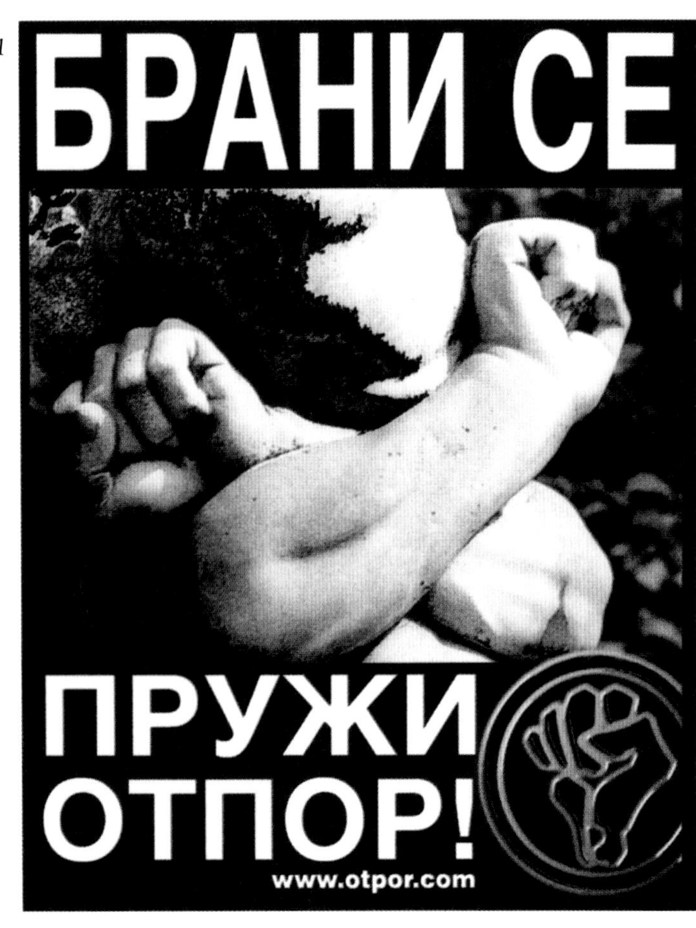
БРАНИ СЕ
ПРУЖИ ОТПОР!
www.otpor.com

B

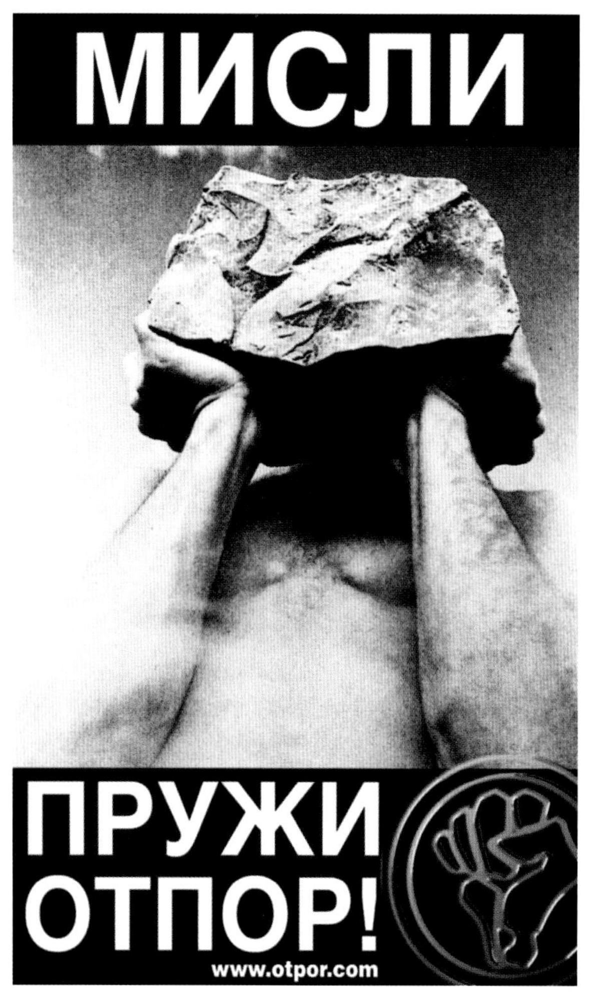
МИСЛИ
ПРУЖИ ОТПОР!
www.otpor.com

C
ОТПОР! ЊЕМУ!
НАША МЕТА

D
2000
ОВО ЈЕ ТА ГОДИНА

E
ГОТОВ ЈЕ!

→ **If Not Elections, Then What?** 2000
Miljenko Dereta, Ivan Valencak and Saki Marinovic
Photograph: V. Miloradovic
Poster (offset)

Otpor! was not the only group campaigning for
change in Serbia's September 2000 elections. This
pre-election poster, carrying a quotation from
the Declaration of Human Rights, was designed
by Miljenko Dereta (Executive Director), Ivan
Valencak and Saki Marinovic: all members of
Gradanske Inicijative (Civic Initiatives), dedicated
to the democratization of Yugoslavia (Serbia).
Civic Initiatives, an NGO or non-governmental
organization, worked to help young people become
aware of the importance of citizens' participation
in the democratic process. It also conducted
educational programmes on human rights and
citizenship. This poster captures the now-or-
never call for change which would eventually vote
Milosevic out of office on 24 September, as well as
spur on the popular revolt that would finally remove
him from power in early October.

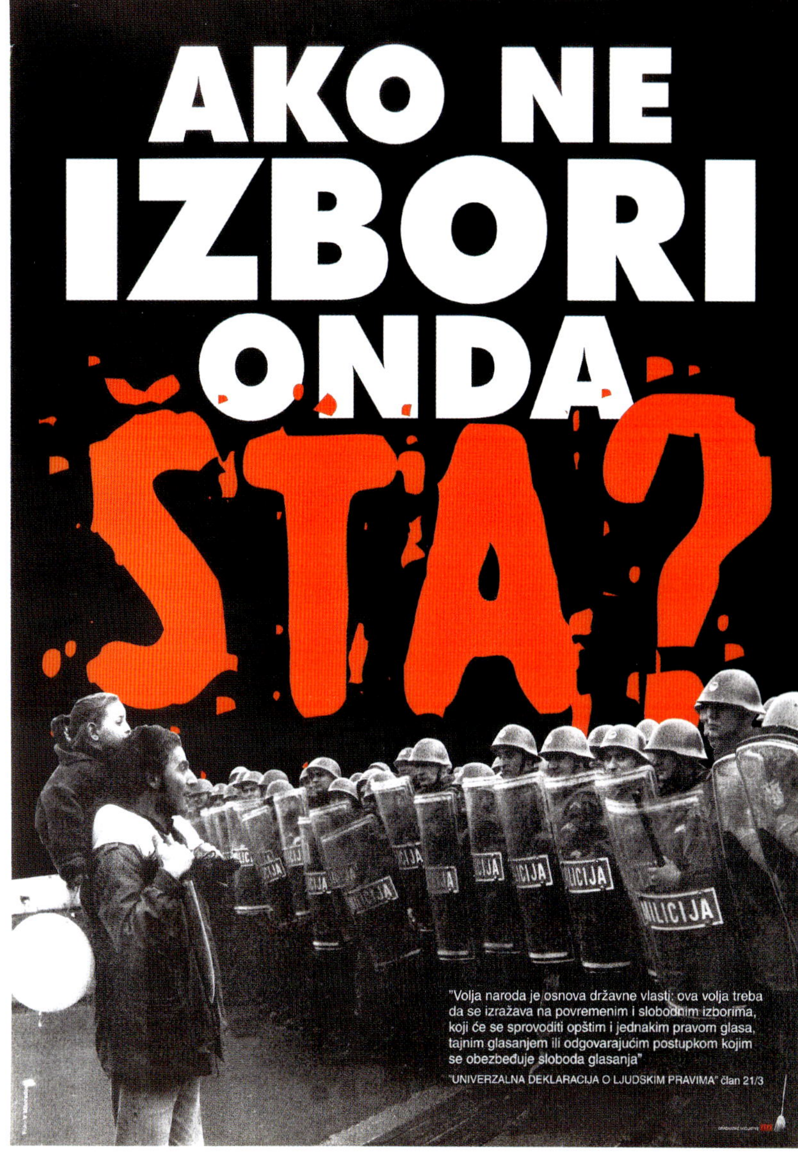

← **Graphics from Otpor!**
(**Resistance!**) *c.*2000
Artists: Otpor!
Poster, leaflets, sticker

Strong resistance to Slobodan Milosevic's
power-hold and war-mongering came from
within Serbia itself. In 1998 the student
movement Otpor! (Resistance!) began to
work towards the democratic overthrow
of Milosevic in the upcoming presidential
elections. Its members (aged 20–21) targeted
young people to vote for change and the
movement grew quickly. It operated a highly
sophisticated marketing campaign with well-
designed graphics similar to an advertising
agency; its 'clenched fist' symbol was treated
like a corporate logo, and appeared all over
Serbia. Confidence and humour gave Otpor!
huge popularity and political edge: crucial
in giving people the courage to act. By July
2000, Otpor!'s membership had reached
40,000. Their most important move came
with the 'He's Finished! campaign, aimed at
the presidential elections of 24 September
2000. Although the opposition (supported
by Otpor!) won the election, Milosevic
didn't budge and a popular revolt finally
removed him on 5 October and sent him
on his way to a 'holiday in The Hague' (the
International Court in The Hague, where
he was imprisoned for the rest of his life).
The strength and energy of the Otpor!
movement can even be felt in the small
selection of graphics shown here.

Translations, all material *c.*2000:

(Image A)   Defend Yourself – Resist!, leaflet
(Image B)   Think – Resist!, leaflet
(Image C)   Resistance! To Him! – Our
        Target, leaflet (showing the
        head of Slobodan Milosevic)
(Image D)   2000 – This is the Year, poster
(Image E)   He's Finished!, sticker

International Solidarity: Global Struggles

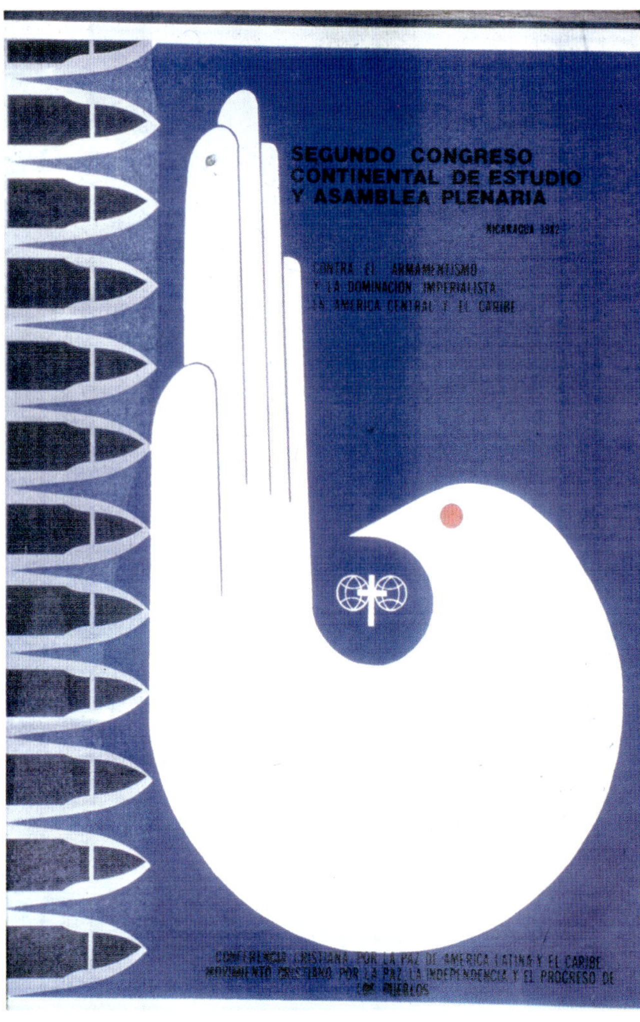

← **Second Continental Congress for Study and Plenary Assembly…** 1982
Artist unknown
Poster

The full title of this Nicaraguan poster announces its mission: 'Second Continental Congress for Study and Plenary Assembly, Against the Arms Race and Imperialist Domination in Central America and the Caribbean'. The poster's design – the peace dove stopping a wall of bullets – is a dramatic depiction of determination and strong resolve. The poster was produced by the Christian Conference for Peace in Latin America and the Caribbean, and the Christian Movement for Peace, Independence and Progress for the People.

→ **Women in Chile** 1987
Greenwich Mural Workshop, London
Poster (silkscreen)

After the overthrow of their democratically-elected (Marxist) president in a CIA-backed coup d'état, Chile was ruled by a brutal military junta led by General Augusto Pinochet from 1973 to 1990. Thousands of so-called dissidents were murdered or 'disappeared' and an estimated 200,000 Chileans were exiled. This poster was produced for the British-based support group 'Chilean Women in Exile', which was determined to oppose the dictatorship. The poster declares International Women's Day as a day of National Protest against Pinochet's regime, and depicts various demonstrations taking place, including women banging on saucepans, a form of protest through noise.

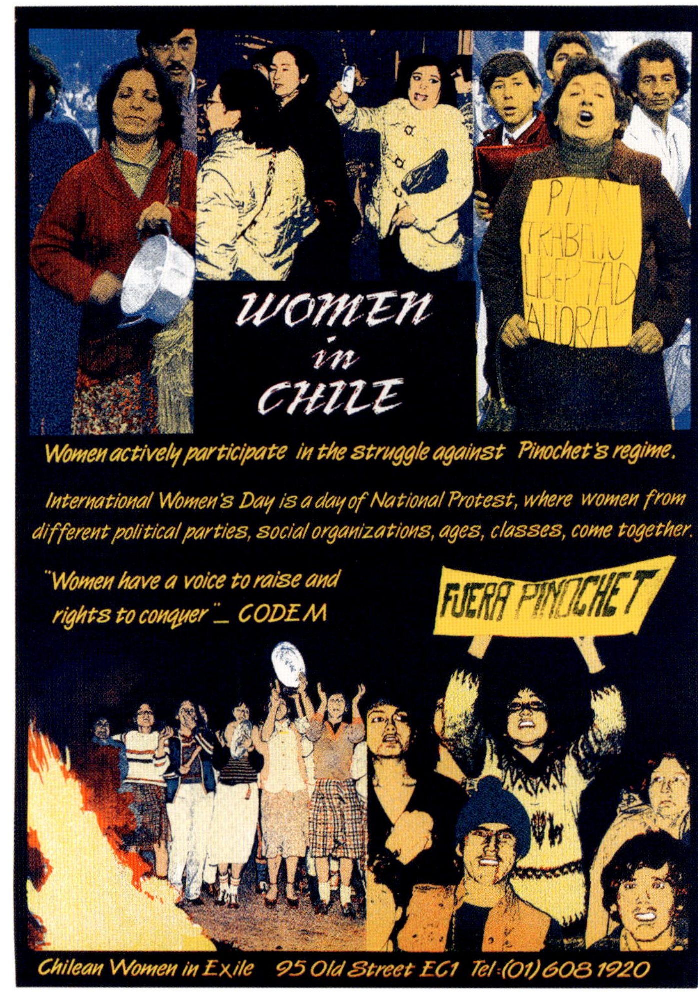

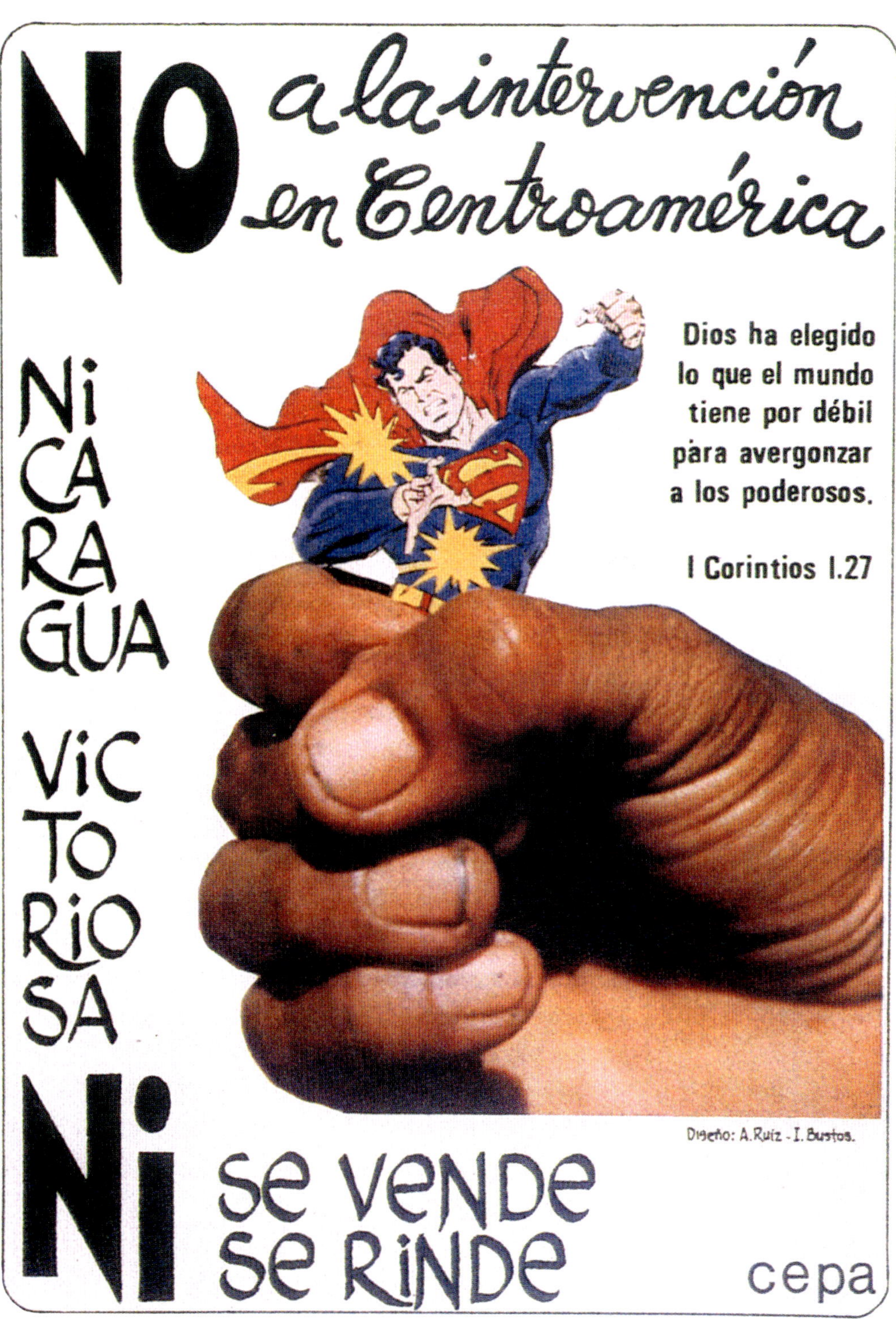

**No Intervention in
Central America** *c.*1985
Design: A. Ruiz and I. Bustos for CEPA
Poster

Throughout the 1980s solidarity and educational campaigns existed in support of Central and South American countries attempting to deal with US interference or military dictators. In Nicaragua, after the overthrow of the Somoza dictatorship in 1979, the victorious Sandinista Revolution and its government employed the production of posters to address self-determination and the country's need for infrastructure and literacy programmes. The posters also encouraged people to mobilize and defend themselves against the US-backed Contras aiming to destabilize the country; and in a broader sense, often warned other Central American countries to resist US intervention, as seen in El Salvador (1982) and the West Indian island of Grenada (1985). The full translation of the poster shown here is 'No intervention in Central America; victorious Nicaragua will neither sell out, nor surrender'. It was produced by CEPA, the Agrarian Education and Promotion Centre in Nicaragua, which encouraged peasant organizations to engage in political action.

Anti-Globalization

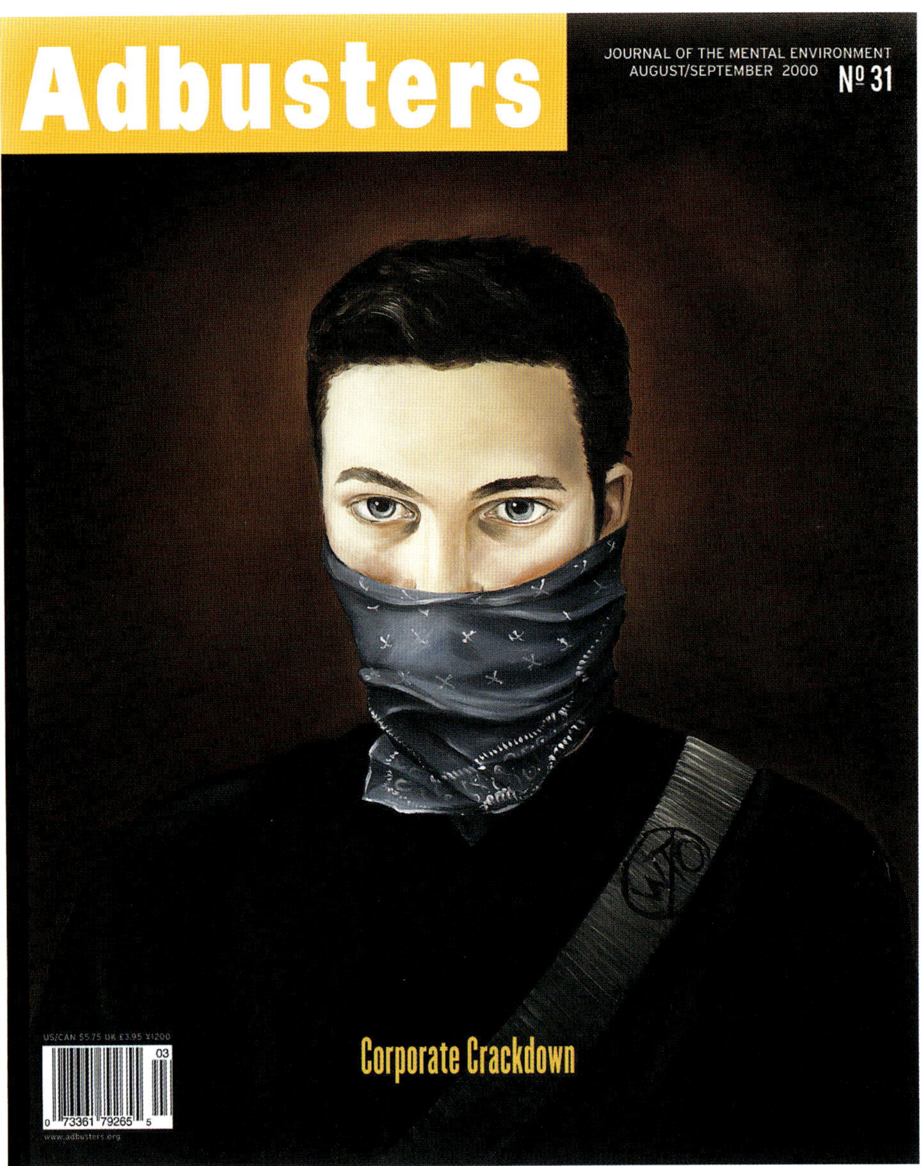

***Adbusters* No. 31 2000**
Artist: Evie Katevatis, painting entitled
'Unidentified (Activist, Seattle)'
Magazine: front cover

In the decade approaching the 21st
century, 'anti-globalization' became a
global resistance movement that had
its roots in anti-corporatism and anti-
capitalism, thereby rejecting the power that
multinational corporations wielded over
world economies and ordinary people's
lives. An important ignition point was the
1994 rebellion staged in the Chiapas region

of Mexico by the Zapatistas, a collective
taking their name from early 1900s rebel
icon and land reformer Emiliano Zapata.
The Zapatistas fought for land rights,
resources and the rights of the indigenous
people, for the Chiapas region was rich
in resources and ripe for development
by multinationals. News of their uprising
circled the world electronically, generating
global solidarity. The Zapatistas projected an
inspirational image of the guerrilla fighter,
wearing ski-masks to ensure that their ideas
and words emanated from a collective voice.
'The mask' (ski-mask, bandana, scarf)

soon became the international hallmark
of the anti-globalization protester. Mass
anti-globalization protests took place
(London, Seattle) aimed at the International
Monetary Fund (IMF) and the World
Trade Organization (WTO), and 'the mask'
became more useful for hiding identity or
protecting against tear gas or pepper-spray.
The anti-corporate backlash included
'brand subversion' and *Adbusters* (shown
here), a magazine based in Vancouver as
well as a movement, expanded the concept,
developing a global craze for 'subvertising'
(corporate ad spoofs).

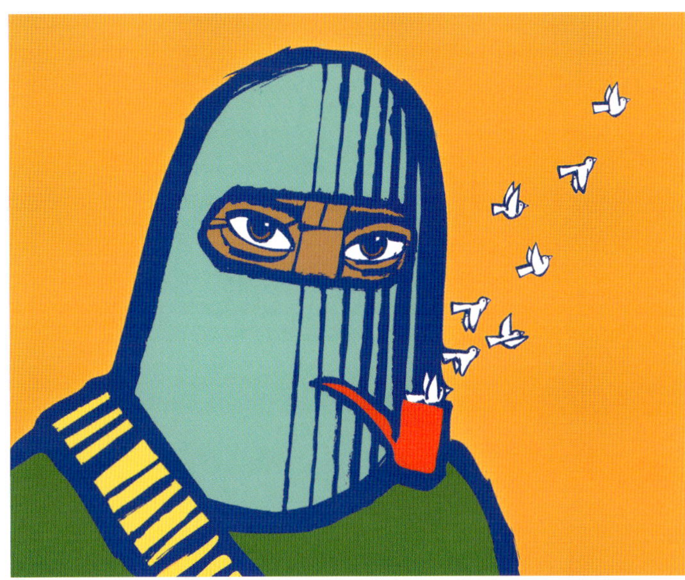

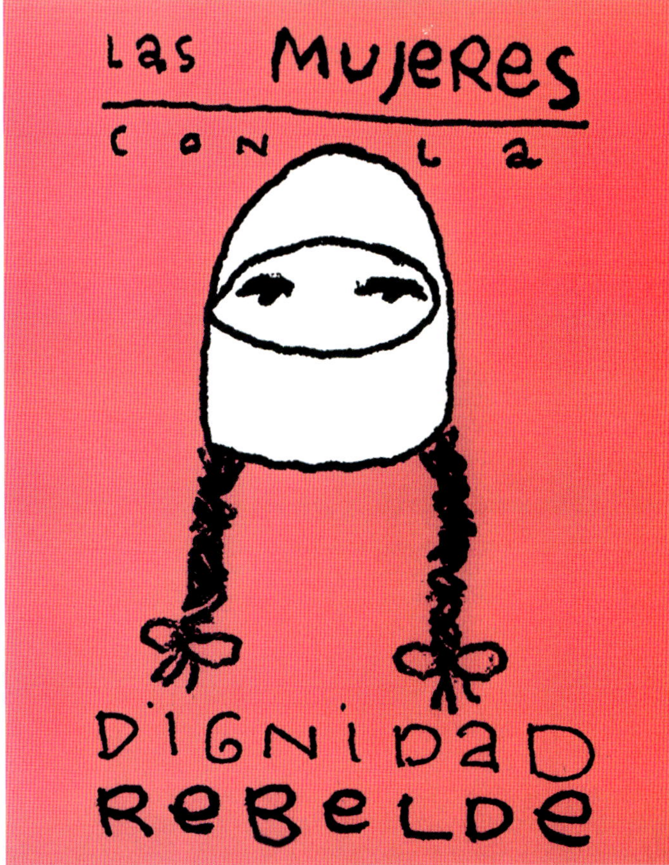

← **Masked Zapatista** 2001
Artist: Ricardo Peláez
Electronic poster

This electronic image shows a masked member of the Zapatista Liberation Army (EZLN), or Zapatistas, smoking a peace pipe. Mexican designers and activists produced images to show solidarity with the Zapatistas and to support the development of a peace process in the Chiapas region.

↙ **Women with Rebellious Dignity** 2001
Margarita Sada
Sticker

In 2001 two groups of designers and agitators in Mexico City – Fuera de Registro (Off the Register) and La Corriente Eléctrica (Electric Current) brought together 15 artists and designers to produce a series of stickers entitled 'Zapata Vive' in support of the peace process in the Chiapas. Margarita Sada's sticker makes the crucial point that women participated at the forefront of the armed resistance; approximately one-third of the Zapatista combatants were women.

↓ *Schnews Annual* 1998
Cover design: Peter Pavement
Book: front and back cover

One of the leading lights of media activism in Britain was *Schnews*. Shown here is a compilation of Issues 101–150 of the renowned free weekly alternative news-sheet, carrying 'the news the mainstream media ignores' as well as information on demonstrations, parties and other events (such as the 'crap arrest of the week') throughout the UK and beyond. It was available in both online and hard-copy form, and was published by the Brighton group 'Justice?'. As their punchy weekly header appropriately barked: 'Wake Up! Wake Up!'

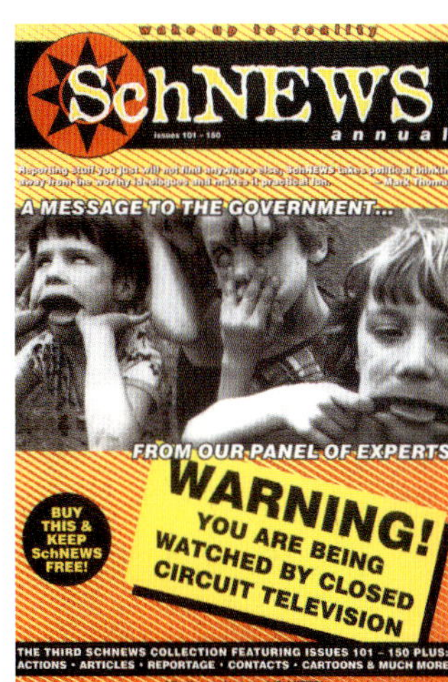

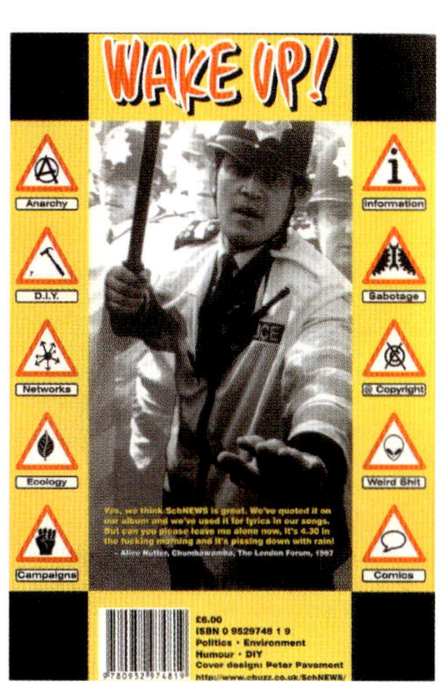

Anti-Corporate Campaigns

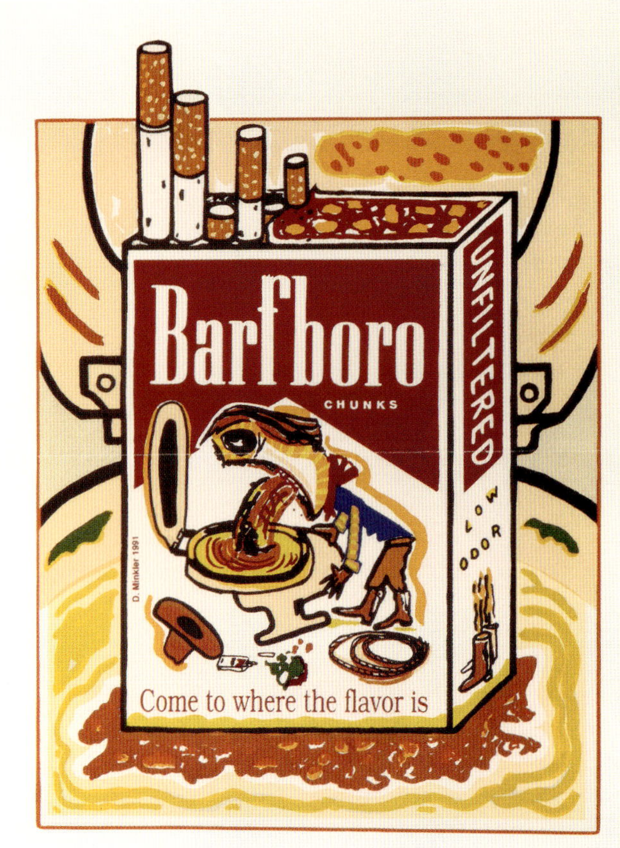

← **Barfboro** 1991
Artist: Doug Minkler
Poster

Throughout the 1990s anti-corporate attitudes were directed against the power of the brands; the frontline of health activism was the tobacco industry. The pioneering US group Doctors Ought to Care (DOC), founded as early as 1977, produced some of the most inventive campaigns against the marketing of tobacco and alcohol to adolescents. Its founder, Dr. Alan Blum, created the Barfboro theme in the 1980s (to barf = to vomit) and collaborated with artist Doug Minkler to create the outlandish campaign that included the Barfboro Barfing Team (1993), Barf Bags and Minkler's sensational posters.

↓ **Bob, I've Got Emphysema** 2000
Asher and Partners (art director Nancy Steinman, photographer Myron Beck, writer Jeff Bossin)
Advertising campaign

As the 1990s progressed, so did the belief that 'smoking kills'. By the end of the decade, the tobacco industry was being forced to pay compensation to health victims and 'reparation payments' by financing anti-tobacco ad campaigns. Ad parodies began to appear that challenged the power and influence of big tobacco, often attacking their brand icons or mascots. In this anti-smoking campaign, created for the California Department of Health Services, Marlboro Man – for so long symbolising a 'tough guy' image – is forced to contemplate emphysema or cancer.

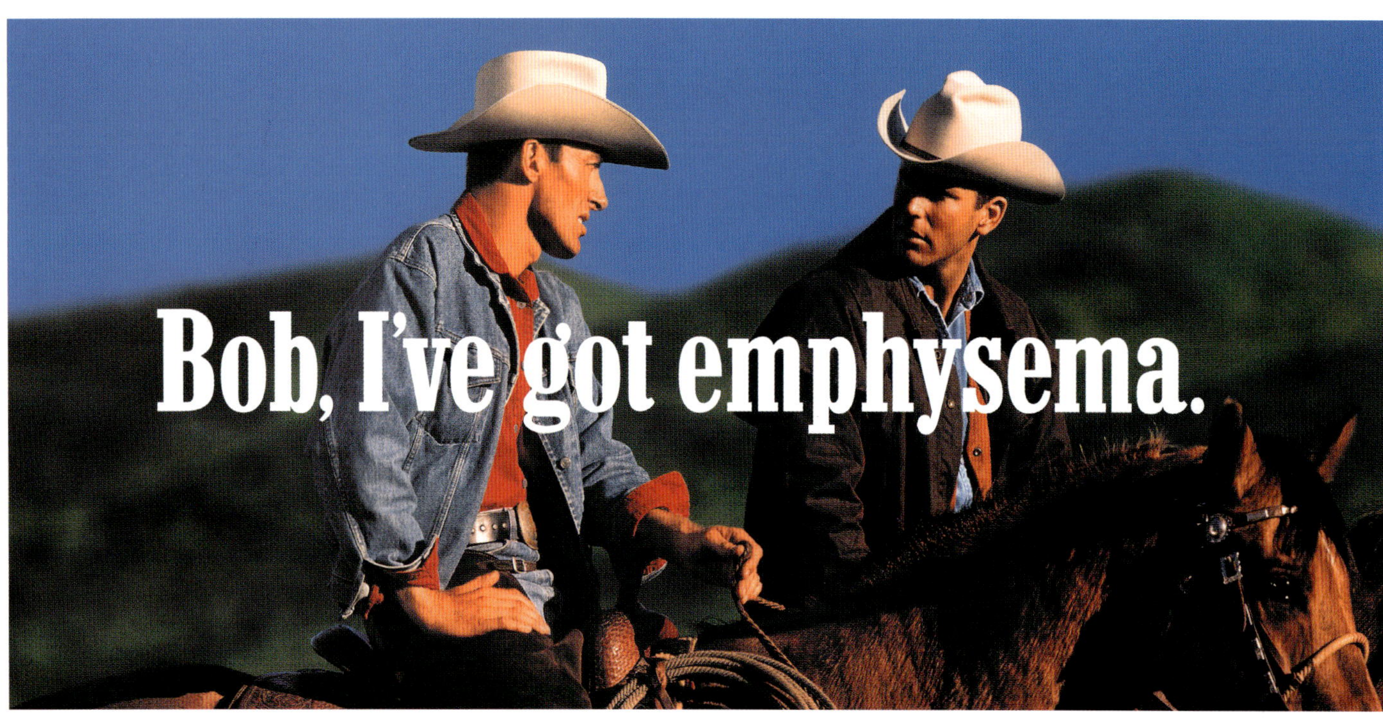

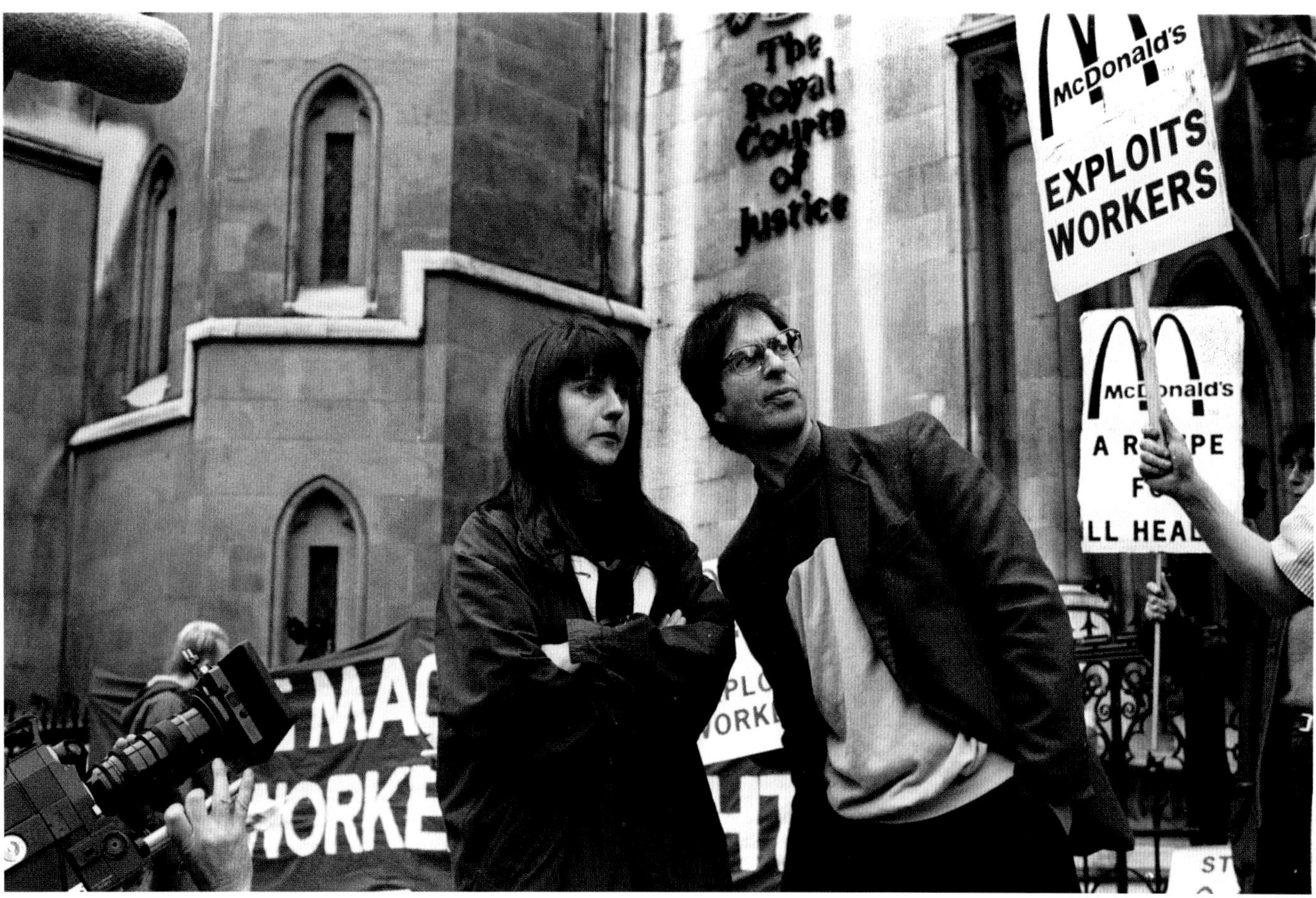

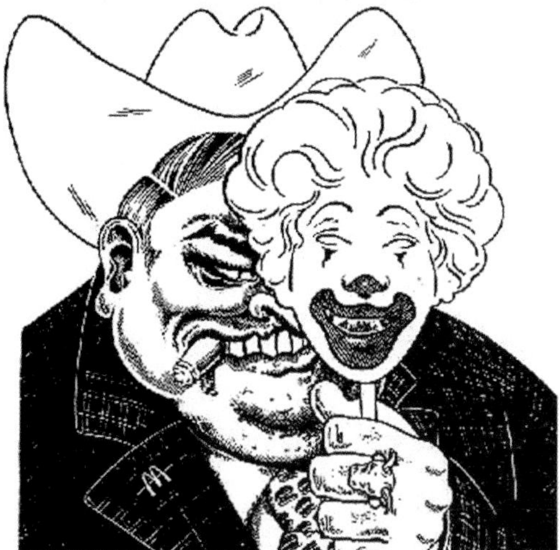

↑ 'The McLibel Two': David
Morris and Helen Steel 1997
Photographer: Nick Cobbing
Photograph

Morris and Steel were the UK activists who went to court to face fast-food corporation giant McDonald's in what became known as the McLibel Trial. This was the photograph shown in the mainstream press at the end of the historic trial (1994–97).

← What's Wrong with McDonald's? 1986–90
London Greenpeace (no relation to Greenpeace International)
Pamphlet: front page

The distribution of this leaflet by London Greenpeace (1986–90), eventually led to the McLibel Trial (1994–97) which remains one of the anti-globalization movement's biggest statements. UK activists David Morris (postman) and Helen Steel (gardener) were taken to court by McDonald's (international fast-food corporation) for distributing 'libellous' information in a pamphlet, resulting in the longest running civil libel case in British history. Morris and Steel were eventually found guilty of libel on a number of counts but the trial was viewed as a public relations disaster for McDonald's and a victory for Morris and Steel. The McLibel Support Campaign co-ordinated the substantial anti-McDonald's publicity, supportive donations and sale of merchandise to help finance legal costs, and a number of well-known protest groups (such as PETA: People for the Ethical Treatment of Animals) ensured that anti-McDonald's campaigning continued for years after.

Animal Rights

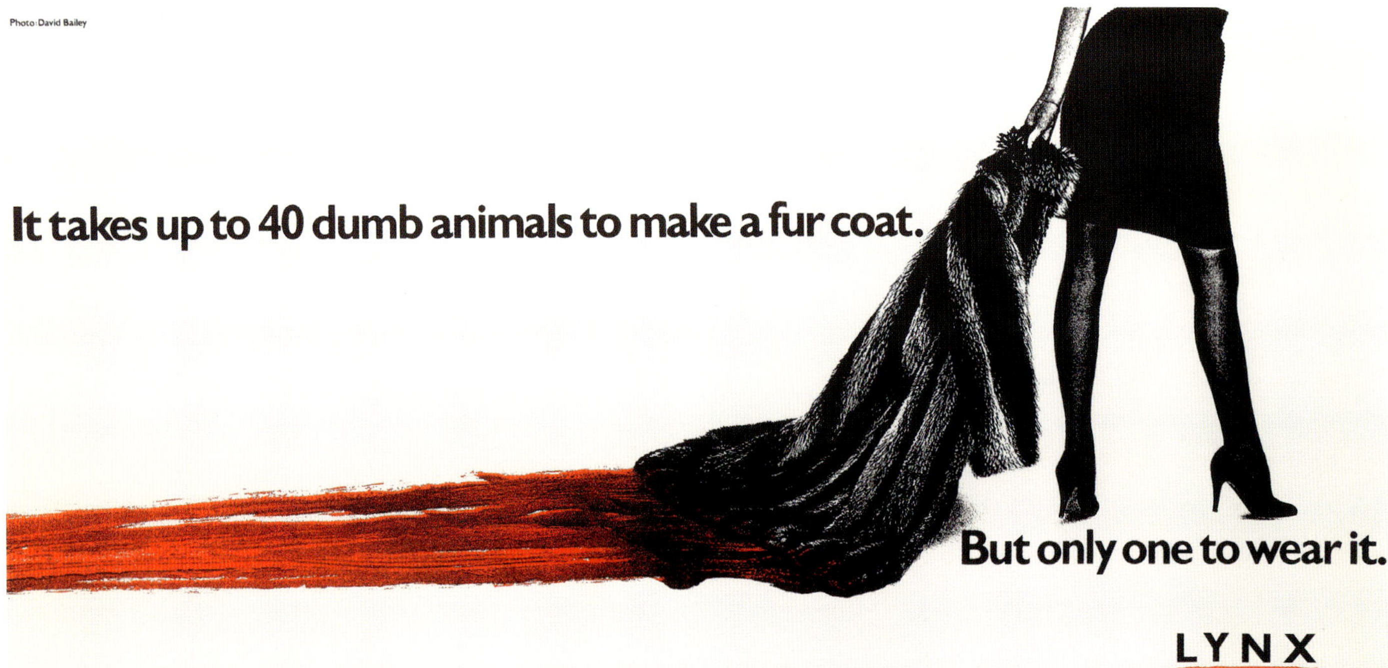

↑ It takes up to 40 dumb animals to make a fur coat. But only one to wear it. 1985
Yellowhammer (art direction Jeremy Pemberton, photographer David Bailey)
Billboard poster

The issue of animal rights became highly popular in the 1980s atmosphere of activism and personal politics, encouraged by the Lynx anti-fur campaign's landmark '40 dumb animals' cinema ad and billboard poster, showing a fashion model dragging a bloody fur coat behind her. It struck a chord, and within months people were wearing fashion designer Katharine Hamnett's t-shirts and badges saying 'Yuck! Your disgusting fur coat'. Shops selling fur were boycotted and fur sales plummeted, creating real damage to the fur industry. Lynx transformed into the Respect for Animals campaign in the 1990s and continued its aggressive visual campaigns. At the same time, PETA (People for the Ethical Treatment of Animals), a large, international US-based organization produced high-profile media campaigns about animal abuse (often involving models or celebrities) and was renowned for its catwalk protests: an attempt to ward off fur-toting designers or models. Together, all of the campaigns mentioned created a stigma against wearing fur that still persists. They also marked a change in attitude, from the caring notion of 'animal welfare' to the forceful call for direct action that demanded animal rights as well as human rights.

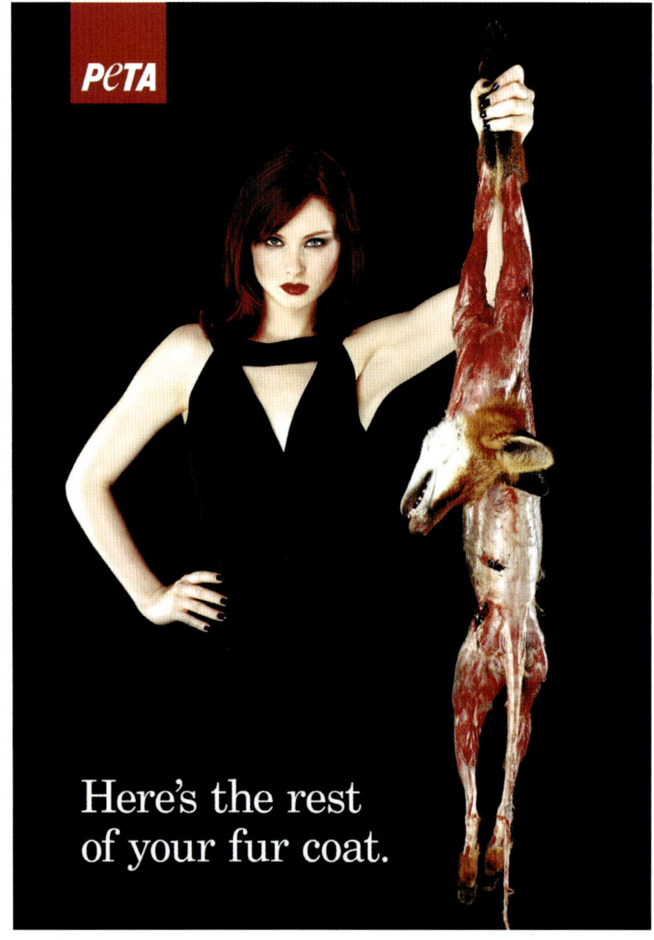

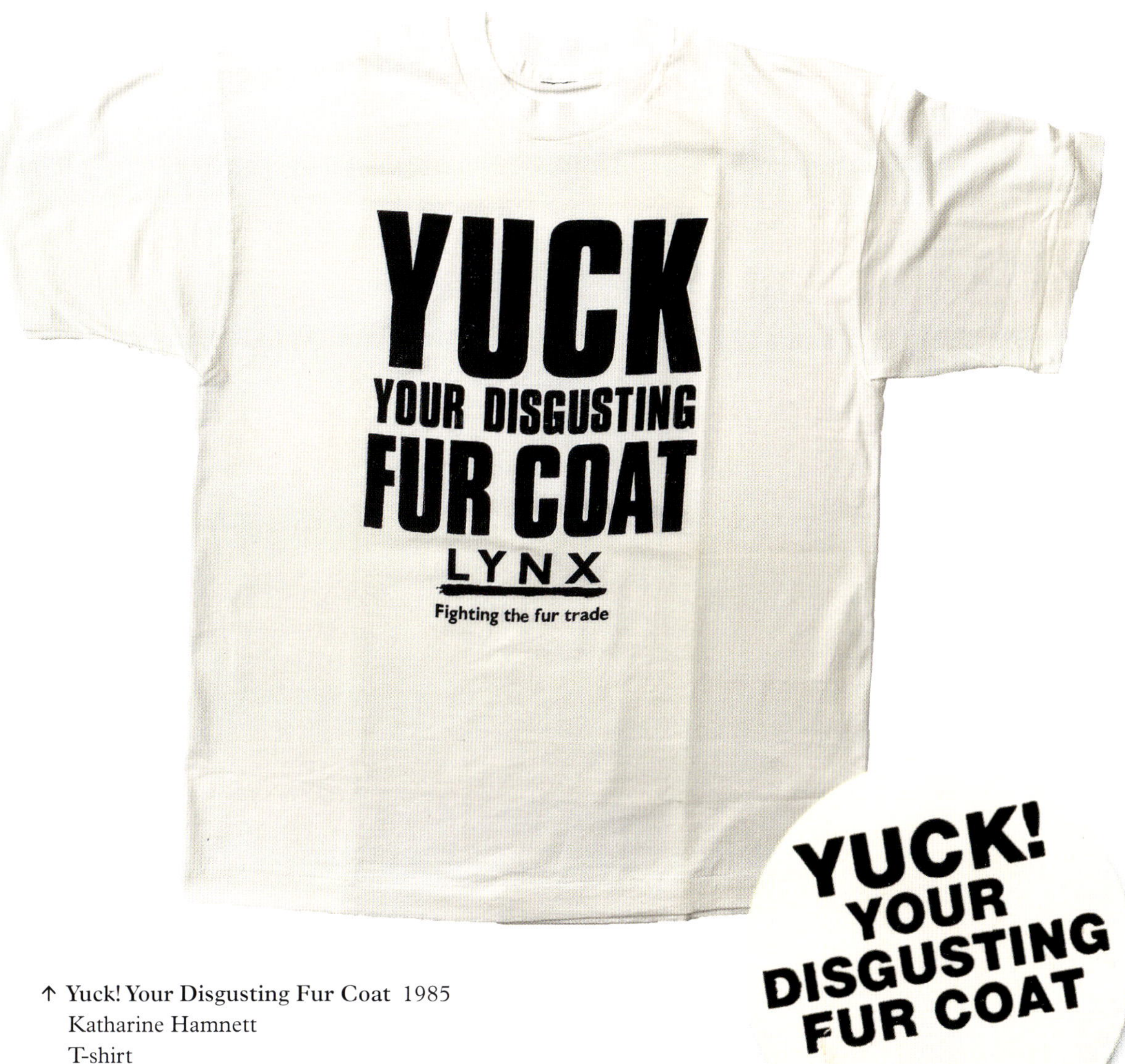

↑ **Yuck! Your Disgusting Fur Coat** 1985
Katharine Hamnett
T-shirt

Fashion designer Katharine Hamnett was known for her
influential 'slogan t-shirts' that caught the vibe of youth
movements in the 1980s and 1990s, and were still effective
with the 21st century anti-war movement. Her slogan for
Lynx, whether on t-shirt or badge, substantially helped to
create a stigma against wearing fur.

→ **Yuck! Your Disgusting Fur Coat** 1985
Lynx
Badge

This badge bears a slogan by fashion designer Katharine
Hamnett, created for Lynx, the anti-fur campaign.

← **Here's the rest of your fur coat** 2002
Photograph: Mary McCartney
Poster

People for the Ethical Treatment of Animals (PETA) created
this anti-fur campaign showing British pop singer Sophie
Ellis Bextor holding up the carcass of a skinned fox. PETA
UK and its affiliates excelled at involving high-profile models,
celebrities and designers in its campaigns in the early 2000s,
as well as producing satirical websites such as http://www.
kentuckyfriedcruelty.com and https://www.seaworldofhurt.com.

Environmental Concerns

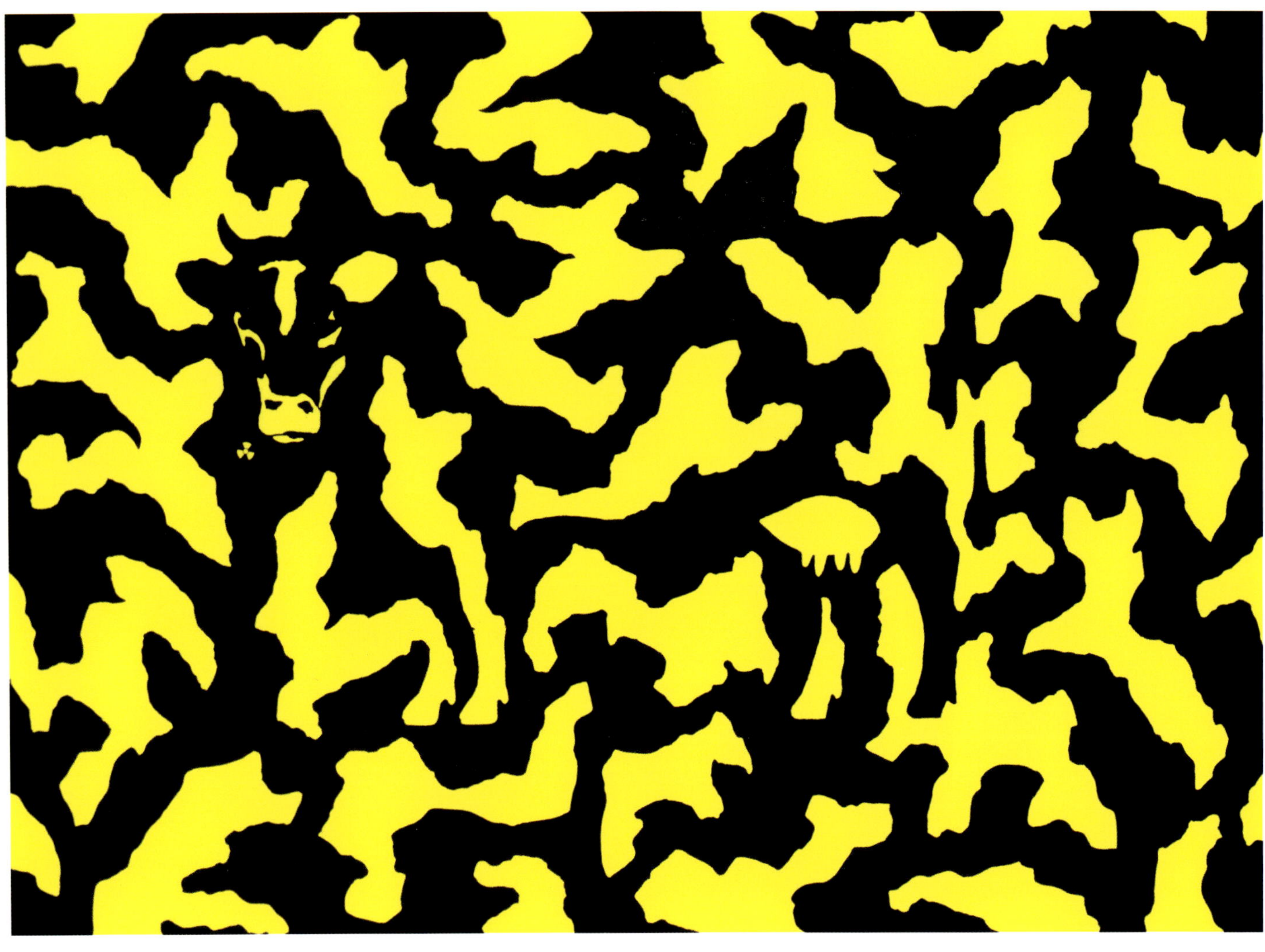

IQ: Radioactive Contamination of the Environment 1986
Uwe Loesch
Poster

In the same way that animal rights activism produced innovative, aggressive visual campaigns throughout the 1980s, environmental statements also produced extreme imagery. Old graphic clichés lost their attraction: no more smiling suns or happy flowers. The destructive forces of pollution, nuclear accidents and massive oil spills demanded shocking images and people willing to engage in direct action. On 26 April 1986, one of four nuclear reactors at the Chernobyl power station in the Soviet Union exploded, producing the world's worst nuclear accident. Due to wind direction, the radioactive 'plume' reached as far as, and badly affected, Scandinavia. In this poster – created at the time of the accident – the spotted irregular pattern of the cow's hide begins to merge with a background of what might be perceived as enlarged, radioactive fallout, or some other poison polluting the air. The lurid yellow simply adds to the horror. Look closely: the cow is chewing a radiation symbol, not clover.

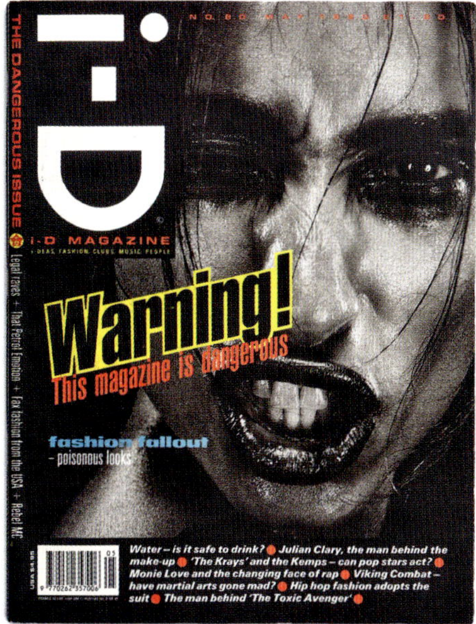

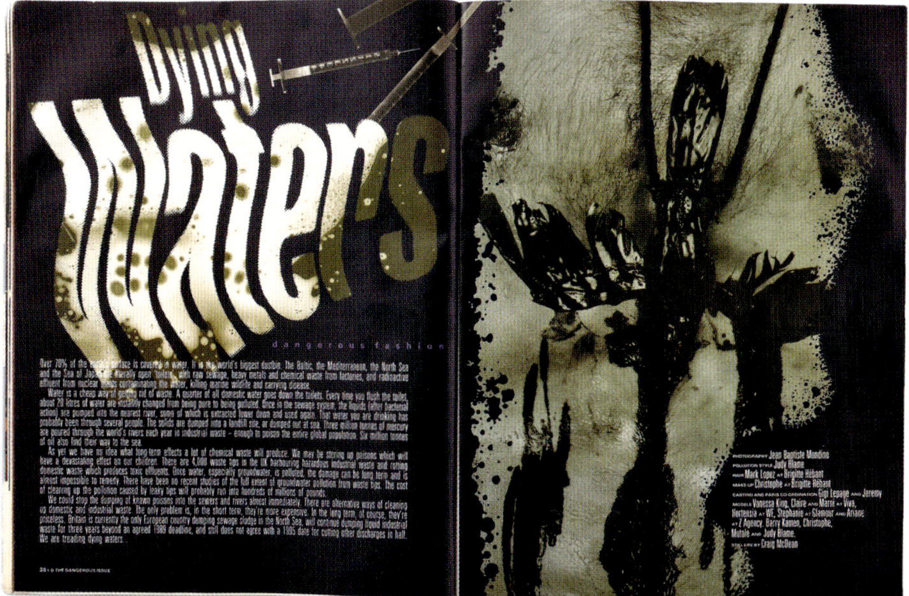

Dying Waters 1990
Artist: Judy Blame
Photographer: Jean Baptiste Mondino
Front cover and style essay: *i-D* No. 80,
May 1990

By the late 1980s, nuclear accidents, oil
spills and reports on the 'greenhouse
effect' (soon to be seen as causing
'global warming'), had all made
environmental issues an urgent matter
of survival. On 24 March 1989, the
Exxon Valdez oil spill occurred in Prince
William Sound, Alaska. The tanker
struck a reef and spilled out 11 million
gallons of crude oil into the water,
which soon also covered the Alaskan
coastline. Maverick fashion stylist Judy
Blame (1960–2018), horrified and
inspired by the *Exxon Valdez* oil spill,
produced this controversial 'pollution
style' essay for youth style magazine *i-D*.
Human models were used to symbolize
oil-slicked birds, and shocking,
informative statements about pollution
appeared throughout the sequence of
pages, threaded through the murky
background. Fashion and style mixed
with politics in an unusual way. (Judy's
'Fuck *Exxon*' necklace, a braided chain
bearing a fake 'dead' bird covered in
oil, is shown on the first double-page
spread.) Three out of seven double-page
spreads are shown here. The *Valdez* spill
was the second largest to take place in
US waters; it was only surpassed by the
2010 Deepwater Horizon spill.

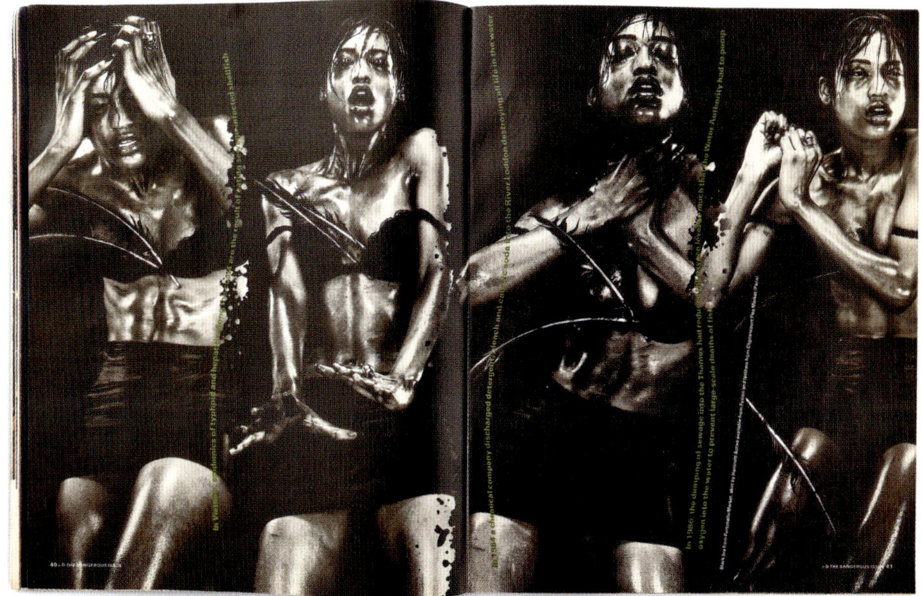

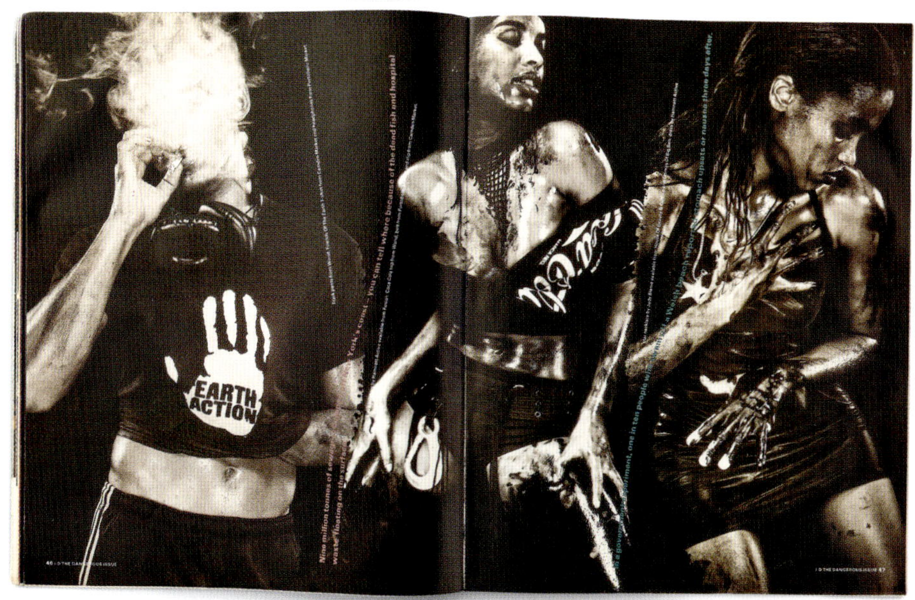

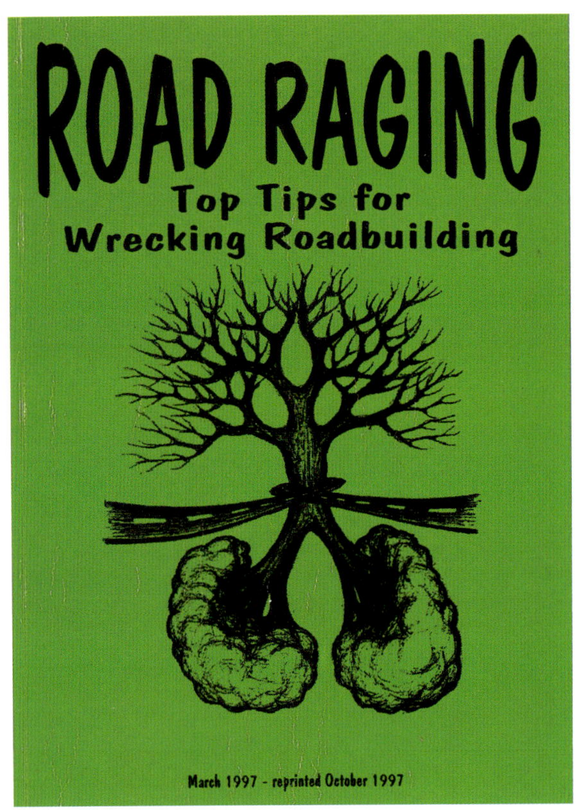

Road Raging: Top Tips for Wrecking Roadbuilding 1997
Road Alert
Handbook

The 1990s saw environmentalism join forces with the new anti-globalization movement, dedicated to people power vs. corporate power. The British roadbuilding protests, held throughout the 1990s, involved militant action against the building of motorways or bypasses through areas of natural beauty (particularly forests), or commuter link roads into London which would add to traffic congestion and pollution. People of all ages and political views joined in, and soon protesters were living in treehouses, tunnelling or devising other ways of stopping the bulldozers sent by developers and big business interests. Such actions pitted the manmade vs. the organic, as well as police vs. protesters. Thus bruised and broken limbs were commonplace, which fuelled the cause of media activism involving video activists, internet hackers and others determined to present an alternative viewpoint to mainstream news, which never showed the brutality of the police or security guards. An excellent example of illustrated information of the time was *Road Raging: Top Tips for Wrecking Roadbuilding*, a resource manual on how to stage an environmental protest campaign, filled with diagrams, instructions and advice, from how to survive a (tree) eviction attempt by security guards in a hydraulic cherrypicker, to what diseases or infections you might suffer in a protest camp.

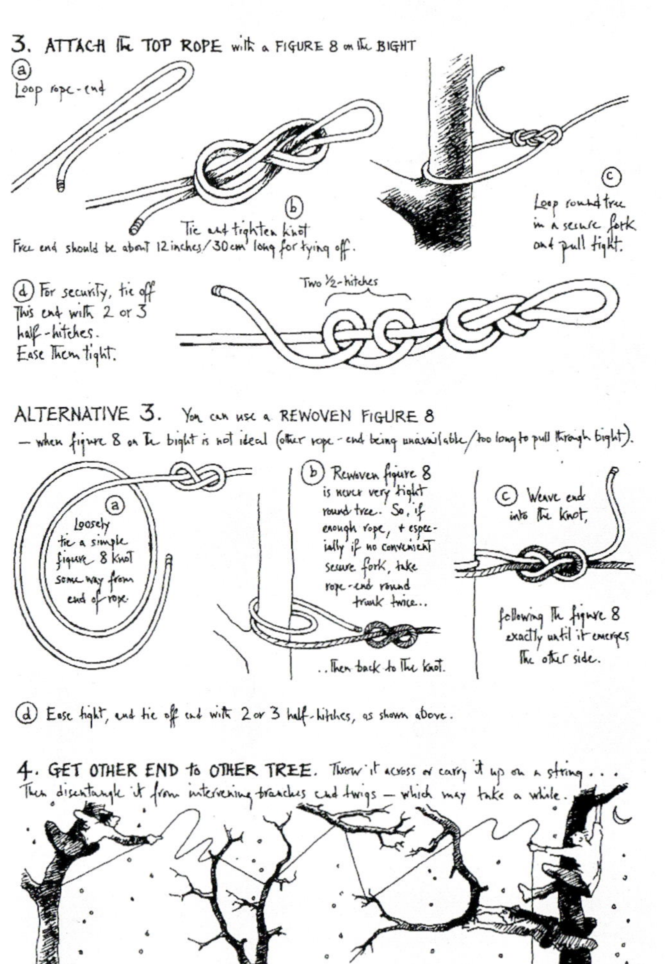

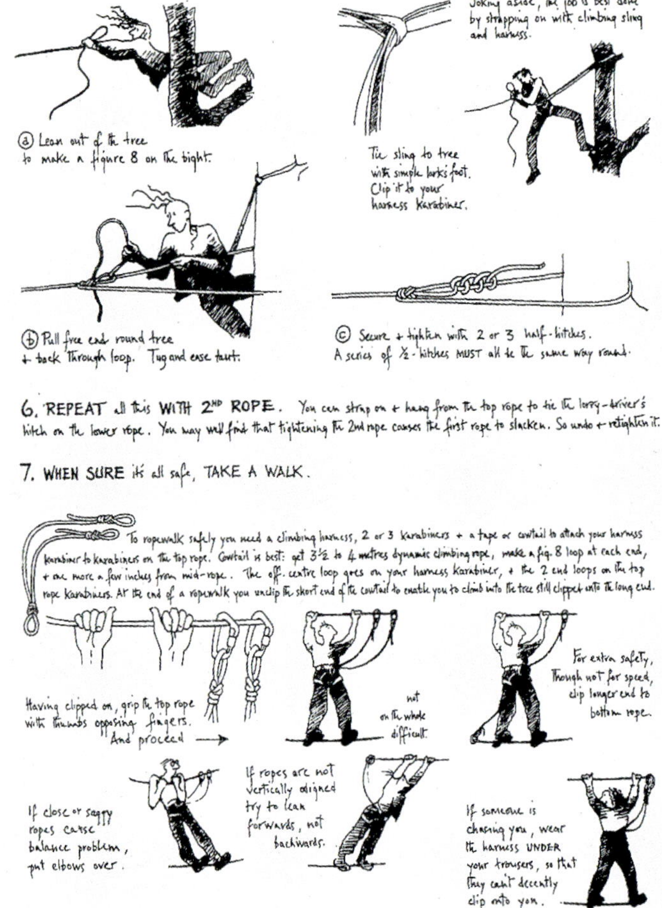

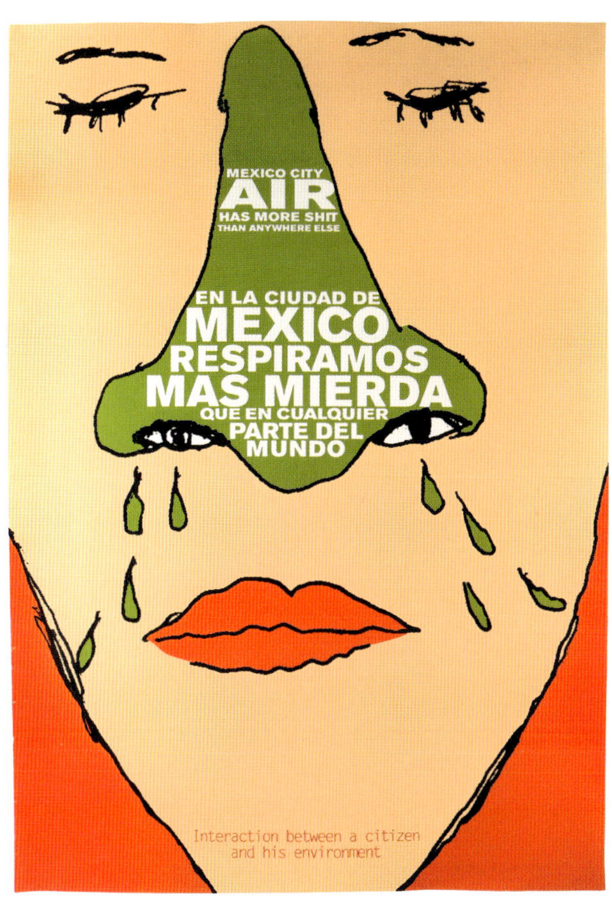

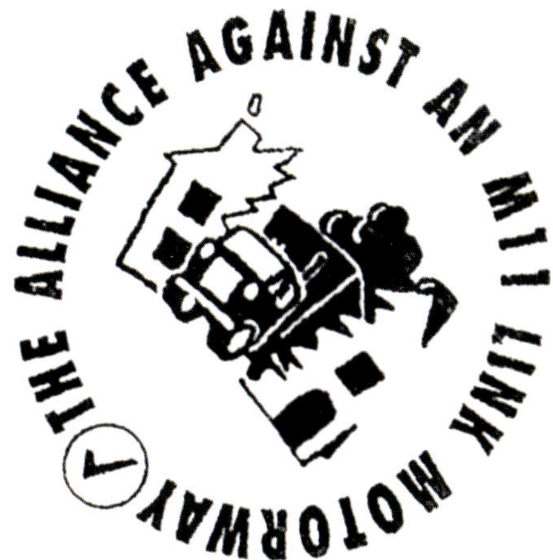

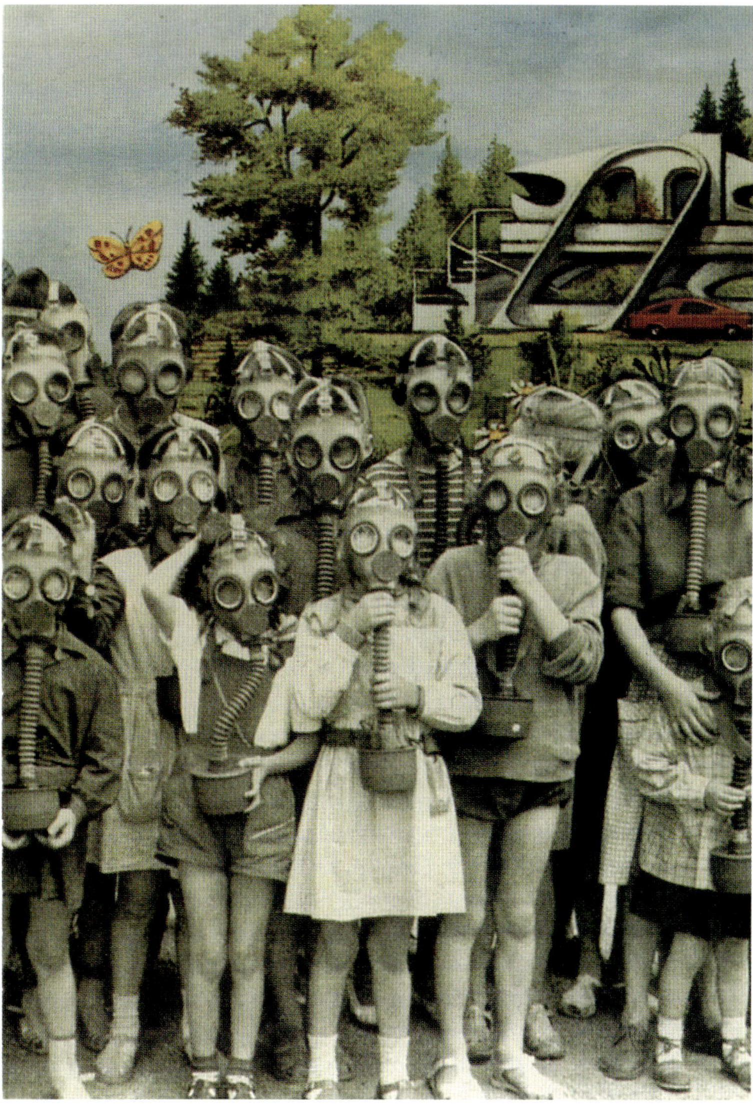

↑ **Mexico City Air** 2001
Alejandro Magallanes
Poster

Pollution began to be recognized as a global disaster
and evoked strong messages from designers around
the world. This poster draws attention to the lack of
clean air in Mexico City – and possibly other major
cities – and asks citizens to interact or deal with the
issue and not be passive.

↗ **The Alliance Against an M11 Link
Motorway** 1993–94
Artist unknown
Logo

This logo belonged to a north London protest
campaign against a link road that caused protesters
to engage in the erection and habitation of a
treehouse in a now-famous chestnut tree which
was to be destroyed.

→ **Children with Gas Masks** 1988
Egon Kramer
Postcard

German photomontagist Egon Kramer has produced
a nightmarish image showing a future where children
are forced to go everywhere in gas masks.

Human Rights, Anti-Racism

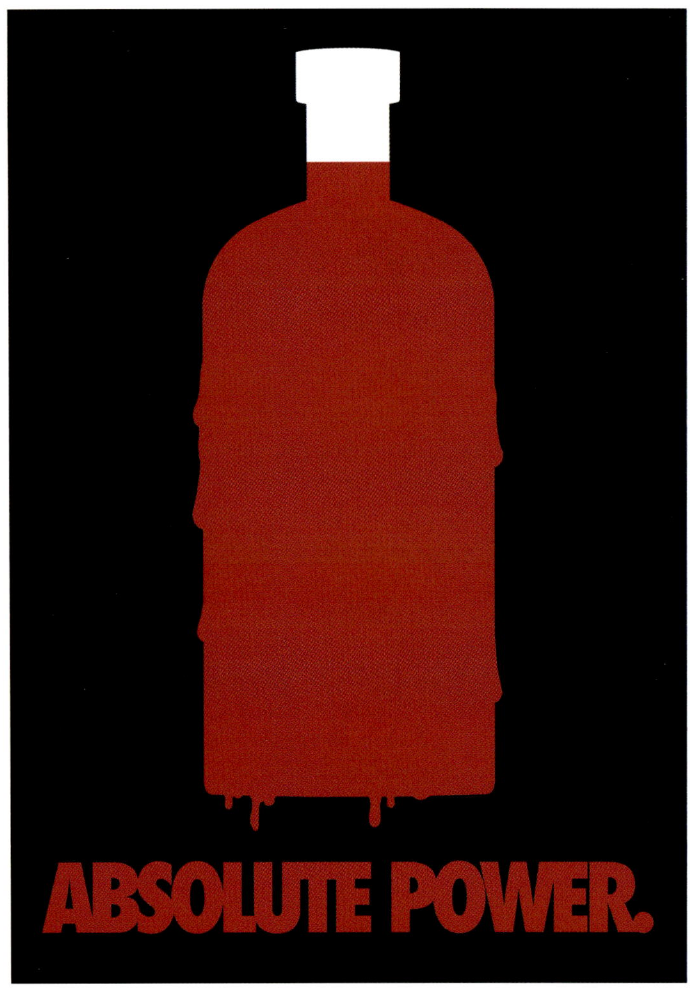

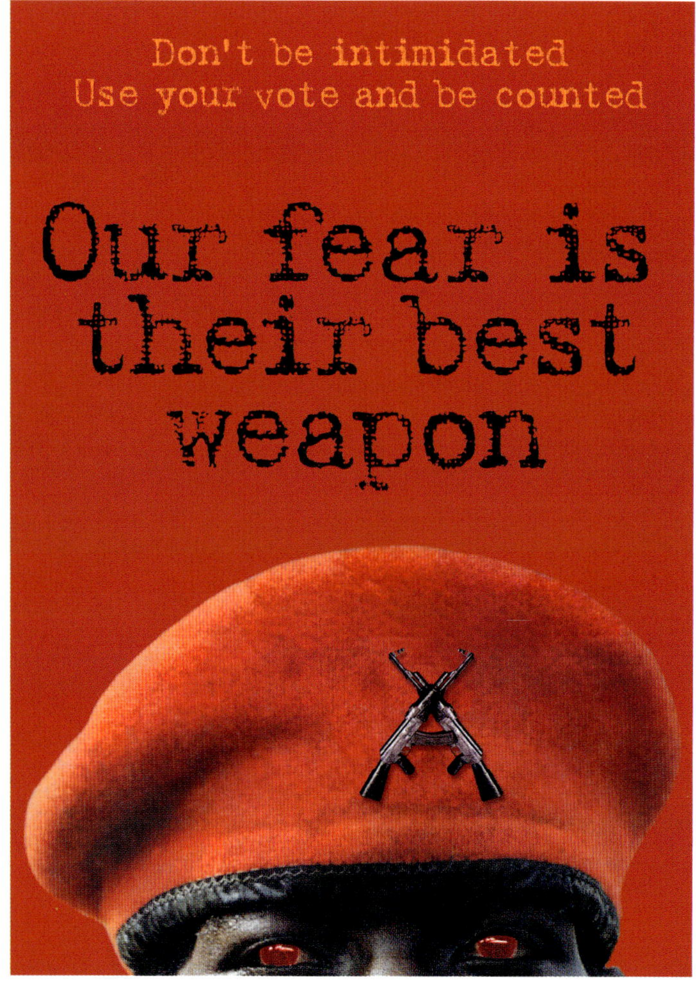

Graphic Commentaries: 30 Days of Activism 2000
Chaz Maviyane-Davies
Emails, electronic posters, texts

By the late 1990s, human rights – in particular, the right to a fair election – were being destroyed in Zimbabwe. President Robert Mugabe, with the help of his ruling party Zanu-PF, was driving the country and its economy to ruin. He maintained a stranglehold on elections through the violence and intimidation of voters, a flawed election process and, by all accounts, a terrorized opposition. In the countdown to the June 2000 general elections, Zimbabwean-born designer Chaz Maviyane-Davies brought Zimbabwe's civil rights abuses and violence to the attention of the world via the internet. He embarked on '30 days of activism' to encourage a vote for change. Creating one or more images per day, he produced 50 Graphic Commentaries (electronic poster images) which were emailed daily to individuals and civic rights groups around the world. They were accompanied by Maviyane-Davies' written texts, African proverbs and quotations, links to additional sites (including the Save Zimbabwe site containing a petition to the UN to mediate elections) and a comic strip entitled 'Shango', intended to help get people to vote for change despite the risks. A request was also made to graphic designers around the world to send designs and join in the creation of an agitprop exhibition/website. Despite all efforts Mugabe still won the election, and tragically Zimbabweans would have to wait until 2018 for a change in leadership.

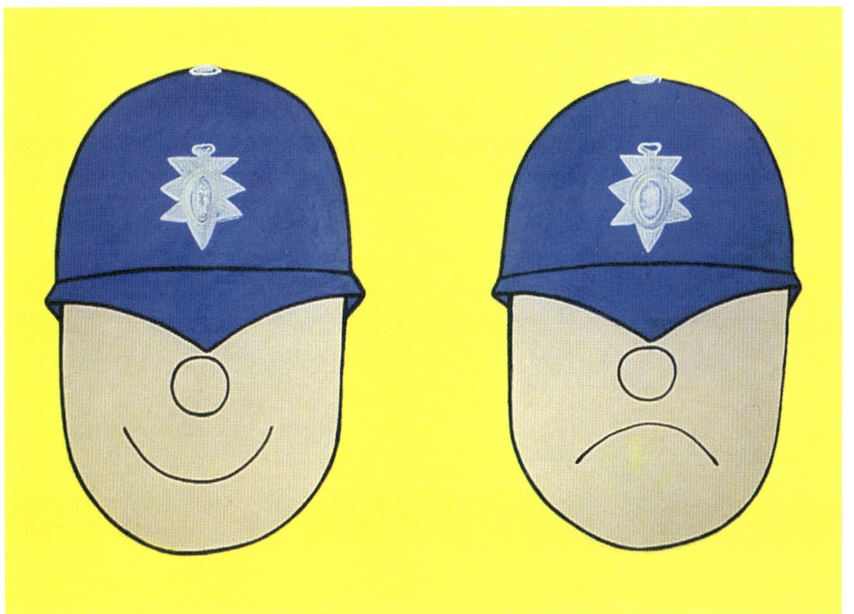

Tam Joseph presents a stark image of the police: comicly simple, or nasty and hard-edged (although both become hypnotically sinister with prolonged viewing). The black community's mistrust of and difficult relationship with the police would continue, coming into sharp focus with the proceedings that followed the tragic death of teenager Stephen Lawrence, murdered in an unprovoked racist attack in 1993. After a bungled murder investigation by police, a public inquiry set up in 1997 resulted in the publication of the Macpherson Report in 1999, which denounced the Metropolitan Police in London for 'institutional racism'.

↓ UK School Report 1980
Artist: Tam Joseph
Painting, postcard, billboard

Despite Britain's strong involvement in the international anti-apartheid movement, it nevertheless had problems with race at home. The extremist National Front was still attempting to march publicly in the late 1970s, only to be met (often in skirmishes in the street) by the opposing Anti-Nazi League. The police presented yet another problem with their targeting of black youths by using heavy-handed 'stop and search' tactics. The anger of the black community finally exploded in 1981 with the Brixton Riots of south London, which then spread throughout the country. Artist Tam Joseph captured the underlying stereotyping and prejudice, by both police and society at large, that developed into assigning the label of 'suspect' to young black men.

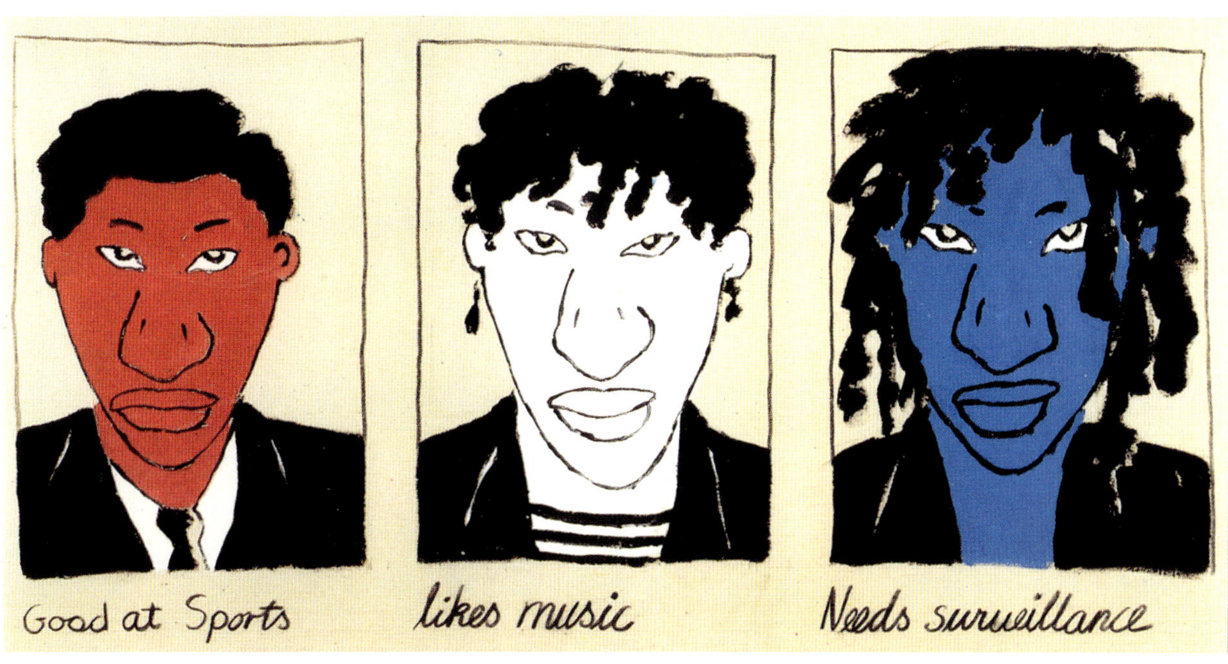

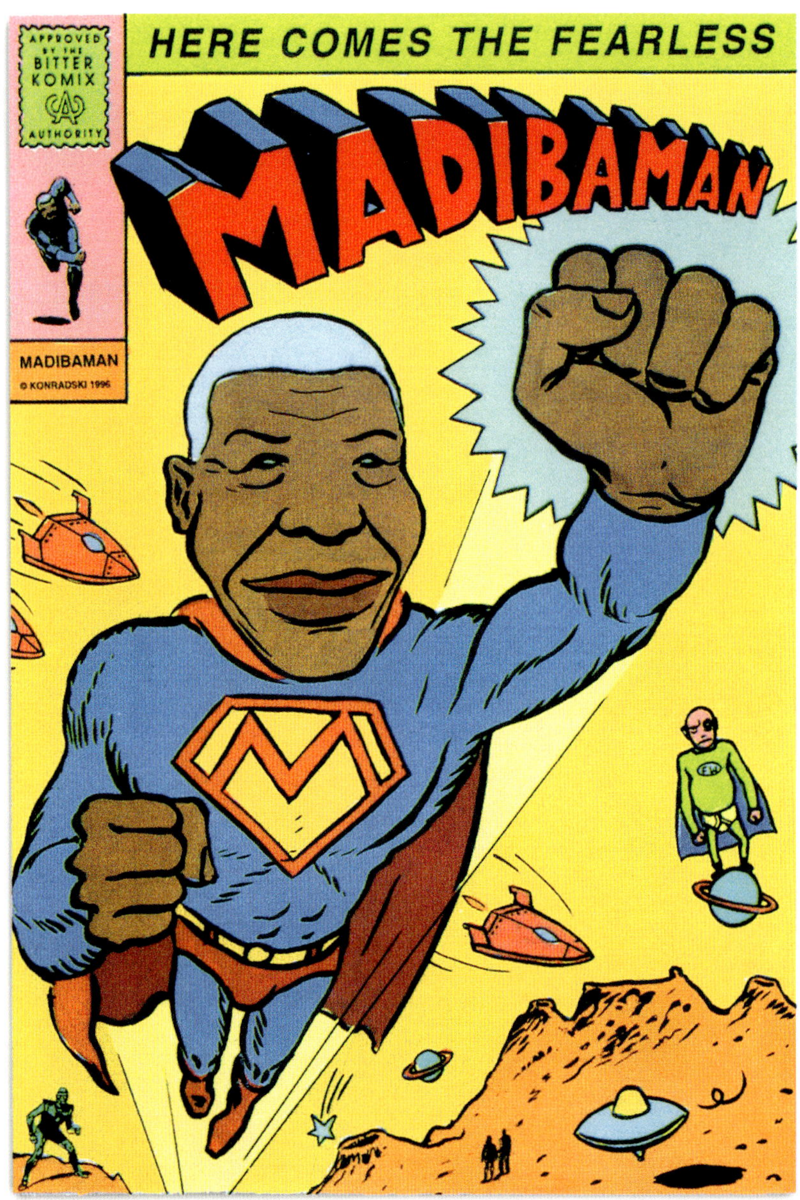

Madibaman 1996
Get Down, Whiteboy! 1998
Conrad Botes
Postcards

Nelson Mandela's victory in the 1994 presidential elections marked the beginning of 'the new South Africa'. It was followed by a period of euphoria, but the shadows of apartheid didn't vanish overnight and old resentments didn't magically disappear. Bitterkomix, founded in 1992 by Anton Kannemeyer (aka Joe Dog) and Conrad Botes, provided a satirical (underground) view of the new South Africa, particularly the fears and obsessions of white South Africans. The image 'Madibaman' comments on the political euphoria that followed the 1994 elections, when Mandela was viewed as Superman, able to save the world and solve all problems. However, 'Get Down, Whiteboy!' depicts a reversal of race and gender roles, as well as power positions, that demand respect, but might really desire revenge, suggesting very different possibilities for the new South Africa.

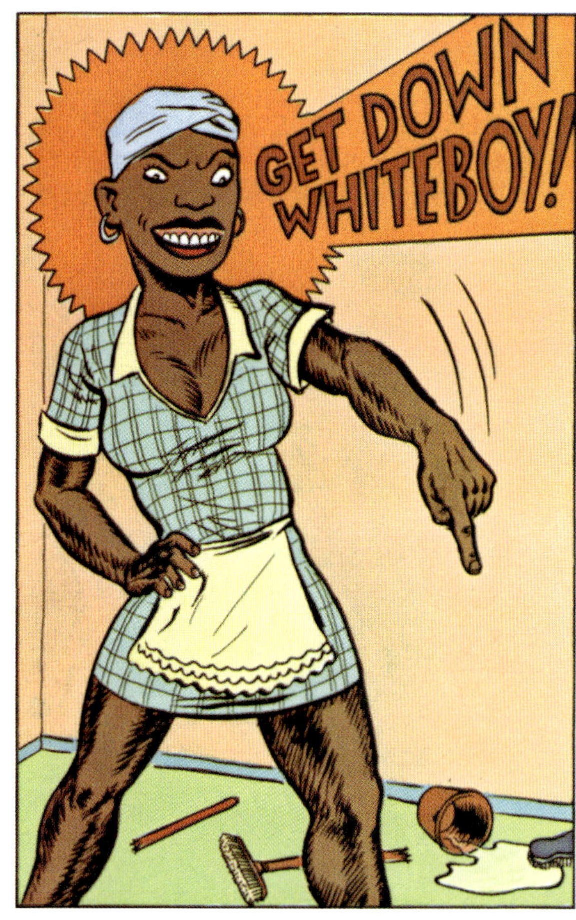

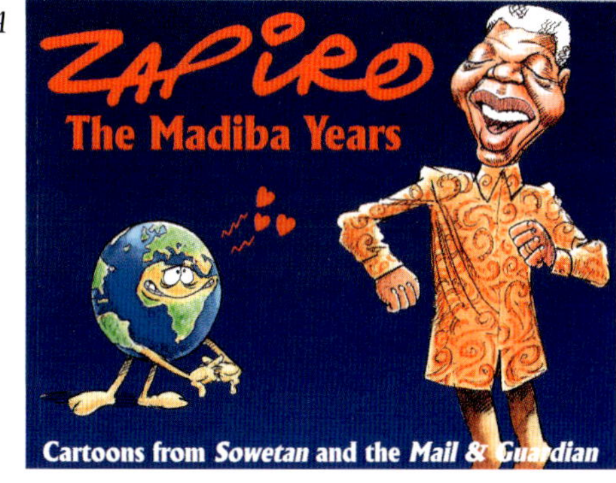

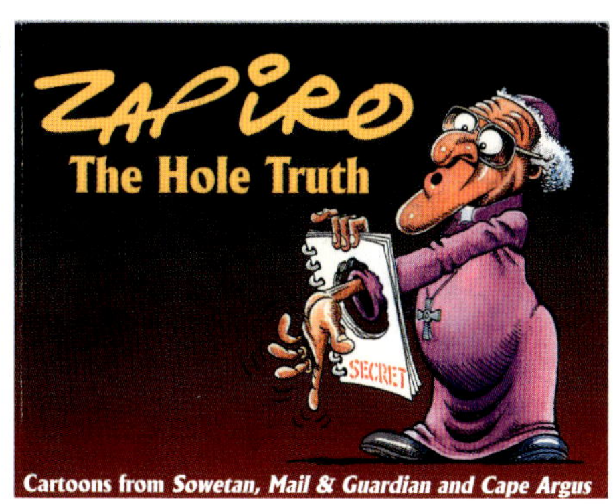

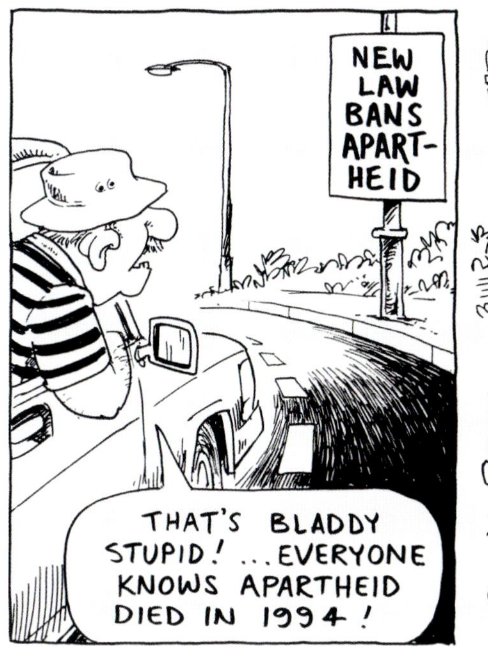

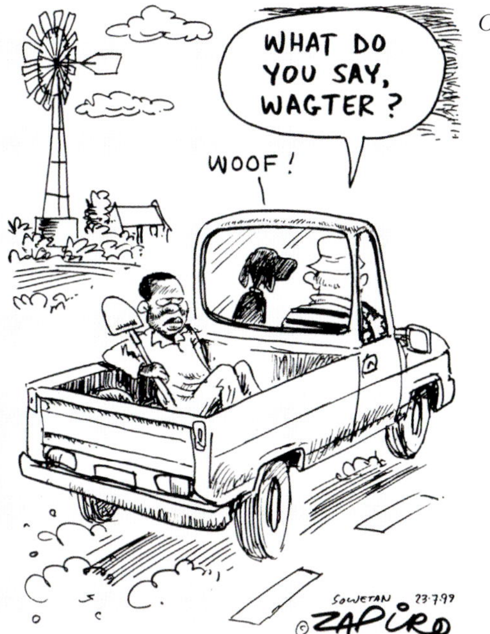

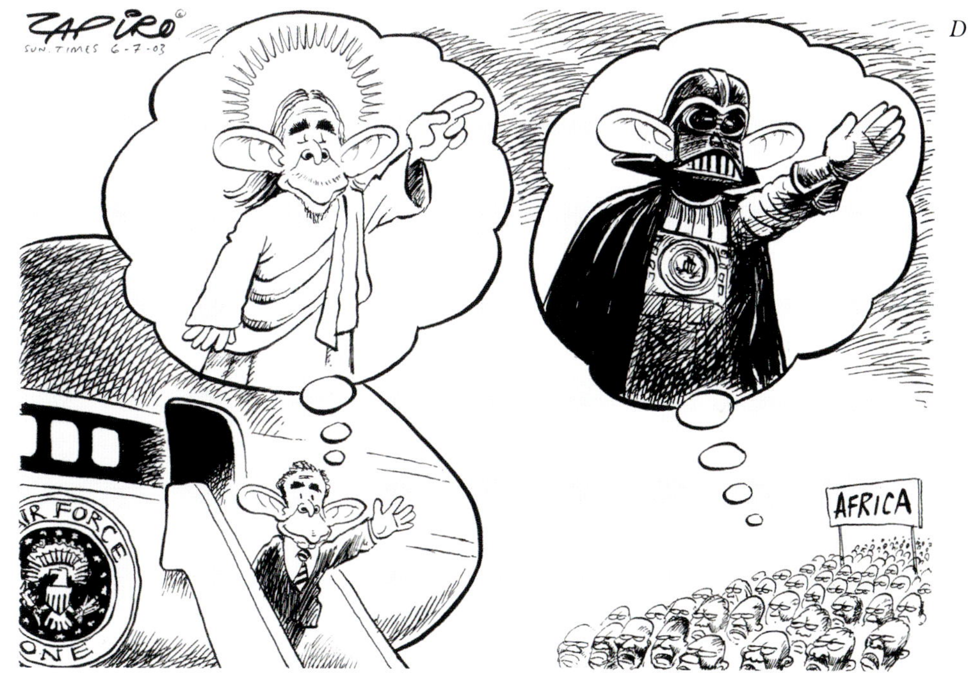

Zapiro
Jonathan Shapiro
Book covers and cartoons

Jonathan Shapiro (aka Zapiro) has been chronicling the social and political developments of South Africa – in cartoons – since 1994. He has worked for a number of newspapers, national and otherwise, while also producing annual collections of his cartoons as books. His collected works amount to a history and commentary of 'the new South Africa', charting the joys,

trials and tribulations of the early years, exposing more recent political mess-ups, and uncovering some of the uncomfortable truths and foibles that exist within the national psyche. Great affection and respect is shown for 'the Madiba Years' (1994–96), when Mandela was president and he and Archbishop Desmond Tutu were uniting the nation and building a new era of reconciliation (for apartheid) that was admired by the world. But many of the politicians that followed didn't measure up and have received sharp treatment from

Zapiro, as only a cartoonist can deliver – we laugh, but also cry. His commentary, however, amounts to an astounding story, depicted by hilarious cartoons, and his critiques of politicians can truly sting: Jacob Zuma (president 2009–18) twice sued him for defamation, but years later dropped the charges.

(Image A)   Zapiro: 'The Madiba Years' 1996
(Image B)   Zapiro: 'The Hole Truth' 1997
(Image C)   Zapiro cartoon 1999
(Image D)   Zapiro cartoon 2003

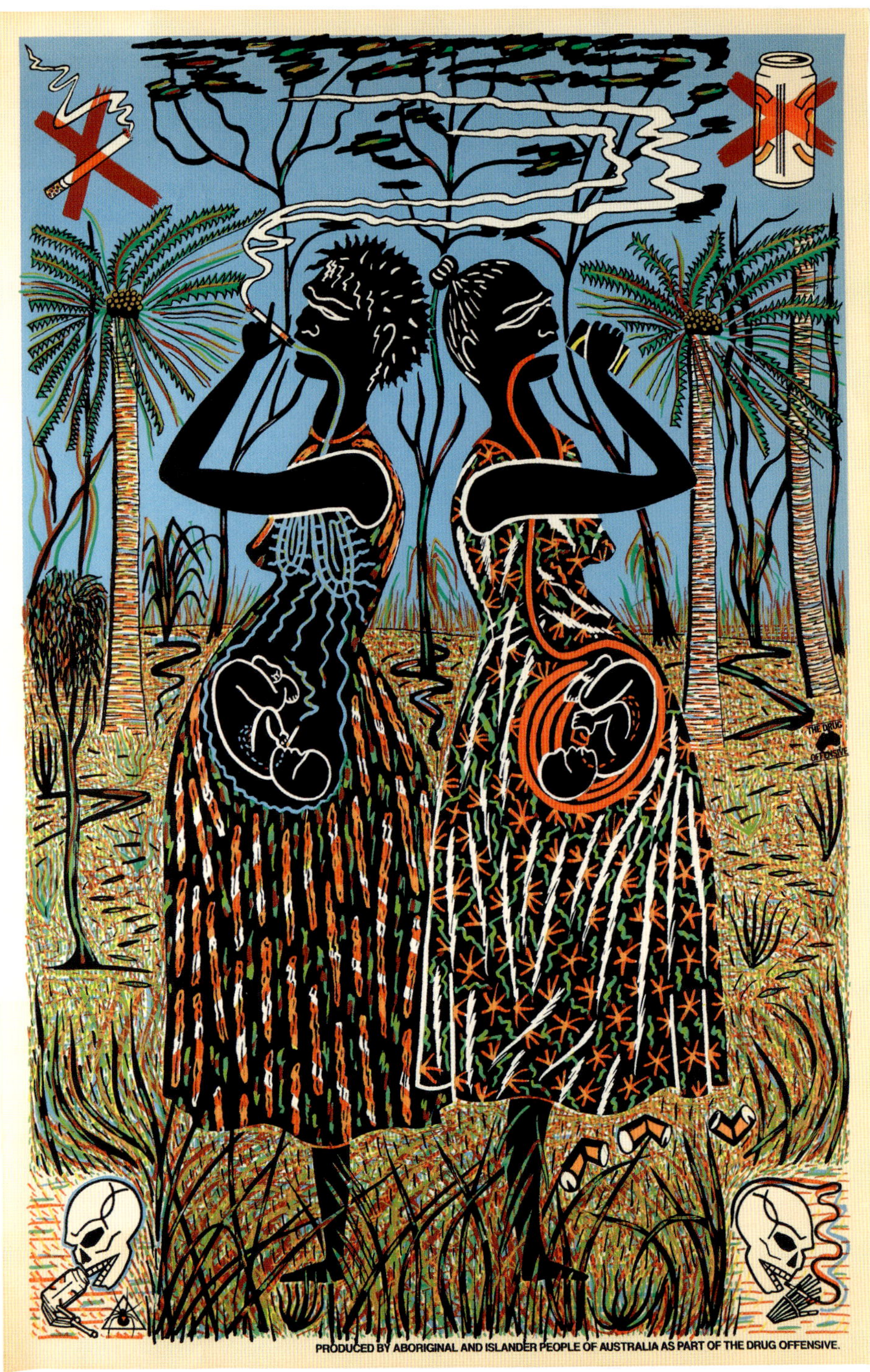

Pregnancy 1988
Redback Graphix
Design: Marie McMahon
Printer: Alison Alder
Poster (silkscreen)

Carrying on Australia's community art tradition of the 1960s and 1970s, a new generation of 1980s activists and graphic arts workshops (including a strong contingent of female artists) continued to produce politically and socially committed work. This included Redback Graphix, Red Planet Arts Workshop, Redletter Community Workshop and individuals such as Pam Debenham and Julia Church. Energized by the graphic style of Punk and advertising, as well as the symbolism and signs of Aboriginal culture, they were dedicated to the politics of the Left. But more specifically they campaigned against nuclear testing in the Pacific Islands (and its effect on Islanders and their environment) and focussed on the needs of the Aboriginal community.

Redback Graphix in particular produced a broad range of educational and informational graphics on safe sex, nutrition and health, the dangers of smoking, drinking and drugs and other subjects, often in consultation or collaboration with Aboriginal communities. 'Pregnancy' (1988), shown here, was produced by Redback Graphix but is also credited as being produced by 'Aboriginal and Islander People of Australia as part of the drug offensive', for the National Campaign Against Drug Abuse in Canberra, Australia.

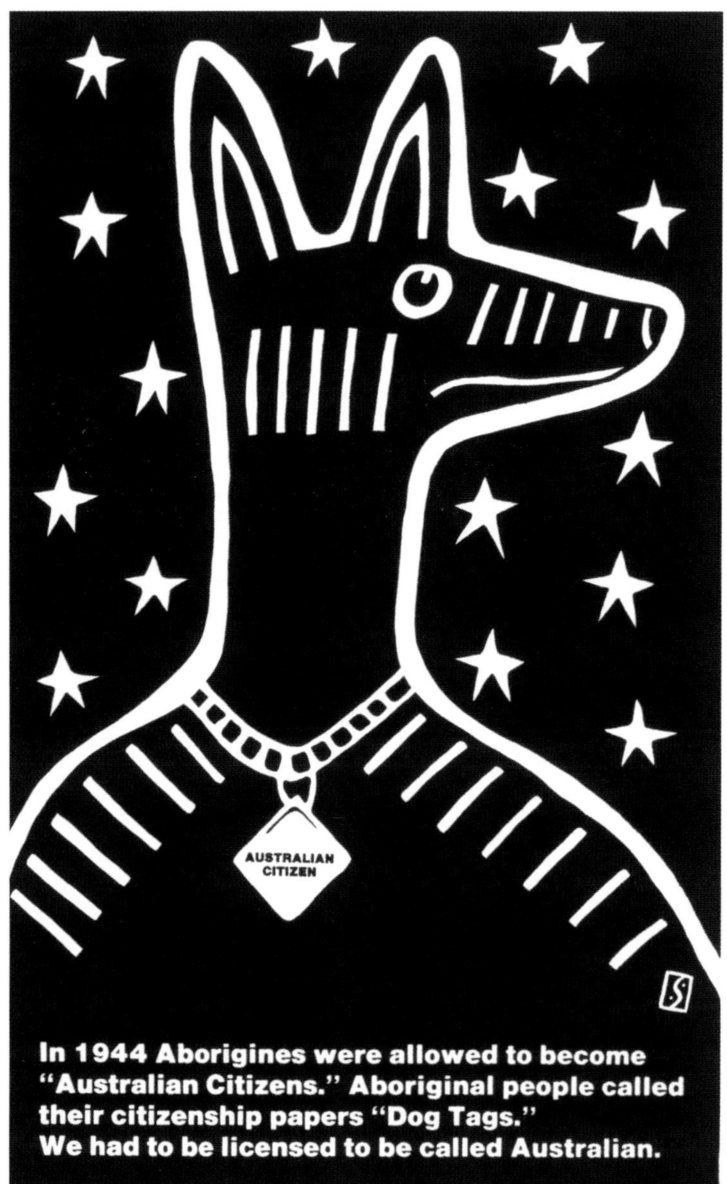

← Citizenship 1987
Sally Morgan
Poster

Aboriginal artist and writer Sally Morgan produced this poster, one of many 'unofficial' art projects created for the Australian Bicentennial of 1988 which placed a sharp focus on Australia's contemporary cultural divisions, resulting in calls for historical reassessment (rather than celebration) with regard to the mistreatment of Aboriginal people. The caption on the poster stating that Aborigines had to 'apply' for citizenship papers from 1944 onwards only tells part of the story: it wasn't until the referendum of 1967 (23 years later) that Aborigines were conferred full citizenship rights. Demanding an end to the oppression of the Aboriginal people continued to be a major theme for the Australian graphic arts workshops of the 1980s, throughout their existence.

↓ History 1987
Pam Debenham
Poster (silkscreen)

Pam Debenham's poster presents a flowing, fabric-like collage of past and present. But its central focus is two policemen or guards marching an Aboriginal out of the picture or towards containment of some sort. And on closer inspection, guns and images of incarceration (fencing, chains, an aerial view of a prison or containment area) weave menacingly through the collage. The past and its cruelties are never far away. The central Aboriginal figure seems ready to emerge from behind bars. But the police or guards grip him tightly. Will he ever escape from white containment?

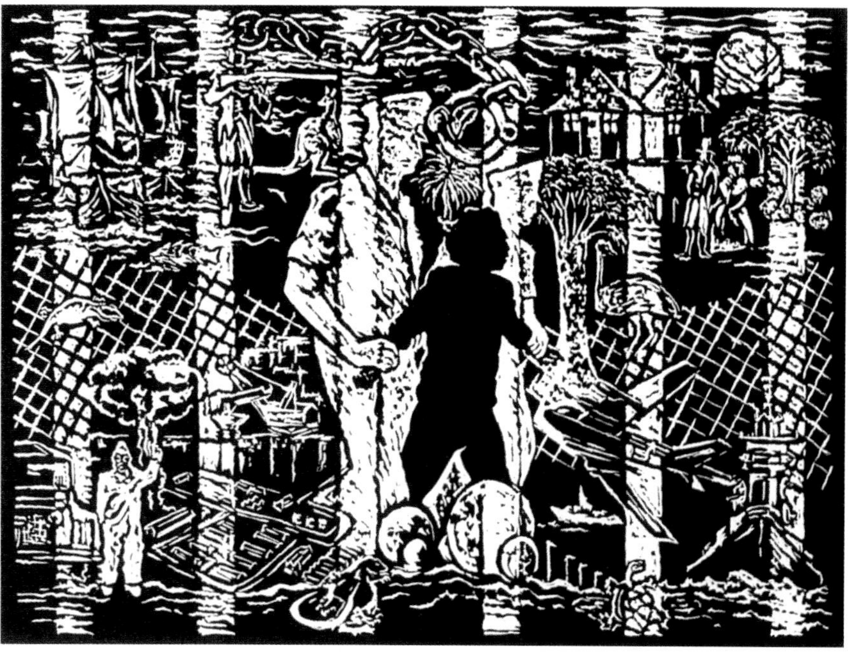

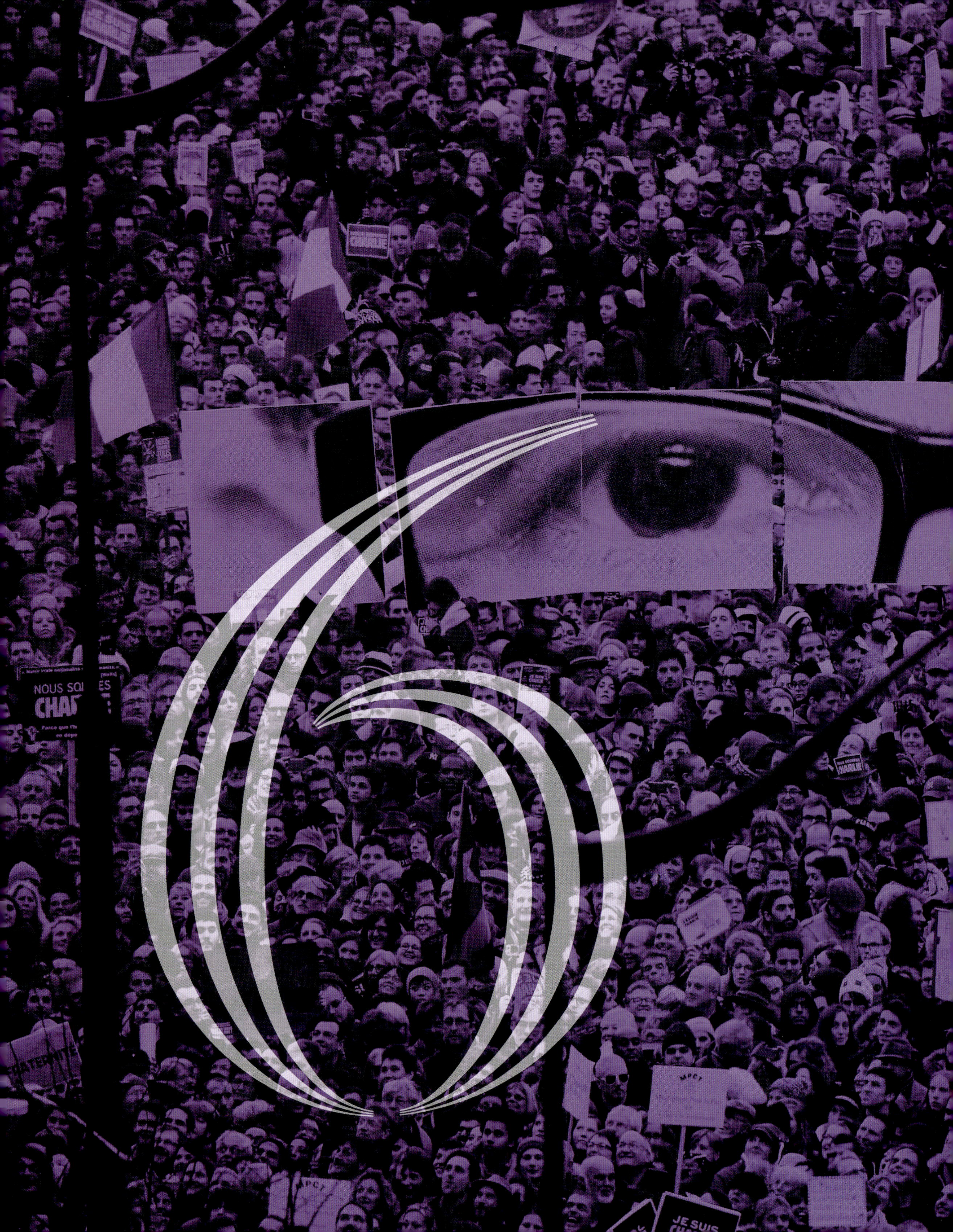

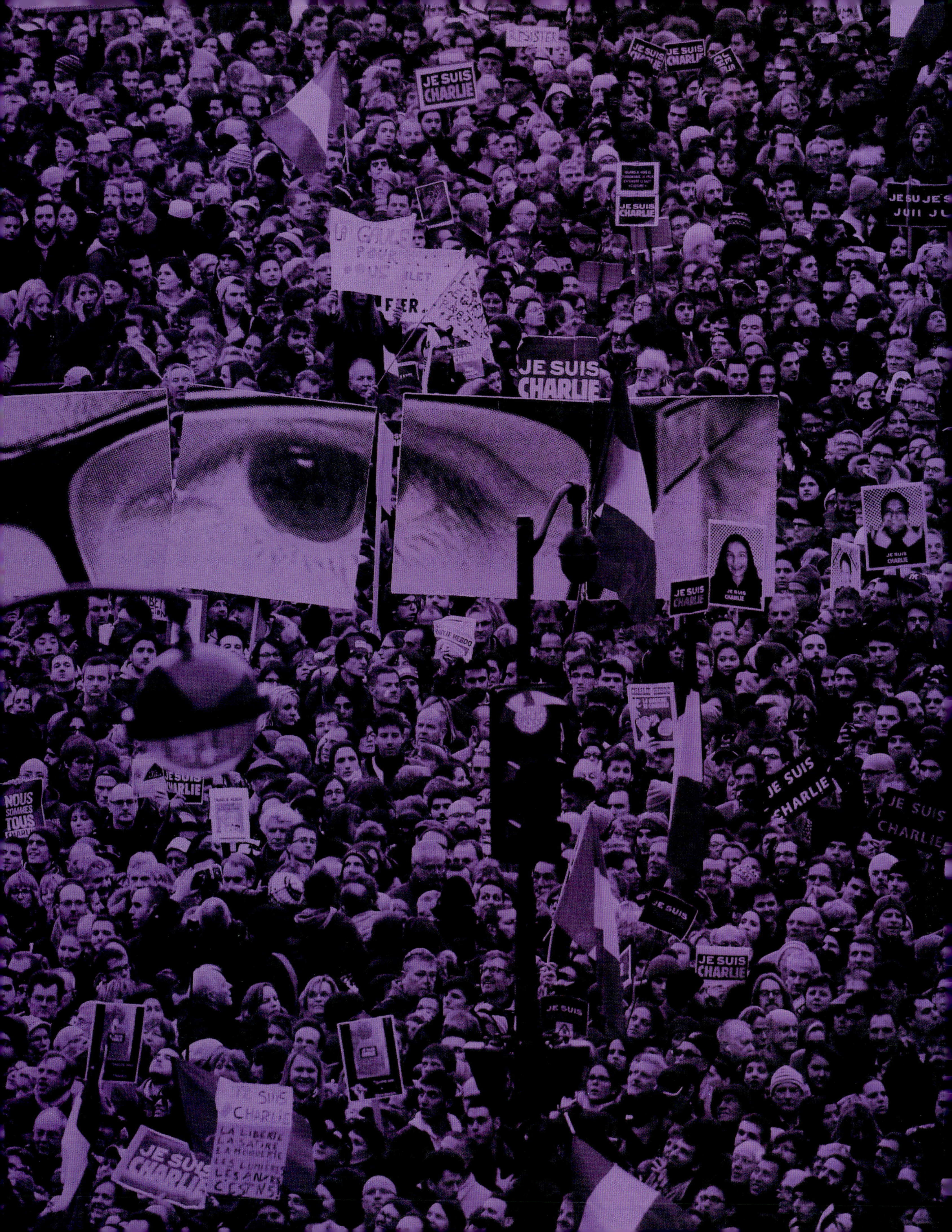

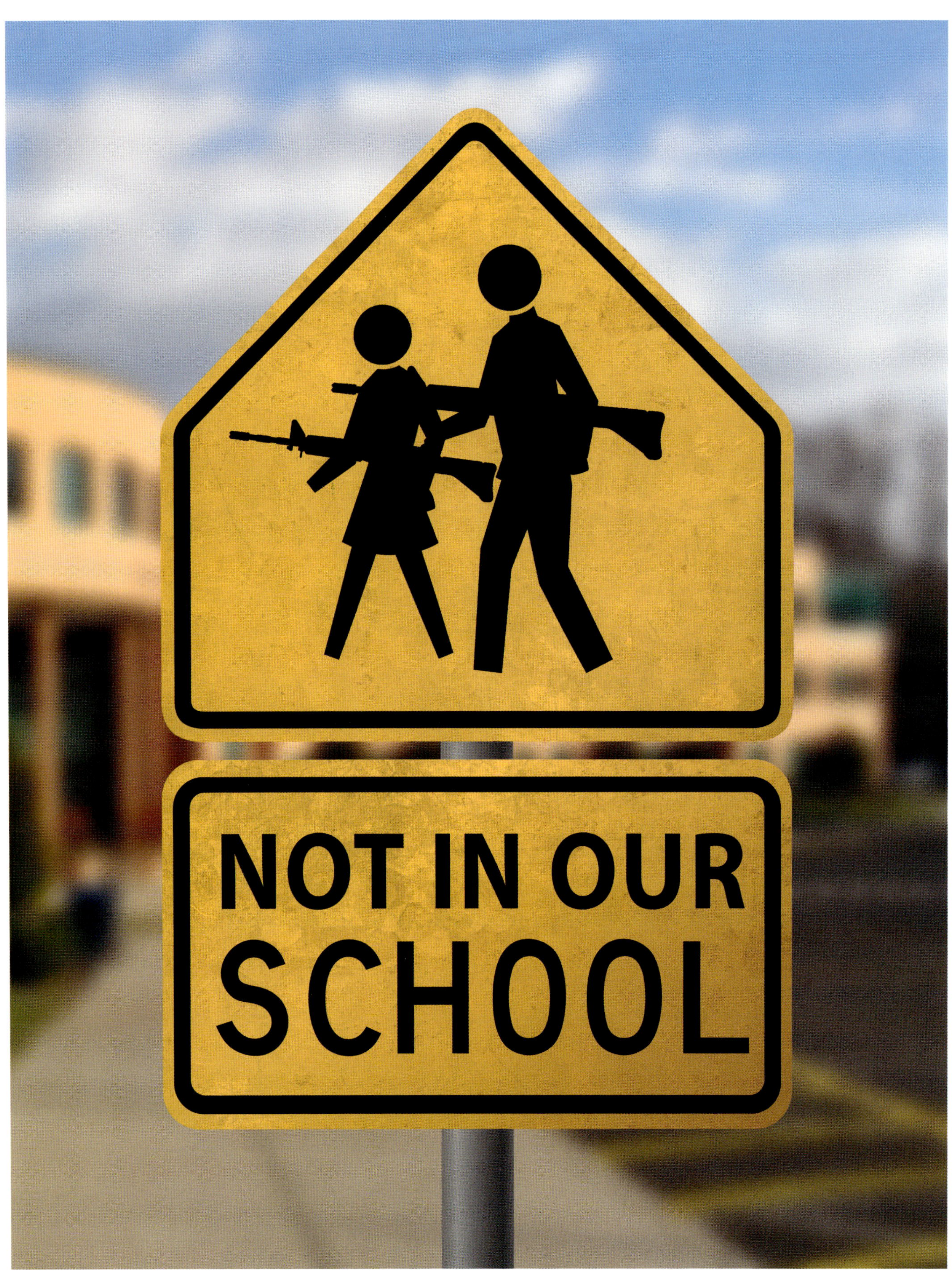

Poster commenting on the problem of arms in schools 2018
BBDO Atlanta

2000–Present

Revolutions and the Demand for Rights

Brian Haw began his ten-year one-man protest in June 2001, targeting the UK-backed United Nations economic sanctions imposed on Iraq prior to the First Gulf War of 1991. Over the following decade (1991–2001) those sanctions had devastated Iraq's economy, causing great suffering and death to Iraqi civilians, particularly children. Haw decided to make a stand and aimed his anger at the callousness of the politicians who backed the UN sanctions. He based his encampment directly across the street from the gates of the Houses of Parliament: an 'exhibition of blame' composed of signs, slogans, texts and shocking images of the horrors inflicted on the children by sanctions and war. Haw's powerful display grew to over 40 metres in length, and was haunted by his round-the-clock presence. It elicited either irritation, or soul-searching, from anyone entering or within the Houses of Parliament.[1]

The new century had started with the destruction of a gigantic symbol of global capitalism. In the terrorist attack of 9/11 (September 11, 2001), two passenger jets hijacked by Al-Qaida terrorists crashed into the twin towers of New York's World Trade Center; another jet came down in Pennsylvania; and a fourth crashed into the Pentagon in Washington, D.C. In the desire for retaliation, US President George W. Bush declared a global 'War on Terror', soon to manifest itself as the War in Afghanistan. In 2002 Bush announced the existence of an 'axis of evil' (Iraq, Iran, North Korea) that harboured 'Weapons of Mass Destruction' (WMDs). By 2003, with still no WMDs in sight, Bush and the UK's Tony Blair felt justified in leading a coalition of countries to invade Iraq.

On 15 February 2003, over one million people (from all over the UK) arrived in London to protest the Iraq War, joined by protests in over 60 countries around the world, including the USA. All were ignored. The military combat operations only lasted from March to May 2003. But the post-war chaos continued. 'Regime change' (the deposition of Iraqi dictator Saddam Hussain) unleashed power struggles between different factions, including Al-Qaida forces. Fighting carried on; coalition and civilian casualties grew. Barack Obama became US president in 2008. The US and UK withdrew troops from Iraq in 2011, but Obama continued the operation of drones. The conflict in Afghanistan remained unresolved.[2]

Both wars, and the events they created, were heavily debated over this time period. The protests were continuous and mourned the killing and the dead, while pointing at the failures of politicians. The protest imagery was often chilling, such as the poster showing the silhouetted image of an Iraqi prisoner undergoing torture in Abu Ghraib prison. Some of it was satirical and funny, at least on initial viewing. But even UK Prime Minister Tony Blair with a tea cup on his head eventually starts to look sinister while holding a Kalashnikov rifle, as shown in the popular protest poster by ad agency Karmarama.

If the events surrounding 9/11 made global capitalism look vulnerable, the economic crash of 2008 would do worse. With the New York stock market in freefall and the USA heading for recession, the interconnectedness of the world's economies meant that other countries soon followed. Severe austerity measures inflicted on some of Europe's citizens brought anger against their politicians and rioting in the streets. In the Middle East and North Africa, wealthy, long-standing dictatorships could no longer keep their people silently suffering in poverty. At the same time, connectivity – between people and countries – had improved massively. Broadband had arrived and mobile technology had leapt ahead; the availability of smartphones and social media allowed for the uploading of images and 'sharing'. Consequently, revolutions, ignited by events or a call to arms, were able to be shared globally.[3]

The 'Year of Revolutions' (2011) started with events in the Middle East, referred to by global media as the Arab Spring. Tunisia was the first to revolt; Egypt soon followed, with Tahrir Square in Cairo as its epicentre, generating brilliant protest imagery (signs, banners) and murals. The spirit of protest spread to Jordan, Bahrain, Morocco, Yemen, Algeria and Libya. In Syria, protests against President Bashar al-Assad turned into outright conflict (still present in 2019) and generated a mass of intense, online protest art by, for example, the poster collective Alshaab Alsori Aref Tarekh (the Syrian People Know Their Way).[4]

Europe was next: On 15 May 2011 thousands of people calling themselves 'Los Indignados' (the Outraged) marched into Madrid's main square, set up a protest camp and showed their anger at an ineffectual government and failing economy. This action sparked off other protests, as well as the creation of an image bank of sophisticated posters for downloading. Greece was suffering from a debt crisis and demonstrating against unemployment, corruption and police violence. August 2011 brought riots and looting to London, sparked by austerity measures and the police-shooting of a 29-year-old black man.[5]

Then the USA joined the revolution: on 17 September 2011 Occupy Wall Street was born. A protest camp was established in New York City's Zuccotti Park, in defiance of corrupt politicians and corporate rule in the midst of a flagging US economy, giving rise to the slogan 'We are the 99%' (a comment relating to reports that 1% of the people owned the majority of the country's wealth). On 15 October 2011 the activist group Occupy London Stock Exchange landed its protest camp on a small area of pavement in front of London's St Paul's Cathedral. It caused the church to question the ethical and spiritual morality of probable eviction and set off heated debates about the modern role of the church. The camp thrived and avoided eviction until Feb 2012.[6]

The Occupy Gezi Park protests of May-June 2013 in Istanbul became a struggle between the will of the Turkish people and the authoritarian power of Prime Minister Recep Tayyip Erdogan. Protesters took over Taksim Square and occupied nearby Gezi Park. A police crackdown was ordered, and images of the excessive use of violence, tear gas and water-cannon filled news reports and social media. Also in 2013, discontent erupted in Brazil when its politicians pushed for the hosting of the 2014 FIFA World Cup and the 2016 Olympics in Rio. The lavish spending on 'FIFA-standard' stadiums clashed badly with the poor medical facilities and high rates of illiteracy in Brazil's cities. Protesters wielding signs demanding 'FIFA-standard hospitals' or 'FIFA-quality schools' were met

with tear gas, stun grenades and rubber bullets, as the games continued inside the stadiums.[7]

Hong Kong's 'Umbrella Revolution' (September–December 2014) began when pro-democracy activists demanded open elections for the Hong Kong chief executive in 2017. Peaceful public demonstrations took place, and protesters formed encampments within one of the world's most important financial centres. The sea of umbrellas, caught in many images appearing on social media, were not only symbolic but of critical use: as protection against riot police, tear gas and pepper-spray, as well as rain or the hot midday sun. The protests also became known for the impromptu art pieces that flourished, and the extraordinary number of solidarity posters appearing on the internet.[8]

Another (on-going) irritation to the Chinese authorities was the artist-activist Ai Weiwei. Recognized as an important figure in global contemporary art, he was also renowned as a blogger, social commentator and constant user of social media (especially microblogging such as Twitter). One of his most crucial art projects dealt with the Sichuan earthquake of 2008 and the collapse of shoddily constructed school buildings that killed over 5,000 schoolchildren. With local officials denying accountability, Ai Weiwei used his blog to invite volunteers to join a 'Citizens' Investigation'. They interviewed families and workers; researched numbers and names of the dead, and threats or payments for families' silence. Ai Weiwei used the resulting information to create artworks that memorialized the children, such as a devastatingly long list of the victims – each listed with a name, date of birth, school class and gender – as compiled by the Citizens' Investigation.[9]

The feminist Punk collective Pussy Riot was formed in 2011 as a reaction to Vladimir Putin's possible return to the presidency of Russia the following year. On 21 February 2012, four members of the collective, wearing their trademark balaclavas, performed 'A Punk Prayer' in front of the altar of Moscow's Cathedral of Christ the Saviour, considered to be the heart of Russian Orthodoxy. Three performers were arrested and charged with 'hooliganism motivated by religious hatred' and sentenced to two years in prison. (One was freed on appeal in October 2012; the other two were also released early.) Their coloured balaclavas became a global symbol of resistance, and the slogan 'Free Pussy Riot' echoed around the world via social media.[10]

Also from Russia: the controversial performance art duo the Blue Noses, founded in 1999 by Alexander Shaburov and Viacheslav Mizin, have continued to produce social critique, mixed with absurdist humour (and nudity), ever since. One of their most notorious projects was 'Era of Mercy' (aka 'An Epoch of Clemency'), 2005, showing two men dressed in the uniform of the Russian military, kissing passionately in a birch forest. It was clearly a satirical statement by the Blue Noses against the intolerance shown towards homosexuality and LGBT culture in Russia.[11]

The Netherlands welcomed the 21st century as the first country to give full rights of marriage to same-sex couples (in

2000). By 2017, over two dozen countries had legalized same-sex marriage, but for some it hadn't come easily. France rejoiced in 2013 but had had a tough time due to worries about right-wing and fundamentalist Catholic groups. In 2014 the USA was still only partially a member of the club, as some of the states lagged behind. But Russia has remained well behind, as prejudice (and often violence) against homosexuality was (and still is) condoned there. Politicians, including Putin himself, felt free to refer to LGBT people in a denigrating manner, both in public and the media. As a result, signs and posters have appeared in protests far and wide, as well as online, showing a variety of portraits of Putin himself wearing heavy make-up and placed against a rainbow (Pride) background.[12]

The USA's recent populist movement to the right also brought worrying signs in the form of the 'Bathroom Bill' which stated that people must only use public toilets of the gender stated on their birth certificate. North Carolina was the first state to pass the Bathroom Bill (March 2016) in the lead-up to the November presidential election. It became a cause célèbre for many people, including LGBT activists, who viewed it as discrimination against transgender people. Another upset for the USA occurred (June 2016) when 49 people lost their lives and 53 were wounded, as a gunman with a military-style assault rifle opened fire on clubbers at 'Pulse', an LGBT nightclub in Orlando, Florida. News of the incident sparked the formation of a collective in New York City calling themselves Gays Against Guns (GAG), which immediately began a campaign of civil disobedience and direct action against gun companies and their supporters.[13]

A black, unarmed, hoodie-clad 17-year-old named Trayvon Martin died in February 2012, shot by neighbourhood watchman George Zimmerman in Sanford, Florida. People took to the streets and signed online petitions, demanding Zimmerman be arrested. He was eventually charged and made to face a jury, who returned a verdict of 'not guilty'. Despite right-wing predictions of racial unrest if Zimmerman was acquitted, there were no riots, only the creation of determined protest groups. Activists Alicia Garza, Patrisse Cullors and Opal Tometi joined together through the posting of solidarity messages online, and Black Lives Matter was founded, a network intended as an affirmation of humanity, while also focusing on the way black lives were systematically and unjustly targeted and ended. The years 2014 and 2015 saw a litany of names of young black men dying at the hands of police who faced little or no accountability, and no punishment, adding a fever to a movement that still calls for social justice.[14]

On Saturday 21 January 2017, the day after President Donald Trump's inauguration as US president, women all over the world marched for women's rights, particularly focusing on his sexist attitudes. During his election campaign, allegations were made that he groped women (which he denied), while comments caught on microphone which he dismissed as 'locker room talk' had caused extreme offence, particularly his alleged comment about women generally: 'Grab them by the pussy. You can do anything.' Over half a million protesters joined

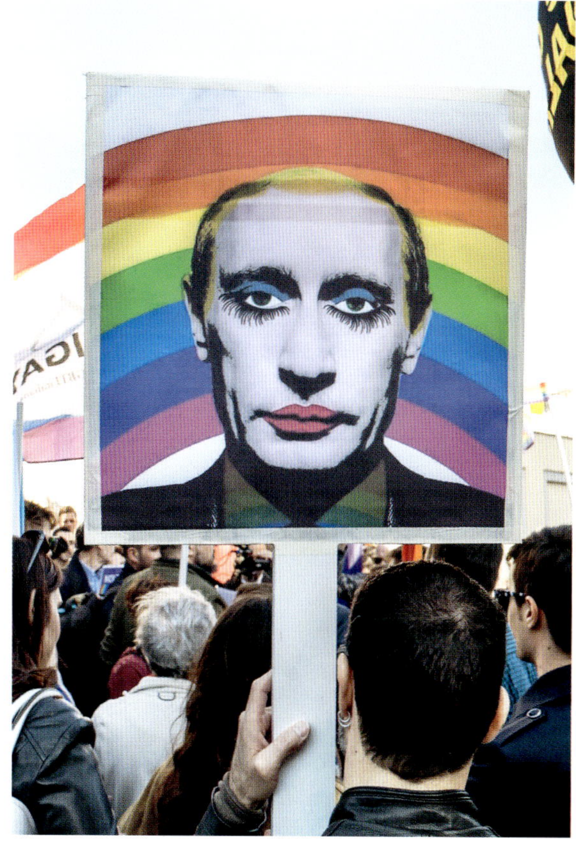

Widely circulated protest image (outlawed in Russia) with many versions, relating to Vladimir Putin's negative attitude to LGBT issues
c. 2013–present
Photograph: Stefano Montesi

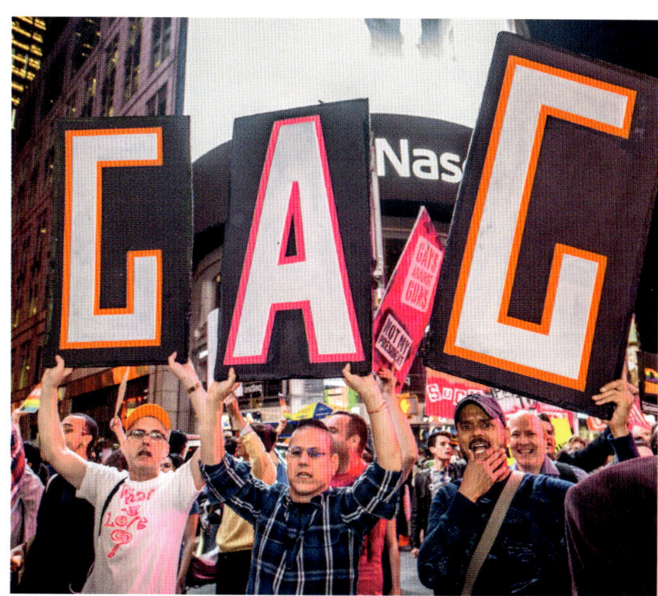

Gays Against Guns (GAG) protest against gun companies and their supporters *c.* 2016
Photograph: Erik McGregor

the March on Washington, an estimated 100,000 marched in London alone, plus 600 'sister marches' took place around the globe. Although celebrities and other notables made speeches in Washington, London and elsewhere, the real stars were the marchers (women, men, families) and the wit and humour they applied to the extraordinary number of messages carried on signs and placards. There were snarling retorts to Trump in 'pussy-grabbing' messages such as 'This Pussy Grabs Back!' or 'Hope Not Grope', as well as seas of pink knitted pussyhats (with cats-ears) worn by the crowd, courtesy of a knitting pattern posted online and translated into twelve languages.[15]

Not long after, and not surprisingly, the #MeToo movement came roaring into global existence. It was initiated by an exposé of sexual harassment allegations against Hollywood mogul Harvey Weinstein. But it became an online call to action by actor Alyssa Milano, who suggested that the real extent of the problem could only be understood if all women who had been sexually assaulted or harassed in their lives took to social media, wrote 'Me Too' as a status, and told their stories. The response was massive. Millions of women from around the world felt empowered to speak out, and engaged in the conversation via Twitter, Facebook and Instagram. Thus #MeToo became a movement allowing ordinary women – and men – to speak out about the harassment and abuse they suffered in everyday life, marking the beginning of a shift in everyday behaviour and power cultures.[16]

Worries about global warming and climate change have made 21st-century citizens take action when natural or manmade disasters strike, or corporations misbehave. In August 2005, when Hurricane Katrina hit the US south coast it obliterated much of the city of New Orleans. The breaching of its levees left 80% of the city submerged, with some areas under eight feet of water and 80–100,000 residents left stranded. The response from federal agencies was slow and shameful; the rescuers were often ordinary people or neighbours. The US design community came to the rescue in their own way. They created the Hurricane Poster Project, an online collection of freshly designed Katrina-related posters for sale: some protesting the inaction of the government, others celebrating the courage of the people involved. Proceeds from the sales went to the American Red Cross in support of the victims of Katrina.[17]

Other angry protests appeared in graphic form in April 2010 when BP's Deepwater Horizon oil rig (in the Gulf of Mexico) exploded, creating the biggest crude oil spill in US-controlled waters to date. Within weeks, the leaked oil had landed on the coastline of Texas, Louisiana, Mississippi, Alabama and Florida, polluting its beaches and wildlife and destroying the fishing and tourist industries. BP's logo was savagely satirized on a logo competition website and again, artists and designers sold angry, but often beautiful, posters to make money for the coastal clean-up. The legacy of both Katrina and Deepwater Horizon, as natural or manmade environmental disasters, haunts the future.[18]

Protest and satire, particularly taking shots at figures of authority, have continued at full tilt in the 21st century. The trio of Tony Blair, along with George W. Bush and his Vice President Dick Cheney, act as reminders of Bush's wars in the Middle East (both Iraq and Afghanistan) operating throughout the Noughties, and a lesson in how badly things can go wrong. David Cameron became the poster-boy for a government of private-school educated, Conservative Party politicians, which dealt out austerity cuts to the rest of the population. The Conservatives continued to be unsteady at the helm, with Theresa May's beleaguered guidance through Brexit procedures: the UK's attempt at withdrawal from the European Union to which it had been a member for at least 40 years. But the biggest target in recent times of both satire and protest has been Donald J. Trump, 45th president of the United States. Trump's distinctive appearance and behaviour, such as his impulsive use of Twitter, make him a prime subject for caricature and a godsend to cartoonists and illustrators. However, his attitudes and divisive presidency, as well as his 'America First' policies, have caused shockwaves and mass protests both inside and outside the USA.[19]

Any satirical laughter stops immediately with the poster/graphic 'Je Suis Charlie' (I Am Charlie) which refers to the incident on 7 January 2015 when two radical Islamist gunmen entered the Paris offices of the satirical comic magazine *Charlie Hebdo*. They killed twelve and injured others on the Hebdo team including office staff, cartoonists, writers and the editor Stéphane Charbonnier. The graphic 'Je Suis Charlie', designed by Joachim Roncin, instantly became a symbol of solidarity, defiance and the right to freedom of speech both in the Twittersphere as well as on marches and demonstrations in Paris, and around the world. Courageously, the magazine went back on sale a week after the killings.[20]

A more recent massacre that also generated a strong movement of resistance was the Parkland, Florida shootings that took place on Valentine's Day, 14 February 2018. A 19-year-old ex-student carrying a legally-purchased assault weapon walked into Marjory Stoneman Douglas High School and opened fire, killing 17 students and staff, and injuring 17 others. The student survivors began what is now a national grassroots movement calling for gun reform and gun safety legislation at local, state and federal level. Five of the survivors organized the March For Our Lives rally held on 24 March in Washington, D.C., which attracted more than 800,000 people. Image banks of posters (for downloading and carrying on the march) were created by the design lab Amplifier, and online magazine *Ad Age* (*Advertising Age*). The student organizers of the March For Our Lives have now claimed the problem as a lifelong mission. A brave undertaking and necessary: from January to May 2018 (barely five months), there have been 16 shootings at US schools resulting in injury or death.[21]

Later that year, another grassroots movement brought shouts of anger in the streets, this time emanating from France. Sparked off in mid-November by a planned tax rise on diesel and petrol, people took to the streets on weekends in violent protests, wearing the yellow high-visibility vests carried in all cars by law. They were called the 'gilets jaunes' (yellow vests),

they included all ages, and their numbers and anger escalated.
They torched cars, smashed windows, threw stones and bricks –
and their fury spread like wildfire; there were protests across the
country. In Paris they carried out much of their destruction in
the richer areas of the city, especially near the Arc de Triomphe
(which they defaced). As the movement became more unified,
their protest broadened to a demand for higher wages, lower
direct taxes and public spending. Their biggest target was
President Emmanuel Macron and his economic policies,
viewed as favouring the rich. The 'gilets jaunes' had become
'the people' versus the government. By mid-January 2019, both
the graffiti and the voices of the protesters called out 'Macron,
Resign!' The front covers of the satirical magazine *Charlie
Hebdo*, throughout this period, caught the mood of frenzy and
chaos. Satire, and satirists, love a revolution.[22]

Now in the 21st century's second decade, globalization –
the interconnectedness of the world – can be seen through a
shattered prism of destabilizing forces. Overly large, wealthy,
global corporations such as Amazon, Apple, Google and
Facebook (likened in a poster by Klaus Staeck to the Four
Horsemen of the Apocalypse) have massive economic control.
We have witnessed more than ten years of rudderless wars in
Iraq and Afghanistan, the destructive force of ISIS, and the
on-going destruction of Syria. The global political pendulum
keeps moving to the right, bringing with it the rise of populism
and divisive social attitudes. Within this – as shown by Kate
Evans' graphic novel *Threads* – we are witnessing a global shift
of populations: refugees and asylum seekers desperate to find
safety, economic migrants in search of a better life. More than
ever before, they call upon our humanity and our creativity, to
recognize the need for change and action.

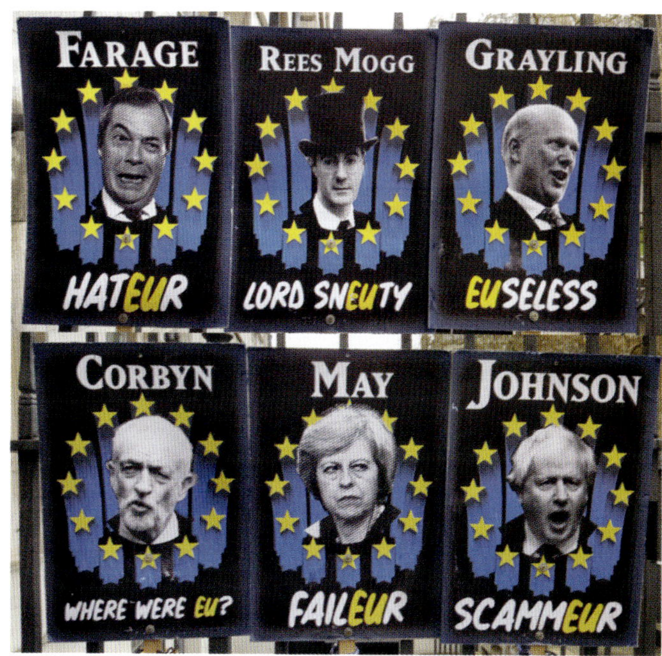

**Poster protest: Politicians' confusion over Leave or
Remain (in the European Union)** 2019
Photograph: Liz McQuiston

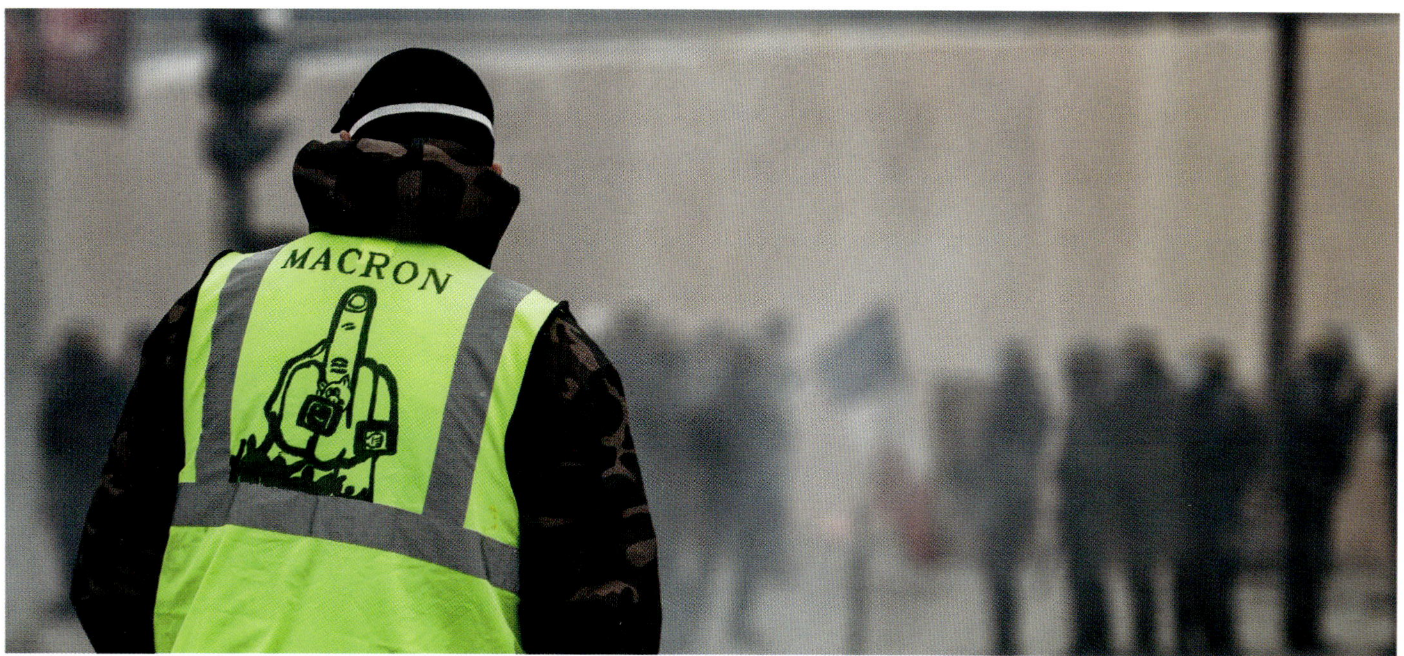

A 'gilet jaune' protester wears a gesture aimed at French President Macron 2018
Photograph: Piero Cruciatti

The War on Terror

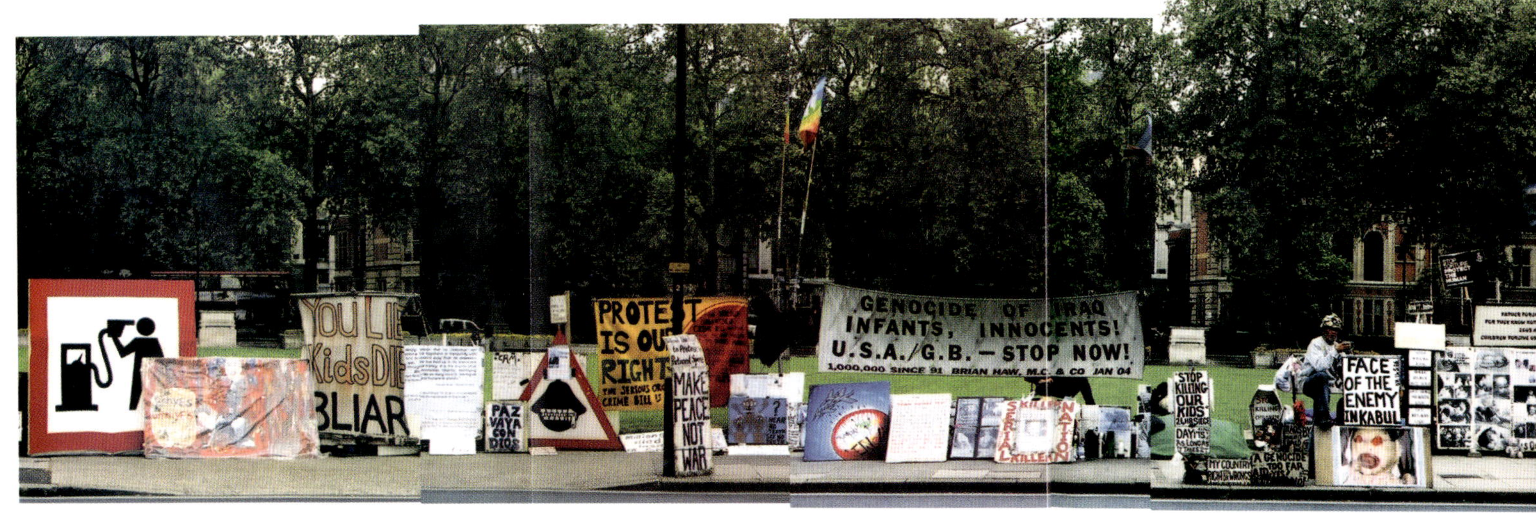

↑ **The Brian Haw Peace Camp** 2001–11
Brian Haw
Photograph of Haw's camp, taken from Mark
Wallinger's 'State Britain'

Brian Haw's ten-year, one-man protest began in
2001. He aimed to make the British government
realise the damage done to Iraqi civilians, especially
children, over the past ten years by UN economic
sanctions imposed on Iraq (and backed by the UK).
He camped across the street from the gates of the
Houses of Parliament, round the clock, displaying
signs, slogans, flags and shocking images. The
installation grew to over 40 metres in length and
well known artists such as Banksy contributed work
to Haw's camp. Although loved by much of the
public, it was considered an eyesore and irritant by
the government. Attempting to rid itself of Brian
Haw's protest, in 2005 the government passed new
legislation – the Serious Organised Crime and Police
Act – designed to curtail freedom of expression
by making it an offense to organise or take part in
a public protest within a one kilometre radius of
Parliament Square (without the authorisation of
the Metropolitan Police). Subsequently 78 police
descended in the early hours of May 23, 2006 to
remove everything in Haw's protest that wouldn't
fit into a 3 x 2 metre space. In 2007 artist Mark
Wallinger produced an installation entitled 'State
Britain' that recreated meticulously Haw's protest
camp at its height – all 43 metres of it – within Tate
Britain; it won the Turner Prize of 2007. Brian Haw
resolutely continued his protest until his death in
June 2011.

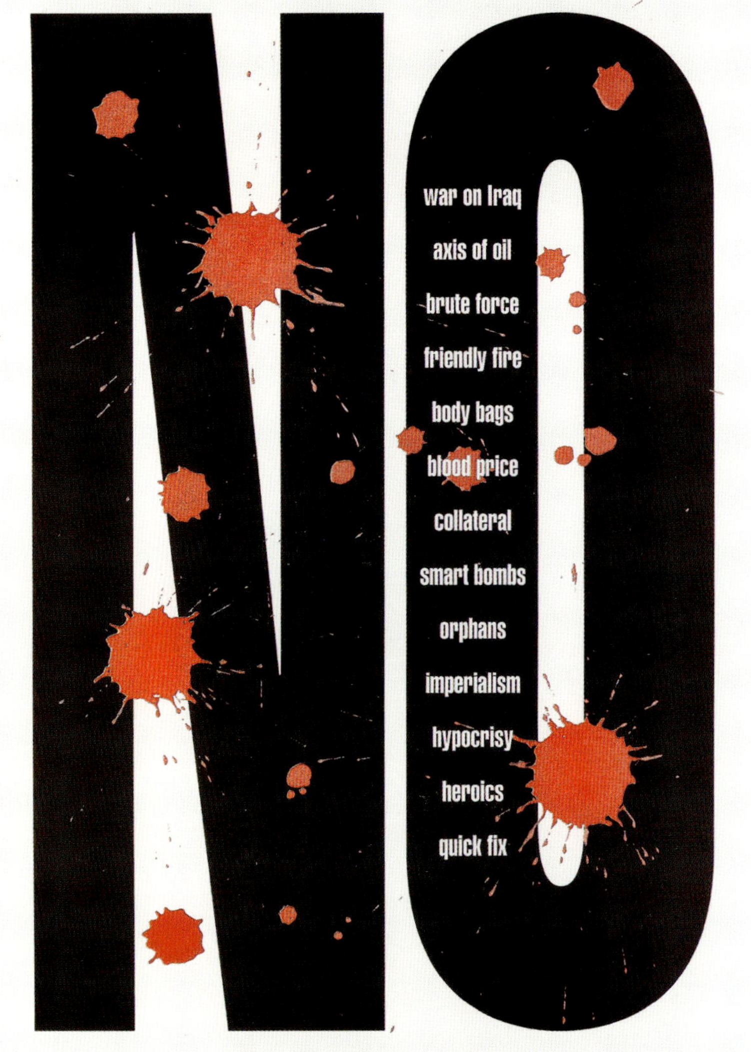

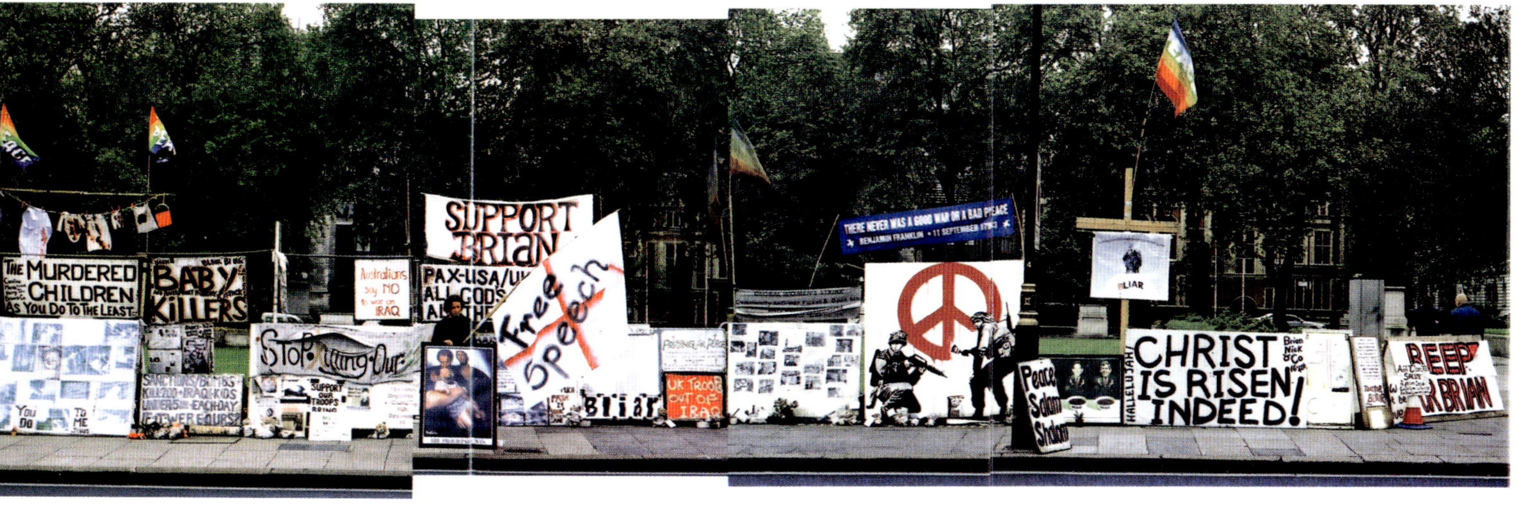

← **NO** 2003
David Gentleman for the Stop the War Coalition
Poster

The Stop the War Coalition was established on 21 September 2001, in the wake of 9/11 and the start of the 'War On Terror'. Over the following ten years, it managed and sustained the massive British public anti-war movement, organising over 40 national demonstrations including London's historic 'Don't Attack Iraq' demonstration of 15 February, 2003. Of all the work contributed by artists supporting its cause over the years, David Gentleman's visual motif of words hit by 'splashes of blood' has been the most relentless and unsettling. Those splashes were present on many 'NO' posters carried in the demo of 2003 and have continued to be seen in installations and on posters up to the present day – a nasty stain that just won't go away, and a reminder of mounting casualties. The Coalition carries on its work, for the threat of war remains ever present.

↓ **Don't Attack Iraq Demonstration, London**
February 15 2003
Photograph: Scott Barbour

The extraordinary variety of slogans and home-made costumes, puppets, placards and other paraphernalia, marching through the streets of London on 15 February, 2003, matched the noise and excitement of that day. David Gentleman's 'NO' poster often dominated, forming a sea of 'NO's and creating a powerfully orchestrated visual shout of anger.

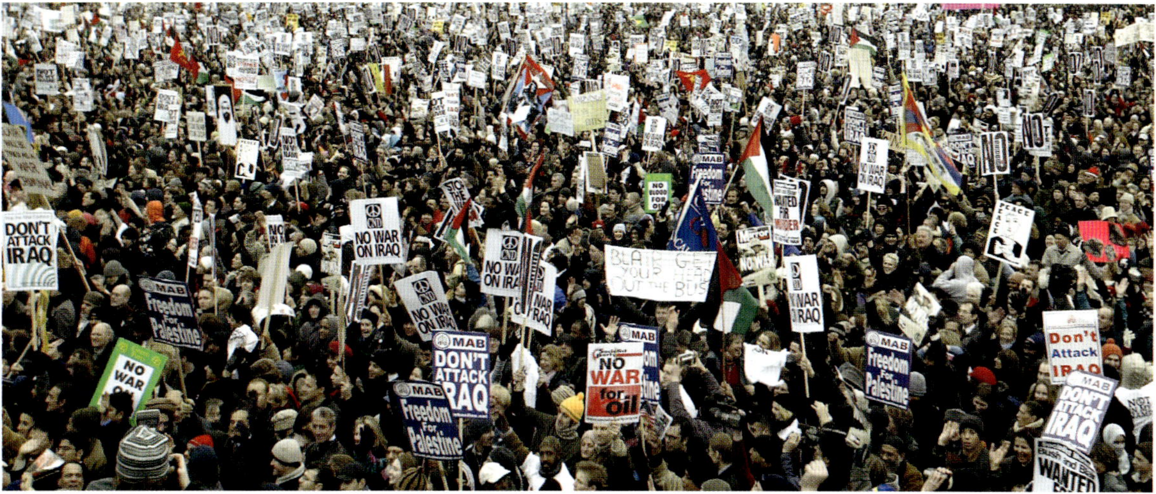

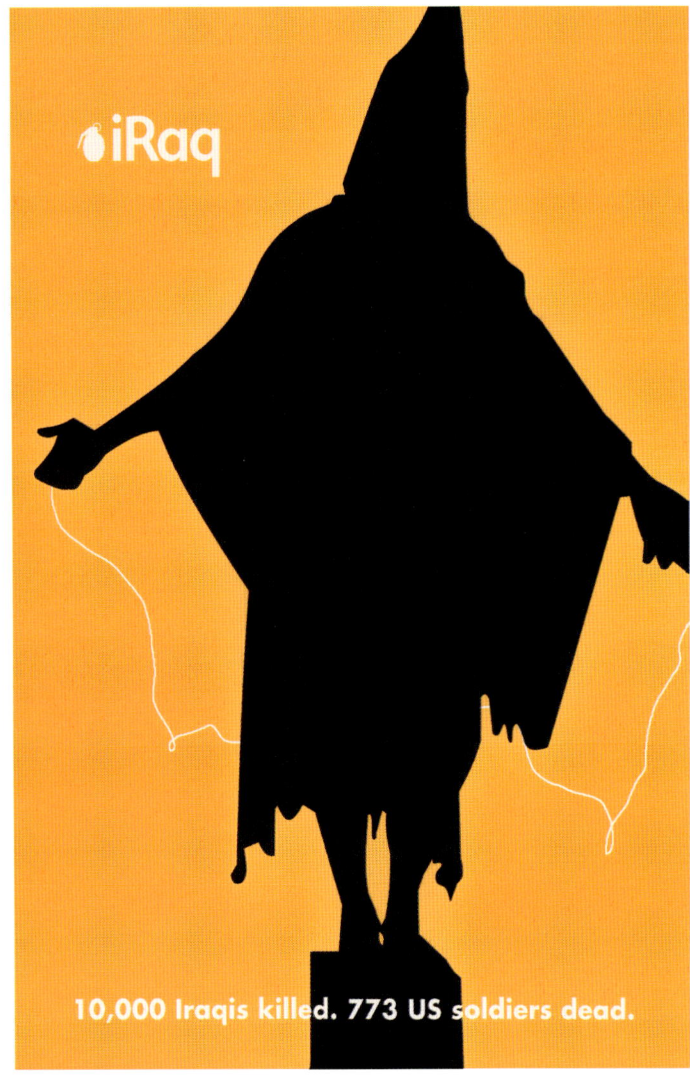

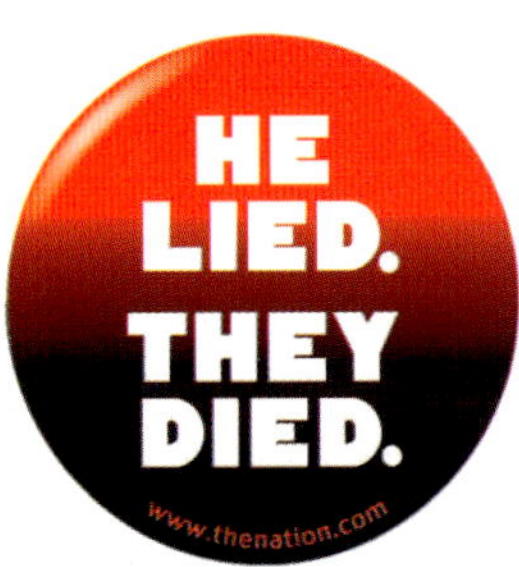

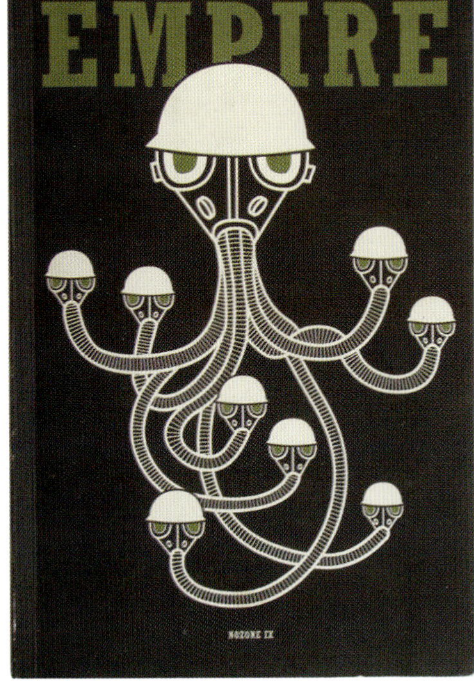

← **iRaq** 2004
Copper Greene and Forkscrew Graphics
Poster

Arguably the most iconic anti-war poster to be produced during the early years of the Iraq War, 'iRaq' combines the stylistic elements of Apple's iPod advertising campaign with the silhouetted image of an Iraqi prisoner undergoing torture. The image of the hooded prisoner was made public following a whistleblower's exposure of atrocities being committed by members of the US military serving at Abu Ghraib prison, and soon became symbolic of everything that had gone wrong with the war, making a heavy impact in both the USA and the UK. The poster was produced (in different versions) by two design collectives, Copper Greene and Forkscrew Graphics, and was available on the internet for downloading by anti-war activists.

↙ **He Lied. They Died.** 2003–04
Milton Glaser for *The Nation* magazine
Badge

The Nation magazine produced a series of anti-Iraq War 'Initiative Buttons' (badges) that it sold to its readers, thus achieving wide circulation. Designed by Milton Glaser, they bore slogans that were both thought-provoking and hard-hitting. But the badge shown here stands out from the rest, mainly (but not only) for its shock value. It suggests that in any war, there are politicians and leaders, and there are inevitably lies. Obviously directed at US President George W. Bush, it could easily have been transported to the UK, where much of the anti-war protest was aimed at Prime Minister Tony Blair. For years after, a rising tide of negative public opinion would continue to haunt Blair for leading the UK into wars in Afghanistan and Iraq, despite overwhelming protest.

← *Empire: Nozone IX* 2004
Knickerbocker
Comic book/journal

The ninth issue of *Nozone* (a comic book of political satire), entitled *Empire*, is a compendium of work by artists, designers, photographers and writers interrogating and protesting against the condition of the USA after 9/11. The front cover illustration, 'Deadly Alliance' by comic artist Knickerbocker, provides a stark indication of the tone of the content.

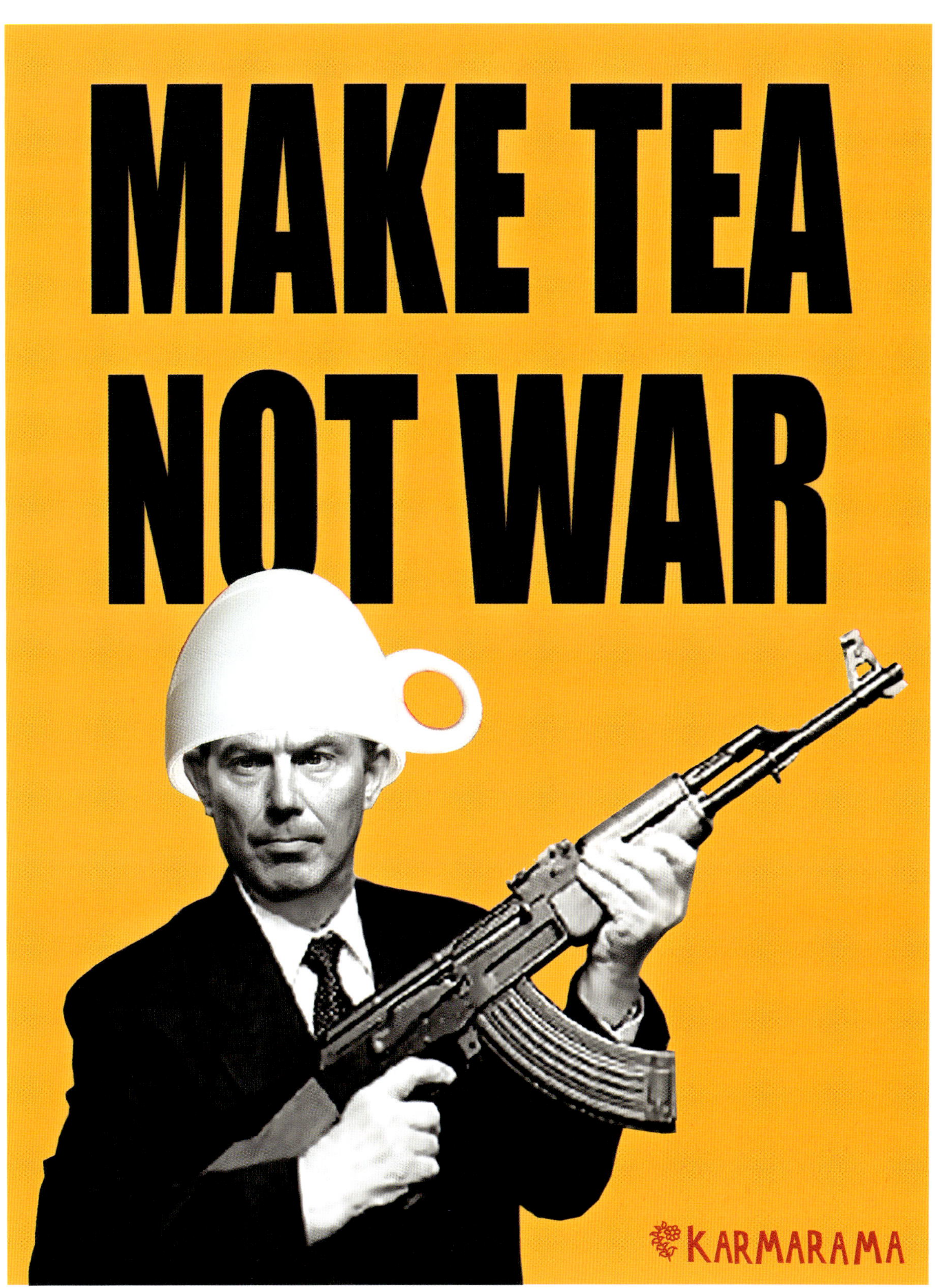

Make Tea Not War 2003
Karmarama advertising and design agency
Poster/placard

On February 15, 2003, over one million people marched through London to protest against Britain's entry into the war in Iraq. At the same time, similar anti-war marches took place around the world in over 300 cities and 60 countries. The British march drew people from around the country: young and old, families with baby buggies, seasoned activists, and first-timers. Karmarama's poster 'Make Tea Not War,' featuring then prime minister Tony Blair holding an assault rifle and wearing a teacup on his head like a helmet, was one of the most popular posters within a stream of placards and slogans, which included 'Not In My Name', 'Regime Change Begins At Home,' and simply 'NO'.

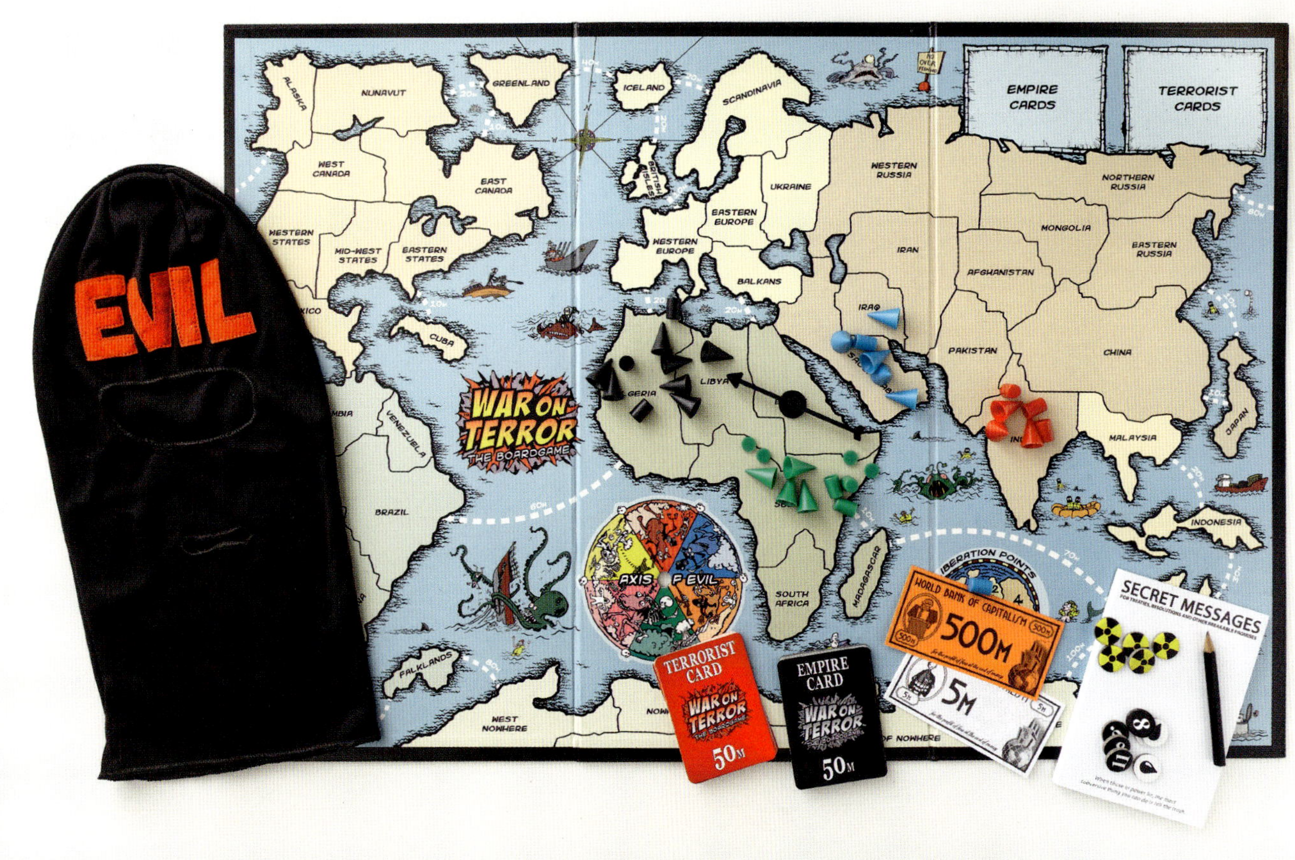

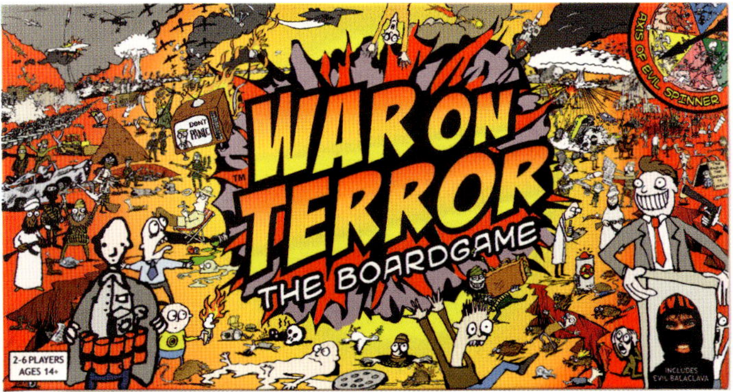

War on Terror: The Boardgame 2006
Andrew Sheerin and Andy Tompkins
Board game

Created by web designers Sheerin and Tompkins, this board game presents a satirical view of the (George W.) Bush Administration and the lead-up to the UK's entry into the Iraq War. The game requires two to six players: each player builds an empire. An empire can decide to become a 'terror state', or it can become one by using the 'Axis of Evil spinner', and the player must then don an enclosed balaclava with 'EVIL' stitched across it. An empire can train terrorists to attack other empires, but the terrorists can use cards such as 'Suicide Bomber' or 'Plane Hijack' to get ahead. In the end, the empires compete and wage war against each other, using such tactics as 'Regime Change'. The game sold 12,000 copies online and through independent stockists and achieved high status when one was seized from protesters by police and confiscated during a raid on a climate change camp, as the balaclava (with 'EVIL' stitched on it) could be used to conceal a person's identity during a criminal act.

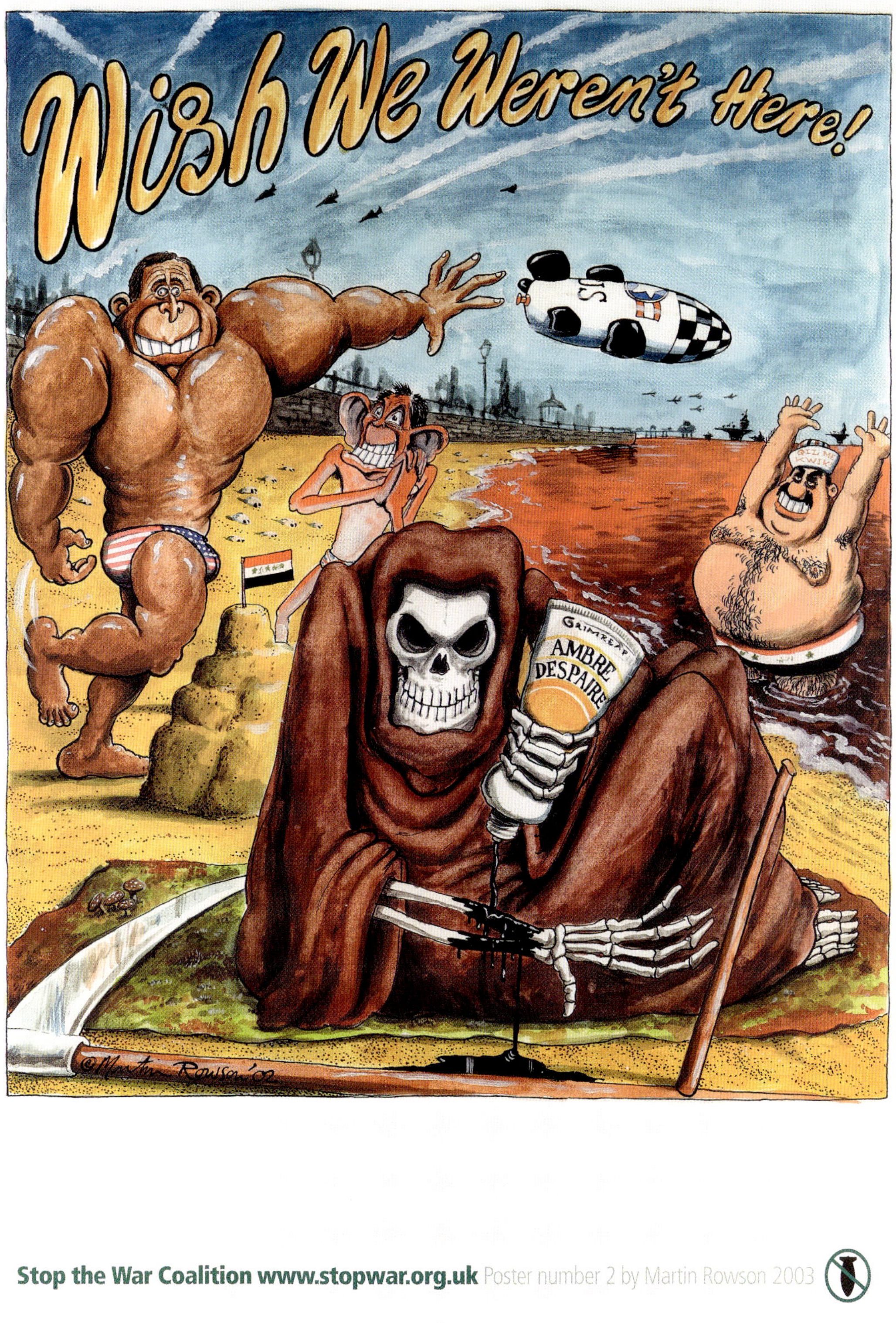

Stop the War Coalition www.stopwar.org.uk Poster number 2 by Martin Rowson 2003 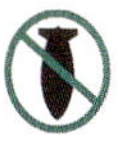

Wish We Weren't Here! 2003
Martin Rowson
Poster (offset)

Martin Rowson's illustration shows a beach scene with all the stereotypical summertime characters, but with a satirical twist. The muscle-man is US President George W. Bush, who is shown throwing an inflatable US missile to Saddam Hussein, President (and despot) of Iraq. The 90-pound weakling, about to join Bush in kicking and destroying Saddam's sandcastle is British Prime Minister Tony Blair. Meanwhile the Grim Reaper, the skeletal symbol of death, is pouring oil on to its arm instead of suntan lotion (hence Ambre Despaire replaces Ambre Solaire.) This is one in a series of posters produced near the start of the Iraq War, intended to oppose the war and raise funds for the Stop the War Coalition. The posters carried images by a number of Britain's leading graphic artists.

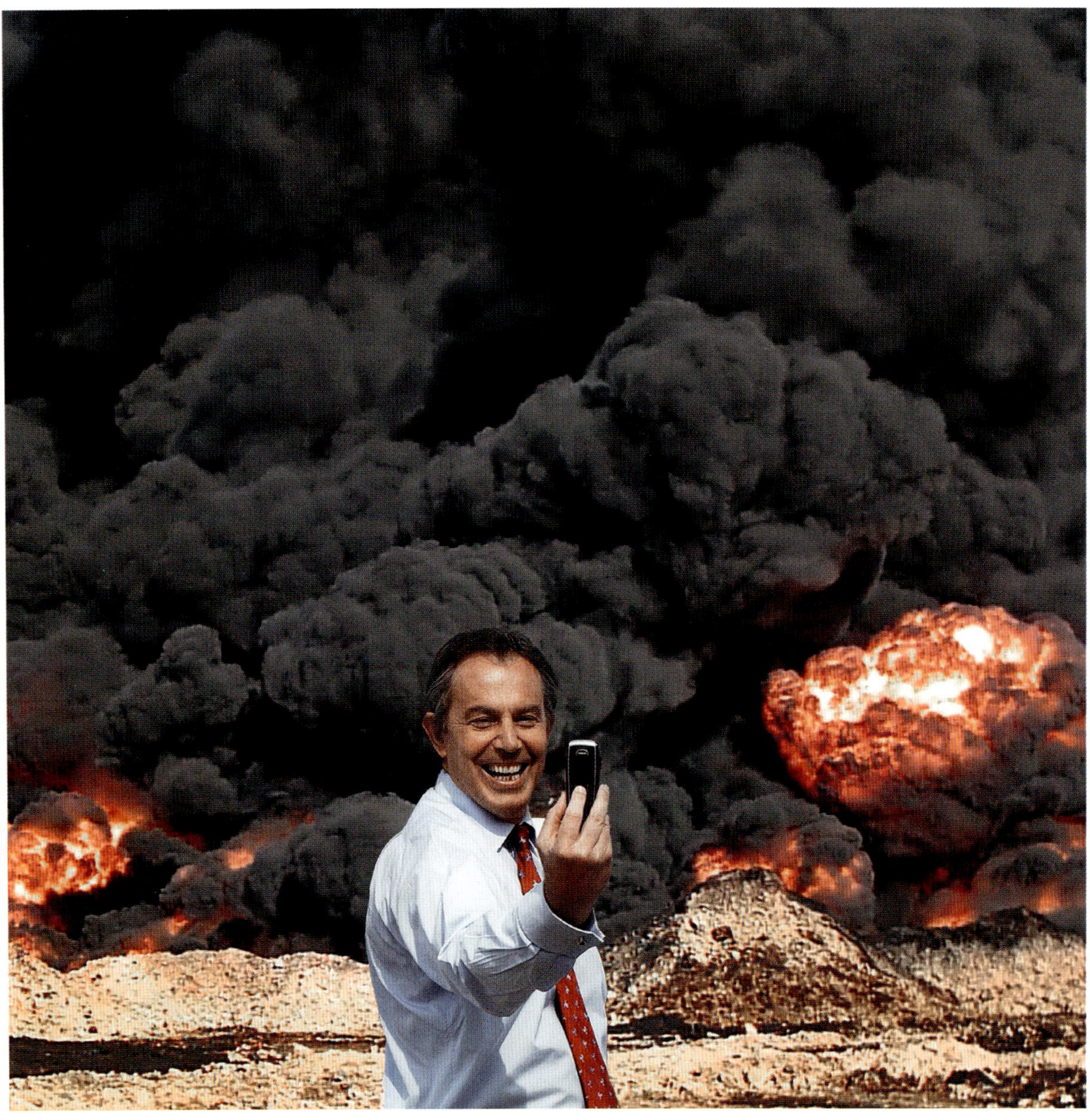

↑ **Photo Op** 2005
kennardphillipps
Photomontage

In this kennardphillipps photomontage,
former Prime Minister Tony Blair is shown
taking a selfie against a background of
burning oilfields. When it first appeared,
it reflected the rising chorus of anger and
disapproval from members of the public,
who blamed Blair for leading Britain into
wars in Afghanistan and then Iraq, despite
London's 'biggest political protest in British
history' which he more or less ignored. The
anger grew as time went on; the Iraq War
extended to nearly eight years of conflict.
British troops finally withdrew from Iraq in
2011. However, in Afghanistan the military
struggled on for over ten years; British
troops finally withdrew in 2014.

→ **The Gray Drape** 2004
Martha Rosler
Poster (silkscreen and offset)

US artist Martha Rosler responded to US involvement in
Afghanistan and Iraq with this photomontage, one of a series
entitled 'Bringing the War Home: House Beautiful (Iraq)'. It
combines the notion of modern home living in the West with the
carnage created by foreign wars. Critiquing the waging of wars in
distant places also informed Rosler's earlier work, when during the
Vietnam War she juxtaposed imagery of model US home interiors,
with photographs of Vietnamese civilians and soldiers, in her series
'Bringing the War Home: House Beautiful' (*c.*1967–72).

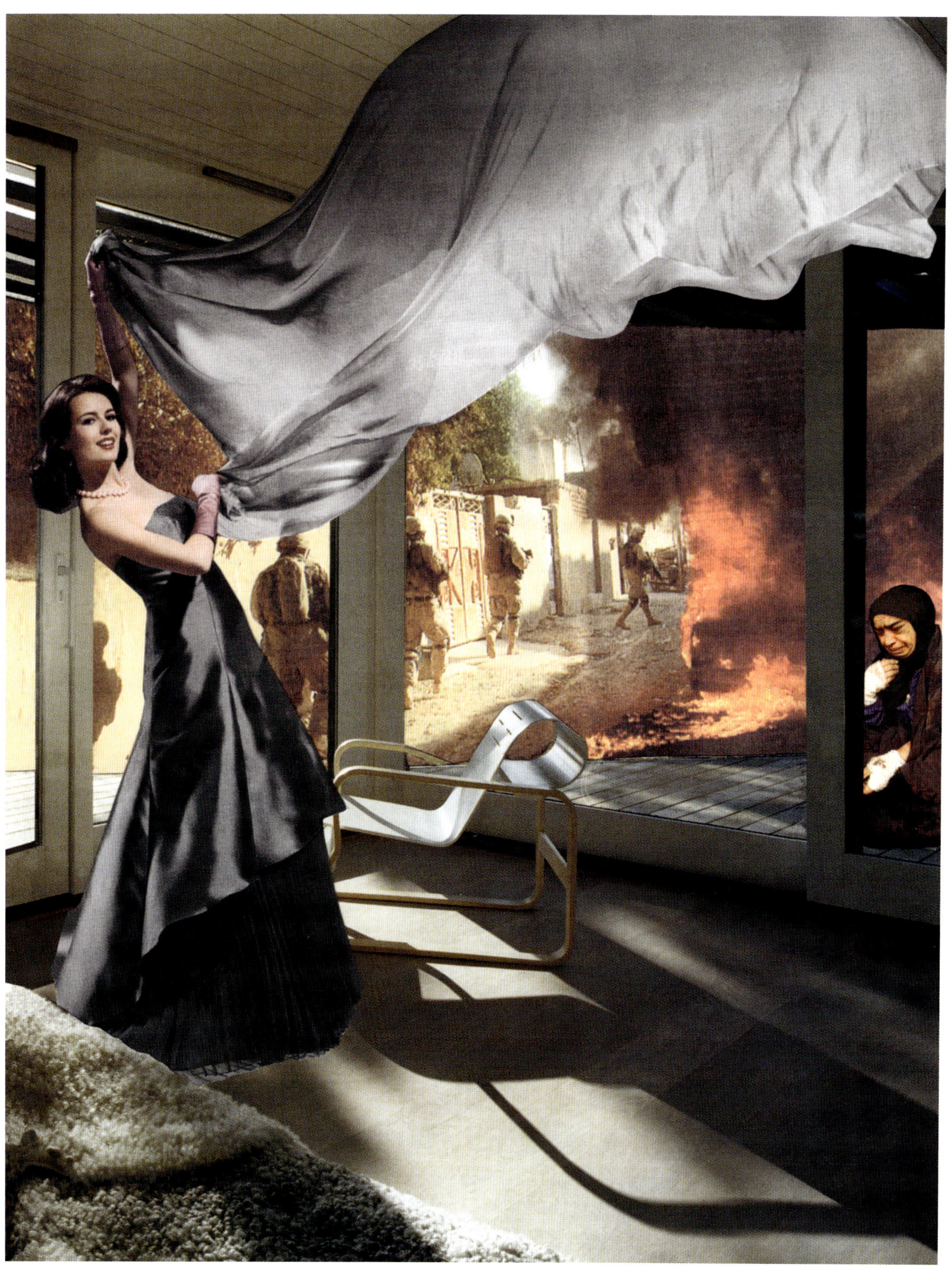

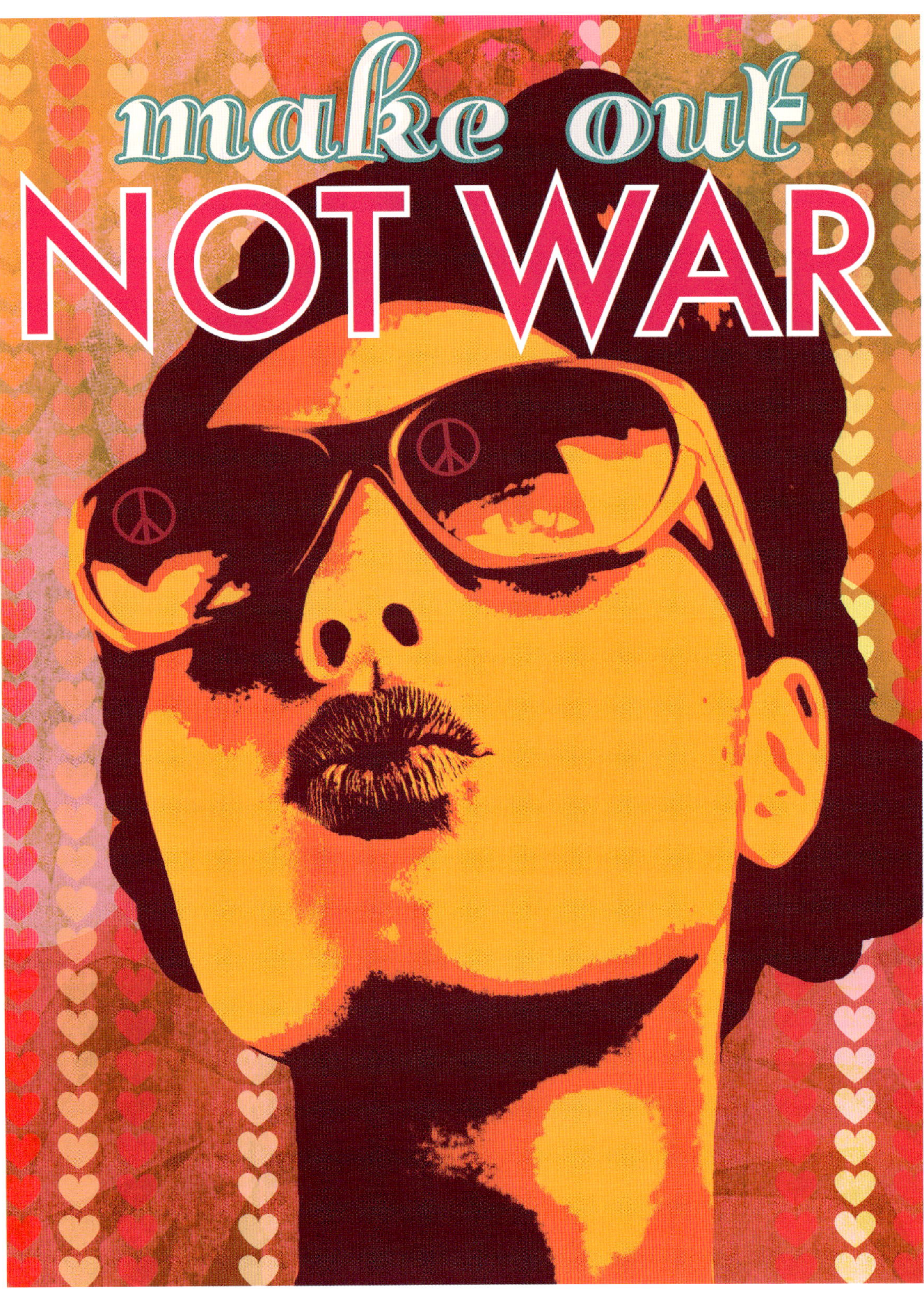

Make Out, Not War 2008
Favianna Rodriguez
Poster

This modern update of a well-worn slogan (Make Love, Not War) sizzles with attitude, in a poster produced for the highly active, women-led peace group known as CODEPINK. Founded by Medea Benjamin and Jodie Evans, their name satirizes the (George W.) Bush administration's Homeland Security colour-coded alert system (yellow, orange, red) warning of a potential terrorist threat. CODEPINK backed Barack Obama in the 2008 presidential elections and his removal of troops from Iraq in 2011. However, it was distressed by his decision to then increase troops in Afghanistan. Obama also engaged in drone warfare soon after his inauguration and continued to favour high-tech weaponry. Shocked by the civilian casualties involved, CODEPINK has continued to campaign against drone warfare.

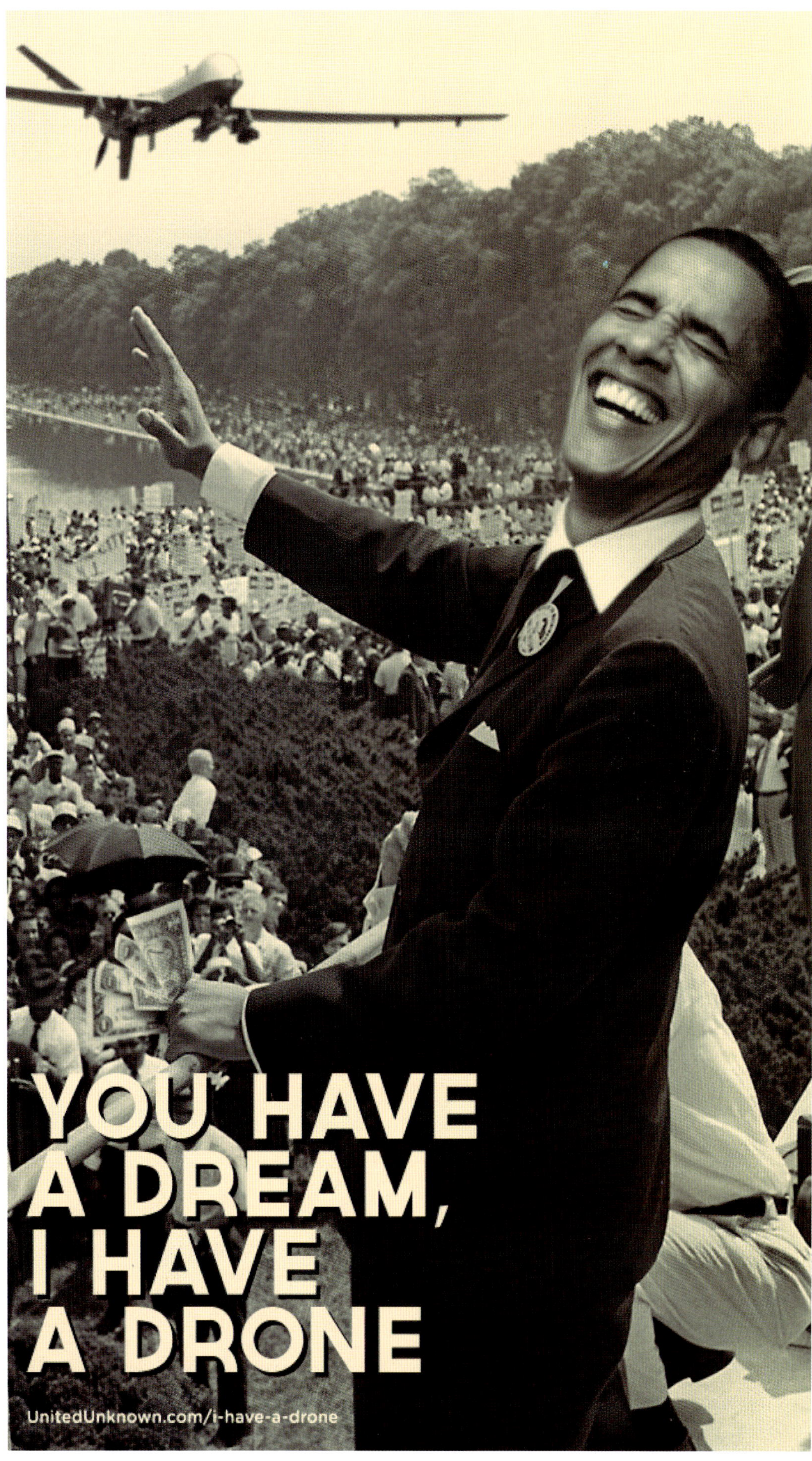

**You Have a Dream,
I Have a Drone** 2013
The United Unknown
Electronic (online) poster

After withdrawing US
troops from the Iraq War
in 2011, Barack Obama
increased the US military
presence in Afghanistan and
ramped up the controversial
use of drones (remotely
piloted, unmanned aircraft)
to pinpoint Al-Qaida and
its associates. The idea of
fighting a sanitized war
from the air, which seemed
to inflict heavy collateral
damage, didn't go down
well with some US citizens
as well as those in US-
friendly countries. This
electronic poster, created
by an anonymous group
of online activists calling
themselves the United
Unknown, manipulates
the famous quote from
Martin Luther King – 'I
Have a Dream' – to protest
Obama's use of drones.

2011–14: Years of Revolution

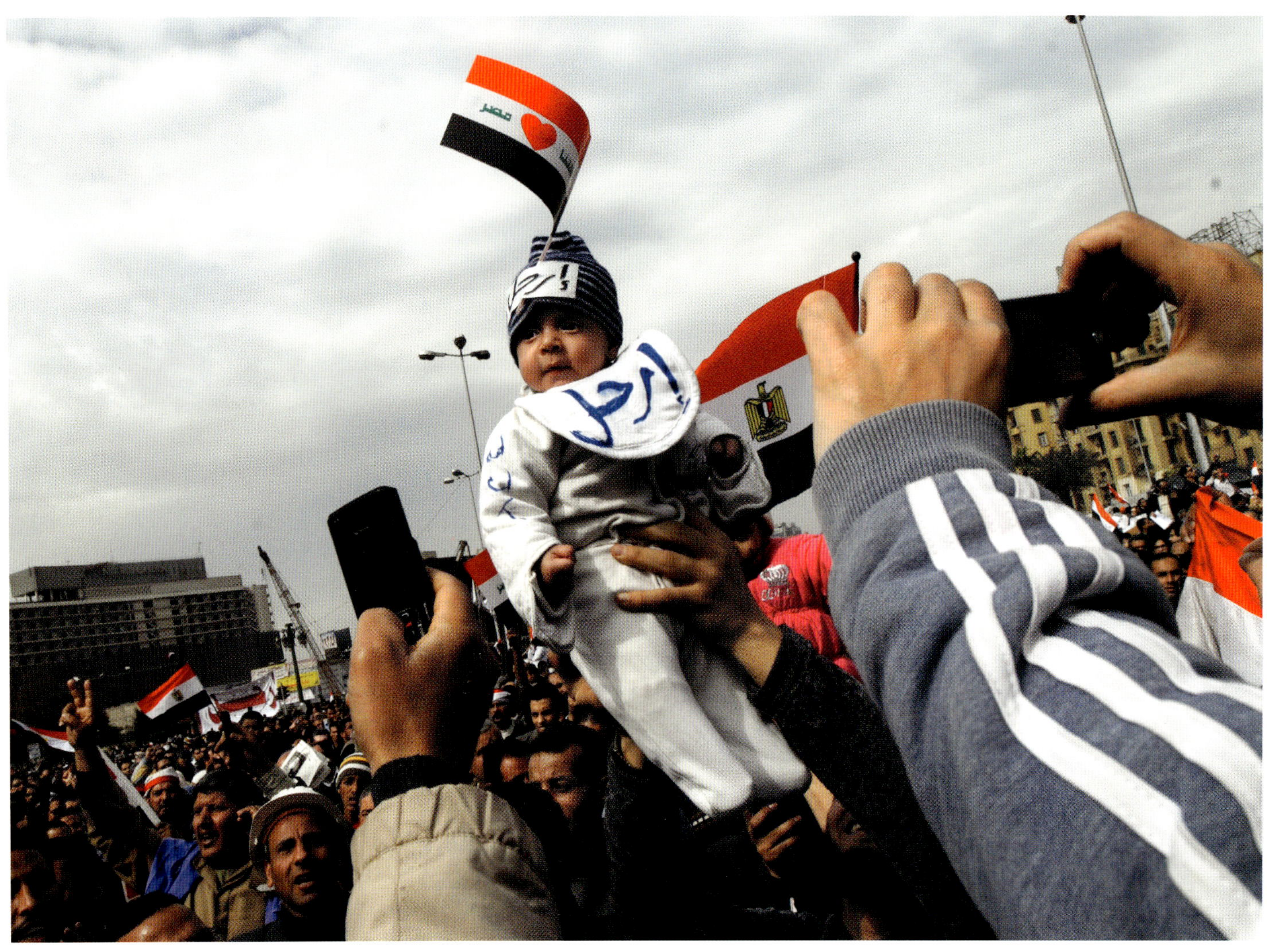

Tahrir Square Protest 2011
Photographer: Mia Gröndahl
Photograph

The 'Year of Revolutions' (2011) had its beginnings in the Middle East. 'The Arab Spring', as it was labelled by the media, owed much of its spread from country to country, to developments in digital technology and its new connectivity. Broadband had arrived in internet cafés and other public computers, and smartphones and social media allowed for the uploading of imagery. Revolutions could now be shared between countries.

So when a poor, oppressed fruit-seller self-immolated in the street in Tunisia, images and videos of the horror were watched by young Egyptians. When the fruit-seller died of his wounds in January 2011, Tunisia revolted and its president fled. Egypt soon followed with its own protests (the heart of its revolution was located in Tahrir Square, Cairo) and by February had ousted its president. The spirit of revolution spread to other countries in the Middle East, including Syria, where protests raged against President Bashar al-Assad. Inspired by this series of events, Europe followed and over the next three years

further protest movements would take place in Spain, Greece, the USA, Russia, Turkey, Brazil, Britain and Hong Kong (2014). All would generate extraordinary street art (murals), photographs, graphics or videos, chronicling protests, spreading information or satirizing brutal leaders. In the images shown here, photographer Mia Gröndahl caught the atmosphere of hope, joy and anger found in the protests in Tahrir Square, as well as people's awareness of the media and the opportunity to send messages to the world. The baby is adorned with a written message to the hated Egyptian president: 'Leave'.

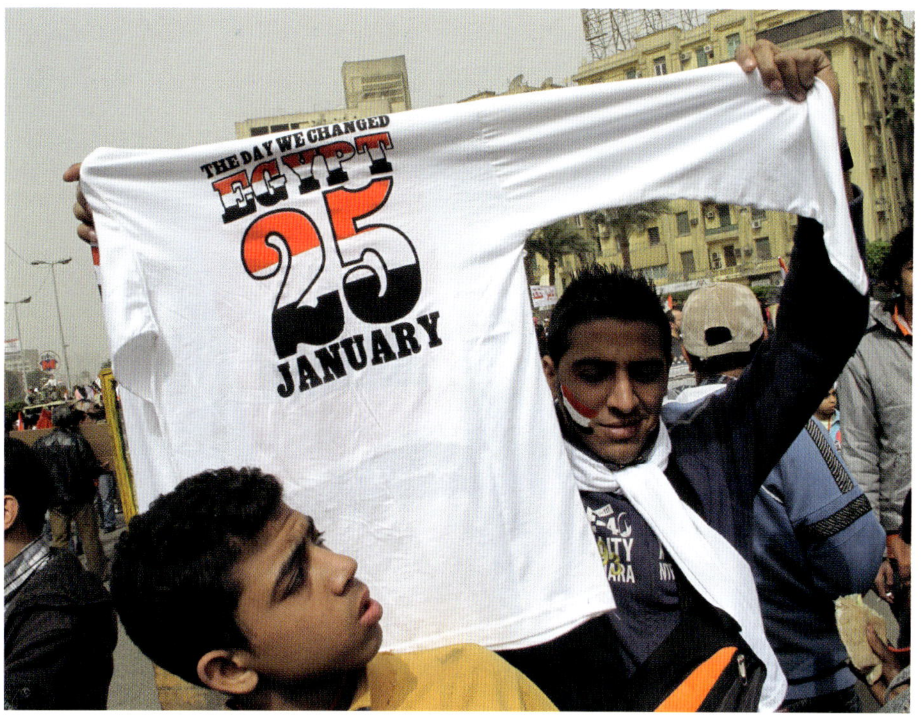

↑ **The Day We Changed Egypt, 25 January** 2011
Photographer: Mia Gröndahl
Photograph

Taking part in the protest in Tahrir Square, a young man proudly holds up a t-shirt saying 'The Day We Changed Egypt, 25 January', while another views it slightly bemused. The twenty-fifth of January, 2011 was the day that revolution erupted in Egypt and thousands of people took to the streets to protest against the current regime.

← **The 2Vth, Anonymous Pharaoh** 2011
Marwan Shahin
Street Art and book cover

When the Egyptian president, Hosni Mubarak, was ousted, illustrator and designer Marwan Shahin produced this brilliant example of street art, drawing the pharaoh Tutankhamun wearing the mask used by hacktivist group Anonymous and adopted by protesters everywhere. The drawing was also used on the cover of the book *Walls of Freedom: Street Art of the Egyptian Revolution* (2014), which chronicles the wealth of street art (murals, stencilling) produced throughout the protests.

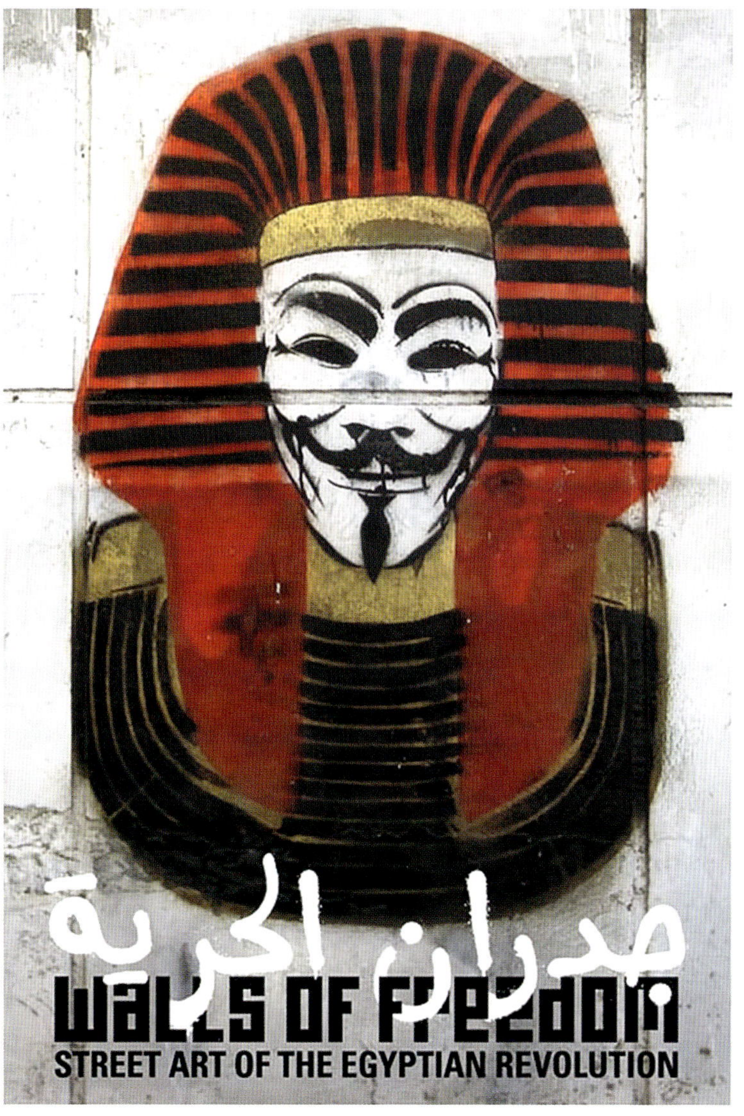

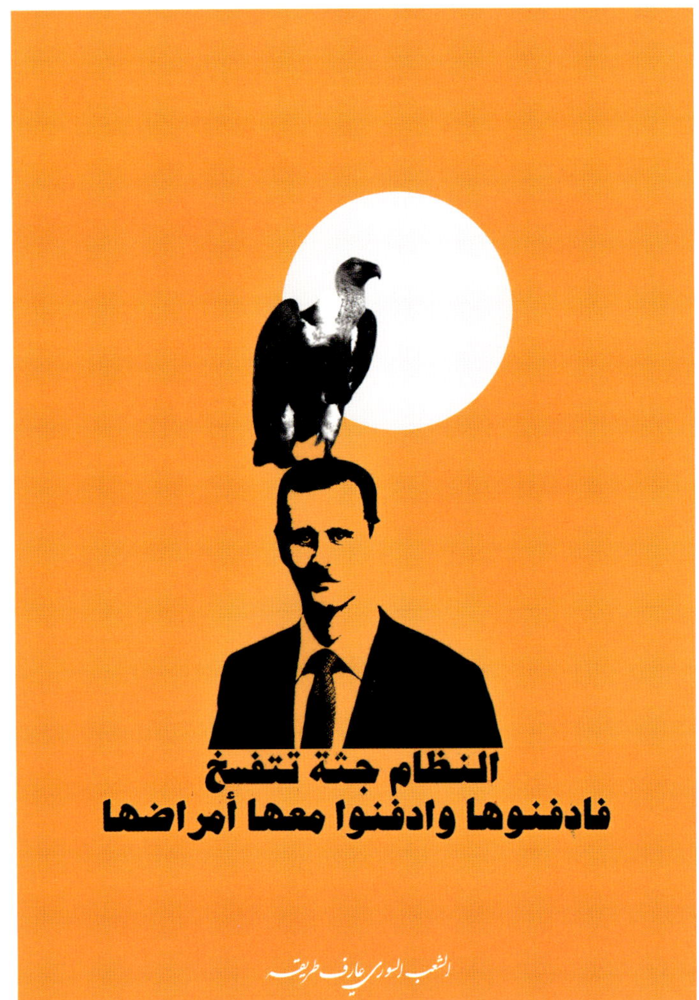

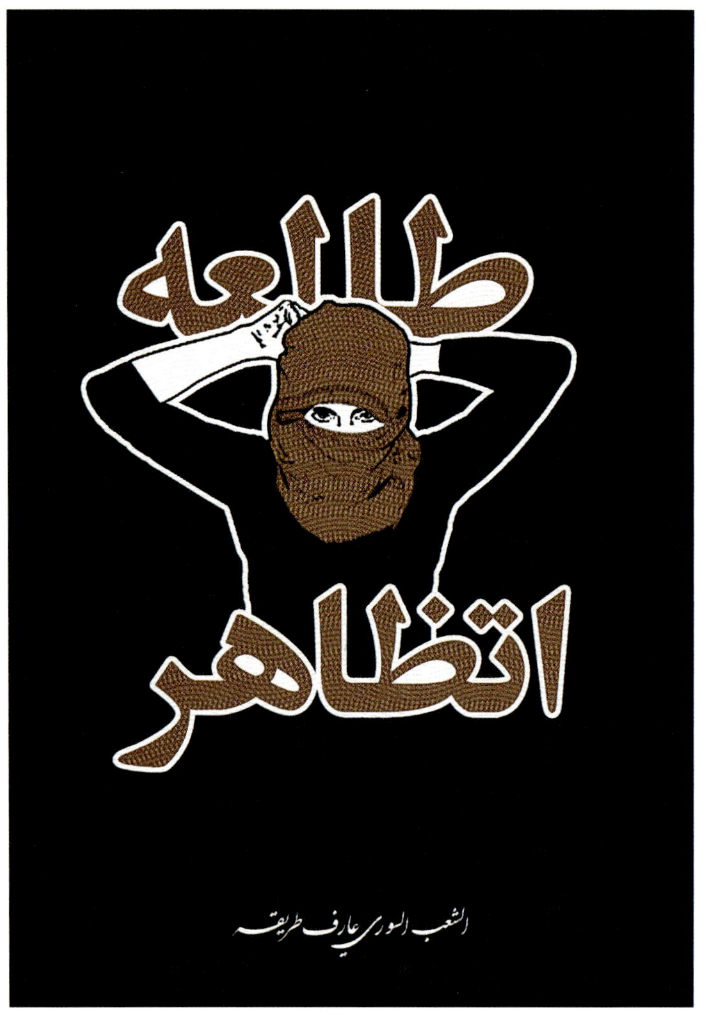

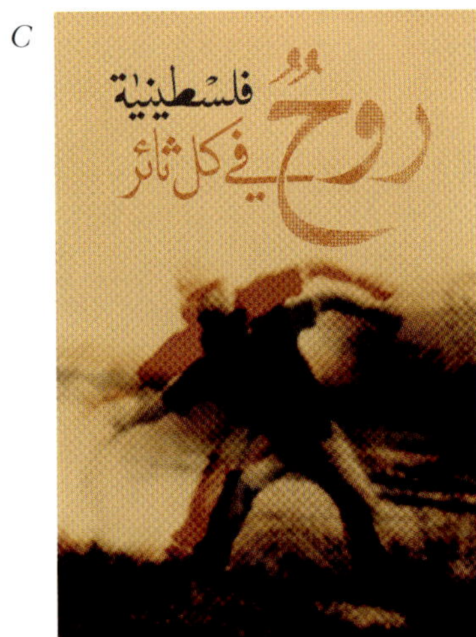

Syrian Revolutionary Posters 2011–12
Alshaab Alsori Aref Tarekh (the Syrian People Know Their Way)
Electronic (online) posters

Syria's uprising against President Bashar al-Assad led to quick, vicious retaliation by the regime followed by a protracted mire of violence, civil war, and fighting between different factions. 'Dissidents' were pursued; the regime's crackdowns and massacres of its own people continued and made world headlines. The earlier years of the conflict produced an outpouring of resistance art, graphics, photography and videos. Some of it was produced by anonymous collectives or people 'on the ground'; some of it was produced by activists in Syria or abroad (the diaspora). Numerous revolutionary posters were created by the anonymous collective Alshaab Alsori Aref Tarekh (The Syrian People Know Their Way), fifteen activists from Syria and abroad. They posted their images to Facebook and Flickr for activists to download and use in demonstrations, as well as to express solidarity and record on-going events in Syria.

Translations:

(Image A) President of Syria Bashar al-Assad is shown with a vulture on his head. The text reads: 'The regime is a rotting corpse. Bury it with its diseases.'

(Image B) The poster reads: 'I'm going to protest'.

(Image C) The poster reads: 'The spirit of Palestine is in the hearts of all revolutionaries'.

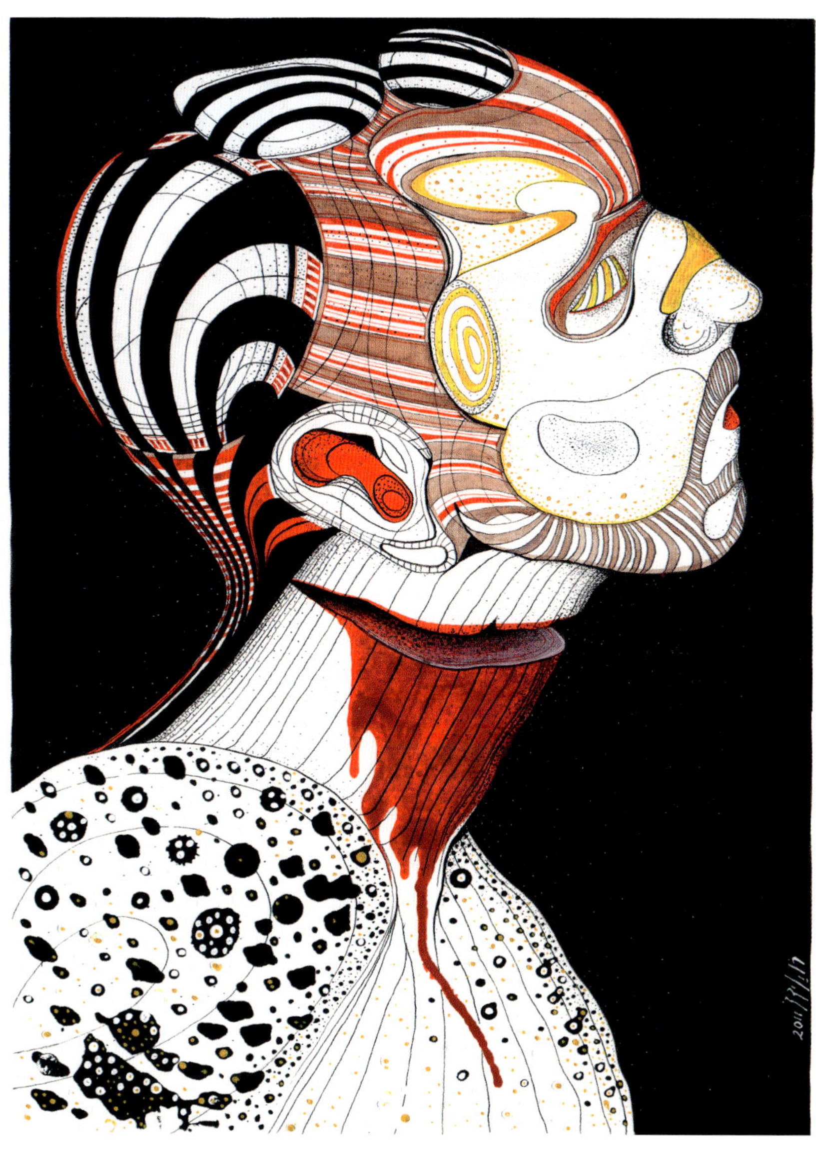

About a Young Man Called Kashoosh 2011
Khalil Younes
Pen-and-ink drawing

Syrian artist Khalil Younes created a series of
drawings entitled *Revolution* 2011, including
iconic images of people and objects from the 2011
revolution, as well as key events from Syria's past.
This drawing from that series is a portrait of the
inspirational singer-songwriter Ibrahim Qashoush
who was critical of the regime, and sang his
revolutionary song 'Yalla irhal ya Bashar!' ('Come
on, Bashar, Get Out!') during mass demonstrations
in Hama and other cities. His portrait represents the
many victims who were brutally murdered in the
2011 uprising.

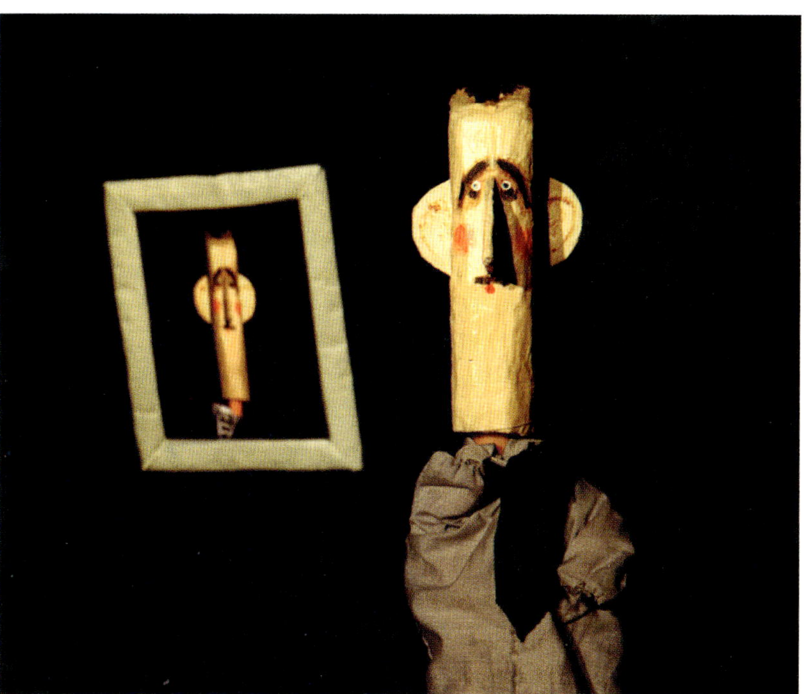

Top Goon: Diaries of a Little Dictator 2011
Masasit Mati
Still of online video (with hand puppets)

During the revolution, the anonymous group
Masasit Mati used hand puppets to create biting,
five-minute videos posted on YouTube, Vimeo and
Facebook. This included the absurdist, satirical
series 'Top Goon: Diaries of a Little Dictator' in
which the puppet 'Beeshu' (a representation of
Bashar) takes the form of a sniffling weakling who
has nightmares, never knows what to do and is
forever taking bad advice from those around him.
The small size of the puppets was intentional; it
allowed them to be easily hidden from the police
when being transported.

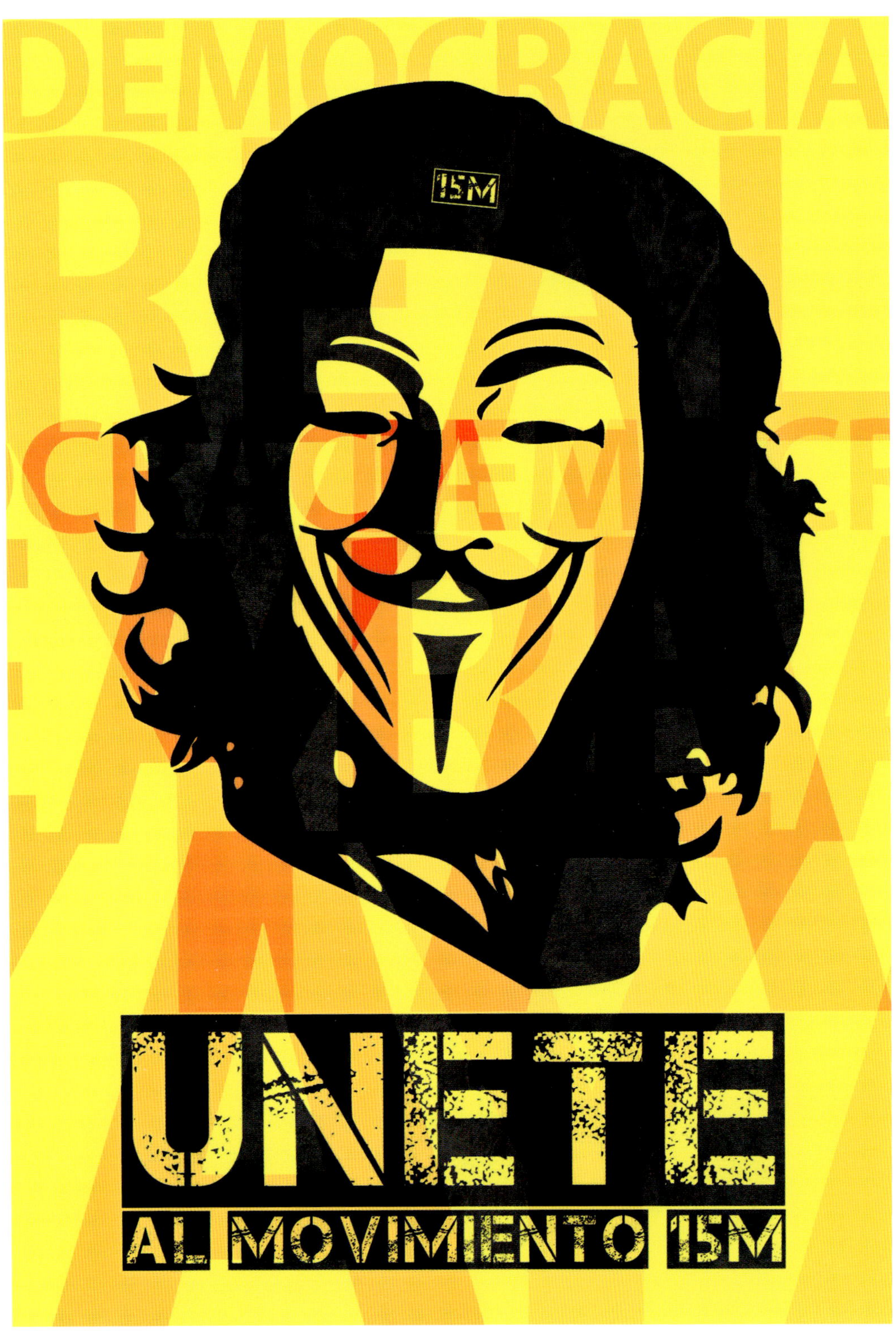

Unete al Movimiento 15M (Join the 15M Movement) 2011
Voces con Futura (Voices of the Future)
Poster (silkscreen and offset)

Inspired by the Arab Spring and angered by austerity measures, a major demonstration was held on 15 May 2011 in Madrid's main square, La Puerta del Sol. Within two days, 200 people were camped in the square; by the end of that week there were 25,000. They were called 'Los Indignados' (the Outraged) or the '15M' movement, after their start date. Although they left the square voluntarily by 2 August, they had forced public debate into the open, and continued to demonstrate throughout the year. They recruited millions of supporters via social networking and made an impact internationally. Also, at the start of the protests, an online image-bank for the movement was created anonymously, entitled Voces con Futura (Voices of the Future). Professional designers, illustrators and graphic artists uploaded signs, banners and posters for free download by activists and demonstrators, creating an impressive archive of high-quality work. In the image-bank poster shown here, Alberto Korda's iconic 1960 photo of Che Guevara has Che wearing an Anonymous mask (the mask of the protester).

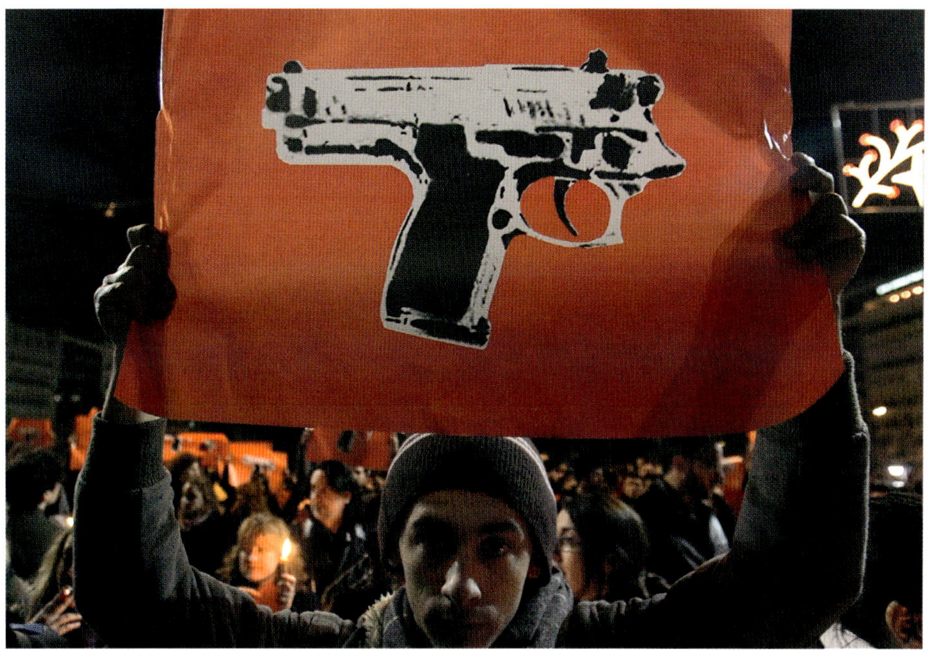

Police Violence in Greece 2008
Artist unknown
Poster

Greece's debt crisis, austerity measures
and high unemployment were
exacerbated by the fatal police-shooting
of a 15-year-old student on 6 December
2008. Six weeks of demonstrations
followed, as well as rioting in Athens
and other cities throughout Greece.
By 2011, not much had improved with
the economy, rioting was still frequent,
police brutality and the murder of
the student was still in mind, and
extremism was on the rise. The poster
image shown here was carried by many
people at the 2008 protests of the
student-shooting.

Dirty Rotten Art Works 2011
Artist: DRB
Postcards

The police-shooting of a 29-year-old black man from north
London was the flashpoint for the rioting and looting that
followed throughout London and spread to at least nine other
British cities. The overriding anger was considered to be rooted
in social and economic inequalities, as well as the obvious
wealth and private school education of the prime minister and
his cabinet (the 'ruling class', who dealt out austerity cuts to
the rest of the country); the heat of that August simply fanned
the flames. The profile of the rioters was confused, from angry
adults (no job, no prospects, no future) to opportunistic looters
and nine-year-old kids. The riots calmed down after a week,
but the anger of a divided society stayed – waiting for the next
opportunity for pay back. The satirical postcards produced
by artist DRB (parodies of matchbox illustrations) depict the
attitude of the time, with colourful but unsettling images.

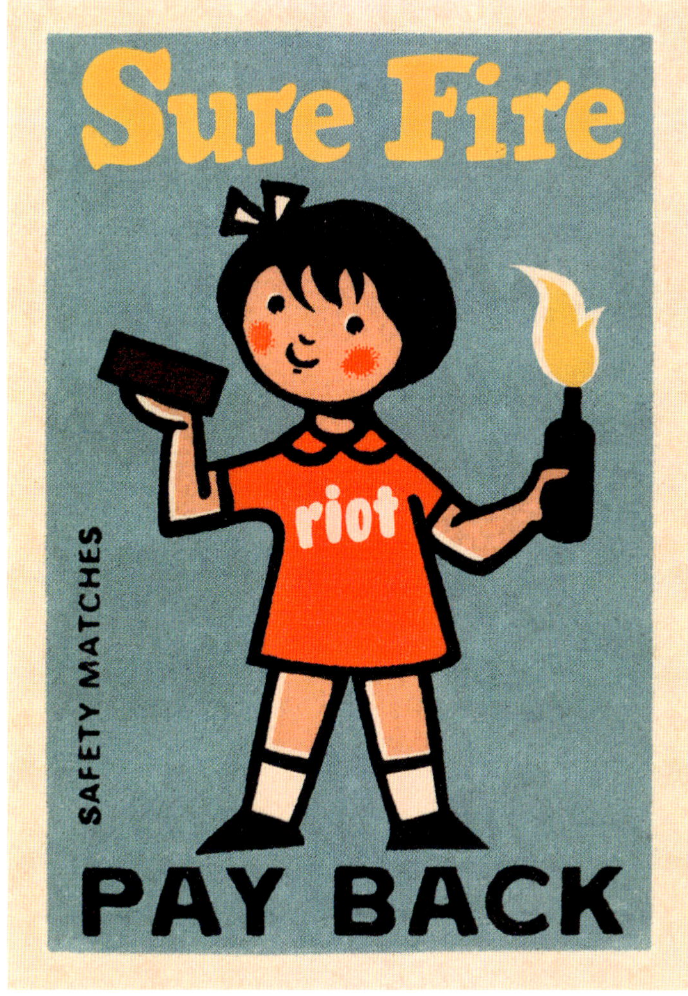

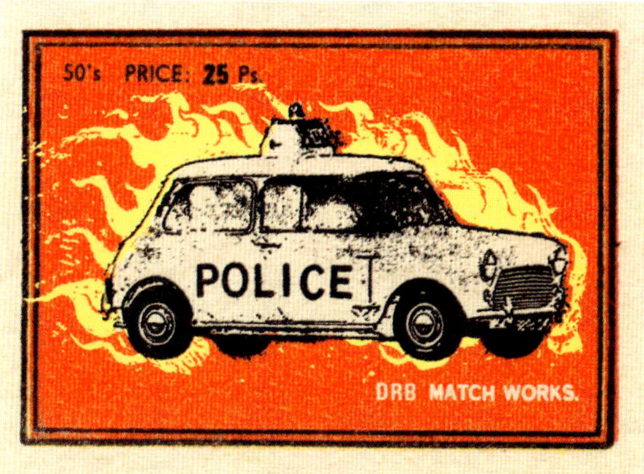

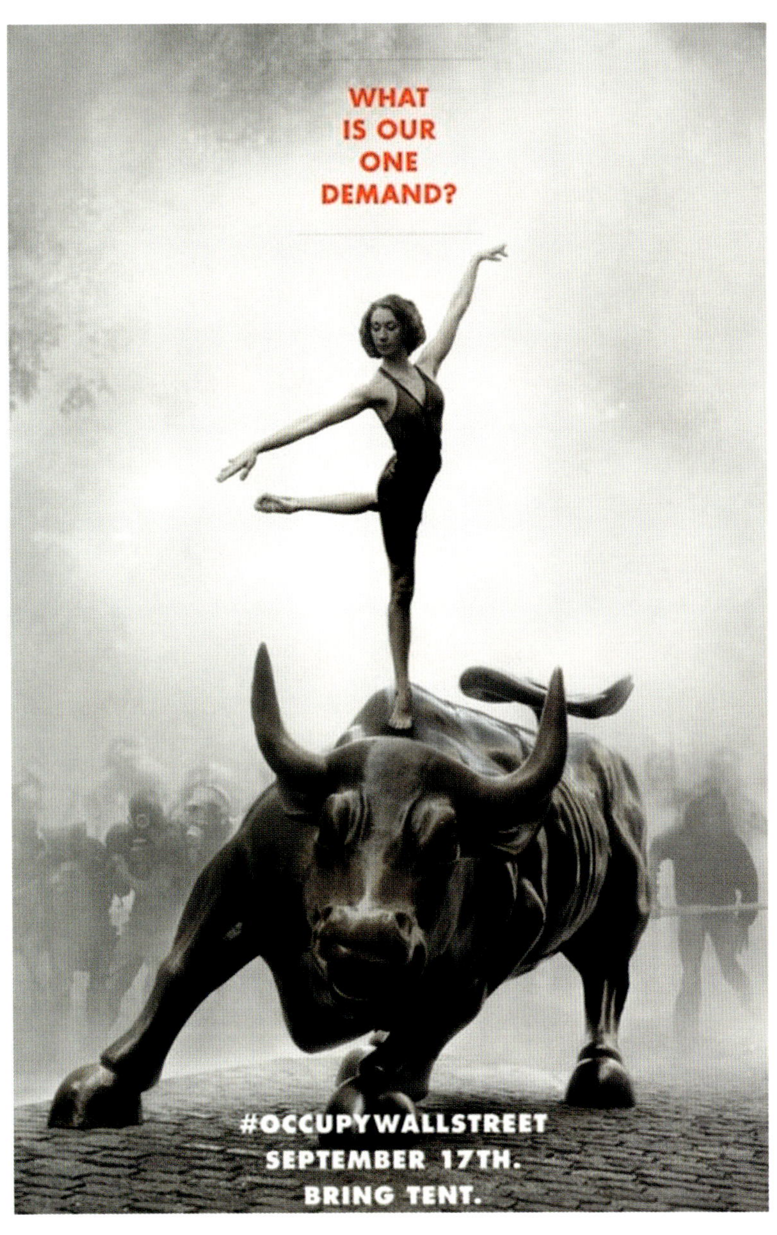

← **What is Our One Demand?** 2011
Concept: Kalle Lasn
Art direction: Pedro Inoue and Will Brown
Poster

This *Adbusters* poster, featuring in the July 2011 issue of the magazine, announced the 17 September meeting in Zuccotti Park that kickstarted the 'Occupy Wall Street encampment. Angry at corrupt politicians, the financial institutions that caused the 2008 crash and the austerity measures which followed, nearly 300 slept in the park and established the protest camp, acquiring the slogan 'We are the 99%', relating to reports that the majority of the country's wealth was owned by only 1%. The camp generated its own newspaper, *The Occupied Wall Street Journal*, and offered discussions, meetings, free food and medical care. Although the protesters were evicted by 15 November, the Occupy movement staged 'Day of Action' protests in cities throughout the USA and the movement spread throughout the world, carrying with it the slogan 'We are the 99%'.

↓ **Occupy George currency stamp** 2011
Artists: Ivan Cash and Andy Dao (Occupy George)
Hand-stamps

Activists Cash and Dao produced a set of hand-stamps bearing messages and infographics about the disparity of wealth in the USA, which were used to stamp dollar bills as an accompaniment to the Occupy protests, hence their name: George Washington appears on the one dollar bill). The notes were then put back in circulation, and remained legal as long as security features on the bills were avoided. The designs were placed on the internet for use by all.

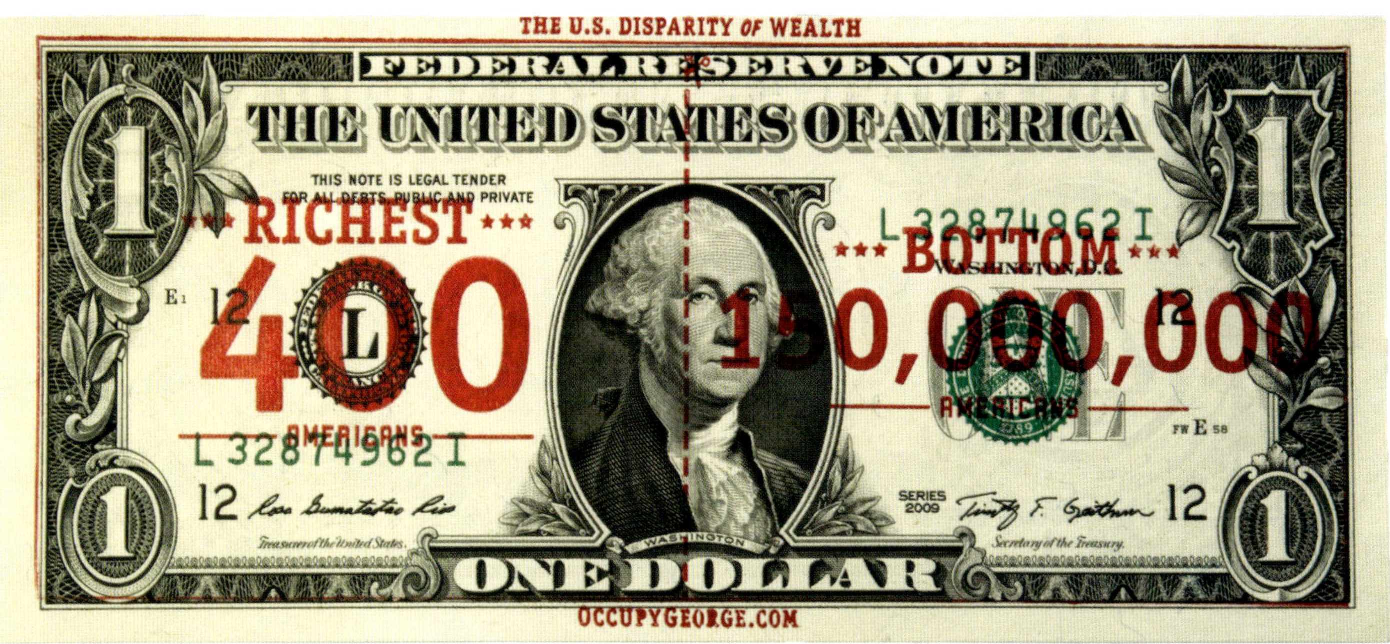

     Revolutions and the Demand for Rights | 2000–Present

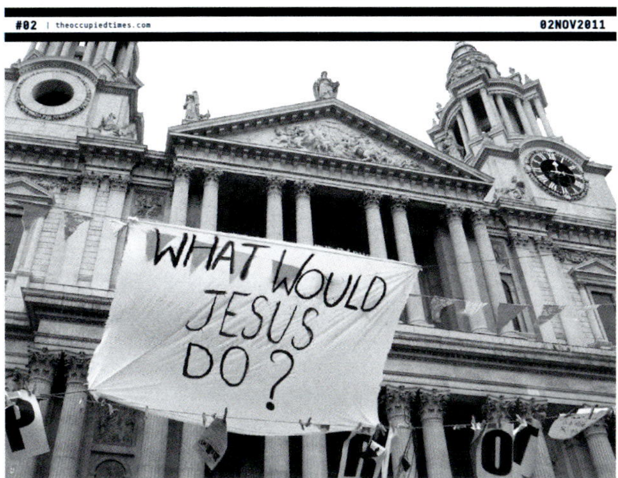

The Occupied Times

~ OF LONDON ~

#02 | theoccupiedtimes.com   02NOV2011

FEARS OF A VIOLENT EVICTION

STACEY KNOTT

Relations between OccupyLSX and St Paul's Cathedral took another twist last Monday when the Dean of St Paul's, Graeme Knowles, resigned amid the controversy of St. Paul's handling of the occupation.

Last week the cathedral sought legal action to evict occupiers, which has caused three clergy to quit.

In a statement, Knowles said he had resigned to "give the opportunity for a fresh approach to the complex and vital questions facing St Paul's, I have thought it best to stand down as dean, to allow new leadership to be exercised. I do this with great sadness, but I now believe that I am no longer the right person to lead the Chapter of this great cathedral."

With Knowles stepping down, the Cathedral has asked the Bishop of London Dr Richard Chartres to assist in providing an independent voice on the ongoing situation at St Paul's.

Two other St Paul's clergy quit their posts in solidarity with the protesters.

The first was the canon chancellor of St Paul's Cathedral, Dr Giles Fraser. He said he could not support the possibility of "violence in the name of the church", then the Rev Fraser Dyer, who worked as a chaplain at St Paul's, stepped down because he was "left feeling embarrassed" by the cathedrals eviction decision.

Knowles' announcement came one day after he and Chartres met with the occupiers to listen to and speak to them about their concerns.

At the public meeting, they said they did not want the eviction to be violent, and that they were willing to open dialogue over the issues the movement was trying to address.

However, many protesters told the Occupied Times they felt the clerics were evasive of their questions, and did not say anything of real substance.

Many in the movement were concerned about a violent eviction, after it was announced on Friday that St Paul's and the City of London Corporation were planning on getting high court injunctions to remove the protesters.

Chartres told the occupiers "nobody wants to see violence." Musician and occupier Ben Doran felt the men were contradictory with their intentions to evict, but also not wanting violence.

"An eviction would apply violence. As a logical process you can't be against one and for the other," he said.

Occupier Tanya Paton, who was part of a working group responsible for liaising with the cathedral, told the Occupied Times she had been trying to open dialogue with the cathedral for the past two weeks, and was pleased they had finally started talking to occupiers.

However, she was also concerned about a violent eviction and hoped the church would commit to protecting the occupiers from one.

CHURCH & STATE SEEK LEGAL ACTION

RORY MACKINNON

Camp residents voiced anger this week as clergy and councillors alike threatened legal action to force them from a public square.

Between 200-300 campers from Occupy London Stock Exchange have held St Paul's Square for more than a fortnight after police barred them from the privately-owned Paternoster Square directly outside the exchange.

But both St Paul's Cathedral and the City of London confirmed late last week they were seeking an eviction order to break up the camp on grounds of obstructing a public highway.

City of London said in a statement they believed protest was "an essential right" in a democracy – "but camping on the highway is not."

"We believe we will have a strong highways case because an encampment on a busy thoroughfare clearly impacts the rights of others," it read.

Meanwhile the Cathedral said only that legal action had "regrettably become necessary."

"The Chapter only takes this step with the greatest reluctance and remains committed to a peaceful solution," the Cathedral's ruling Chapter said in a statement. >>

The Occupied Times of London (#02) 2011
Artists: Tzortzis Rallis and Lazaros Kakoulidis
Newspaper

On 15 October 2011 the activist group Occupy London landed its protest camp in the small area of pavement in front of St Paul's Cathedral. It was greeted with confused reactions from the Anglican Church (some soul-searching was required before the camp was allowed to stay) and irritation from the City of London as well as the news media. Nevertheless, the camp thrived – it staged organized debates and lectures, offered food to visitors and produced occasional performances – and sustained a long-term presence, with a final eviction date of 28 February. It was also a very visual affair, with posters and placards stuck to tents in the camp, on trees and surrounding buildings. Plus *The Occupied Times of London* newspaper was produced, starting as a weekly of 12 A4 pages and eventually growing to a 24-page monthly. Designed by Rallis and Kakoulidis, the newspaper was shortlisted for the 'Designs of the Year 2013' award staged by the London Design Museum.

Occupy London Protester with Anonymous Mask 2011
Photographer: Jeremy Barr
Photograph

Occupy London protesters often wore masks when facing the media, but not necessarily when facing the British public and tourists who were usually very friendly.

Occupy London 2011
Artist unknown
Flyer/leaflet

This Occupy London leaflet was very much in evidence at the start of the protest, as it announced the camps' arrival to anyone wishing to be involved, and carries the (now international) slogan 'We are the 99%'.

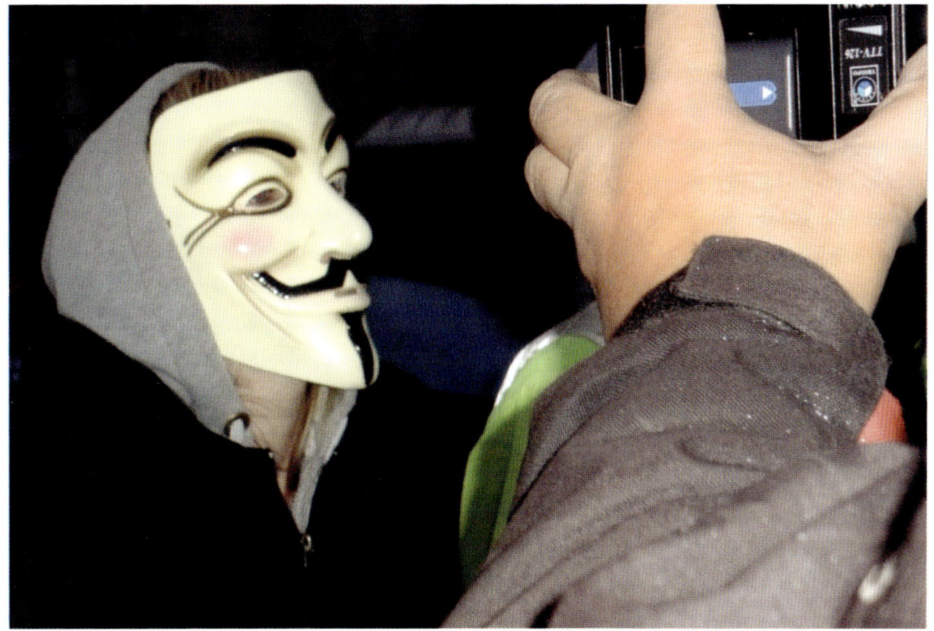

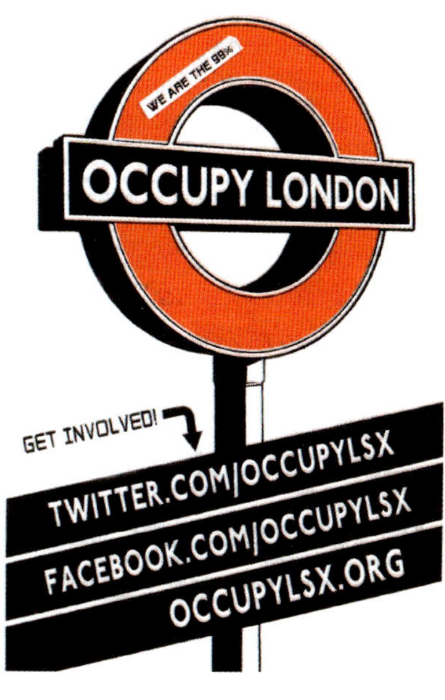

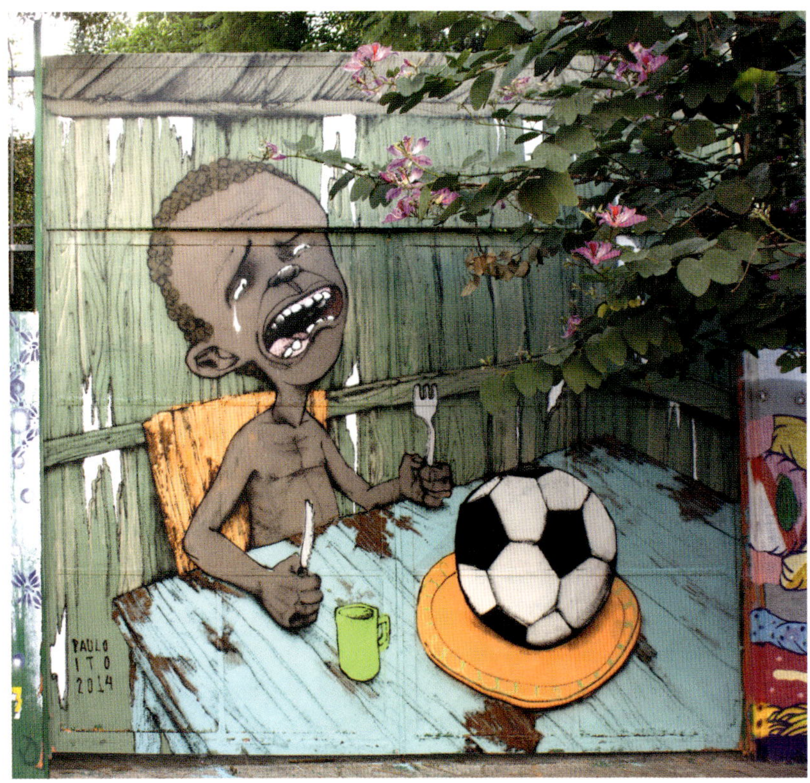

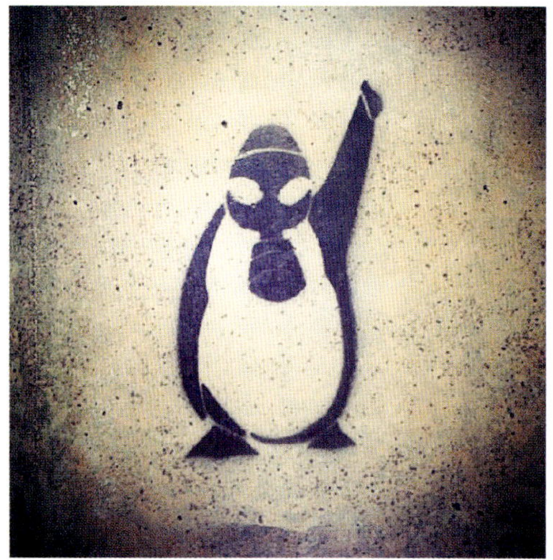

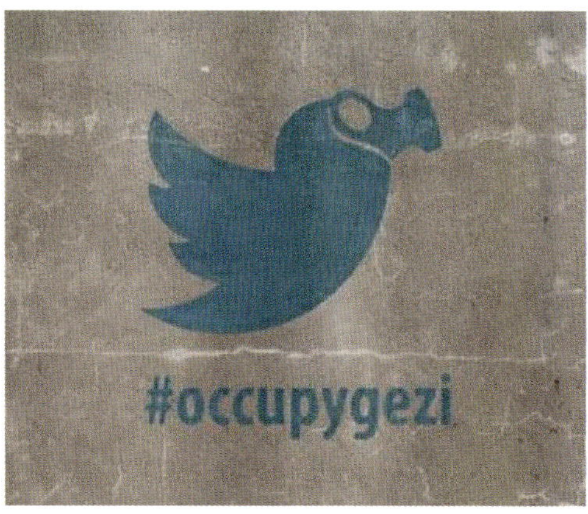

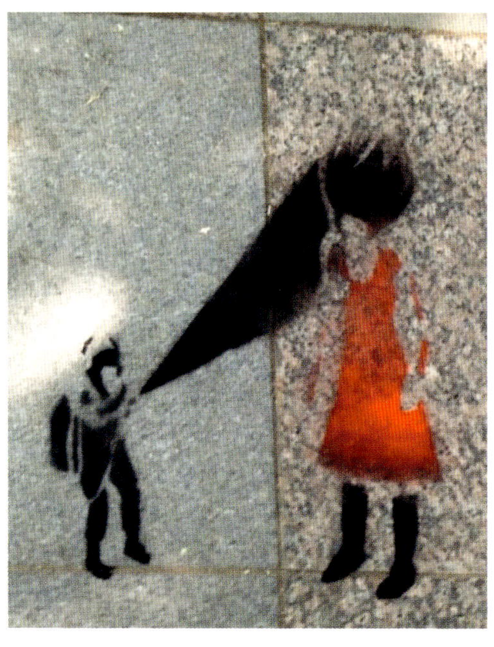

 Anti-World Cup Mural 2014
Artist: Paulo Ito
Mural and electronic image

Discontent erupted in Brazil in 2013 when its politicians pushed for the hosting of the 2014 FIFA World Cup and the 2016 Olympics in Rio. At the time its main cities suffered from overcrowding, weakened social services and low living standards. The lavish spending on 'FIFA-standard' stadiums clashed badly with cries of political corruption, poor medical facilities, overcrowded hospitals and high rates of illiteracy. Protesters wielding signs outside the stadiums during the Confederations Cup games, the precursor to the World Cup, June 2013, demanding 'FIFA-standard hospitals' and 'FIFA-quality schools', were met with tear gas, stun grenades and rubber bullets. Protests against the World Cup were present throughout the run-up to the event. This mural painting by São Paulo street artist Paulo Ito, of a starving child eating a football, went viral on social media in the run-up to the World Cup in May 2014.

 Stencilled Memes 2013
 Artists unknown
Stencils sprayed in the city

The gas mask became a sign of honour in Istanbul's Gezi Park protests, and was depicted on the Twitter bird logo, as Twitter was crucial to the protesters for information dissemination. It also appeared on the face of a defiant penguin, a symbol of anger felt when a major news channel broadcast a bird documentary (with penguins) and ignored an extremely violent protest. From thereon, birds and penguins were depicted as having joined the protesters. A photo of a policeman pepper-spraying a woman in a red dress also became a social media icon, as well as being stencilled throughout Istanbul.

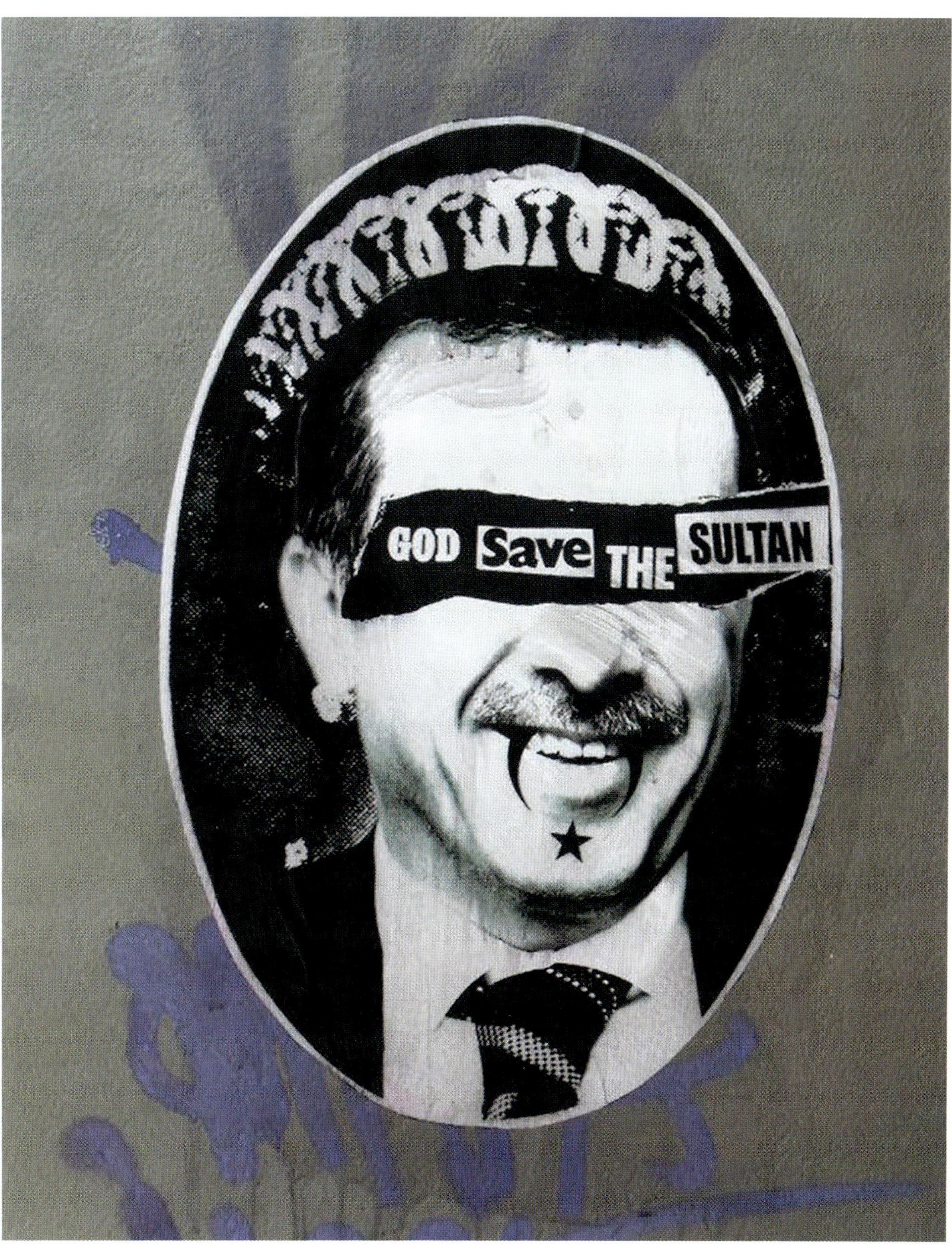

God Save the Sultan 2013
Artist unknown
Poster

When Istanbul's Gezi Park was due for demolition and development (as a shopping centre), mass protests to save the park took place. The Occupy Gezi Park protests of May–June 2013 involved protesters taking over Taksim Square and occupying nearby Gezi Park, setting up food stalls, a library, a stage and so on while sending invitations via social media to a wide range of activists to join in. However, authoritarian Prime Minister (now President) Recep Tayyip Erdogan denounced the protesters and ordered a police crackdown on 31 May. Anti-government protests spread throughout the country. From thereon, reports and images emerging from the Taksim Square protests showed excessive use of violence including tear gas and water cannon. Protesters responded with innovative home-made gas masks, and satirized the violence through imagery which was spread through posters, social media or stencilled in the streets. The power struggle between Erdogan and his people ended with eight dead and thousands injured. In the protest poster shown here, Jamie Reid's Sex Pistols cover for 'God Save the Queen' is manipulated to show Prime Minister Erdogan with the words 'God Save the Sultan', a comment on his growing authoritarianism.

Hong Kong's Umbrella Revolution

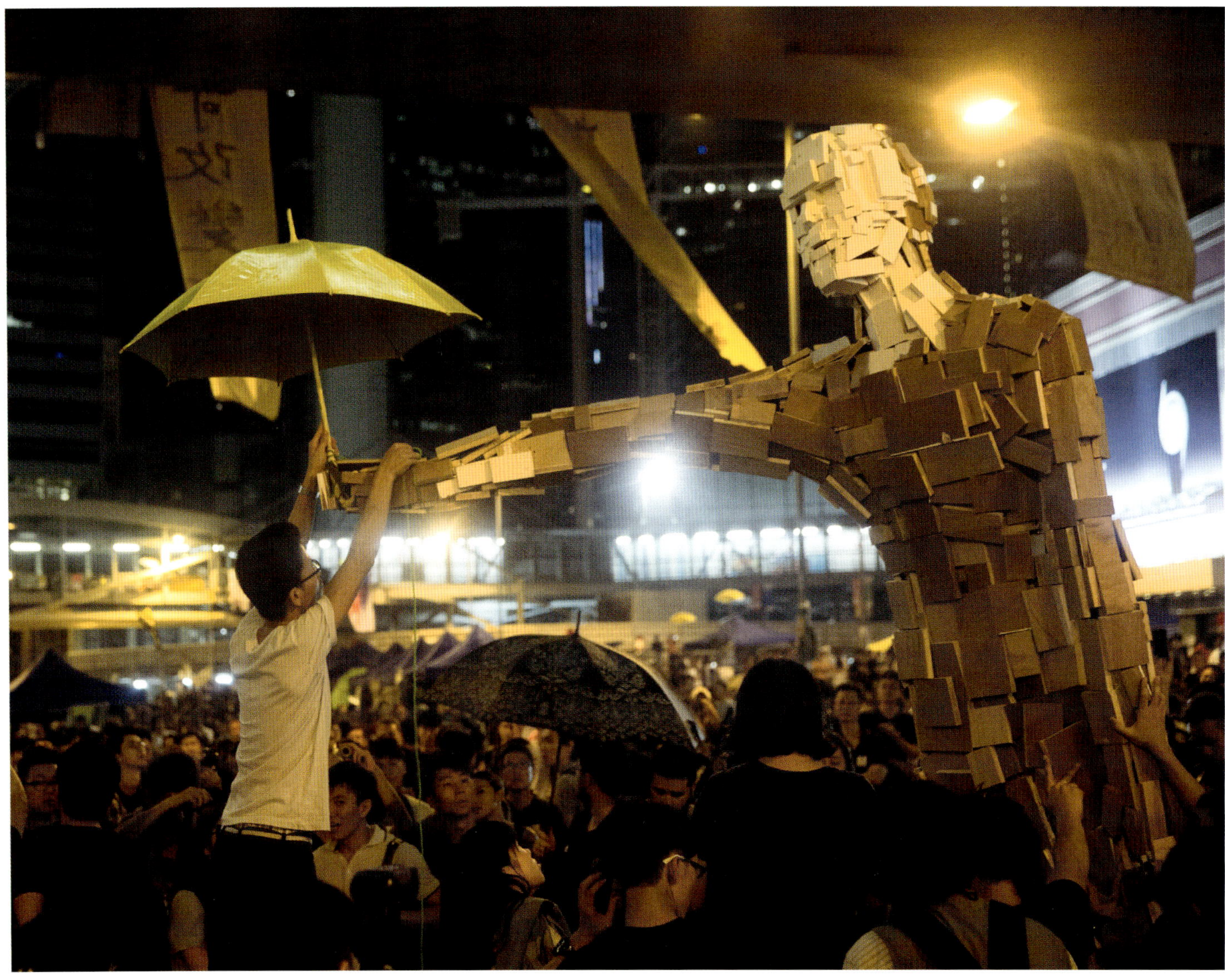

Umbrella Man 2014
Artists unknown
Impromptu sculpture

After nearly a century of British governance, Hong Kong (on lease to Britain from China) was returned to its owner. Hopes of achieving a democratic system slowly faded under the repression of mainland China. In 2014, when announcements were made about the upcoming 2017 elections for the Hong Kong chief executive, it became clear that the Beijing authorities would insist on three pre-screened candidates. Hong Kong's pro-democracy activists demanded open elections and held the 'Umbrella Revolution' (September–December 2014). Peaceful public demonstrations took place, initiated by a protest group entitled 'Occupy Central with Peace and Love'. Encampments were formed, and tens of thousands of protesters blocked thoroughfares and transport to Central, one of the world's most important financial centres, often holding umbrellas. It was not always a calm affair. The sea of umbrellas, caught in many images appearing on social media, were of critical use: as protection against riot police brutality, tear gas and pepper-spray, as well as rain or the hot midday sun. Ribbons were worn in the adopted colour, yellow, symbolising universal suffrage and serving as identifiers of the movement and its sympathizers. The protests also became known for the impromptu art pieces that flourished, and the extraordinary number of solidarity posters appearing on the internet. 'Umbrella Man', shown here, was a 3.6 m (12 ft) tall sculpture made of wood and set up by students outside the city government headquarters. Sadly, public support eventually waned and in mid-December the central protest site was shut down. Defiance has continued – online and in other ways – ever since.

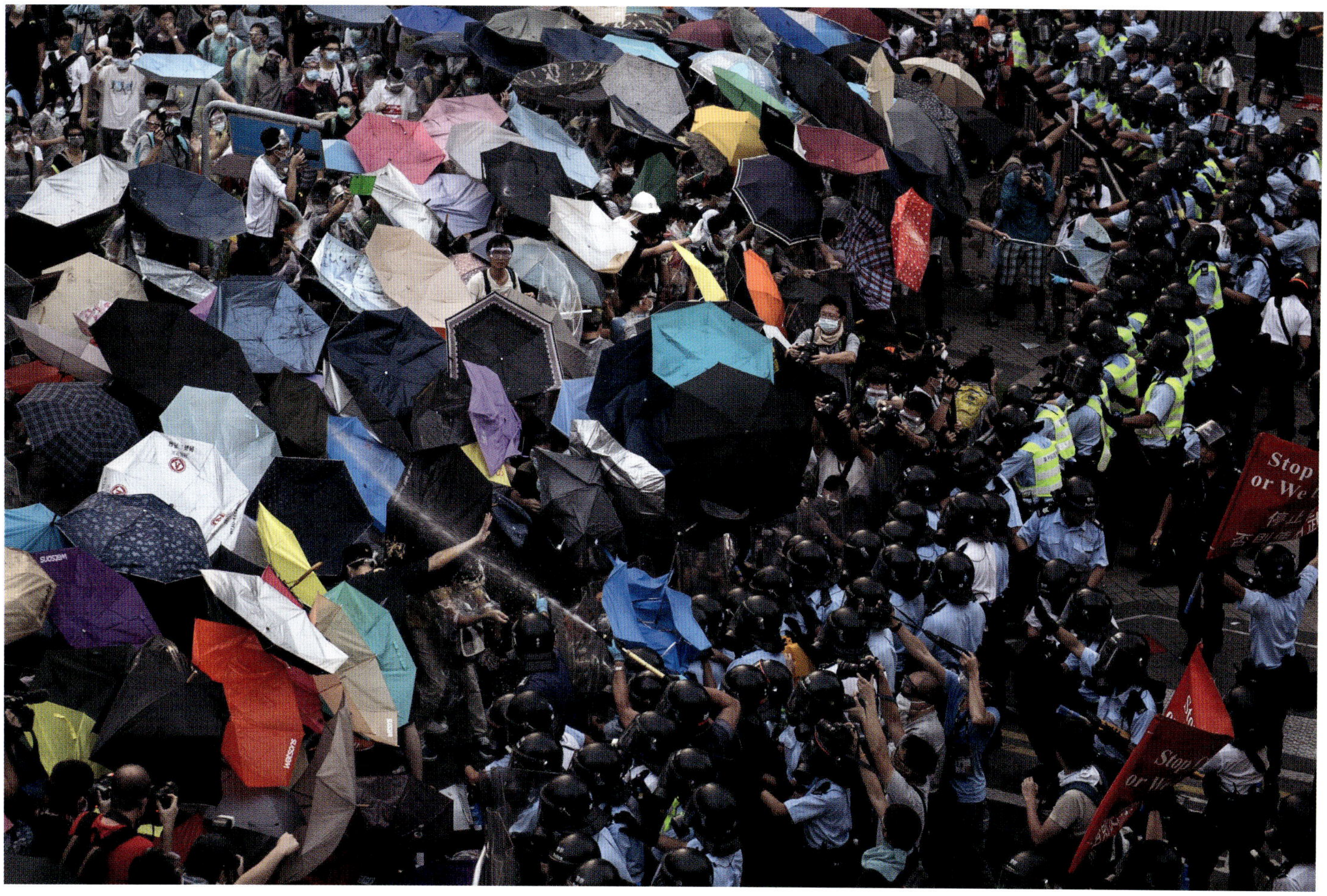

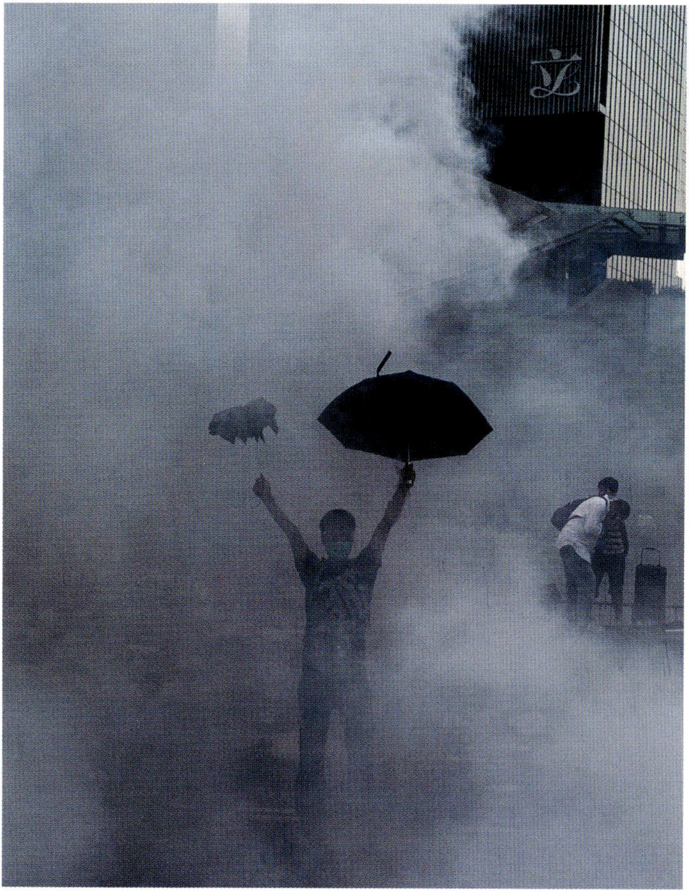

↑ **Umbrella Revolution Protest** 2014
Photographer unknown
Photograph

Protesters used umbrellas to protect themselves from
the indiscriminate use of tear gas and pepper-spray by
Hong Kong's riot police, as shown here. Many without
gas masks wore goggles and wrapped cling film around
their heads (like a cap) or around their arms.

← **Umbrella Revolution Protest** 2014
Photographer: Xaume Olleros
Photograph

A lone protester gestures defiantly through a fog of tear
gas near the Hong Kong government headquarters.
Finally tens of thousands of pro-democracy protesters
brought parts of central Hong Kong to a standstill on
September 28, 2014, after an escalation of protests that
had lasted for days.

A

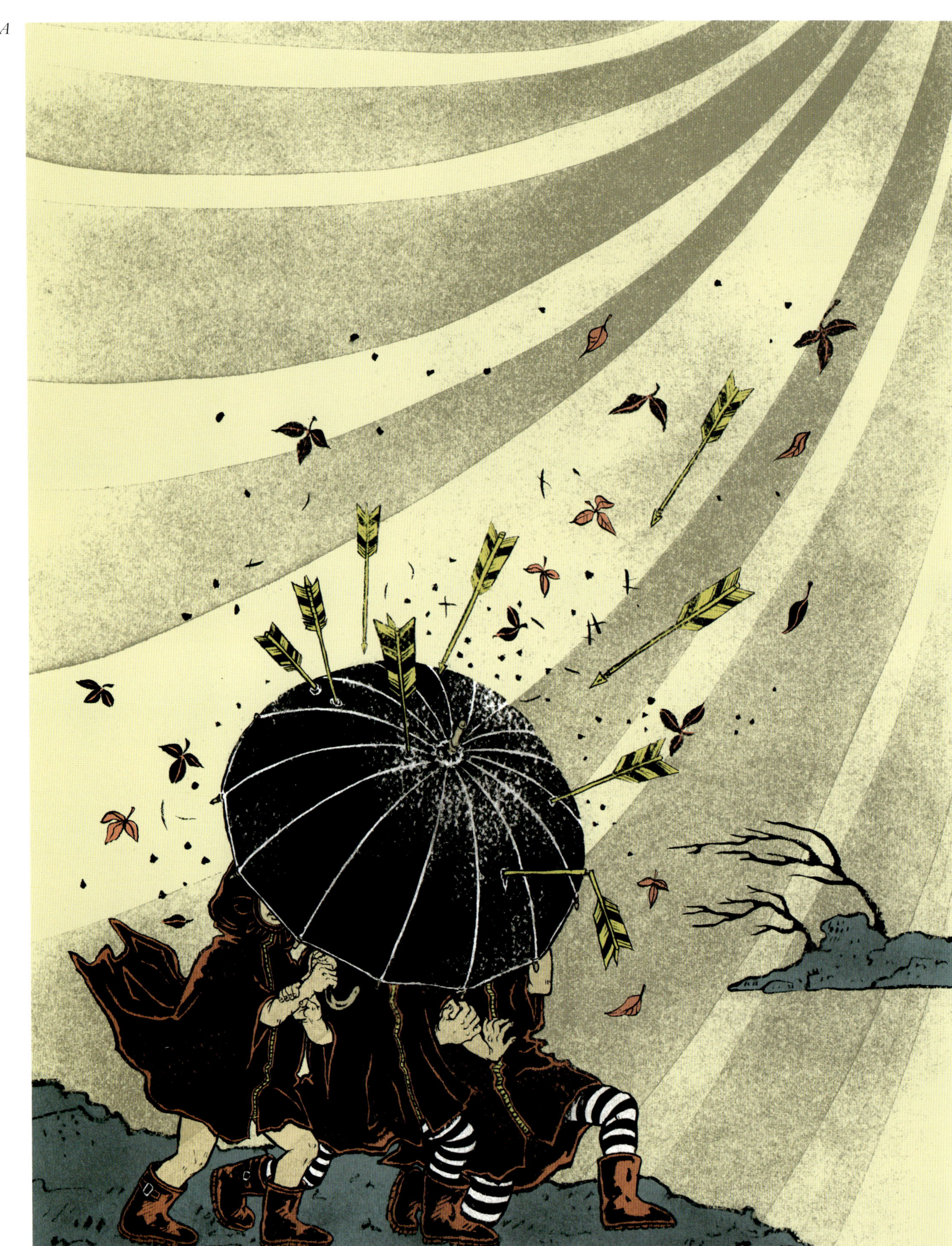

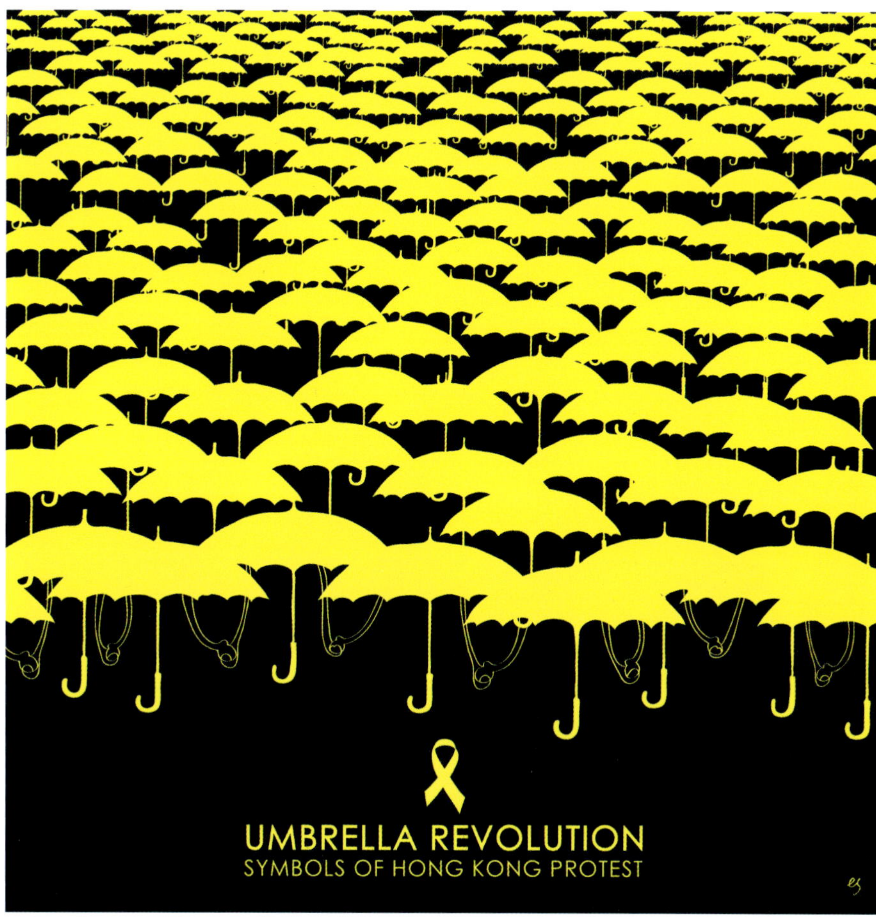

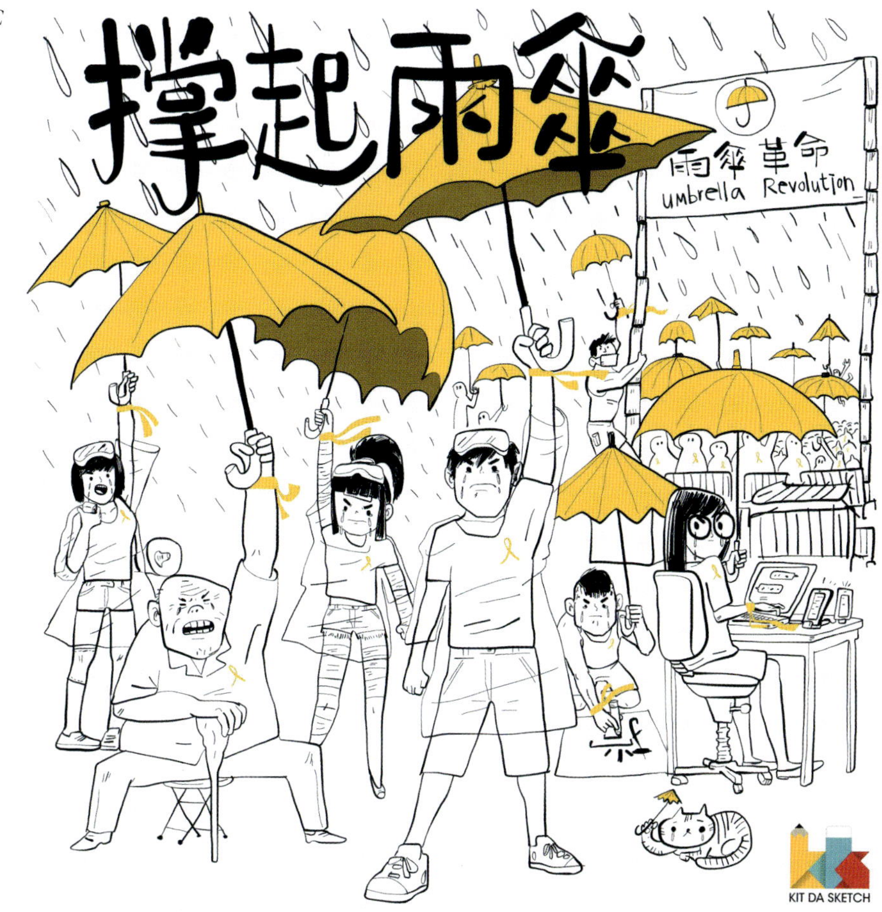

**Umbrella Revolution Solidarity
Posters** 2014
Various Artists
Electronic (online) posters

Many solidarity posters appeared on the
internet, often using the visual identifier of
yellow umbrellas or yellow ribbons. Three of
the artists involved are listed here:

(Image A)   Yuko Shimizu, Japanese
illustrator, New York City

(Image B)   Raven H. Ma

(Image C)   Kit Da Sketch – Kit Man; the
lettering at the top of the poster
reads 'Let's Keep the Umbrella
Up' (the title of a song in Hong
Kong, 2014, with lyrics about the
Umbrella Revolution)

Russia: Pussy Riot, The Blue Noses

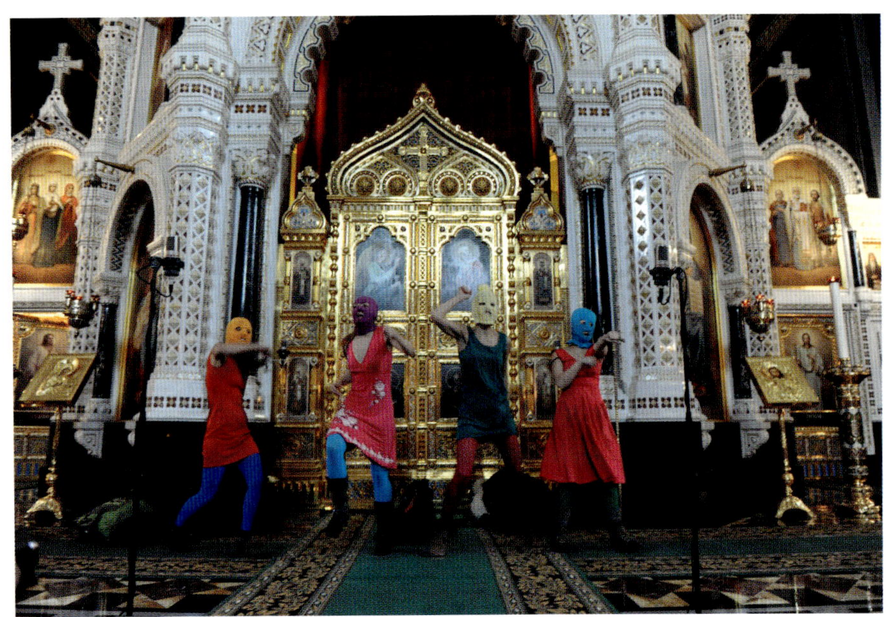

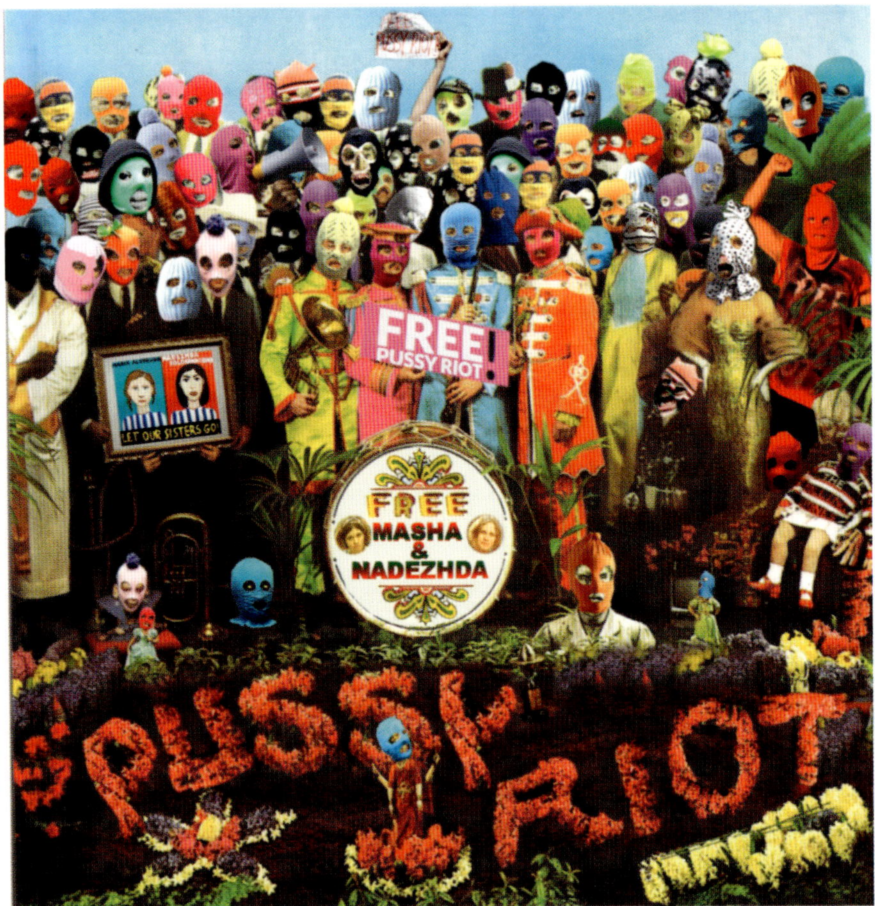

Pussy Riot's Performance, 'A Punk Prayer' 2012
Photographer unknown
Photograph

The feminist Punk collective Pussy Riot was formed in 2011 as a reaction to Vladimir Putin's possible return to the presidency of Russia in 2012. As Putin was about to regain the presidency, they planned an outrageous performance. On 21 February 2012, four of the collective's members – wearing their trademark coloured balaclavas – performed 'A Punk Prayer' in front of the altar of Moscow's Cathedral of Christ the Saviour, considered to be the heart of the Russian Orthodoxy. The song was laden with profanities, with a chorus of 'Virgin Mary, drive Putin out'. Within 30 seconds the performance was stopped by church officials. Maria Alyokhina, Yekaterina Samutsevich and Nadezhda Tolokonnikova (who came to be known as Masha, Katya and Nadya) were arrested and charged with 'hooliganism motivated by religious hatred'. A worldwide solidarity movement operated throughout their trial, sentencing and incarceration, and their coloured balaclavas became a global symbol of resistance. All were sentenced to two years in prison, but were eventually released early.

Free Pussy Riot with a Little Help from My Friends *c.*2012
Artist: Jorge Artajo
Electronic (online) poster

During their trial and imprisonment, the slogan 'Free Pussy Riot' echoed around the world via internet or social media, often accompanied by colourful and/or outrageous posters and art pieces. This image is an appropriation of The Beatles' 1967 *Sgt. Pepper's Lonely Hearts Club Band* album cover, designed by artist Peter Blake and his wife Jann Haworth. Only two Pussy Riot members are mentioned as Katya was freed on probation on appeal in October 2012; the other two were released in December 2013.

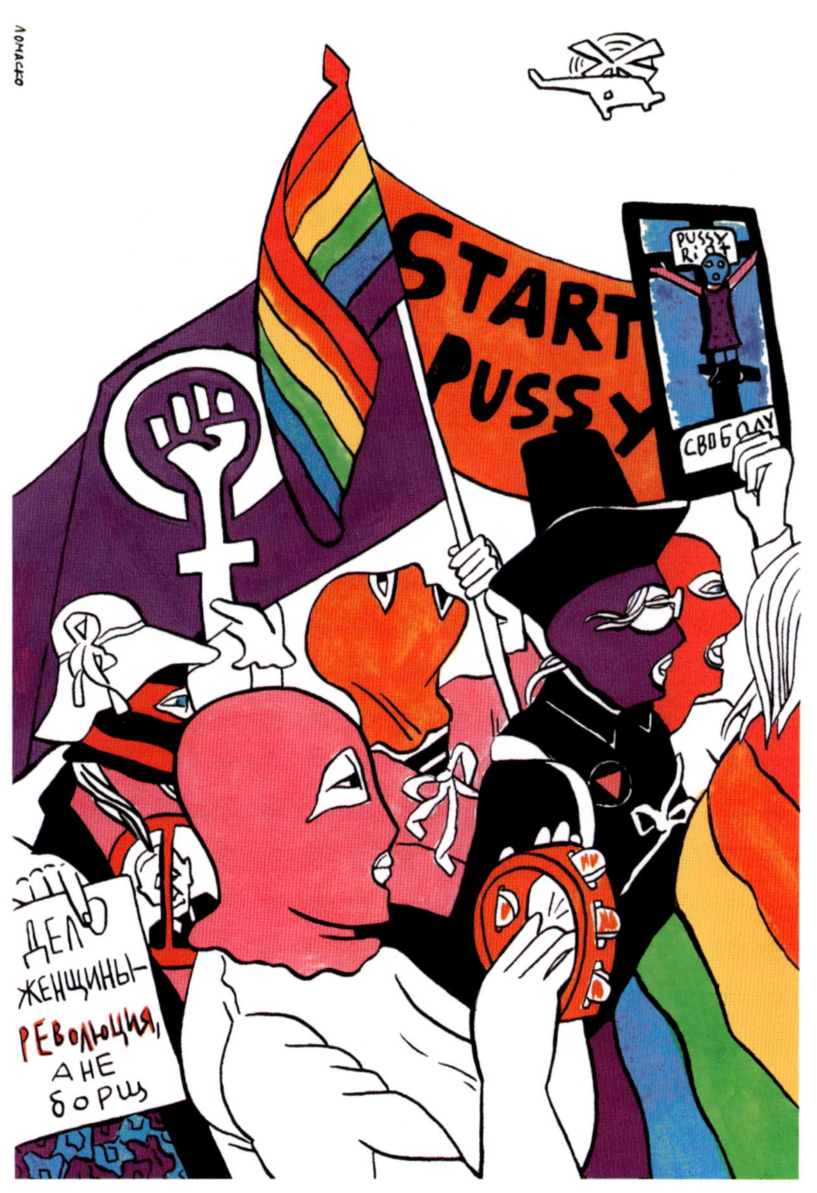

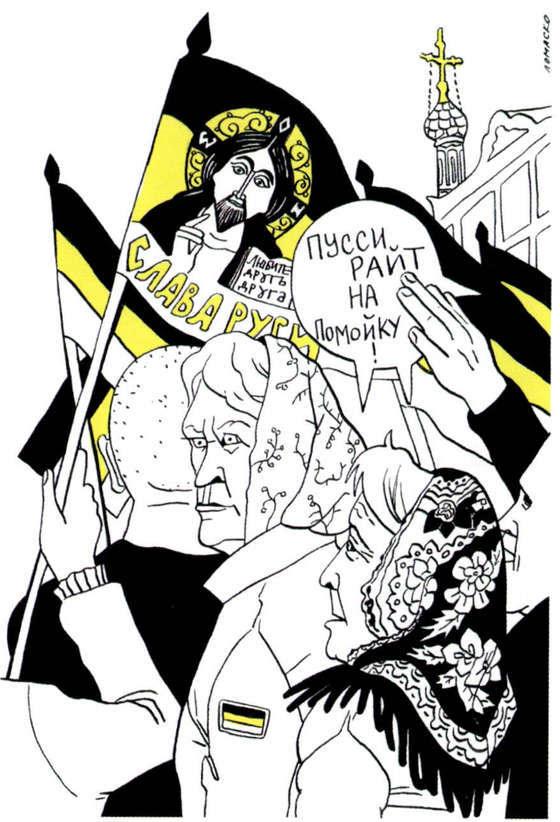

↑ **Pussy Riot Support Column** 2012
↗ **Nationalists' Column**
   Artist: Victoria Lomasko
   Drawings

Both images are from the series 'Chronicle of the Resistance', which show different perspectives on support (or not) for Pussy Riot during the 'March of Millions', a series of mass anti-government rallies held in May, June and September 2012 in Moscow. In the image on the left (6 May) the woman's poster reads: 'Women's business is a revolution, not a soup.' In the image on the right (15 September), the women are chanting 'Pussy Riot – in the trash!' The flag reads 'Glory to Russia!'

A

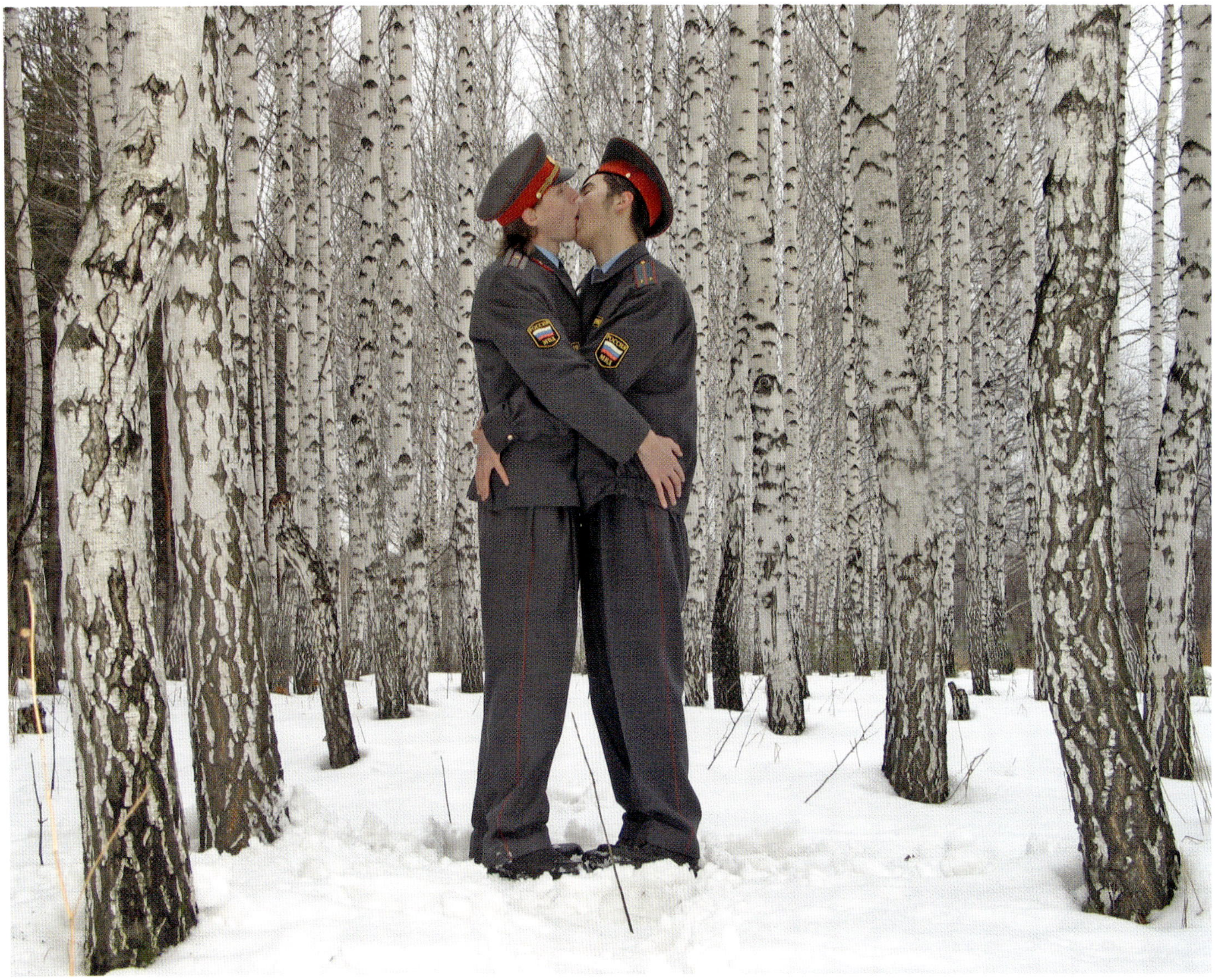

B

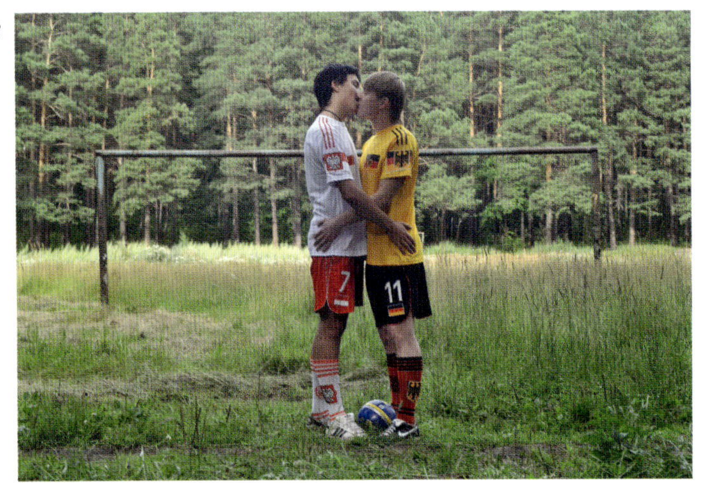

C

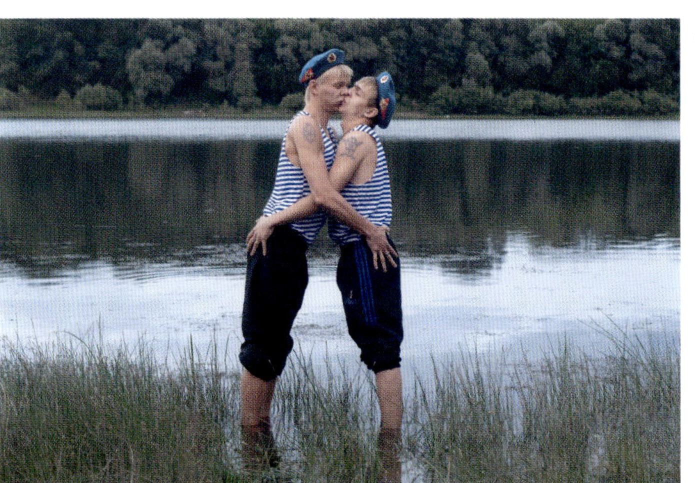

An Epoch of Clemency (Kissing Policemen) 2005–09
Artists: The Blue Noses
Photographers: The Blue Noses
Photographs

The controversial performance art duo the Blue Noses was founded in 1999 and consists of Alexander Shaburov and Viacheslav Mizin. Being from Siberia, they are crucial members of the Siberian separatist movement: solely an invention in the minds of artists from Siberia, but enough to cause worry to the authorities.

They excel at social critique mixed with self-deprecation, irreverence, absurdist humour (with a great deal of nudity), and have been inclined to take the occasional poke at Vladimir Putin as well as other global leaders along the way. One of their classic pieces was 'An Epoch of Clemency (Kissing Policemen)', created in 2005 and labelled 'pornographic' in 2007 by the Minister of Culture, who denied it permission to be part of an exhibition in Paris. Influenced by Banksy's 'Kissing Coppers' (2004), it showed two men dressed in the uniform of the Russian military kissing passionately in a birch forest. But they then proceeded to ensure that they had included all of Russia's most favoured icons (the military, ballet, sport) by adding Kissing Airbornemen, Kissing Ballerinas and Kissing Football Players. It's a satirical as well as a confrontational statement, created in a country deeply intolerant of LGBT culture.

(Image A)   Kissing Policemen
(Image B)   Kissing Football Players
(Image C)   Kissing Airbornemen
(Image D)   Kissing Ballerinas

D

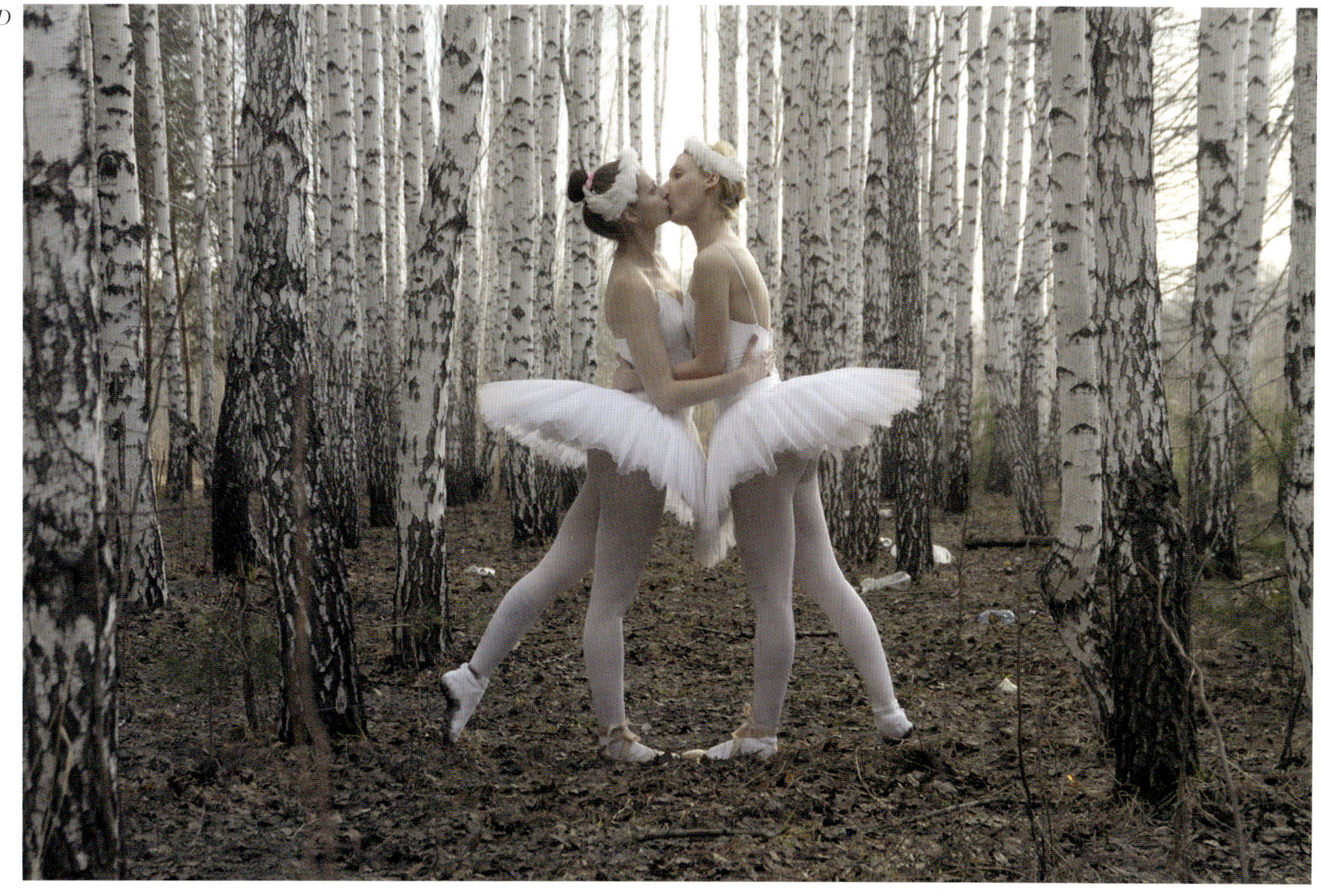

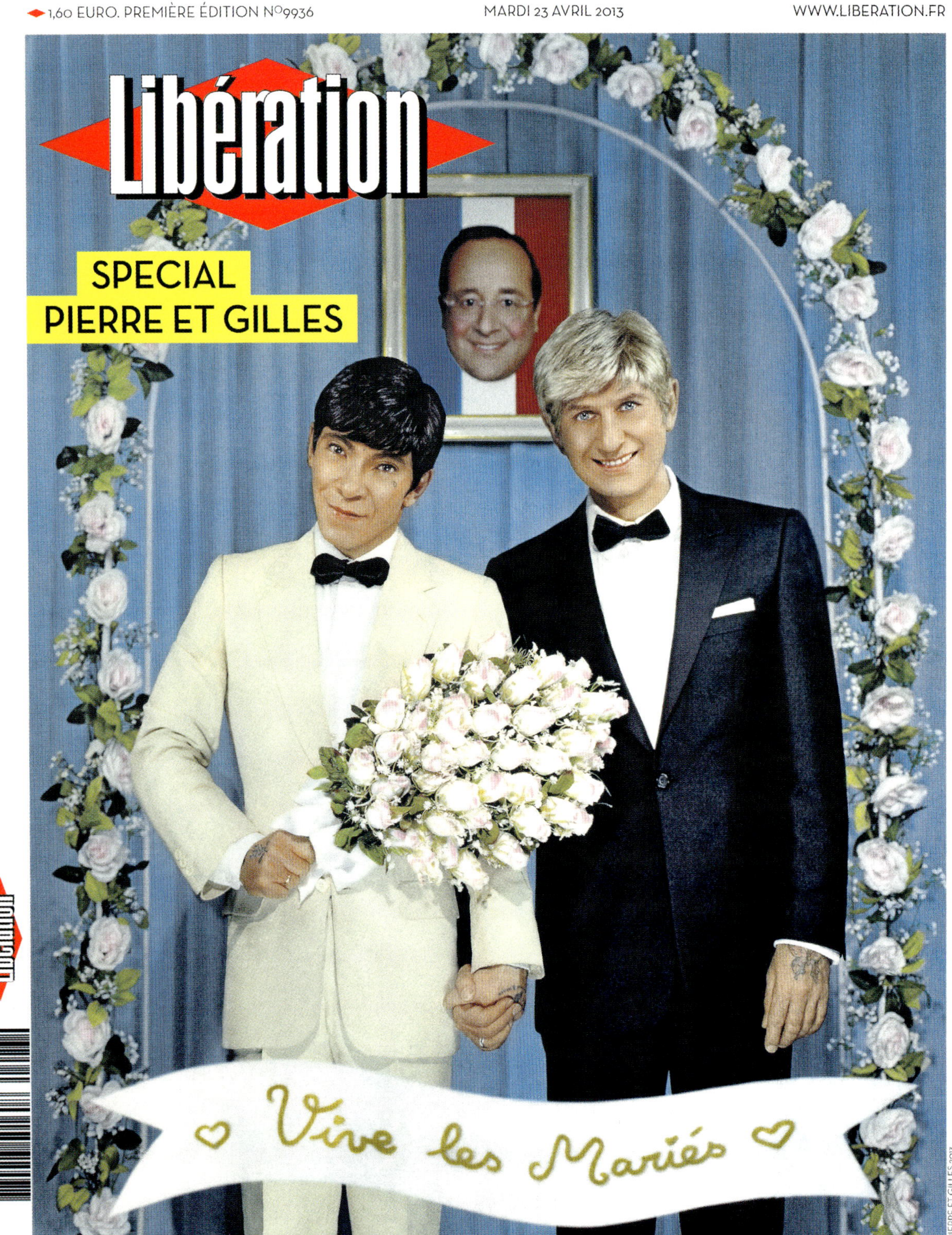

1,60 EURO. PREMIÈRE ÉDITION N°9936
MARDI 23 AVRIL 2013
WWW.LIBERATION.FR
Libération
SPECIAL
PIERRE ET GILLES
♡ Vive les Mariés ♡
PIERRE ET GILLES 2013
M 00135 - 423 - F: 1,60 €
IMPRIMÉ EN FRANCE / PRINTED IN FRANCE Allemagne 2,30 €, Andorre 1,60 €, Autriche 2,80 €, Belgique 1,70 €, Canada 4,50 $, Danemark 27 Kr, DOM 2,40 €, Espagne 2,30 €, Etats-Unis 5 $, Finlande 2,70 €, Grande-Bretagne 1,80 £, Grèce 2,70 €, Irlande 2,40 €, Israël 20 ILS, Italie 2,30 €, Luxembourg 1,70 €, Maroc 17 Dh, Norvège 27 Kr, Pays-Bas 2,30 €, Portugal (cont.) 2,40 €, Slovénie 2,70 €, Suède 24 Kr, Suisse 3,20 FS, TOM 420 CFP, Tunisie 2,40 DT, Zone CFA 2 000CFA.

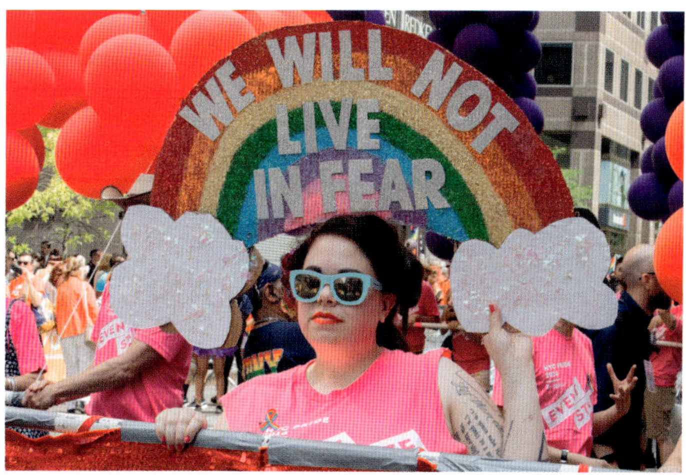

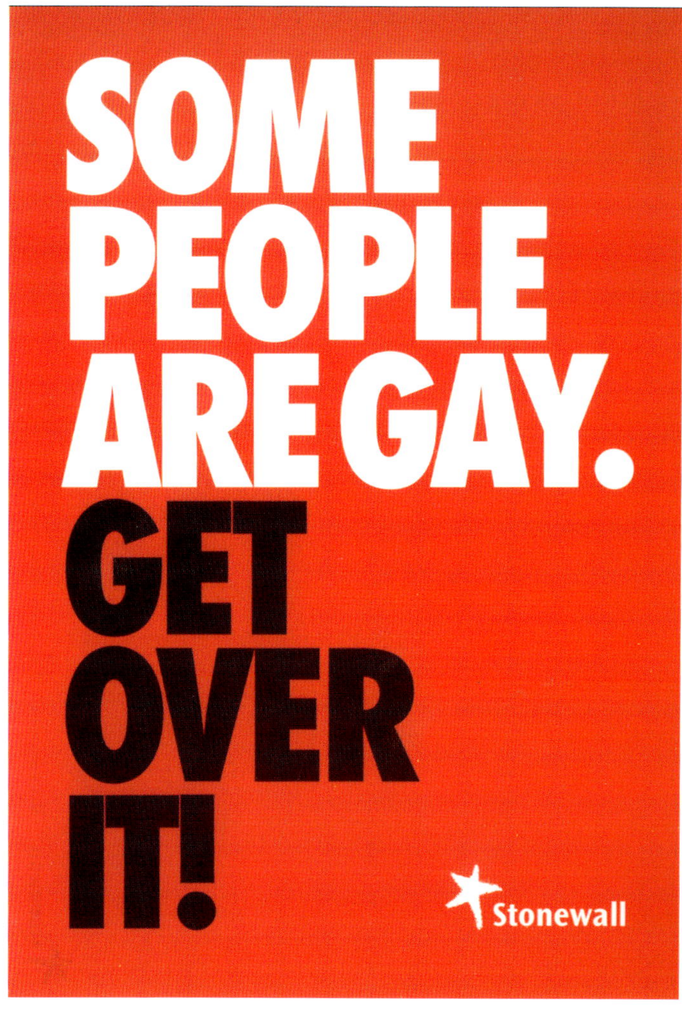

← *Libération* (Vive les Mariés),
23 April 2013
Artists: Pierre et Gilles
Newspaper: front page

The year 2001 brought full rights of marriage to same-sex couples in the Netherlands, instilling the possibility that more countries would follow. So they did, although it wasn't necessarily easy. France achieved it in 2013, despite protests from right-wing groups. The newspaper, *Libération*, celebrated with a front-page art portrait by famed duo Pierre et Gilles: Pierre Commoy, photographer and Gilles Blanchard, painter. Produced in their fantasy-style, with a touch of the erotic, the image presents a life-size portrayal of the two figurines that stand on top of the wedding cake. The face floating behind them is the then French President François Hollande, who signed the legislation into law. The UK soon followed, with the first same-sex marriages taking place in March 2014. Finally, on 25 June, 2015, the White House was illuminated with the rainbow colours, as a Supreme Court ruling sanctioned same-sex marriage in all 50 states. By 2017, over two dozen countries had legalised same-sex marriage.

↗ **We Will Not Live In Fear (the Pride**
↗ **Parade)** date unknown
Photographer unknown
Photograph

The first Gay Pride March took place in New York City in 1970, the year following the Stonewall Riots. As time went on, it was copied in other countries: an opportunity to assert not only LGBT presence, but also to celebrate it in a colourful and joyful way. It is now a massive celebration in many countries around the world; 'Pride London', normally held in June, now expects to attract an estimated one million visitors. The great international connector is the use of the rainbow gay pride flag designed by San Francisco artist Gilbert Baker in 1978, which remains the modern LGBT flag of six coloured stripes.

→ **Some People Are Gay. Get Over It!** *c.*2014
Stonewall
Poster, postcard, sticker

Stonewall (named after the 1969 riots) is a forceful LGBT rights charity in the UK, founded in 1989. Its attitude, with regard to promotional material, is necessarily aggressive and confident, and matches its motto: 'Acceptance Without Exception'.

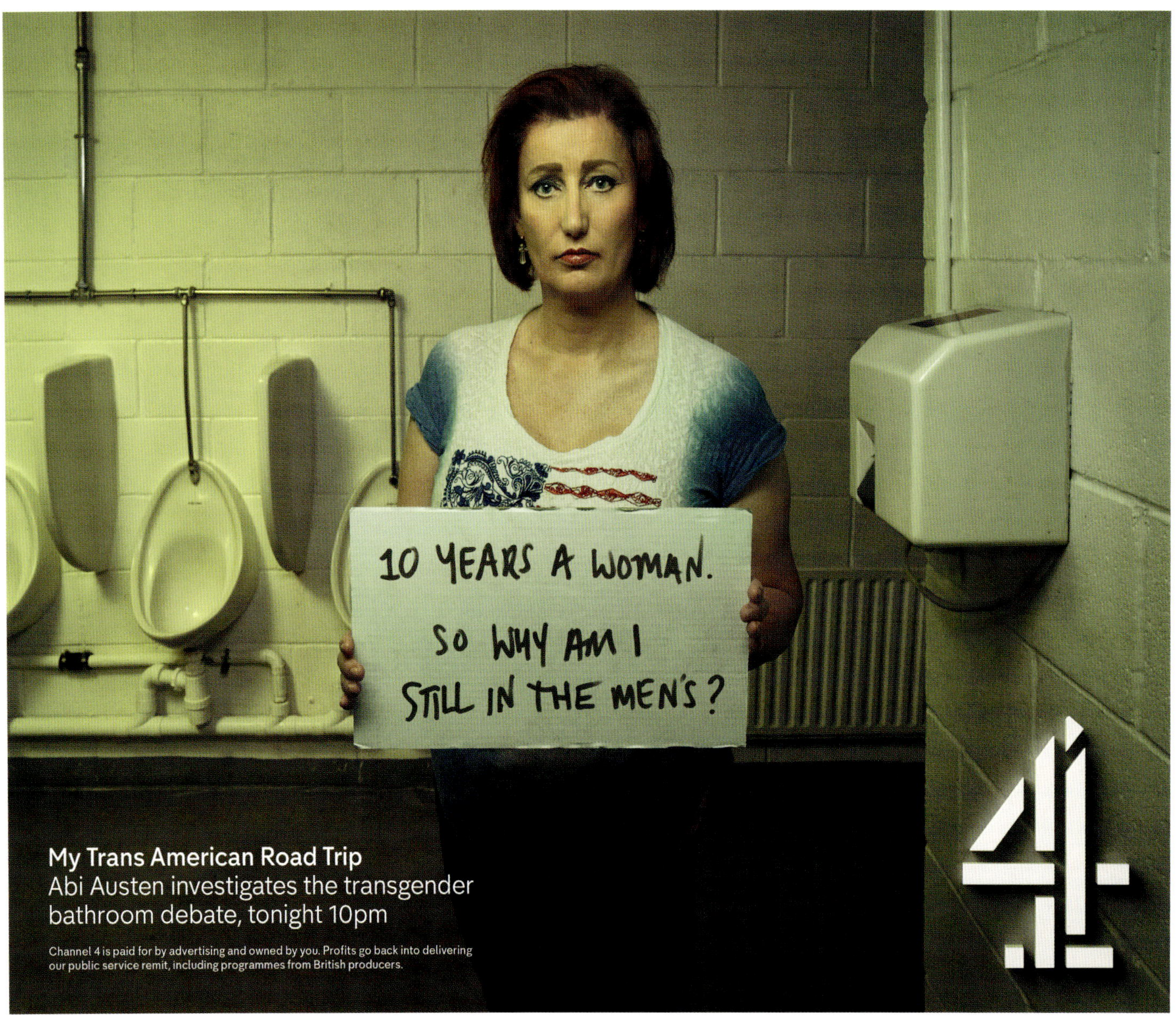

My Trans American Road Trip 2016
Channel Four and Documentary Filmmaker Abigail Austen
Television promotion and newspaper
advertisement

As America's mood was shifting slowly
to the right in the lead-up to the 2016
presidential election, North Carolina
became the first state to pass the Bathroom
Bill in March of that year. The controversial
Bathroom Bill stated that people must only
use public toilets of the gender stated on
their birth certificate. It became a cause
célèbre for many people including LGBT
activists who viewed it as discrimination
against transgender people. It would
also become an element in the political
battleground of the presidential election, as
North Carolina was a 'swing state' (capable
of shifting the country's majority-vote
from Democrat to Republican). Armed
with a film crew, Abigail Austen – British
foreign affairs correspondent, transgender
woman and LGBT activist – travelled
through North Carolina, confronting the
prejudiced attitudes that gave birth to such
discrimination and the lives being damaged
by it. The resulting documentary, 'My
Trans American Road Trip', presented an
emotional, and at times frightening, view of
an America that is rarely seen by the rest of
the world.

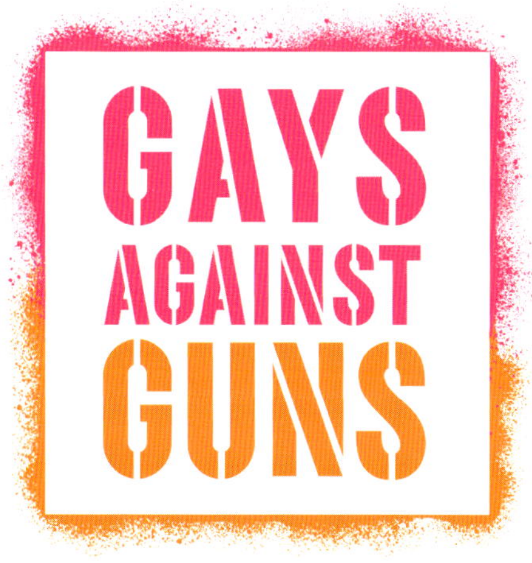

**Gays Against Guns (GAG) Logo
and 'Die-In' Action** 2016
Logo Artists: Gays Against Guns
Photograph: Photographer unknown

In June 2016, a gunman with a military-style assault rifle opened fire on clubbers at Pulse, an LGBT nightclub in Orlando, Florida: 49 people lost their lives, 53 were wounded. News of the incident sparked the formation of a collective in New York City calling themselves Gays Against Guns (GAG), founded by John Grauwiler, Kevin Hertzog and Brian Worth. Their members include several veterans of the US activist group known as ACT UP, which in the late 1980s combatted government inaction on AIDS. GAG began a campaign of civil disobedience and direct action against gun companies and their supporters. Campaigns have included 'die-in' actions: for example, a protest including people of all ages, was led by dozens of silent, white-veiled figures carrying placards with the names and faces of victims from Pulse, as well as some of the 20 six- and seven-year olds massacred at Sandy Hook Elementary School, Connecticut in 2012. The procession headed for the offices of BlackRock, one of the biggest investors in gun companies. On arrival, GAG members stormed the BlackRock offices, holding placards saying 'Gun$ sell. People die. $tock soars.' They then performed a 'die-in' in the foyer with 12 protesters lying on the floor to represent 12 people killed in a cinema in Colorado in 2012, with weapons made by gun companies BlackRock supports. GAG also targets brands that partner with the National Rifle Association (NRA), including car rental companies, telling them to end their relationship with the NRA, or the LGBT community would end their relationship with them. GAG's protests are necessarily visceral and direct, in an attempt to take on America's gun death epidemic.

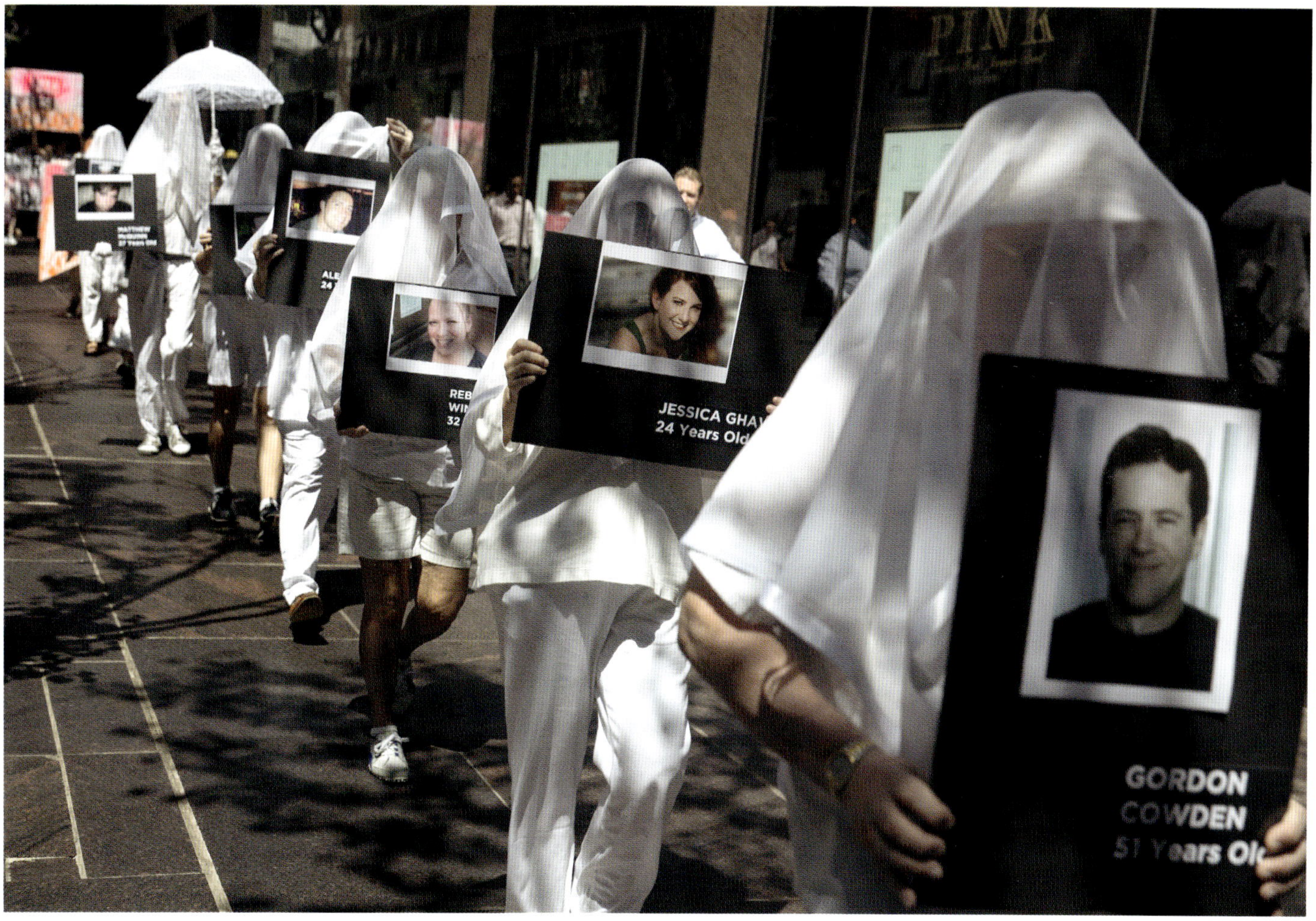

Black Lives Matter

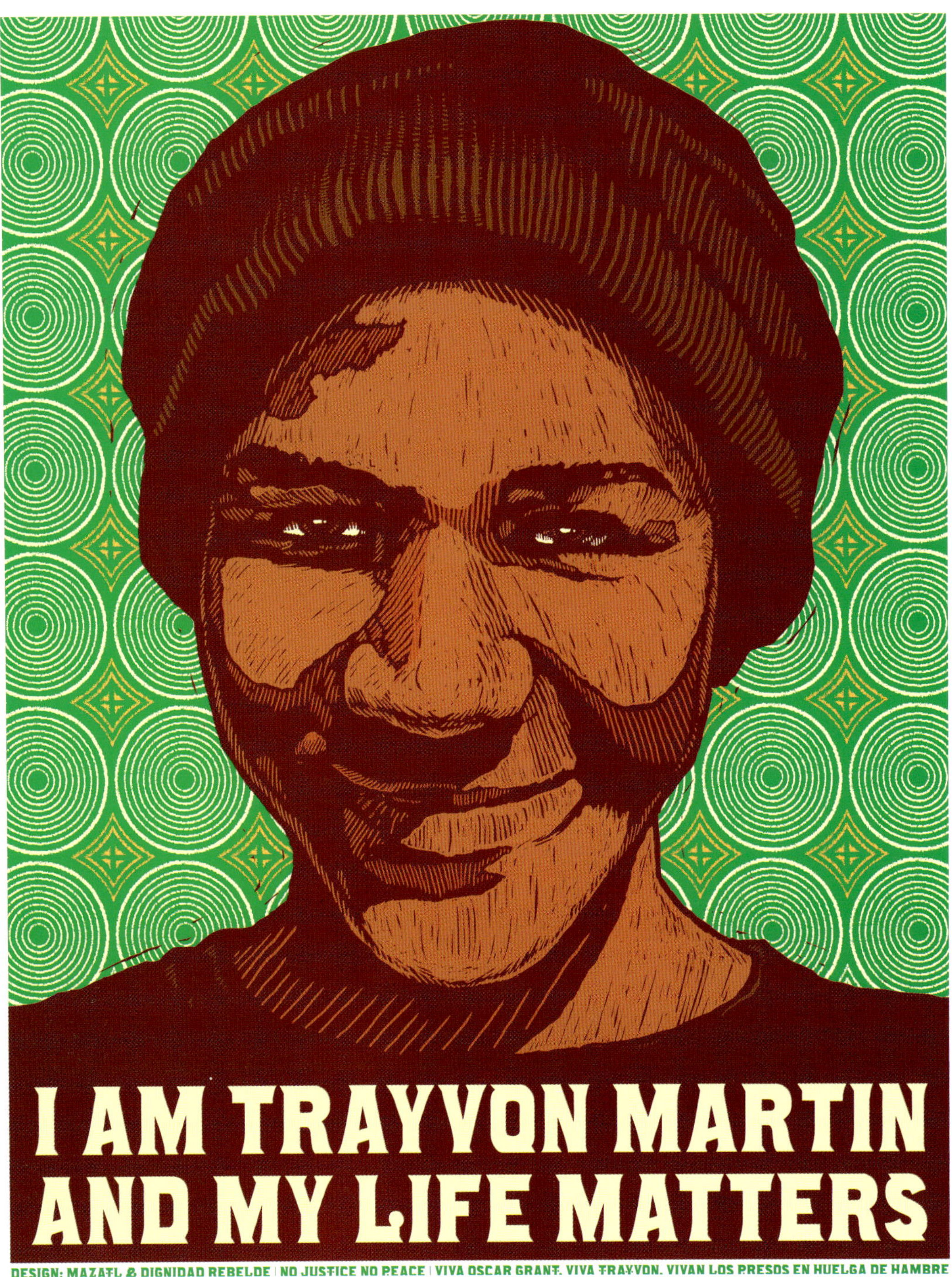

I Am Trayvon Martin 2013
Artists: Jesus Barraza, Mazatl and
Melanie Cervantes
Poster

People took to the streets to protest when a black, unarmed 17-year-old named Trayvon Martin was shot and killed by neighbourhood watchman George Zimmerman in Sanford, Florida in February 2012. Zimmerman was arrested, charged and upon facing a jury, received a verdict of 'not guilty'. This incident and many others sparked the founding in 2013 of the solidarity network #BlackLivesMatter by three radical black organizers, Alicia Garza, Patrisse Cullors and Opal Tometi. It was intended as an affirmation of humanity while also providing a badly needed focus on how black lives were unjustly targeted and terminated. Gathering strength from its activities both online and off (attending protests), it has now become the Black Lives Matter Global Network, a movement with a website carrying actions taking place internationally while sounding a clear call for involvement and activism: Take Action, Fight for Black Lives.

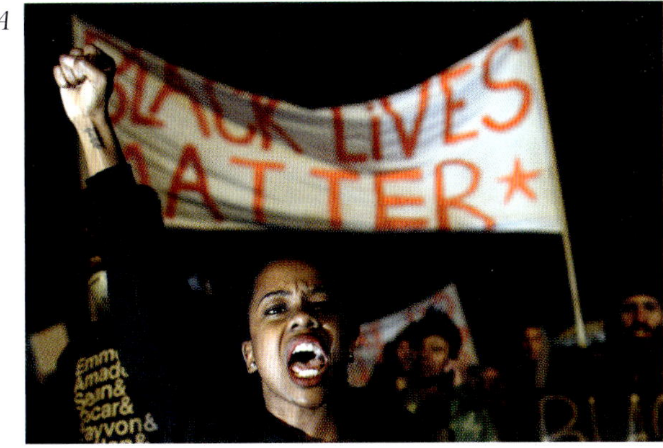

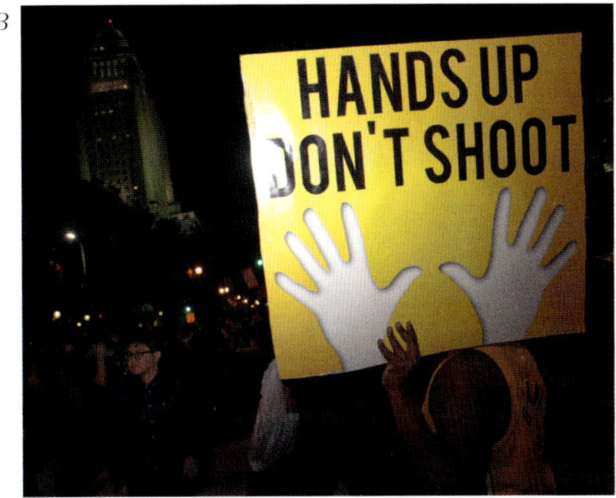

Signs of Protest 2014–15

← *(Image A)* Photographer: Jewel Samad
↙ *(Image B)* Photographer: David Bro
↓ *(Image C)* Photographer: Patrick T. Fallon;
Protester: actress Logan Browning
Photographs

In the summer of 2014, police officer Darren Wilson shot and killed 18-year-old Michael Brown as he left a convenience store in Ferguson, Missouri. Protests ensued, with protesters raising their hands in surrender, chanting 'Hands Up, Don't Shoot', believed to be (and later disputed) the final words spoken by Brown before he was shot. Nevertheless, the phrase became a national rallying cry for both media and protesters thereafter. That same summer, protesters were given yet another focus for their anger when, in New York City, police placed another man, Eric Garner, in a chokehold and held him down while he gasped 'I can't breathe' (allegedly 11 times) and then died. The years 2014 and 2015 saw too many young black men dying at the hands of police who faced little or no accountability or punishment, adding fuel to a movement – Black Lives Matter – that still campaigns for social justice.

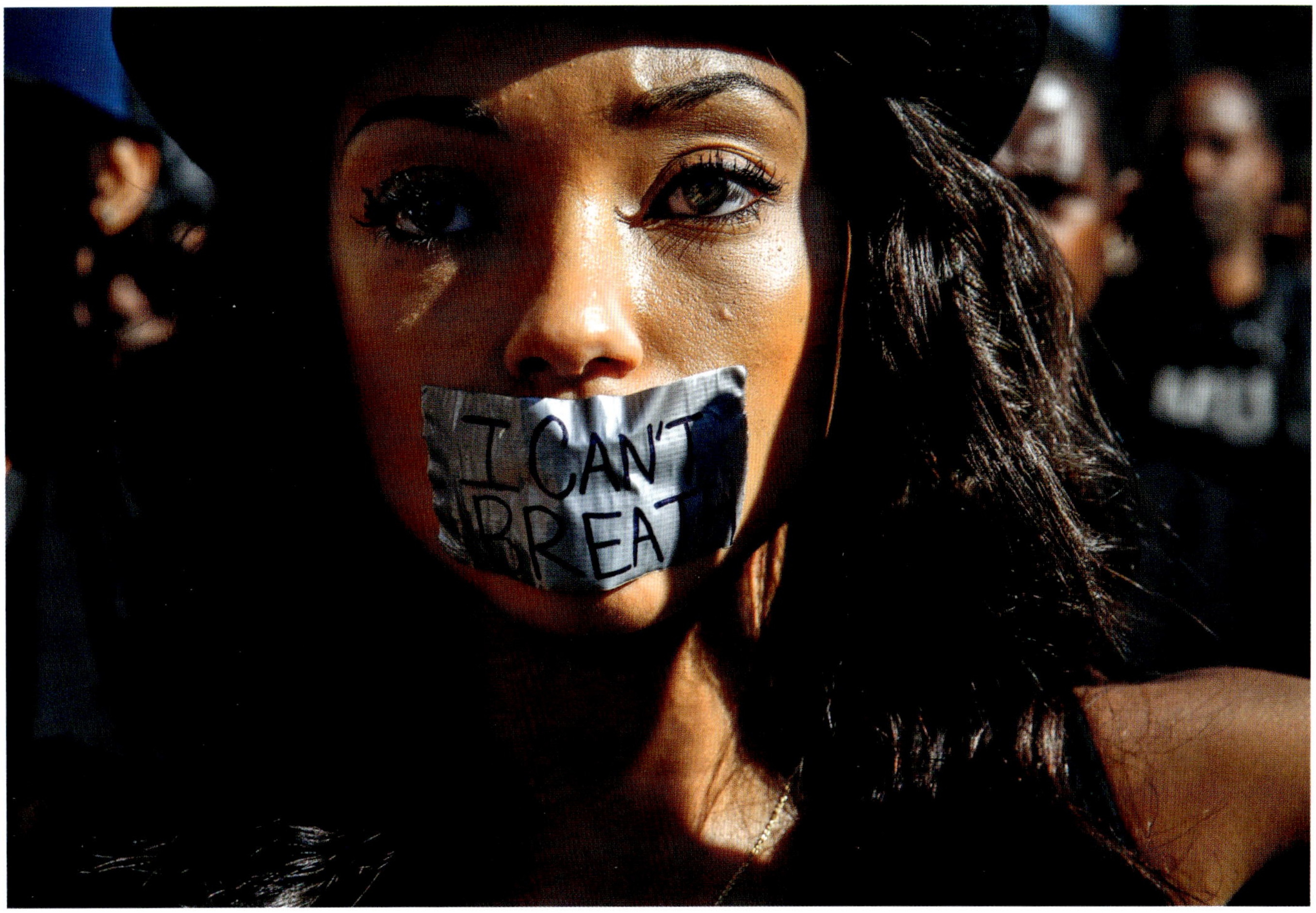

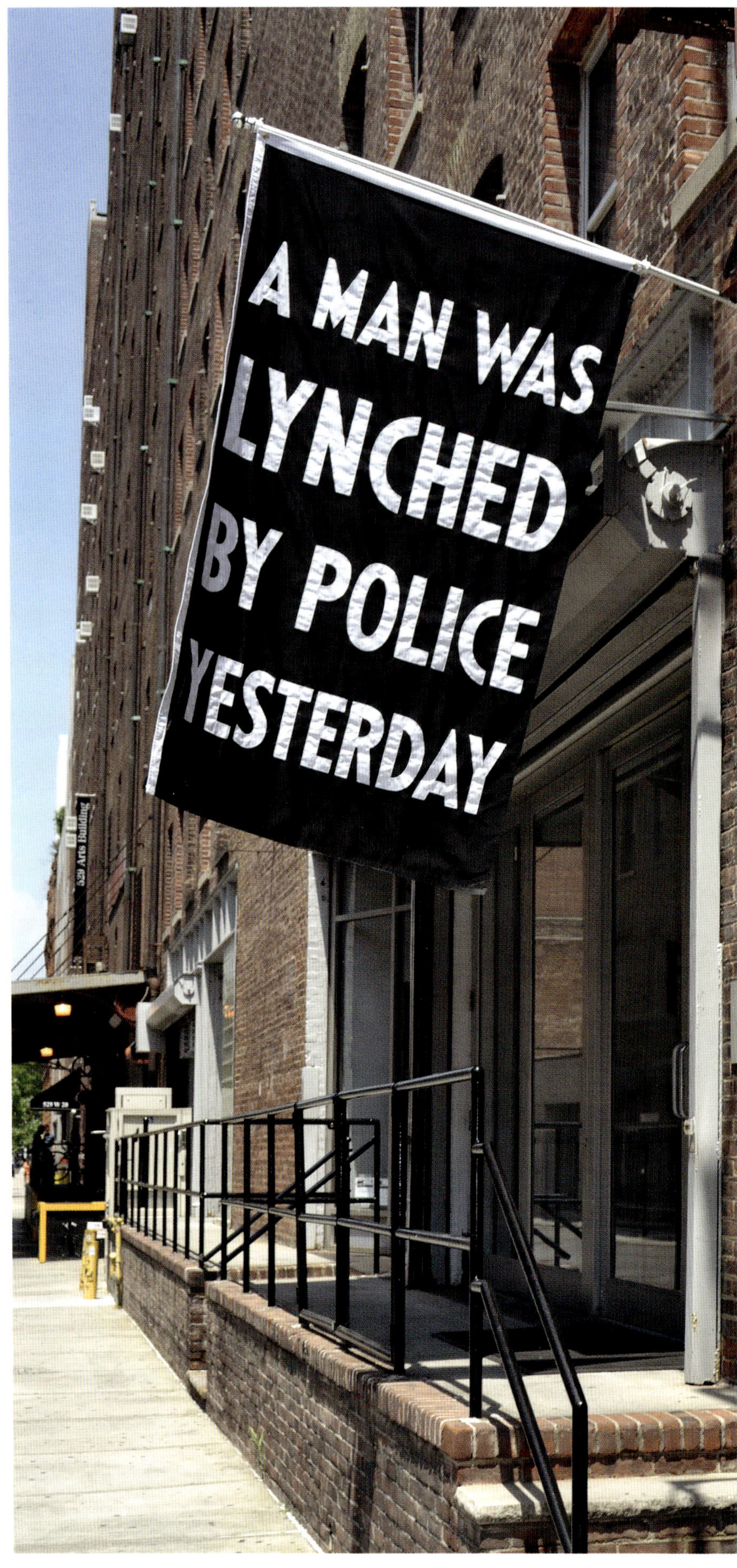

A Man Was Lynched By Police
Yesterday 2015
Artist: Dread Scott
Flag

Dread Scott's political art often references history, which he then relates to the present. Or, in his words, he is 'propelling history forward'. Even his professional name references the historic Dred Scott case of 1857, when Scott (a slave) appealed to the Supreme Court for his freedom but was told that all blacks, slaves or free, were not and could never be citizens of the United States: a highly controversial response that foreshadowed the Civil War. In 2015, unarmed black man Walter Scott (no relation) was stalked and shot dead by a policeman in South Carolina. In response, Dread Scott produced an updated version of a flag that the NAACP (National Association for the Advancement of Colored People) flew from its New York headquarters the day after a race-based lynching (hanging) of a black person. This procedure continued throughout the period 1920–38. The NAACP flag stated simply 'A Man Was Lynched Yesterday'; Dread Scott added the words 'By Police'. Thus the horrors of the past still haunt us today. The updated flag highlights the racist police terror that has prevailed, both then and now, and the importance of resistance.

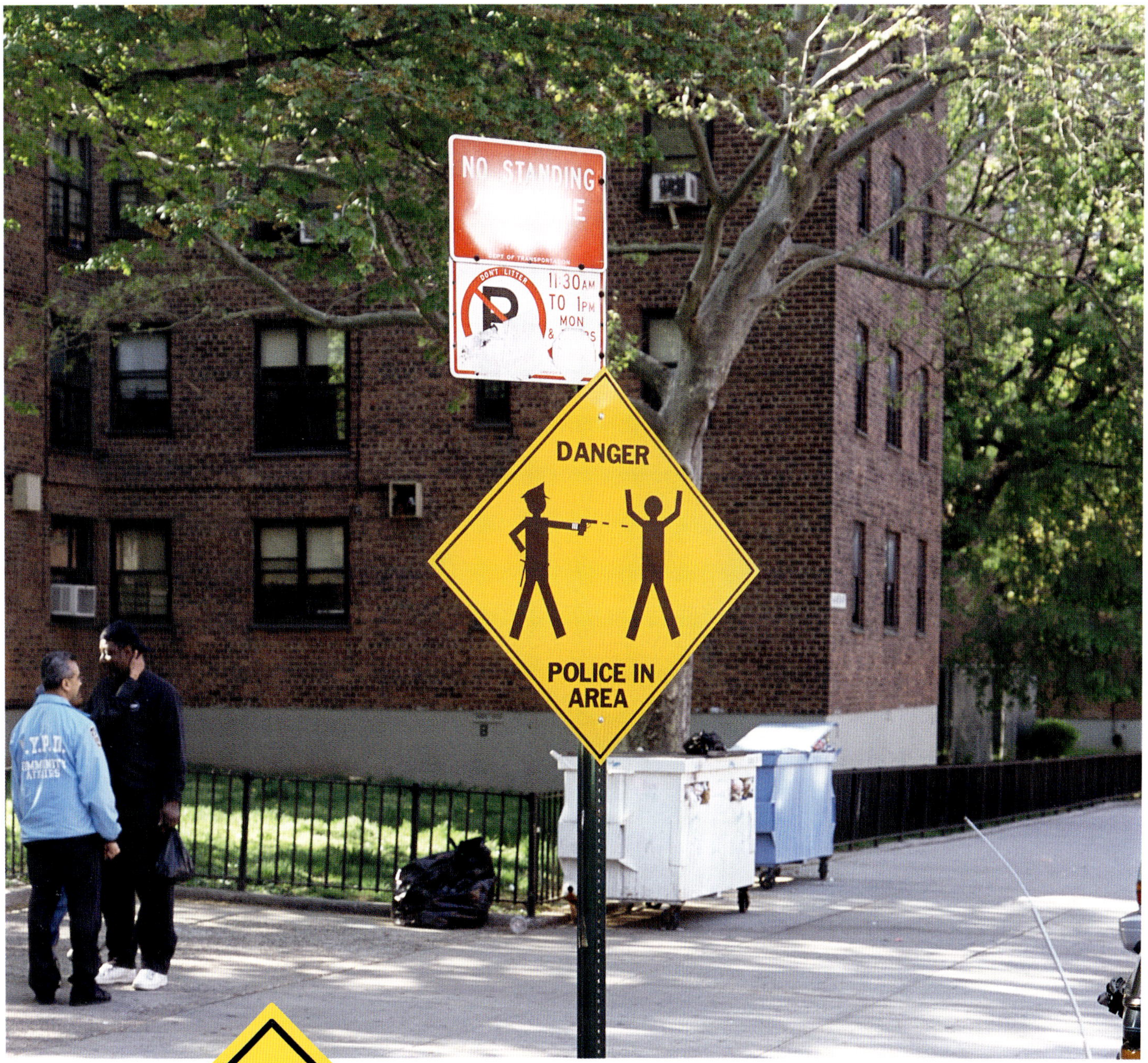

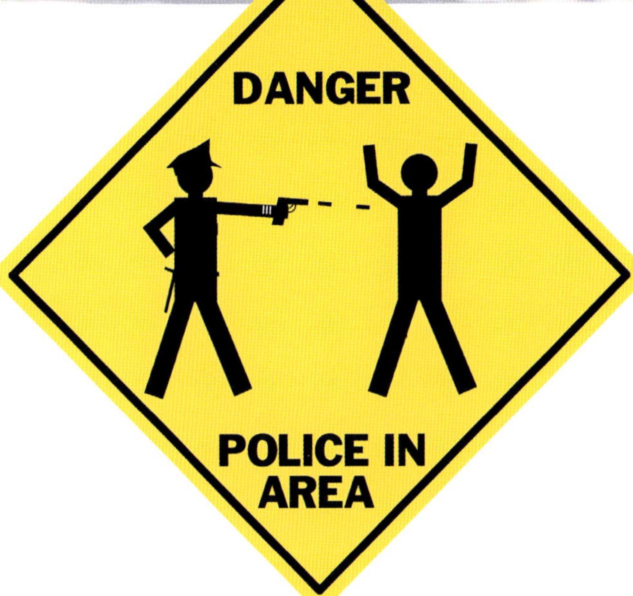

Sign of the Times 2001
Artist: Dread Scott
Screenprint on aluminium
Photograph 2003

Dread Scott installed his 'Sign of the Times' on a street
in Fort Greene, Brooklyn, five days after – and on
the site – where Floyd 'Fly Ty' Quinones was killed in
April 2003. Apparently neighbours loved the project
and suggested 'Danger: Police in Area' stickers. The
work was only on view for eight hours, then removed.
This project preceded Scott's flag project 'A Man Was
Lynched By Police Yesterday' by 12 years: a shocking
reminder of the on-going nature of the problem of
black killings by police.

Women's Rights

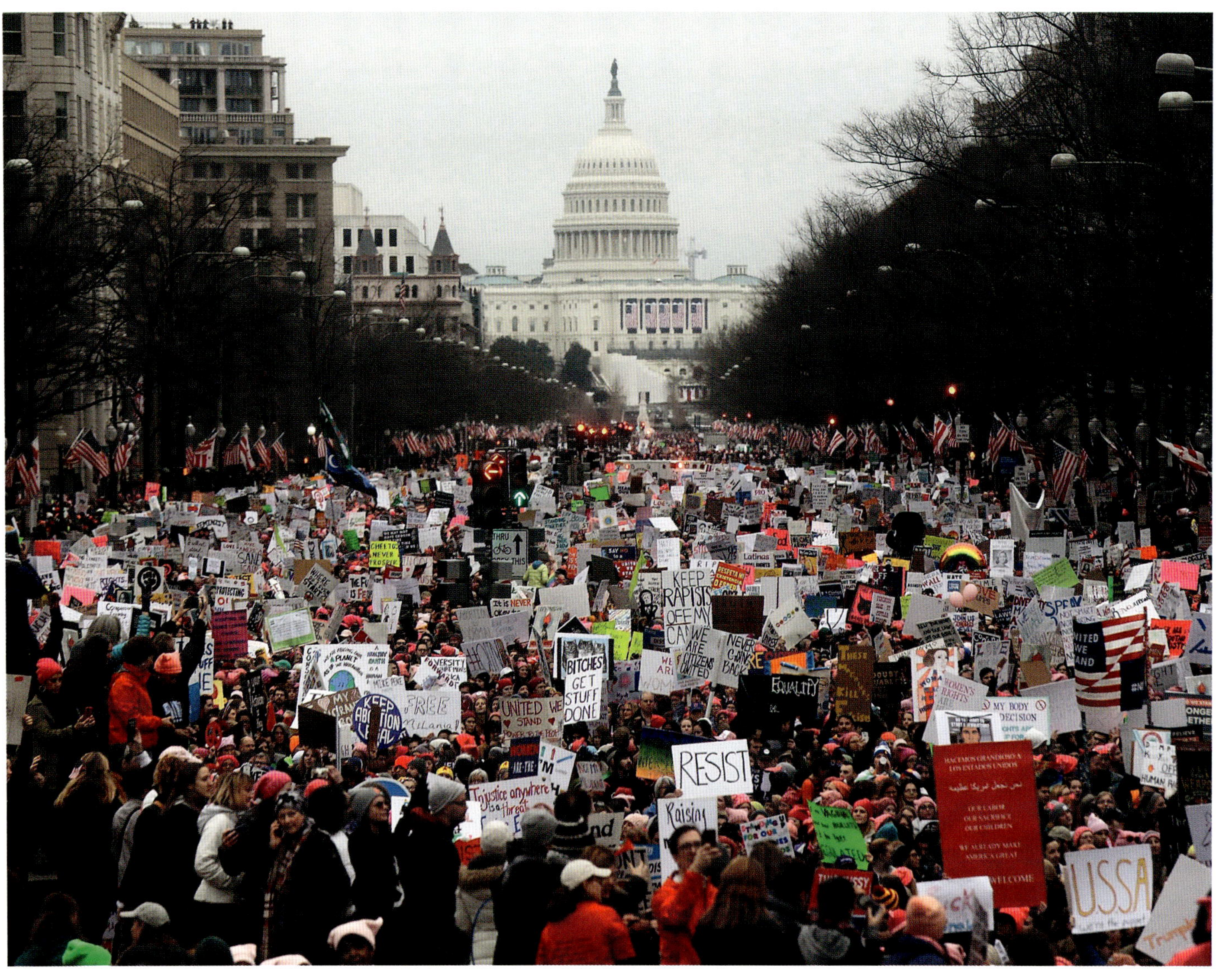

The Women's March on Washington, D.C. January 21 2017
Photographer: Mario Tama
Photograph

The day after President Donald Trump's inauguration as US President (Saturday, 21 January 2017), women all over the world marched for women's rights and in protest against his sexist attitudes. During Trump's election campaign, allegations were made that he groped women (which he denied), while comments caught on microphone that he dismissed as 'locker room talk' had caused extreme offence, particularly his comment about women generally: 'Grab them by the pussy'. Over half a million protesters joined the March on Washington, an estimated 100,000 marched in London alone (with more in nine other British cities), plus 600 'sister marches' took place around the globe in cities reaching from Europe, Africa and Asia to Australia and New Zealand. Groups of travellers even sent photos of themselves holding placards and signs of solidarity from Antarctica. The last global count of protesters reached five million. Although celebrities and other notables made speeches in Washington, London and elsewhere, the real stars were the marchers (women, men, families) and the humour they applied to messages carried on signs and placards. There were 'pussy-grabbing' retorts such as 'This pussy grabs back!' as well as pink knitted pussyhats with cats-ears worn by the crowds, courtesy of a knitting pattern posted online. Some signs hinted at earlier phases of feminism: 'Now you've pissed off grandma' (followed by an obscene gesture), or 'I can't believe we still have to fight for this shit'. Others were just funny – 'Does this ass (drawing of Trump) make my sign look big?' – or threatening: 'History has its eyes on YOU'.

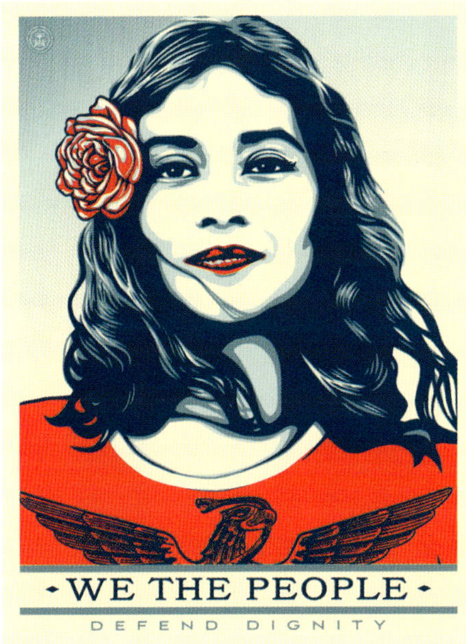
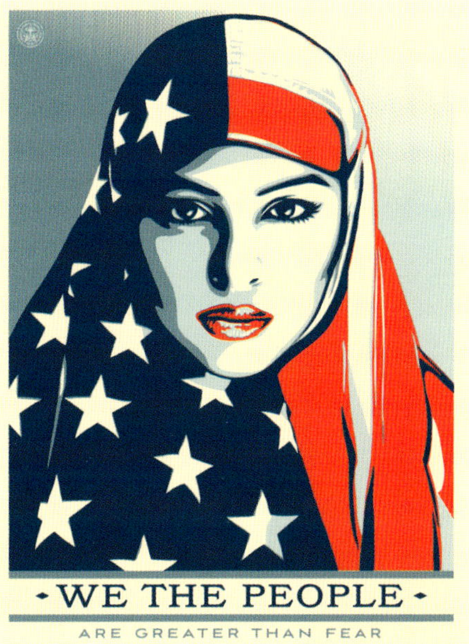
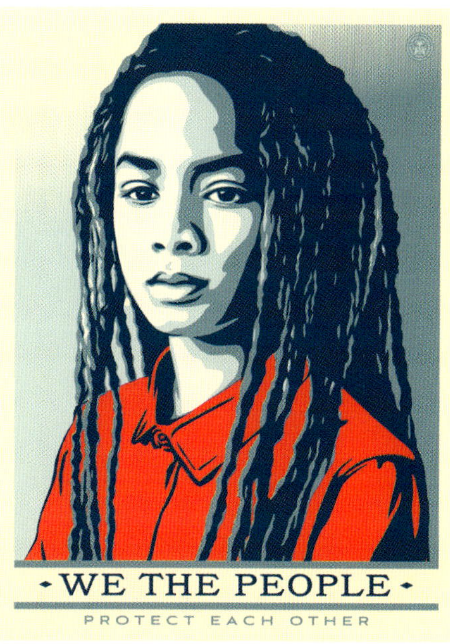

↑ **We the People** 2017
Shepard Fairey
Poster series

Street artist and illustrator Shepard Fairey
designed the 'We the People' series of three posters
for the Women's March of January 2017. Produced
in collaboration with the Amplifier Foundation,
the posters protested against President-elect
Donald Trump by depicting a Muslim woman, a
Latino woman and an African-American girl (one
image per poster). They all represented groups
that Fairey thought might be excluded or have a
hard time in Trump's America. A large number
were crowdsourced and printed, as well as being
downloadable for free. They resonated strongly
with the marchers, and were not only ubiquitous
in the Washington and London marches but also
maintained a strong presence in marches around
the world.

→ **A Woman's Place is in the Resistance** 2017
Hayley Gilmore (Ladies Who Design)
Poster

Graphic designer Hayley Gilmore of 'Ladies
Who Design', based in Mississippi, USA created
this popular poster for the Women's March in
Washington or 'wherever you are' (free and
downloadable). The poster features General/
Princess Leia Organa from the *Star Wars* films as
a source of inspiration, and was also intended as a
tribute to the life and legacy of Carrie Fisher, the
actress who played Princess Leia, who died at the
end of 2016. It featured strongly in the Women's
March: London absolutely loved it.

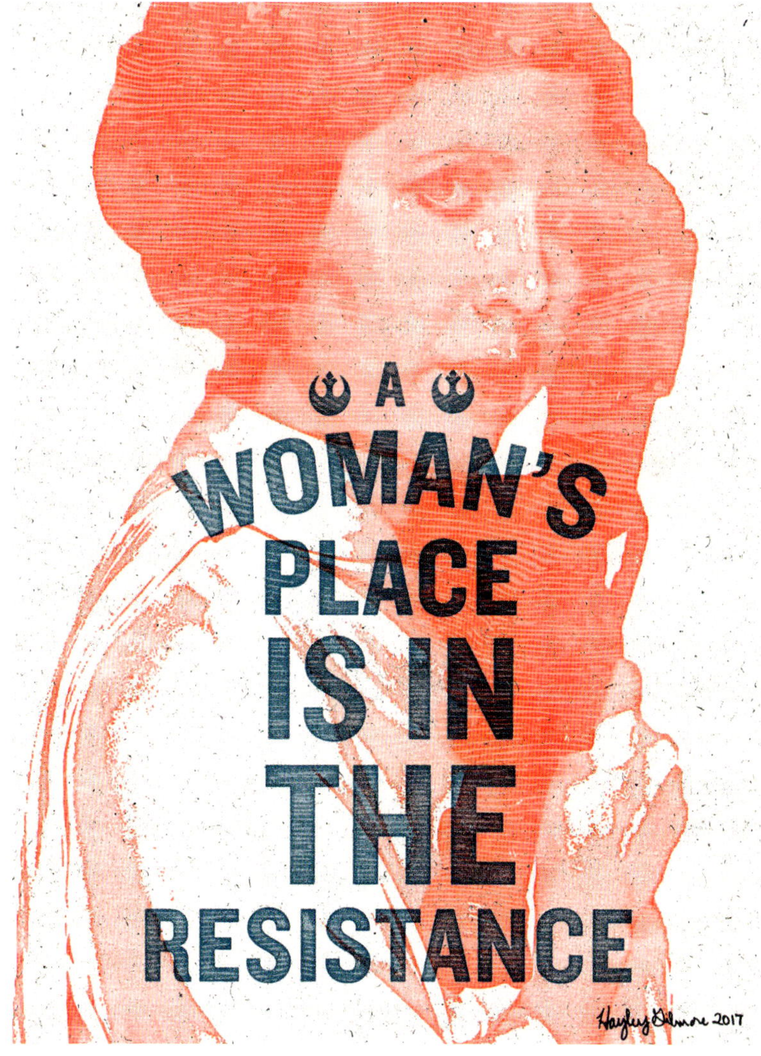

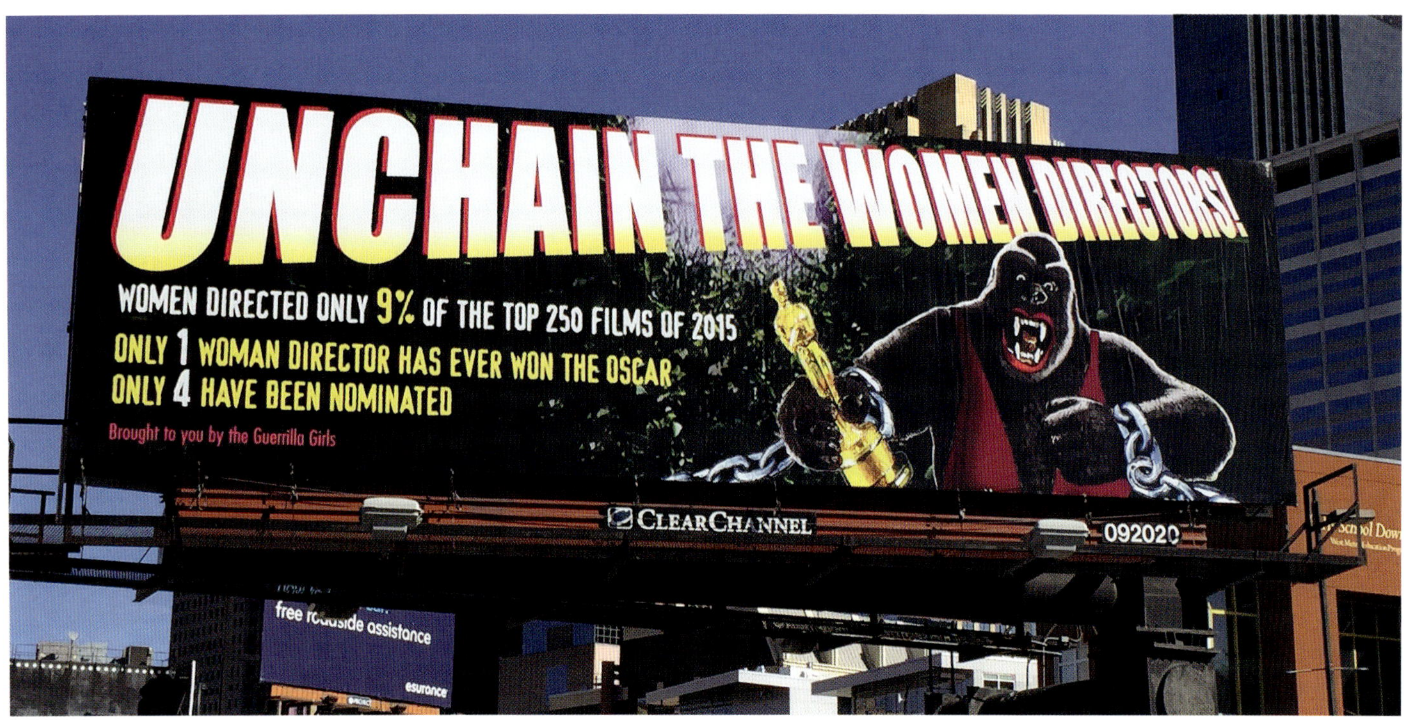

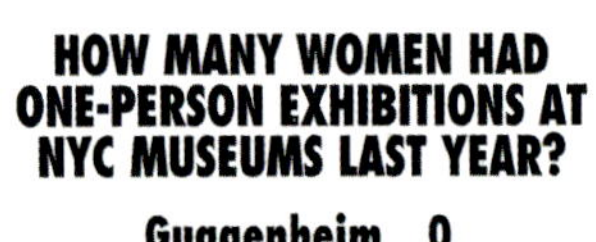

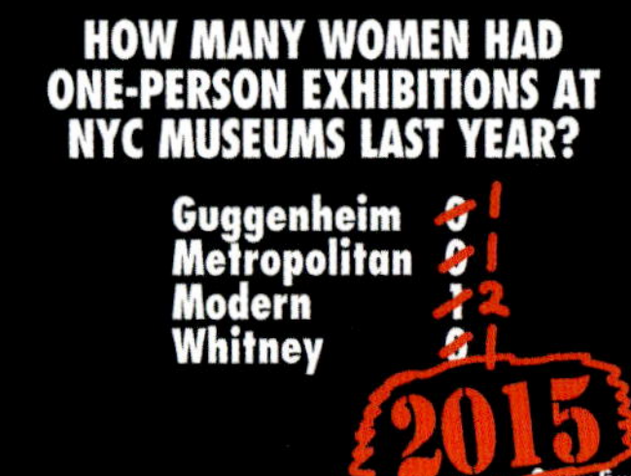

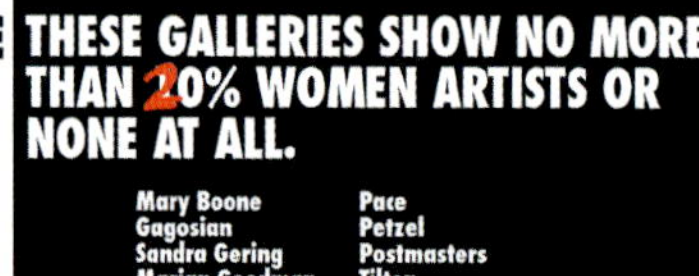

Guerrilla Girls, Art Activism 1985–2018
Guerrilla Girls
Posters and photograph

The US feminist art activist group known as Guerrilla Girls was founded in 1985, producing spontaneous street posters that exposed sexual and racial discrimination in the New York art world. They have managed to carry on their fight against discrimination in the art establishment by expanding their activities and their reach: they produce street projects and exhibitions (with museums) all over the world, publish books, make appearances, give lectures and have an in-your-face online presence. Plus their point of attack has not gone away; they still have good reason to protest against discrimination – with regard to gender, race and other issues – in the global art establishment and creative industries. Their anonymity, preserved by wearing gorilla masks or costumes, has ensured their longevity: apparently over 55 people have been members over the years, for varying lengths of time. Their current work, including the posters shown here, shouts out the lack of improvement. They may still have to wage guerrilla warfare for quite some time.

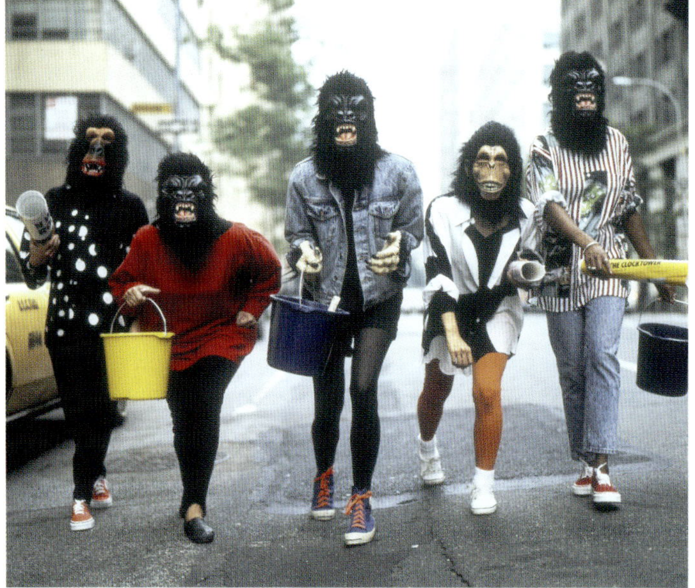

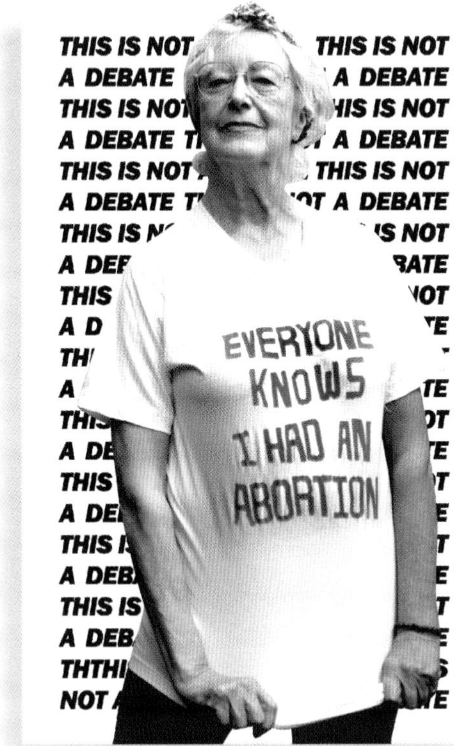

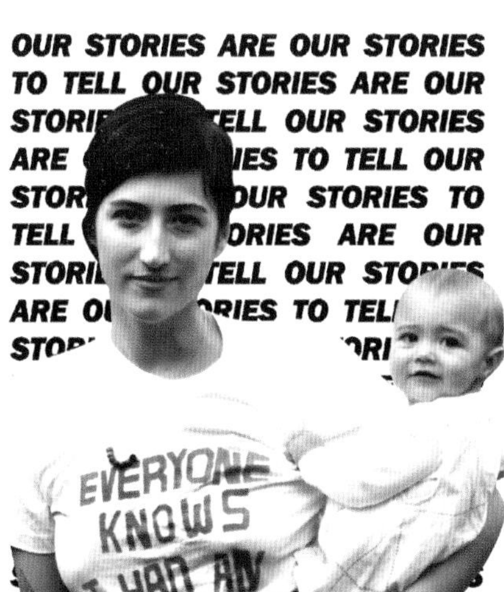

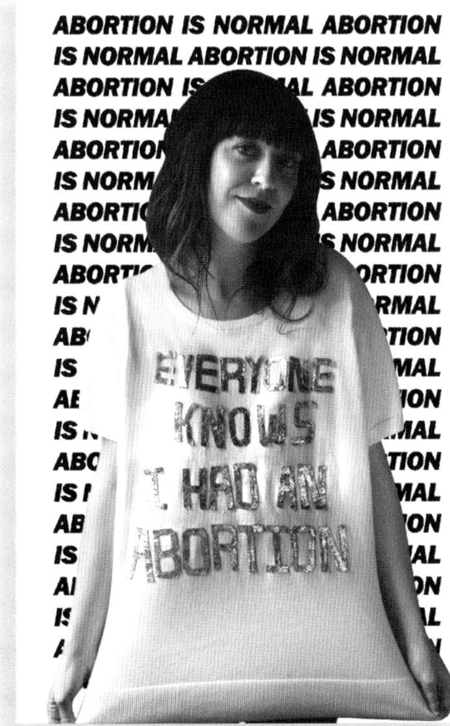

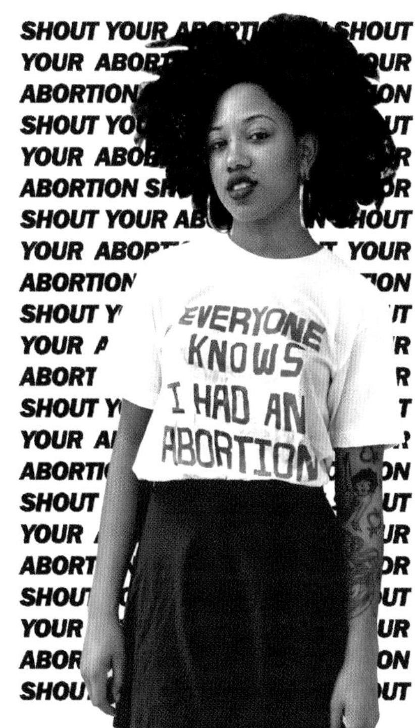

Shout Your Abortion 2015
Civilization
Hashtag, poster campaign and website

The hashtag #ShoutYourAbortion, launched by Seattle design practice Civilization in September 2015, aimed to create an empowering communication line where people could discuss their abortion experiences without fear or shame. Since then it has been used more than 250,000 times, some possibly discussing their experiences without shame for the first time in their lives. Civilization also designed a poster campaign and a website where visitors could upload videos, write, download material and learn.

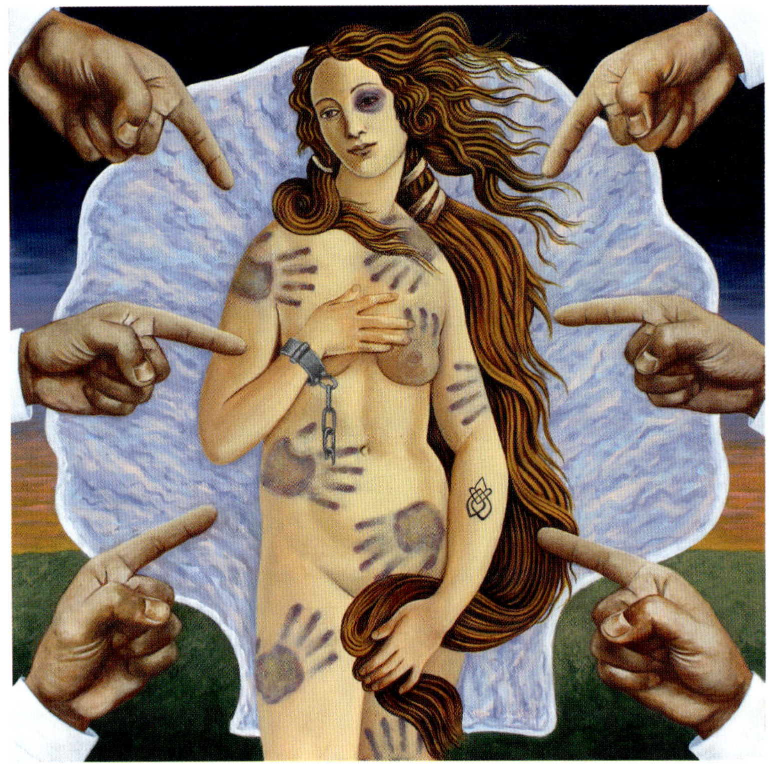

A Prisoner No More 2018
Artist: Laura Dumm
Painting / Digital image

The empowering flood of (verbal) responses generated on social media by the #MeToo movement also encouraged supportive visual statements. Suddenly the internet was full of #MeToo art: logos, illustrations and other imagery that called for an end to sexual abuse and demanded a review of the power imbalances that still existed in society. One of the most intriguing of these internet images was Cleveland artist Laura Dumm's surreal composition 'A Prisoner No More', in which a graphic rendering of Botticelli's *Venus* was plagued by timeless (including modern) symbols of male domination and physical assault. It signalled that such behaviour has been going on for centuries. Now it's time for change!

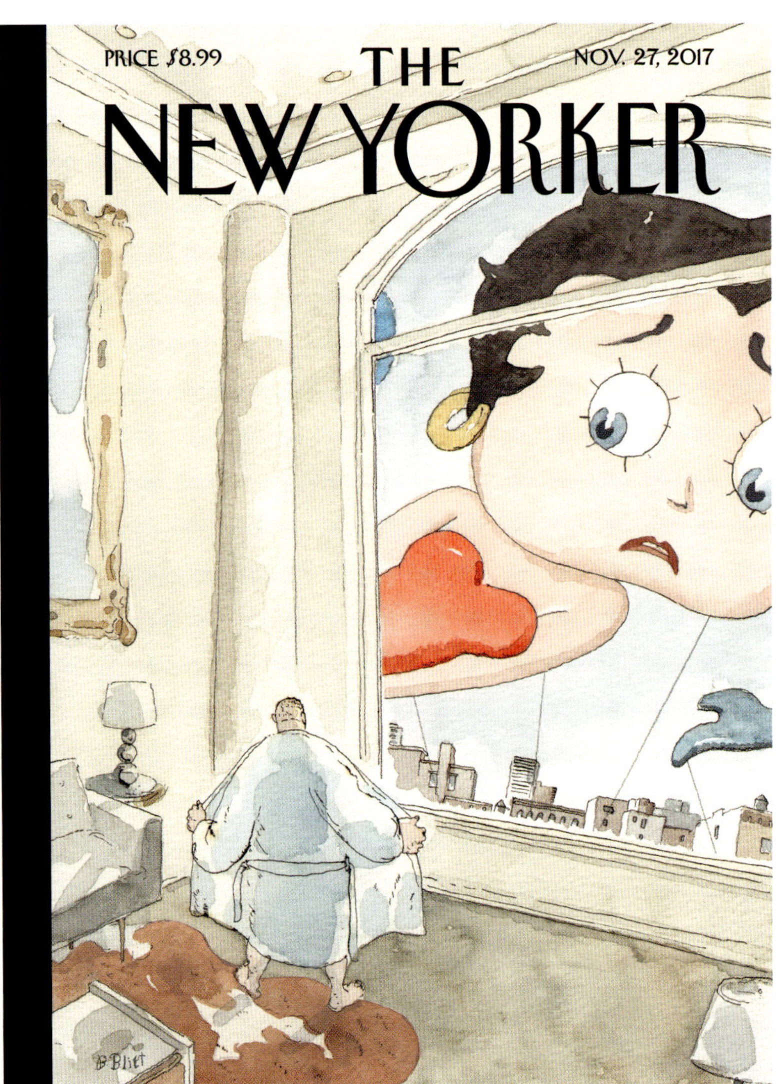

Nowhere to Hide 2017
Illustrator: Barry Blitt
Front cover: *The New Yorker*, 27 November, 2017

The #MeToo movement was initiated by an exposé of sexual assault allegations (by Hollywood actresses) against Hollywood mogul Harvey Weinstein. When actress Alyssa Milano made a call to action on social media, millions of women – and some men – felt empowered and used Twitter, Facebook and Instagram to disclose the harassment or abuse they faced in their own lives. It became a global discussion about men's behaviour towards women and the power imbalances regarding gender still present in society. This illustration harks back to the events that kicked off the movement: accounts, given by women, of Harvey Weinstein's misbehaviour (including where he would excuse himself from a one-to-one 'business' meeting and then return, to their shock, wearing nothing but a robe). The traditional annual New York Thanksgiving Day Parade, held at the end of November, is known for its massive balloons of cartoon characters, five or six storeys high. Here Betty Boop, the sexy, cinematic cartoon character of the 1930s and a well-loved Hollywood symbol, peers into a hotel window as she floats past and is 'flashed', to her dismay, by a figure resembling Harvey Weinstein.

And Nevertheless She Persisted 2017
Artist: Peter O. Zierlein
Poster

Here Peter O. Zierlein's sharp and colourful paper-cut technique packs a punch for the feminist cause. It relates to an incident in the US Senate in 2017, when Democratic Senator Elizabeth Warren objected to Trump's nomination of Senator Jeff Sessions as US Attorney General. She began reading out a rather long letter from 1986 by Coretta Scott King (wife of Martin Luther King), who opposed Sessions' earlier appointment as a federal judge. Senate Majority Leader Mitch McConnell interrupted Warren's speech, accusing her of violating a Senate rule that said, more or less, a Senator cannot demean another Senator. The Senate then voted along (Republican) party lines to stop Warren from continuing to speak during the debate. Following the vote, McConnell defended the action of the Senate by saying that Warren had violated a rule, had been warned and had been given an explanation … 'nevertheless, she persisted'. Warren later read King's letter in its entirety outside the Senate chamber. Produced as a Facebook video, it was viewed nearly 13 million times. At the same time, 'Nevertheless, she persisted' became a feminist rallying cry. To many it represented the age-old practice of silencing women, thereby excluding them from political discourse.

Eco-Disasters, Eco-Crimes

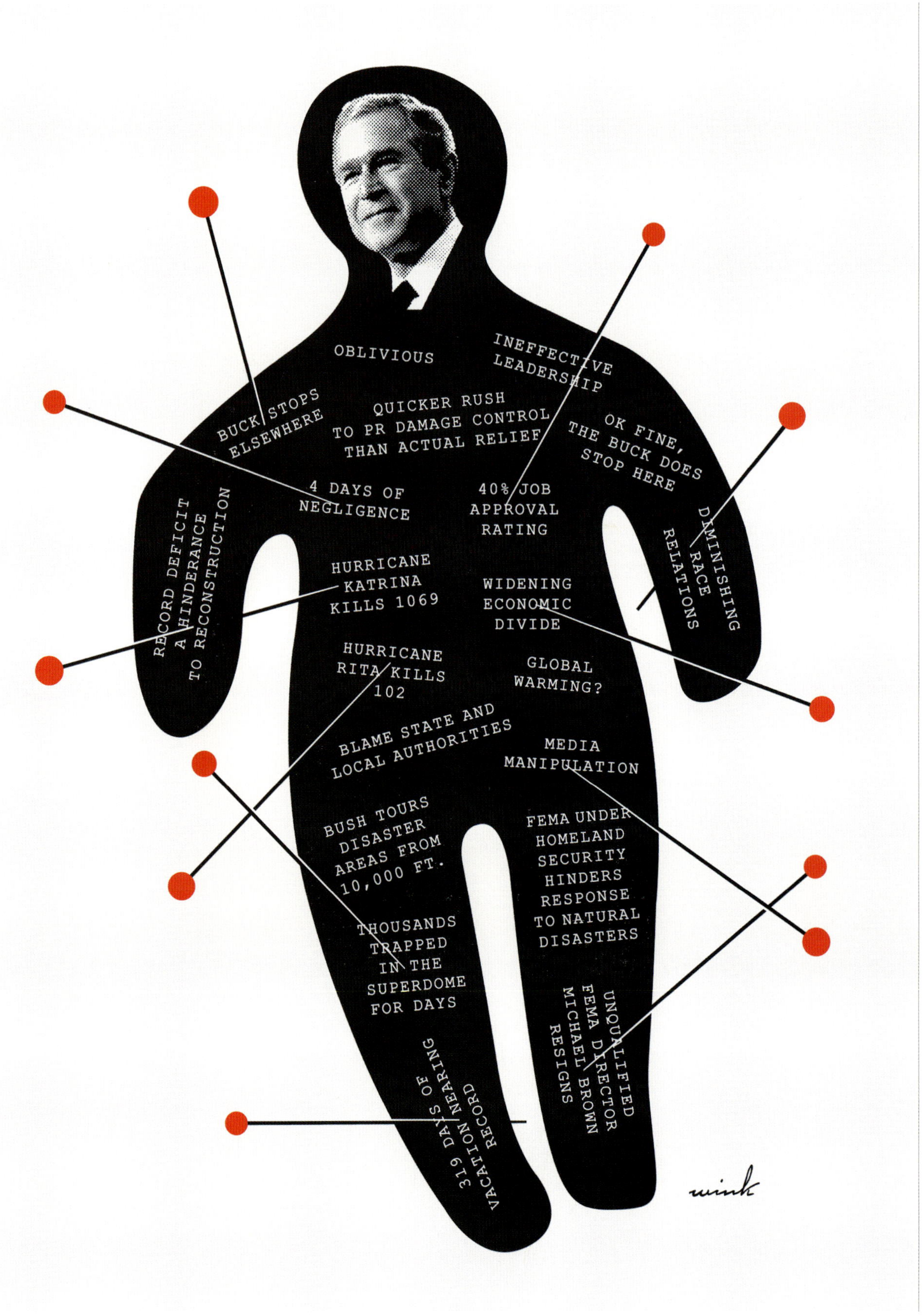

← **Voodoo** 2005
Artist: Richard Boynton (Wink design firm)
Poster

Environmentalism in the 21st century is no longer about warnings of what may happen; it is now more about how to deal with consequences. The roll call of disasters includes global warming (the rise of the earth's temperature resulting from human abuse of the earth's natural resources); the extinction of insects and animals; the pollution of air and water; the ubiquity of plastics in the ecosystems of both nature and the home; the changing weather patterns that bring overwhelming storms resulting from phenomena related to global warming; and more. Most, if not all, of the issues listed are now considered to be at crisis level. All can be said to involve human error or selfishness. The graphics on the following pages might initially appear satirical or humorous but they are all, in the end, damning in their call to action. When the monstrous Hurricane Katrina hit the US south coast in 2005, it obliterated much of New Orleans; the breaching of its levees left over 80% of the city submerged (often the poorer sections) and 80–100,000 residents stranded. Richard Boynton's poster aims harsh criticism at the shamefully slow response of President George W. Bush and federal agencies. The poster was part of the Hurricane Poster Project, raising funds to support Katrina's victims.

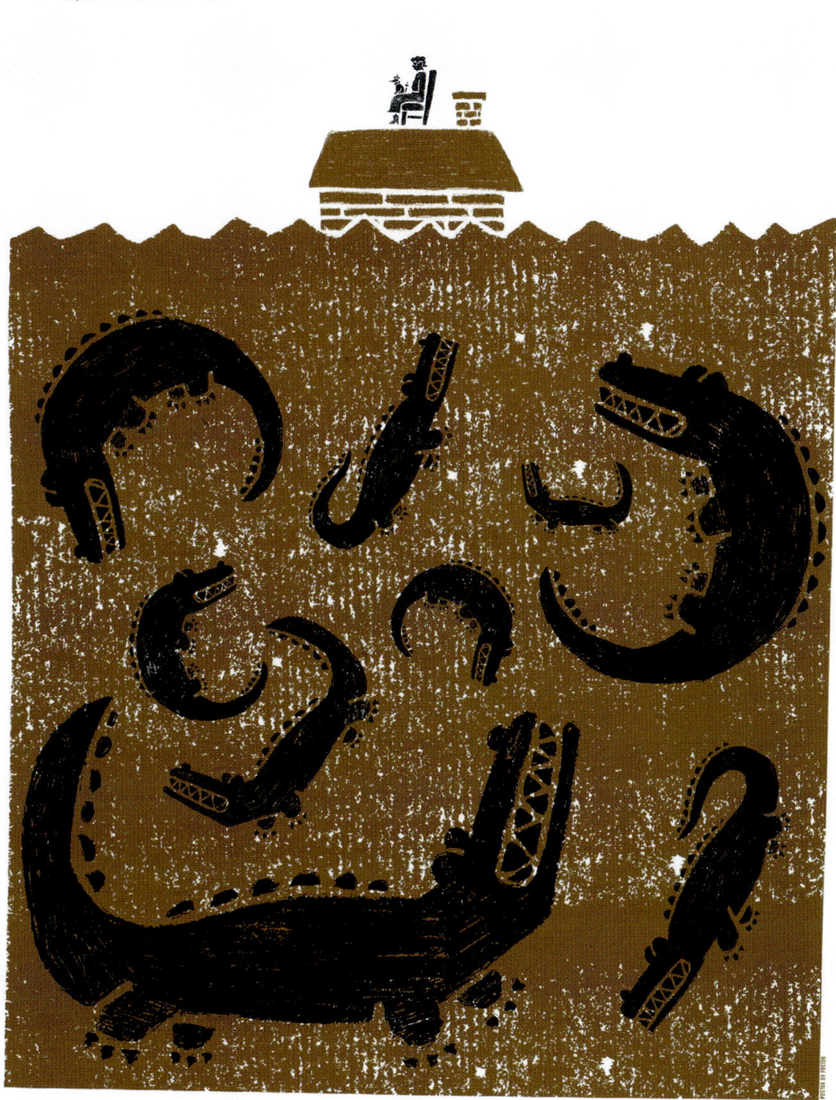

↑ **The Hurricane Poster Project** 2005
Artist: John Foster (Bad People Good Things)
Poster

This poster, designed and illustrated by John Foster, is another product of the US design community's Hurricane Poster Project, which raised money for the American Red Cross through sales of its posters. The quote that appears within the poster (in the top left corner) is recording artist Kanye West's famous statement to the media, 'George Bush doesn't care about black people', as some of the areas worst hit by Katrina were poor, black neighbourhoods. This poster was extremely popular, raised significant funds for the Red Cross, and hung in the Louisiana Statehouse.

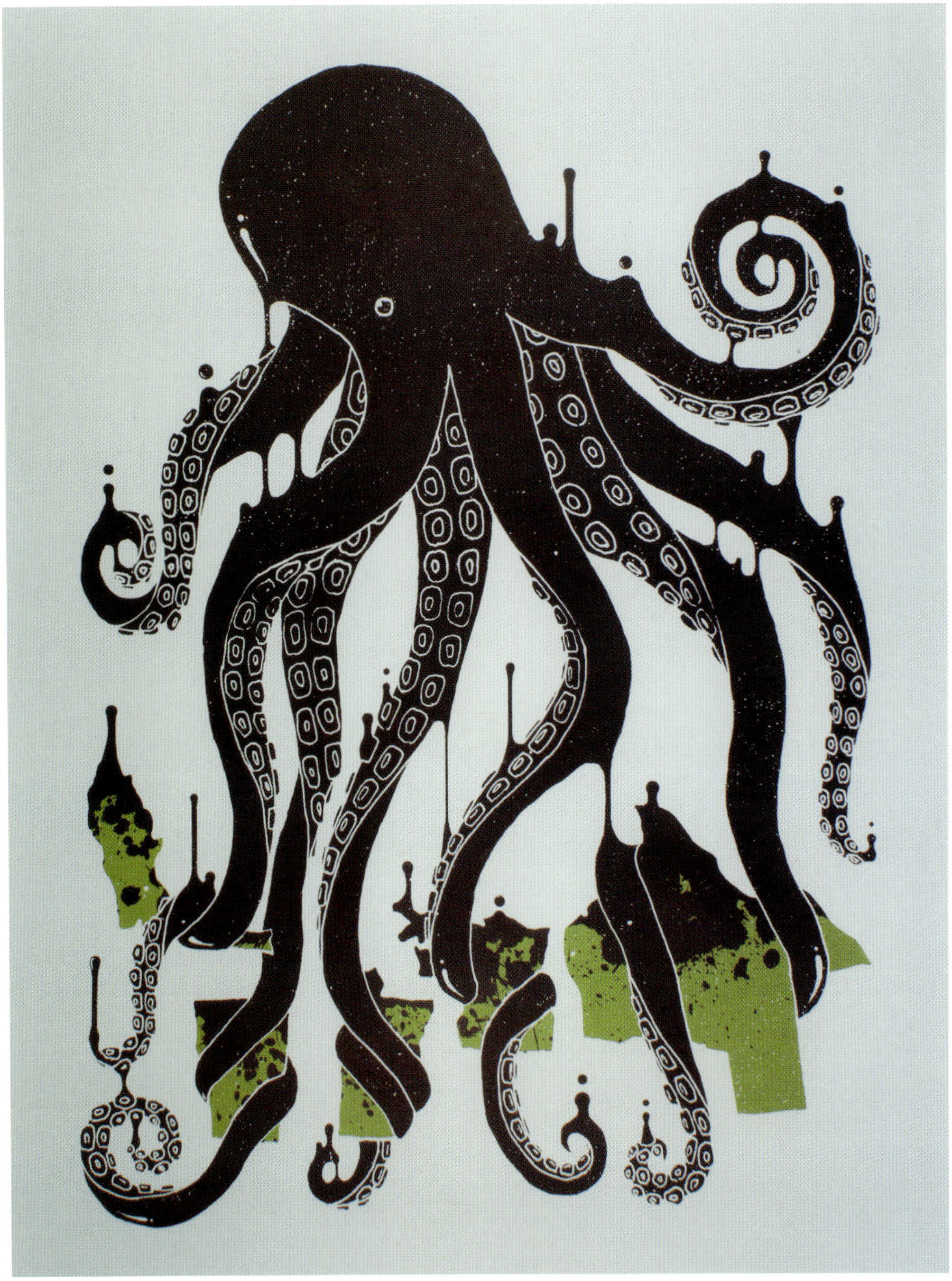

The octopus poster image, followed by the caption text.

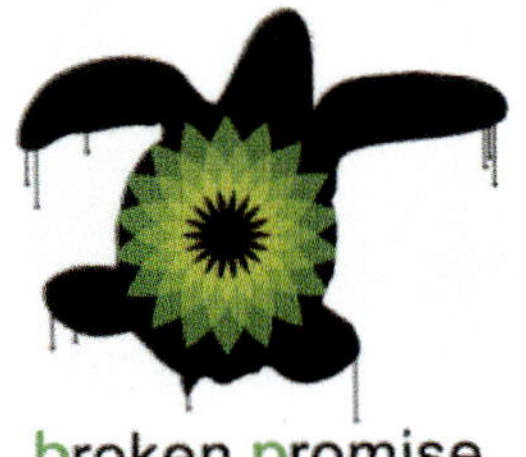

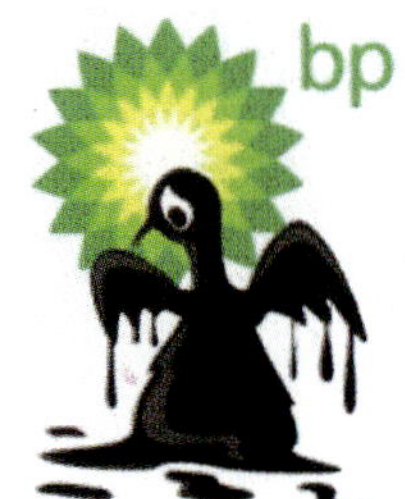

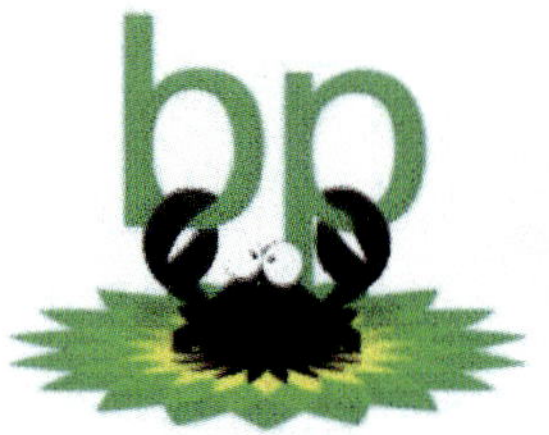

← **Octopus Vulgaris** 2010
Jude Landry
Poster

In April 2010, BP's Deepwater Horizon oil rig in the Gulf of Mexico exploded, producing the biggest crude oil spill in US-controlled waters to date. Jude Landry created this poster to raise awareness and funds for the oil spill clean-up. The leaked oil landed along the coastline of the Gulf States: Louisiana, Mississippi, Alabama, Florida and Texas. The poster also remarks on the fragility of the Gulf States' economies and the USA's dependence on feeding its oil needs.

↓ **Redesigns of BP's Logo** 2010
Varied artists
Logos

At the time of the BP Deepwater Horizon oil spill, a website that normally generated competitions for designing business logos created a competition to redesign BP's logo, as a 'culture-jamming' experience. A vast number of design contributors piled on to the site to (very skilfully) vent their ire. The exercise became one of the website's most successful competitions – ever.

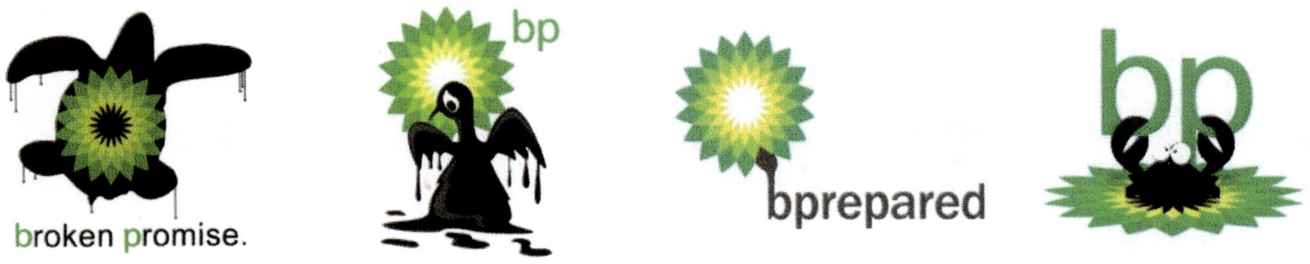

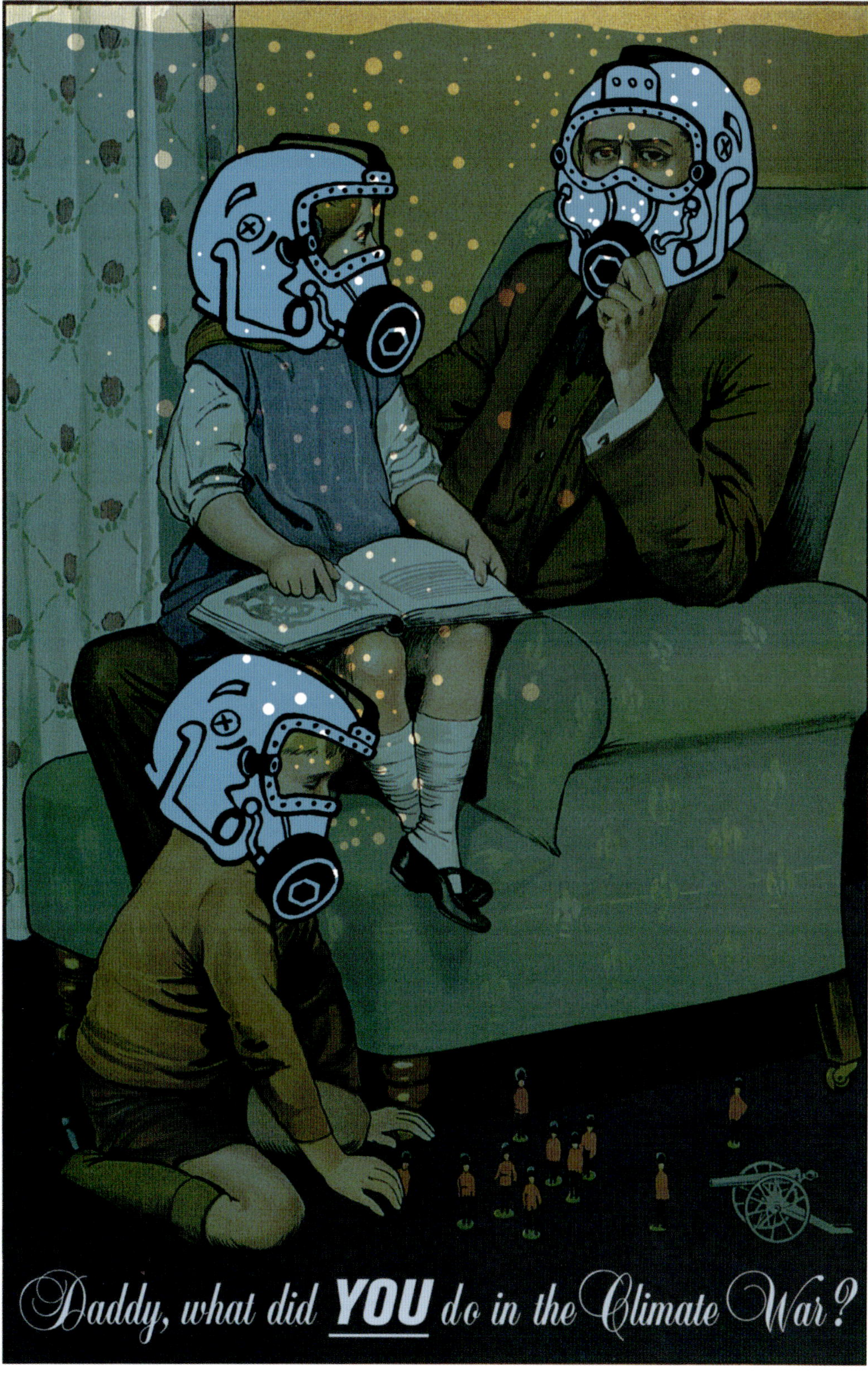

Climate War 2017
Josh MacPhee
Poster

In this parody of a well-known First World War British recruitment poster, the little girl is asking her father what he (and his generation) did to try to stop the global warming that resulted in the rising seas, as they all sit together underwater. It's a nightmarish vision of the future, and was mass-produced and distributed at the 2017 People's Climate March in Washington, D.C.

Political Satire: In Your Face

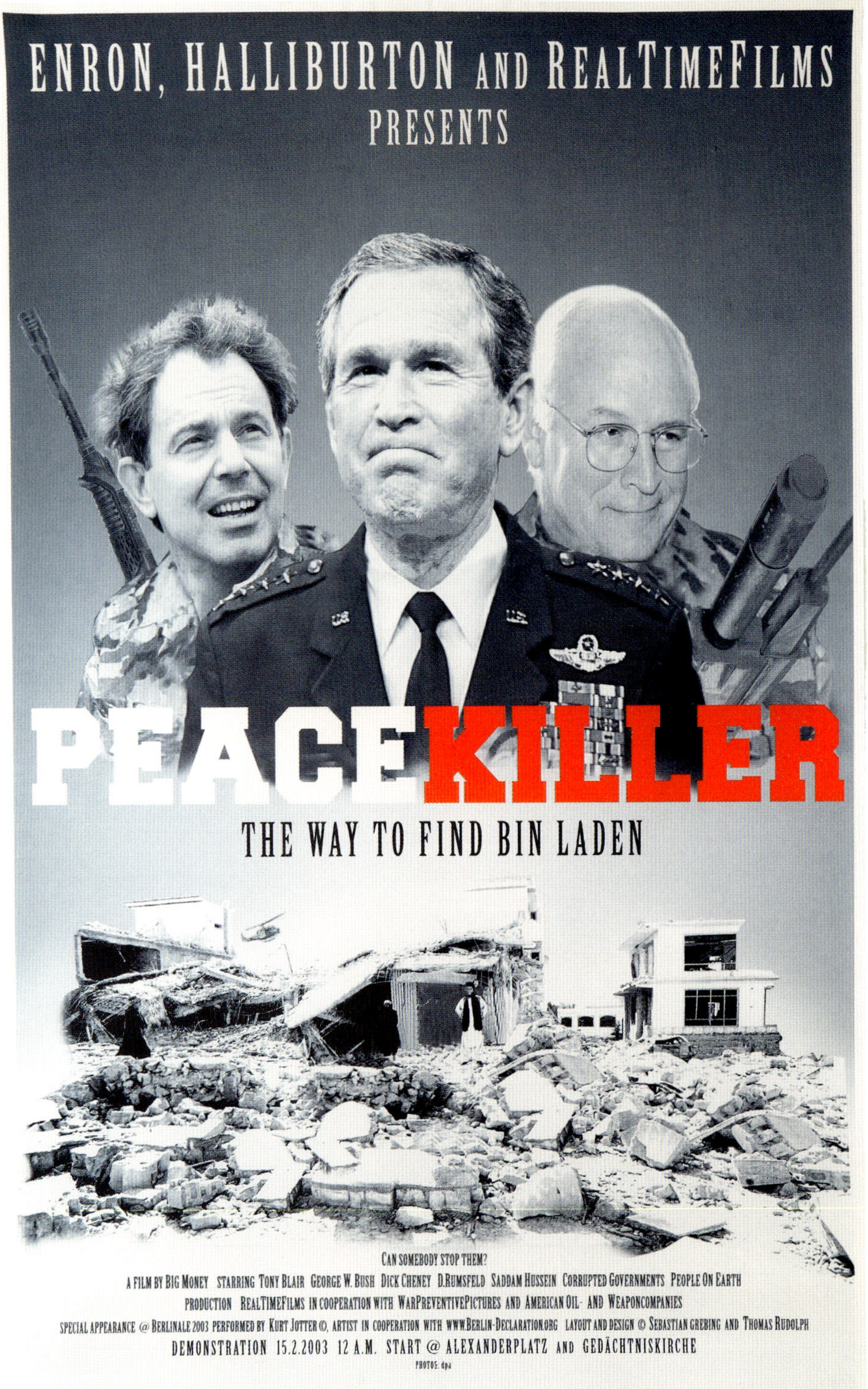

Peacekiller: The Way To Find Bin Laden 2003
Kurt Jotter, Sebastian Grering and Thomas Rudolph
Poster (offset)

The 21st century has been a turbulent time for Britain and the United States – and their 'special relationship'. Both countries were locked together in extended wars (Afghanistan and Iraq); both were suffering from the extreme rise of social divisions between the 'haves' and the 'have nots'; and in both artists, designers and the general population exercised their right to freedom of speech and protested, against these and many other issues, targeting their leaders. Political satire has been brutal and brilliant through the first two decades and shows no sign of easing up. This German parody of a war-film poster is actually announcing a demonstration, with date and time at the bottom. Pictured is the triumvirate of Tony Blair, on the left, acting the part of the young(ish), ready-for-anything hero; US Vice-President Dick Cheney, on the right, the knowing veteran with big guns; and President George W. Bush, centre, as the over-confident, bullying leader. In their desire to find Osama Bin Laden, they have bombed Afghanistan to rubble (although that might be him, very small, teasingly standing in the ruins). References are also made to Halliburton, one of the largest US civilian contractors in Iraq and closely connected to Dick Cheney, and Enron, the massive US energy trading corporation that collapsed after a scandal relating to 'fraud and conspiracy' in 2001.

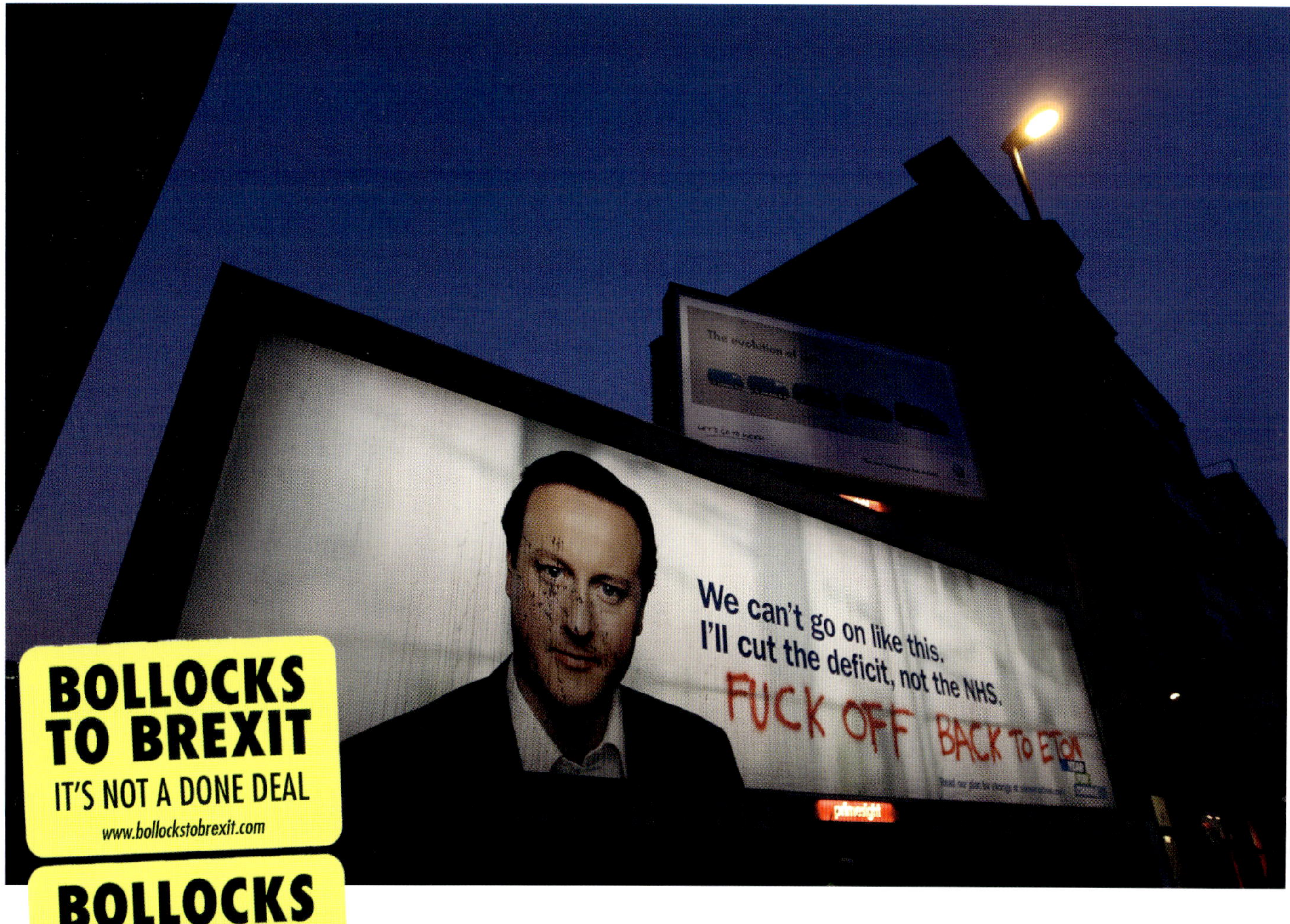

↑ **Conservative Party Election Poster (With Graffiti)** 2010
Graffiti artist unknown
Billboard poster

A billboard from the British general election campaign of 2010 shows David Cameron, head of the Conservative Party and soon-to-be newly elected prime minister. The graffiti relates to the view that Cameron and his cabinet – all private-school educated politicians – were a well-heeled, political elite who dealt out austerity cuts to the rest of the population. The school mentioned, Eton, is considered very upper-class.

← **Bollocks to Brexit** 2018
Artist unknown
Stickers

Following a referendum held on 23 June 2016 (voting 'Leave' or 'Remain'), the UK population voted to 'Leave' the European Union. UK Prime Minister Theresa May triggered the process on 29 March 2017, with a scheduled leave date of 29 March 2019. The referendum results had been very close, and the negotiations of 'Brexit' (Britain + exit) have been very challenging. The process has seen constant public protests from both sides – those who wanted it, as well as those who didn't – and British politicians have fought like cats and dogs over it. By summer 2018, the date this sticker appeared, 'Bollocks to Brexit' could have many interpretations. It might be seen as the continuing argument of the 'Remain' campaign still wishing to remain in the EU, but could also be seen as a statement of exhaustion by the general public, who have grown tired of the bickering and wish it would just go away.

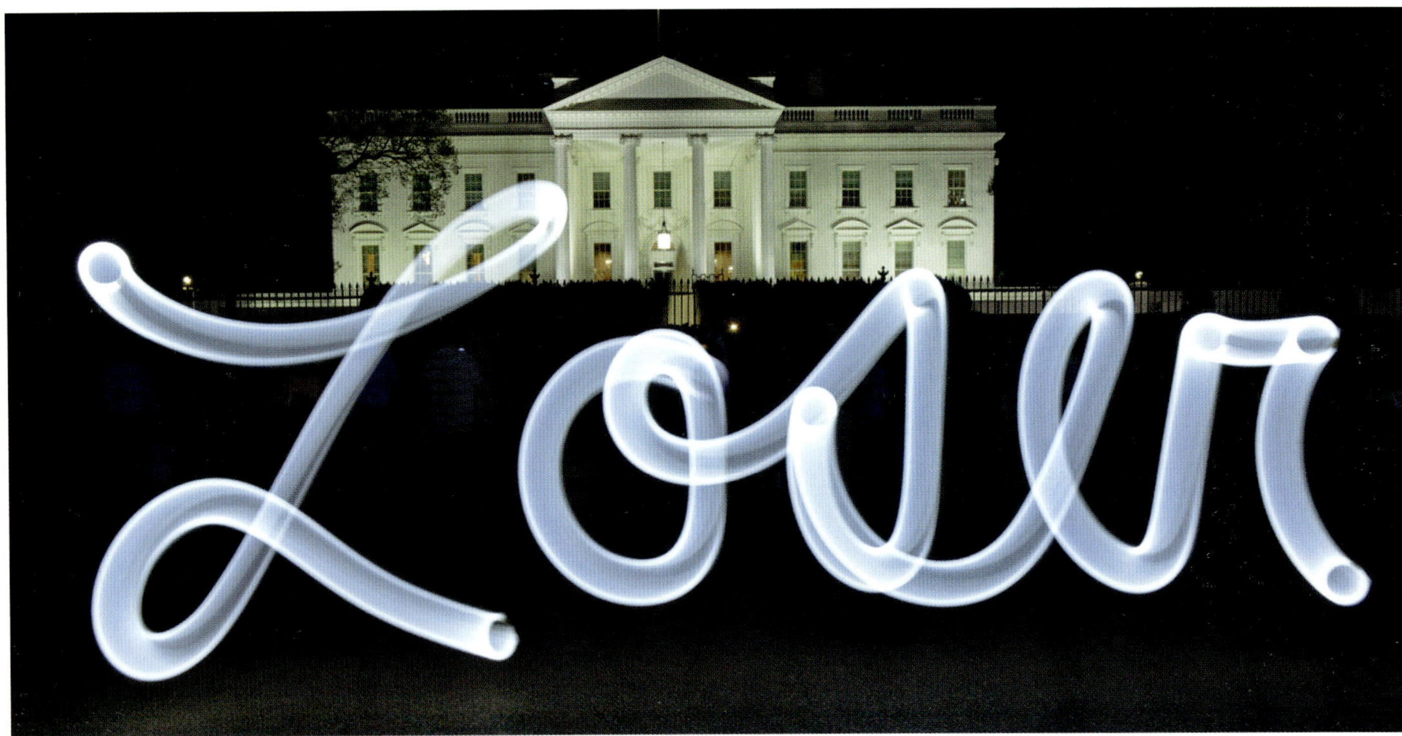

Loser 2016–17
Artist: Vicki DaSilva
Photograph

Donald Trump's victory in the 2016 presidential election brought a wide variety of strong, immediate reactions. American 'light painter' and 'light graffiti' artist Vicki DaSilva exploded with words such as 'Loser' or 'Delusional' slammed in light across the White House, making powerful single frame time exposure photographs at night.

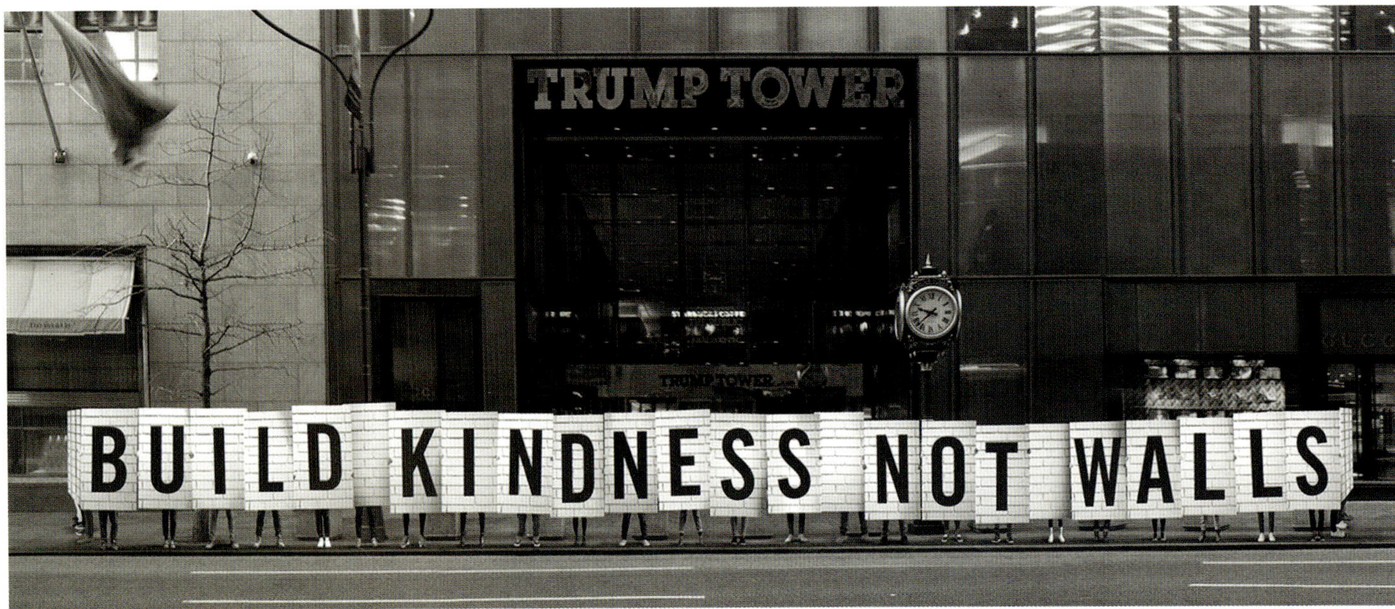

Build Kindness Not Walls 2016
Artists: Jessica Walsh, Timothy Goodman and students of the School of Visual Arts
Photograph

In the long run-up to the 2016 US presidential election, Jessica Walsh (of Sagmeister + Walsh, a New York design firm) and collaborator Timothy Goodman decided to react to Trump's pre-election threat to build a wall between the USA and Mexico. They involved graphic design students at the School of Visual Arts in designing a kindness 'wall' around Trump Tower in New York City. On 15 March 2016 approximately 100 volunteers stood in front of the entrance for three hours, holding 101.5 x 152.5 cm (40 x 60 in) boards that spelled out 'Build Kindness Not Walls'. As of March 2019, President Trump's desire to 'build the wall' still remains a threat, not reality.

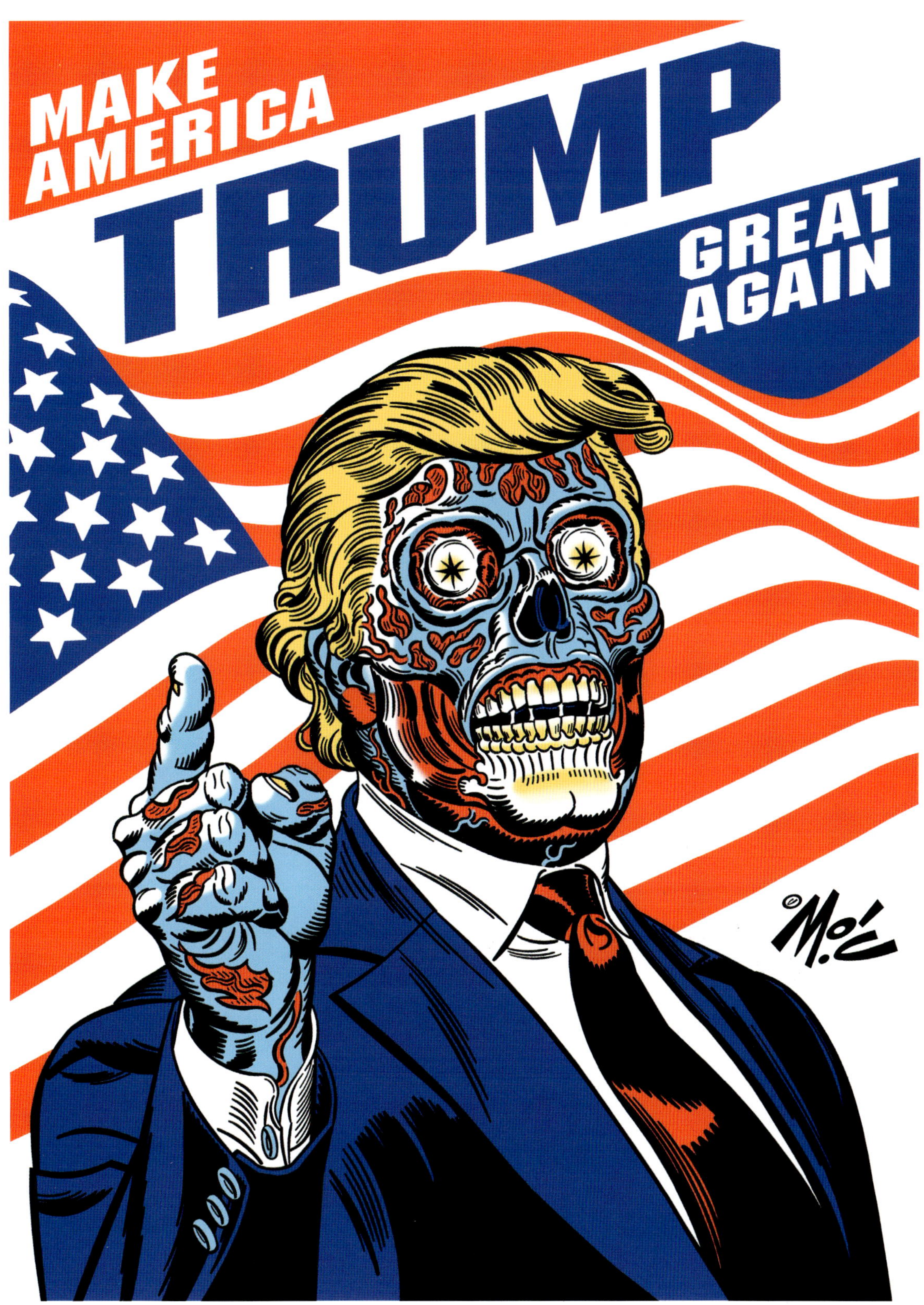

Trump: Make America Great Again 2016
Mitch O'Connell
Poster and t-shirt

Before, during and after the 2016 US presidential election, Trump was caricatured in a variety of formats, usually by artists in defiance of all he was and stood for, but also – at times – just for fun. His highly identifiable visual characteristics were a gift to artists and satirists around the world: the strange, blond quiff, the permanent orange tan, the huge bulk in a dark suit. Mitch O'Connell's wonderfully surreal, monster-like Trump-zombie matched the feeling of Armageddon experienced by those appalled at his election victory, while also offering a spark of humour as a welcome survival tactic for the future.

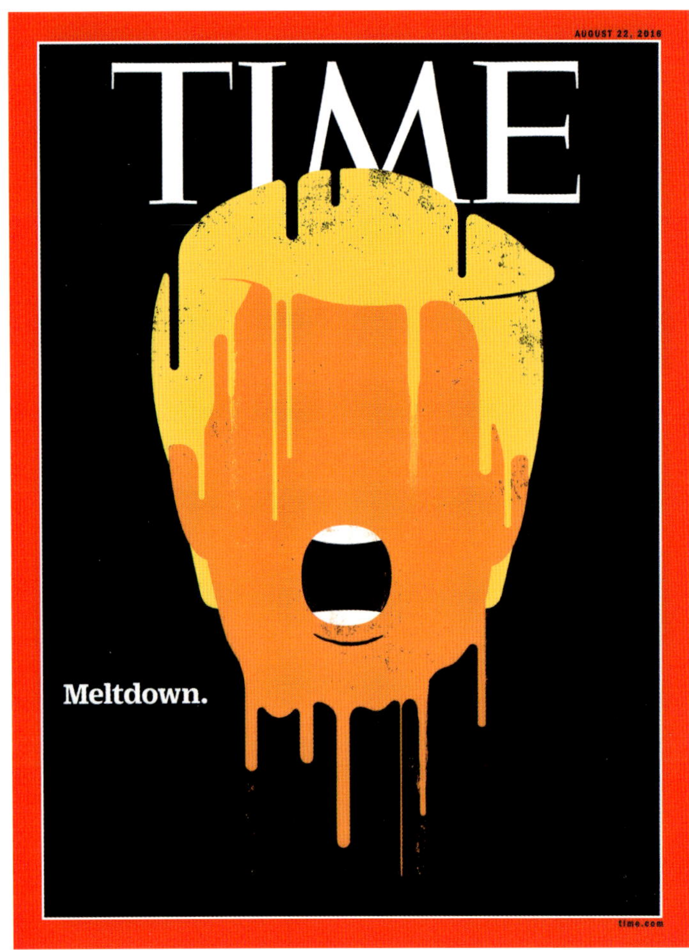

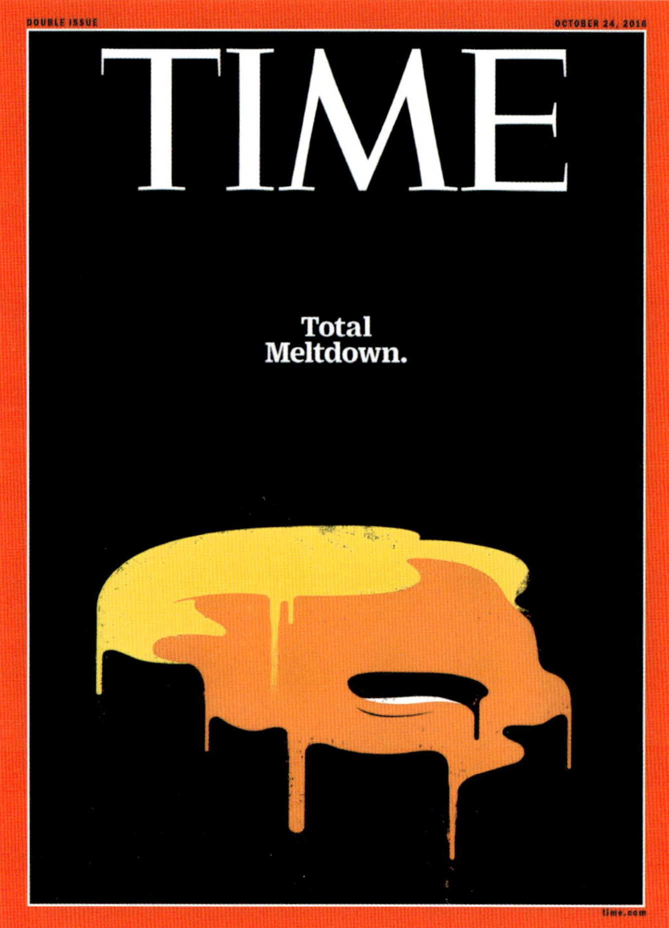

↑ **Meltdown and Total Meltdown** 2016
Edel Rodriguez
TIME magazine: two front covers

During the 2016 election campaign, *TIME* magazine's
front cover of 22 August carried a portrait by Edel
Rodriguez of Trump (and possibly the Republican
Party) in meltdown, due to his bombastic statements
and disrespectful attitudes to women, the press and
others. By 24 October, the Republican Party was even
more worried about Trump, and *TIME* asked the artist
to illustrate an even greater state of collapse.

→ **Coward In Chief** 2016
James Victore
Poster (silkscreen and offset)

Poster artist James Victore is renowned for being
extremely direct and outrageously forceful. He shocks,
he surprises, he is politically astute and on the side of
social justice – and he (obviously) is against Trump.
This poster shouts out a list of nasties, scrawled on what
might be a dark, grim shadow of evil doing. Victore
doesn't allow Trump the joy of colour or emotion. The
poster was originally designed for MoveOn.org, which
campaigns for gun control, against war and other issues
including resistance to Trump.

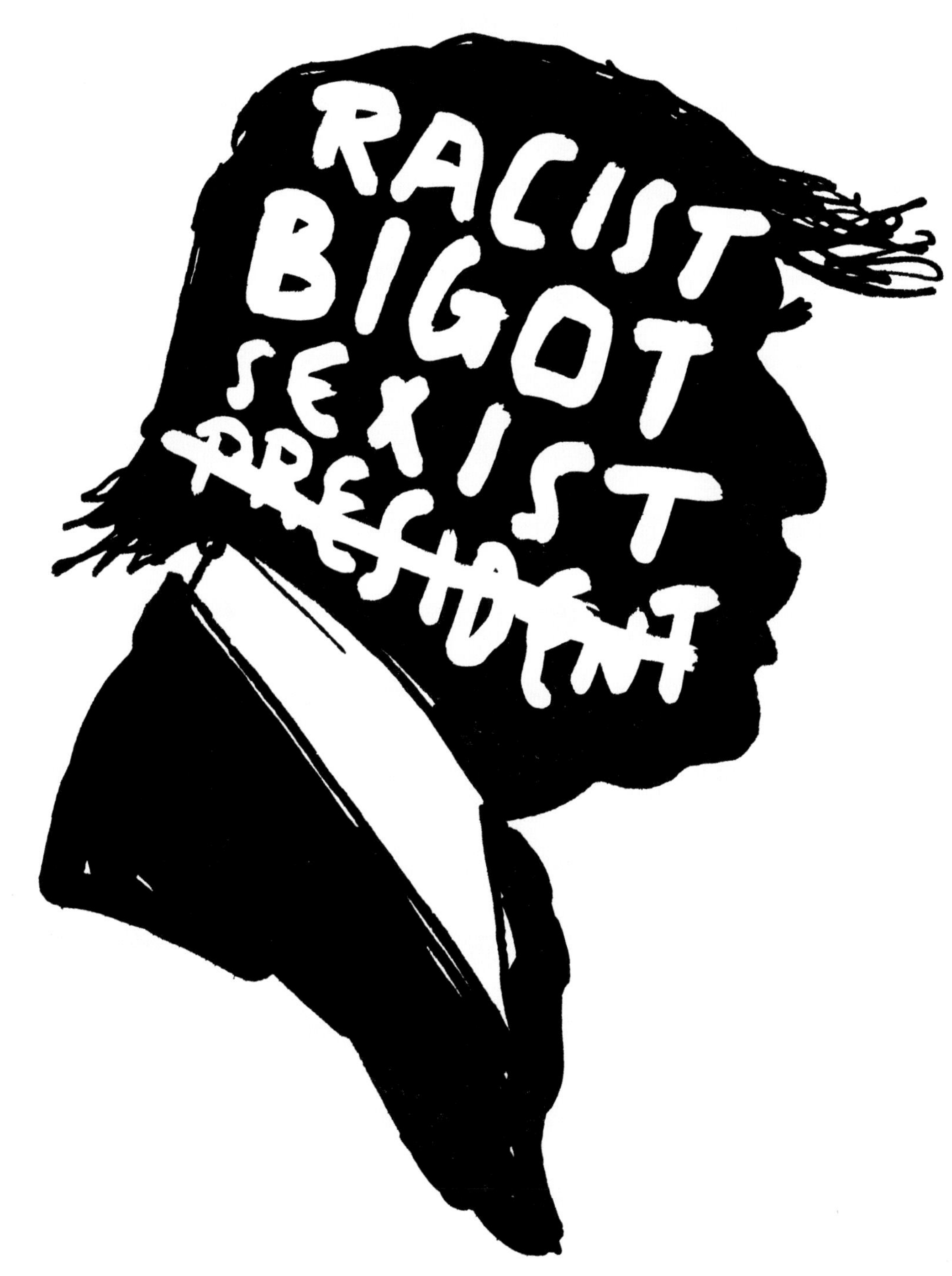
RACIST
BIGOT
SEXIST
PRESIDENT

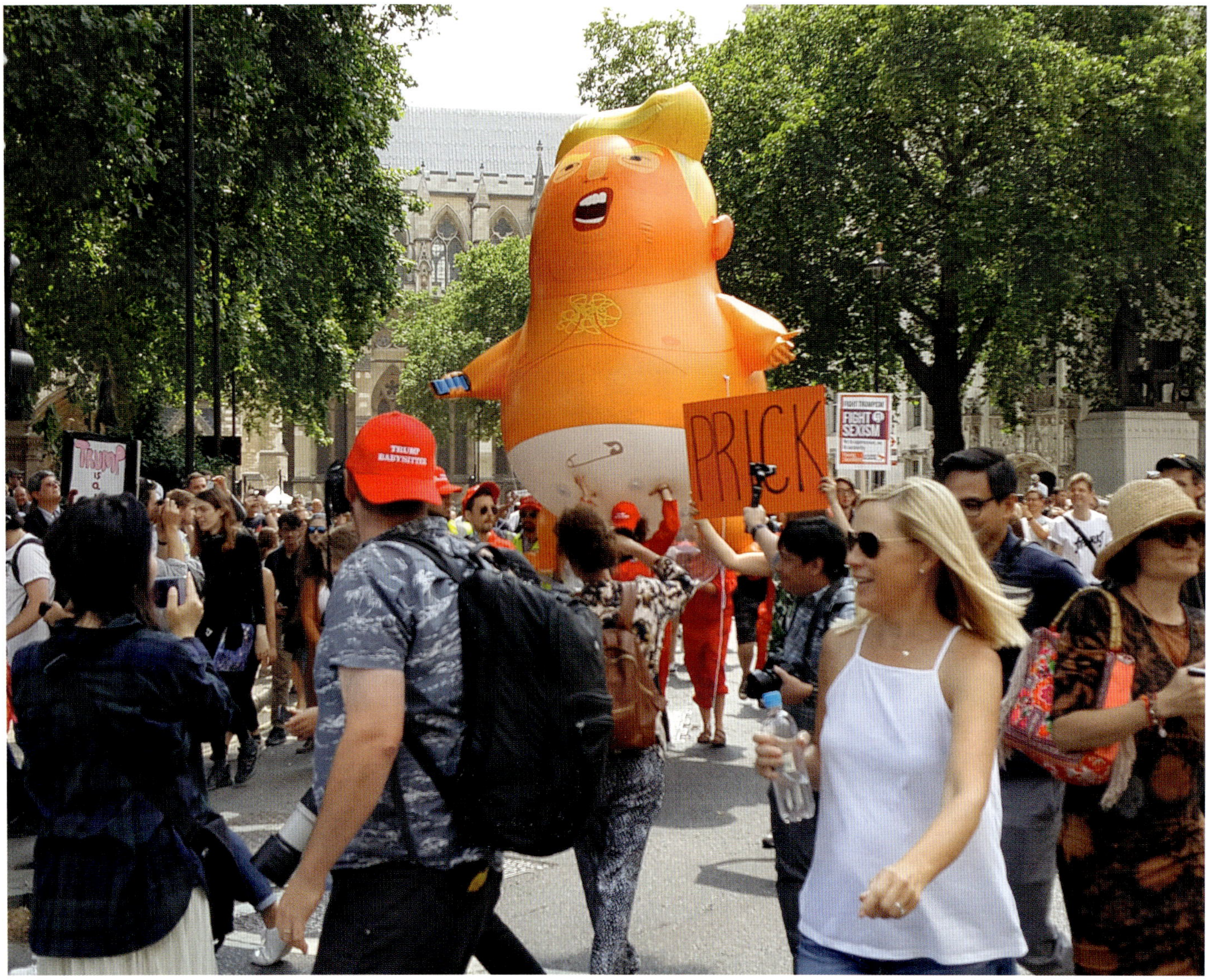

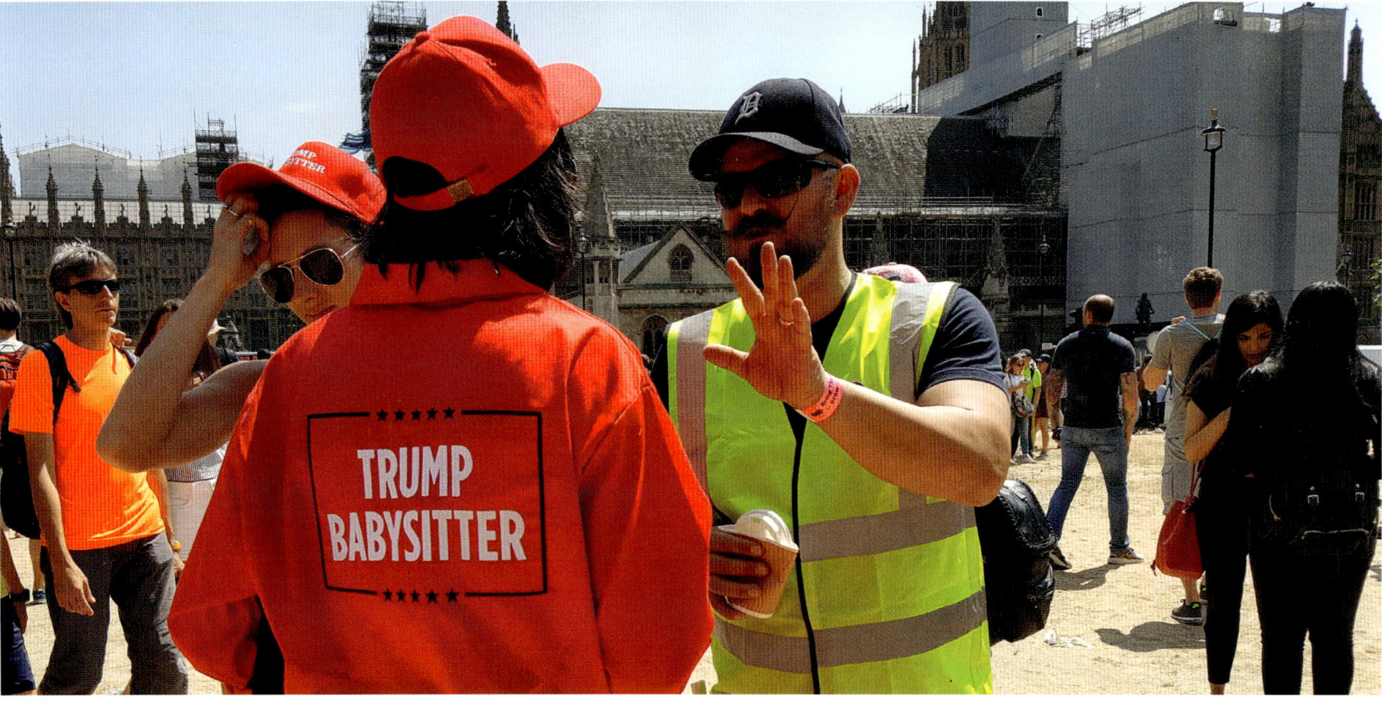TRUMP
BABYSITTER
PRICK
FIGHT TRUMPS
FIGHT
SEXISM
TRUMP
BABYSITTER

← **Trump Baby** 2018
↘ Artists: Leo Murray and colleagues
Photographer: Liz McQuiston
Inflatable blimp, stickers

When Donald Trump arrived for his three-day visit to the UK (beginning
13 July 2018), London was ready for him. Crowdfunded by over 10,000
people, 'Trump Baby' – a 20-ft-high inflatable blimp of Trump wearing
a diaper, clutching a cellphone and throwing a temper tantrum – was
created by British activist Leo Murray and his colleagues, the 'Trump
Babysitters'. The blimp was given permission by the Mayor's office to fly
for two hours (no higher than 100 feet) anchored to a spot in Parliament
Square, across the street from Big Ben. After its descent, Trump Baby was
inflated again a few hours later and held above the heads of protesters
gathering in Parliament Square. Meanwhile two mass demonstrations, with
different starting points, marched through London, aiming to coalesce
in the Trafalgar Square/Whitehall area. The 'Together Against Trump'
demonstration brought massive representation from political parties and
unions, and some of their leaders, packed together in Trafalgar Square to
hear talks from guest speakers. The other demonstration, 'Bring the Noise',
organized by the Women's March London coalition, marched with pots,
pans, drums and other instruments to 'protest with noise', often in costume.
They were headed down the middle of Whitehall, when the protesters from
Parliament Square suddenly hurried towards them, carrying Baby Trump
jubilantly over their heads. The two groups met for a 'showdown' in the
middle of Whitehall, with those who 'brought the noise' blasting away at
Baby Trump and finally forcing him back into Parliament Square: a joyous
piece of street theatre. In the end, the real Trump avoided London on his
visit, but an estimated 250,000 protesters made their voices heard.

↓ **'Bring the Noise' Demonstration** 2018
Photographer: Liz McQuiston
Photographs

During the events of 13 July 2018 – Trump's visit to the UK – the 'Bring
the Noise' demonstration was accompanied by a sea of signs and placards
with angry, but more often humorous statements, ranging from 'Knitters
Against Trump' to 'Feed Him to the Corgis' (the Queen's dogs).

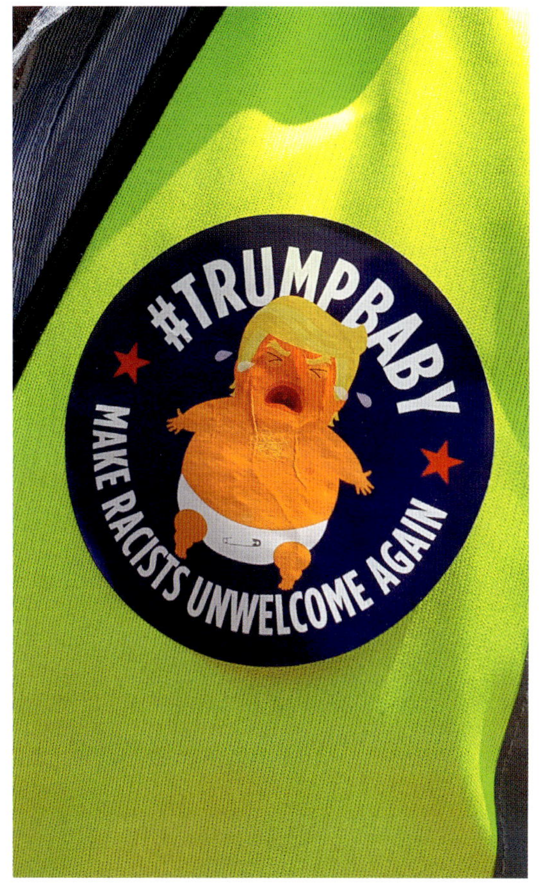

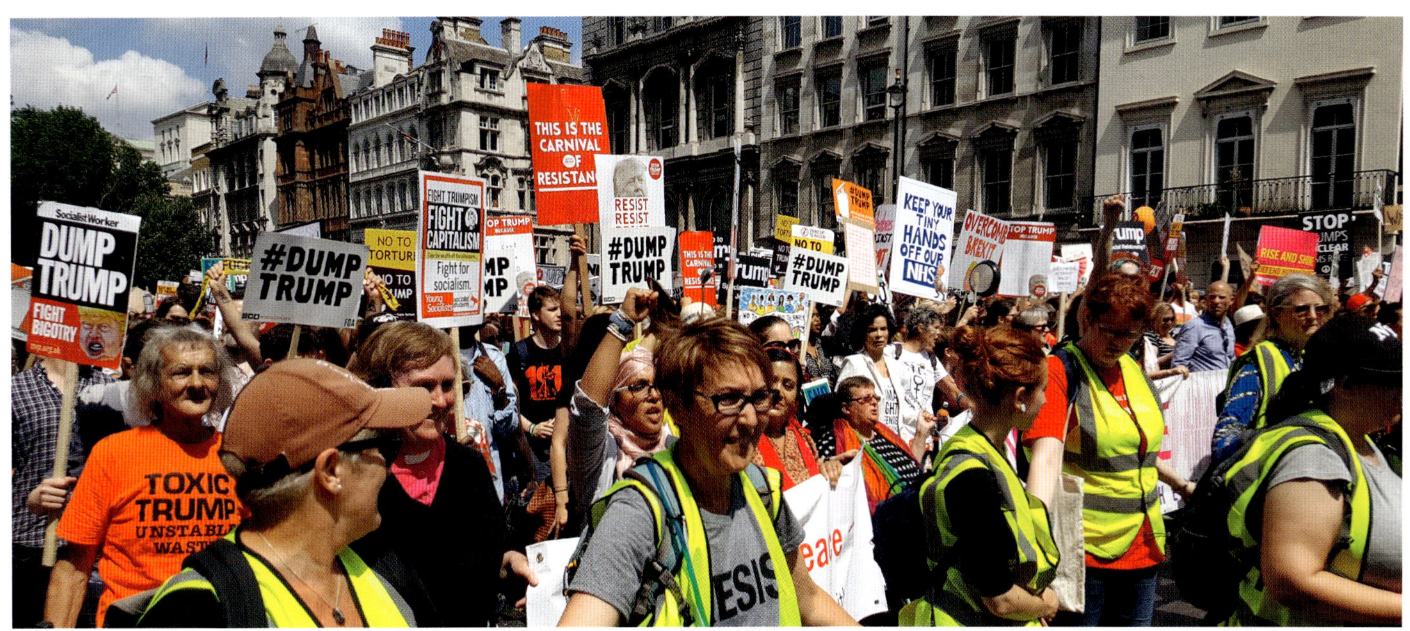

Human Rights, Social Struggles

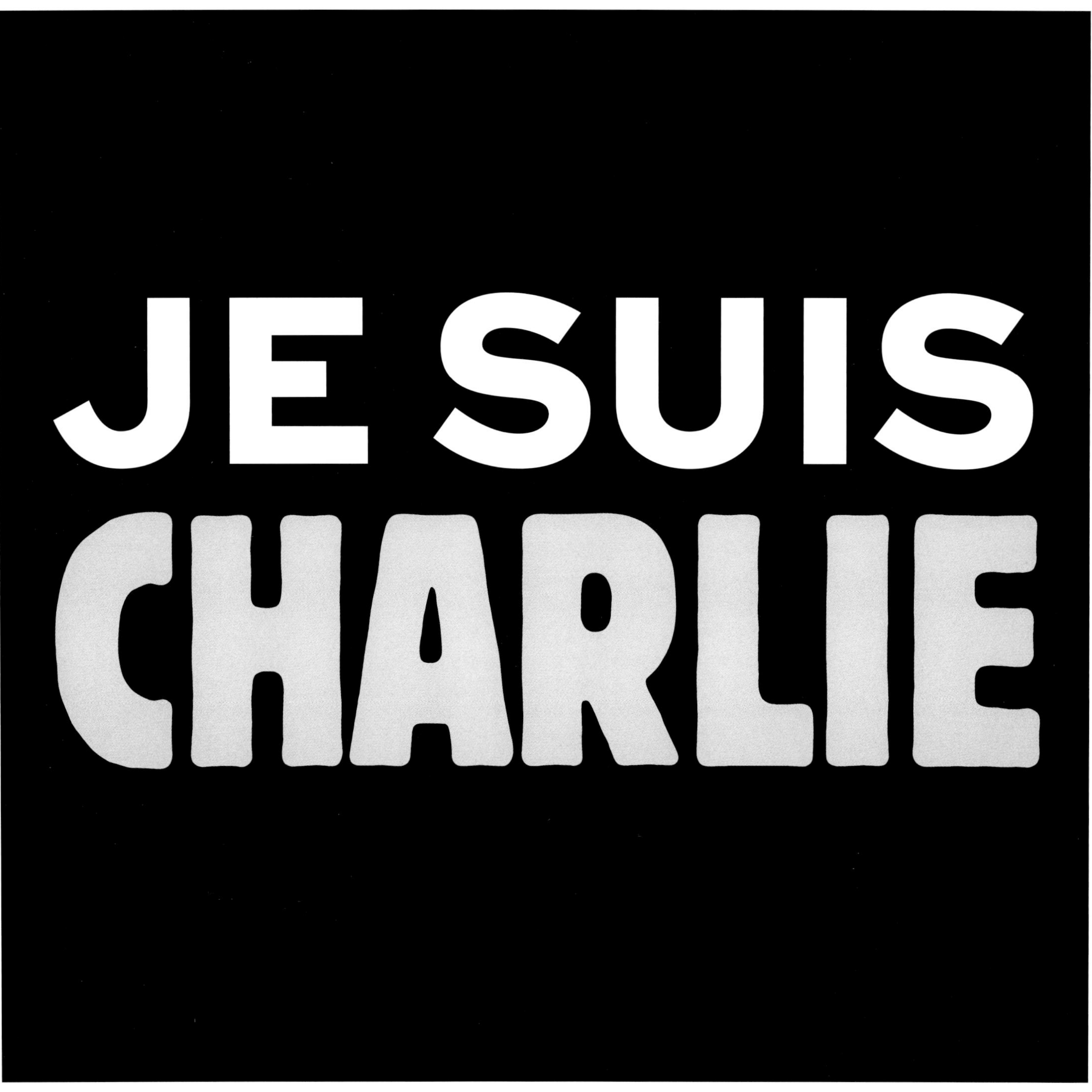

Je Suis Charlie (I Am Charlie) 2015
Artist: Joachim Roncin
Electronic poster (online) and print

The weekly French satirical comic magazine, *Charlie Hebdo*, could be viewed as the descendant of the 19th century French comic papers that excelled at 'going too far'. Founded in 1969, it made its reputation over the years by outrageously mocking religious and political authority. In recent years, it continued to lampoon radical Islam, despite threats and government appeals for restraint, arguing that France's freedom of speech gave it the right to criticize any religion. Then on 7 January 2015, two radical Islamist gunmen entered their Paris offices, killing twelve – including the editor, Stéphane Charbonnier – and injuring office staff, cartoonists and writers on the Hebdo team. This poster/graphic (Je Suis Charlie), designed by Joachim Roncin immediately after hearing the shock news of the massacre, instantly became a symbol of solidarity, defiance and the right to freedom of speech. It appeared in strength on social media and on marches and demonstrations.

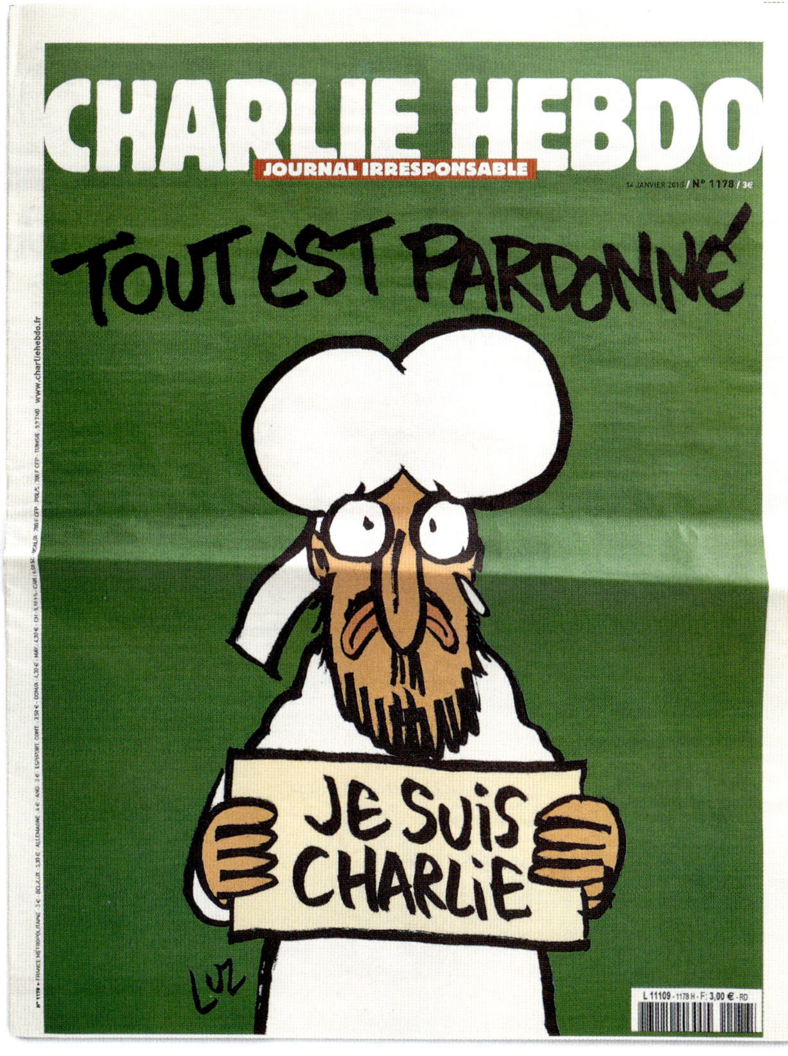

← *Charlie Hebdo: The Survivors' Issue*
14 January 2015
Cartoonist: LUZ
Magazine: front cover

Charlie Hebdo: The Survivors' Issue was defiantly
back on sale a week after twelve people
were killed in its offices, including its editor.
Controversially, the cover bears a cartoon of the
Prophet Muhammed, weeping and holding a 'Je
Suis Charlie' sign. Above him is the statement
'All is forgiven', apparently intended to be a
message from the survivors to the terrorists.

↓ *Charlie Hebdo* Unity Rally, Paris
10 January 2015
Artist: JR
Photographer unknown
Photograph

In solidarity, French artist and photographer JR
and his studio produced a photographic image of
the eyes of Stéphane Charbonnier (aka 'Charb'),
editor and chief cartoonist of *Charlie Hebdo*
magazine and one of the twelve killed in the attack
on the Hebdo offices. The image was divided
across eight placards and carried by the marchers,
as shown here in one of the many Unity Rallies
held in France on Sunday, 10 January, 2015.

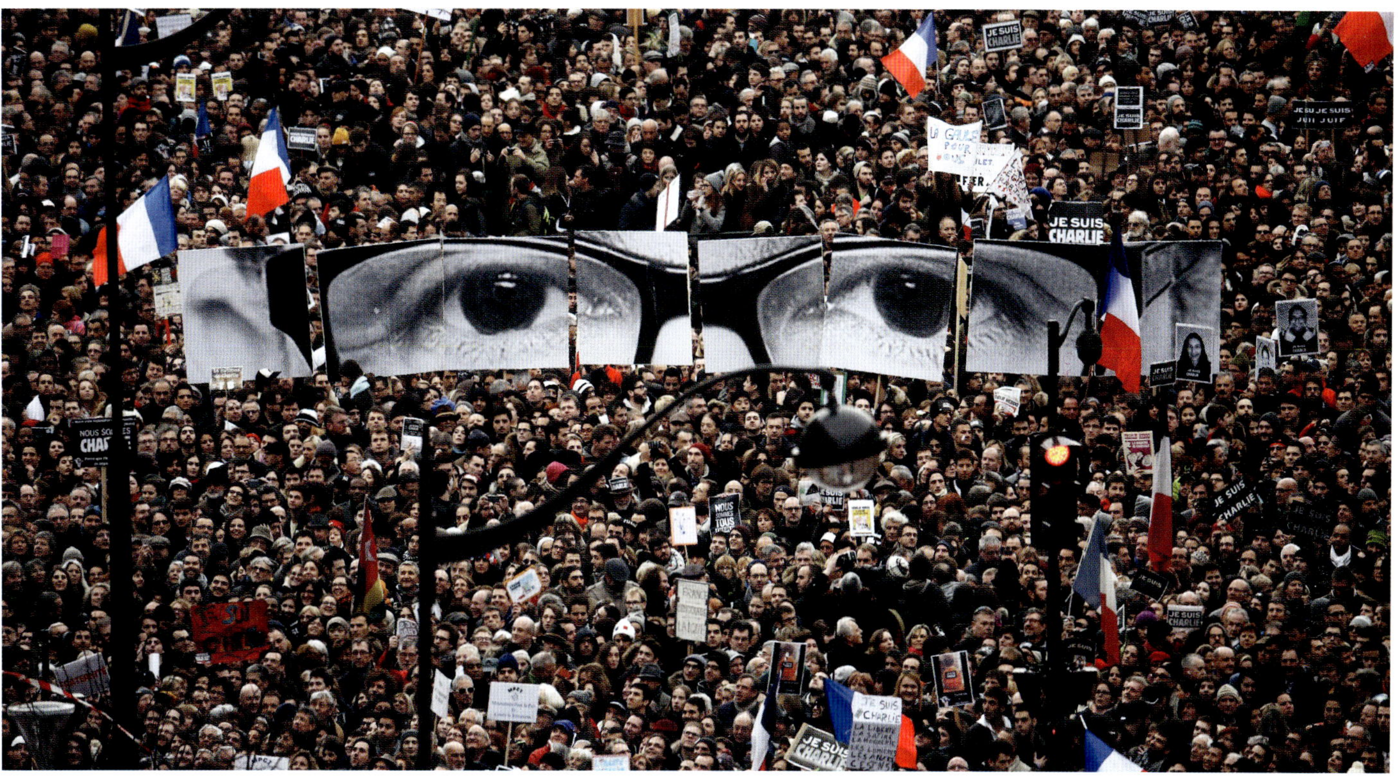

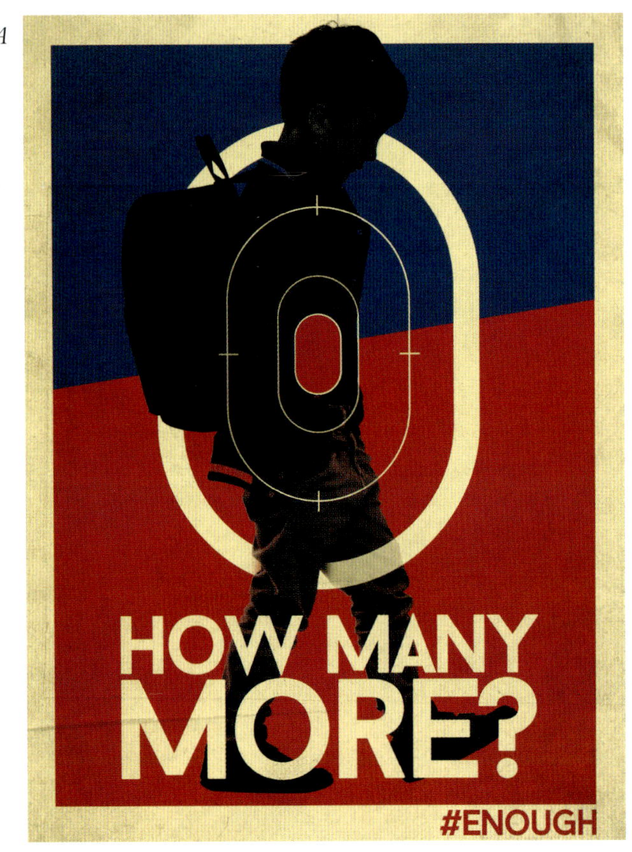
HOW MANY
MORE?
#ENOUGH

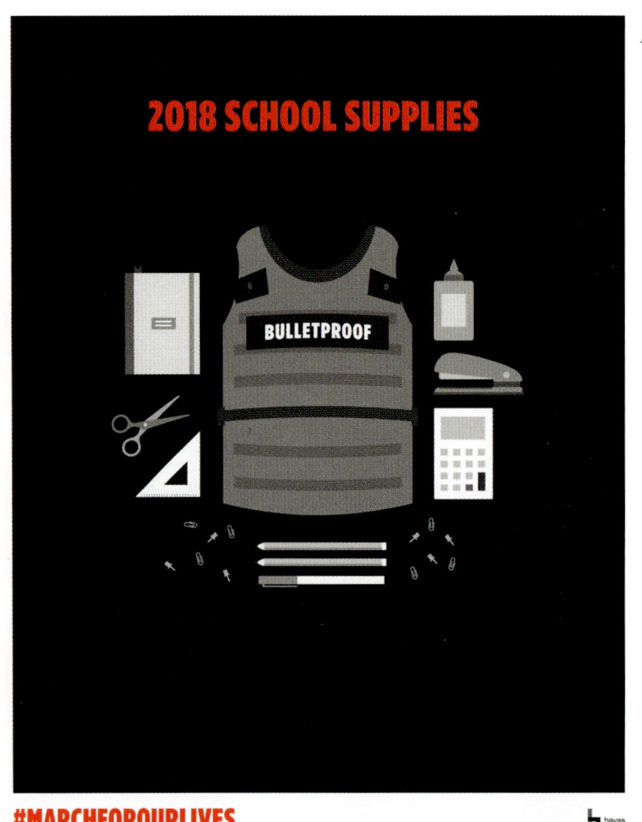
2018 SCHOOL SUPPLIES
BULLETPROOF
#MARCHFOROURLIVES
havas

C

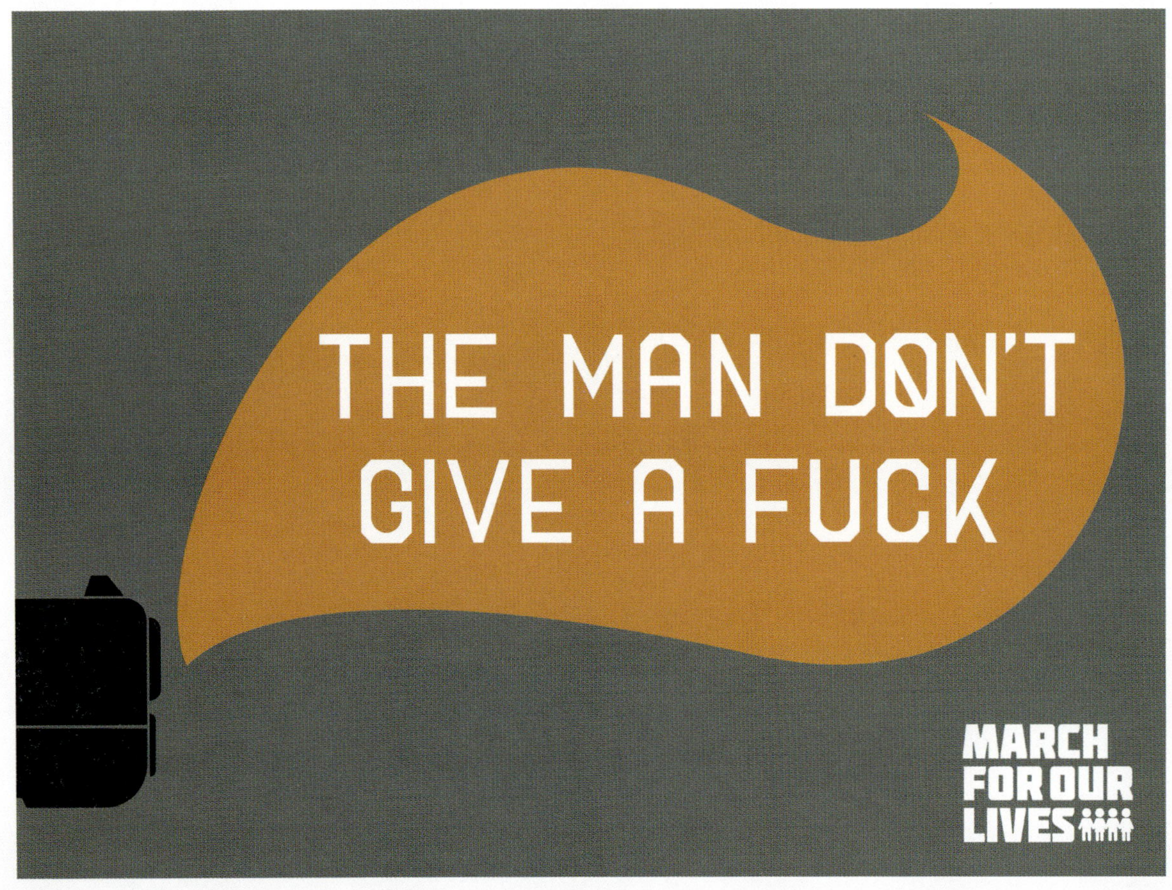
THE MAN DON'T
GIVE A FUCK
MARCH
FOR OUR
LIVES

Advertising Age magazine and various artists
Posters (for downloading)

On Valentine's Day (14 February) 2018, a 19-year-old ex-student walked into Marjory Stoneman Douglas High School carrying an assault rifle and killed 17 students and staff, and injured 17 more. The students immediately began a resistance movement calling for gun reform and gun safety legislation, protesting over social media as well as taking their cause to local, state and federal government. Five of the survivors also organized (and spoke at) the 'March for Our Lives' rally in Washington D.C. held on 24 March, attended by over 800,000 people. Before the march, online magazine *Ad Age* (*Advertising Age*) addressed the advertising community, which then created 1,000 billboards across the country (including two huge ones in Times Square) devoted to magnifying the students' messages. *Ad Age* also briefed its readers, in partnership with the Gun Safety Alliance, to produce a bank of downloadable posters for carrying on the upcoming march, calling for an end to gun violence in the USA and particularly in schools. A number of those posters are shown here, along with the names of their creators.

(Image A)   Dave Nieves

(Image B)   Shane Smith

(Image C)   Adam Ledbury, Assoc. Creative Director, M/H VCCP ad agency

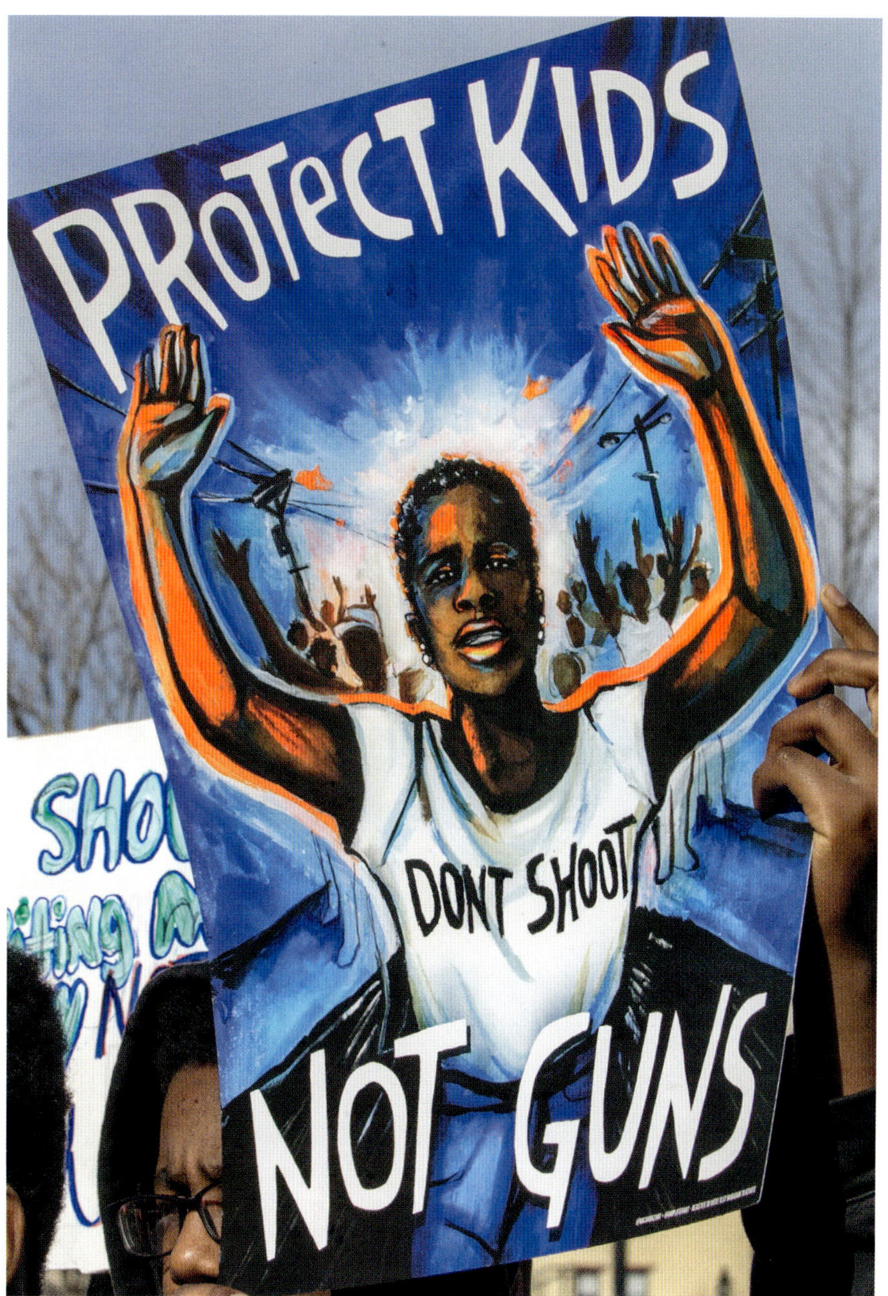

↑ **Protect Kids, Not Guns** 2018
Artist: Micah Bazant; Photographer: Alex Edelman
Poster (offset)

When design lab Amplifier hosted an open call for the creation of poster art to be carried through the streets during the March For Our Lives rally, trans artist Micah Bazant produced this poster. It communicates a number of issues: it is an open call for gun reform, but its message could also be relating to Trump, who 'protects guns' in that he resists supporting gun reform and instead supports the National Rifle Association (NRA), a very strong gun lobby with voting power. Bazant also intended the poster to act as a reminder of the number of black youths killed by guns. The character in the poster has their 'hands up' and wears a t-shirt saying 'don't shoot'. This is a direct reference to the protest chant 'hands up, Don't shoot', the shooting of 18-year-old Michael Brown in Ferguson, Missouri, and the targeting of black youths by the police. Amplifier printed 40,000 of these posters for distribution at the March For Our Lives rally.

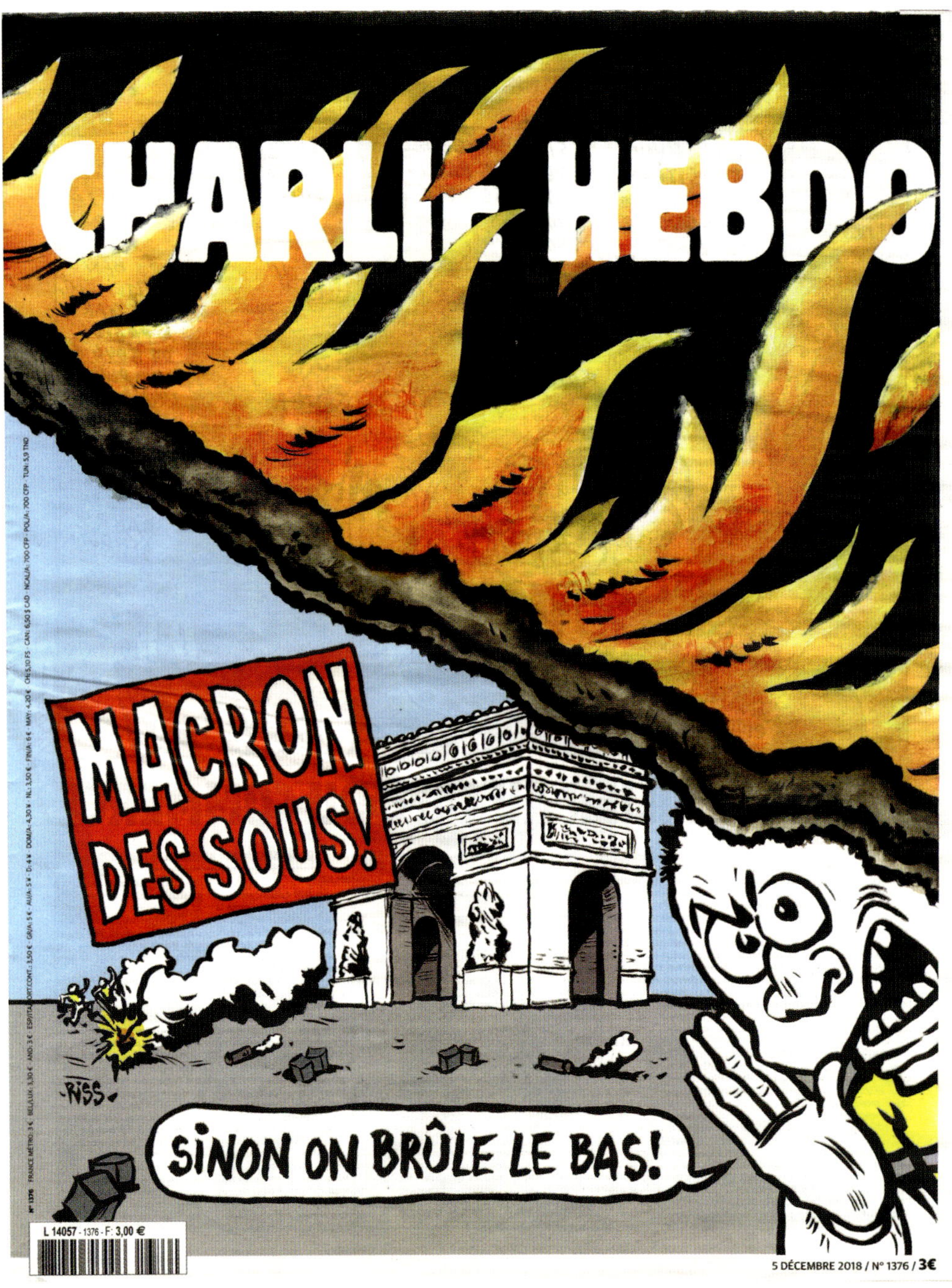

Charlie Hebdo **magazine**
5 December 2018
Cartoonist: **RISS**
Front cover

By 2018 the pendulum of European politics was swinging to the right, with the election of new, 'populist' leaders and the growth of right-wing parties in previously stable, liberal countries such as Germany. But if some of Europe's discontent with government was showing itself in political elections, the anger of the French was pouring out into the street. It began with a planned fuel tax rise. In mid-November, people protested on the weekends showing identification and solidarity by wearing the 'gilet jaune' (yellow vest) that all French carry in their car by law. The weekend protests spread through France, and grew in numbers and in violence. In Paris, they torched cars, smashed windows and defaced the Arc de Triomphe. The protests, at their peak numbering 300,000 across the country, gradually became more unified and transformed into a broader demand for higher wages, lower direct taxes and public spending increases. The 'gilets jaunes' movement became 'the people' versus the government, with all ages involved and criticism that President Emmanuel Macron acted 'like a king'. By Saturday, 12 January, 2019 (the 9th consecutive weekend of unrest) there were still 80,000, across the country, taking part in protests against Macron's economic policies, and the violence was still present in the streets. Early on in the protests, the satirical comic magazine *Charlie Hebdo*, never missing a chance to stir things up, produced this 5 December front cover in lurid yellow, with flames licking across its masthead, and a thuggish protester yelling (roughly translated) 'Macron, give us the money! Or we'll burn the Underpass!' (meaning they'll burn the structure on which society sits).

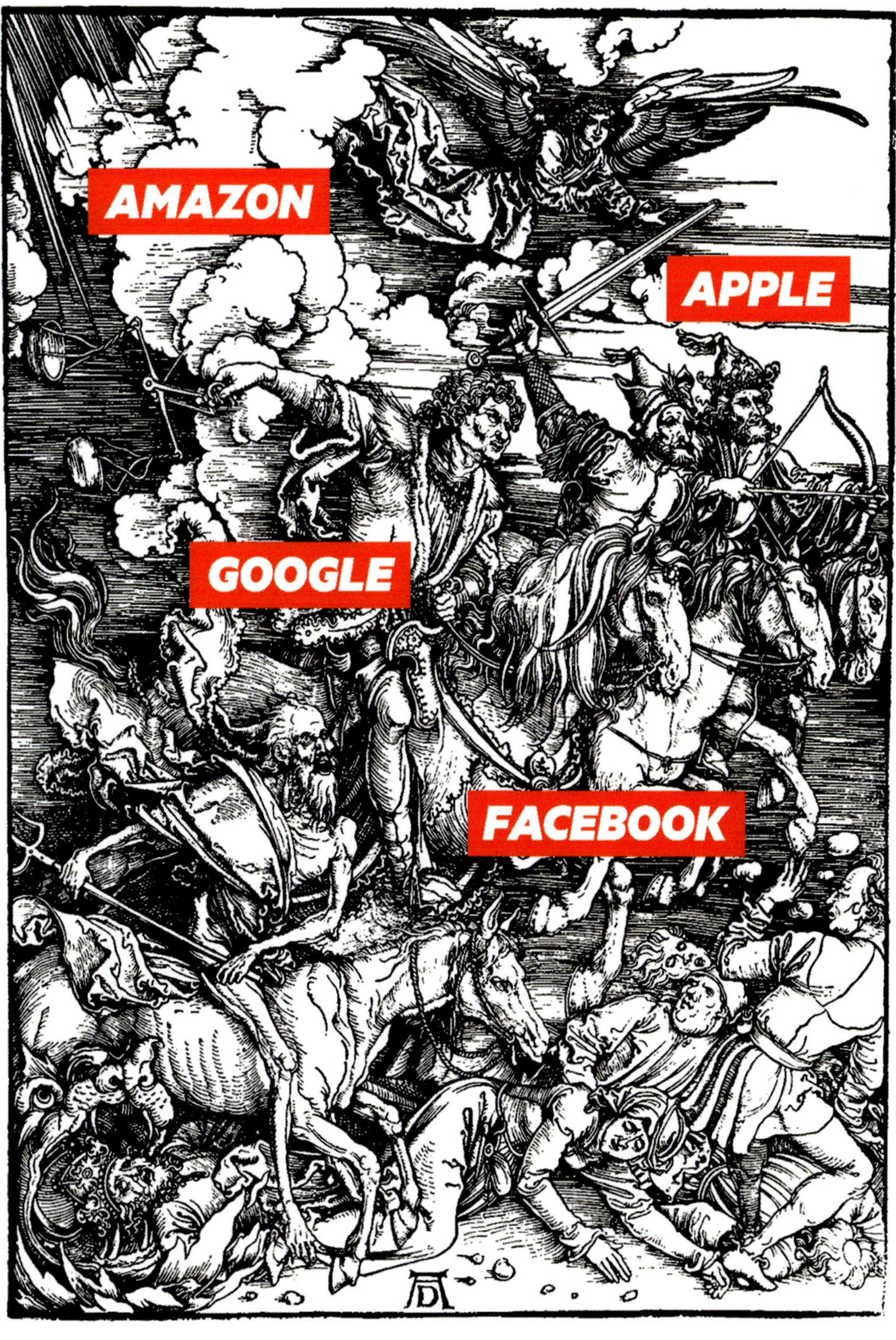

**The Apocalyptic Riders
(after Albrecht Dürer)** 2014
Klaus Staeck
Poster and postcard

In a warning of impending doom, Klaus Staeck places the names of four 21st century global corporations upon Albrecht Dürer's familiar woodcut, 'The Four Horsemen of the Apocalypse', created in 1498. The four horsemen represent (from left to right) death, famine, war and conquest: a warning of evils to come at the end of the world. There are plenty of misgivings about the size (and arguably low tax payments) of the global corporations mentioned, and their tendency to keep expanding into new areas of operation, while hiding under new names. In the 21st century, 'big' can feel threatening and controlling. We have been warned.

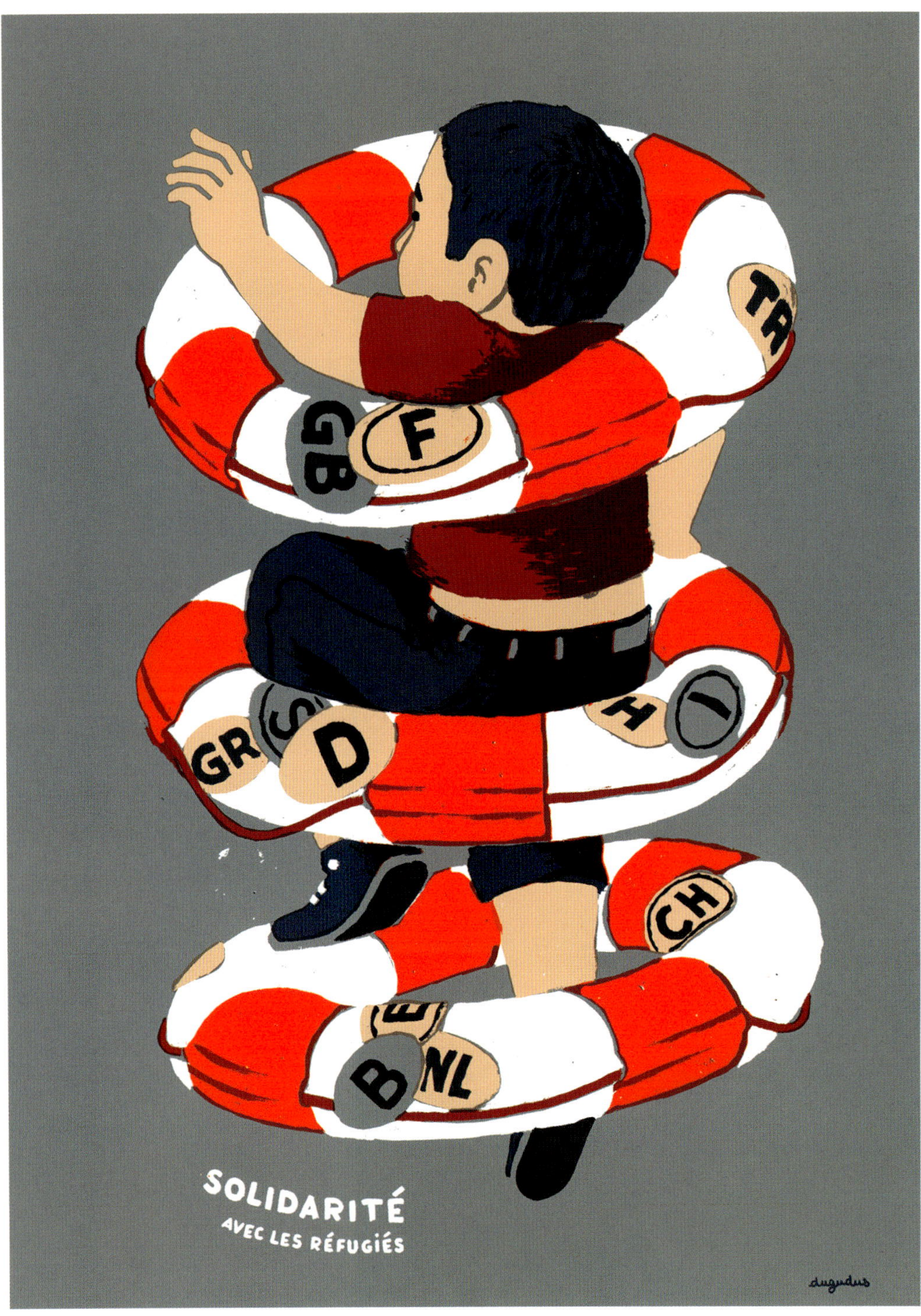

Solidarité avec les Réfugiés (Solidarity with Refugees) 2016
Dugudus
Poster

French graphic designer and illustrator Dugudus produced this poster as a call to all countries,
especially European – some of which are labelled on the lifebuoys – to help refugees fleeing
the war and misery of their countries at the risk of their lives. It also depicts a small boy
attempting to scramble to safety within the lifebuoys, calling to mind a terrible tragedy. From
the appearance of his clothes, the boy represents three-year-old Aylan Kurdi from northern
Syria whose lifeless body was washed up on a beach in Turkey in September 2015. He was
one of twelve Syrians who drowned when their boat capsized while attempting to reach the
Greek island of Kos; all were escaping the war in Syria, and its occupation by Islamic State,
at that point in time.

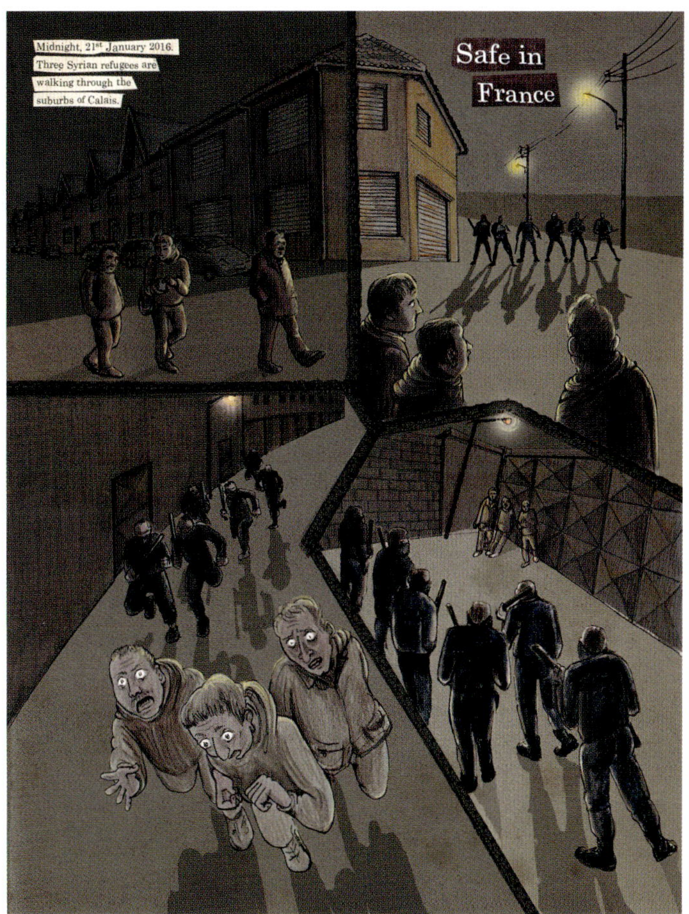

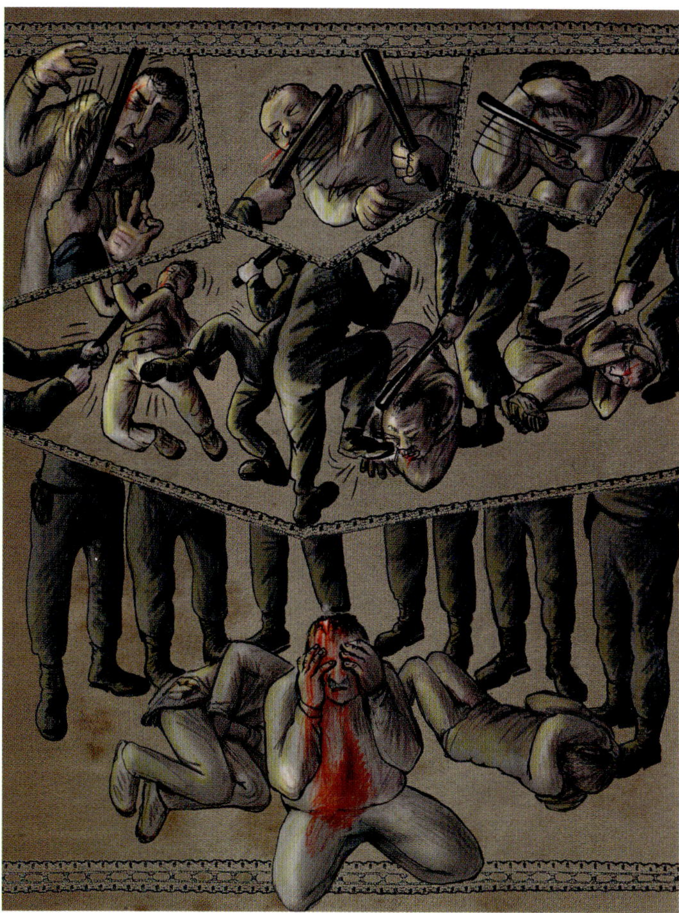

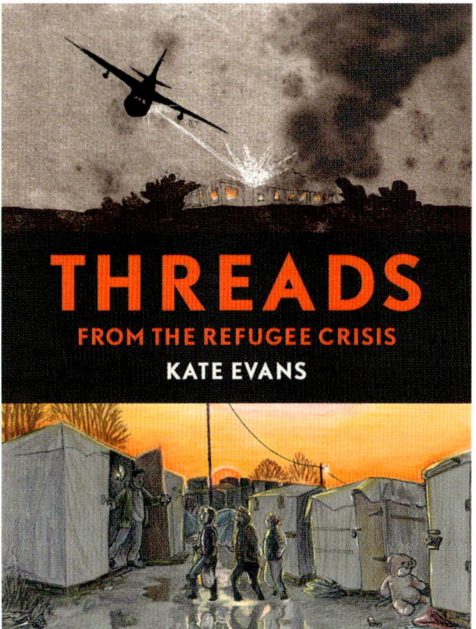

Threads: From the Refugee Crisis 2017
Author and artist: Kate Evans
Front cover and two inside pages

Over the past ten years, the displacement of populations from the Middle East
– largely due to conflicts in Iraq, Afghanistan and Syria – and the instability of
various countries in Africa, have led to what is now referred to as 'the refugee
crisis'. Some of these groups, on leaving home, headed towards neighbouring
'friendly' countries and settled, often in refugee camps; some headed for Europe by
what became well-worn but dangerous routes (often involving travel by sea). Those
refugees travelling to Europe comprised two groups: asylum-seekers, escaping
injury or death in their home country, or economic migrants, forced to find a new
home or in search of work and a better life. Many died travelling by overloaded
boats to reach Europe. In 2011 an 'unofficial' migrant camp began to grow outside
Calais on the northern coast of France, filled with refugees from the Middle East
and Africa, all with a hope of reaching Britain. The camp grew and grew, and
became known as 'the Jungle' (by both news media and its inhabitants) largely due
to its lack of facilities and poor conditions with regard to food, water, sanitation
and health services. By the time the camp was finally dismantled (October 2016)
and its inhabitants transported to housing and processing centres, up to 10,000
refugees were living there. British artist Kate Evans' graphic novel *'Threads'* gives a
journalistic account of her visits to the Jungle, and relays her experiences from all
angles: the friendliness and difficulties of the inhabitants, the attitudes and actions
of the police and authorities, the terror felt by children involved, her motherly guilt
at leaving her 12-year-old son to go on her trips, some of the angry responses she
gets from the British public, and the incredible people she meets trying to do good.
It is an incredible and frightening journey, drawn with passion.

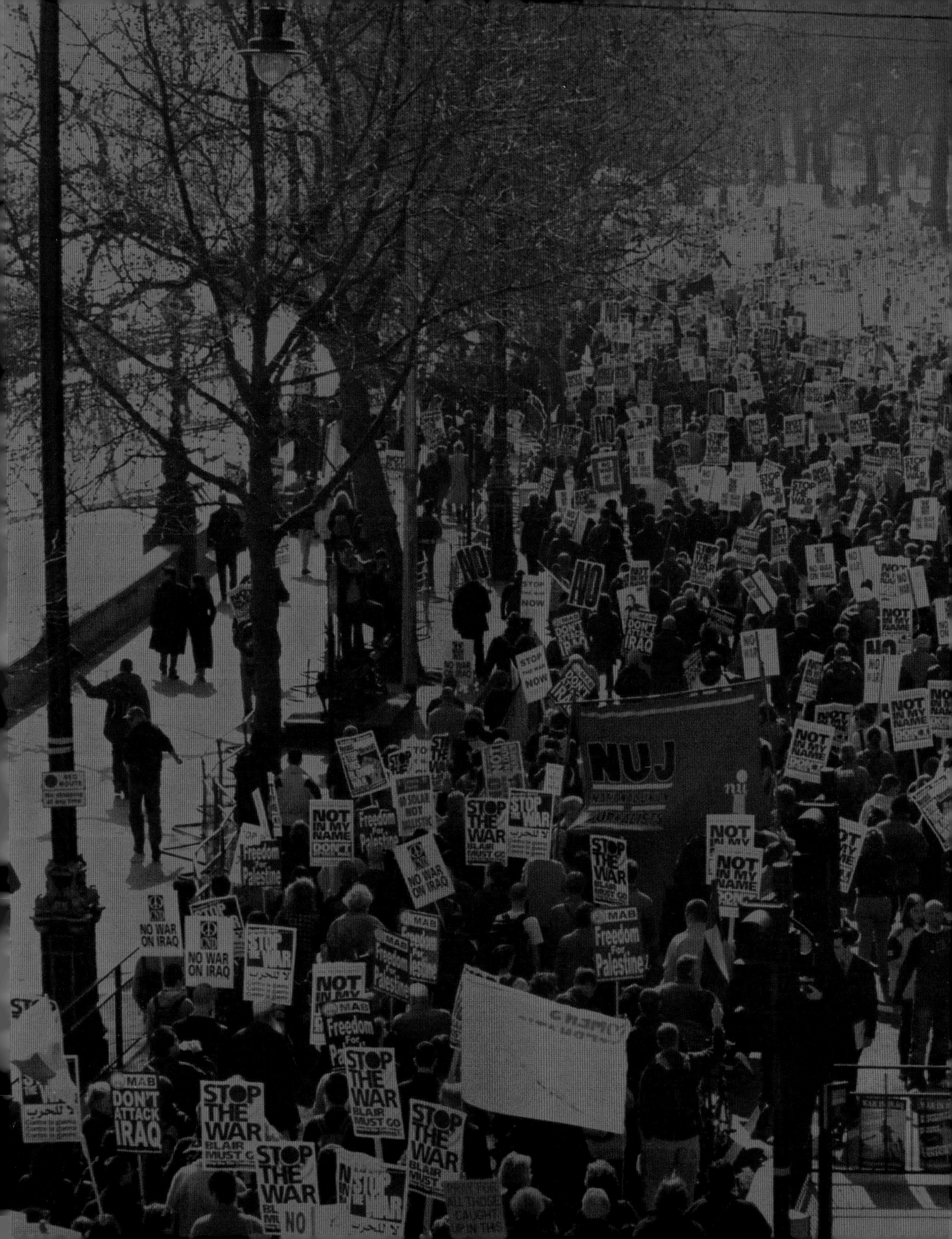

NO
NO
NO
NOT IN MY NAME
NOT IN MY NAME
NOT IN MY NAME
NUJ
STOP THE WAR
STOP THE WAR BLAIR MUST GO
NOT IN MY NAME
MAB Freedom for Palestine
NO WAR ON IRAQ
NO WAR ON IRAQ
STOP THE WAR BLAIR MUST GO
STOP THE WAR BLAIR MUST GO
STOP THE WAR
MAB DON'T ATTACK IRAQ
DON'T ATTACK IRAQ
NO

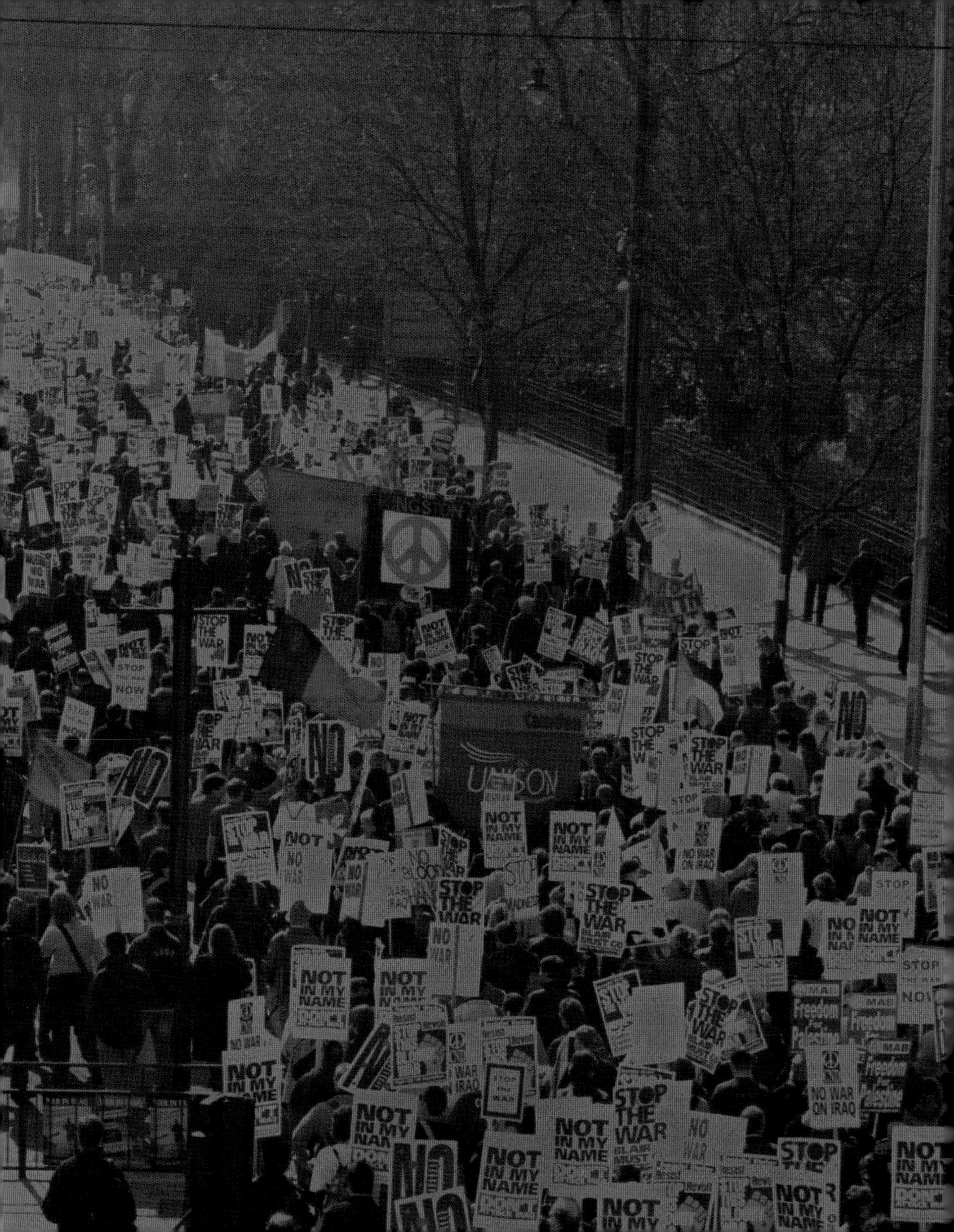

KINGSTON
STOP THE WAR
NOT IN MY NAME
NO WAR
NO WAR ON IRAQ
STOP THE WAR NOW
NO
NOT IN MY NAME
NO BLOOD FOR OIL
STOP THE MADNESS
BLAIR MUST GO
FREEDOM
UNISON
STOP

Endnotes

CHAPTER 1

1 Robert Philippe, *Political Graphics: Art as a Weapon*, Phaidon Press 1982, pp9–12.
2 Ibid, p52 and p12.
3 Ibid, p44. And Richard Harris Art Collection, Jacques Callot, The Miseries and Misfortunes of War, http://www.richardharrisartcollection.com/portfolio-view/jacques-callot/
4 Art Gallery New South Wales, Collection: 'The Hanging', from the suite *The Miseries and Misfortunes of War 1633*, Jacques Callot, Essay by Peter Raissis, Prints & Drawings Europe 1500–1900, 2014, https://www.artgallery.nsw.gov.au/collection/works/DO10.1963.11/
5 A.J.P. Taylor, *How Wars Begin*, Book Club Associates/Hamish Hamilton 1979, pp18-33; Gordon Kerr, *A Short History of Europe*, Pocket Essentials 2013, pp98–100. And Sylvia Neely, *A Concise History of the French Revolution*, Rowman & Littlefield Publishers 2008, 'Women and the Revolution', p147–151.
6 Robert Philippe, *Political Graphics: Art as a Weapon*, Phaidon Press 1982, pp122 and 126–128.
7 Mark Bills, *The Art of Satire: London in Caricature*, Philip Wilson Publishers 2006, pp18–19 and 42–49.
8 Vic Gatrell, *City of Laughter: Sex and Satire in Eighteenth-Century London*, Atlantic Books 2006, pp258–287. And Mark Bills, *The Art of Satire: London in Caricature*, Philip Wilson Publishers 2006, pp106-112.
9 Patricia Wright, *Goya*, Dorling Kindersley/The National Gallery London 1993, pp38–43 and 28–29.
10 Ibid.
11 William Feaver, *Masters of Caricature: From Hogarth and Gillray to Scarfe and Levine*, Weidenfeld and Nicolson 1981, pp11, 24, 70–71. And Steven Heller and Gail Anderson, *Graphic Wit: The Art of Humor in Design*, Watson-Guptill Publications 1991, pp16–18.
12 Museum of the City of New York, *MCNY Blog: New York Stories*. Article by Anne DiFabio, Print collection, 2013. https://blog.mcny.org/2013/09/24/thomas-nast-takes-down-tammany-a-cartoonists-crusade-against-a-political-boss/
13 Ibid. And John Adler with Draper Hill, *Doomed by Cartoon: How Cartoonist Thomas Nast and The New York Times Brought Down Boss Tweed and His Ring of Thieves*, Morgan James Publishing 2008, pp46-47 and 126–127.
14 Museum of the City of New York, *MCNY Blog: New York Stories*. Article by Anne DiFabio, Print collection, 2013. https://blog.mcny.org/2013/09/24/thomas-nast-takes-down-tammany-a-cartoonists-crusade-against-a-political-boss/

CHAPTER 2

1 Julian Rothenstein (ed.), *Posada: Messenger of Mortality*, Redstone Press/South Bank Centre 1989, Introduction by Peter Wollen, pp14–23. And *Graphic: 500 Designs That Matter*, Phaidon Press 2017, Item 303: Calaveras.
2 Liz McQuiston, *Suffragettes to She-Devils: Women's Liberation and Beyond*, Phaidon Press 1997, pp24–28.
3 Ibid.
4 Kurt Rowland, *A History of the Modern Movement: Art Architecture Design*, Van Nostrand Reinhold/Looking and Seeing 1973, pp129–135 and 144.
5 Ibid, pp140-147. And Hans Richter, *Dada: Art and Anti-Art*, Oxford University Press 1965 (reprinted 1978), pp11–38.
6 David Elliott (ed.), *Alexander Rodchenko*, Museum of Modern Art Oxford 1979, Essay 'Productivist Life' by Szymon Bojko, pp78–81.
7 Ibid. And M. N. Yablonskaya, *Women Artists of Russia's New Age 1900-1935*, Thames and Hudson 1990, pp141–156.
8 Kurt Rowland, *A History of the Modern Movement: Art Architecture Design*, Van Nostrand Reinhold/Looking and Seeing 1973, pp201–203.
9 Toby Clark, *Art and Propaganda in the Twentieth Century: The Political Image in the Age of Mass Culture*, The Everyman Art Library/George Weidenfeld and Nicolson 1997, p48. And William Feaver, *Masters of Caricature: From Hogarth and Gillray to Scarfe and Levine*, Weidenfeld and Nicolson 1981, pp130–132, 137, 150, 154.

CHAPTER 3

1 Joy Hakim, *Freedom: A History of US*, Oxford University Press 2003, pp271–281.
2 Ibid.
3 Social Realism https://www.theartstory.org/print_new_design.html?id=social_realism&name=Social%20Realism&type=movement And Ben Shahn, American Artist https://www.theartstory.org/print_new_design.html?id=shahn_ben&name=Ben%20Shahn&type=artist
4 Joy Hakim, *Freedom: A History of US*, Oxford University Press 2003, pp281–283.
5 *Photomontages of the Nazi Period: John Heartfield*, Gordon Fraser/Universe Books 1977, Essay 'John Heartfield's Photomontages' by Peter Selz, pp7–16.
6 John Tisa (ed.), *The Palette and the Flame: Posters of the Spanish Civil War*, Collet's Publishers 1980, Foreword by Luigi Longo, ppIX–XII.
7 Susan Roy, *Bomboozled! How the US Government Misled Itself and Its People into Believing They Could Survive a Nuclear Attack*, Pointed Leaf Press 2010, pp13–14.
8 Ibid, pp14-27. And Steve Ryfle, *Japan's Favorite Mon-star: The Unauthorized Biography of 'The Big G'*, ECW Press 1998, pp20-21 and 41–45.
9 Ibid. And Barry Miles, *Peace: 50 Years of Protest 1958-2008*, Collins & Brown 2008, pp54 and 74–75.
10 Ibid, pp55-78 and 87–94.
11 Ibid, pp106–107.
12 Maggie Andrews and Janis Lomas, *A History of Women in 100 Objects*, The History Press 2018, pp325–327.
13 The Posterbook Collective of the South African History Archive, *Images of Defiance: South African Resistance Posters of the 1980s*, Ravan Press Johannesburg 1991, p14. And South African History Online: Pass Laws in South Africa 1800-1994 https://www.sahistory.org.za/article/pass-laws-south-africa-1800-1994; and South Africa: Overcoming Apartheid, Building Democracy http://overcomingapartheid.msu.edu/multimedia.php?id=65-259-3
14 Ibid.

CHAPTER 4

1 Lincoln Cushing, *Revolución! Cuban Poster Art*, Chronicle Books 2003, pp23–24. And BBC News: Timeline: US-Cuba relations: https://www.bbc.co.uk/news/world-latin-america-12159943
2 Lincoln Cushing, Revolución! Cuban Poster Art, Chronicle Books 2003, pp15–18.
3 Liz McQuiston, *Graphic Agitation*, Phaidon Press 1993, pp142–147.
4 Ibid.
5 Humphrey Carpenter, *That Was SATIRE That Was: The Satire Boom of the 1960s*, Victor Gollancz 2000, pp93–110 and 155–183.
6 Tariq Ali and Susan Watkins, *1968: Marching in the Streets*, Bloomsbury 1998, pp124–128, 172–175 and 183-184.
7 Stephen Shames and Bobby Seale, *Power to the People: The World of the Black Panthers*, Abrams 2016, pp10–14. And Stephen Shames, *The Black Panthers: Photographs by Stephen Shames*, Aperture 2006, pp11–13 and 138–145.
8 The Stonewall Riots http://web-static.nypl.org/exhibitions/1969/stonewall.html And the Gay Liberation Front (USA) http://web-static.nypl.org/exhibitions/1969/liberation.html
9 The Gay Liberation Front (Britain) https://timeline.com/this-is-what-britains-gay-liberation-front-movement-looked-like-in-the-1970s-c8583401a209
10 Johan Kugelberg and Philippe Vermés, *Beauty is in the Street: A Visual Record of the May '68 Paris Uprising*, Four Corners Books 2011, pp13–15, 34–36 and 76–81.

11 Terry Jones (ed.), *Not Another Punk Book*, Aurum Press 1978, pp7–30 and 56–74 and 92.

12 *Graphic: 500 Designs That Matter*, Phaidon Press 2017, Item 496: Whole Earth Catalog: Access to Tools (1968-75).

13 Three Mile Island Nuclear Accident, http://www.world-nuclear.org/information-library/safety-and-security/safety-of-plants/three-mile-island-accident.aspx

14 Giancarlo Ceraudo, *Destino Final*, Schilt Publishing 2017, pp10–23, 41–48 and 73–80. And Steve Crawshaw, *Street Spirit: The Power of Protest and Mischief*, LOM Art/Michael O'Mara Books 2017, pp80–81.

CHAPTER 5

1 Liz McQuiston, *Suffragettes to She-Devils: Women's Liberation and Beyond*, Phaidon Press 1997, pp226–229.

2 Bill Rolston, *Drawing Support: Murals in the North of Ireland*, Beyond the Pale Publications 1994, ppi-viii. And Mike Simons, *Striking Back: Photographs of the Great Miners' Strike 1984-85*, pp6–12 and 72–77.

3 Liz McQuiston, *Graphic Agitation 2*, Phaidon Press 2004, pp172–177.

4 The Posterbook Collective of the South African History Archive, *Images of Defiance: South African Resistance Posters of the 1980s*, Ravan Press Johannesburg 1991, pp14–15 and 181. And *Art from the Frontline: Contemporary Art from Southern Africa*, Frontline States and Karia Press 1990, Article by Ernest Harsch 'Frontline Resistance ', pp17–22.

5 Liz McQuiston, *Suffragettes to She-Devils: Women's Liberation and Beyond*, Phaidon Press 1997, pp114–123, 140–147, 150–161.

6 Douglas Crimp with Adam Rolston, *AIDS Demo Graphics*, Bay Press 1990, p12–36.

7 Carrie Moyer and Sue Schaffner, *Straight to Hell: 10 Years of Dyke Action Machine!*, Exhibition Brochure (Yerba Buena Center for the Arts, San Francisco) 2002.

8 Scott Minick and Jiao Ping, *Chinese Graphic Design in the Twentieth Century*, Van Nostrand Reinhold 1990, p150–151. And *Today* newspaper (front page) Monday 5 June 1989, Article by Louise Branson re massacre on 4 June 1989.

9 Dana Bartelt and Marta Sylvestrová, *Art as Activist: Revolutionary Posters from Central and Eastern Europe*, Thames and Hudson 1992, Essay by Marta Sylvestrová 'The Art of the Street', pp13–24, and timeline of revolutions by Gale Stokes 'Comrades Adieu!', pp151–158.

10 Philip M. Taylor, *War and the Media: Propaganda and Persuasion in the Gulf War*, Manchester University Press (Second Edition) 1998, Introduction: 'Image and Reality in the Gulf War', pp1–30.

11 Liz McQuiston, *Graphic Agitation 2*, Phaidon Press 2004, pp123–126.

12 Ibid. And Matthew Collin, *This is Serbia Calling: Rock'n'Roll Radio and Belgrade's Underground Resistance*, Serpent's Tail 2001, pp199–234.

13 Barricada International Collective, *Barricada USA: 10th Anniversary Celebration Calendar*, Barricada USA 1989. The calendar celebrated 10 years since the Nicaraguan revolution (July 19, 1979) and was annotated throughout.

14 Emma Bircham and John Charlton (eds.), *Anti-Capitalism: A Guide to the Movement*, Bookmarks Publications 2001, Essay by Susan George 'Corporate Globalisation', pp11–24.

15 Ibid. And John Vidal, *McLibel: Burger Culture on Trial*, Macmillan 1997, pp3–20. And Adbusters Media Foundation (adbusters.org).

16 Bitterkomix review http://www.stripkap.net/sa2.html

17 'A discussion with Jonathan Shapiro on 29th November 2017' (Interviewed by Nastassia Arendse) https://www.zapiro.com/e-store/contact-us/interviews/178-a-discussion-with-jonathan-shapiro

18 1988 Australian Bicentennial https://www.theaustralian.com.au/50th-birthday/bicentennial-and-beyond/story-fnlkofie-1226936978775

CHAPTER 6

1 Mark Wallinger, *State Britain*, Tate Publishing (pamphlet) 2007, Essay by Clarrie Wallis.

2 'Millions March for Peace' (front page), *The Independent on Sunday*, 16 February 2003, No. 679, Special Section 'The People's Protest', pp2-5.

3 Symon Hill, *Digital Revolutions: Activism in the Internet Age*, New Internationalist Publications 2013, pp23-24, 30-34 and 74-76.

4 Kurt Andersen, 'The Protester', *TIME* magazine, Vol.178 No.25, December 26, 2011-January 2, 2012, pp70-72.

5 Ibid, p72.

6 Ibid, p73.

7 Yaman Kayabali, 'Protest Art in Real Time', *Creative Review*, August 2013, pp66-68. And Dave Zirin, *Brazil's Dance with the Devil: The World Cup, The Olympics and the Fight for Democracy*, Haymarket Books 2014, pp205-2011.

8 Ying Chan, 'People Power', Jon Henley 'Protesting with Brollies at the Ready' and Archie Bland 'The App That Helps Beat Censorship', *The Guardian* (G2 section), Tuesday 30 September 2014, pp6-9.

9 Ai Weiwei, *Ai Weiwei's Blog: Writings, Interviews and Digital Rants 2006-2009*, The MIT Press 2011, Section beginning 'Citizen Investigation', pp209-225.

10 Emely Neu and Jade French in collaboration with Pussy Riot, *Let's Start a Pussy Riot*, Rough Trade 2013, Section 'The History of Pussy Riot, by Pussy Riot, pp22-23.

11 Éléa Baucheron and Diane Routex, *The Museum of Scandals: Art That Shocked the World*, Prestel Verlag 2013, pp128-129.

12 Robert Aldrich (ed.), *Gay Life and Culture: A World History*, Thames and Hudson 2006, pp360-363. And Pew Research Center, 'Gay Marriage Around the World', August 8, 2017, http://www.pewforum.org/2017/08/08/gay-marriage-around-the-world-2013/#netherlands

13 Tal Kopan and Eugene Scott (CNN), 'North Carolina governor signs controversial transgender bill', CNNPolitics, March 24, 2016, https://edition.cnn.com/2016/03/23/politics/north-carolina-gender-bathrooms-bill/index.html And Rupert Neate, 'Gays Against Guns' (Special Report), *The Observer Magazine*, 22 January 2017, pp22-29.

14 Wesley Lowery, *'They Can't Kill Us All': The Story of Black Lives Matter*, Penguin Books 2017, pp81-88.

15 Robert Mendick (London), Harriet Alexander and David Lawler (Washington), 'From Africa to London, the world protests', *The Sunday Telegraph*, Sunday 22 January 2017, pp6-7. And the original Pussyhat Project Manifesto with pattern, https://www.pussyhatproject.com/print/

16 Nadia Khomami, '#MeToo: how a hashtag became a rallying cry against sexual harassment', *The Guardian*, Friday 20 October 2017, https://www.theguardian.com/world/2017/oct/20/women-worldwide-use-hashtag-metoo-against-sexual-harassment

17 Kelly Knauer (ed.), *TIME: The Year in Review (2005)*, Special Report: Hurricane Season, 'It Struck the Gulf Coast, But It Ruined a Nation: Katrina', Time Books 2005, pp12-21.

18 David Usborne, 'BP, the Gulf Oil Spill and 87 days that changed the World', *The Independent*, Saturday 17 July 2010, pp6-7. And Alice-Azania Jarvis, 'Disaster By Numbers', *The Independent*, Tues 14 September 2010, pp12-13.

19 'PM facing Cabinet rebellion as she finalises Brexit deal' (front page) and Richard Vaughan, 'May faces revolt in Cabinet over Brexit backstop', 'i', Friday 9 November 2018, pp6-7. And Kim Hjelmgaard, 'Diaper-clad "Trump Baby" blimp to fly over London during President's visit', *USA Today*, July 6, 2018, https://eu.usatoday.com/story/news/world/2018/07/05/trump-baby-blimp-approved-london-mayor-sadiq-khan-trump-uk-visit/760669002/

20 John Lichfield, 'Nation defiant after terrorists kill 12 people in assault on satirical magazine' and Cahal Milmo, 'Dark reflection in the City of Light and then burning anger', *The Independent*, Thursday 8 January 2015, pp4-5.

21 Guardian Staff, 'How many school shootings have there been in 2018 so far?', *The Guardian*, Friday 18 May 2018, https://www.theguardian.com/world/2018/ Diaz, 'feb/14/school-shootings-in-america-2018-how-many-so-far And Sarah Gray, 'The March for Our Lives Protest Is This Saturday. Here's Everything to Know', *TIME* magazine, March 23, 2018, http://time.com/5167102/march-for-our-lives-parkland-school-shooting-protest/

22 Andrew Hussey, 'Macron's Crisis Without End', *New Statesman*, 4-10 January 2019, pp13-14. And Angelique Chrisafis, 'Can Macron turn back the French tidal wave of discontent?, *The Guardian Weekly*, 7 December 2018, Vol.200 No.1, pp15-17

Bibliography

Adler, J. (2008) *Doomed By Cartoon: How Cartoonist Thomas Nast and The New York Times Brought Down Boss Tweed and His Ring of Thieves*, Morgan James Publishing, Garden City, New York, USA.

Adriani, G., Krieger, P., Roters, E. and Thomas, K. (1985) *Hannah Hoch 1889-1978 Collages*, Institute for Foreign Cultural Relations, Stuttgart, West Germany.

Ai, W. (2011) *Ai Weiwei's Blog: Writings, Interviews and Digital Rants, 2006-2009*, The MIT Press, Cambridge, MA, USA.

Ali, T. and Watkins, S. (1998) *1968: Marching in the Streets*, Bloomsbury Publishing, London.

Aldrich, R. (ed.) (2006) *Gay Life and Culture: A World History*, Thames and Hudson, London.

Andrews, M. and Lomas, J. (2018) *A History of Women in 100 Objects*, The History Press, Stroud, Gloucestershire, UK.

Anikst, M. (ed.) (1987) *Soviet Commercial Design of the Twenties*, Thames and Hudson, London.

Atkinson, D. (1992) *The Purple, White & Green: Suffragettes in London 1906-14*, Museum of London.

Baker, D. (2017) *Nuclear Weapons: 1945 onwards (strategic and tactical delivery systems)*, Haynes Publishing, Yeovil, Somerset, UK.

Bartelt, D. and Sylvestrová, M. (1992) *Art as Activist: Revolutionary Posters from Central and Eastern Europe*, Thames and Hudson, London.

Batchelor, T., Lewisohn, C. and Myrone, M. (2010) *Rude Britannia: British Comic Art*, Tate Publishing, London.

Bills, M. (2006) *The Art of Satire: London in Caricature*, Museum of London/Philip Wilson Publishers, London.

Bircham, E. and Charlton, J. (eds.) (2001) *Anti-Capitalism: A Guide to the Movement*, Bookmarks Publications, London.

Burgin, A. (ed.) (2011) *Stop The War: A Graphic History*, Francis Boutle Publishers/Stop The War Coalition, London.

Bury, S. (ed.) (2007) *Breaking the Rules: The Printed Face of the European Avant Garde 1900-1937*, The British Library, London.

Carpenter, H. (2000) *That Was SATIRE That Was: The Satire Boom of the 1960s*, Victor Gollancz, London.

Ceraudo, G. (2017) *Destino Final*, Schilt Publishing, Amsterdam, NL.

Coe, S. and Metz, H. (1983) *How to Commit Suicide in South Africa*, Raw Books & Graphics, New York, New York, USA. (Illustrations by Sue Coe, text by Holly Metz.)

Conal, R. (1992) *Art Attack: The Midnight Politics of a Guerrilla Artist*, HarperCollins Publishers, New York, New York, USA.

Crawshaw, S. (2017) *Street Spirit: The Power of Protest and Mischief*, LOM Art/Michael O'Mara Books, London.

Crimp, D. and Rolston, A. (1990) *AIDS Demo Graphics*, Bay Press, Seattle, Washington, USA.

Crowley, D. (2008) *Posters of the Cold War*, V&A Publishing, London.

Cushing, L. (2003) *Revolución! Cuban Poster Art*, Chronicle Books, San Francisco, California, USA.

Editors of TIME (2005) *Hurricane Katrina: The Storm That Changed America*, TIME Books, New York, New York, USA.

Elliott, D. (ed.) (1979) *Alexander Rodchenko*, Museum of Modern Art, Oxford, UK.

Evans, D. and Gohl, S. (1986) *Photomontage: A Political Weapon*, Gordon Fraser, London.

Evans, K. (2017) *Threads: From the Refugee Crisis*, Verso Books, London.

Feaver, W. (1981) *Masters of Caricature: From Hogarth and Gillray to Scarfe and Levine*, Weidenfeld and Nicolson, London.

Flood, C. and Grindon, G. (eds.) (2014) *Disobedient Objects*, V&A Publishing, London.

French, J. and Neu, E. (2013) *Let's Start a Pussy Riot*, Rough Trade, London.

Garrigan, J. *et al* (1975) *Images of an Era: The American Poster 1945-75*, National Collection of Fine Arts, Smithsonian Institution, Washington, D.C.

Gatrell, V. (2006) *City of Laughter: Sex and Satire in Eighteenth-Century London*, Atlantic Books, London.

Glaser, M., Ilic, M., Civilization and Elbers, D. (eds.) (2017) *The Design of Dissent*. Exhibition held at Graphic Matters, Breda, NL, Sept-Oct 2017. [Exhibition catalogue]

Godfrey, M. and Whitley, Z. (2017) *Soul of a Nation: Art in the Age of Black Power*, Tate Publishing, London.

Grondahl, M. (2011) *Tahrir Square: The Heart of the Egyptian Revolution*, The American University in Cairo Press, Cairo, Egypt.

Hakim, J. (2003) *Freedom: A History of US*, Oxford University Press, New York, New York, USA.

Halasa, M., Omareen, Z. and Mahfoud, N. (2014) *Syria Speaks: Art and Culture from the Frontline*, Saqi Books, London.

Harris, R. (no date) *Jacques Callot, The Miseries and Misfortunes of War*. Available at: http://www.richardharrisartcollection.com/portfolio-view/jacques-callot/ (Accessed: 17 March 2019)

Hastings, M. (2018) *Vietnam: An Epic Tragedy 1945-1975*, William Collins Books, London.

Hayden, T. (2017) *Hell No: The Forgotten Power of the Vietnam Peace Movement*, Yale University Press, London.

Hill, S. (2013) *Digital Revolutions: Activism in the Internet Age*, New Internationalist Publications, Oxford, UK.

Jones, T. (ed.) (1978) *Not Another Punk Book*, Aurum Press, London.

Kugelberg, J. and Verm s, P. (2011) *Beauty Is In The Street: A Visual Record of the May '68 Paris Uprising*, Four Corners Books, London.

Loesch-Quintin, L. and Terragni, E. (eds.) (2017) *Graphic: 500 Designs That Matter*, Phaidon Press, London.

Lomasko, V. (2017) *Other Russias*, Penguin Books, UK.

Lowery, W. (2017) *They Can't Kill Us All: The Story of Black Lives Matter*, Penguin Books, UK.

McQuiston, L. (1997) *Suffragettes to She-Devils: Women's Liberation and Beyond*, Phaidon Press, London.

Miles, B. (2008) *Peace: 50 Years of Protest 1958-2008*, Collins & Brown, London.

Neely, S. (2008) *A Concise History of the French Revolution*, Rowman & Littlefield Publishers, Lanham, Maryland, USA.

Philippe, R. (1982) *Political Graphics: Art as a Weapon*, Phaidon Press, Oxford, UK.

Photomontages of the Nazi Period: John Heartfield (1977) Gordon Fraser/Universe Books, London.

Poster Collective of the South African History Archive (1995) *Images of Defiance: South African Resistance Posters of the 1980s*, Ravan Press, Johannesburg, South Africa.

Richter, H. (1978) *Dada: Art and Anti-Art*, Thames & Hudson, London.

Road Raging: Top Tips for Wrecking Roadbuilding (1997) Road Alert!, Newbury, UK.

Roberts, L., Shaw, D., Wright, R. and Cubbage, M. (2018) *Hope to Nope: Graphics and Politics 2008-18*, The Design Museum, London.

Rolston, B. (1994) *Drawing Support: Murals in the North of Ireland*, Beyond the Pale/BTP Publications, Belfast.

Rolston, B. (1998) *Drawing Support 2: Murals of War and Peace*, Beyond the Pale/BTP Publications, Belfast.

Rothenstein, J. (ed.) (1989) *Posada: Messenger of Mortality*, Redstone Press/Southbank Centre, London.

Rowland, K. (1973) *A History of the Modern Movement: Art Architecture Design*, Looking and Seeing, London.

Roy, S. (2010) *Bomboozled! How the US Government Misled Itself and Its People into Believing They Could Survive a Nuclear Attack*, Pointed Leaf Press, New York, New York, USA.

Ryfle, S. (1998) *Japan's Favorite Mon-Star: The Unauthorized Biography of 'The Big G'*, ECW Press, Toronto, Ontario, Canada.

Sacco, J. (2002) *Safe Area Gorazde: The War in Eastern Bosnia 1992-95*, Fantagraphics, Seattle, WA, USA.

See Red Women's Workshop (2016) Four Corners Books, London.

Shames, S. (2006) *The Black Panthers: Photographs by Stephen Shames*, Aperture Foundation, New York, New York, USA.

Shames, S. and Seale, B. (2016) *Power to the People: The World of the Black Panthers*, Abrams, New York, New York, USA.

Simons, M. (2004) *Striking Back: Photographs of the Great Miners' Strike 1984-1985*, Bookmarks Publications, London.

Smith, Lyn (2017) *People Power: Fighting for Peace from the First World War to the Present*, Thames & Hudson, London.

Strizenova, T. (ed.) (1987) *Costume Revolution: Textiles, Clothing and Costume of the Soviet Union in the Twenties*, Trefoil Publications, London.

Taylor, A.J.P. (1979) *How Wars Begin*, Book Club Associates, London.

Taylor, P. M. (1998) *War and the Media: Propaganda and Persuasion in the Gulf War*, Manchester University Press (Second Edition), Manchester, UK.

Tickner, L. (1987) *The Spectacle of Women: Imagery of the Suffrage Campaign 1907-14*, Chatto & Windus, London.

Tisa, J. (1980) *The Palette and the Flame: Posters of the Spanish Civil War*, Collet's Publishers, London.

Vidal, J. (1997) *McLibel: Burger Culture on Trial*, Macmillan, London.

Welch, D. (2013) *Propaganda: Power and Persuasion*, The British Library, London.

Wright, P. (1993) *Goya*, Dorling Kindersley (in association with The National Gallery), London.

Wye, Deborah (1988) *Committed to Print: Social and Political Themes in Recent American Printed Art*, The Museum of Modern Art, New York, New York, USA.

Yablonskaya, M. N. (1990) *Women Artists of Russia's New Age 1900-1935*, Thames and Hudson, London.

Zirin, D. (2014) *Brazil's Dance with the Devil: The World Cup, The Olympics, and the Fight for Democracy*, Haymarket Books, Chicago, Illinois, USA.

Picture Credits

Chapter Openers

8–9 (& 23 t) Fashionable Contrasts, 1792 by James Gillray, Private Collection/Bridgeman Images
34–35 'Don Quixote', 1900–13 by Jose Guadalupe Posada, INTERFOTO/Alamy Stock Photo
62–63 CND protest march through Scarborough in North Yorkshire, 1960, Edward Miller/Keystone/Getty Images
86–87 (& 105 t) Striking Sanitation Department Workers, 1968, Bettmann/Getty Images
130–31 Lesbian Protesters at New York City Board of Education, 1992, Photo by Charles Wenzelberg/New York Post Archives /© NYP Holdings, Inc. via Getty Images
200–01 & 263 b Charlie Hebdo Unity Rally, Paris, 2015, Artist: JR.

Main spreads

6 t Anti-Nuclear Power sticker: logo by Anne Lind and Søren Lisberg; 6 b McLibel Support Campaign; 7 Extinction Rebellion; 11 The British Library Board/ Scala, Florence; 13 t Lebrecht Music & Arts/Alamy Stock Photo; 13 b The Granger Collection/Alamy Stock Photo; 14 © British Library Board. All Rights Reserved/Bridgeman Images; 15 Fine Art Images/Heritage Images/Getty Images; 16–17 Miss Média/Flickr/CC BY 2.0; 18 l Pictorial Press Ltd/Alamy Stock Photo; 18 r Musee de la Ville de Paris, Musee Carnavalet, Paris, France/Archives Charmet/Bridgeman Images; 19 t Niday Picture Library/Alamy Stock Photo; 19 b The History Collection/Alamy Stock Photo; 20 Yomangani (public domain); 21 t James Gillray, Courtesy of the Warden and Scholars of New College, Oxford/Bridgeman Images; 21 b Universal History Archive/UIG via Getty Images; 22 t Artokoloro Quint Lox Limited/Alamy Stock Photo; 22 b Wellcome Collection; 23 b Guildhall Library & Art Gallery/Heritage Images/Getty Images; 24–25 Museo del Prado; 26 Granger Historical Picture Archive/Alamy Stock Photo; 27 t Honoré Daumier; 27 b The History Collection/Alamy Stock Photo; 28 World History Archive/Alamy Stock Photo; 29 l Racconish (public domain); 29 r Racconish (public domain); 30 Library of Congress; 31 t Library of Congress; 31 b © CORBIS/Corbis via Getty Images; 32 via HathiTrust digital library; 33 l Granger Historical Picture Archive/Alamy Stock Photo; 33 r Metropolitan Museum of Art/Harris Brisbane Dick Fund, 1928; 36 Museum of London/Heritage Images/Getty Images; 39 age fotostock/Alamy Stock Photo; 40–41 José Guadalupe Posada; 42 Bob Thomas/Popperfoto/Getty Images; 43 b Museum of London, UK/Bridgeman Images; 43 t Hilda Dallas; 44 t Museum of London/Heritage Images/Getty Images; 44 b © Museum of London; 45 © The March of the Women Collection/Mary Evans Picture Library; 46 t Museum of London/Heritage Images/Getty Images; 46 b Museum of London/Heritage Images/Getty Images; 47 Time Life Pictures/Mansell/The LIFE Picture Collection/Getty Images; 48 l Museum of London/Heritage Images/Getty Images; 48 r © Museum of London; 49 r Museum of London/Heritage Images/Getty Images; 49 tl LSE Library/Flickr; 49 bl: LSE Library/Flickr; 50 Fine Art Images/Heritage Images/Getty Images; 51 r Tallandier/Bridgeman Images; 51 l The Picture Art Collection/Alamy Stock Photo; 52 l Bibliotheque Litteraire Jacques Doucet, Paris, France/Archives Charmet/Bridgeman Images; 52 r Apic/Getty Images; 53 Hannah Höch © DACS 2019. Photo: Scala, Florence/bpk, Bildagentur fuer Kunst, Kultur und Geschichte, Berlin; 54 © The Heartfield Community of Heirs/DACS 2019. Photo: SeM/UIG via Getty Images; 55 t © Estate of George Grosz, Princeton, N.J./DACS 2019. Photo: Private Collection/The Stapleton Collection/Bridgeman Images; 55 b © The Heartfield Community of Heirs/DACS 2019. Photo: Private Collection/Joerg Hejkal/Bridgeman Images; 56 © Rodchenko & Stepanova Archive, DACS, RAO 2019. Photo: Digital image, The Museum of Modern Art, New York/Scala, Florence; 57 bl © Rodchenko & Stepanova Archive, DACS, RAO 2019. Digital Image, Fine Art Images/Heritage Images/Scala, Florence; 57 r © Rodchenko & Stepanova Archive, DACS, RAO 2019. Photo: Fine Art Images/Heritage Images/Getty Images; 57 tl © Rodchenko & Stepanova Archive, DACS, RAO 2019. Digital image, The Museum of Modern Art, New York/Scala, Florence; 58 t © Rodchenko & Stepanova Archive, DACS, RAO 2019. Photo: Private Collection/Calmann & King Ltd/Bridgeman Images; 58 b DEA PICTURE LIBRARY/De Agostini/Getty Images; 59 Fine Art Images/Heritage Images/Getty Images; 60 tl Private Collection/Bridgeman Images; 60 m Art Media/Print Collector/Getty Images; 60 bl Fine Art Images/Heritage Images/Getty Images; 60 br Everett Collection Inc/Alamy Stock Photo; 61 Universal History Archive/UIG via Getty images; 64 Photo Scala, Florence/bpk, Bildagentur fuer Kunst, Kultur und Geschichte, Berlin; 67 t Buyenlarge/Getty Images; 67 b Keystone-France/Gamma-Keystone via Getty Images; 68 l © Estate of Ben Shahn/VAGA at ARS, NY and DACS, London 2019. Digital image: The Museum of Modern Art, New York/Scala, Florence; 68 tr © Estate of Ben Shahn/VAGA at ARS, NY and DACS, London 2019. Photo: Granger Historical Picture Archive/Alamy Stock Photo; 68 br © Estate of Ben Shahn/VAGA at ARS, NY and DACS, London 2019. Photo: K.J. Historical/CORBIS/Corbis via Getty Images; 69 © Estate of Ben Shahn/VAGA at ARS, NY and DACS, London 2019. Photo: Fotosearch/Getty Images; 70 r Karl Arnold, © DACS 2019.; 70 l © The Heartfield Community of Heirs/DACS 2019. Photo: Scala, Florence/bpk, Bildagentur fuer Kunst, Kultur und Geschichte, Berlin; 71 © The Heartfield Community of Heirs/DACS 2019. Photo: Peter Horree/Alamy Stock Photo; 72 © The Heartfield Community of Heirs/DACS 2019. Image Provided By The John Heartfield Exhibition Website; 73 © The Heartfield Community of Heirs/DACS 2019. Image Provided By The John Heartfield Exhibition Website; 74 Photo 12/ UIG via Getty Images; 75 Fotosearch/Getty Images; 76 b Fotosearch/Getty Images; 76 t Fototeca Gilardi/Getty Images; 77 Universal History Archive/UIG via Getty Images; 78 Digital image, The Museum of Modern Art, New York/Scala, Florence; 79 r Mary Evans Picture Library/ONSLOW AUCTIONS LIMITED; 79 l Everett Collection Inc/Alamy Stock Photo; 80 Bettmann/Getty Images; 81 FHK Henrion; 82 Mary Evans/Marx Memorial Library; 83 t ©TopFoto.co.uk; 83 b Popperfoto/Getty Images; 84 Bureau of Prisons/Getty Images; 85 Source: Historical Papers Research Archive, University of the Witwatersrand, Johannesburg, South Africa.; 88 CSPG; 91 t Spanish Women's Liberation Movement; 91 b Alison Fell; 92 Fine Art Images/Heritage Images/Getty Images; 93 all Library of Congress/OSPAAL; 94 tl Reproduced by kind permission of PRIVATE EYE magazine/Gerald Scarfe; 94 bl University of Wollongong, Australia/Felix Deniis; 94 br University of Wollongong, Australia/Felix Deniis; 95 Contraband Collection/Alamy Stock Photo; 96 b Kim Nowacki/Flickr; 96 t Sudent Movement 1968, Mexico; 97 Klaus Staeck, © DACS 2019; 98 Seymour Chwast Archive; 99 b Kiyoshi Kuromiya. Photo: University of Michigan Library (Special Collections Research Center, Joseph A. Labadie Collection; 99 t Art Workers Coalition, USA/Bridgeman Images; 100 l Library of Congress/Tomi Ungerer; 100 r Napalm Graphic. Digital image: Whitney Museum of American Art/Licensed by Scala; 101 Digital image, The Museum of Modern Art, New York/Scala, Florence; 102 Library of Congress; 103 t & b: International Times; 104 Stephen F. Somerstein/Getty Images; 105 b Library of Congress; 106 Library of Congress; 107 t Private Collection/Penrodas Collection; 107 b Popperfoto/Getty Images; 108 © Emory Douglas/DACS 2019. Photo: Library of Congress; 109 © Emory Douglas/DACS 2019. Photo: Contraband Collection/Alamy Stock Photo; 110 Chicago Women's Graphics Collective; 111 l See Red Women's Workshop; 111 r © Monica Sjöö; 111 m Private Collection/Contraband Collection/Alamy Stock Photo; 112 © See Red Women's Workshop; 113 t C. Clement/Los Angeles Women's Center; 113 b Pen Dalton: "Women's Posters"; 114 b Chicago Women's Graphics Collective; 114 t Jill Posener; 115 Sheila Levrant de Bretteville; 116 The Image Works/TopFoto; 117 tr © Gay Liberation Front. Photo: Bishopsgate Institute; 117 tl © Gay Liberation Front. Photo: Bishopsgate Institute; 117 bl Penrodas Collection; 118–19 API/Gamma-Rapho via Getty Images; 120 l Pictorial Press Ltd/Alamy Stock Photo; 120 r TheCoverVersion/Alamy Stock Photo; 121 all Aurum Press; 122 t Private Collection/boredteenagers.co.uk; 122 b M&N/Alamy Stock Photo; 123 © Linder Sterling. All rights reserved, DACS 2019.; 124 all The Last Whole Earth Catalog; 125 © Robert Rauschenberg Foundation/VAGA at ARS, NY and DACS, London 2019.; 126 tl Rand Holmes Estate/comixjoint.com; 126 br Die Grünen; 126 tr Poster, Critical Mass 74, 1974; Designed by Arnold Saks (1931); USA; Gift of Various Donors; 1981-29-69; 127 Chips Mackinolty and Toni Robertson; 128–29 DANIEL GARCIA/AFP/Getty Images; 132 Artwork © Bureau, Marlene McCarty and Donald Moffett; 135 t The Women's Press; 135 b © Guerrilla Girls, courtesy guerrillagirls.com; 137 t Trio design group; 137 b Trio design group; 138 l © Peter Kennard; 138 r © Peter Kennard; 139 l © Edward Barber; 139 r Bob Light and John Houston; 140 b Christer Themptander, © DACS 2019; 140 t Designed by Yusaku Kamekura/Organized by Japan Graphic Designers Association Inc.; 141 Christer Themptander, © DACS 2019; 142 Library of Congress; 143 br Photographer: Brenda Prince; 143 tl The Greenham Factor; 143 tr The Greenham Factor; 143 mr © Campbell Collection on loan to The Peace Museum; 144 bl © Robbie Conal; 144 tl © Robbie Conal; 144 br © Steve Bell; 145 Spy magazine; 146 Bill Rolston; 147 ml In Pictures Ltd./Corbis via Getty Images; 147 tr Stephen Dorley-Brown; 147 bl An Phoblacht; 148 Andrew Barr; 149 b Bishopsgate Institute; 149 t John Harris/reportdigital.co.uk; 150 t & b: David Tartakover; 151 t & b: Yossi Lemel, Israel; 152 l Federation of South African Women; 152 r © Paul Weinberg/South Photos/Africa Media Online; 153 Private Collection/AF Fotografie; 154 t & b: Knockabout Comics; 155 l Wild Plakken (Frank Beekers, Lies Ros, Rob Schröder); 155 r Paul Peter Piech (The Taurus Press); 156 Contraband Collection/Alamy Stock Photo; 157 b Keith Haring artwork © Keith Haring Foundation; 157 t John Cole/Alamy Stock Photo; 158 all © Guerrilla Girls, courtesy guerrillagirls.com; 159 Women's Action Coalition (WAC)/Bethany Johns Design, New York; 160 Barbara Kruger, Courtesy the artist and Sprüth Magers; 161 t Helaine Victoria Press, Indiana; 161 b Helaine Victoria Press, Indiana; 162 Shocking Pink; 163 all © SisterSerpents; 164 t Contraband Collection/Alamy; 164 b Gran Fury; 165 l ACT UP/THE SILENCE = DEATH PROJECT/Wellcome Trust; 165 r ACT UP; 166 l Big Active; 166 tr Big Active; 166 br Big Active; 166 mr Big Active; 167 bl ACT UP; 167 tr Swedish Federation for Gay and Lesbian Rights; 167 br Foto: Jörg Reichardt/Grafik: Detlev Pusch; 167 tl Swedish Federation for Gay and Lesbian Rights; 167 bm Redback Graphix; 168–69 Dyke Action Machine!; 170 t Outrage!; 170 b Neville Elder/Corbis via Getty Images; 171 t Manik Design South; 171 b Mother City Queer Projects; 172 t Tomasz Sarnecki (1966-2018) © Monika Sarnecka; 172 b Jerzy Janiszewski; 173 l István Orosz; 173 r István Orosz; 174 Péter Pócs; 175 t Dusan Zdimal; 175 b Feliks Büttner; 176 Steven Lyons; 177 l Copyright by Stephen Kroninger/Library of Congress; 177 r Copyright © Joe Sacco. Courtesy of Fantagraphics Books (www.fantagraphics.com); 178 Ranko Novak; 179 tl Asim Djelilovic; 179 tr Trio design group; 179 mr Trio design group; 179 br Trio design group; 180 all Otpor!; 181 Miljenko Dereta, Ivan Valencak and

Acknowledgements

First and foremost I wish to express my heartfelt thanks to my colleagues at White Lion Publishing – Philip Cooper, Publisher; Nicki Davis, Senior Commissioning Editor; Laura Bulbeck, Senior Editor; and Josse Pickard, Designer – for their passion, skill, hard work and enthusiastic support throughout the making of this book. Their encouragement and kindness sustained me through a very long haul, and for that I am deeply grateful.

My thanks also go to the Staff of the Library at the Institut Français in South Kensington, London for their help with translations, and to Dan Gilbert, Librarian, at Ravensbourne, London for help with an urgent search for material.

Encouragement and solidarity came from a number of directions over the past few years.

From family, and particularly my nephew Alex McQuiston, whose eye for collecting sharp satire is even better than mine. And from newly found friends and colleagues at the Graphic Matters festival in Breda, The Netherlands, in September 2017, including: Dennis Elbers, founder and director of Graphic Matters; Thomas Dahm, founder of Neon Moiré, an online 'meeting place' for design and designers; and Michael Ellsworth and Corey Gutch, founders of Civilization studio in Seattle. I owe thanks to my friend and colleague of many years, the fine art photographer Verdi Yahooda, for meaningful conversations and another view of the world. And extend my thanks to the many artists, designers and activists whose work inspired me, and who kindly gave permission for their work to be reproduced in this book.

My final, and deepest, note of gratitude for help in the making of this book, must go to my partner, Professor Jeremy G H Barr, for his intellect, his humour, his unending support, and his poetry.

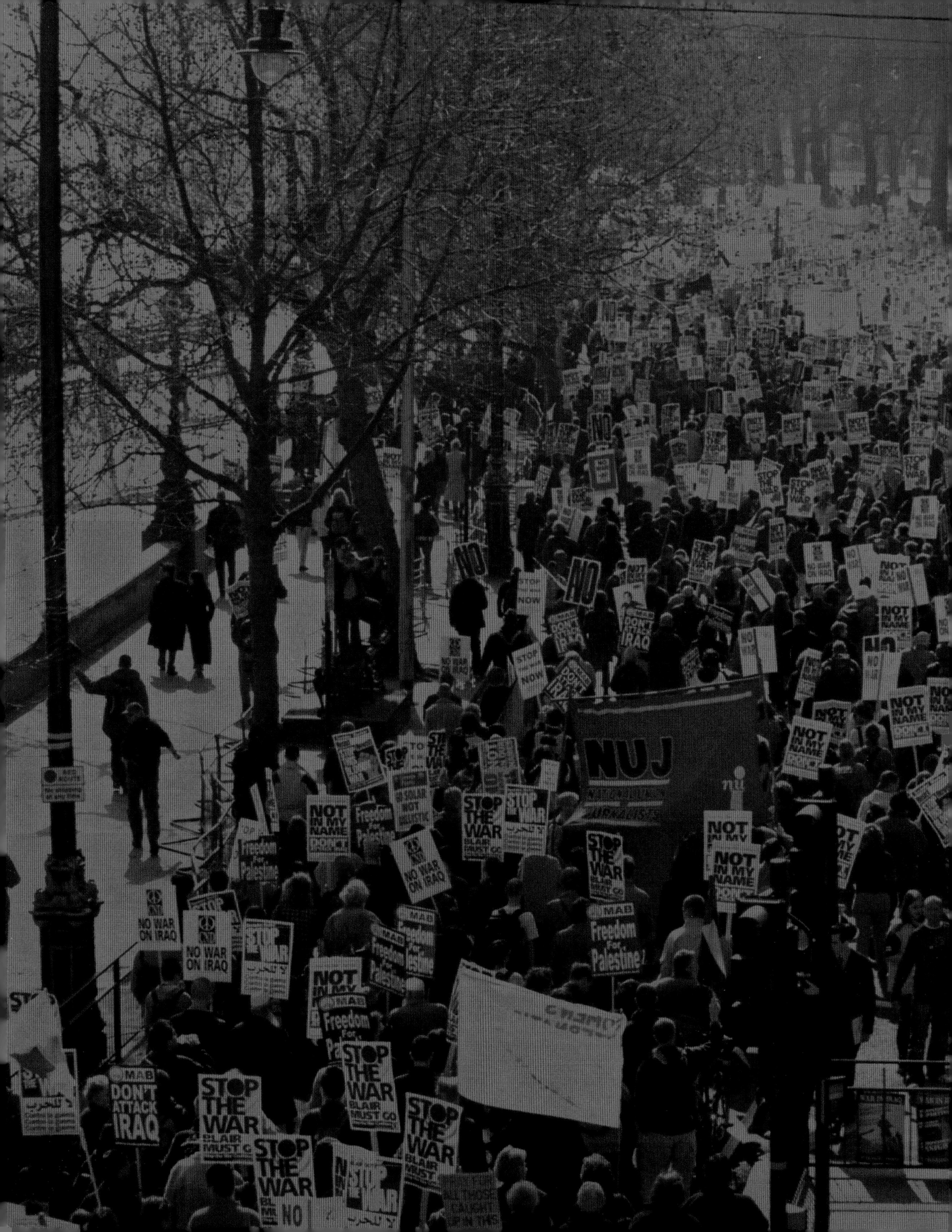

NO
NO
NO
STOP THE WAR
NOT IN MY NAME
NUJ
NATIONAL UNION OF JOURNALISTS
STOP THE WAR BLAIR MUST GO
NOT IN MY NAME
NOT IN MY NAME
MAB Freedom for Palestine
NO WAR ON IRAQ
NO SOLAR NOT BALLISTIC
STOP THE WAR
NO WAR ON IRAQ
MAB DON'T ATTACK IRAQ
STOP THE WAR BLAIR MUST GO
STOP THE WAR BLAIR MUST GO
STOP THE WAR
DON'T ATTACK IRAQ
STOP NOW

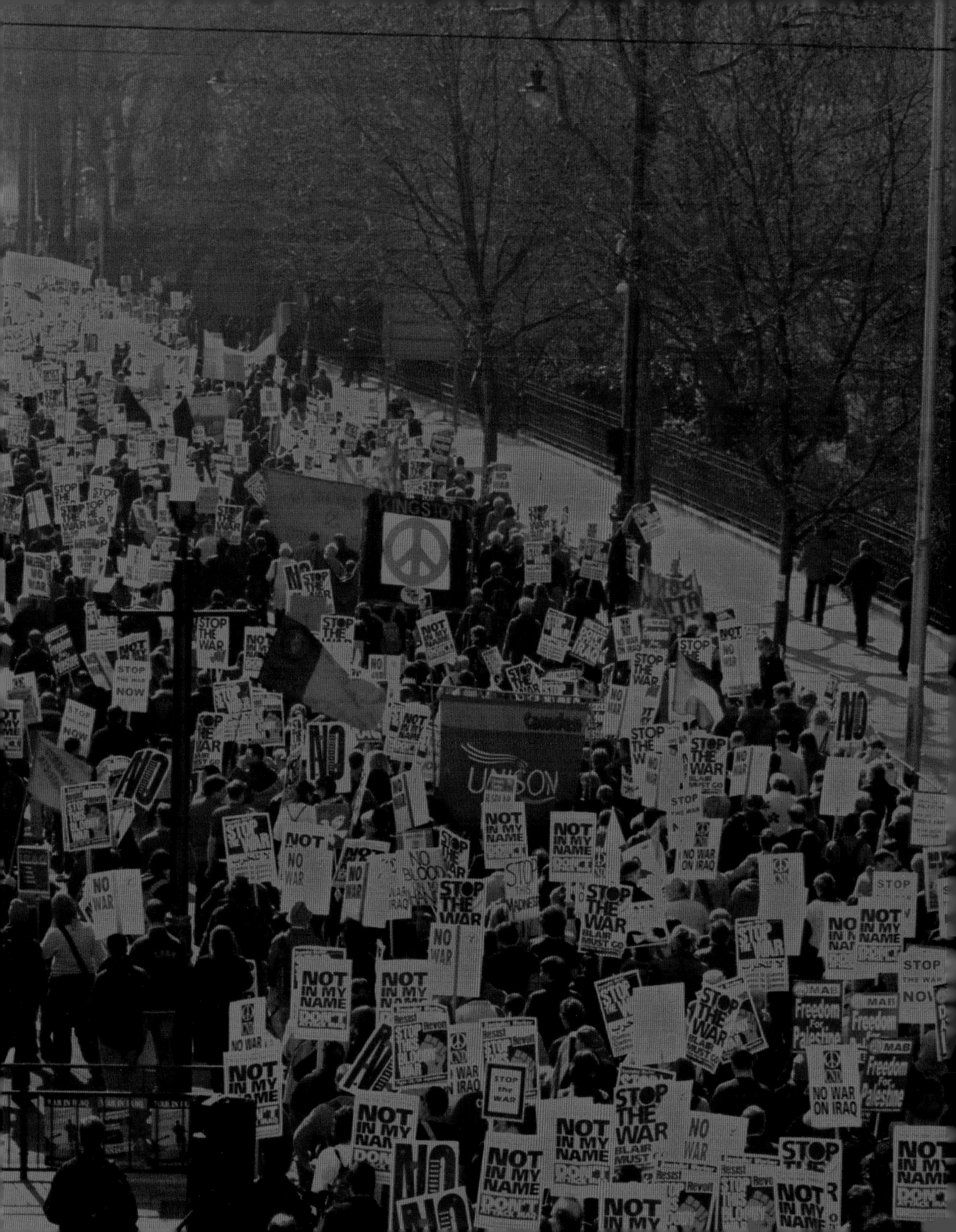

KINGSTON
STOP THE WAR
NOT IN MY NAME
NO WAR
NO WAR ON IRAQ
UNISON
STOP THE WAR BLAIR MUST GO
NO BLOOD FOR OIL
STOP THE MADNESS
MAB Freedom for Palestine
RESIST
Revolt